Music and Esotericism

Aries Book Series

Texts and Studies in Western Esotericism

VOLUME 9

Music and Esotericism

Edited by

Laurence Wuidar

BRILL

LEIDEN • BOSTON
2010

Cover illustration: Detail from "Aurora consurgens", Zurich Zentralbibliothek (MS. Rhenoviensis 172), v. 1420.

This book is printed on acid-free paper.

Library of Congress Cataloging-in-Publication Data

Music and esotericism / edited by Laurence Wuidar.
    p. cm. — (Aries book series. Texts and studies in Western esotericism)
    Includes index.
    English (chiefly); some articles in French or Italian, with English summaries.
    ISBN 978-90-04-18267-7 (hardback : alk. paper)
    1. Music and occultism. 2. Music and magic. 3. Music—Philosophy and aesthetics.
I. Wuidar, Laurence, 1978– II. Title. III. Series.

    ML3800.M83 2010
    780'.013—dc22

                                                                    2010013402

ISSN 1871-1405
ISBN 978 90 04 18267 7

Printed and bound in Great Britain by
CPI Antony Rowe, Chippenham and Eastbourne

CONTENTS

ACKNOWLEDGEMENTS

I am grateful to the members of the scientific board of the conference "Music and Esotericism: Art and Science of Sounds Facing the Occult Knowledge" (Rome, Academia Belgica, 14–18 April 2008) Brenno Boccadoro, Charles Burnett, Walter Corten, Paolo Gozza, David Juste and Steven Vanden Broecke. I would also like to thank Wouter J. Hanegraaff, editor of the Aries Book Series and Marjorie Roth for rereading some of the articles of this volume.

INTRODUCTION

Laurence Wuidar

This volume developed out of the Conference "Music and Esotericism: Art and Science of Sounds Facing the Occult Knowledge", organized at the *Academia Belgica* in Rome (14–18 April 2008). The concept for the Conference was to bring together scholars working on magic, astrology, alchemy, divination and cabbala in order to study the relationship of these to music. Its aim was to understand and break down the barriers between the history of art, music, science and ideas. Its purpose was to act as a multidisciplinary dialogue on music, as studied in the light of specific historical and scientific contexts, in order to both deepen and share our knowledge of the cultural background of the musical world in terms of science and belief.

These epistemological issues bring historians of science and ideas into a dialogue with musicologists, facilitating a network of the various relationships which exist between music and esotericism in order to view afresh the interpenetration of disciplines. Each paper focused on either the use of music within cultural and occult scientific traditions, or on the presence of these traditions in music. The subject matter of the papers reflected two complementary parts of the question. The first regards the viewpoint of philosophers and the way their theories integrate music; the second, the viewpoint of musicians, composers and theoreticians who are either interested in or have sought to integrate esoteric knowledge into their theories or compositions. A wide chronological range, stretching from antiquity to the twentieth century, raises the problem of continuity and rupture in the definition of esotericism, and maybe even of music.

At every point in our journey to comprehend "Music and Esotericism", our enquiry must focus its energies on two questions. First how do music and esotericism actually function together? And, second, how do their functions, status and even their very definitions coevolve?

The perspective adopted is a historical one. Up to the time of Kepler, astrology, magic, the cosmological conception of music and the musical conception of the cosmos were still influencing cultural developments, including those of science. Historians have been, and often still are, reluctant to recognize the vital role of esoteric philosophy in the formative period of modern science. Yet it is recognized that esotericism had a influence on the visual and musical arts, as witness the astrological iconographies of the Schifanoia Palace in Ferrara and Villa Farnesina in Rome, or the importance of music in Ficino's magical rites. Music has always had a function far beyond that of entertainment. It constitutes a significant link in the intertwining of analogical correspondences that underlie the esoteric concept of the world and of the cosmos.

From music in the magico-astral theories of Ficino to music in Kepler's astronomy, the interactions between music, esotericism and science have been brought to light by members of the Warburg Institute since the 1950s. There are still numerous individuals within the historical purview of music and esotericism who should be probed with respect to their unique features, their traditionalism or their innovation. One should also think about a historical synthesis on a national and European level. Only once these two tracks are completed will we be able to have a synthetic and nuanced look at the interactions between music and esotericism.

The present book maintains a focus on the individual level, taking stock of recent research on such crucial authors as Marsilio Ficino, Tommaso Campanella, Athanasius Kircher, Johannes Kepler and Marin Mersenne. It also reveals some views on less studied authors, at least with respect to music, such as Abu Ma'shar and Giovanni Battista della Porta. It also reveals some views on less studied composers, at least in terms of their relationship to esotericism, such as Orlando di Lasso, John Dowland, Ferruccio Busoni, Aleksandr Skrjabin and Anton Webern.

Omnes affectus species nostri pro sua diversitate habent proprios modos in voce atque cantu quorum occulta familiaritate excitantur (Augustine, *Confessions*, X, 33). Music, thinking in terms of the antique Greek *ethos* theory, powerfully represents human characters and passions. Therefore the question is how to manipulate sound so as to have an impact on man. The occult is the sympathetic invisible link between things.

The Pythagorean-Platonic concept of music holds that mathematical ratios rule the human soul and body as well as celestial bodies. If it is true that the same numerical relations are found in the configurations of the planets, the human soul and body, and the harmonies of music, then the latter can be seen as a privileged and pragmatic interface between above and below and can play a role in the quest for the felicitous union of heaven and earth. Mathematics is made flesh in the material vibrations of musical instruments and sounds that are thus thought of in terms of sympathies and antipathies. A determined sound corresponds to a determined planet, the skin use to build a drum corresponds to the animal and the music played on this instrument still produces effect on the animal's word. The very corporality of music is also at stake.

The elements of the musical composition – voices, modes, scales – were not compared to natural and celestial elements just by metaphor but by analogy, which renders these comparisons practical. Each voice corresponds to an element, fire, air, earth and water, and each mode to a planet, therefore natural magic and its medical application as well as astrology and its applications can operate musically.

The composer manipulates the divine mathematical proportions expressing and bringing harmony on earth. Music was called a *divine science* not only because one of its aims was to glorify God, but also because the composer was a creator representing on earth the harmony of his Creator, having received a divine gift. If He arranged everything in numbers, weights and measures, so does the composer.

In the eighteenth century, the epistemology of music changes as the categories of arts and sciences change. The fundamental breaking point in the eighteenth century modifies the relation between music and esotericism.

Esotericism itself is transformed. The occult is the hidden dimension of nature, the power of words, sounds and things. Esotericism and its reflections in musical practice must be approached differently in the pre- and post-Rationalist historical contexts. Magic, astrology and alchemy are practical and philosophical systems with very precise aims. Nature and the celestial world hide things from human understanding. But there is nothing hidden that will not be revealed, and there is nothing secret that will not become known and come to light (Luc 8, 17). It is sufficient to know how to use the occult world to see its effects manifested. Magic, astrology and alchemy are ways to investigate and act on realities. These ways are concealed from the profane, or the unlearned. The learned are able to illuminate the occult world and he or she knows the principles of action within this reality and can read, without being dazzled, the vast book of the worlds above and below. Such knowledge is called 'esoteric', because it is reserved for those who can decipher the signs in this book.

This double notion – to decipher and to use – is central to esotericism, and helps us understand its special relationship with music.
The intangible is clothed in the sensory, and humans in collaboration
with nature, or with the divine, can act wisely. Magic, astrology and
alchemy, in mutual support, serve this end. Their actions may lead to
the unification of terrestrial and celestial natures within either good
or evil moral frameworks, a matter that is troubling to the arbiters of
morality.

Black magic and deterministic astrology are in conflict, respectively
with ethics and with the divine freedom to choose the future. In contrast, natural magic and natural astrology can effectively draw from the
benefits of their knowledge into human life. By turning to the powers
of elements and understanding of celestial dispositions, we can move
beyond the raw suffering of the human condition. Heaven and nature
can carry us to a better future. Natural astrology serves agriculture
and relationships. Blessed sights and smells and magical rites heal our
wounds with their hidden virtues.

The philosopher, the magician and the musician establishes a framework of thinking about the world and the relationships of man with
man and of man with elemental and celestial nature. They include
the various form of esotercisim in their search for the pragmatic and
philosophical actions on intellectual and sensible substance, from an
action of one on an another to an action on destiny.

Music, because of its corporeal but invisible nature, holds a specific position within this invisible relation. Because of its structure and
natural similitude – invisible as the occult, aerial as the *spiritus* of the
man and the world, corporeal as the human and as the celestial bodies – music magnifies its effects on the animate and inanimate things.
The power of sounds, even more the power of musical sound, lies in
its ability to transform the person, to repair a broken harmony in her
soul, to temper the constitution of her body, to help her spirit to find
peace, to help her reach the divine word; the power of musical sound
also attracts spiritual and celestial force on earth, music being a potent
invocator.

The musical, magical and philosophical pragmatism is understand-
able only through the position of the sign within modern society. Each
element is a sign of another element which is the sign of another reality which is the sign of another element etc. Once the interpretative
and analogical logic is engaged, no element escapes it. The root tells
the organ that tells the planet. The flower tells the star that tells the

divine. Stone, plant, root, leaf, metal, fruit, musical note, one thing tells another thing the content of which is the echo of a superior content.

Man remains the object of the dialogue. As microcosm, the centre of all analogies, man is the focal point where, finally, all disciplines meet. The result of these disciplines, from the effective to the speculative power, is valid only in terms of the measure of the zodiacal, musical and elemental human being. Nature and the superior world are inhabited by a crowd of animate and inanimate beings that man tries to understand and with whom he would like to converse. In this conversation, when natural and not demoniac, man does not infringe upon divine rules. The primary cause dictates its willpower to the secondary causes, so that when man speaks to the stars, through magical rites or through music, he performs a sacred act.

If in the large book of the world everything is a sign, then the sign, the bearer of spirit, must be strictly respected. The exact enunciation of the word, its vowels and consonants, its rhythm, and complete respect for the formula, magical or musical, are the indispensable operating tools. The betrayal of the sign breaks the link with the universe. In the best case, it only negates the effect of the sign. At worst, the betrayal counteracts it. The betrayed sign then becomes inoperative or harmful. Here musical stakes are also magical stakes. The musical sign, from the interval to the mode, comprises a significant and efficient force that can be used in astro-magical rites for divinatory or medical outcomes. The twofold meaning of the term "character" becomes evident, and the character as sign reverberates with the planetary and musical character. Any given song is spangled with a constellation of signs: words, melody, rhythm, mode, interval, the components of the composition are as many ingredients to the service of a spiritual recipe and of a speculative action.

Music in relation with other epistemic modes begs new questions of definition. Within the magical and astrological frame, what are the basic features of music? As an aspect of ritual, music is a material reality that is as much fixed as gestural, as much verbal as it is acoustic and rhythmic. The key importance of the word in these rites is the magical echo of the debates on the interactions between text and music that were a focal point for the Renaissance period and still are for musicologists.

Esotericism and its links with music changed radically in the latter half of the eighteenth century. Music was no longer the celestial reality reflected in the earthly one, *musica mundana* with its analogical architecture was no longer the cognitive scaffolding of science such as astronomy. During the nineteenth and twentieth centuries, "esotericism" still covers a knowledge hidden from being understood by the profane. But the world of the individual, profane or initiated, is no longer the same. Magic is an object of ethnological and anthropological study. Astrology is no longer a science – possibly criticised as vain – but a superstition.

The second part of this book, dedicated to music and esotericism in the nineteenth and twentieth centuries, focuses more on technical aspects of music and turns more systematically to musical analysis. Single compositions are considered with regard to the esoteric preoccupations of the composer, whether he or she was affiliated or not with an esoteric society. The debate on cosmic correspondences is part of organisations where composers meet other artists, scientists, scholars and other thinkers. Once again they seek the ancient ideal – a certain union or reunion with a superior world. In the process, the value of the artist is affirmed. The composer reaches for an all-embracing artistic expression, perhaps, in which extra-musical references are encoded. The composer creates a work in which he seeks, possibly, an ideal of total art.

Pragmatism has become more ethereal, even though some facets have survived. The philosophers, magicians and musicians of the early modern period used aroma, image and song in personal and planetary patterns in order to focus these powerful attributes upon the attainment of a specific effect. Following in their stead, the composer aims for a mystical experience. He or she interacts with the world through music, ruled by extra-musical features, from the golden mean to the planetary sigils, or by ineffably superior gestures.

The sacred dimension of the musico-magic act has endured into the nineteenth and twentieth centuries, as is evident from the case studies presented in this book. The sacred gesture continues to be set through musical and artistic creation even if the origin, the practices and possibly the significance of this gesture have undergone irrevocable mutations. The question of the need for an absolute remains and passes through the search of the sacred, through the prism of music.

Noting the influences of esoteric ideas (Rosicrucian and Pythagorean number symbolism, for example) is nothing new in musicology – hermeneutists have interpreted and even overinterpreted this material for some time. But by surveying these influences chronologically one can help to map the smooth and rough transitions in their development. It is not a mere reprocessing or re-actualisation of the past occult knowledge for the sake of a new philosophy. Nether is it a simple appropriation of an esoteric tradition to upgrade the artistic creation. The chronological course of the cases presented in this book shows the persistence and the transformations of the interactions between music and esotericism.

The book is divided into three parts. The first part, "Early Modern Occult Knowledge and Music", chronologically arranged, offers a multifaceted point of view taking into account two different aspects. The first aspect is the link between music, magnetism, medicine, magic and astrology. The opening chapter deals with the attractive power of music and magnetism discussed in Adelard of Bath's *On the Same and the Different* and his account on music's effects on human beings and animals. The attractiveness of music and of the magnet is then considered as two aspects of the same natural phenomenon. The starting point of this analysis is the *Great Introduction to Astrology* of the medieval Arabic scientist Abu Ma'shar. The same question is than analyzed in the works of the Roman baroque polymath Athanasius Kircher and leads to a reflection on the power of music as a medicine. The next chapter deals with medicine, magic and music within the *Le Livre des eschez amoureux moralisés* of Évrart de Conty, Charles V's physician. The use of speculative music within metaphysical, cosmological and human questions is developed and the originality of the Évrart de Conty determined. This fourteenth century glimpse at music, magic and medicine are completed by the chapters of Concetta Pennuto and Marta Moiso dealing with these disciplines in the sixteenth and seventeenth centuries. The chapter by Pennuto gives a comprehensive understanding of music in Giovanni Battista della Porta's *Magia Naturalis*: the power of music, from sounds to the material of the musical instrument, as seen in the light of Renaissance theory and the utilization of music in medicine. The chapter by Moiso offers a deep analysis of Tommaso Campanella's use of music within the *De Sensu rerum et magia* and the *Theology*. Marsilio Ficino and Bernardino Telesio's musico-magical theories are first stated so that Campanella's works are re-evaluated within their cultural background. The evolution of Campanella's thoughts about music, notably comparing the two mentioned works, is also analysed. These chapters present a kaleidoscope of the links between music, magnetism, magic and medicine through various authors from varied cultural, linguistic and religious backgrounds. They clarify the European and extra-European dimension of the tradition of the association between music, magnetism, magic and medicine. This offers the reader, at the same time, a synthesis of the problematic along with a very precise and deep look at some known and lesser known individuals.

The chapters by Brigitte Van Wymeersch and David Juste are dedicated to René Descartes, Marin Mersenne, Nicolas-Claude Fabri de Peiresc, Pierre Gassendi and Johannes Kepler. These two chapters shed a new light on the interactions between science, esotericism and music. The first offers an overview of the famous mystery of the sounding of cords on a musical instrument without it being touched. This is but an emblematic case that reveals the fundamental change in the epistemologic concepts during the seventeenth century. The transformation from a magical explanation of the mysterious sounds of the cords to an acoustic explanation of the same phenomena, in terms of physical sciences, is one of the most important examples of how music was used as an object of experimentation leading to new scientific meaning. The last chapter gives a new look at Kepler's theory by demonstrating how music – which was intrinsically linked to aspects in astrology since Ptolemy – has been used by Kepler in his reform of astrology. This new light on Kepler's reform of astrology is of particular importance to the understanding of the place of musical theory in the seventeenth century scientific mind.

The second approach consists of chapters dealing with composers and their relation to esotericism. The chapter by Marjorie Roth is a fully documented investigation on Orlando di Lasso's motet cycle *Prophetiae Sibyllarum*. This musical enigma, unsolved by musicologists, is given a new interpretation. The starting point is to clarify some still unexplained musical and textual components of the motet cycle in the Sibylline tradition and some of their developments in Italian Renaissance esotericism. It takes into account the tradition of the spiritual alchemy, as well as the biblical tradition of prophecies, to reach a fresh interpretation of di Lasso's music and its context. The chapter by Anthony Rooley deals with John Dowland's music, examining the private circle of lyrics from Elizabethan times, at the English 'School of Night', and the Hermetic poetry within seventeenth century England. The article points out the interest in this esoteric art shown by patrons and noble families, as well as by artists, and thus gives a twofold reading of the sources – on the esoteric meaning of text and context. The chapter by Barbara Kennedy analyses the figure of Orpheus, the musician and healer, within seventeenth century poetry. Ficino's view on Orpheus and the interpretation of Orpheus as a precursor of Christ, whose musical power maintains universal harmony, introduces an analysis of John Dowland and of the poet-composer and physician Thomas Campion's uses of Orpheus. Campion's poetry shows his multifaceted concept of music not only as an access to God but also as an instrument for astrology. In this respect, the point of view of some composers meets the physical and philosophical attempts of theoreticians showing how these two approaches are complementary.

The short middle section of the book, entitled "Philosophical intermezzo", is composed of two chapters on music in the theosophical wisdom of the Ancients and on music for its esoteric value in the thinking of some nineteenth century philosophers. The first chapter (Maël Mathieu and Daniel Cohen) is a precise account of music in the works of the Neo-Platonist Proclus's *Commentary on the Republic* and *Commentary on the Timaeus* leading to the central place of music being considered as the higher form of philosophy. The musical structure has structural and symbolical sympathies with the universe, reality and soul. The diatonic mode is shown to have singular affinities with the dialectic method, thus music is seen as the purest rational method to reach divine principles. The second chapter (Jacques Amblard) deals with the nineteenth century German philosophers Hegel, Schopenhauer and Nietzsche and their approach to music and, or as, an esotericism. This chapter gives a definition of "esotericism" for the nineteenth and twentieth centuries, and is therefore also an introduction to the second part of the book, which is also arranged chronologically.

The first chapter of the second part of the book (Tim Rudbøg), introduces the power of sound in Helena Petrovna Blavatsky's 'Esoteric Instructions'. It begins, in continuation of the reflection of the last chapter of the "Philosophical intermezzo", with a definition of "music" and "Western esotericism". This is followed by a nineteenth century echo of the notion analyzed in the first part of the book. The relation between music and the cosmos as well as the Platonic-Pythagorean tradition are explained within the nineteenth century prospective in terms of similitude and difference with the Antique and Renaissance points of view. Sound, as a number, is then analysed in Blavatsky's cosmology and "Esoteric Instructions", her esoteric instrument and method addressed to students of Theosophy with the aim of developing spiritual powers and relations with the divine.

The chapter by Judith Crispin introduces Ferruccio Busoni's musical esotericism by giving a reading of his opera *Doktor Faust*, the symbol of his mystical concept of music. It portrays how the act of composition itself is, for Busoni, an occult practice similar to magic. The sacred, spiritual, magical and mystical dimensions of composition are revealed in numerous ways, from literary testimonies (in the writings of Busoni for example) to musical ones. The chapter by Barbara Aniello is on the esoteric influences in Aleksandr Skrjabin's works, mainly *Poem of Extase, Prometheus* or the poem of fire, *The Mystherium* and their theosophical content. The artistic context, from poetry to dance, is traced to show a common theosophical thought. The chapter by Wouter Hanegraaff, echoing the one by Rudbøg, also focuses on the definition of "Western esotericism" dealing with musical esotericism within the works of Anton Webern and the second Viennese school. The interest for esotericism in Arnold Schönberg's works and writings is demonstrated, first through anecdotal influences of the composer, for example his interest for the Jewish cabbala, and then within his compositions, including his opera *Moses and Aron*. Schönberg's and primarily Webern's musical esotericism is analyzed in terms of the belief they share in music as a privileged method of gnosis and as part of cosmic law. The musical esotericism of Webern, influenced by Schönberg, Swedenborg and Goethe, is then analysed in depth through his work, and through his belief in the correspondence between natural, spiritual and musical hidden laws to build an image of the universal order in the quest of the Absolute. The last chapter closes the loop by inserting the post-modern musical novel of Helmut Krausser, *Melodien oder Nachträge zum Quecksilbernen Zeitalter*, published in 1993. From Orlando di Lasso or John Dowland to Busoni or Webern, from Abu Ma'shar or Évrart de Conty to Ficino or Kepler, this collection of essays on music and esotericism offers a framework in which to to ponder the multifaceted relationships between music and esotericism, as well as the impact of these relationships within cultural history.

PART ONE

EARLY MODERN OCCULT KNOWLEDGE AND MUSIC

MUSIC AND MAGNETISM, FROM ABU MA'SHAR TO KIRCHER

Charles Burnett

I would like to start with a story. A peasant is in the fields in Puglia, on the heel of Italy, on a hot summer's day, taking his siesta in the open air, without any boots or gloves protecting his hands and feet. Along comes a spider, and bites his exposed flesh. He notices it hardly more than he would notice the sting of a fly. The poison gradually spreads through his body, until eventually he loses his appetite; he becomes feverous, and his skin pales to a jaundiced colour. Eventually, after a whole year has passed and the same season returns, in the heat of the sun, he throws away all modesty and dances like a maniac. The doctors try out all kinds of remedies, the Theriac, the Orvietan potion, the great Mithridatum, the dust of an eagle's stone; all to no avail. Only a musical note or a melody which contains the same ratios as the original poison has any effect: it forces the man, willy nilly, to dance and dance until he sweats out the venom, and collapses from exhaustion.

The story, or rather a series of case histories, can be found in the *Magnes* or *De arte Magnetica* ('on the magnet', or 'on the magnetic art') of the Jesuit polymath, Athanasius Kircher (1601–1680), which was published in Rome in 1641. Kircher is, of course, describing the phenomenon of tarantism, but what is striking is that this occurs within a section on 'Musical magnetism' in this vast text. What does music share in common with magnetism?

The most obvious way in which music and a magnet resemble each other is that they both attract. The attractive power of music is described frequently enough in Western literature from Plato's *Republic* to the pied piper of Hamlyn. Among these is the discussion in Adelard of Bath's *On the Same and the Different*, a text on the moral value of the seven liberal arts, which gives a very sympathetic account of the fifth liberal art – music. Having described music's effects on human beings (including his own experience of a little boy moving his hands and fingers in time to the music when he himself played a 'cithara'), he describes music's influence on brute animals (in this instance, perhaps significantly, calling them 'mute animals' rather than 'brute animals', i.e. living beings which simply do not have the powers of speech):

> In mute animals the force of music has a not inconsiderable effect. Among the English the very fish are driven into nets by the sweet sound of a bell floating on the surface of the water. Among the Parthians the songs of men lull the deer into sleep so that there is no need for nets. Birds, too, are led into snares by songs.[1]

From ancient times the magnet, or more precisely, the lodestone, was also known for its powers of attraction, specifically its ability to attract iron. Plato, again, in his dialogue *Ion*, writes that '...the stone which Euripides named a magnet, but most people call the "Heraclea stone", not only attracts iron rings, but also imparts to them a power whereby they in turn are able to do the very same things as the stone, and attract other rings'. Galen compared the lodestone to cathartic drugs that attract certain qualities, and to drugs that remove thorns and arrowpoints and draw out animal poisons or arrow-tip poisons. Dioscorides recommended the lodestone for 'drawing out gross humors'.[2]

It would seem natural to see the attractiveness of music and of the magnet as two aspects of the same natural phenomenon. This, however, as far as I know, was rarely stated. Something that comes close to this, however, occurs in the cosmology of the astrologer, Abu Maʿshar.

Abu Maʿshar (787–886) wrote a *Great Introduction to Astrology*, the first book of which includes a detailed discussion on how the stars cause effects in the sublunar world (Book 1, chapter 3). It is in this context that he mentions both the magnet and music. The relevant sections consist of two paragraphs, which follow one another, but are not entirely consistent with each other. First, he differentiates between the two ways in which one thing can act upon another: action by direct contact (e.g., fire burning wood) and action through a medium. Action through a medium, in turn, is divided into three: voluntary action (a man throws a stone and hits something), proximate medium (fire warms water through the medium of the cauldron) and distant medium. Abu Maʿshar illustrates this last action primarily by means of the magnet:

---

[1] Adelard of Bath, *Conversations with His Nephew*, 52–53.
[2] For these references see Roller, *The De magnete of William Gilbert*, 13–20.

> Like the magnet stone which naturally moves iron and draws it towards itself from a certain distance by the mediation of the air, because this stone has the nature to move and attract iron, and iron has the nature to receive movement from the stone and be drawn towards it because of its connection to it by nature.... Sometimes the iron which is adjacent to the stone is attracted to it, and brings with it whatever of its kind happens at that time to be attached to it or close to it (compare the passage of Plato's *Ion* just quoted).... Many kinds of substances and drugs may be found which produce by their nature movement and attraction of something else towards them from nearby or from a distance. It is in accordance with this third kind of action that the celestial bodies move the terrestrial bodies and change them and their conditions from one to another....[3]

A paragraph later Abu Ma'shar turns to the question of the difference between something being *caused* by and something *resulting from* something else. 'Cause' and 'effect' can be seen in voluntary action (standing and sitting) and natural action (fire burning wood). But:

> What results from another thing is different from this: it is the movement and change that occurs in one thing as a result of something else, when the two things are separated by a certain distance, such as blushing as a result of shame, and pallor as a result of fear, and the effect on the man's movement of soul and limbs of the song of a singer skilled in singing, and the movement, tremor, surprise and confusion in the lover when he sees the beloved, and the bashfulness in the beloved when he sees the lover, and the result of movement and attraction in iron as a result of the magnet-stone.[4]

So here we have the effect of music (as in the story of the little boy in Adelard's *On the Same and the Different*) described as analogous to that of the magnet (and analogous again to the effects of the stars). Abu Ma'shar, however, is not being completely consistent (it is as if he got the two paragraphs from two different sources). In the first paragraph the last division is *action at a distance*, in the second it is *consequent activity*. So, in the second division, blushing and pallor can only with difficulty be described as being 'action at a distance'. It can be noted that Abu Ma'shar's work was translated into Latin twice in the mid-twelfth century – once in a very literal way by John of Seville, and a second time in an intelligent paraphrase by Hermann

---

[3] Abu Ma'shar, *Liber introductorii maioris ad scientiam judiciorum astrorum*, II, 21 (Arabic original), and V, 24 (John of Seville's translation).
[4] Ibid., II, 22 (Arabic) and VI, 410–411 (revision of John of Seville's translation).

of Carinthia. And Hermann, significantly, omits the mention of the magnet in the second paragraph perhaps because he was aware of a certain inconsistency between the two paragraphs.[5]

The realisation that a magnet did not only attract iron (or repel it) but also would orient in a north-south direction when set free to turn does not appear in Europe until the late twelfth century. Thereafter, much was written on the powers and uses of the magnet. The greatest medieval work on the magnet in the Middle Ages was that of Peter Peregrinus of Maricourt (1269). This was a source of the even greater work of the early modern period, William Gilbert's *De magnete* (1600). Neither of these works, however, as far as I can see, brought music into consideration.[6]

It is, rather, the massive work of Athanasius Kircher which addresses the question of music and magnetism.[7] His *Magnes* is one of the earliest of his large compositions. It deals with every aspect of the magnet. A translation of the tortuous title would go something like this:

> 'The Magnet' or 'On the Magnetic Art': a three-part work which, aside from explaining by a new method the whole nature of the magnet and its use in all the arts and sciences, includes many hitherto unknown secrets of nature from among the forces and prodigious effects of magnetic and other hidden motions of nature in physical, chemical and mathematical experiments of every kind.[8]

---

[5] Ibid., VIII, 10–11 (Hermann's translation): acciditque dum lapis ferrum trahit et materiam aliam plerumque ferro coherentem trahit. Hicque modus alterum in alterum nature proprietate quadam agendi in multis tam herbis quam lapidibus invenitur...hoc ergo modo celestis essentia in inferioris mundi naturam agere omnino videtur.... Quod vero propter aliud fit ab hiis diversum. Nec enim faciente alio fit, sed alio precedente nature quadam cognatione sequitur ut verecundiam rubor, timorem pallor, musica modulamina animi corporisque motus consoni. Ad hunc igitur modum celestia corpora cum super hunc mundum motu naturali ferantur, consequuntur alligati sibi inferioris mundi elementorum motus naturales generationes rerum et corruptiones producentes.

[6] Petrus Peregrinus de Maricourt, *Opera*, 13–109, Gilbert, *De magnete*.

[7] For an introduction to this less-studied work of Kircher, see Baldwin, 'Kircher's Magnetic Investigations'.

[8] *Magnes sive De Arte Magnetica: opus tripartitum quo praeterquam quod universa magnetis Natura, eiusque in omnibus Artibus et Scientiis usus nova methodo explicetur, e viribus quoque et prodigiosis effectibus Magneticarum, aliarumque abditarum Naturae motionum in Elementis, Lapidibus, Plantis et Animalibus elucescentium, multa hucusque incognita Naturae arcana per Physica, Medica, Chymica, et Mathematica omnis generis experimenta recluduntur.*

And indeed, in its 900 odd pages it covers: the names of the magnet, what the ancients knew about it, the invention of the nautical compass (*pyxis nautica*), terrestrial magnetism, the variations in the direction in which the needle points, depending on location, the influence of the shape of the magnet, the magnetic astrolabe, a magnetic instrument for measuring heights, breadths and depths, magnetic onomancy by which whatever noun, verb or letter anyone conceives in his/her mind is shown by the magnetic statue in those things which are inscribed on the brim, a magnetic instrument by which a conversation can be carried on between participants who are a league away from each other, and so on.

The third of the three books of the *Magnes* is entitled 'Mundus sive catena magnetica' ('the universe or the magnetic chain' – with an obvious allusion to the Golden Chain) and addresses questions of whether the elements are attracted and repulsed because of magnetism and whether it is magnetism that causes the Sun and the Moon to effect the tides and by which plants draw their nourishment from the soil. Like the classical medical writers Kircher discusses the use of the magnet in medical cures, but adds a chapter on the magnetism of the elixir of life. But the vast book reaches its climax and conclusion with three significant sections (*partes*): 'on the attractive force of the imaginative power', 'on the magnetism of music', and 'on the magnetism of love'.[9] What more can be added after that, other than the 'The magnet epiloque of the magnetic universe: namely God, the magnet at the centre of all things. The End'.[10]

What then, is the magnetism of music? Kircher explains at the beginning of this section that 'There is so much magnetism in musical modulation (*moduli*) – so much efficacy of the attractive virtue (*tractiva virtus*) that it is not without reason that the Ancients presented Orpheus the musician as attracting animals, trees and even the stones themselves by the sound of the lyre'.[11] Kircher explains this efficacy as being due to Orpheus's knowledge of the harmony of the celestial spheres. Thus he was able to call down (*devocare*) their influence and

---

[9] Kircher, *Magnes*, unpaginated list of chapter headings: De vi attractiva potentiae imaginativae; De Magnetismo Musicae; De Magnetismo Amoris.

[10] Ibid., Synopsis totius operis, sig. b8v: Mundi Magnetici Magnes Epilogus, idest, Deus rerum omnium centralis magnes. Finis.

[11] Ibid., 840: Tantus inest Musicis modulis Magnetismus, tanta tractivae virtutis efficacia, ut non sine ratione Prisci Orpheum Musicum animalia, sylvas, atque adeo ipsa saxa lyrae sono trahentem produxerint.

force and, relying on this, attract whatever he wished. For, by knowing by what ratio and harmony (*concentus*) each thing in nature was constituted and composed and which planet it obeyed and was subject to, Orpheus could accommodate musical ratios to both them and their planets, and entice even inanimate things into motion. For there are seeds of harmony (*semina harmoniae*) in all things, like hidden sparks which iron entices out of the flint stone.[12]

The magnetic force of music, moving everything (*magnetica vis musicae omnia movens*) is obvious in man too. Here Kircher discusses music's powers of attraction *and* repulsion, so distinctive of the magnet:

> Apt *moduli* and songs (*cantilenae*) which soothe the mind, refresh and calm the heart, inept and unharmonious sounds make him agitated and uneasy.[13]

And (echoing Adelard) it is not only man who is affected in this way, but also beasts:

> Animals themselves are captured by musical *moduli*. Elephants are enticed (on the authority of Strabo) by drums, swans by the cithara, birds by the sweet flute in the hands of the deceptive fowler...[14]

'Let us see', then, Kircher continues, 'what magnetism there is in music for attracting souls'.[15] In fact, 'some sounds are so apt and harmonious, so sweetly influencing, that they seem even to draw the soul out of itself'.[16] The influence of the first chapter of Boethius's *De institutione musica* is clear in Kircher's arguments and examples. But Kircher interprets Boethius's words on the powerful effects of music in terms of his own very broad concept of magnetism. Another subtlety he adds is that music does not influence the soul directly, since the soul is immortal and immaterial. Rather, it moves the *spirit*, which is the soul's instrument and, since it is the 'most subtle vapour of the blood, it is very moble and thin, and so is easily aroused by air that

[12] Ibid., 841.

[13] Ibid., 842: aptis modulis et cantilenis animum delinientibus <cor> non remittatur, contra indecentibus et inconcinnis angatur et restringatur.

[14] Ibid., 842: Musicis modulis non homines tantum, sed et animalia ipsa capiuntur, alliciuntur Elephantes, Strabone teste, tympanis, Cygni cithara, fistula dulce canit volucrem cum decipit auceps....

[15] Ibid., 843: videamus quis Musicae ad trahendos animos insit magnetismus.

[16] Ibid., 843: quidam <soni> adeo apti et concinni, ita suaviter influentes, ut animam extra se rapere videantur.

has been struck harmonically'.[17] Kircher manages to incorporate a lot of contemporary music theory into this section: on consonances and dissonances (e.g., he follows the just intonation advocated by Zarlino, in which 3rds and 6ths are consonances), and on the *tonoi* (Dorian, Lydian, Mixolydian, Aeolian, and the Greek 'first, second, third' and 'fourth' *tonoi*). Of all musical forms 'fugues' are the sweetest.[18]

Kircher goes on to describe a series of experiments designed to show the effects of music: strings vibrating in sympathy (which demonstrate how the human spirit moves when the outside air vibrates in harmony), and sounds augmented when sung within a vaulted building. But the rest of the section – indeed, half the entire length of the section – on the magnetism of music, is devoted to one subject alone: tarantism.[19]

This is a condition thought to be caused by the bite of a tarantula spider, and prevalent in the area of Tarento in the heel of Italy. According to Kircher, the bite affects different people in different ways depending on the nature of the spider, and the different temperaments of the victims. One 'tarantatus' will run about continuously, another will laugh, another will cry, another will shout out, another will sleep, another will not be able to sleep, another will be bilious, another will jump around, another will sweat, another will fall into fits of shivering. In each case the musical ratios in the individuals' ears will be attracted to corresponding ratios in the venom. But there are visual correspondences too: the victim will be pathologically attracted to the colour of the spider that bit him. Some crave for green, others for yellow, others for red. When they come across an object of the desired colour they are so obsessed by it that, like famished lions, they tear it with their teeth, but then they embrace it like men madly in love, with their mouths gaping and their eyes streaming with tears.[20]

---

[17] Ibid., 846: Spiritus enim huiusmodi cum subtilissimus quidam sanguinis vapor sit, admodum mobilis ac tenuis, facile ab aere harmonice concitato incitatur.

[18] Ibid., 849: Primo artificiosa tonorum mistura, variaeque sonorum ad arsin et thesin se syncopantium colligationes, quibus consona dissonis adeo strictis amicitiae legibus connectuntur, ut nihil suavius percipi possit, quas variae vocum diminutiones fugarumque artificiose contextarum mutuae amicaeque insecutiones plurimum adaugent.

[19] Among the large literature on tarantism, the most relevant and complete are Ernesto de Martino, *La terra del rimorso*, and Gentilcore, 'Ritualized Illness'.

[20] Kircher, *Magnes*, 868.

The most obvious differences in reaction depend on the preva-
lence in the *tarantatus* of one of the four elements: fire, water, air
and earth. Those of a fiery temperament when aroused by music rush
about swinging (*gestientes*) a drawn sword or some other shimmer-
ing, flame-coloured weapon; throwing their bodies around in different directions and gesticulating crazily, they now catch the sword in
their right hand, now in their left, and now in their mouths. Those of
a watery temperament desire eagerly to see in the middle of the dance
floor, basins full of water surrounded by green foliage, into which they
plunge their arms and their whole head and splash about like ducks
flapping their wings in a pond. Those of an airy temperament, affect
to speak Spanish to make themselves seem grand and noble, with their
heads in the air, or they dangle from trees, especially those who are
bitten by tarantulas spinning a thread. Those of an earthy disposition,
after dancing for a while, slump to the ground and hug their knees
with their arms so tightly that they seem wrapped in sorrow and grief,
while others stretch out on the ground and strike the earth with their
hands and feet like epilectics or lunatics.[21]

All these reactions are aroused, compounded and resolved according to the ratios and the harmonies of the pitch or the melody. These
affect the soul and the body of the *tarantati* with such a passion that
immediately on hearing the musical instrument they are absorbed into
its sweetness. They halt as if stunned, and then, full of joy, they repeat
the dancing and in extraordinary gestures (*gesticulationes*) show forth
their happiness and great delight in the compatible harmony. But if
whilst they are dancing, discord or a harmony which is incompatible
with the poison arises, whether by mistake, or because of the mischief
of the musicians, they contort their heads and necks, and roll their
eyes, as if they are suffering from great violence and pain.[22]

Kircher then describes the different melodies that are used for different kinds of poison, most of which agree in the *tonus* called the 'L'aria
Turchesca'. The songs are made to fit the obsessions of the *tarantati*:
for those who are affected by green, the songs refer to flowering gardens, fields and pleasant glades; for those affected by red, martial melodies, iambic, bacchic and dithyrambic metres are used; for those who
rejoice in water, songs of love, evoking rivers, springs and waterfalls,

---

[21] Ibid., pp. 869–870.
[22] Ibid., p. 870.

are composed. These melodies not only cure sufferers from tarantism, but also anyone afflicted with feelings of melancholy, excessive love, anger and revenge.[23] Examples of the melodies follow.[24]

Kircher explains in detail how music has the force to expel the poison of the tarantula. The plucked or bowed strings arouse the air into that mode in which they themselves move, and by this proportional mixture of sounds they arouse a pleasant harmony in the ears and mind. The air moves the spirit, thinning it out; the spirit, becoming less dense, acts upon the muscles, arteries and innermost fibres, so that they unlock the hidden force of the poison. In the same process the spirit, muscles and arteries become warm and a certain itchiness and ticklishness arises. The patient, pleasurably affected by this tickling sensation, breaks out into dancing. Movement of the whole body and the humours follows the dancing; heat follows the movement; a relaxation of the whole body and the opening of the pores follows the heat; and, finally, the breathing out of the venomous breath follows the opening of the pores.[25]

What makes tarantism relevant to magnetism, I suppose, is that the music is *drawing out* the poison, as the lodestone draws the iron, and that this is possible because of the sharing of the same ratios between the patient's complexion and the music: the sympathy between what draws and what is drawn, though this is never explicitly stated.

At the end of the section Kircher writes, with a rare touch of humour: 'Now at last, tired out by the tarantine dancing, let us betake ourselves to love, as a sure stopping place, an end to our agitation and a centre of quiet.'[26] And here it is appropriate to end this article too.

---

[23] Ibid., 871.

[24] Several performances of tarantellas based on the melodies provided by Kircher have been recorded: e.g., Ensemble L'Arpeggiata (Christina Pluhar), La Tarantella: Antidotum Tarantulae (Alpha SA503) and Ensemble Terra d'Otranto, Tarantule Antidoti et Follie, produced by the Museo Provinciale "S. Castromediano" of the Provincia di Lecce. I am grateful to Sietske Fransen and Margherita Fiorello for introducing me to these two CDs.

[25] Kircher, Magnes, 882–883.

[26] Ibid., 891: Sed iam tandem saltu Tarentino defatigati, ad Amorem veluti ad fidam stationem et agitationis nostrae terminum centrumque quietis nos conferamus.

BIBLIOGRAPHY

Abu Ma'shar, *Liber introductorii maioris ad scientiam judiciorum astrorum*, ed. R. Lemay, 9 vols., Naples: Istituto universitario orientale 1996–1997.

Adelard of Bath, *Conversations with His Nephew*, ed. and trans. C. Burnett et al., Cambridge: Cambridge University Press 1998.

Baldwin, M., 'Kircher's Magnetic Investigations', in Daniel Stolzenberg, *The Great Art of Knowing: The Baroque Encyclopedia of Athanasius Kircher*, Stanford and Fiesole: Stanford University Libraries and Edizioni Cadmo 2001, 85–92.

De Martino, E., *La terra del rimorso*, Milan: Il Saggiatore, 1961.

Gentilcore, D., 'Ritualized Illness and Music Therapy: Views of Tarantism in the Kingdom of Naples', in: Horden, P., *Music as Medicine: The History of Music Therapy since Antiquity*, Aldershot: Ashgate 2000, 255–272.

Gilbert, William, *De magnete*, London: The Chiswick Press 1600.

Kircher, Athanasius, *Magnes sive De Arte Magnetica*, Rome: Sumptibus Hermanni Scheus, ex typographia Ludovici Grignani 1641.

Petrus Peregrinus de Maricourt, *Opera: Epistula de magnete, nova compositio astrolabii particularis*, ed. L. Sturlese and R. B. Thomson, Pisa: Scuola Normale Superiore 1995.

Roller, D. H. D., *The* De magnete *of William Gilbert*, Amsterdam: Hertzberger 1959.

LE MÉDECIN ET LES SONS : MUSIQUE ET MAGIE DANS 'LE LIVRE DES ESCHEZ AMOUREUX MORALISÉS' D'ÉVRART DE CONTY

Amandine Mussou

English summary: In this paper, I will focus on the *De Musica* Évrart de Conty, Charles V's physician, inserts in *Le Livre des eschez amoureux moralisés* (ca. 1400). He actually rewrites about one thousand verses from the poem *Les Eschés amoureux* (ca. 1370–1380) but adds a long digression about magic. Danielle Jacquart has interpreted this addition in political terms. I would like to go one step further and claim that music is a way to include reflexions on esotericism in this encyclopedia. Considered as a science of proportions and an art of sounds, music can be a model to think universal harmony but can also be linked to more polemical kinds of knowledge.

Évrart de Conty, médecin de Charles V, commente avant 1405, année de sa mort, le récit en vers des *Eschés amoureux* dans un long ouvrage en prose, *Le Livre des eschez amoureux moralisés*[1]. S'inscrivant dans la trame narrative du *Roman de la Rose*, *Les Eschés amoureux* relatent notamment une partie d'échecs allégorique au cours de laquelle le narrateur est maté par une jeune fille dont il s'éprend. L'attribution du poème est actuellement discutée. La critique le considérait jusque-là comme anonyme ; désormais, il est permis de penser qu'Évrart de Conty en soit également l'auteur[2]. Si *Le Livre des eschez amoureux moralisés* semble limiter son entreprise de moralisation à environ un cinquième du poème initial – c'est-à-dire à l'épisode de la partie d'échecs –, le commentaire inclut néanmoins certains développements

---

[1] Aucune édition intégrale du récit en vers n'est disponible à ce jour. Il existe cependant des éditions partielles dont celles de Kraft et de Raimondi qui permettent d'avoir accès aux neuf mille premiers vers du texte. Pour le commentaire en prose, voir l'édition de Guichard-Tesson et de Roy.

[2] Voir notamment, au sujet de cette attribution, Guichard-Tesson, « Évrart de Conty, poète, traducteur et commentateur ». Dans l'édition des *Eschés amoureux* qu'ils préparent, à paraître chez Droz, O'Sullivan et Heyworth s'opposent toutefois à cette attribution.

présents dans le poème au-delà de cet épisode narratif. Le récit en vers est en effet bipartite : une première partie retrace les pérégrinations du narrateur jusqu'au Verger d'Amour et à sa défaite aux échecs – il s'agit des neuf mille premier vers. La déesse de l'entendement Pallas survient ensuite et délivre un long discours de plus de vingt mille vers, abordant des sujets aussi variés que la distinction entre vie voluptueuse, vie active et vie contemplative, un éloge de la ville de Paris, les bienfaits de la musique *etc.* Ce dernier passage[3] est largement amplifié dans *Le Livre des eschez amoureux moralisés*, et le commentateur justifie s'être attardé sur ce sujet en renvoyant notamment à l'intérêt qu'il y porte[4]. Dans son commentaire, Évrart de Conty propose un véritable *De musica*, intégré dans une description des sept arts libéraux : il s'agit de l'un des nombreux « petits traités » inclus dans la trame de cet ouvrage encyclopédique[5].

Après avoir rapidement évoqué le *trivium* – la grammaire, la logique et la rhétorique –, le commentateur s'attarde davantage sur les arts du *quadrivium* – l'arithmétique, la géométrie, l'astronomie et la musique. Si cette dernière occupe traditionnellement la deuxième place dans l'enseignement quadrivial[6], l'auteur la fait figurer en ultime position et lui attribue le plus important volume textuel. Il se livre à une relecture détaillée du passage sur la musique des *Eschés amoureux*[7] et conserve tous les éléments présents dans la version en vers en réorganisant quelque peu le propos et en le glosant largement[8]. Un ajout important est immédiatement repérable : dans *Le Livre des eschez amoureux moralisés*, Évrart de Conty clôt son *De musica* par une lon-

---

[3] La seule édition disponible de ce passage – de nos jours difficilement lisible dans l'unique manuscrit l'ayant conservé (Dresden, Sächsische Landesbibliothek, Oc. 66, fol. 130v°–137r°) – est celle d'Abert.

[4] « Et se je y suis arresté longuement, ce m'a fait la matere, qui en est sy plaisans que cellui qui s'y applique a envis s'en depart, et ce aussi que l'acteur du livre rimé dessusdit longuement s'y arreste [...]. » [Et je m'y suis longuement attardé en raison du sujet, qui est si plaisant qu'on ne s'en sépare qu'à contrecœur ; je m'y suis attardé également parce que l'auteur du livre en vers mentionné précédemment s'y est lui-même longuement attardé.], Évrart de Conty, *Le Livre des eschez amoureux moralisés*, 207. Les traductions, dans la suite de l'article, sont les nôtres.

[5] Badel, *Le Roman de la rose au XIVᵉ siècle*, 311.

[6] Voir Meyer, « Mathématique et musique au Moyen Âge ».

[7] Pour une table comparée des deux versions du développement sur la musique, voir l'introduction proposée par Hyatte et Ponchard-Hyatte, dans Évrart de Conty (attribué à), *L'Harmonie des sphères*, x–xi.

[8] Évrart de Conty, *Le Livre des eschez amoureux moralisés*, 135–208. La digression sur la magie occupe les pages 197 à 208 de l'édition.

gue digression sur la magie, absente du texte original. La version en vers contenait quelques remarques éparses sur les méfaits de la magie en matière d'amour, mais nulle trace – du moins dans les deux manuscrits inachevés que nous avons conservés[9] – d'un développement théorique comparable à celui du glossateur[10]. Le commentaire se propose certes d'élucider le poème initial et amplifie à cet égard souvent sa source, comme en témoignent les tout premiers mots du texte :

> Ce present livre fut fait et ordené principalment a l'instance d'un autre, fait en rimes nagueres, et de nouvel venu a cognoissance, qui est intitulé *Des Eschez amoureux* ou *Des Eschez d'amours*, aussi come pour declairier aucunes choses que la rime contient qui semblent estre obscures et estranges de prime face[11]. [Ce livre fut écrit principalement à l'instar d'un autre ouvrage, écrit naguère en vers et récemment découvert, qui s'intitule *Des Échecs amoureux* ou *Des Échecs d'amour*, afin d'éclaircir certains passages en vers, qui paraissent obscurs et étranges de prime abord.]

Malgré cette justification, l'insertion d'un tel codicille sur la magie à cet endroit ne laisse pas de surprendre. Dans la version en vers, Pallas intégrait son «petit traité» sur la musique dans un passage concernant l'éducation des enfants. En commentant *Les Eschés amoureux*, Évrart de Conty a choisi d'extraire ces réflexions théoriques de leur décor initial pour les insérer au sein d'une étude systématique des sept arts libéraux. L'accent se déplace ainsi de l'une à l'autre des versions: si le contenu est globalement le même – à l'exception notable de la digression sur la magie –, le cotexte charge ce passage d'un sens nouveau. Le statut de la musique au sein des différents types de savoirs convoqués par cette œuvre à visée encyclopédique est à examiner.

Homme de science et de cour, puisqu'il a été maître régent de la faculté de médecine de Paris pendant plus de cinquante ans et médecin particulier de Charles V[12], Évrart de Conty accorde à la musique une place primordiale. Dans le sillage de son texte-source, il fait de cet

---

[9] Le manuscrit le plus complet est celui de Dresde, précédemment cité. Le manuscrit de Venise, Biblioteca Marciana, fr. app. 23, est fragmentaire.

[10] L'une des sources possibles de ce développement nous semble être la seconde moitié de la deuxième partie du *De configurationibus qualitatum et motuum* de Nicole Oresme (chapitres XXV à XL). L'auteur introduit des réflexions sur la magie également après avoir évoqué les pouvoirs de la musique.

[11] Évrart de Conty, *Le Livre des eschez amoureux moralisés*, 2.

[12] Nous ne disposons pas de renseignements très nombreux au sujet d'Évrart de Conty. Toutefois, pour plus de précisions biographiques, voir notamment l'introduction d'Évrart de Conty, *Le Livre des eschez amoureux moralisés*, liv–lvi.

art un modèle de pensée universel, permettant de comprendre et de rendre compte de l'ensemble du monde en le mesurant à l'aune de la consonance. En ajoutant le développement sur la magie, il semble également considérer la musique comme un point de passage privilégié entre discours scientifiques autorisés et mise en question de certaines pratiques. Les liens entre musique, magie et médecine sont très sensibles chez cet homme dont la vision du monde est imprégnée d'un savoir médical[13]. Entre recours à l'explication scientifique et reconnaissance de certains pouvoirs magiques de la musique, le commentateur construit sa théorie musicale en confrontant l'art des proportions et des sons à d'autres types de discours plus ou moins savants[14].

Des échecs à la musique : la musique comme clé de lecture

La musique est avant tout affaire de proportions pour Évrart de Conty et son *De Musica* s'inscrit d'emblée dans cette perspective, en définissant le dernier des arts quadriviaux comme ce « qui traicte et determine des differences et des diversités de sons et des proporcions qu'ilz ont les uns as autres »[15]. Ce rapport étroit entre la musique et le nombre n'a évidemment rien de nouveau, et Évrart de Conty se place sous l'autorité de Pythagore en relatant la légende, évoquée par Boèce dans le *De institutione musica*, selon laquelle le philosophe aurait découvert les rapports des consonances en écoutant les sons produits par des marteaux dans une forge. Après de longs passages concernant les proportions des différents intervalles et la division du monocorde, l'auteur reprend à son compte la tripartition boécienne entre musique mondaine, musique humaine et musique instrumentale. Cet héritage boécien exhibé par l'auteur ouvre ainsi la musique à l'homme et au monde.

---

[13] Jacquart, *La Médecine médiévale dans le cadre parisien*, 284. Il faut toutefois noter, ajoute Danielle Jacquart, que malgré sa forte représentation dans *Le Livre des eschez amoureux moralisés*, la médecine n'y fait qu'une entrée discrète en tant que discipline à part entière.

[14] Sur les rapports entre musique et médecine, voir notamment la deuxième partie de Horden (ed.), *Music as Medicine*, « Medieval Europe », 101–144. Sur les rapports entre musique et magie, voir Godwin (ed.), *Music, Mysticism and Magic: a sourcebook*.

[15] Évrart de Conty, *Le Livre des eschez amoureux moralisés*, 135.

Le premier point sur lequel l'auteur du *Livre des eschez amoureux moralisés* revient est la théorie de l'harmonie des sphères. La possibilité que le mouvement des planètes puisse produire des sons, niée par Aristote, est discutée tout au long du Moyen Âge. Évrart de Conty met en regard les différentes doctrines relatives à l'existence d'une musique céleste, puis prend ses distances en affirmant :

> Mais que les cieulx par leurs mouvemens facent sons ne noise quelconques melodieuse ou aultre, ainsy qu'il semble que aucunes escriptures veuillent dire, selon la verité, ce n'est pas chose a croire ne chose qui se puist par raison soustenir, que les cieux ne sont pas de matiere sonnable[16]. [Mais que les cieux produisent des sons ou quelque bruit mélodieux par leurs mouvements, comme ce que certains ouvrages semblent vouloir dire, en vérité, on ne peut le croire ni l'affirmer raisonnablement, car les cieux ne sont pas d'une matière capable d'émettre des sons.]

Les Eschés amoureux suggéraient également qu'il ne fallait pas « entendre a la lettre » cette théorie et relevaient sa fonction allégorique[17]. De même, Évrart, dans le commentaire en prose, insiste sur la valeur métaphorique de la musique céleste :

> Ce doubz son donc et celle melodie des esperes du ciel n'est pas chose sensible ne reele, ainz est tant seulement chose intellectuelle et chose qui ne peut estre comprise fors de l'entendement[18]. [Ce doux son et cette mélodie des sphères n'est pas quelque chose de sensible ni de réel, il s'agit plutôt d'une chose intellectuelle, qui ne peut être comprise que par l'entendement.]

C'est en raison des proportions qui régissent les rapports entre les différents corps célestes que l'on peut parler d'une musique cosmique, et non en raison de la réalité sensible d'une véritable musique des sphères. Thomas d'Aquin mettait en doute la réalité de la *musica mundana*[19]. Chez Évrart de Conty, elle est réduite à « une sorte de métaphore sensible d'une donnée purement intellectuelle »[20].

---

[16] Ibid., 160.

[17] « Sans faille, beaulx filz, ceste chose/ du son du ciel que je t'expose/ n'est pas a entendre a la lettre. », Abert, « Die Musikästhetik der *Échecs amoureux* », 896, v. 413–415. Voir également les vers 704–711 où le terme de « metaphoire » est employé au sujet de la « melodie celestre », ibid., 903.

[18] Évrart de Conty, *Le Livre des eschez amoureux moralisés*, 161.

[19] Tomas d'Aquin, *In Aristotelis « De coelo et mundo »*, II, lect. 14.

[20] Fritz, *Paysages sonores au Moyen Âge*, 145.

La musique n'en conserve pas moins son pouvoir métaphysique, qui consiste à mettre en relation les différents éléments de l'univers.[21] Le médecin de Charles V décline en effet, de façon systématique, les différents domaines pour lesquels la musique peut servir de modèle. Conformément à la tradition pythagoricienne, Évrart de Conty utilise l'harmonie musicale pour penser les harmonies. La théorie de l'harmonie universelle est notamment appliquée, de façon relativement originale, aux relations entre les êtres humains. La proportion double, appelée *dyapason* – c'est-à-dire l'octave –, sert à concevoir les rapports entre l'homme et la femme. Un exemple de cette harmonie régie par l'intervalle musical le plus parfait[22] est la différence qui existe entre leurs voix : celle de l'homme, « grosse, grave et pesant », entretient un rapport relevant de cette proportion double avec celle de la femme, « gresle, ague et soutille »[23]. L'union amoureuse est pensée en termes musicaux et la parfaite concorde des amants est envisagée dans ses manifestations physiques : c'est parce que leurs voix sont *consonantes* que l'homme et la femme peuvent s'aimer. De même, l'harmonie des quatre éléments est appréhendée selon la *musical mesure* :

> Finablement, pour ce que les philosophes anciens se esmerveilloient come se porroit estre que les .iiij. elemens se acordoient ainsy pour leur diversité et contraires natures, et ilz veoient oultre que les musicaulx nombres font acorder les sons de diverses manieres et presenter ensemble plaisaument a l'oye, pour ce disoient ilz que nature assembloit aussi les elemens et les mesloit ensemble par les musicaux nombres dessus-diz[24]. [Finalement, comme les anciens philosophes se demandaient comment les quatre éléments pouvaient ainsi s'accorder en raison de leur diversité et de leurs natures contraires, et qu'ils voyaient que les proportions musicales accordaient les sons différents et les rendaient plaisants à l'oreille, ils disaient que Nature assemblait aussi les éléments et les mêlait en fonction de ces proportions musicales.]

C'est également en raison de la faculté de la musique à faire cohabiter harmonieusement les contraires que le médecin introduit des réflexions sur le pouls :

---

[21] Sultan, « *En conjunction de science* », t. I, 355. L'ensemble de ce développement est largement inspiré des réflexions d'Agathe Sultan.

[22] « Se nous voulons aussi les dessusdites consonancies ensemble comparer, en tant que elles sont consonantes, nous trouverons que dyapason est sur toutes la meilleur et la plus excellente. » Évrart de Conty, *Le Livre des eschez amoureux moralisés*, 149.

[23] Ibid.,179.

[24] Ibid., 164.

Du poulz donc dessusdit dit Avicennes que la nature de musique y est trouvee car tout aussi que les chans de musique sont composés de sons agus et graves, tres ordeneement enssuiant l'un l'autre et par proporcion deue et convenable entremellé souvent, tout aussi est le poulz de divers mouvemens et pluseurs composé qui ainsy s'entressuient tres ordeneement[25]. [Avicenne dit qu'on trouve la nature de la musique dans le pouls, car tout comme les chants se composent de sons aigus et graves, se succédant de façon très ordonnée, et généralement mêlés selon des proportions appropriées et convenables, de même le pouls est composé de mouvements différents qui se succèdent de façon ordonnée.]

En l'absence d'une compréhension totale de la circulation du sang, les médecins médiévaux ont souvent utilisé le *topos* antique de la comparaison avec la musique. Ce mystérieux phénomène, comparable aux marées ou aux mouvements des astres, est ainsi expliqué par l'art des sons et des proportions[26]. Le recours à la musique permet de décrire, selon un principe analogique – les formules de comparaison comme «tout aussi» sont légion dans le texte –, un fait naturel dont le fonctionnement de détail demeurait obscur.

La musique intervient donc comme comparant pour rendre compte de phénomènes macrocosmiques – les positions des astres, les éléments, le rythme des saisons… – et microcosmiques – le pouls, les voix des hommes et des femmes… Malgré sa prise de distance épistémologique à l'égard de la réalité de la *musica mundana*, qui le conduit à métaphoriser cette dernière, Évrart de Conty postule l'antique universalité de la musique. Le lien entre macrocosme et microcosme est rendu évident par la juxtaposition de la réflexion sur les proportions musicales régissant le monde planétaire et d'un développement sur l'enfant dans le ventre de sa mère. L'auteur affirme que trois périodes sont distinctes pendant la grossesse: la première est le temps de la formation corporelle de l'enfant, la deuxième le rend «parfaiz quant a son mouvement» et la troisième est le moment où «il doit estre meur et tout parfait pour naistre»[27]. Les trois temps sont liés entre eux par des proportions mathématiques renvoyant à des consonances musicales.[28] Cette constatation de départ est suivie d'une série d'exemples mettant en application ce principe de proportion. Si la conclusion du

---

[25] Ibid., 179.
[26] Voir sur ce point l'article de Siraisi, «The music of pulse».
[27] Évrart de Conty, *Le Livre des eschez amoureux moralisés*, 177.
[28] «De ces troiz temps dient les philosophes que le second est le double au premier et le tiers d'autre part est trebles au second», *idem*.

paragraphe revient sur le lien qui unit la grossesse à la musique, l'auteur utilise cette dernière comme un prétexte pour relater certaines de ses observations en tant que médecin :

> Et pour ce, s'aucunes fames dient que elles sentent souvent et ont senty leurs enfans remouvoir a .xl. jours, nous y povons dire – supposé qu'il soit voir, ce qui n'est pas bien raisonable a croire – qu'il n'avient pas souvent, ou que par aventure elles sont deceues[29]. [Et pour cette raison, si certaines femmes disent qu'elles sentent fréquemment et ont senti leur enfant bouger à quarante jours, nous pouvons dire – à supposer que ce soit vrai, ce que l'on ne peut pas raisonnablement croire – que c'est un cas très rare, ou qu'il est possible que ces femmes soient victimes d'illusions.]

De même, lorsque l'auteur affirme, se réclamant notamment d'Al Kindi que les proportions musicales sont trouvées « es degrés medicinaulx »[30], il poursuit en décrivant la réalité médicale des quatre degrés de toxicité des médicaments, bien plus qu'en en analysant les ressorts musicaux. La musique est donc un modèle de pensée, mais elle permet également de faire valoir de nombreux savoirs et, plus particulièrement, de légitimer certaines compétences médicales. La rigueur mathématique de la musique autorise un emploi médical et moral de la comparaison. L'insistance sur la *musical mesure* est en effet intimement liée à la fois à la qualité de médecin du commentateur et à la morale qu'il souhaite transmettre : Danielle Jacquart a montré que l'appel à la vertu de modération, constante dans toute son œuvre, va de pair avec la recherche d'un équilibre entre les qualités contraires, qui constitue l'objectif principal de l'art médical et qu'incarne la musique[31].

Le dernier art du *quadrivium* occupe ainsi une place centrale dans le réseau de savoirs présents dans cet ouvrage à visée encyclopédique. Au cœur d'une relation entre microcosme et macrocosme héritée de la tradition platonicienne, la musique intervient en tant qu'abstrac-

---

[29] Ibid., 178. Ce type de remarques est absent du texte initial : l'auteur des *Eschés amoureux*, s'il s'agit bien d'Évrart de Conty, se met moins en scène en tant que médecin dans la version en vers que dans la version en prose. Il faut toutefois préciser qu'on ne peut déterminer dans *Le Livre des eschez amoureux* s'il s'agit d'une « anecdote colportée dans le milieu médical », d'un « exemple universitaire » ou d'une « observation personnelle dissimulée derrière une tournure impersonnelle », Ducos, « Évrart de Conty, médecin et vulgarisateur à la cour de Charles V », 67.

[30] Évrart de Conty, *Le Livre des eschez amoureux moralisés*, 180–181 : « la double proporcion et la quadruble aussi qui en musique sont dyapason et double dyapason sont entre les degrés et les vertus medicinaulx trouvees ».

[31] Voir sur ce point Jacquart, « Médecine et morale », 369.

tion mathématique rendant intelligible ce qui ne l'est pas *a priori*. Ce n'est pas la musique comme art des sons, mais davantage la musique comme science des proportions qui est alors convoquée – comme le souligne bien la longue comparaison que mène Évrart de Conty entre la musique et les figures géométriques[32]. Clé pour penser et comprendre l'univers, les relations mathématiques établies entre les sons deviennent un modèle herméneutique, à l'instar du jeu d'échecs dans *Le Livre des eschez amoureux moralisés*. Dans son prologue, l'auteur insiste sur la richesse métaphorique des échecs, qui peuvent à la fois représenter la société civile, être une image réduite de la stratégie militaire, être comparés aux mouvements des planètes et enfin, offrir un miroir aux batailles amoureuses. La présence d'un même comparé – le mouvement des planètes – pourrait légitimer le rapprochement entre les échecs et la musique. La comparaison avec les échecs, si elle est répétée à plusieurs reprises au sujet de l'astronomie[33], n'est jamais mentionnée explicitement à propos de la musique. Un même système de combinatoire gouverne néanmoins ces deux jeux sur les nombres et autorise un tel rapprochement. La rithmomachie, jeu didactique inventé pendant la première moitié du XIe siècle qui s'inspire des mathématiques pythagoriciennes, se joue par exemple sur un double échiquier. Le premier traité à avoir fourni une description détaillée du jeu, vers 1130, aborde la question de ses relations avec la musique. Son auteur, Fortolf, a montré que toutes les proportions numériques pouvaient être transposées en correspondances entre les sons[34]. Évrart

---

[32] Évrart de Conty, *Le Livre des eschez amoureux moralisés*, 181–189. Ce développement est une illustration parfaite du travail de commentateur auquel se livre Évrart de Conty : en effet, dans le poème, ce sujet est traité de façon très allusive en une dizaine de vers et le glossateur propose à partir de là une réflexion ordonnée et nettement amplifiée.

[33] Voir par exemple : « Et c'est semblable chose a ce que j'ay dit ailleurs du gieu des eschés, car qui aroit parfaite cognoissance de cest gieu et il veist deux personnes jouer, dont chascun a son tour feist le meilleur trait qui simplement seroit lors possible a fere, il n'est pas doubte, veu le premier trait que l'un d'eulx feroit, il saroit bien [...] a quel fin le gieu devroit venir. [...] Briefment, ainsy est il du ciel, qui bien parfaitement le congnoistroit, car les estoilles traient et se meuvent tousdiz tres ordeneement. » [Et c'est comparable à ce que j'ai dit ailleurs au sujet des échecs : imaginons quelqu'un qui connaîtrait parfaitement ce jeu, s'il voyait deux personnes jouer et que chacun des deux faisait à son tour le meilleur coup possible, nul doute qu'ayant vu le premier coup de l'un des joueurs, il connaîtrait l'issue du jeu. En somme, ainsi en va-t-il du ciel pour qui le connaîtrait parfaitement, car les étoiles se meuvent de façon très ordonnée.], Évrart de Conty, *Le Livre des eschez amoureux moralisés*, 114–115.

[34] Le but du jeu est de placer au moins trois pièces sur la moitié du champ adverse, de façon à ce qu'elles aient des distances égales entre elles et une ou plusieurs moyen-

de Conty, s'il n'établit pas un parallèle aussi net entre la musique et le
jeu qui lui sert de support, les conçoit tous deux comme une langue
symbolique rendant compte du monde dans sa diversité.

Au terme de ce parcours, il semble que le médecin de Charles V n'ait
recours à la musique que de façon figurée. Il ne faudrait cependant pas
figer le statut qu'il lui assigne dans ce type d'emploi. Sa pensée oscille
entre une utilisation allégorique de la dernière science du *quadrivium*,
à la manière de l'allégorie échiquéenne, et un usage plus littéral[35]. Ces
deux attitudes paraissent déterminer une utilisation d'une part herméneutique de la musique, liée à des savoirs autorisés – en tant qu'allégorie d'une harmonie universelle réglée par un système de proportions.
D'autre part, en tant qu'art des sons altérant les corps et les âmes, la
musique permet à ce médecin d'intégrer des réflexions concernant des
savoirs plus polémiques au sein de son *De Musica*.

LA MAGIE EN QUESTION : LA MUSIQUE COMME POINT DE BASCULE

L'universalité de la musique est, dans la logique du texte, ce qui explique et justifie ses effets sur l'homme et les animaux. Après avoir énuméré tous les domaines régis par des proportions musicales, Évrart
de Conty insiste sur les effets de la musique. Sans encore évoquer de
possibles pouvoirs magiques de cette dernière, l'auteur met en relief
sa puissance d'*alteracion* du corps et de l'âme : elle «altere et transmue [l'âme humaine] d'un propos en un autre moult souvent et d'une
affection en l'autre»[36]. [La musique altère et transmue très souvent
l'âme humaine d'un état en un autre et d'une affection en une autre.]
Cette idée est exprimée par l'auteur dans des termes proches, dans
la traduction des *Problemata* pseudo-aristotéliciens qu'il établit à la
demande de Charles V[37] :

---

nes mathématiques (arithmétiques, géométriques, harmoniques). Voir Breidert,
«Arithmomachia» et Folkerts, «La rithmomachie et le manuscrit Avranches 235».
[35] Sultan, «*En conjunction de science*», t. I, 356.
[36] Évrart de Conty, *Le Livre des eschez amoureux moralisés*, 190–191.
[37] Il semble en effet acquis que cette traduction des *Problemata* aurait fait l'objet
d'une commande de Charles V. Cette commande daterait de 1372 et il est certain
qu'Évrart de Conty y travaille encore en 1377 puisqu'il fait référence dans son texte
à Nicole Oresme, évêque de Lisieux. Ce dernier accéda à cette fonction en 1377 et
mourut en 1382. Pour plus de détail, voir notamment le volume collectif édité sous
la direction de De Leemans et Goyens, *Aristotle's* Problemata *in different times and
tongues*.

Pour ce devons nous encore oultre savoir que ceste musique qui ainsi est en sons et en chans excercee, selonc les phylosophes anciens, ha diverses vertus et diverses efficaces en la transmutation desus dite de l'ame et aussi du cors[38]. [Nous devons par ailleurs savoir que cette musique qui est produite par des instruments et des voix, selon les philosophes anciens, a divers pouvoirs dans la transformation évoquée ci-dessus de l'âme et du corps.]

L'influence de la musique ici soulignée relève de la production de véritables sons. Il ne s'agit plus de *musica mundana* ni de *musica humana*, mais de *musica instrumentalis*, «qui est la droite propre et la vraie musique»[39].

Pour traduire et commenter les *Problemata*, Évrart de Conty se fonde notamment sur l'*Expositio Problematum Aristotelis* de Pietro d'Abano. Or, par rapport à ce dernier, il amplifie nettement le développement relatif aux pouvoirs de la musique. Alors que cet aspect était résumé en quelques lignes chez le premier commentateur du texte, il devient chez Évrart un répertoire d'exemples traditionnels[40]. Ce type d'amplification le conduit à verser dans la fable et à multiplier les récits. La musique et ses pouvoirs présentent un intérêt poétique pour l'amateur de mythologie qu'était le médecin de Charles V, même dans un texte de vulgarisation scientifique comme la traduction des *Problemata*. Dans *Le Livre des eschez amoureux moralisés*, l'auteur fait également référence aux figures d'Orphée, d'Amphion, de Midas, d'Arion et de David, dont il relate les histoires sans chercher à les moraliser. Cette encyclopédie apparaît alors comme une synthèse des matériaux narratifs et discursifs présents à la fois dans *Les Eschés amoureux* et la traduction du traité pseudo-aristotélicien. Insérées dans le «petit traité» de théorie musicale, ces *ficcions* – le terme est employé dans le texte en vers[41] – établissent un lien très étroit entre le narratif et le discursif, caractéristique de l'écriture d'Évrart de Conty. Joëlle Ducos interprète ce type d'échos littéraires et poétiques au sein d'une œuvre scientifique comme autant de déviations par rapport au modèle

---

[38] Évrart de Conty, *Les Problèmes*, manuscrit B.N. fr. 24282, fol. 28r°. Il s'agit d'un manuscrit autographe. Une édition de la traduction des *Problemata* est actuellement en préparation, sous la direction de Ducos, Goyens et Guichard-Tesson, à paraître chez Champion.

[39] Évrart de Conty, *Le Livre des eschez amoureux moralisés*, 165.

[40] Voir Mauro, «La musica nei commenti ai *Problemi*».

[41] «Qui trouva d'Amphion/ et d'Orpheus la ficcion…», Abert, «Die Musikästhetik der *Échecs amoureux*», 913, v. 1109–1110.

scolastique, signant par là l'ambition vulgarisatrice du texte[42]. Dans le
cas que nous étudions, les *fables*[43], exhibées en tant que telles, caution-
nent la réalité des effets de la musique. Néanmoins, les potentialités
narratives des pouvoirs de la musique n'empêchent pas le médecin de
Charles V de s'y intéresser d'un point de vue scientifique.

Dans *Le Songe du vergier*, dialogue entre un clerc et un chevalier
adapté d'un texte latin en 1378 sur commande de Charles V et attribué à Évrart de Trémaugon, les effets thérapeutiques de la musique
sont discutés. Le clerc affirme que «lez herbes et lez melodies si puent
grandement changier et muer la disposicion du corps». Le chevalier
répond cependant que les mélodies ne peuvent pas guérir mais uni-
quement *mitiguer* [apaiser] les malades[44]. Quelques années plus tard,
Évrart de Conty relit également le *topos* des pouvoirs de la musique à
la lumière du discours médical qui lui est cher et affirme que la musique guérit certaines maladies:

> Finablement, elle garist de pluseurs maladies, mesmement de celles qui
> sourviennent par les accidens de l'ame, et par especial de la melancolie
> qui vient aucunesfoiz de par amours amer trop excessivement, laquelle
> maladie est appelle en medicine *amor hereos*[45]. [En dernier lieu, elle
> soigne plusieurs maladies, surtout celles qui sont liées aux accidents de
> l'âme, et notamment la mélancolie, provoquée parfois par un amour
> excessif; cette maladie est appelée par les médecins *amor hereos*[46].]

---

[42] Ducos, «Lectures et vulgarisations du savoir aristotélicien», 222.

[43] «Les grans merveilles dessusdites et les autres semblables que musique peut faire
nous sont trop bien segnefiees par la *fable* ancienne qui de Amphion et de Orpheus
est *fainte*», Évrart de Conty, *Le Livre des eschez amoureux moralisés*, 191. C'est nous
qui soulignons. Sur les rapports entre fiction et explicitation, voir Guichard-Tesson,
«'Parler par figure et fabuleusement'».

[44] *Le Songe du vergier*, vol. I, 391.

[45] Évrart de Conty, *Le Livre des eschez amoureux moralisés*, 191. On retrouve une
phrase très similaire dans la traduction des *Problemata* par Évrart: «Finablement elle
garist de pluseurs maladies et par especial de celles qui sourviennent par les accidens
de l'ame, si que de la melancolie qui vient aucune fois par amer par amours trop
curieusement et de pluseurs autres, et de ce, avons nous en pluseurs escriptures moult
de examples que je trespasse par cause de briefté.», Évrart de Conty, *Les Problèmes*,
B.N. fr. 24282, fol. 27v°. Dans la version en vers des *Eschés amoureux*, ces vertus de
la musique sont à peine esquissées: «et si saichez bien somme toute/ que la musical
melodie/ garist de mainte maladie.», Abert, «Die Musikästhetik der *Échecs amoureux*», 914, v. 1163–1165.

[46] Voir Klibansky, Panofsky et Saxl, *Saturne et la mélancolie. Études historiques et
philosophiques: nature, religion, médecine et art*, notamment le chapitre «La mélancolie dans la médecine, la science et la philosophie du Moyen Âge», 123–197.

La musique est une forme de médecine. Ces deux disciplines produisent des effets sur le corps et l'âme. Le discours sur l'éthos des modes est ainsi expliqué par la *complexion* de chacun :

> car chacun se delite plus par nature en ce qui ly est semblable et qui plus se conforme a sa complexion et a une occulte nature que chascun a en soy[47]. [car naturellement, on préfère ce qui nous est semblable et ce qui est conforme à notre complexion et à notre occulte nature.]

L'analyse des effets de la musique repose sur des considérations physiques – la théorie des complexions –, qui n'évacuent cependant pas toute la part de mystère sur laquelle se fonde cette théorie – l'auteur parle d'une *occulte nature*. La pensée d'Évrart de Conty se construit donc entre volonté d'élucidation scientifique par l'étude des effets de la musique sur le corps et maintien d'un certain flou quant à leurs fondements. La volonté de «combler le vide dans l'explication»[48], caractéristique de l'esprit scolastique, se heurte ici à l'obscurité du corps humain pour un médecin médiéval.

Ces mystérieux effets de la musique permettent la transition vers la magie. Après avoir énuméré les différents animaux sensibles à la musique, l'auteur mentionne, sans toutefois cautionner *a priori* ce jugement, le fait que les esprits eux-mêmes puissent être émus par la musique. Ce glissement du chant à l'incantation introduit la digression consacrée à la magie, absente du poème initial, et que Danielle Jacquart est, à notre connaissance, la seule à avoir relevée[49]. Afin de mettre cette insertion en perspective, il est utile de rappeler que le *De musica* est précédé d'un *De astronomia* dans *Le Livre des eschez amoureux*. L'auteur décline cet art libéral en deux parties : l'*astrologie* est la science relative aux mouvements des astres et l'*astronomie* concerne les jugements qui en découlent[50]. Il n'est guère étonnant que le médecin de Charles V se proclame amateur passionné d'astrologie. Ce domaine bénéficie d'une promotion socioculturelle et politique à la fin du Moyen Âge[51] et Charles le Sage, plus particulièrement, passait

---

[47] Évrart de Conty, *Le Livre des eschez amoureux moralisés*, 193.

[48] Weill-Parot, «Encadrement ou dévoilement», 153 *sqq*.

[49] Jacquart, «Médecine et morale», 372 notamment. Danielle Jacquart analyse cette digression en termes, entre autres, politiques.

[50] «et ceste science a deux principaux parties : l'une des mouvemens, laquelle est appellee communement des anciens astrologie, l'autre des jugemens, qui s'en enssuit, et ceste aussi des anciens le plus communement est astronomie appellee», Évrart de Conty, *Le Livre des eschez amoureux moralisés*, 108.

[51] Voir la deuxième partie de l'ouvrage de J.-P. Boudet, *Entre science et nigromance*.

pour « tres expert et sage en ycelle [l'astrologie] »[52]. Évrart de Conty quant à lui est convaincu que les influences célestes régissent les phénomènes naturels et que l'astrologie permet de les prévoir. Toutefois, il prend soin de préserver le libre arbitre et l'hégémonie divine sur le cours des astres[53]. Le rapport entre faculté de prévoir l'avenir et doctrine chrétienne demeure néanmoins problématique. En évoquant les magiciens et leurs pratiques de divinations, l'auteur affirme :

> ilz se metent en grant peril de l'ame et en encourent l'indignacion de Dieu a qui, ce semble, ilz veulent oster sa seignourie, quant ilz veulent savoir les choses a venir et les choses secretes qui seulement appartiennent a ly[54]. [Ils mettent leur âme en grand péril et encourent l'indignation de Dieu à qui ils veulent, semble-t-il, ravir la puissance, quand ils veulent savoir le futur et les secrets qui appartiennent à lui seul.]

Cet argument théologique clôt la digression sur la magie. L'introduction d'une réflexion sur ces pratiques est de toute évidence délicate dans un texte à tonalité chrétienne et Évrart maintient une ferme distinction entre recours à l'astrologie naturelle pour connaître l'avenir et pratique magico-astrale à visée divinatoire. Il défend la science des images si elle reste strictement astrologique, mais il en proscrit tous les ajouts magiques[55]. On retrouve ici une posture adoptée par d'autres auteurs de l'époque. L'auteur du *Songe du vergier* se fait l'écho de cette ligne de partage, comme en témoigne le titre du chapitre CLXV : « Le Clerc met plusieurs especes et manieres de divinacions et appreuve lez unes, come sont celles qui se font par Astrologie, en aucuns cas, et si repreuve lez aultres, come celles qui se font par Nygromancie, Geomancie et par semblables sciences deffendues »[56].

Si certaines formes de divination sont condamnées, la magie n'en occupe pas moins une place importante dans *Le Livre des eschez amoureux moralisés*. Elle y désigne « tout phénomène dans la production duquel l'homme intervient d'une façon ou d'une autre et dont le processus n'obéit pas à la causalité habituelle et est donc occulté à la

---

[52] Christine de Pisan, *Le Livre des fais et bonnes meurs du sage roi Charles V*, t. II, 16.
[53] Voir sur ce point Jacquart, *La Médecine médiévale dans le cadre parisien*, 312.
[54] Évrart de Conty, *Le Livre des eschez amoureux moralisés*, 207.
[55] Évrart de Conty condamne « les ymages que on fait par incantacion et par l'art de magique ou on use de conjuracions et de sacrefices appartenans a esperis malignes, car telx ymages ne sont pas recevable en l'escole de philosophie naturele, ainz en sont et doivent estre a bon droit degecté et banny », ibid., 131–132. Voir sur ce point Jacquart, *La Médecine médiévale dans le cadre parisien*, 315.
[56] *Le Songe du vergier*, vol. I, 363.

perception et à la compréhension ordinaires – à l'exclusion des miracles »[57]. Évrart de Conty reconnaît l'existence des esprits. Il disqualifie
la partie de la magie qu'est la *nigromancie*, qui consiste à invoquer ces
derniers, car, ils ne peuvent pas être contraints. En revanche, la science
appelée *magique* est reconnue[58], car elle ne fait pas appel aux esprits
mais qu'elle :

> use d'aucunes autres choses trouvees en nature qui ont vertus secretes
> et de grant efficace […], sy come sont les estoilles du ciel, les pierres
> precieuses, les herbes et les plantes, et aussi les paroles et les sons musi-
> caulx qui sont de grant vertu, come dit est[59]. [se sert de certaines choses
> naturelles, qui ont des vertus secrètes et de grands pouvoirs, comme les
> étoiles, les pierres précieuses, les herbes et les plantes, et les paroles et les
> sons musicaux, qui ont, comme on le dit, de grandes vertus.]

S'il affirme que cette science produit plus de mal que de bien, l'auteur
lui assigne cependant une certaine efficacité, qu'il illustre notamment
par des exemples mythologiques en faisant appel aux figures de Circé,
Médée ou Déjanire. Ces récits remplissent une fois de plus le rôle de
caution narrative, mais sont également agrémentés d'un développement cherchant à analyser d'un point de vue scientifique ces métamorphoses. Tout comme ces magiciennes ont altéré les corps des
hommes chacune à leur manière, l'altération des *vertus sensitives* peut
être entraînée par une maladie. Évrart évoque, comme exemple d'altération des sens, les transformations en loup garou. De telles maladies
provoquent des *mutacions* et *alienacions des senz et de pensee* ; de la
même façon, la magie peut sembler dénaturer les corps. De ce fait, l'art
des magiciens est reconnu et crédité d'un degré de réalité. C'est à la
lumière de la scientificité médicale qu'est examinée la magie. Le même
type d'explication rend en effet compte des métamorphoses magiques
et de certaines maladies affectant les sens. Cette confrontation entre
magie et médecine met bien en évidence « qu'il serait donc erroné de
croire la magie privée de rationalité »[60]. Évrart de Conty tente de déce-
ler les réseaux de causalité responsables des illusions magiques.

---

[57] Nous empruntons cette définition à Weill-Parot, « Science et magie au Moyen
Âge », 530.
[58] Nicole Oresme ouvre son développement sur la magie par cette même distinction
dans son *De configurationibus qualitatum et motuum*.
[59] Évrart de Conty, *Le Livre des eschez amoureux moralisés*, 198.
[60] Weill-Parot, « Science et magie au Moyen Âge », 536.

Lorsqu'il s'efforce d'étudier les liens qui unissent la musique à la
magie, l'auteur du *Livre des eschez amoureux moralisés* doit constater
que la faculté de transformation des corps et des âmes par les sons est
une croyance partagée par tous. Il semble même que les paroles, qui
sont pourtant éphémères et intangibles, aient des pouvoirs plus étendus que les pierres précieuses et les herbes :

> les magiciens tiennent et croient que les paroles les ont assez plus gran-
> des [les vertus a cest art profitables], car en toutes les œuvres de ceste
> science ou on œuvre des pierres dessusdites et des herbes, on adjouste
> voulentiers aussi communement aucunes oroisons ou aucunes paroles,
> aussi come se tout ne vaulsist riens sans elles[61] [les magiciens pensent
> et croient que les paroles ont des pouvoirs magiques bien plus grands,
> car à chaque fois que l'on utilise des pierres et des herbes dans un but
> magique, on ajoute volontiers habituellement des oraisons ou des paro-
> les, comme si tout ne valait rien sans elles.]

Comme les animaux se montrent sensibles aux pouvoirs de ces orai-
sons, il faut convenir que ce n'est pas en raison de leur signification
que les paroles agissent, mais en vertu du son qu'elles produisent.
Afin d'augmenter leur efficacité, les magiciens prononcent souvent
ces paroles en chantant : il s'agit alors d'*incantacions*[62]. L'auteur reste
prudent tout au long de cette description des pouvoirs magiques de la
musique, en modalisant constamment son discours à l'aide d'incises
du type « se nous voulons les escriptures croire », « si comme Aristote
veult dire » *etc.*

La position personnelle d'Évrart au sujet de la magie n'est donc guère
aisée à percevoir. Cependant, lorsqu'il délivre les trois jugements couramment portés sur la magie, il fait valoir sa propre opinion, résidant
dans une voie moyenne, comme à l'habitude de ce penseur imprégné
d'aristotélisme. Les théologiens pensent d'une part que toute pratique
magique est liée aux esprits malins, certains philosophes anciens considèrent d'autre part que c'est en Nature qu'il faut trouver la cause et la
raison de ces manifestations magiques. L'opinion la plus raisonnable
est selon l'auteur une voie moyenne : Évrart ne réfute ni l'existence
des esprits, ni la présence dans la Nature de potentialités magiques.
Malgré cette reconnaissance de la magie comme possible exploitation

---

[61] Évrart de Conty, *Le Livre des eschez amoureux moralisés*, 202.
[62] « Sans faille, aussi sont les paroles dessusdites dont ceste science use aucunesfoiz
en chantant pronuncies, aussi come ce fut pour avoir plus grant veru et plus grant
efficace. », *idem.*

de données réellement existantes, il met cependant en garde son lecteur contre les *illusions, faulses apparences* et *decepcions* qui y sont attachées. Pour donner plus de force à son propos, il donne l'exemple de pratiques consistant à observer l'apparition d'images dans des surfaces réfléchissantes – comme les ongles, les miroirs, des épées.... Ces pratiques illusionnent les sens de leur victime en leur donnant à voir des images de fantaisie. Évrart de Conty décrit le mécanisme qui mène à la formation de ces images : l'âme de l'illusionné se referme sur elle-même et crée des images décevantes en s'efforçant de faire apparaître ce que lui suggère le magicien. S'il reconnaît une certaine efficace de la magie, l'auteur met cependant en garde son lecteur contre les fausses apparences[63]. Dans ce passage, l'auteur du *Livre des eschez amoureux moralisés* surmonte le conflit entre magie et explication et discrédite de ce fait les pratiques qu'il décrit. En effet, ses explications détruisent la part de « non-encore-connu » sur laquelle elles reposent en le mettant au jour[64]. Il s'agit de montrer que ces tours sont faussement magiques. Par ailleurs, en tant que médecin, il n'oublie pas de mettre en garde contre les dommages provoqués sur l'âme et le corps : la distraction provoquée peut entraîner des dommages irrémédiables, et les enfants, victimes de ces magiciens, peuvent devenir aveugles[65].

Évrart de Conty semble hésiter entre intérêt pour des expérimentations magiques, dont il cherche à comprendre le fonctionnement en détail, et condamnation de celles-ci. Cet homme de science du tournant des XIVe–XVe siècles est manifestement intrigué par de telles pratiques et le défi qu'elles opposent à l'entendement, mais il demeure prudent. Son embarras se comprend à la lumière du contexte de production de l'œuvre. En effet, en 1398, l'affaire de Jean de Bar avait incité la Faculté de théologie, à l'instigation de Jean Gerson, à condamner vingt-huit articles relatifs à l'usage de la magie[66] et Évrart ne pouvait ignorer les rumeurs circulant sur l'ensorcellement de Charles VI et les différentes

---

[63] « Ja soit ce donc que le magicien puist bien aucunesfoiz, par ce qu'il ly appert en usant de son art, savoir la verité des choses qu'il demande par responce ou par signes, ceste chose neantmoins ne avient mie souvent ne ce n'est pas chose aussi bien sceure, ainz treuve on que ce sont le plus communement illusions et faulses apparences ou responces doutables et de double sentence », ibid., 206.

[64] Nous nous inspirons ici des remarques très éclairantes de Weill-Parot, « Encadrement ou dévoilement », 155 notamment.

[65] Cette remarque est déjà présente chez Nicole Oresme, *De configurationibus qualitatum et motuum*, II, chap. XXX.

[66] Évrart de Conty fait allusion à ces articles : « Sans faille, ceste opinion est reprouvee des theologiens et est un des articles condanpnés a Paris », *Le Livre des eschez*

tentatives pour traiter sa folie[67]. Cette dimension politique peut sans
doute expliquer l'ajout par rapport au poème initial, composé sous
le règne de Charles V[68]. Par ailleurs, pour un médecin, reconnaître
de façon univoque la fréquence et l'efficacité des interventions surna-
turelles «aurait amené nécessairement à abandonner les patients aux
mains de désenvoûteurs de tous ordres et à renoncer à défendre l'efficacité d'un art fondé sur les principes de la philosophie naturelle»[69]. La
position complexe de l'auteur du *Livre des eschez amoureux moralisés*,
peut ainsi être éclairée par sa fonction sociale et le contexte politique
dans lequel il écrivait. La magie était alors une question cruciale, qui
méritait un développement dans un texte à visée encyclopédique[70] et
Évrart choisit de l'intégrer à la fin de sa réflexion sur la musique. Cette
dernière, si elle est parfois un peu oubliée au moment où il insère sa
digression sur la magie, fournit néanmoins le cadre nécessaire à cette
digression.

Les hommes de lettres ayant vécu sous les règnes de Charles V et Charles VI ont bien souvent pris position autour de la question des sciences
occultes. Philippe de Mézières fait surgir dans son récit allégorique du
Songe du vieil pelerin une figure représentant Superstition, qui s'op-
pose en tout point au personnage de Bonne Foy[71]. La répartition axio-
logique entre les deux figures va dans ce texte de pair avec l'orientation
chrétienne défendue par l'auteur. Nicole Oresme condamne l'astrologie dans son *Livre de divinacions*, mais défend la magie naturelle dans

---

amoureux moralisés, 59. Voir sur ce point Veenstra, *Magic and Divination at the
Courts of Burgundy and France*, 351–355.

[67] Voir Autrand, *Charles VI. La folie du roi*.

[68] On situe la rédaction du poème entre 1370 et 1380 en raison d'une allusion à Du
Guesclin dans le manuscrit de Dresde, fol. 100b. C'est en 1370 que Du Guesclin accède
au rang de connétable; il meurt en 1380. Voir l'introduction de Kraft à son édition de
l'épisode du Verger d'Amour, *Liebesgarten-Allegorie der «Echecs amoureux»*, 31.

[69] Jacquart, *La Médecine médiévale dans le cadre parisien*, 321.

[70] Il est à cet égard intéressant de relever que dans un manuscrit de la traduction
des *Problemata* par Évrart de Conty, Jena, Thüringer Universitäts und Landesbibliothek, ms El.f.81, fol. 1r°, l'enlumineur a représenté des figures masculines renvoyant
aux domaines de savoirs abordés par le texte (un médecin, un musicien *etc.*) et a
ajouté un homme semblant représenter le mage ou l'alchimiste, supposant sans doute
qu'Aristote n'aurait pas omis une science aussi importante, Cadden, «Preliminary
observations on the place of the *Problemata* in medieval learning», 5.

[71] «Comment une vieille horrible et deguisee soudainement se treuva ou milieu du
parquet du consistoire appareillie de defendre les jugemens d'astrologie sus les choses
a avenir [...]», Philippe de Mézières, *Le Songe du Vieil Pelerin*, t. I, 595 *sqq*.

son *De configurationibus qualitatum et motuum*[72]. Évrart de Conty quant à lui déclare être un amateur d'astrologie et se montre, malgré toutes ses précautions rhétoriques, fort intéressé par les expérimentations magiques et leurs fondements.

La longue digression sur la magie ajoutée par l'auteur du *Livre des eschez amoureux moralisés* permet, semble-t-il, de penser la musique selon deux pôles. Elle est d'une part la science des proportions – caractéristique qui l'intègre dans le *quadrivium*. Elle autorise la mise en relation entre elles de toutes les choses. Postulant une universalité de la musique, l'auteur en fait une clé de lecture et de compréhension du monde. S'il critique l'utilisation littérale des concepts de *musica mundana* et de *musica humana*, il emploie néanmoins le dernier art du *quadrivium* comme un modèle intellectuel. La musique est d'autre part l'art des sons et c'est ce qui la fait basculer vers un usage plus pratique. Des pouvoirs antiques de la musique, l'auteur passe à ses potentialités magiques intrinsèques. À la fois sensible et intelligible, à la fois instrumentale, humaine et mondaine, la musique permet ainsi l'articulation de savoirs autorisés, comme la délivrance d'une compétence médicale, et de discours plus polémiques, comme une prise de position, certes complexe et ambiguë, sur les pratiques magiques.

> Si soit pris en gré ce qui en est dit, se aucune chose y ha qui soit bien dite, et la deffaute soit aussi amendee au bon plaisir du miex considerant ceste matere[73]. [Que l'on agrée ce qui a été dit, si l'on y trouve quelques paroles bien dites, mais que les défauts soient corrigés au bon plaisir de qui connaîtra mieux cette matière.]

C'est ainsi que se clôt l'une des sections des *Problemata*, dans leur traduction par Évrart de Conty, consacrée à l'harmonie. L'auteur ne cesse d'affirmer que le texte qu'il traduit est obscur, et les passages relatifs à la musique sont précisément saturés de ces remarques. La musique semble ainsi être un domaine que l'auteur ne pense pas complètement maîtriser. Cette qualité de *terra incognita*[74] peut expliquer son statut

---

[72] Voir Lefèvre, *Rhétorique et divination chez Nicole Oresme* et Thorndike, *A History of Magic and Experimental Science*, vol. III, chap. XXV, « Oresme on astrology » et chap. XXVI, « Oresme on magic and fascination ».

[73] Évrart de Conty, *Les Problèmes*, manuscrit B.N. fr. 24282, explicit de la XIXe partie, consacrée à l'harmonie, fol. 56v°.

[74] Voir sur ce point Agathe Sultan, « *En conjunction de science* », tome I, p. 340. Agathe Sultan parle davantage à ce sujet de la séparation des métiers de compositeur et de poète à la fin du Moyen Âge. Il semble cependant intéressant d'appliquer cette hypothèse à l'auteur à caractère encyclopédique qu'était Évrart de Conty.

d'intermédiaire dans *Le Livre des eschez amoureux moralisés*: science aux facettes multiples, la musique permet l'articulation de plusieurs types de discours.

BIBLIOGRAPHIE

Abert, H., « Die Musikästhetik der *Échecs amoureux* », *Romanische Forschungen*, t. 15 (1904), 884–925.

Autrand, F., *Charles VI. La folie du roi*, Paris: 1986.

Badel, P.-Y., *Le Roman de la rose au XIVᵉ siècle. Étude de la réception de l'œuvre*, Genève: 1980.

Boèce, *Traité de la musique*, introduction, traduction et notes par C. Meyer, Turnhout: 2004.

Boudet, J.-P., *Entre science et nigromance. Atsrologie, divination et magie dans l'Occident médiéval (XIIᵉ–XVᵉ siècle)*, Paris: 2006.

Breidert, W., « Arithmomachia », in *Quadrivium. Musiques et sciences*, colloque conçu par Lustgarten, D., Joubert, C.-H., Pahaut, S. et Salazar, M. [Metz, 8–10 mars 1991], Paris: 1992, 169–178.

Cadden, J., « Preliminary observations on the place of the *Problemata* in medieval learning », in De Leemans, P., et Goyens, M. (eds.), *Aristotle's* Problemata *in different times and tongues*, Leuven: 2006, 1–19.

Christine de Pisan, *Le Livre des fais et bonnes meurs du sage roi Charles V*, Solente, S. (éd.), Paris: 1940, 2 volumes.

De Leemans, P., et Goyens, M. (eds.), *Aristotle's* Problemata *in different times and tongues*, Leuven: 2006.

Ducos, J., « Évrart de Conty, médecin et vulgarisateur à la cour de Charles V », in Cabanès, J.-L., (dir.), *Eidôlon, Cahiers du Laboratoire Pluridisciplinaire de Recherches sur l'Imaginaire appliquées à la Littérature*, n°55, *Littérature et médecine II*, juillet 2000, 63–74.

——, « Lectures et vulgarisations du savoir aristotélicien: les gloses d'Évrart de Conty (sections XXV–XXVI) », in De Leemans, P., et Goyens, M. (eds.), *Aristotle's* Problemata *in different times and tongues*, Leuven: 2006, 199–225.

Évrart de Conty (attribué à), *L'Harmonie des sphères: encyclopédie d'astronomie et de musique extraite du commentaire sur les* Échecs amoureux *(XVᵉ siècle)*, édition critique d'après les manuscrits de la BNF, Hyatte, R., Ponchard-Hyatte, M., New York, Berne, Frankfurt am Main: 1985.

Évrart de Conty, *Le Livre des eschez amoureux moralisés*, édition de Françoise Guichard-Tesson et de Bruno Roy, Montréal: 1993.

Folkerts, M., « La rithmomachie et le manuscrit Avranches 235 », Louis Callebat et Olivier Desbordes (éds.), *Science antique, science médiévale (autour d'Avranches 235). Actes du Colloque International (Mont-Saint-Michel, 4–7 septembre 1998)*, Hildesheim-Zürich-New York: 2000, 347–357.

Fritz, J.-M., *Paysages sonores au Moyen Âge. Le versant épistémologique*, Paris: 2000.

Godwin, J., (ed.), *Music, Mysticism and Magic: a sourcebook*, London-New York: 1986.

Guichard-Tesson, F., « Évrart de Conty, poète, traducteur et commentateur », in De Leemans, P., et Goyens, M. (eds.), *Aristotle's* Problemata *in different times and tongues*, Leuven: 2006, 145–174.

Guichard-Tesson, F., « 'Parler par figure et fabuleusement' dans les *Eschez amoureux* », *Le moyen français*, n°60–61 (2007), 257–290.

Horden, P., (ed.), *Music as Medicine. The History of Music Therapy since Antiquity*, Aldershot-Burlington USA-Singapore-Sydney: 2000.

Jacquart, D., *La Médecine médiévale dans le cadre parisien*, Paris: 1998.

——, «Médecine et morale: les cinq sens chez Évrard de Conty († 1405)», *Micrologus*, X (2002) «I cinque sensi. The Five Senses», 365–378.

Klibansky, R., Panofsky, E., et Saxl, F., *Saturne et la mélancolie. Études historiques et philosophiques: nature, religion, médecine et art*, traduit de l'anglais et d'autres langues par Durand-Bogaert, F., et Évrard, L., Paris: 1989 (1ère édition en anglais, 1964).

Kraft, C., *Liebesgarten-Allegorie der «Echecs amoureux», Kritische Ausgabe und Kommentar*, Frankfurt am Main: 1977.

Lefèvre, S., *Rhétorique et divination chez Nicole Oresme (c. 1322–1382). Étude et édition du Livre de divinacions*, thèse pour le doctorat, sous la direction de D. Poirion, Université de la Sorbonne-Paris IV: 1992, 3 volumes.

Mauro, L., «La musica nei commenti ai *Problemi*: Pietro d'Abano e Évrart de Conty», in Mauro, L., (a cura di), *La Musica nel pensiero medievale*, Ravenna: 2001, 31–69.

Meyer, C., «Mathématique et musique au Moyen Âge», in *Quadrivium. Musiques et sciences*, colloque conçu par Lustgarten, D., Joubert, C.-H., Pahaut, S. et Salazar, M. [Metz, 8–10 mars 1991], Paris: 1992, 107–121.

Nicole Oresme, *Nicole Oresme and the Medieval Geometry of Qualities and Motions. A treatise on the uniformity and difformity of intensities known as Tractatus de configurationibus qualitatum et motuum*, Marshall Clagett (ed.), Madison, Milkauwee and London: 1968.

Philippe de Mézières, *Le Songe du Vieil Pelerin*, éd. G. W. Coopland, Cambridge: 1969, 2 volumes.

Raimondi, G., «*Les Eschés amoureux*. Studio preparatorio ed edizione (I. vv. 1–3662)», *Pluteus*, 8–9 (1990–1998), Alessandria: 67–241.

——, «*Les Eschés amoureux*. Studio preparatorio ed edizione (II. vv. 3663–5538)», in *Pluteus*, 10 (1999), Alessandria: 2007, 39–158.

Siraisi, N. G., «The music of pulse in the writings of italian academic physicians (fourteenth and fifteenth century)», *Speculum*, n°50 (1975), 689–710.

Le Songe du vergier, Schnerb-Lièvre, M. (éd.), Paris: 1982, 2 volumes.

Sultan, A., «*En conjunction de science». Musique et rhétorique à la fin du Moyen Âge*, thèse de doctorat sous la direction de Madame le professeur J. Cerquiglini-Toulet, Université de Paris IV-Sorbonne: 2005, 2 volumes.

Thorndike, L., *A History of Magic and Experimental Science*, New York: 1958, 8 volumes.

Veenstra, J. R., *Magic and Divination at the Courts of Burgundy and France. Text and Context of Laurens Pignon's Contre les devineurs (1413)*, Leiden-New York-Köln: 1998.

Weill-Parot, N., «Science et magie au Moyen Âge», in Hamesse, J. (éd.), *Bilan et perspectives des études médiévales (1993–1998). Actes du IIe Congrès Européen d'Études Médiévales [1999]*, Turnhout: 2004.

——, «Encadrement ou dévoilement. L'occulte et le secret dans la nature chez Albert le Grand et Roger Bacon», in *Micrologus*, XIV, «Il Segreto», Firenze: 2006, 151–170.

PROPHECY, HARMONY, AND THE ALCHEMICAL TRANSFORMATION OF THE SOUL: THE KEY TO LASSO'S CHROMATIC SIBYLS

Marjorie A. Roth

Orlando di Lasso's Latin motet cycle *Prophetiae Sibyllarum* is an endur-ing puzzle of the Renaissance repertoire. More than a century after its discovery, the Sibyl cycle's unusually pervasive chromaticism, uncom-mon subject, unique texts, and unconfirmed provenance continue to challenge our music-theoretical assumptions, and thwart our attempts to situate the work within the context of sixteenth-century musical culture.[1] Several modern analyses of the prologue motet, *Carmina*

---

[1] Little can be said with certainty about the *Prophetiae Sibyllarum*. The facts are as follows: Four manuscript partbooks represent the only version of the cycle to survive from Lasso's lifetime (b. 1530/32–d. 1594). Originally part of the private collection of Duke Albrecht V of Bavaria, under whose auspices the manuscript was copied and illuminated, it is not known why, when, or how the work left Munich prior to being listed as missing from the archive in the mid-eighteenth century. Purchased from an anonymous owner in 1854 by an Augsburg agent representing the Wiener k. und. k. Hofbibliothek, the Sibyl codex is now catalogued as Mus. Hs. 18.744 at the Österreichische Nationalbibliothek. The partbooks measure 187 mm × 260 mm, are copied on parchment, bound in red velvet, and are embellished with enameled metal clasps. The musical notation for each Sibylline motet begins with a small portrait of the Sibyl whose oracle comprises its text (Figure 1b, soprano partbook, Persian Sibyl, fol. 24r. Image credit Österreichische Nationalbibliothek, ÖNB/Wien E 28.421-C). An identifying nameplate appears on the facing page (Figure 1a, soprano partbook, fol. 23v. Image credit ÖNB/Wien E 28.420-C). The prologue motet, *Carmina chromatico*, carries no illustration and no nameplate (Figure 1c, tenor partbook, fol. 23r. Image credit ÖNB/Wien E 29.980-C). There is general agreement that the illuminations were executed by Munich court artist Hans Mielich, who supplied each Sibyl with a Christological attribute and a number (presumably indicating her age). These features bear no relationship to the motet texts that follow. A portrait of the composer 'at 28 years of age' originally appeared at the end of each partbook (the cantus portrait is now missing). Lasso's sons published the *Prophetiae Sibyllarum* after his death, dedi-cating it to Abbot Paul Widmann of Tegernsee (Munich: Nikolaus Heinrich, 1600). This print contains no Sibylline imagery, no portrait of the composer, and survives incompletely (see RISM a I: L 1016). The motets of the *Prophetiae Sibyllarum* were never included in the *Magnum Opus Musicum*, the collected edition of Lasso's motets published by his sons (Munich: Nikolaus Heinrich, 1604). No other musical settings of the Sibyl cycle's texts have been identified. The earliest scholarly mention of the work appeared in 1864, when August Wilhelm Ambros wrote of its extravagant chromati-cism: 'Die angewendete Chromatik ist aber auch hier kein willkürliches Experiment,

Figure 1a. Soprano partbook, Persian Sibyl, fol. 23v. Image credit Austrian National Library, Vienna E 28.420-C.

Figure 1b. Soprano partbook, Persian Sibyl, fol. 24r. Image credit Austrian National Library, Vienna E 28.421-C.

Figure 1c. Tenor partbook, Prologue, fol. 23r. Image credit Austrian National Library, Vienna E 29.980-C.

chromatico, have been published, but while they do explore the technique of Lasso's harmony they fail to address sufficiently the questions of historical context and interpretation that are of primary interest here.[2] More pertinent to this essay are studies that have grappled with

---

sondern hat ihren äesthetischen Grund, den Prophetenliedern eine besondere, ungewhonte und wunderbare Farbung zu geben' (The shifting chromaticism here is no arbitrary experiment, but instead has its aesthetic basis in giving the songs of prophecy an unusual and wonderful coloring). See Ambros, *Geschichte der Musik*, 357–358; Leuchtmann, *Orlando di Lasso*, 124–134; Owens, *Mus. Hs. 18.744*, v–ix; Bergquist, 'The Poems', 516–521; Schlötterer, *Neue Reihe*, 11, 21; and Leuchtmann and Schaefer, *Prachthandschriften*, 40–41.

[2] No complete analysis of the *Prophetiae Sibyllarum* has been published, nor is one necessary in order to grasp Lasso's basic chromatic technique. As several scholars have noted, the harmonic shifts that so astonish the ear throughout the cycle comprise variations on one relatively simple voice-leading procedure (see Schlötterer, *Neue Reihe*, xvii–xx; and Hübler, 'chromatische Kompositionen', 29–34). Analytical attention has focused primarily on the prologue, the words of which announce and demonstrate the chromaticism to follow (see Example 1 and Figure 7). Each published analysis takes a unique approach to the prologue's harmony, revealing perhaps as much about the authors' pre-analytical assumptions as they do about Lasso's precompositional ones. See Berger, *Chromatic and Enharmonic*, 104–117, 'Tonality and Atonality', 484–504, and 'Common and Unusual', 61–73; Lake, 'A Comparison', 1–19; Crook, 'Tonal Compass', 286–306; Lowinsky, *Tonality and Atonality*, 38–41; Mitchell, 'The Prologue', 264–273; Klumpenhouwer, 'Cartesian', 15–37; and Boetticher, *Lasso*

questions of origin and function by examining the limited amount of documentary and biographical evidence available.[3] Peter Bergquist's identification of the Italian humanist source of Lasso's Latin Sibyl poems and their subsequent print history is foremost among such work.[4] Other important studies have confirmed that the *unica* set of illuminated manuscript partbooks – the musical notation of which is not in Lasso's hand – was produced by Munich court artisans, probably as part of Duke Albrecht V's effort to raise the artistic prestige of his court.[5]

But from what exemplar those artisans were copying, and from where that exemplar came, is not known, nor has the question ever been raised and explored in earnest. Moreover, there is no liturgical or ceremonial context with which the Sibyl cycle can be linked unambiguously, no record of a complete contemporary performance, and no reception history.[6] Even the popular assumption that the *Prophetiae Sibyllarum* was originally conceived and composed for Albrecht

---

und seine Zeit, 71–79. An unpublished analysis by this author, read before the New York-St. Lawrence Chapter of the American Musicological Society in 2004, suggests a connection between the prologue's chromatic harmony and its formal structure, context, and interpretation. See Roth, "Musical Model?'; see also Roth, 'The Voice of Prophecy', 320–348.

[3] Few facts about Lasso's early life survive. Born in the Franco-Flemish province of Mons, Lasso believed until late in his life that 1530 had been the year of his birth. He came to Italy as a youth and by 1551 was settled in Rome, serving as *maestro di cappella* at St. John Lateran from the spring of 1553 until the summer of 1554, at which time he returned briefly to Mons. Lasso was in Antwerp in 1555, and by 1556 was associated with Albrecht V's chapel at Munich. The partbooks of the Sibyl cycle were probably copied in 1558, (which, at the time, Lasso would have believed was his '28th year'). In addition to the sources mentioned in fn. 1, see also Haar, 'Lassus', 295–97; Roche, *Lassus*; van den Borren, *Orlande de Lassus*, 1–14; Langlois, 'Con bien fou', 8–10; Cardamone, 'Salon as Marketplace', 64–90, and 'Pro-French Factions', 23–47; Bossuyt, 'Lassos erste Jahre', 55–67; and Coeurdevey, *Roland de Lassus*.

[4] Bergquist, 'The Poems', 516–538.

[5] The question of scribal hand was settled by Helmut Hell, who identified that of Jean Pollet in the notation of the manuscript (Hell, 'Lasso-Autograph?', 51–64). See also Sandberger, 'Mitteilungen', 36; Leuchtmann, *Orlando di Lasso*, 124–125, fn. 144; and Owens, *Mus. Hs. 18.744*, vii–viii. On the *Prophetiae Sibyllarum*'s relationship to Munich, the opinions of Sandberger, Boetticher, Leuchtmann, Bergquist, and Schlötterer have had a significant impact on subsequent scholarship (see Bibliography).

[6] The only occasion upon which excerpts from the Sibyl cycle are known to have been heard took place in France in 1574. The publisher Le Roy reported to Lasso that King Charles IX had been favorably impressed with 'some Sibyls plus the prologue' (see Schlötterer, *Neue Reihe*, xxi; and Haar, "Composer and Entrepreneur', 135). Establishing a viable context for performance of the *Prophetiae Sibyllarum* is challenging. In 1990 Reinhold Schlötterer advanced the theory that it might have been linked to private devotional practices at Munich (Schlötterer, *Neue Reihe*, xii–xiii). In 1937 Hans Joachim Therstappen noted in his first modern edition of the work that

V's Bavarian court cannot be confirmed as fact. We know that Lasso lived in Italy for almost a decade before moving to Munich, and that he passed the year immediately prior to that move elsewhere in the north. The *Prophetiae Sibyllarum* could, therefore, have come from Naples (where he spent his youth near the legendary Cumaean Sibyl's cave), or from Rome (where he lived and worked in close proximity to Michelangelo's Sistine Chapel Sibyls), or from Antwerp (the base from which he began to publish after leaving Italy).[7] Thus it is clear that despite decades of research, we have grasped only isolated parts of Lasso's Sibylline enigma; parts that do not unite to form a coherent vision of the whole. Old questions remain to be answered, and new questions have yet to be asked.

For example, although the literature is filled with comment on the unusual text and chromaticism of the prologue, there is a remarkable absence of curiosity regarding the extreme peculiarity of a prologue being present at the opening of a motet cycle in the first place. During the Middle Ages and the Renaissance, prologues belonged typically to works of the theater, to literary romances, to pseudo-dramatic musical works like the madrigal comedy and, a bit later on of course, to opera. But prologues were not, as a rule, associated with the motet.[8] Yet we have never asked why Lasso's Sibylline motet cycle has one, and whether its anomalous presence conveys any useful information about the original performance context, meaning, and patronage of the work. Moreover, the traditional explanation of the *Prophetiae Sibyllarum's* intense chromaticism as "tone-painting" has never been examined critically, even though the majority of the cycle's chromatic shifts do not derive from any specific text imagery. And finally, the incongruous fact that the prologue motet – as it stands in the single surviving manuscript source, at least – carries no illustration and indicates no speaker, while all the other motets are assigned to specifically named and illustrated characters, has yet to be probed. It is

---

the series of prophetic motets had an almost 'Advent-like' character (Therstappen, *Das Chorwerk*, 2).

[7] Scholarly opinion on the cycle's provenance has been divided between Italy and Germany. Those favoring a southern origin emphasize aspects of musical style and *topos*, while those inclined toward the north cite the production of the partbooks at Munich. Given Lasso's mobility in the 1550s we should keep in mind that the copying of the manuscript at the Bavarian court cannot and must not be interpreted as proof that the cycle was originally intended for that context.

[8] See Cusick, 'Prologue', 302–303; Carter, 'Prologue', 424–425; and Woolf, *English Mystery Plays*, 158 and 164.

possible that a character was once intended for the *Carmina chroma-tico*, too, and that his or her identity is related to the prologue's curi-ous text and music.

In short, we have yet to comprehend fully what the marvelous fusion of oracular text to chromatic tone would have meant to the composer who created it, to the listeners who experienced it, and to the patron or patrons who desired it; and why that meaning was ultimately made manifest in a cycle of chromatic Latin motets. Unlike previous ana-lytical and documentary studies of the *Prophetiae Sibyllarum*, this essay takes the Sibyls themselves as a point of departure, examining points of intersection between Sibylline tradition and various trends in Western esotericism as they coexisted in mid-sixteenth-century Italy. Viewed from this perspective, Lasso's Sibyl cycle emerges as an artifact that is less a purely musical achievement than it is a profound and multi-faceted meditation upon the message and the meaning of Sibyl-line prophecy during the Renaissance. In the discussion that follows, a new source for the *Prophetiae Sibyllarum's* texts will be identified and the ramifications of that discovery will be explored in terms of a viable speaker for the prologue, a new interpretation of the chromatic harmony, and a proposed original audience and performance context for the work.

TEXT SOURCES: OLD AND NEW

Example 1: Prologue, Prophetiae Sibyllarum, *Text & Translation*

Carmina chromatico quae audis modulata tenore	These are the polyphonic songs that you now hear in a chromatic tenor;
Haec sunt illa quibus nostrae olim arcana salutis	[The songs] by which the twice-six Sibyls once sang, with intrepid mouths
Bis senae intrepido cecinerunt ore Sibyllae.	the mystery of our salvation.

In 1979, Peter Bergquist identified the source of Lasso's twelve Latin Sibyl poems.[9] The texts first appeared in an early sixteenth-century

---

[9] The Sibyl poems only, that is; the *Prophetiae Sibyllarum* is still the only known source for the prologue text (see Bergquist, 'The Poems', 529. Example 1 provides

Venetian edition of the *Discordantiae sanctorum doctorum Hieronymi et Augustini*, a humanistically-inspired theological treatise by Filippo de Barbieri (d. 1487), first published at Rome in 1481.[10] The twelve Sibyls of the *Discordantiae* are named in column 4 of Appendix 1.[11] Barbieri's treatise opens with a theological dispute between St. Jerome and St. Augustine, the subject of which is the validity of prophecy coming from outside Christian tradition. Among the many pagans noted and quoted in the text, right alongside the Church Fathers and the Old Testament Prophets, the Sibyls are singled out as the most authoritative. Barbieri gives them their own special sub-section in the text, complete with a set of illustrations portraying each Sibyl as she delivers her prophecy.

The woodcuts in Figure 2, Figure 3a, and Figure 3b come from two different editions of the *Discordantiae*. Figure 2 is Sibylla Persica from an early Roman edition of 1482.[12]

---

the original Latin and an English translation of the prologue. Many thanks to Peter Forshaw for this translation.

[10] Philippus de Barberiis, *Discordantiae sanctorum doctorum Hieronymi et Augustini*, Rome: J. P. Lignamine, 1481 (two versions of the 1481 edition exist, one with Sibyl illustrations only and one with images of both Sibyls and Prophets). A second Roman edition by another publisher followed in 1482 (*Discordantiae sanctorum doctorum Hieronymi et Augustini, tractatus sollemnis et utilis*, Georg Herold & Sixtus Reissinger), featuring more sophisticated Sibyl illustrations and no Prophets. Summary descriptions of the various prints can be found in Sheehan, *Bibliothecae Apostolicae*, reference numbers B-50-53, 380–383; and Bergquist, "The Poems', 522–529.

[11] Appendix 1 summarizes the most famous historical lists of Sibyls up to and including Lasso's group. The standardization of these twelve Sibyls originated with their depiction on the entrance hall wall of Giordano Orsini's palazzo Monte Giordano in Rome (c. 1432; destroyed 1470s or 1480s). To Varro's ancient list of ten Orsini added Sibylla Europaea and Sibylla Agrippa (See Bergquist, 'The Poems', 523; and Mode, 'Monte Giordano', 22–35). Unlike the other Sibylline names, Orsini's "Agrippa" is problematic in that it does not indicate a specific geographic region. Art historian Emile Mâle, however, has noted that in a manuscript version of the *Discordantiae* copied in the early 1480s (Paris, Bibliothèque nationale, Arsenal ms. no. 78, f. 67), the name "Agrippa" appears instead as "Aegyptia". See Mâle, *L'art religieux*, 261, fn. 2.

[12] Herold & Reissinger, 1482; used here because of its superior imagery. The list of Sibyls and the texts beneath them are essentially the same as those of the slightly earlier, less decorative Lignamine editions of 1481. Figure 2 is reproduced from the Bibliothèque nationale de France "gallica" website, public domain [remove underlinings, etc.](http://catalogue.bnf. fr/ark:/12148/ cb372825722/description, accessed September 4, 2008). The Bibliothèque nationale copy is dated 1481, with no publisher given. Comparison with a Biblioteca Apostolica Vaticana copy of the treatise (Inc. IV .280) shows that the text and illustrations are identical to those of the Herolt & Reissinger edition of 1482, and not the Lignamine editions of 1481.

Sibylla perfica ueſtita ueſte aurea cũ uelo albo i
capite. Dicens ſic Ecce beſtia cõculcaberis et gig
netur dominus in orbē terrag.et gremiũ uirginis
erit ſal⁕gẽtiũ.et pedes ci⁕ i ualitudie. hominum

Figure 2. Barbieri (1482), Persian Sibyl, public domain.

As is the case with all Barbieri's Sibyls, the caption below Persica's
image provides her name, a description of her clothing and a quotation
from the prophecy traditionally assigned to her in the art, literature,
and theology of the Middle Ages and the Renaissance. This common
prophecy is repeated on the scroll she holds in her hands. Figures 3a
and 3b show Sibylla Persica again, pictured in a later Venetian edition
of the *Discordantiae*.[13] By this time each Sibyl has acquired her own
two-page chapter, the woodcuts are considerably more elaborate, and
the Sibylline dossiers have been expanded and moved to the facing
page. Most important with respect to the *Prophetiae Sibyllarum*, however, is the addition of a new and much longer prophetic text for each

---

[13] Philippus de Barberiis, *Discordantiae sanctorum doctorum Hieronymi et Augustini, Quattuor hic compressa opuscula*, Venice: Bernardinum Benalium, c. 1500–1525.
Figures 3a and 3b (verso and recto sides of the Persian Sibyl's new presentation).

Figures 3a and 3b. Barbieri, c. 1500–1525. Figures 3a and 3b. Reproduced with permission of the National Gallery of Art Library, David K. E. Bruce Fund.

Sibyl. As figures 3a and 3b show, opposite Persica's image and beneath her expanded biography is the earliest known appearance of the six-line Latin poem that would later become her text in Lasso's motet cycle. Peter Bergquist has noted that these new oracular poems appear out of nowhere for the sixteenth-century Venetian edition, with no indication of their origin.[14]

My study of Sibylline Tradition and its relationship to the cultural context of Barbieri's treatise has, however, revealed an earlier source of the poems. In 1990 Reinhold Schlötterer noted that three of Lasso's Latin motet texts resembled three Italian theatrical verses from a popular Florentine Annunciation play by Feo Belcari.[15] The solid line connecting the right and left columns of Example 2 indicates the text correspondence mentioned by Schlötterer. The center column of Example 2, however, shows the new, earlier source for Barbieri's complete set of poems: a series of engravings from the 1470s attributed to Baccio Baldini, containing twelve Italian Sibylline verses that correspond exactly, in terms of their striking text imagery, to all twelve Latin Sibyl poems in the Venetian *Discordantiae*.

Example 2: Text Source Comparisons

Belcari, *Sacre Rappresentazione* (Late fifteenth century)	Baldini Engravings (c. 1470)	Barbieri/Lasso Poems (c. 1500–1525)
Persica (3)_____	Persica (1)_____	Persica (1)
	Libyca (2)_____	Libyca (2)
	Delphica (3)_____	Delphica (3)
	Cimmeria [Chimica] (4)_____	Cimmeria (4)
Samia (5)_____	Samia (6)_____	Samia (5)
Cumaea (8) - - - - - - - - - -Cumaea (7)_____		Cumaea (6)

[14] Bergquist, 'The Poems', 528. The author traces the print history of the poems in Italy and Germany, ultimately choosing as Lasso's most likely text source a northern edition of the sixth-century Greek *Oracula Sibyllina*, to which Barbieri's set of Latin Sibyl poems were appended (Sixt Birken and Sebastien Castellion, ed., *Sibyllinorum oraculorum Libri VIII*, Basel, 1555). Bergquist acknowledges that his conclusion is not grounded in the textual superiority of this print to any of the earlier Italian or German possibilities. See Roth, 'The Voice of Prophecy,' 298–303, for a critique of Bergquist's argument.

[15] Schlötterer, *Neue Reihe*, xiii–xiv.

Hellespontica (4) - - - - - -	Hellespontica (8)_____	Hellespontica (7)
	Phrygia (9)_____	Phrygia (8)
	Europaea (11)_____	Europaea (9)
Tiburtina (9) - - - - - - - - -	Tiburtina (10)_____	Tiburtina (10)
Erythraea (1)_____	Erythraea (5)_____	Erythraea (11)
	Agrippa (12)_____	Agrippa (12)
Sophonia (2)*		
Michea (6)*		
Osea (7)*		

Key: _____ Same poems
 - - - - - - - - - - Different poems
 * Sibyls not known to standard Western lists
 ( ) Order in which Sibyls appear

Figures 4 and 5 illustrate that Baldini, like Barbieri, depicted each Sibyl in the act of delivering her oracle, the full text of which appears in close visual proximity to her image.[16] And like Barbieri, Baldini was careful to include a quotation from each Sibyl's familiar traditional prophecy, either placed on her scroll, in her book, or simply floating in the air beside her. Art historians agree that Baldini's engravings commemorate the elaborate costumes and speeches of a popular theatrical production, probably an early version of Belcari's play.[17]

Example 3: Text Comparisons, Delphic Sibyl

Example 3a: Standard Delphic Prophecy in the Middle Ages &
Renaissance

Nascetur propheta absque matris coitu ex virgine eius.
A prophet will be born without his mother's coition, from a virgin.

Example 3b:	*Example 3c:*
Baldini/Belcari Delphic Prophecy,	*Lasso/Barbieri Delphic Prophecy,*
c. 1470	*c. 1500–1525*

---

[16] In Baldini's case the oracles are beneath the images, while Barbieri's Sibyls are pictured opposite their prophecies. Figures 4 and 5 are found in Hind, *Early Italian Engraving*, plates 246 and 247.

[17] Mâle, 'Une influence', 89–90. A modern edition of an abridged version of Belcari's play can be found in d'Ancona, *Sacre Rappresentazione*, vol. 1, 167–89. D'Ancona notes that the play was first published in the late fifteenth century and went through a series of reprints from 1528 until the early seventeenth century.

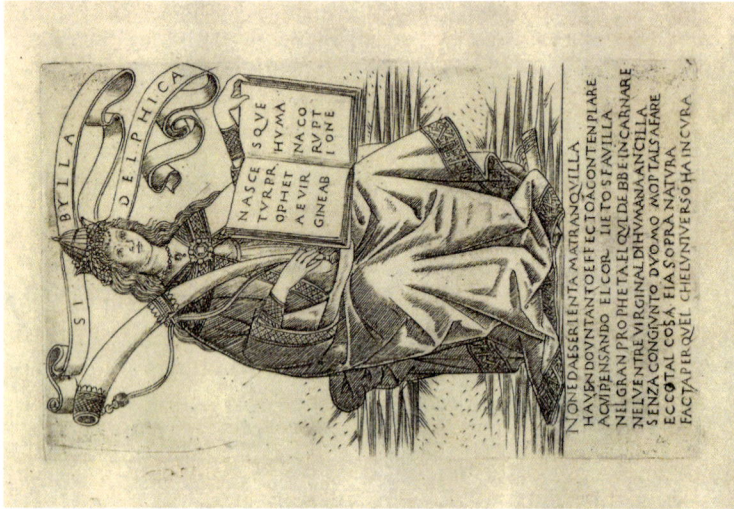

Figures 4 and 5. Baldini (c. 1470), Cimmerian Sibyl (Chimicha) and Delphic Sibyl. Reproduced with permission of the Trustees of the British Museum.

None daeser lenta ma tranquilla Havendo un tanto effecto a contenplare A cui pensando el cor lieto sfavilla Nel gran propheta el qui debbe incarnare Nel ventre virginal di humana ancilla Senza congiunto d'uomo mortal sa fare Ecco tal cosa fia sopra natura Facta per quel che l'universo ha in cura.	Non tarde veniet, tacita sed mente tenendum Hoc opus. hoc memori semper qui corde reponet, Huius pertentant cur gaudia magna prophetae Eximii, qui virginea conceptus ab alvo Prodibit, sine contactu maris. Omnia vincit Hoc naturae opera: ad fecit, qui cuncta gubernat.
She is not to be <u>slow but quiet,</u> being so effective in <u>contemplation.</u> In this thinking her heart happily sparks, through the great prophet who will become incarnate in the virgin womb of a human handmaid. She knows how to do this without Union of a mortal man. <u>Behold, this is a thing above nature,</u> done by the one who cares about the universe.	*He shall not come <u>slowly</u> (but this work must be held with <u>quiet thought</u>), he who will ever store this in a mindful heart, why his prophets may announce great joys of this exalted one, who shall come forth conceived from the virginal womb without taint of man. <u>This conquers all the works of nature:</u> yet he has done this who governs all things.*

The texts of the Delphic Sibyl provide a case in point. Example 3a is the short prophecy traditionally assigned to her throughout the Middle Ages and the Renaissance. When compared with Examples 3b and 3c, the unusual poetic imagery shared by the Italian verse and the Latin poem is clear. Both go far beyond Delphica's conventional oracle in terms of length and memorable wording, describing the Virgin's conception of Christ as 'a thing above nature' that requires 'slow and quiet contemplation' to occur. Nowhere else in Sibylline tradition are such unique turns of phrase attributed to Sibylla Delphica (or to any other Sibyl, for that matter). As Example 2 indicates, each of the *Discordantiae's* Latin sacred poems represents a careful preservation of the remarkable poetic imagery originating with the slightly earlier Italian theatrical verses.[18] Thus while it is true that the earliest source for the *Prophetiae Sibyllarum's* Latin poems is indeed the theological

---

[18] A comparison of all twelve Italian and Latin texts, as well as all twelve traditional Sibylline prophecies, can be found in Roth, 'The Voice of Prophecy', Appendix VI, 387–398 (Latin translations taken from Bergquist, 'The poems', 532–537; Italian translations by Amerigo Fabbri).

treatise identified by Bergquist, the original poetic content, context, and spirit of those poems belongs to Italian sacred theater. The *Discordantiae's* Venetian editor evidently felt that the popular theatrical verses would make a fitting contribution to the Sibylline dossiers that had been a feature of the treatise since its first edition. To preserve the scholarly tone of the work, he simply transposed Italian secular verse into Latin sacred poetry. The results are not literal translations; but the care with which the text imagery is preserved suggests that the editor had the Italian verses before him as he worked, that he intended his readers to recognize their distinctive wording, and to recall their theatrical origin as well.

A SPEAKER FOR THE *PROPHETIAE SIBYLLARUM'S* PROLOGUE

Knowing that Lasso's motet texts have their roots in the theater raises the intriguing possibility that the *Prophetiae Sibyllarum* was conceived originally as a dramatic (or semi-dramatic) work. If so, then the presence of a prologue is explained and the question of an intended speaker comes to the fore.[19] Traditionally, the character chosen to deliver a prologue is recognized as an expert on the subject to follow. He summarizes it for the audience and helps them understand its meaning. An appropriate speaker for Lasso's prologue, then, would surely have confirmed ties to Sibylline tradition. Ideally, he would be a Prophet himself; or if not, then he would be someone who, like the Sibyls, played an important part in human salvation history. And if not a musician or composer, then this speaker should at least be knowledgeable about some process or practice that can be reasonably described as "chromatic".[20] And finally, since he draws themes of prophecy, salvation, and chromaticism together with such remarkable efficiency in the *Carmina chromatico's* short text, perhaps this speaker is alluding

---

[19] We must keep in mind that the exemplar from which the Munich artisans worked when copying and illuminating the manuscript has not survived. It is possible that this exemplar originally indicated a character for the prologue whose name was omitted, for whatever reason, in the Munich manuscript partbooks. Both prologues and epilogues were flexible entities during the sixteenth and seventeenth centuries, designed to be adapted to suit the needs of each new performance. See Duffin, *Shakespeare's Songbook*, 13.

[20] Since Antiquity the word "chromatic" was used with reference to gradations of color as well as musical pitch.

to an aspect of Lasso's harmony that conveyed a special meaning to listeners of a particular kind. The chromaticism is musical, certainly; but the prologue's speaker may also be hinting that it is a metaphor for some other "chromatic" process or experience upon which he is himself an authority, and which is also embedded within the substance of Sibylline prophecy.

Readers familiar with esoteric trends in Italian Renaissance humanism will recognize Hermes Mercurius Trismegistus in this brief character sketch. In addition to his established ties to the art of music,[21] from the time of Lactantius Hermes was acknowledged by the Church as companion to his fellow pagan Prophets of Christ, the Sibyls.[22] During the Renaissance, Marsilio Ficino celebrated the Sibyls and their Sage in his *De religione Christiana* and *Theologica Platonica*,[23] and Hermes even appears in an edition of Barbieri's *Discordantiae*, mentioned in a substantial quote from Lactantius placed just before the Sibyl and Prophet illustrations appear in the text.[24] But surely the most spectacular proof of the historical and theological ties between Hermes and the Sibyls comes from the mosaic pavement of the Siena Cathedral. Here it is Hermes himself who welcomes Christians at the door, and ten of his Sibyls who flank the path leading up to the altar on both sides of the nave (Example 4).[25]

---

[21] Ancient legend names Hermes as the inventor of musical instruments, which he imprinted with symbols of the seven planets and their metals. Greek myth transmits the story that Hermes created his older brother Apollo's famous lyre as a peace offering for having stolen his cows. See Cary, *The Oxford Classical Dictionary*, 417.

[22] Lactantius, *Divine institutes*, first published in 1465. See Books I and IV on the legitimate prophetic status of the Sibyls and Hermes.

[23] Ficino, *De religione Christiana*, XXV (1576), and *Theologica platonica*, (1482), Book 13.2.8 (On Seers and Prophets) and 13.2.31 & 36 (The Seven Kinds of Emptiness or Release).

[24] No illustration of Hermes is included in this second Lignamine edition of 1481. It does, however, include an interesting image of "Plato Philosophus" among the Prophets, with this caption: "Plato dicit: In principio erat verbum & verbum erat apud deum U deus erat verbum. Usquae ibi & verbum caro factum est, etc." (Plato said: In the beginning was the word, and the word was with God and the word was God and the word was made flesh). See de Barberiis, *Tractatus est de discordantia*...(University of Michigan, Harlan Hatcher Graduate Research Library, Incun. 134). Plato's image occurs last in the series (with more discussion of Hermes in the subsequent text), following illustrations of the Sibyls and Prophets, Christ, John the Baptist, and a Nativity scene.

[25] See Appendix 1 (column 5). Figure 6 reproduces the mosaic of Hermes (public domain).

Example 4: Hermes and the Sibyls, Siena Cathedral Pavement

Altar

Tiburtina	Persica
Samia	Erythraea
Phrygia	Cumaea
Hellespontica	Cimmeria
Libyca	Delphica

Entrance: Hermes Mercurius
Trismegistus

The Siena pavement was completed in the 1480s, and is contemporary
with the first published version of Lactantius's *Divine institutes*, with
Ficino's writings on Hermes and the Sibyls, with the first editions of
Barbieri's treatise, with Belcari's Annunciation play, and with the set
of theatrical engravings I have shown to be the earliest known incarnation of the *Prophetiae Sibyllarum's* poems. It is therefore reason-
able to suggest that the named Pre-Christian Prophet who introduces
viewers to Sibylline images on the Siena cathedral floor is also the
unnamed character who introduces listeners to Sibylline songs in Lasso's motet cycle. Their connection is clear in the theology, art, and literature of the Renaissance, and I believe Lasso's *Prophetiae Sibyllarum*
to be the only musical manifestation of their partnership identified
thus far.

CHROMATIC HARMONY AS SPIRITUAL TRANSFORMATION

If we accept the "thrice-great" Hermes as master of ceremonies for
his "twice-six" Sibyls in the *Prophetiae Sibyllarum*, then we are free
to explore the effect of his identity upon contemporary interpretation of the cycle's pervasive chromaticism. Up to this point Lasso's
harmonic shifts have been explained simply as "tone-painting," the
musical counterpart to the contorted postures and facial expressions
used typically to express prophetic agony in the visual arts. Musical
analysts point to moments in the cycle when chromatic progressions
occur in conjunction with words in the text that invite such treatment.
The harmonies accompanying the word "chromatico" at the opening

Figure 6. Hermes Trismegistus, Siena Cathedral (public domain).

of the prologue (G-major/B-major/c#-minor/E-major) are one such example (see Figure 7).[26]

---

[26] The overall modal assignment of the prologue is mode 8; the opening and closing harmonies on G, with the main internal cadence on C, match the final and reciting tone normally associated with the Hypomixolydian mode. The low clef, no signature, and G final configuration also correspond to the tonal type that is used in Renaissance polypony to represent Mode 8 (See Powers, 'Tonal Types', 428–470). Use of the terms "major" and "minor" here reflect only the nature of the individual vertical sonorities; no reference to common practice tonality is intended. The five chromatic semi-tone

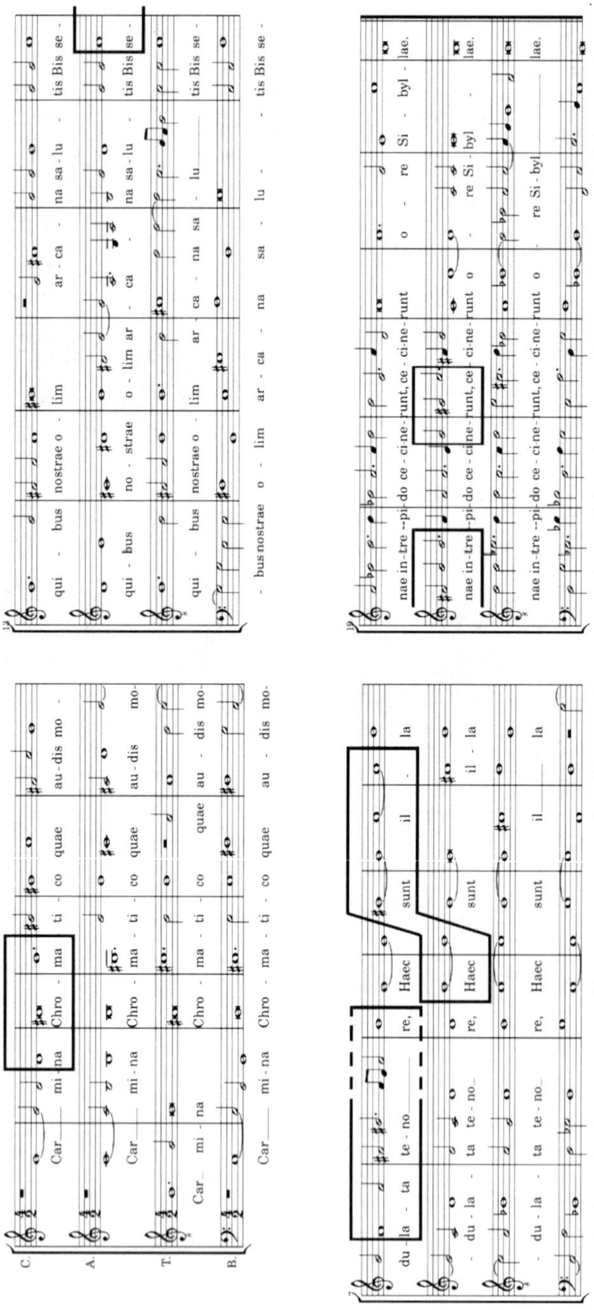

62   MARJORIE A. ROTH

Figure 7. Orlando di Lasso, *Prophetiae Sibyllarum*, Prologue motet, *Carmina chromatico.*

But while such moments do draw attention toward obvious word-tone correspondences, they also deflect it away from the fact that throughout the cycle as a whole, the majority of Lasso's chromatic gestures are not tied to specific words or phrases. The uniformly oracular tone and Marian orientation of the twelve Sibyl poems render them so similar in general content that the isolation of any particular poetic image for purposes of musical highlighting seems almost fortuitous. Moreover, the continual repetition of the same harmonic device – whether setting important words, unremarkable words, or fragments of several words within the same gesture – further dilutes the argument that Lasso's chromaticism can be explained exclusively as text-generated "tone-painting".[27]

Indeed, in most cases the Sibyl cycle's frequent chromatic shifts appear to follow a logic all their own, operating far beneath the textual surface of the music. As such it is possible that Lasso's listeners experienced them on two separate interpretive levels. On the most superficial plane the chromaticism would have been recognized as expressive of specific poetic imagery since, at times, Lasso's chromatic progressions do coincide with evocative words in the texts. And on this most "exoteric" level, the mention Hermes makes of chromaticism in the prologue would certainly have been taken as referring to a purely musical kind of chromaticism. But at a deeper interpretive level, the *Prophetiae*

---

progressions in the prologue are bracketed in Figure 7. The one accompanying the word "chromatico" seems a clear case of tone-painting. The chromatic setting of "tenore" may be, as well, since that word is linked grammatically to "chromatico". The three subsequent chromatic progressions are harder to explain as explicit word-tone correspondences, however, without referring them back to the ideas expressed in the first line of text. Many thanks to Steve Smith for Figures 7 and 8.

[27] A complete account of the chromatic semi-tone progressions in all the motets of the *Prophetiae Sibyllarum* is impractical here, but a few general remarks can be made. Outside of the prologue, instances of unambiguous chromatic "tone-painting" are relatively rare (see the multiple repetitions of 'per saecula vivus', Sibylla Libyca, mm. 46–51; and 'myrrham, aurum, thura Sabaea', Sibylla Cimmeria, mm. 37–43). Less obvious but still possible instances of chromatic "tone-painting" may occur on 'virgine matre', Sibylla Persica, mm. 1–4 and Sibylla Erythraea, mm. 30–32; and 'virgine magnus', Sibylla Persica, mm. 43–45. Since the cycle is full of references to the Virgin, however, it is unclear why these few would have been singled out for harmonic highlighting. Instances when "tone-painting" seems an unlikely explanation for a chromatic event resemble mm. 17–18 of the Libyan Sibyl's motet, when the chromatic progression occurs over fragments of several words and two grammatical units. The majority of Lasso's chromatic progressions fit this last description.

Sibyllarum's chromatic harmony would also have been understood as the embodiment of an essentially "esoteric" idea: the Platonically-derived goal of "imitation" that all creative artists of the Renaissance sought to achieve in their literary, artistic, and musical works.[28] I propose that Lasso's striking harmonic shifts, when not inspired by one specific word or phrase in a single Sibyl's prophecy, were intended to imitate the actual experience promised by all Sibylline prophecy. Mid-sixteenth-century listeners interested in avant-garde musical trends and also in questions of spiritual reform would have been capable of interpreting Lasso's chromaticism as a musically appropriate manifestation of the essential meaning of the Sibylline message – that is, the transformation and salvation of the human soul.

It is the overarching theme of transformation that connects the general prophetic *topos* of the *Prophetiae Sibyllarum* to its main characters, and to Lasso's chromatic technique. Ever since their entrance into Church doctrine during the early centuries CE, the Sibyls had devoted themselves solely to predicting the transformation of mankind from a condition of sin to one of grace through the birth, death, and resurrection of a Savior. Formulated in late Antiquity and passed on to the Middle Ages, this Christian reorientation of Sibylline prophecy toward the goal of salvation continued into the Renaissance, where it acquired a characteristically humanistic twist toward the blending of pagan Antiquity with modern Christianity.[29] The inherently transformational

---

[28] Armen Carapetyan has pointed out that realistic copying of the words, as in conventional "tone-painting," was only one of the ways music could imitate a text during the sixteenth century (Carapetyan, '*Imitazione della Natura*', 52). Theories of imitation and the semi-divine role of the imitative artist during the Renaissance rested largely on Plato (*Timaeus, Phaedrus, Republic, Ion*), Aristotle (*Poetics, Politics*), and the Pythagorean concept of the "harmony of the spheres" as interpreted and applied in the poetics of men like Giraldi Cinthio (*Discorsi [...] intorno al comporre dei romanzi*, Venice: 1554) and Francesco Patrizi (*La deca ammirabile*, Ferrara: 1587). See Henninger, *Touches of Sweet Harmony*; Sörbom, 'Aristotle,' 40; Wightman and Bryce, *Essays*, 187–207; Wightman, 'On the Nature', 205–232; Schwartz, 'Poetry as Imitation', 298–289; Platt, 'Never Before', 387–393.

[29] In addition to Lactantius, many other Fathers of the Church made use of the Sibyls in their efforts to define doctrine and bring in new converts. Moreover, several books of the sixth-century Byzantine collection of Sibylline prophecies, the *Oracula Sibyllina*, either adapted Jewish Sibyllines to Christian purposes (Books 1, 2, and the first part of book 8), or introduced completely new Christian material (the second part of book 8). See Cohn, *Pursuit*, 30–35; Momigliano, 'From the Pagan,' 7–12; Dronke, 'Hermes and the Sibyls', 1–38; and Thompson, 'Patristic Use', 127–128; and Grafton, 'Higher Criticism', 155–170. See also Parke, *Sibyls and Sibylline Oracles*; Tixeront, *Handbook*; and Coxe, *Ante-Nicene*.

properties of the *Prophetiae Sibyllarum's* harmonic style, too, had a long and venerable pedigree. Ancient Greek music theory recognized the chromatic inflection of pitch as a transformative process, likening it to the purifying physical and ethical effects attributed to the alchemical transformation of metals.[30] During the Renaissance, humanism's influence on music encouraged further exploration of this notion. The sixteenth-century theorist and composer Don Nicola Vicentino (d.1576),[31] for example, developed the idea of chromaticism as a kind of transformation. In his treatise *L'antica musica ridotta all moderna prattica* (Rome, 1555), Vicentino used the word *tramutatio* (transmutation) to describe the process of moving from the diatonic *genus* to the more ethically elevated chromatic *genus*.[32] Certainly he was thinking primarily in musical and compositional terms; but it is nonetheless true that in many humanistic circles of Vicentino's time the word *tramutatio* carried unmistakable overtones of another art grounded in the process of transformation, similarly marked by gradations of "color" and also dedicated to spiritual and material improvement.[33] This was,

---

[30] For example, the Greek text 'On the Making of Gold' by Pseudo-Zosimus in *Codex Marcianus 299 (M)* preserves material dating back to the first century CE and contains a discourse comparing musical and alchemical processes. The four musical "elements" (*stoiceioi*) of the tetrachord are equated with the four material elements comprising the egg from which the Philosopher's Stone is born (Wellesz, 'Music in the Treatises', 145–158). See also Henderson, 'Ancient Greek Music', 343–344; Winnington-Ingram, 'Greece: Ancient', 663–664; Taylor, 'The Alchemical Works', 135, fn. 23, 25–26; Meinl, "Alchemie und Musik', 209–212.

[31] Vicentino's famous disagreement with papal singer Vicente Lusitano over the practicality of singing non-diatonic music led, in June of 1551, to a series of public debates in Rome, with Vicentino ultimately the loser. It is not known whether Lasso was present for the event, but as the repercussions from it continued for years afterward – well into the time of Lasso's residence in Rome – the young composer could not have failed to be influenced by the issue.

[32] Vicentino, *Ancient Music*, 48; Berger, *Chromatic and Enharmonic*, 10, 15–16, and 126, fn. 27. Latin forms of the word "transmutation" appear in theory treatises prior to and contemporary with Vicentino's treatise. The majority of Medieval works use the word with reference to alteration of a rhythmic mode. During the sixteenth century, instances of "transmutation" being used with reference to musica ficta and alterations of mode become more frequent. See for example Franchino Gaffurio, *De harmonia instrumentorum opus* (Milan, 1518) and Stephano Vanneo, *Recanteum de musica aurea* (Rome, 1533).

[33] Since the earliest alchemical literature (Bolos of Mendes, *Phusika kai mustica*) color has marked the stages of transmutation during the alchemical process. See Holmyard, *Alchemy*, 26. In terms of music and the idea of color change during the Renaissance, the word "chromatic" was known to derive from the Greek *chroai*, a term that described subtle tonal colorations with the melodic *genera* achieved through

of course, the art of alchemy, the esoteric process by which base metal was transformed into gold.[34] In the *Prophetiae Sibyllarum*, then, we have an artwork in which several "transformational" themes dear to sixteenth-century Roman humanism converge: an abiding interest in prophecy and salvation, an acute concern for spiritual reform, much philosophical and practical curiosity about chromatic music, and the habitual use of alchemical language to describe the incremental phases of improvement in religious, political, social, and musical spheres.[35]

But were the Sibyls who sang Lasso's transforming harmonies themselves alchemists, or were they ever associated historically with the art? It is a fact that Sibylline prophecy had been linked to the process of metallic transformation since Antiquity. In his famous Fourth *Eclogue*, the Roman poet Virgil made the Cumaean Sibyl predict an Age of Iron giving way to a new Age of Gold. This famous "Cumaean Song" made such an impression on the Middle Ages that a quotation from it entered Church doctrine and became the Cumaean Sibyl's standard prophecy in Christian art, theater, and literature. Moreover, since the early Christian era persons inclined toward a spiritual interpretation of alchemy had associated Christ with the Philosopher's Stone, the catalyst necessary for the purifying process of salvation to begin. It is possible that the Sibyls, as acknowledged Prophets of that Stone, might

---

intervallic alteration. See Levin, 'Aspects', 283, and Hendersen, 'Ancient Greek Music', 343–344.

[34] The most recent translation of Vicentino's treatise (M. R. Maniates, 1996) gives the title as *Ancient Music Adapted to Modern Practice*. The English word "adapted" is perhaps inadequate to capture important shades of meaning inherent in the Italian *ridotta*, which suggests the process of "boiling down". Moreover, when describing how the diatonic and chromatic *genera* relate to one another, Vicentino notes that the chromatic is already present in the untransformed diatonic, needing only to be drawn out of it. Once accomplished, the transformed chromatic *genus* is an improved resource for setting ethically elevated texts and creating more spiritually edifying music. The similarities of this description to the alchemical process of drawing the inherent gold out of base metals are striking. I do not mean to imply that Vicentino was a practicing alchemist seeking to equate that art with the art of musical composition in his treatise (although I do not rule out the possibility). But the parallels that exist between Vicentino's musical language and the language of contemporary alchemy are worth remarking.

[35] Smith, 'Language of Mediation', 1–25; Brann, 'Alchemy and Melancholy, 127–148; Baldwin, 'Strange Bedfellows?', 41–64; Rowland, *Culture*; Schuler, 'Spiritual Alchemies', 293–318; Linden, 'Alchemy and Eschatology, 79–88; Crisciani, 'Conception of Alchemy,' 165–81; Sheppard, 'Redemption Theme', 42–46; Newman, 'Prophecy and Alchemy', 97–115; Keller, 'Science of Salvation', 486–493.

have been associated at least peripherally with spiritual alchemy.[36] And finally, although the early Church Fathers granted the Sibyl an unassailable position in Christian doctrine, a secularized and somewhat magical interpretation of her grew up alongside her sacred persona during the Middle Ages and Renaissance. Transferred to the realm of romance literature, the Virgin Sibyl's great age and unattractiveness were reinvented as youth and a dangerous beauty, while her prophetic gift was redefined as sorcery.[37] While I have discovered no unequivocal report of a Sibyl engaged in specifically alchemical work, it is nonetheless true that by Lasso's day educated people would have recognized the Sibyl as a figure possessed of both divine and magical gifts.

Indirect evidence of ties to alchemy might be drawn, however, from a few technical details in Baldini's engravings and in Lasso's *Prophetiae Sibyllarum*. First, since the art of alchemy was understood as existing above or outside of nature in that it enhanced or accelerated a natural process, the Baldini Delphic Sibyl's reference to Christ's conception as being 'a thing above nature' (see Examples 3b and 3c) comes across with a distinctly alchemical ring. The same can be said of her reference to 'slow and quiet contemplation', since it was common knowledge that an alchemist must work with patience and devotion. Second, there is the curious personal name attributed to Baldini's Cimmerian Sibyl in the upper left corner of her image (Figure 4). "Sibylla Chimica" (Chimicha) is an intriguing appellation, especially in light of her costume's suggestive headpiece. And finally, a moment of particularly striking and prolonged harmonic drama at the end of Lasso's Cimmerian Sibyl motet seems to recall Baldini's Sibylla Chimica and her decidedly

---

[36] See Mattingly, "Virgil's Fourth Eclogue', 14–19; Eliot, 'Christian World', 3–13; Kinter and Keller, *The Sibyl*, 35–36; Fairclough, *Virgil*; Comparetti, *Vergil*. The term "spiritual alchemy" is often fraught with Jungian associations for modern readers, but no such specific associations are intended here. I refer only to the fact that as early as Pseudo-Zosimos (*On the Making of Gold*, 300 CE) a close relationship existed between the transformative processes of physical alchemy and that of spiritual purification. This relationship continued through the early modern period in works like Petrus Bonus's *Margarita pretiosa novella* (written c. 1330, published Venice, 1546), the papal court speeches of Giles of Viterbo (d. 1532), and the sermons of John Donne (d. 1631). See also Coudert, 'Spiritual Alchemy', 46–47.

[37] Waegeman, 'Medieval Sibyl'; Kinter and Keller, *The Sibyl*; Dietachmayer, 'das Bild der Sibyllen'; Haffen, *Contribution*; McGinn, 'Sibylline Tradition'; Barto, *Tannhäuser*; Desonay, *Le Paradis*; Neri, 'Le tradizione italiane'; Patton, *Fairy Mythology*; Weiss, *Sibyllen*.

mercurial hat. One wonders if it can really be a coincidence that the slow chromatic progression, extending through the word *aurum* (gold), is followed by the most wrenching harmonic twist in the entire cycle, as Lasso's Cimmeria (alias Chimica?) describes the nativity gifts of the Magi from the East (Figure 8).

While these details are intriguing, the evidence for the Sibyls themselves as practicing alchemists is inconclusive, circumstantial at best. But about their long-time companion and the speaker for Lasso's prologue proposed above, there can be no doubt. Hermes Trismegistus was recognized by sixteenth-century humanists as the father of spiritual/philosophical alchemy and of practical/magical alchemy as well. If Hermes is the speaker in the *Prophetiae Sibyllarum's* prologue, then we can be sure the chromaticism he announces there – and the chromaticism his twelve companions echo ceaselessly throughout the cycle – was never intended to be understood as exclusively musical. By its very nature, the harmony of the *Prophetiae Sibyllarum* is alchemical. Like the colorfully chromatic process of physical alchemy, the musically chromatic process of Lasso's harmony imitates perfectly the transfor-

Figure 8. Orlando di Lasso, *Prophetiae Sibyllarum*, Cimmerian Sibyl excerpt, mm. 33–45.

mational experience of the soul as it undergoes the process of its own salvation.

SPECULATIONS ON PATRONAGE AND PERFORMANCE CONTEXT

The new information and ideas about the *Prophetiae Sibyllarum* discussed above suggest a re-evaluation of the work in terms of its generic assignment. Understood narrowly as a cycle of motets the *Prophetiae Sibyllarum* remains problematic since, in addition to its distinctly unmotet-like inclusion of a prologue, no conventionally para-liturgical or ceremonial context has ever emerged for its performance. Even Lasso's sons seem to have doubted its generic purity, excluding it from their complete edition of their father's motets. As a theater piece, however, the Sibyl cycle presents more felicitous possibilities. When understood as the musical setting of an Annunciation play, Lasso's motets acquire a satisfying sub-generic categorization and an automatic para-liturgical connection as well, being associated with a major feast and the sacred dramas commonly performed on that occasion. Moreover, during some calendar years the Annunciation (March 25) overlaps Holy Week. It is interesting that in 1554, Lasso's final year in service as *Maestro di cappella* at St. John Lateran, the Annunciation happened to fall on Easter Vigil,[38] the one day in the Church year upon which the reading of twelve Hebrew prophecies constitutes the main liturgical event. Lasso's twelve Sibylline motets parallel the twelve Biblical prophecies of Holy Saturday nicely, in a way that would have satisfied a Renaissance humanist's penchant for synthesizing the pagan and Hebrew forerunners of Christ.

I propose that the *Prophetiae Sibyllarum* was originally conceived as a private, un-staged musical drama, a sacred parallel – in form, musical style and function – to the slightly later secular genre of the madrigal comedy. Although madrigal comedies eschewed costumes, sets, and stage action, they were still "dramatic" in that they borrowed well-known characters and scenarios from staged theater or literature. The familiar costumes and postures of these borrowed characters were represented by stationary images included with the musical notation,

---

[38] Marcos J. Montes, *Calculation of the Ecclesiastical Calendar*, http://www.smart/ net/~mmontes/ec-cal.html (accessed May 12, 2005).

and their well-known personality traits and speech accents were conveyed through appropriate musical means.

Orazio Vecchi's madrigal comedy *L'Amfiparnasso* provides a case in point.[39] The second stanza of the prologue's text makes it clear that the singers themselves were the intended audience, and that the place of performance was not the physical stage of the worldly theater, but instead the visionary stage of the theater of the imagination.[40] Vecchi borrowed figures from the *commedia dell'arte* and used musical means to recreate the gestures, moods and actions the singers would have expected of each beloved character. He also provided images of the characters at the beginning of each madrigal, to enhance the performers' recollection of them.[41] Similarly, the Sibylline miniatures included in the manuscript partbooks of the *Prophetiae Sibyllarum* may indicate that, like Vecchi's *L'Amfiparnasso*, Lasso's Sibyl cycle also was created for an audience of singers who knew the personalities of their famous prophetic characters well; an audience who understood the nature and content of their typical speeches, and required only visual images – and appropriately transformative harmonies – to raise in imagination the message, meaning, and magic inherent in the music.[42]

But what kind of a contemporary audience would have required so singular a work of art? What kind of listener, patron, or singer would have been equipped to recognize Hermes as the speaker in the Pro-

---

[39] Venice: Gardano, 1597.

[40] *L'Amfiparnasso's* prologue is delivered by the *commedia dell'arte* character Lelio, who says in the second stanza: 'And the city where this story takes place is the great theater of the World, therefore everyone desires to hear it. But yet you should know that this spectacle of which I speak is seen in the mind, where it enters through the ears, and not through the eyes. But be silent, and instead of seeing, now listen.'

[41] The image of Lelio used at the head of the prologue in *L'Amfiparnasso* is reproduced in Nutter, 'Madrigal Comedy", 482–483, along with the image of Gratiano and Pantalone that precedes their madrigal in Act I, scene 3.

[42] Michael Maier's *Atalanta Fugiens* (Oppenheim, 1618) comes to mind here as well, as a work that combines music, poetry, visual imagery, and alchemy in a composition not designed for public performance but instead for the private contemplation and edification of the performers. For more on the *Atalanta Fugiens* see Manfred Kelkel, 'A la recherche d'un art total: musique et alchimie chez Michael Maier', *Analyse Musicale* 8 (1987), 49–55; Jacques Rebotier, 'L'art de la musique chez Michael Maier', *Revue de l'Histoire des religions* (1972), 29–51; Domenico Canzoniero, *L'Atalanta fugiens (1617) di Michael Maier*, tesi di laurea [inedita], Università degli Studi di Bologna, 1996–1997. Many thanks to Laurence Wuidar for these references. See also Joscelyn Godwin, 'A Context for Michael Maier's *Atalanta Fugiens*', *The Hermetic Journal* 29 (1995), 4–10.

logue, and to appreciate the alchemical overtones of Lasso's chromatic harmony? The original audience I envision for the *Prophetiae Sibyllarum* would have been humanistically-educated, trained in theology, and well-versed in the literature, lore, art, and theater of a Sibylline Tradition that connected the pagan Antiquity that was their private dream to the glories and griefs of the High Renaissance culture that was their public reality. They would have been musically sophisticated, able to sing polyphony, and familiar with the fierce chromatic debates raging around them. They would have enjoyed discussing the ethical potential of chromatic music, and the ways in which they might make practical use of it to better their world. They would have been concerned with questions of human salvation, and dedicated to the slow and difficult process of reforming their souls and their religious institutions.

Imagine a private gathering of Roman humanists in the early 1550s: lovers of music, art, and poetry; scholars and reformers of the Church, dedicated to the past and future glory of their beloved city; devotees of Hermes and his perennial wisdom; enamored of the Sibyls and all their Classical past. They would have met for conviviality, spiritual contemplation and entertainment, much as their forebears had done in the golden days of Italian Humanism, before the effects of the Protestant Reformation and the Sack of Rome had combined to dissolve the world of wonders they knew and loved. Lasso's *Prophetiae Sibyllarum* would have been an eminently suitable entertainment for such an audience. They might have sung the motets themselves, opening their souls to the experience of salvation by filling their eyes with images of the Sibyls who promised it, and their ears with the chromatic harmonies that imitated it. As Romans and humanists with their hearts and minds anchored in the past – but as reformers and leaders facing an uncertain future – an evening's experience of Sibylline prophecy in sight and in sound would have restored their wounded pride, renewed their flagging faith, and offered warmth and consolation as the chill of the Counter-Reformation set in.

APPENDIX 1: HISTORICAL LISTS OF SIBYLS

	I. Lactantius DI (4th c)[43]	II. Orsini Palace frescoes[44] (1432)	III. St. Gallen woodcuts[45] (1470)	IV. Barbieri treatise[46] (1481/1482)	V. Siena pavement[47] (1480s)	VI. Barbieri treatise[48] (c. 1500–25)	VII. Lasso Prophetiae Sibyllarum (c. 1550–60)
0.	-0- (H.M.T.)	-0-	-0-	-0- (H.M.T.)	H.M.T.	-0-	Prologue (H.M.T)
1.	Persica	Persica	Persica	Persica	Lybica (L)	Persica	Persica
2.	Libyca	Libyca	Libyca	Libyca	Delphica (R)	Libyca	Libyca
3.	Delphica	Dephica	Erythraea	Delphica	Hellespontica (L)	Delphica	Delphica
4.	Cimmeria	Cimmeria	Cumaea	Cimmeria/Chimica	Cimmeria (R)	Cimmeria/Chimica	Cimmeria
5.	Erythraea	Erythraea	Samia	Erythraea	Phrygia (L)	Samia	Samia
6.	Samia	Samia	Cimmeria	Samia	Cumana (R)	Cumaea/Cumana	Cumaea
7.	Cumaea	Cumaea	Europaea	Cumaea/Cumana	Samia (L)	Hellespontica	Hellespontica
8.	Hellespontica	Hellespontica	Tiburtina	Hellespontica	Erythraea (R)	Phrygia	Phrygia
9.	Phrygia	Phrygia	Agrippa	Phrygia	Tiburtina (L)	Europaea	Europaea
10.	Tiburtina	Tiburtina	Delphica	Europaea	Persica (R)	Tiburtina	Tiburtina
11.	-0-	Europaea	Hellespontica	Tiburtina	-0-	Erythraea	Erythraea
12.	-0-	Agrippa	Phrygia	Agrippa	-0-	Agrippa	Agrippa

[43] Lactantius, *Divine Institutes*, 4th c. BCE. (published 1465); based on Varro's list of Sibyls in the (now lost) *Antiquitates rerum divinarum*, 1st century, BCE.

[44] From fifteenth-century manuscript descriptions of the Orsini palace frescoes at Monte Giordano in Rome: Liège ms. 6 F (*Grand Séminaire de Liège*, c. 1430's); Tongerloo ms. HB I 16 (*Abbey of Tongerloo*, c. 1450); Munich Staatsbibliothek cod. Lat. Mon. 19859, fol. 187v–189v, 1478). Liège and Tongerloo are virtually identical. The Munich manuscript is an abridged version of the other two sources. In all three the order of the Sibyls is the same.

[45] See facsimile edition by P. Heitz (ed.), *Oracula Sibyllina*, Strassburg: Heitz & Mündel, 1903.

[46] Philippus de Barberiis, *Discordantiae sanctorum doctorum Hieronymi et Augustini*, Rome: J. P. Lignamine, 1481 (Biblioteca Apostolica Vaticana, Membr. IV. 29); and Barberiis, *Discordantiae.... Tractatus sollemnis et utilis*, Georg Herold & Sixtus Reissinger: Rome, 1482 (Biblioteca Apostolica Vaticana, Inc. IV. 280). A second Lignamine edition of Barbieri's treatise, also published in 1481 (*Tractatus est de discordantia inter Eusebium Heironium & Aurelium Augustinum approbatus Sibyllarum & propheatum*, Rome) lists the Sibyls in this same order, but pairs them with prophets (University of Michigan, Harlan Hatcher Graduate Research Library, Incun. 134). This edition also quotes Lactantius on Hermes Mercurius Trismegistus in the text before the images of the Sibyls and Prophets appear (H.M.T., above).

[47] The Siena Cathedral's ten Sibyls occur in two columns on the right and left sides of the nave. Any sense of narrative or chronology, if indeed one was ever intended, is difficult to construct from this arrangement. The Cathedral's Cimmerian Sibyl is misnamed as 'Cumaea'.

[48] Philippus de Barberiis, *Discordantiae sanctorum doctorum Hieronymi et Augustini, Quattuor hic compressa opuscula*, Venice: Bernardinum Benalium, c. 1500–1525. (National Gallery of Art Library, BR50 B34 1520). The copy held by the Folger Shakespeare Library (Inc. B107) reverses the order of the last two Sibyls, and mislabels the image of Sibylla Libyca.

BIBLIOGRAPHY

Ambros, A.W., *Geschichte der Musik*, vol. 3, Leipzig: 1868. Photographic reprint, Hildesheim: G. Olms, 1968.

Baldwin, M., 'Alchemy and the Society of Jesus in the Seventeenth Century: Strange Bedfellows?', *Ambix* 40:2 (1993), 41–64.

Barto, P., *Tannhäuser and the Mountain of Venus: A Study in the Legend of the Germanic Paradise*, New York: Oxford University Press, 1916.

Berger, K., *Theories of Chromatic and Enharmonic Music in Later Sixteenth Century Italy*, Ann Arbor: UMI Research Press, 1976, 1980.

——, 'Tonality and Atonality in the Prologue to Orlando di Lasso's Prophetiae Sibyllarum: Some Methodological Problems in the Analysis of Sixteenth-Century Music', *The Musical Quarterly* 66 (1980), 484–504.

——, 'The Common and Unusual Steps of Musica Ficta: A Background for the Gamut of Orlando di Lasso's Prophetiae Sibyllarum', *Revue belge de musicologie* 39–40 (1985-6), 61–73.

Bergquist, P., 'The Poems of Orlando di Lasso's Prophetiae Sibyllarum and Their Sources', *Journal of the American Musicological Society* 32 (1979), 516–538.

Boetticher, W., *Orlando di Lasso und seine Zeit: 1532-1594*, vol. 1, Kassel: Bärenreiter, 1958.

Bossuyt, I., 'Lassos erste Jahre in München (1556-59): Eine "cosa non riuscita"? Neue Materialen aufgrund unveroffentlicher Briefer von Johann Jakob Fugger, Antoine Perrenot de Granville, und Orlando di Lasso', in: Stephen Horner and Bernhold Schmid (eds.), *Festschrift für Horst Leuchtmann zum 65. Geburtstag*, Tutzing: Schneider 1993, 55–67.

Brann, N., 'Alchemy and Melancholy in Medieval and Renaissance Thought: A Query into the Mythical Basis of Their Relationship', *Ambix* 32:3 (1985), 127–148.

Carapetyan, A., 'The Concept of Imitazione della Natura in the Sixteenth Century,' *Journal of Renaissance and Baroque Music* 1 (1946), 47–67.

Cardamone, D. G., 'The Salon as Marketplace in the 1550s: Patrons and Collectors of Lasso's Secular Music', in: P. Bergquist (ed.), *Orlando di Lasso Studies*, Cambridge: Cambridge University Press 1999, 64–90.

——, '"Orlando di Lasso and Pro-French Factions in Rome', in: I. Bossuyt (ed.), *Orlandus Lassus and His Time*, Belgium: Alamire 1995, 23–47.

Carter, T., 'Prologue', in: S. Sadie (ed.), *The New Grove Dictionary of Music and Musicians*, 2nd edition, vol. 20, London & New York: Macmillan 2001, 424–425.

Cary, M., et al., *The Oxford Classical Dictionary*, Oxford: Clarendon Press, 1949.

Coeurdevey, A., *Roland de Lassus*, Paris: Fayard, 2003.

Cohn, N., *The Pursuit of the Millennium*, New York: Oxford University Press, 1972.

Comparetti, D., *Vergil in the Middle Ages*, trans. E. Benecke, New York: G. E. Stechert, 1929.

Coudert, A., 'Spiritual Alchemy' in W.J. Hanegraaff, (ed.): *Dictionary of Gnosis and Western Esotericism*, Leiden: Brill 2005, 46–47.

Coxe, A. C., ed., *The Ante-Nicene Fathers: Translations of the Writings of the Fathers Down to AD 325*, vol. 2, New York: Scribners, 1926.

Crisciani, C., 'The Conception of Alchemy as Expressed in the *Pretiosa Margarita Novella* of Petrus Bonus of Ferrara', *Ambix* 20:3 (1973), 165–181.

Crook, D., 'Tonal Compass in the Motets of Orlando di Lasso', in: D. Pesche (ed.), *Hearing the Motet*, Oxford: Oxford University Press 1998, 286–306.

Cusick, S. G., 'Prologue', in: S. Sadie (ed.), *The New Grove Dictionary of Music and Musicians*, vol. 15, London & New York: Macmillan 1980, 302–303.

D'Ancona, A., *Sacre Rappresentazione*, vol. 1, Florence: Successori le Monnier 1872, 167–189.

Desonay, F., *Le Paradis de la reine Sibylle d'Antoine de la Sale*, Paris, 1930.

Dietachmayer, G., 'Das Bild der Sibyllen im Mittelalter,' Diplomarbeit, Universität Wien, 1988.

Dronke, P., 'Hermes and the Sibyls: Continuations and Creations', inaugural lecture delivered March 9, 1990, Cambridge: Cambridge University Press, 1990.

Duffin, R. W., *Shakespeare's Songbook* (Foreword by Stephen Orgel), London: W. W. Norton, 2004.

Eliot, T. S., 'Virgil and the Christian World', *Sewanee Review* 61:1 (1953), 1–14.

Fairclough, H. R., Virgil, vol. 1, *Eclogues, Georgics, Aeneid I-IV*, London: William Heinemann, 1935.

Ficino, M., *de religione Christiana* in: Marsilius Ficinus, *Opera*, chapter 25, Basel, 1576.

——, *Platonic Theology*, trans. M. J. B. Allen, ed. J. Hankins, vol. 4 & vol. 6, London: Harvard University Press, 2004.

Grafton, A., 'Higher Criticism Ancient and Modern: The Lamentable Deaths of Hermes and the Sibyls,' in: C. Dionisetti, et. al. (eds.), *The Uses of Greek and Latin: Historical Essays*, London: The Warburg Institute 1988, 155–170.

Godwin, J., 'A Context for Michael Maier's *Atalanta Fugiens*', *The Hermetic Journal* 29 (1995), 4–10.

Haar, J., 'Orlande de Lassus', in: S. Sadie (ed.), *The New Grove Dictionary of Music and Musicians*, 2nd edition, vol. 14, London & New York: Macmillan 2001, 295–297.

——, 'Orlando di Lasso, Composer and Print Entrepreneur', in: Kate van Orden (ed.), *Music and the Cultures of Print*, New York: Garland 2000, 125–162.

Haffen, J., *Contribution a l'Etude de la Sibylle Mediévale*, Paris: Université de Besançon, 1984.

Hell, H., 'Ist der Wiener Sibyllen-codex wirklich ein Lasso-Autograph?', *Musik in Bayern* 28 (1984), 51–64.

Henderson, I., 'Ancient Greek Music' in: E. Wellesz (ed.), *The New Oxford History of Music*, London: Oxford University Press 1957, 336–397.

Henninger, S. K., *Touches of Sweet Harmony: Pythagorean Cosmology and Renaissance Poetics*, San Marino, CA: Huntington Library, 1974.

Hind, A. M., *Early Italian Engraving*, London: B. Quartich, Ltd., 1938.

Holmyard, E. J., *Alchemy*, Harmondsworth, England: Penguin Books, 1957.

Hübler, K.-K., 'Orlando di Lasso's Prophetiae Sibyllarum oder über chromatische Kompositionen im 16. Jahrhundert', *Zeitschrift für Musiktheorie* 1 (1978), 29–34.

Kassler, J. C., 'Music as Model in Early Modern Science', *History of Science* 20 (1982), 103–139.

Keller, J. R. 'The Science of Salvation: Spiritual Alchemy in John Donne's Final Sermon', *Sixteenth Century Journal* 23:3 (1992), 486–493.

Kinter, W. L., and Keller, J. R., *The Sibyl: Prophetess of Antiquity and Medieval Fay*, Philadelphia: Dorrance, 1967.

Klumpenhouwer, H., 'The Cartesian Choir', *Music Theory Spectrum* 14:1 (1992), 15–37.

Lake, W., 'Orlando di Lasso's Prologue to Prophetiae Sibyllarum: A Comparison of Analytical Approaches', *In Theory Only* 11 (1989–91), 1–19.

Langlois, F., *Con bien fou tu serais Orlando: Commentaires et traduction*, Paris: Bernard Coutaz, 1998.

Leuchtmann, H., *Orlando di Lasso*, vol. 1, Wiesbaden: Breitkopf & Härtel, 1976.

Leuchtmann, H., and H. Schaefer, *Orlando di Lasso: Prachthandschriften und Quellenüberlieferung aus dem Beständen der Bayerische Staatsbibliothek München*, Tutzing: Hans Schneider, 1994.

Levin, F. R. 'Aspects of Ancient Greek Music' in D. R. Fideler (ed.), *Alexandria*, vol. 1, Grand Rapids: Phanes Press 1991, 251–291.

Linden, S.J., 'Mystical Alchemy and Eschatology in Seventeenth Century Religious Poetry', *Pacific Coast Philology* 19 (1984), 79–88.

Lowinsky, E., *Tonality and Atonality in Sixteenth Century Music*, Berkeley and Los Angeles: University of California Press, 1962.

Mâle, E., 'Une influence des mystères sur l'art italien de XV siècle', *Gazette des beaux-arts* 35 (1906), 89–94.

——, *L'art religieux de la fin du môyen age en France*, Paris: Librarie A. Colin, 1925.

Mattingly, H., 'Virgil's Fourth Eclogue', *Journal of the Warburg and Courtauld Institutes* 10 (1947), 14–19.

McGinn, B., 'Teste David cum Sibylla: The Significance of the Sibylline Tradition in the Middle Ages' in: J. Kirshner and S. Wemple (eds.), *Women of the Medieval World*, New York: Basil Blackwell 1985, 7–35.

Meinl, C., 'Alchemie und Musik', in: *Der Alchemie in der europaischen Kultur- und Wissenschaftsgeschichte, 16th Wolfenbüttler Symposium, Herzog August Bibliothek*, Wiesbaden: O. Harrass 1984, 201–227.

Mitchell, W., 'The Prologue to Orlando di Lasso's Prophetiae Sibyllarum', *Music Forum* 2 (1970), 264–273.

Mode, R. L., 'The Monte Giordano Famous Men Cycle of Cardinal Giordano Orsini and the *Uomini Famosi* Tradition in Fifteenth-Century Art', PhD. dissertation, University of Michigan, 1970.

Momigliano, A., 'From the Pagan to the Christian Sibyl' in: C. Dionisetti, et. al. (eds.), *The Uses of Greek and Latin*: Historical Essays, London: The Warburg Institute 1988, 3–18.

Neri, F., 'Le Tradizione italiane della Sibylla', *Studi medievali* 4 (1912–13), 213–230.

Newman, W., 'Prophecy and Alchemy: The Origin of Eirenaeus Philalethes', *Ambix* 37:3 (1990), 97–115.

Nutter, D., 'Madrigal Comedy', in: S. Sadie (ed.), *The New Grove Dictionary of Music and Musicians*, vol. 11, London & New York: Macmillan 1980, 482–483.

Owens, J. A., ed., *Vienna Österreichische Nationalbibliothek, Musiksammlung, Mus. Hs. 18.744*, New York: Garland, 1986.

Parke, H.W., *Sibyls and Sibylline Prophecy in Classical Antiquity*, London: Routledge, 1988.

Partner, P., *Renaissance Rome 1500–1559: A Portrait of a Society*, Berkeley & Los Angeles: University of California Press, 1979.

Patton, L. A., *Studies in the Fairy Mythology of Arthurian Romance*, Boston, 1903.

Platt, P. G., '"Never Before Known or Dreamt of": Francesco Patrizi and the Power of Wonder in Renaissance Poetics', *Review of English Studies* 43:171 (1992), 387–394.

Powers, H. S. 'Tonal Types and Modal Categories', *Journal of the American Musicological Society* 31:3 (1981), 428–470.

Roche, J., *Lassus*, Oxford Studies of Composers, vol. 19, London: Oxford University Press, 1982.

Roth, M. A., 'The Song of the Prophets: A Musical Model for Orlando di Lasso's Carmina Chromatico?', unpublished paper read before the New York – St. Lawrence Chapter of the American Musicological Society, 3 April, 2004.

——, 'The Voice of Prophecy: Orlando di Lasso's Sibyls and Italian Humanism', unpublished dissertation, University of Rochester, Eastman School of Music, 2005 (Ann Arbor, Michigan: UMI Dissertation Services, Microform #3186973).

Rowland, I. D., *The Culture of the High Renaissance: Ancients and Moderns in Sixteenth Century Rome*, Cambridge: Cambridge University Press, 1998.

Sandberger, A., 'Mitteilungen über ein Handschrift und ein neues Bildnis Orlando di Lasso's', in: A. Sandberger (ed.), *Ausgewählte Aufsätze zur Musikgeschichte*, vol. 1, Munich: Drei Masken Verlag 1921, 34–40.

Schlötterer, R., ed., *Orlando di Lasso, Neue Reihe*, vol. 21, 'Prophetiae Sibyllarum', Kassel: Bärenreiter, 1990.

Schwartz, D., 'Poetry as Imitation' in: J. Rahn (ed.), *Perspectives on Musical Aesthetics*, New York: W. W. Norton 1994, 297–301.

Schuler, R. M., 'Some Spiritual Alchemies of Seventeenth-Century England', *Journal of the History of Ideas* 41:2 (1980), 293–318.

Sheehan, W. J., ed., *Bibliothecae Apostolicae Vaticanae Incunabula, Studi e testi*, vol. 2, Vatican City, 1997.

Sheppard, H. J., 'The Redemption Theme and Hellenistic Alchemy', *Ambix* 7 (1959), 42–46.

Smith, P., 'Alchemy as a Language of Mediation at the Hapsburg Court', *Isis* 85:1 (1994), 1–25.

Sörbom, G., 'Aristotle on Music as Representation', *Journal of Aesthetics and Art Criticism* 52:1 (1994), 37–46.

Taylor, S.F., 'The Alchemical Works of Stephanos of Alexandria', *Ambix* 1 (1937), vol. 1, 116–139; vol. 2, 39–49.

Thompson, B., 'Patristic Use of the Sibylline Oracles', *Review of Religion* 16 (1952), 115–136.

Van den Borren, C., *Orlande de Lassus*, 3rd edition, Paris: Librarie Fèlix Alcan, 1982.

Vicentino, N., *Ancient Music Adapted to Modern Practice*, ed. C. V. Palisca, trans. M. R. Maniates, New Haven: Yale University Press, 1996.

Waegeman, A., 'The Medieval Sibyl' in: L. J. R. Milis (ed.), *The Pagan Middle Ages*, trans. T. Guest, Woodbridge: The Boydell Press 1988, 83–107.

Wellesz, E., 'Music in the Treatises of Greek Gnostics and Alchemists,' *Ambix* 4 (1951), 145–158.

Weiss, J., 'Sibyllen und sibyllinische Weissagungen in der Literatur des Mittelalters', Diplomarbeit, Universität Wien, 1995.

Whiteman, W. P. D., 'Adam Smith: On the Nature of that Imitation which Takes Place in What are Called the Imitative Arts, Part II', *Musiktheorie* 15:3 (2000), 205–223.

Whiteman, W. P. D, and J. C. Bryce, eds., *Adam Smith: Essays on Philosophical Subjects*, Oxford: Clarendon Press, 1980.

Winnington-Ingram, R. P., 'Greece, I: Ancient' in: S. Sadie (ed.), *The New Grove Dictionary of Music and Musicians*, vol. 7, London & New York: Macmillan 1980, 663–664.

Woolf, R., *The English Mystery Plays*, Berkeley and Los Angeles: University of California Press, 1972.

DWELLING IN DARKNESS:
DOWLAND'S DARK SONGS AS HERMETIC PESSIMIST GNOSIS, AND COULD THIS BE 'EVIDENCE' OF THE ESOTERIC 'SCHOOL OF NIGHT'?

Anthony Rooley

In darknesse let me dwell, the ground shall sorrow be,
The roofe Dispaire to barre all cheerfull light from mee,
The wals of marble blacke that moistned still shall weepe,
My musicke hellish jarring sounds to banish friendly sleepe.
Thus wedded to my woes, and bedded to my tombe,
O let me living die till death doe come.
In darknesse let me dwell...[1]

Indubitably John Dowland's song 'In Darkness let Me Dwell' (*A Musical Banquet, 1610*)[2] is one of the most profound, most sublime and most enigmatic songs of that Age. 'Profound' because the performers and listeners are transported to an exquisitely cavernous space, at

---

[1] In every case when quoting original poetry or lyrics I refer to the original printed source. In each of the quotations I make, I have chosen to represent the poetry in original spelling and original punctuation (although modernizing the 'long "*s*"', and the "*u*"/"*v*" and "*i*"/"*j*" interchangeability). The inconsistency that the Elizabethans applied to first letter capitalization for personification (this was applied so much more sensibly and thoroughly in the 18thC, for example), and their wanton punctuation leaves controversial alternative readings. Nevertheless, the attentive reader can make individual judgments of their own, not filtered by editors who inevitably work from their own 'frame of reference', not an Elizabethan or Jacobean one. With the present topic 'obscurity' is the name of the game, and it would be a brave (or foolish) scholar who pronounced that one interpretation only is correct. The use of *tropes*, refined to a high degree of subtlety was engendered by such works as Peacham, Henry *The Garden of Eloquence*, 1577 (facsimile edition, *The Scolar Press Ltd.* Menston, England, 1971) where specifically the rhetorical figures of *Antithesis, Paradox* and *Antiphrasis* are explored in all the writers I refer to in this essay. 'Black' means 'White' and 'White' means 'Black', and all the World is at sea!

[2] In every instance of quoting original books, both poetry and music, I have had the pleasure of exploring the original image via the facility of *EEBO* ('Early English Books Online') a facility that allows access to the most obscure publications, and of course to all the valuable prefatory material often set aside when editorial work on poetry has been published in scholarly editions focused on the poetry alone. A topic such as 'Dwelling in Darkness' is inevitably enriched by 'contextual' material that can only be considered when consulting the original image. I urge the interested reader to contact his or her nearest participating institution that allows access to EEBO.

once un-nerving, chilling, yet resonant with deep familiarity; 'Sublime' because one is transported to subtle realms of hinted insights as yet undefined; and 'Enigmatic' because 'What the *Hell* is this *really* all about?' The meaning is actually 'secret', but an open secret understood by those who wish to look (or listen) from a certain angle; a certain 'trick of the light' reveals a chink or narrow window that glances into another parallel universe. It is not unlike a Phillip Pullman fantasy, played out in an Oxford familiar yet disturbingly strange.[3] When Sting performs 'In Darkness Let me Dwell' in his DVD version of his 'Dowland Affair'[4] it is shot in the gloomy cellar of his Tuscan Villa, and the glancing light reveals a tear, a true tear, falling from Sting's eye onto his cheek. This is not neo-Gothic Special Effects, but a genuine result of a man searching, and in his life-long search he stumbled on Dowland, and found a resonance beyond intellect, beyond belief, because it tumbled him into that parallel universe. That tear describes better than a thousand words or a hundred songs the power of *Insight*, the power of real esoteric understanding. From Alfred Deller's early 1960s 'other-worldly' countertenor recording (with plangent lutenist Desmond Dupre as accomplice)[5] through the several varied versions of the 1970s explosion of 'Early Music' enthusiasm, to the 21st century contributions of an edgy, post-modern new generation, hardly a one misses out on this power, as the final note unexpectedly but inevitably plunges us into an abyss of silence... (and, darkness).

I perceive sufficient impetus in the best poetry and music of this period of a generally 'Hermetic' kind (and a more precise definition of that will emerge as this essay unfolds), and with a circle of 'patrons' with the education and inclination to enjoy art forms where 'layered interpretations' are supportable, that it is possible to claim a 'school' of the most open kind. A circle of cognoscenti (a better label than 'school', anyway perhaps) who mostly knew each other, or certainly knew of each other, and who enjoyed the intellectual thrill of the deep delight afforded by complex devices. The 'School of Night' is hardly tenable as a precise 'gentlemen's club' with membership, rules, and rituals – where members came and went.[6] But a circle or fraternity of the most open kind that developed certain 'significations' (such as

---

[3] Pullman, *His Dark* Material, 1995.

[4] Sting, *Songs from the Labyrinth*, 2006 (CD and DVD).

[5] Deller, *Flow my tears* (with Desmond Dupre) recorded by HMV, 1953.

[6] The most valuable survey of 'The School of Night is found in Bradbrook', *The School of Night; A Study in Literary Relationships of Sir Walter Raleigh*, 1936. This

'Dwelling in Darkness') that provided a link to a body of thought, a philosophy that lent itself to certain artistic expressions and modes of thinking is not only feasible, but it is hardly credible that such a circle would not develop under the strange ethos that underpinned the Elizabethan court.

'In Darkness let me dwell' does not exist in a vacuum, of course. It has mates – there are other songs to keep its doleful company. There is an inner circle of lyrics from Elizabethan/Jacobean times that espouse the same strange repugnance at a seductive familiar world of sense – and not all of these songs are by John Dowland. First and foremost is the setting of the same words by John Coperario, in a work that fairly claims to be the first true song-cycle in the English language: *Funeral Teares, 1606*. At the heart of this elegiac cycle of seven songs lies the symbolic fourth song, whose first verse is exactly that of Dowland's published several years later (but for the noteworthy change in the last line (*Oh let me dying live* in stead of Dowland's *Oh let me living die!*). It begins with a lute 'prelude' that plays on the well-known folk tune of the time, 'How should I your true love know?', here a touching reference to the dedicatee of the cycle, the Lady Penelope, famed in poetry and song (with herself being a renowned singer), and recently famed in *fama malum* – ill-intended gossip.[7] As if imitating shadowy conversation, the *Cantus* (Lady Penelope's outward thoughts) duets in pungent dissonance and extended polyphony with the *Altus* (perhaps her *Soul* in dialogue; or more fancifully, a dialogue with her deceased lover's *Ghost* – Charles Blount, Earl of Devonshire). Rumour was rife, and it started from the top – King James was jealous, envious, and deeply disturbed by Blount's 'secret' work. Something is alluded to in the long rhyming preface to the songs:

> Lov'd he? And did not he nath'less assist
>   Great Britaines counsils, and in secret cells
> The Muses visite? And alone untwist
>   The riddles of deepe Philosophic spels?
> Did Dev'nshire love? And lov'd not Dev'nshire so

---

work engendered much heated exchange amongst Shakespeare scholars, and I hope this present essay might re-ignite some of that searching.

[7] Freedman, *Poor Penelope: Lady Penelope Rich, an Elizabethan Woman*, 1983. An excellent study of the nature of the 'gossip' surrounding a noble woman who was renowned for 'her fineness of Wit', and beauty of voice, yet who died in pathetic circumstances.

Throughout the cycle topical references are made – some we can perceive today, but others, more subtle are undoubtedly lost after a four-
century gap. But the second verse of Song 4 is as though the direct
thoughts of Penelope wracked in her bereavement, and in her public
shaming through manipulated gossip-mongering:

> My dainties griefe shall be, and teares my poisned wine,
>   My sighes the aire, through which my panting hart shall pine:
> My robes my mind shall sute exceeding blackest night,
>   My study shall be tragicke thoughtes sad fancy to delight.
> Pale Ghosts and frightful shades shal my acquaintance be:
>   O thus my hapless joy I haste to thee.

'Joy' in the last line refers to her man, Charles, one of whose many
noble names included 'Mountjoy' – an embarrassing sobriquet for the
gossips to feed on, with its unfortunate vulgar sexual implications!

There are other, more fragmentary quotations of 'In Darkness Let
Me Dwell': also in *A Musicall Banquet, 1610* – in John Dowland's
'Farre from triumphing Court', a four-stanza epic, the last from the
aged hands of Sir Henry Lee (the oldest of the old Elizabethan retain-
ers) he writes at the end of the first stanza: *And hee on earth, In darknesse left to moane.* This complex work, redolent of Lee's life spent in
allegorical play centred around his 'goddess' (Queen Elizabeth, and
latterly Queen Anne, and more particularly her son next in line for the
throne, Prince Henry) is a summation of at least 20 years of symbolic
interplay between the artisan, John Dowland, and the 'Queen's Champion', and 'spin-doctor', publicist, and esoteric manipulator of the lore
of Elizabeth (Belphoebe, Astraea, Diana, Virgin Goddess) – and all
that went with the most incredible maneuvering in creating the 'Cult
of Elizabeth'.[8] Lee was at the heart of all that, and at the heart of what
followed after Elizabeth's death in 1603. He died in 1610, and with
his death much of the power of esoteric thought and activity, artistic
interchange and 'Protestant Brotherly Love' of a mystically fired creative energy also died.

Perhaps the earliest mention, in Dowland's songs, of 'In darkness let
me dwell' occurs in Song 5, from *The Second Booke of Songs, 1600*. This
is much the earliest mention of these potent words, but used as though

---

[8] For more on the rich allegory associated with Sir Henry Lee, see Yates, *Astrea:
The Imperial Theme in the 16th Century*, 'Elizabethan Chivalry: The Romance of the
Accession Day Tilts', 1975, 88.

they were already a quotation from some pre-existing reference. What could that be, I wonder?

> Mourne, mourne, day is with darknesse fled,
>   What heaven then governs earth,
> O none but hell in heavens stead,
>   Chokes with his mistes our mirth.
> Mourne, mourne, looke now for day nor night, but that from hell,
> Then all must as they may in darknesse learn to dwell,
> But yet this change must needs change our delight,
>   That thus the Sunne should harbour with the night.

Although not stated openly, this song number five is in fact the last of a powerful trilogy that begins with the famous 'Sorrow stay, lend true repentant tears', followed by the 'Lady Hope', urging a cheerful, worldly alternative to sable-coloured melancholy, 'Die not before thy day, poor man condemned'.[9] It is a piece of musical alchemy.

In the same volume of songs, embedded in perhaps the most famous lyric of that Age, Song 2 is none other than 'Flow my tears' (or *Lachrimae*). The third section of this 'pavan-form' song is:

> Hark you shadowes that in darknesse dwell,
>   Learne to contemne light,
> Happie, happie they that in hell
>   Feele not the worlds despite.

This, I think is the public source of all the later quotations. We can be sure of this because of this song's outstanding popularity – familiar on the lips of every playwright of the time, 'published in nine cities of Europe' (according to Dowland himself) and the words and music quoted in uncountable instances. Who wrote the words? We cannot now know – perhaps Dowland, or one of the circle he moved in, served, or courted for patronage? It is a mystery, a secret – but an open one, since the *Lachrimae* poem became common parlance. Why then do we today not really understand it? It is enigmatic, hints at sublime ideals, yet appears to be 'pseudo-profound' – yes, we listen to its reiteration in performance, but feel not dejected as the superficial

---

[9] For more on the opening songs in Dowland's second book, see Rooley, "I saw my Lady Weepe: *The First Five Songs of John Dowland's* Second Book of Songs", 1982, 197.

reading of the words might suggest, but rather uplifted, relieved, and pleasured! The experience is *cathartic*.[10]

In truth what the vibrant attentive listener hears creates *catharsis*. 'Flow my tears' is medicinal, as indeed it was intended to be; as the dying cadence closes one is relieved of the burden of personal grief, pain, anguish, and our 'weary days'. This is the inner language of 'pessimist gnosis' – knowledge of the Divine (and therefore of Man's origins also) – in fact the Hermetic-neo-Platonic philosophy that engaged at least in some measure most of the thinking poets, artists, patrons of the late-Elizabethan era. The beauty of the paradox creating opposing yet uniting forces that lead to gnosis (knowledge of 'the Divine') is sweet simplicity itself.[11] In Dowland's text the two are personified, as was standard in allegorical metaphor, as two female entities: 'Hope, thy keeper', and the 'Hag, Despair' (see his 'Die not, before thy day, poor man condemned' Book Two, No. 4). The battle over Man's attentions between the wonderful, seductive world of sensual appetite (*Optimist Gnosis* – seeing the world of sense as a sign-post to the divine realm – *As Above, So Below* – the essence of Platonic Philosophy) and understanding that world as being the source of illusion, pain and suffering, because false (*Pessimist Gnosis* – seeing the world of sense as a trap, filled with false light, and ruled by *Ignorance* – a male personification of most gruesome sight and nature, perhaps to be understood as a manifestation of Edmund Spenser's horrifying *Blatant Beast*, with its rusty iron teeth).[12]

This, our earthly embodiment, is a shadow, a seeming not the being, of true existence, and much of the finest output of poets, composers and their understanding patrons in the time roughly between 1590 to 1620 was impulsed from such an awareness. The esoteric reading of the best of this work is clear – seen through a certain 'play of light'. With all the forgoing in mind, reading the lyric of this song of Dowland's, printed in his *First Booke of Songes, 1597 [No. 14]* perhaps allows us to penetrate the mystery more thoroughly:

---

[10] For more on 'Flow my Teares' and Dowland's other darkly melancholy songs, see Rooley, "New Light on John Dowland's songs of darkness", 1983, 6.

[11] Much on the complex neo-Platonic philosophy in Elizabethan England can be found in French, *John Dee: The World of an Elizabethan Magus*, 1972.

[12] For more on 'the Blatant Beast' of Spenser, see *The Spenser Encyclopedia*, 96.

All ye whom whom love or fortune hath betraide,
   All ye that dreame of blisse but live in greif,
Al ye whose hopes are evermore delaid,
   Al ye whose sighes or sicknes wants releife:
Lend eares and teares to me most hapless man,
   That sings my sorrowes like the dying Swanne.

Care that consumes the heart with inward paine,
   Paine that presents sad care in outward view,
Both tyrant-like enforce me to complaine,
   But still in vaine, for none my plaints will rue,
Teares, sighes, and ceaseless cries alone I spend,
   My woe wants comfort, and my sorrow end.

The opening 'invocation' calls to all men and women with ears to hear who are in like state to the poet/composer/performer. In fact the performance stands in as spokesman, or more properly, as 'orator' for Everyman – indeed almost as interceding 'high priest', so formally intoned is the language. The listeners are witnesses to this 'ceaseless cry', and the cry is for them also, wailing by proxy. If this is the 'invocation', then 'Flow my tears' becomes the 'credo' of this ardent band of believers:

Flow my teares fall from your springs,
   Exilde for ever: Let mee morne
Where nights black bird hir sad infamy sings,
   There let mee live forlorne.
Downe vaine lights shine you no more,
   No nights are dark enough for those
That in despaire their last fortunes deplore,
   Light doth but shame disclose.
Never may my woes be relieved, since pitie is fled
   And teares, and sighes, and grones
My wearied dayes, of all joyes have deprived.
From the highest spire of contentment, my fortune is throwne,
   And feare, and griefe, and paine
For my deserts, are my hopes since hope is gone.
Harke you shadowes that in darknesse dwell,
   Learne to contemne light,
Happie, happie they that in hell
   Feele not the worlds despite.

The colon placed after 'ever' in line two serves as a warning – Dowland's setting continues with a melodic flow that hardly allows the singer to express that colon, yet the shift of meaning is probably of

considerable significance. But did the printer mean it, or was it care-
lessness? We shall never know – and so our interpretations needs must
proceed with caution. However, this caution in mind, the general sense
of the whole poem allows for several interpretations. If you were the
Earl of Essex, or putting poetry into his mouth, mind and heart, in
1600, this poem would be very much how you might have expressed
matters. Spurned by Elizabeth yet again (how many 'complaint' poems
can a man write to his unyielding 'goddess'?) these words reflect accurately the condition he was in, hence soon after, the 'Essex Rebellion'
that was to be his fatal downfall. But there were many who supported
him – some openly, others covertly.[13] 'Dwelling in darkness' is a con-
venient cloak for various and possibly nefarious activities dangerous
to reveal openly.

It would be unwise, though, to search for a specific interpretation
that reflects 'biographical matters' pure and simple, especially within
an artistic context. Allegory and metaphor abound in all poetry of this
age, and sometimes quite convoluted in its use and purpose. A number of Essex supporters were also inclined to arcane devices – so that
matters such as 'constitutional stability' with regard to Royal Succession, worldly though that may be, got thoroughly bound up in devices,
designs and desires expressed in complex allegory.

With the few song-texts I have presented so far, a number of personalities have been implicated – Dowland's hoped for patrons, and
the noble families with much to win or lose that they represent. Most
of these people have not really been linked with the highly esoteric and
vaporous 'School of Night' by any previous writers (either those for or
those against the shadowy proposal of an 'esoteric club'). My position,
after working with this body of performing material for a number of
years, is that I perceive links between not only the artists (poets and
composers, primarily though visual imagery carries ample support
for these links), but also, and perhaps most pertinently between the
patrons responsible for commissioning these works.

It is the purpose of this essay to establish the veracity of this position. Take two unlike personalities: the elderly Sir Henry Lee – author
of much of the complex allegory associated with Elizabeth I, and in
his dotage, supporter of the young Prince Henry, next in line for the
throne (almost the most urgent perception Lee had was for the impor-

---

tance of stability in transition for the benefit of the Nation, and to assure the maintenance of the wealth of the Noble Families); and, in complete contrast, the young, beautiful, educated, spend-thrift Lucy, Countess of Bedford (a representative of the Noble Families whose future Lee wanted secured).[14] We do not know that they met, or got on at all, but neither could possibly have been ignorant of the other – and both had, despite much diversity, a great deal in common – not least, John Dowland. Lee throughout his life had cultivated elaborate pastimes – and one of his adopted personas was that of a hermit, with the name varying from *Lelius*, and later, *Loricus*. This hermit enjoyed dwelling in a dark cell, or cave in chosen contrast to the bright light of Court. That this was a device, a 'play', is obvious – living at Court and close to the Queen (he described himself as 'The Queen's Champion' at the Annual Accession Day Tilts – their elaborate form was almost entirely due to Lee's designs and desires). The symbolic opposition of the bright 'light' of court, and the pensive, thoughtful gloom of the hermit's cell is all-important to understanding Henry Lee's complicated imagery; but it is also important more generally for our understanding, as it is an easier reference point for us not schooled in esoteric thinking of the late-Renaissance. Much lies behind the 'light' and the 'dark' of 'court' and 'cell'...

This enquiry will return to Sir Henry Lee in a moment, but first a little more on the chosen opposite, Lucy Countess of Bedford. Her symbolic role at court and at her chosen cell ('Twickenham Gardens', by the Thames to the west of London was her version of the Leelian 'cell', an altogether more practical choice than Lee's estate at Ditchley, north of Oxford for its closer proximity to court events). She had joined Elizabeth's retinue of Ladies-in-waiting whilst a very young thing in the late 1590s, and used in the dual role of youthful reminder of Elizabeth as a young princess, but more painfully as a reminder of the fact: the Queen was aging, and growing more cantankerous. Lucy was not long in favour, as her husband was closely implicated with the Essex Rebellion, was fined £10,000 and spent some time in jail. With Elizabeth's death Lucy's fortunes changed as she and her husband were amongst the first to greet Queen Anne and King James, and indeed accompanied them on their journey to London in late 1603. Lucy was

---

[14] For more on Lucy, Countess of Bedford, see Rooley, 1982 and the *Dictionary of National Biography*.

to remain one of the Queen's favourites and close companion in a number of the Royal Masques.

Lucy Harington's marriage to Edward Russell, 3rd Earl of Bedford actual took place on the 12th December 1594, when Lucy was but 12 years old (or at least, just turned 12!). It was already a 'symbolic marriage' with layers of meaning: 12th December is the patronal Saint's Day for Saint Lucy, the Christian Martyr's namesake of the young Harington bride, obviously a carefully chosen arrangement, for Lucy employed imagery relating to the 2nd century saint at 'tortuous' length: it was all to do with 'eyes', 'weeping', 'darkness' (as in blindness) for St Lucy apparently had the most beautiful eyes, admired by a Pagan Prince who so desired her. She was committed to Jesus, and to show her determination her eyes were gouged out and sent on a platter, skewered, to her admirer (they were, it is said, miraculously restored the next day, according to the Martyrology written several centuries later). In mediaeval iconography this is how St Lucy was depicted, holding the platter proudly – it was a common symbol to all in young Lucy's day, and the reason the saint's day was the 12th December was this started the week of shortest days, longest nights in the annual calendar, ending with Doubting Thomas' Day on the 21st – the Winter Solstice. So though 'Lucy' is from the Latin 'lucis', meaning light, the paradox of celebrating 'darkness' is not difficult to understand. The 12 year old bride was thoroughly immersed in such symbolic thinking, as were the many poets encircling her, dedicating their complex allegories to her. In the year of her marriage several 'dark works' were printed and dedicated to her; Michael Drayton's contributions are particularly noteworthy, for they are part of a lengthy complex allegorical story.

Drayton had dedicated a work in the previous year, 1593 to Robert Dudley, Earl of Essex, lamenting one of the earl's frequent banishments from court. It is cast in the Spenserian style of Nine Shepherd's 'Eclogues', with the shepherd 'Rowland' being the Earl. It begins in this manner:

The First Eglog.

When as the joyull spring brings in
  The Summers sweet reliefe:
Poor Rowland malcontent bewayles
  The winter of his griefe.

As yet the reader has only a mild suggestion that Rowland is unhappy. The second stanza of the poem gently brings in 'night' imagery, in a suitably rustic style:

Fayre Philomel, night-musicke of the Spring,
   Sweetly recordes her tunefull harmony,
And with deepe sobbes, and dolefull sorrowing,
   Before fayre Cynthya actes her Tragedy:
The Throstlecock, by breaking of the day,
   Chants to his sweete, full many a lovely lay.

But consider how utterly distressed this has become by the ninth
eclogue; and the burden and function of the poem is now crystal clear:

The Ninth Eglog.

When cole-blacke night with sable vaile
   Eclipsd the gladsome light,
Rowland in darksome shade alone,
   Bemoanes his wofull plight.

This is how sad a state Rowland has declined into, because his Cynthia
(Elizabeth, of course) has so abused him:

All is agone, such is my endless griefe,
   And my mishaps amended naught with moane,
I see the heavens will yield me no reliefe:
   What helpeth care, when cure is past and gone,
And teares I see doe me avayle no good,
   But as great showres increase the rising flood.

With folded armes, thus hanging downe his head,
   He gave a groane as though his heart had broke,
Then looking pale and wan as he were dead,
   He fetcht a sigh, but never a word he spoke:
For now his heart wax'd cold as any stone,
   Was never man alive so woe begone.

The poet thus weaves biography and fiction together, and in doing so
skillfully hopes to affect the outcome for his patron. With these last
'woe begone' stanzas, the listening Cynthia is pricked into action:

With that fayre Cinthya stoups her glittering vayle,
   And dives adowne into the Ocean flood,
The easterne brow which erst was wan and pale,
   Now in the dawning blusheth red as blood:
The whistling Larke ymounted on her wings,
   To the gray morrow, her good morrow sings.

And indeed Elizabeth re-called Essex (from his 'wilds of Wanstead',
in the east!) back to the Court 'light', and all was forgiven.[15] Drayton's

---

[15] Dowland's song (to Essex's poetry) 'Can she excuse my wrongs with virtue's

work was done…but he had set a precedent, and next he embraced
Lucy's marriage to Edward Russell, employing the imagery of darkness,
tears, eyes – seemingly inappropriate references for 'joyous Hymen's'
day!

Amour 1.

Reade here (sweet Mayd) the story of my wo,
   The drery abstracts of my endless cares:
With my lives sorrow enterlyned so,
   Smok'd with my sighes, and blotted with my teares.

By the end, after 50 sonnets, almost everyone revolving around either
'eyes' or 'tears', he comes to this summation:

Amour 51.

Goe you my lynes, Embassadors of love,
   With my harts tribute to her conquering eyes,
From whence, if you one teare of pitty move
   For all my woes, that onely shall suffice.

I have to say, does this not point up the vast gulf between our time
and theirs? Here is a 12 year-old being presented with verse that, to say
the least, is at the leading-edge of socio-political philosophical utterance…and that she thrived on it! (Her father gave her 'the education
of a boy' – having had several daughters, each educated as a male). By
the age of 12, childish things were put firmly aside – you were either
an infant, or a young adult, nothing in between.

   Now what these verses parade, in common, no matter to whom they
are addressed, nor from whom the poet's patronage stems, is a vocabulary of 'darkness', of opposition to common light. They are an expression of *melancholy*, black, sable melancholy – and all are drawing on
the established convention: in art – poetry, music, performance – (all
reflections directly of court life, therefore political life). The Earl of
Essex might well have established the melancholy guise most adroitly,
but in so doing he was merely a man of his time.

---

cloak' (Book I, n° 6) makes Wanstead 'famous' for being out in the Styx, as in the 'C'
section of the galliard form in which the piece is cast (the galliard being Elizabeth's
favourite dance) Dowland puts in the lute part a counter-melody which is in fact the
famous folk-tune of the time 'Shall I go walk the Woods so Wild'. See Poulton, *John
Dowland*, 227.

The idea of 'inspired melancholy' had an authoritative pedigree, ultimately stretching back to the Florentine philosopher, Marsilio Ficino, with his understanding of the influence of *Saturn*, who ruled his own horoscope. But saturnine melancholy pervaded the best artists – Dürer, in his *Melancholia I* engraving gave a new archetype for artistic melancholy. The philosophy was expressed, at great length, in Cornelius Agrippa, brought to English awareness by such as John Dee – a true *Magus* and philosopher, who in the 1570s had the ear of all the most mighty, including Elizabeth herself, and indeed, Sir Henry Lee. That Dee fell from favour in the 1590s – the very decade that saw such an explosion of 'inspired melancholy', only serves to prove the fickleness of society (and the power of politics) – definitely not to be trusted.

That the Earl of Essex chose to adapt the 'weeds of woe', dressing in black sable, and creating the archetype of *melancholy,* only shows how adroit the man was at sensing the mood of the time – he was a consummate posturer, entirely alert for how he 'looked', or came across. His power, though, on those 'acolytes' around him was tremendous, and although the chief architects of 'inspired melancholy' were either disgraced (John Dee), or recently retired (Sir Henry Lee), or too young to be of much worth (Lucy, Countess of Bedford), or merely artisans obedient to the nobility (John Dowland, George Chapman, and legions of others) Essex paraded the *affect* as though it was entirely of his own creation.

Essex complicated the plot extensively in the 1590s and mainly for his own ends – political conniving and artistic endeavor are always uneasy partners. It is a shame, but a fact, that some of the most highflown dressing of deep philosophy in artistic guise was manipulated for short-term political gain. His 'sable black' attire suited his posturing, aimed at the somewhat pliant Elizabeth (at least, she was pliant towards Essex in the early 1590s), for what does sable black represent but the Night? The Night's only light are the Stars ('Astraea') and of course the Moon ('Cynthia') – both symbolic images personified in Elizabeth, carefully manufactured and massaged by Sir Henry Lee ever since the Accession, and most fully explored in the elaborate presentation for 1590, when Lee wore a suit of white armour, emblazoned with a sun in gold on the right shoulder, representing the active life and service, and a moon in silver on the left, for the contemplative life of devotion and prayer. He stepped out of a 'Temple to Vesta', a tent erected by his instruction, made in white taffeta, with its door festooned with white eglantine – the Queen's favoured flower emblem – whiteness was the order of this display; the eternal white light of Lee's 'goddesse', ever pure, ever virginal. The poem he wrote for this precise moment, as he emerged from the 'Temple' and advanced towards the Queen and her Ladies, was performed by John Dowland playing the lute, and the Queen's favourite tenor, Robert Hales, singing the verse: 'His golden locks time hath to silver turned'. Here is a skillfully manipulated piece of 'optimist gnosis' (knowledge of the Divine through the medium of the senses: colours, words, music, gesture, symbolism – all uniting in praise); the munificence of the Divine Goddess bestowed blessings on all her subjects. Her 'light' cast all else into the shade. Devereux, the Earl of Essex, could therefore only wear black sable, and his precocious artistic genius found succour in expressing the opposite: 'pessimist gnosis' – how hard it is, in the travail of the long night, to let genius find the exactly refined mode of 'complaining'. There is an exquisitely beautiful madrigal by John Wilbye that profoundly embraces this curious form:

> Draw on sweet night, best friend unto those cares,
>   That do arise from painfull melancholy,
> My life so ill through want of comfort fares,
>   That unto thee I consecrate it wholly.
> Sweet night draw on, O sweet night draw on, sweet night draw on.
> My griefes when they be told
>   To shades and darknes, find some ease from paining,
> And while thou all in silence dort enfold,
>   I then shall have best time for my complaining

John Wilbye's refined setting of these words – a 'hymn' to Inspired Melancholy – was not published until 1609, in 'The Second Set of Madrigales', but the evocation could have been voiced any time in the previous 15 years. This fine collection is dedicated to the Lady Arbella Stuart, a lady-in-waiting to Queen Anne, and a close confidant to Lucy, Countess of Bedford. It would appear that Arbella was a true member of the *cognescenti*:

> Madame.
>
> The deepe understanding you have in all the Artes, and particular excellency in this of Musicke, doth by a certaine kinde of right, challenge the Dedication of the better sort of Labours in that Facultie; especially in these times when Musicke sits solitary among her sister Sciences…

By 1609, long after the execution of Essex, and after Elizabeth 'the Goddesse' had gone to Heaven, artistic circles explored new areas of patronage: Sir Henry Lee was still able to effect considerable influence – from his distant Hermit's Cell, and his schooling of the young Prince Henry established an extraordinary potent alternative court where poets and musicians gathered in dense numbers.[16] Queen Anne enjoyed this display, and loved the show engendered by the regular Court Masques; but King James remained suspicious of anything and everything that smacked of secrets, Hermetic Wisdom, and subtle symbolic imagery – it all looked too much like witchcraft! He was jealous of his son's popularity, and his discomfort deepened even as the arts grew ever more elaborate, and 'artificial'; and their potency only high-lighted his impotency. A dangerous and tense atmosphere enveloped the entire court circle.

One of the most brilliant and individual minds of the day was locked in the Tower, from trumped-up charges in 1603 – Sir Walter Raleigh, one of a group of 'atheists' feared by King James, a typical example of his paranoia. Indeed, Prince Henry exclaimed 'None but my Father would keep such a bird in a cage'. Raleigh's espousing of the Hermetic outlook reflects well in his so-called 'atheistic' poetry. A setting of a typical, poem whose central imagery is of the hermit, was published also in 1609, in a volume of songs by Alfonso Ferrabosco the Younger, and dedicated to Prince Henry:

> Like hermit poore, in place obscure
>   I meane to spend my dayes of endlesse doubt,
> To waile such woes as time cannot recure,
>   Where none but Love shall find mee out,
> And at my gates dispaire shall linger still,
>   To let in death when Love and Fortune will.

The imagery of darkness, and all the associated emblems are potent significations of the inspirational 'pain' associated with artistic labours. The apotheosis of this point of view is most completely represented back in 1594, with the first major publication of the work of George Chapman – aimed at Elizabeth, the new bride Lucy, the court of Essex, the followers of Dee, Raleigh, and all those 'melancholic lovers in sable-coloured robes', the essence of the Hermetic School: 'The Shadow of Night: Containing Two Poeticall Hymnes', Devised by G. C.

---

[16] The nature of the artistic milieu around young Prince Henry is well explored in Strong, *Henry Prince of Wales and England's Lost Renaissance*, 1986.

Gent', 1594.[17] A more abstruse epic it is hard to conceive, and that is its point! It is for the 'cognoscenti', and they alone will understand. Here is a taste of what this pair of poems is about:

Hymnus in Noctem.

Great Goddess to whose throne in Cynthian fires,
  This earthly Altar endless fumes expires,
Therefore in fumes of sighes and fires of griefe,
  To fearefull chances thou sendst bold relief,
Happie, thrice happie type, and nurse of death,
  Who breathless feeds on nothing but our breath
In whom must virtue and her issue live,
  Or die for ever, let humor give
Seas to mine eyes, that I may quicklie weepe
  The shipwracke of the world: or let soft sleepe
(Binding my sences) lose my working soule,
  That in her highest pitch, she may controule
The court of skill, compact of misterie,
  Wanting but franchisement, and memorie
To reach all secrets: then in blissful trance,
  Raise her (dear Night) to that perseverance,
That in my torture, she all earths may sing,
  And force to tremble in her trumpeting
Heaven's christall temples: in her powr's implant
  Skill of my griefs, and she can nothing want.

A modern reader might not understand a word of this, but remember, this is but the first 20 lines of a poem that unfolds slowly, deliberately over 400 lines; and then continues a second poem, 'Ad Cynthiam', in like abstruse vein. Close on to 1,000 lines of abstract philosophizing on the nature of night and inspiration, and the good of mankind expressed in art, and Hermes' dark Cave.

Indeed, Chapman's own words of dedication to his fellow Hermetic friend, Matthew Roydon, sets out the position with poetic prose loaded with mythological reference, but with clarity also:

It is an exceeding rapture of delight in the deepe search of knowledge, (none knoweth better then thy selfe sweet Mathew) that maketh men manfully indure th'extremes incident to that Herculean labour: from flints must the Gorgonean fount be smitten. Men must be shod by Mer-

---

[17] Chapman and the diverse 'occult' influences influencing him is best explored through Yates, *The Occult Philosophy in the Elizabethan Age*, 1979. See particularly the Chapter XIII, 135.

curie, girt with Saturnes Adamantine sword, take the shield from Pallas,
the helm from Pluto, and have the eyes of Grea (as Hesiodus armes Per-
seus against Medusa) before they can cut the viperous head of benumb-
ing ignorance, or subdue their monstrous affections to most beautifull
judgement.

Likewise, later in this opening epistle, Chapman makes it very clear
which noblemen he is indebted to – a trio of some of the most influential men of the land, forming a circle who 'strike fire out of darknesse,
which the brightest Day shall envie for beautie':

> I remember my good Mathew how joyfully oftentimes you reported unto
> me, that most ingenious Darbie, deepe searching Northumberland, and
> skill imbracing heire of Hunsdon had most profitably entertained learn-
> ing in themselves, to the vital warmth of freezing science, and to the
> admirable luster of their true Nobilitie

The conclusion of the *Hymnus ad Noctem* makes it clear that the light
of ordinary day (the world of sense experience) should be shunned by
all followers of Night, in order that the True Light can be perceived:

> Which grant for ever (oh eternall Night)
> Till virtue flourish in the light of light.

The general vocabulary, and specific word-choice employed throughout this extended epic suggests that this is the 'quarry', the source for
the ideas and words used in all the lyrics relating to 'dwelling in darkness' set to music in the following years after 1594.

England's flowering of hermetic-inspired advanced inspirational art
in poetry and music was hi-jacked by Arrogance for short-term political ends. Nevertheless, Essex is now known to a relatively small number of specialists, but the art created for his temporary *furor politicus*
survives and is available to all. If we look carefully, we can see the wood
for the trees. What an Age; what Wit; what a Vision of Humanity lies
behind that panoply of devices, allegory and abstruse philosophy.

BIBLIOGRAPHY

Chapman, G., *The Shadow of Night*, London, William Ponsonby, 1594.
Coperario, J., *John Funeral Teares*, London, John Browne, 1606.
Daniel, S., *Samuel Delia and Rosamunde*, London, Simon Waterson, 1594.
——, *A Panegyricke*, London, Edward Blount, 1603.
——, *The Masque of Blacknesse*, London, Edward Allde, 1604.
——, *The Vision of the 12 Goddesses*, London, Simon Waterson, 1604.
——, *A Funeral Poem*, London, 1606.

Danyel, J., *Songs*, London, Thomas Adams, 1606.
Donne, J., *Poems*, London, John Marriott, 1633.
Dowland, J., *The First Booke of Songes*, London, Peter Short, 1597.
——, *The Second Booke of Songs*, London, Thomas Este, 1600.
——, *The Third and Last Book of Songs*, London, Thomas Adams, 1603.
——, *A Pilgrimes Solace*, London, Thomas Snodham (et al.), 1612.
Dowland, R., *A Musicall Banquet*, London, Thomas Adams, 1610.
Drayton, M., *The Shepherd's Garland*, London, Thomas Woodcocke, 1593.
——, *Idea's Mirrour*, London, Nicholas Linge, 1594.
——, *Matilda*, London, John Busby, 1594.
Ferrabosco, A., *Ayres*, London, John Brown, 1609.
Nashe, T., *The Terrours of Night*, London, William Jones, 1594.
Peacham, H., *The Garden of Eloquence*, London, William Jones, 1577.
Peele, G., *Polihymnia*, London, Richard Jhones, 1590.
Spenser, E., *The Faerie Queen*, London, William Ponsonbie, 1596.
Ward, J., *A First Set of Madrigals*, London, Thomas Snodham, 1613.
Wilbye, J., *A Second Set of Madrigals*, London, Thomas Este, 1609.

Modern Works

Bradbrook, M. C., *The School of Night*, London, Cambridge University Press, 1936.
Burckhardt, T., *Alchemy*, London, Stuart and Watkins, 1967.
Freedman, S., *Poor Penelope*, London, Kensal Press, 1983.
French, P. J., *John Dee*, London, Routledge and Kegan Paul, 1972.
Poulton, D., *John Dowland*, London, Faber, 1972.
Pullman, P., *His Dark Materials*, London, Scholastic, 1995.
Strong, R., *Henry Prince of Wales*, London, Thames and Hudson, 1986.
Rooley, A., 'I Saw My Lady Weep: The First Five Songs of John Dowland's 'Second Book of Songs', *Temenos* Vol. 2, London, 1982, pp. 197–216.
——, 'New Light on John Dowland's Songs of Darkness', *Early Music* Vol. 11, No. 1, 1983, pp. 6–21.
Yates, F. A., *Astraea*, London, Routledge and Kegan Paul, 1975.
——, *Giordano Bruno and the Hermetic Tradition*, London, Routledge and Kegan Paul, 1964.
——, *The Occult Philosophy in the Elizabethan Age*, London, Routledge and Kegan Paul, 1979.

ORPHEUS "RECURED":
THE HEALING ART OF THOMAS CAMPION

Barbara Kennedy

The identification of Marsilio Ficino with Orpheus was recorded by his oldest friend, Naldo Naldi in a poem that traced the journey of Orpheus' soul from Homer to Ficino.[1] Each recipient of the soul received some aspect of Orpheus' gifts: Homer received song, Pythagoras ethical teaching and Ennius, piety. Naldi writes that after Ennius' death, Orpheus' soul had to wait 1600 years until its next reincarnation:

> Marsilius donec divina e sorte daretur
> Indueret cuius membra pudica libens.
> Hinc rigidas cythara quercus et carmine mulcet
> Atque feris iterum mollia corda facit.[2]

This is neither a literary conceit nor a metaphor to describe Ficino's Neoplatonic philosophy. The spirit of Orpheus permeates the writings of Ficino who aroused devotion with his singing of the Orphic hymns. The story of Orpheus, while appearing superficially simple, belies a deep psychological and philosophical complexity: art enters life as a means of dealing with death. It is a story that amalgamates myth, folklore and legend and it lends itself to many interpretations through different eras and cultures although certain key motifs remain unchanged: the musician who can tame the wildness of nature, the shaman who visits the underworld and the prophesying severed head that symbolized the dichotomy between the body and soul. As it survived into the Christian age, Orpheus the musician, teacher, healer and shepherd becomes a Christ-like figure whose musical power maintains universal harmony. For the Christian Church the most important aspect of this

---

[1] Naldo Naldi was Professor of Poetry and Rhetoric at Florence University form 1485 and a member of Ficino's Florentine Academy. Marsilio Ficino, *The Letters of Marsilio Ficino, Volume 5 being a translation of Liber VI*, trans. Fellowship of the Language Department of the School of Economic Science, London: Shepheard-Walwyn Publishers, 1994, p. 179. All citations are to this edition.

[2] Until Marsilius should be granted by divine fate, whose chaste limbs he may willingly put on. Hence he soothes the unyielding oaks with his lyre and his song and softens once more the hearts of wild beasts. Warden, 'Orpheus and Ficino', 86.

legend was Orpheus' descent into the labyrinth of darkness (Hades) and "rebirth." Thus he becomes the saviour, signifying the magical power of music to redeem love from the dead. It is only through works such as Boccaccio's *Genealogia deorum gentilium* and Coluccio Salutati's *De laboribus Herculis*, that Orpheus is reborn as the incarnation of the power of music, the champion of humanism, the accepted face of paganism and the prophet of mysticism for the Neoplatonists.[3] It was this recovered Orpheus that Ficino strongly identified with. By painting an image of Orpheus on his lyre, Ficinian singing appealed to both the visual and auditory senses, providing an ideological construct for Ficino's Orphic belief in the power of music to heal body and soul, leading mankind back to the higher spiritual realms. For Ficino divine music was twofold:

> One kind, they say, exists entirely in the eternal mind of God. The second is in the motions and order of the heavens by which the heavenly spheres and their orbits make a marvellous harmony.[4]

Ficino strove to imitate God and express the music of the soul through the Orphic hymns. Their aim was to bring the *spiritus* of man into harmony with the *spiritus mundi* by love, song and light. Through song the singer creates a God-inspired frenzy whereby he raises himself and the listener to God. Ficino divides the divine frenzy or Platonic furor into four kinds: love, poetry, the mysteries and prophecy. It is love however, that unites the frenzies because it underpins the relationship between microcosm and macrocosm, man and God. Ficino believed that Orpheus embodied the platonic furor: as the theological poet, lover and musician, Orpheus re-harmonizes creation, curing not just the individual but the cosmos as a whole. Through emulating the Orphic furor in his own hymns, Ficino reclaimed Orpheus from the prototypical medieval lover, to the musician, civiliser and theologian of an ancient hermetic tradition.

The impact of Ficino's recuperation of the classical Orpheus can still be detected fifty years after his death in the musical compositions of John Dowland and Thomas Campion who where striving to emulate the Orphic vision of love as Platonic assuagement and spiritual purga-

---

[3] Vicari calls Boccaccio and Salutati humanists in the Renaissance sense of the word because they were concerned with the art of poetry and had the historian's intellectual interest in the ancients and their pagan religious practices. Warden, *Orpheus*, 79.

[4] Ficino, *The Letters*, vol. I. 42–44.

tion in line with the rapidly evolving progression of sixteenth century music.[5] Known posthumously as England's "musical poet," Thomas Campion was a sixteenth century physician, poet and composer and while he was concerned with prosody, that is, uniting the music to the poetry through the coalescence of melody to the sense of the stanza, it was the legend of Orpheus that formed the centrality of Campion's philosophy and musicality. He strove to portray universal harmony in his lyrics, masques and Latin poetry endeavouring to capture the equilibrium between God and man that Orpheus represented.[6] With his references to Orpheus and the healing power of song, Campion persuades us that music is "an emblem of creativity and order," it is a microcosmic imitation of the music of the spheres, endorsing the Pythagorean viewpoint that music could be viewed as a mathematical model of universal order and incorporating the Ficinian speculations that defined self-consciousness in philosophical terms.[7] For Campion it is love that 'chaines the earth and heaven/Turnes the spheres.'[8] In John Dowland's *First Booke of Songes or Ayres* published in1597, Campion wrote a dedicatory epigram comparing Dowland as a musician with Orpheus, a plaudit that Campion also deserved. He developed a musico-poetic aesthetic where each art compliments but does not dominate the other: 'I have chiefly aymed to couple my Words and Notes lovingly together, which will be much for him to doe that hath not power over both.'[9]

Percival Vivian acknowledges that Campion was the first author to state the harmonic ideas that were replacing the contrapuntal theory of the Middle Ages, although his idea of marrying music and poetry was not unique: the majority of Elizabethan and Stuart lyrics were

---

[5] Wilfred Mellers argues that two basic modifications in music's nature and function were necessary: one was the evolution of the "Western" notion of harmony as progression in time; the other was the partial subservience of music to words, not, as in the Middle ages, as invocation, but as communication from one human being to another. Mellers, *The masks of Orpheus, Seven stages in the story of European music*, 9.

[6] Catherine Ing argues that the lyrics of the Elizabethan age were the products of highly conscious artists, often working to rule, always well aware of the effect they wished to produce, and deliberately choosing certain means towards their chosen ends. Ing, *Elizabethan Lyrics A study in the development of English metres and their relation to poetic effect*, 9.

[7] Irwin, 'Thomas Campion and the Musical Emblem,' 136.

[8] Vivian, *The Works of Thomas Campion*, 23. All citations are to this edition.

[9] Ibid., 115.

written to be set to music and presented as airs or madrigals.[10] Both
music and poetry provide an aesthetic experience that can be either
independent or interdependent on each other. They share a common
root in classical mythology: it is thought that the first poetry was sung
and tradition told how Orpheus and Arion enchanted their listeners
by words accompanied by the lyre.[11] With the Renaissance's renewed
interest in classical Greek culture, the knowledge that Greek lyrics had
been sung strengthened the cultural impetus in trying to unite these
two art forms although the relationship between them was always to
remain complex.

Although England had no formal academy in developing humanist
and Platonic theories, English literary and musical culture was influenced by music from the Netherlands, and the work of the Italian and
French academies, especially the French *Plèiade* and Florentine *Cam-
erata*.[12] As a Latin scholar Campion believed that he could incorporate
classical metres in vernacular poetry, thus, he argues, the verse line
should be the unit of time and the metrical feet fractions of this unit.
Following the French Academicians theories of measuring music to
the quantity of the words, Campion argued:

> But when we speake simply of number, we intend only the disseuer'd
> quantity; but when we speake of a Poeme written in number, we con-
> sider not only the distinct number of the sillables, but also their value,
> which is contained in the length or shortnes of their sound.[13]

The idea of amalgamating verse with mathematical metre to achieve
poetic harmony was not unique to Campion, but rather he follows in
a tradition where the divine mathematics is believed to be the root of
universal proportion and concord. The importance of number, derived
from classical sources, had been expounded by philosophers such as
St Augustine, Boethius and Ficino and its significance on cosmological and religious theories had already made an impact in English literature by the end of the sixteenth century. As poet-composer and
physician, Campion held the conviction that in nature and art, order

---

[10] Pattison, *Music and Poetry of the English Renaissance*, 36.
[11] Mathiesen, *Apollo's Lyre Greek Music and Music Theory in Antiquity and the
Middle Ages*, 74.
[12] The left wing of the *Plèiade* interpreted Ronsard's view on the close relationship
between music and poetry as a justification for using music to solve the problems of
quantitative metre. Pattison, *Music and Poetry of the English Renaissance*, 122.
[13] Vivian, *The Works of Thomas Campion*, 35.

and harmony must be similar to accommodate the Divine symmetry of the universe. Up until the sixteenth century music theory has been strongly influenced by Boethius' *De Musica* where music was seen as a mirror to universal order, an idea upheld by Campion who argues: 'The world is made by Simmetry and proportion, and is in that respect compared to Musick, and Musick to Poetry.'[14] As a physician he would have been familiar with the theory concerning the correlation between the harmony of music to the four elements and bodily humors, and that the seven steps of the musical scale represented the circling of the celestial spheres, the seven spirits around the throne of God and the seven days of creation.[15] But music also reflected the life of man: both have a beginning, middle and end. Music was believed to reflect human emotion and its cadences reflected the highs and lows of human feeling, but most importantly it articulated the inevitability of death.[16] For Campion, number in poetry and music is the essence and functions on two levels: it meant the actual number by counting of syllables in a line but also it had a philosophical dimension which distinguishes it from its concrete quality. Numbers in music represented order, proportion and mysticism.[17] Campion asks, 'What music can there be where there is not proportion observed?'[18] Music, like the Geometrical structures of the universe was thought to be immutable and this immutability allowed mankind to dwell on God in a harmonious relationship.[19] Music revealed God and the working of nature; it allowed mankind access to the Divine:

> Come, let vs sound with melody, the praises
> Of the kings king, th' omnipotent creator,
> Author of number that hath the entire world in Harmonie framed.[20]

---

[14] *Idem.*

[15] Finney, *Musical Backgrounds for English Literature: 1580–1650*, 34.

[16] Ibid., 41.

[17] Finney argues that metaphysical interpretation of number as revealed in music was basic to occult practices in England. John Dee, in his preface to Euclid's *Elements of Geometry*, recommended music, as had Saint Augustine, as a key to number, Ibid., 36–37.

[18] Vivian, *The Works of Thomas Campion*, 35.

[19] Finney defines nature in relation to music as the essential property of soul and music. It assumed an immutable characteristic that makes soul or music what it is. The soul of man and of the world is by nature harmony and music itself has by nature an identical harmony. Finney, *Musical Backgrounds*, 62.

[20] Vivian, *The Works of Thomas Campion*, 17.

Campion fits the words to a tune that is in Sapphic metre.[21] While imitating the Latin and Greek poets 'both diligent obseruers of the number and quantity of sillables, not in their verses only but likewise in their prose,' he is also composing a metrical rhythm compatible with the mood of the poem.[22] Through choosing this metrical form, Campion recalls the ancient Greece world, suggesting that number equates to harmony, a gift from the god Apollo:

> Their browes with great Apollos bayes are hid.
> He first taught number and true harmony.[23]

The use of the Sapphic metre also recalls Orpheus whose severed head was honoured on the isle of Lesbos, an island closely associated with the poetess, Sappho. Ficino, expanding on the Hermetic belief of the effect of music on the natural, vital and animal spirits, included the notion of a cosmic spirit, or *pneuma*: a spirit that pervaded and gave life to everything in the universe.[24] Ficinian theory, based on Pythagorean and Platonic philosophy, believed that music transmitted a celestial influence. Since the universe was conceived in musical proportions Ficino argued, its *spiritus* must also be musical: 'the world both lives and breathes, and it is possible for us to draw its spirit. It is actually drawn by man through his own spirit'[25] This cosmic breath, or pervading universal music, not only correlated with the power of the breath of God but was also believed to reflect the dominant emotion of each planet since each heavenly body possessed specific characteristics, an idea Campion endorses, 'Though, when her sad planet raignes, Froward she bee' adding an astrological dimension to his work.[26] The planets' moods could be imitated in man-made music because both shared the world spirit. Philosophers such as Ficino believed that by inhaling this cosmic spirit, human emotion and characteristics could be influenced and even changed.[27] Associated with the belief in the power of a world spirit, was the belief that the power of a singer's

---

[21] Lowbury, Salter and Young, *Thomas Campion Poet, Composer, Physician*, 85.
[22] Vivian, *The Works of Thomas Campion*, 35.
[23] Ibid., 41.
[24] Ficino, *The Book of Life*, trans. Charles Boer, 91. All citations are to this edition.
[25] Ficino, *The Book of Life*, 96.
[26] Vivian, *The Works of Thomas Campion*, 13.
[27] Finney suggests that a deluge of occult writing believing in the efficacy of music to call down celestial spirit followed the translation of Agrippa's *Occult Philosophy* in 1651. Finney, *Musical Background*, 112.

spirit was associated with the power of the breath of God. The motion of air set up by sound had the ability to move the body and spirits: emotion was believed to be accompanied by motion of the spirits.[28] The power of voice is one of the recurring themes in Campion's lyric poetry: 'The eare is a rationall sence and a chiefe judge of proportion.'[29] The sound of English poetry, dependent on stress, language, metrical feet, word syllables, type of verse and organisation of time in relation to speech sounds, are all subjects Campion engages with in his treatise, *The Art of English Poesie*. As a musician he had a strong sense of time which enabled him to choose words whose syllables came close to meeting the needs of classical feet.[30] Campion's poetry does not rely on visual imagery but rather he uses music to develop his poetic form and underpin his philosophy, for music was not merely about composition but also a way to understanding the universe.[31] He allows aural perception to dominate over the other senses so that the listener feels the movements and emotions of his work. His poetry 'sounds', thus mourning will 'speake', lips 'swell', 'sad notes fall' and 'sighes want ayre'. For Campion, 'He that the eares of ioy will euer pearse, Must sing glad notes.'[32] The idea of nature as an aural experience extends to the Divine cosmos where:

> To his sweet Lute Apollo sung the motions of the Spheares;
> The wondorous order of the Stars, whose course diuides the yeares;
> And all the Mysteries aboue.[33]

The organisation of sound into rhythm was essential to Campion's lyric poetry to provide the correct harmonic, melodic and rhythmical nature essential to both art forms.[34] Rhyme appears to take secondary

---

[28] Ficino, *The Book of Life*, 161.

[29] Vivian, *The Works of Thomas Campion*, 36.

[30] Ing argues that many of Campion's rules about quantity in syllables are confused and impracticable, but this should not obscure his sense of rhythm. Ing, *Elizabethan Lyrics*, p. 60.

[31] Finney defines music in this sense as speculative music which deals with the nature of sound, with the position and function of music in the entire system of human knowledge and with music's usefulness to man. It included metaphysical speculation on the harmony of the universe, for it was widely taught in the Renaissance that the whole cosmos operates according to musical law. Finney, *Musical Backgrounds*, ix.

[32] Vivian, *The Works of Thomas Campion*, 27.

[33] Ibid., 178.

[34] Plato describes harmony as the reconciliation of opposites, "Music, like medicine, creates agreement by producing concord and love between these various opposites." Plato, *Symposium*, 187c in: Cooper (ed.), *Plato Complete Works*, 471.

importance to the cadence and rhythm of Campion's work. Thus poetry was spoken in 'measured sounds' and music in poetic language.

Campion's ideas on love in his lyric poetry are the expansion of a single literary conceit: the contrast between heavenly joy and earthly love. However his work does not merely replicate the contemporaneous poetic conceits of his time but also describes the impact love can have on the human body: he describes the signs and symptoms and the lover's chills, fevers, paleness, erratic behaviour and moods and the consequences this has on the body, such as loss of appetite and malaise. Love, Campion suggests, can bring both joy and anguish. He admonishes the listener to 'Tune thy Musicke to thy hart' so that joy and sorrow can both be expressed through music.[35] Ultimately the musical articulation of human emotion is used in praising the glory of God, 'Thy power, O God, thy merices, to record, Will sweeten eu'ry note and eu'ry word'[36] His poetry acknowledges that music is love because love is harmony and harmony is music.[37] Campion's work occasionally substitutes the word 'music' with melody and harmony to balance the music and mood of his words, displaying a Platonic idealisation of music, love and harmony.[38] Plato argues that poetry and music are similar to medicine because the three are guided by the god of Love in the search for physiological and spiritual harmony. The physician's task is to 'effect a reconciliation and establish mutual love between the most basic bodily elements.'[39]

The idea of music as a healing motif is one Campion believes in. He qualified as a physician between 1602 and 1606 and his use of medical terminology and music as a healing metaphor substantially increases in his four *Books of Ayes*, published from 1602–1617.[40] In his *Second Booke of Ayres*, Campion describes the physiological effects of old age. In one of his most famous lyrics he writes, 'Cold age deafes not there our eares, nor vapour dims our eyes'.[41] By the time this volume was

---

[35] Vivian, *The Works of Thomas Campion*, 121.
[36] Ibid., 120.
[37] Finney, *Musical backgrounds*, 77.
[38] Plato writes, 'Music, like medicine, creates agreement by producing concord and love between these various Opposites. Music is therefore simply the science of the effects of Love on rhythm and harmony.' Plato, *Symposium*, 187c, in Cooper, op. cit., 471.
[39] Plato, *Symposium*, 186d, Ibid., 470.
[40] Vivian, *The Works of Thomas Campion*, xxxix.
[41] Ibid., 122.

written, his work was showing a depth of understanding about the physical effects that emotions can have on the body. Thus jealousy is compared to 'a sicke mans rest, its soone diseased.'[42] By his *Fourth Booke of Ayres*, Campion is using words such as "plague", "weeping wounds" and "Maladies", and Galenic theory is inherent in his lyrics, for example, the belief that the left side of the body is associated with weakness:

> Yet me thinkes, a heate I finde,
> Like thirstlonging, that doth bide
> Euer on my weaker side,
> Where they say my heart doth moue.
> Venus, grant it be not loue.[43]

His images of wounding and healing by beauty and love, features of his later poetry, are prevalent in this last book of Ayres. One of the words that consistently appears in his lyric poetry is "cure" or "recure", thus 'Their sinne-sicke soules by him shall be recurred' reveals God as the Divine physician healing the physical and spiritual needs of mankind.[44] Campion's use of alliteration highlights how evil, the 'poisoned baytes of sinne' can warp the soul.[45] However, if we are punished by God, there is no cure except through Him:

> If Powres Celestiall wound vs
> And will not yield reliefe,
> Woe then must needs confound vs,
> For none can cure our griefe[46]

Campion uses the idea of curing to evoke one of his favourite medical metaphors: hidden wounds cannot heal, 'A wound long hid growes past recure.'[47] The forsaken lover's tears reach out for a cure, for an action that 'Proud of a wound the bleeding Souldiers grow' and the lover endures 'Griefe that knows nor cause, nor cure.'[48] For Campion this emotional grief cannot simply be cured by medicine and he implies that it is time and nature that is required to heal psychological wounds, 'Griefes past recure fooles try to heale,/That greater harmes

---

[42] Vivian, *The Works of Thomas Campion*, 136.
[43] Vivian, *The Works of Thomas Campion*, 179.
[44] Ibid., 118.
[45] Ibid., 121.
[46] Ibid., 133.
[47] Ibid., 135.
[48] Ibid., 162.

on lesse inflict".[49] Yet as love can cause pain so it has the power to
enchant and music, as an image of divine harmony, has the power to
refine the soul – it could "recure" the beloved, 'But with one touch of
grace cure all my paine.'[50] Thus, his words 'have charm'd her' suggesting the power of words and sound.[51] Campion elaborates on the idea
of enchanted music to melt his mistress' heart when he sings:

> Then come, you Fayries, dance with me a round;
> Melt her hard hart with your melodious sound

His use of assonance and alliteration at the beginning of the poem
signals his intent to convey the idea of magic, music and charms to
woo his mistress and his use of 'thrice three times' evokes the magical
power of number that will cure the pain of his mistress' hard heart:

> Thrice tosse these Oaken ashes in the ayre
> Thrice sit thou mute in this inchanted chayre
> And thrice three times tye vp this true loues knot
> And murmur soft, she will, or shee will not.[52]

This poem has nuances of an incantation; Campion takes on the role of
magician, who appeals for a transformation in his beloved's response.
As lyric poet he has a dual role – his Orphic power is used to animate
his beloved's feelings and his song transports the listener to a dimension where the song is part of the harmonic whole.

Campion's lyric poetry also includes the contemporaneous idea that
lovesickness in women was associated with sexual frustration due to a
'wandering womb' and could be cured by intercourse:[53]

> Maids are full of longing thoughts that breed a bloudlesse sickenesse,
> And that, ofty I heare men say, is onely cur'd by quicknesse.[54]

The image of 'bloudlesse sickenesse' is a favoured metaphor used by
Campion as an indicator of turbulent emotions such as sexual anguish,
unrequited love or mourning. Untreated grief can lead to melancholy
or madness, a theme he develops in his *Fourth Booke of Ayres* where

---

[49] Ibid., 177.
[50] Ibid., 167.
[51] Ibid., 172.
[52] Ibid., 169.
[53] Greenblatt, *The Norton Shakespeare*, 3266.
[54] Vivian, *The Works of Thomas Campion*, 187.

the poetry displays a psychological dimension and understanding of the human condition:

> The first step to madnesse
> Is the excesse of sadnesse.[55]

The best medicine for rejected love is the ability to forget. Although Campion's lyric poetry is moulded in the generalized conventions of late Elizabethan and Jacobean writings, they also reveal a personal level: it is Campion's grief and love that we witness. This personalization of his lyric poetry extends to his use of medical imagery that appears repeatedly, particularly in the later years. His practice of medicine appears to give him a deeper understanding of human nature and the lyric poetry expresses a wide range of human emotion and expression of moods ranging from depression and madness to love and euphoria.[56] Campion longs for water from the mythological Lethe because 'Tis their best med'cine that are pain'd/All thought to loose of past delight.'[57] By recalling the river of Oblivion from the underworld of Greek myths Campion evokes the memory of Orpheus and poetically they share anguish for lost love.

Campion derives his melody from the inflection of the spoken word and from his marrying of these two art forms he emerges as a great musical poet with a profound understanding of the complexities of human nature.[58] His work is a reflection of the change in Elizabethan and Jacobean philosophical thought and demonstrates a new and penetrating vision in the history of ideas. His works may be seen as a product of the convergence of foreign and English cultural traditions where words and notes form a 'couple lovingly together,' to achieve a perfect union. The vitality of cultural expression at the end of the sixteenth century reflected a transitional period of an era where a tension existed between a growing humanism that contemplated an

---

[55] Ibid., 182.
[56] Lowbury, Slater and Young suggest that it is significant that in the twenty-one poems by Campion in Rosseter's *Booke of Ayres*, which was published several years before he took his medical degree, there are no references to wounds or healing, and very few images to suggest the impact of medical experience. Lowbury, Slater and Young, *Thomas Campion*, 182.
[57] Vivian, *The Works of Thomas Campion*, 183.
[58] Kastendieck argues that Campion had learned the secret that could only be known in an age where the air rang with music, an age where people where endowed with a musical consciousness. Kastendieck, *England's Musical Poet, Thomas Campion*, 161.

awareness of individual consciousness – the belief in the power of the
individual to control their own destiny versus the Christian hierarchy
of the Middle Ages. There was no sharp delineation in this transitional
process but rather, what Wilfrid Mellers termed "interpenetration"
between the old and the new.[59] This new individualism was echoed
in music through new values in musical notes and a change in how
songs were sung. The marriage of poetry and music thus provided the
perfect means of expression for this imitation of *musica universalis* –
the listener was persuaded that the audible sounds of music was an
expression of a divine intelligence manifesting through the various
dimensions of creation. Campion was one of the forerunners in exploring the musical imagination within the confines of human experience:
he deals with man's potentialities and explores man's essential nature.
His poetic rhythms although varied, never lose the inflections of the
speaking voice, yet, at the same time, they flowed spontaneously with
the accompanying music because the word structure in many of his
lyrics follows a similar pattern of imagery and rhythm and emotional
contours to that of the melody.[60] While his lyrics are unpretentious
and simple, scholars are still unsure if Campion wrote the words to
fit the music or vice versa, but each art form has the ability to stand
alone as a separate entity from the other. His chief originality is the
musical quality of his lyric poetry because it strives to achieve perfection between the words and the "sound" of the poems and the magic
of his work lies largely in Campion's ability to achieve this.

Most studies on Campion focus on his melodious coupling of words
and music, but his attempt to "recure" physical and psychological
"wounds" to create a harmonious whole, may be seen as his interpretation of the Ficinian desire of the human soul to ascend to the Original
One. Certainly, his interest in the divine music and mathematics of
Platonic theology is prevalent throughout his work and suggests that
the purpose of music is to elevate the listener. By enabling the listener
to have access to divine harmony through his musico-poetics, Campion
"heals" the soul. This overriding desire for harmony in conjunction

---

[59] Mellers, *Harmonious Meeting: A study of the Relationship between English Music,
Poetry and Theatre, c. 1600–1900*, 19.
[60] Mazzaro argues that in aiming to achieve the exact union of words and music,
there is nothing in the words which encourages the auditor to linger. The poetry
appears deliberately designed to allow for the anticipatory drive of music. Mazzaro,
Transformations in the Renaissance English Lyric, 129.

with his suggestive use of prophecy and magic, allows Campion to wear the Orphic mantle. It was not until the rebirth of lyricism in the Romantic Period that music and poetry were united again in a manner that Campion had achieved in Renaissance England.

BIBLIOGRAPHY

Campion, T., *The Works of Thomas Campion*, ed. Percival Vivian, Oxford: Clarendon Press, 1909.

Cooper, J. M., *Plato Complete Works*, Indianapolis and Cambridge: Hackett Publishing Company, 1997.

Ficino, M., *The Letters of Marsilio Ficino, Volume 1 being a translation of Liber V1*, trans. Fellowship of the Language Department of the School of Economic Science, London: Shepheard-Walwyn Publishers, 1975.

——, *The Letters of Marsilio Ficino, Volume 5 being a translation of Liber V1*, trans. Fellowship of the Language Department of the School of Economic Science, London: Shepheard-Walwyn Publishers, 1994.

——, *The Book of Life*, trans. Charles Boer of *Liber de Vita* (or *De Vita Triplica*), Texas: Spring publications, Inc., 1980.

Finney, G. L., *Musical Backgrounds for English Literature: 1580–1650*, New Brunswick, New Jersey: Rutgers University Press, 1961.

Friedman, J. B., *Orpheus in the Middle Ages*, Cambridge, Massachusetts: Harvard University Press, 1970.

Greenblatt, S., *The Norton Shakespeare*, London: W.W. Norton & Company Ltd. 1997.

Ing, C., *Elizabethan Lyrics A study in the development of English metres and their relation to poetic effect*, London: Chatto & Windus, 1968.

Irwin, J. T., "Thomas Campion and the Musical Emblem", *Studies in English Literature, 1500–1900*, Vol. 10, No. 1, The English Renaissance. (Winter, 1970), pp. 121–141.

Kastendieck, M. M., *England's Musical Poet, Thomas Campion*, New York, Russell & Russell, 1963.

Lowbury, E., Salter, T. and Young, A., *Thomas Campion Poet, Composer, Physician*, London: Chato & Windus, 1970.

Lindley, D., *Thomas Campion*, Leiden, The Netherlands: E.J. Brill, 1986.

Mathiesen, T. J., *Apollo's Lyre Greek Music and Music Theory in Antiquity and the Middle Ages*, Lincoln and London: University of Nebraska Press, 1999.

Mazzaro, J., *Transformations in the Renaissance English Lyric*, Ithaca and London: Cornell University Press, 1970.

Mellers, W., *Harmonious Meeting: A study of the Relationship between English Music, Poetry and Theatre, c. 1600–1900*, London: Dobson Books Ltd., 1965.

——, *The masks of Orpheus. Seven stages in the story of European music*, Manchester: Manchester University Press, 1987.

Pattison, B., *Music and Poetry of the English Renaissance*, London: Methuen & Co. Ltd., 1948.

Smith, G., *Elizabethan Critical Essays, Volume 11*, Oxford: Oxford University Press, 1904.

Spink, I., *English Song Dowland to Purcell*, London: B.T. Batsford Ltd, 1974.

Warden, J., *Orpheus, The Metamorphoses of a Myth*, Toronto, Buffalo and London: University of Toronto Press, 1982.

GIOVAMBATTISTA DELLA PORTA E L'EFFICACIA TERAPEUTICA DELLA MUSICA

Concetta Pennuto

English summary: Giovambattista della Porta analyses the powers of music on the body and soul of listeners in *Magia Naturalis* XX 7. The aim of this paper is to study this chapter in order to focus on the search of the relationship between music and medicine in Della Porta's philosophical and medical thought. Since sound depends on the material of musical instruments, namely strings, woods and skins, Della Porta conceives music as able to produce its influence on the body and soul of people and patients. In fact, musical instruments material is the same used by physicians in their pharmaceutical remedies, though in animal, herbal and mineral forms. Thus, it is possible to read Della Porta's theory of the medical power of sounds in the light of the Renaissance debate about the therapeutic use of music in medicine.

Il legame antico tra musica, medicina e filosofia è testimoniato, nella cultura greco-romana, da una vasta letteratura sul potere che musica strumentale e canto mostrano nell'allontanare pestilenze, curare sciatiche, sedare o incitare gli animi, restituire l'udito ai sordi, curare il morso velenoso dei serpenti, condizionare il temperamento, i caratteri, i costumi e la morale di interi popoli e così via[1]. Durante l'età medievale, sebbene alcuni studi abbiano messo in luce un calo d'interesse per gli effetti della musica in campo medico, soprattutto nell'Occidente cristiano[2], non si possono trascurare influenti pagine di certa trattatistica, in particolare filosofica, in cui si commenta la capacità della musica di condizionare l'anima e il corpo degli ascoltatori[3]. Lo studio delle relazioni tra musica e medicina si arricchisce nel Rinascimento, come testimoniano gli scritti di medici e filosofi quali Marsilio Ficino, Cornelio Agrippa e Girolamo Fracastoro. L'intento di questo contributo è leggere le pagine che Giovambattista Della Porta dedica

---

[1] West, 'Music Therapy in Antiquity'; *Idem, Ancient Greek Music*, chap. 1, 31–33.
[2] Horden, 'Commentary on Part II', 104–107; Burnett, 'Spiritual medicine'.
[3] Boccadoro, 'La musique, les passions, l'âme et le corps'.

nella *Magia Naturalis* agli effetti meravigliosi della musica su colui che
l'ascolta. Nel contesto di un importante sviluppo del pensiero rinascimentale sul legame tra musica e medicina, per Della Porta l'impiego
terapeutico del suono è basato sul nesso tra suoni, materiali degli strumenti musicali, parti del corpo e malattie.

Il capitolo settimo del ventesimo libro della *Magia Naturalis* (ultima
versione 1589)[4] è dedicato alla *lyra* e alle sue proprietà meravigliose
(*mirae proprietates*)[5]. Siamo ormai in conclusione di un volume che
si era aperto con la definizione di *magia* quale sinonimo di sapienza e
completa conoscenza della natura. Maghi sono i sapienti, in accordo
alla ricca tradizione platonica, neoplatonica, pitagorica, ermetica, filosofica e medica citata da Della Porta a supporto e autorità di tale definizione[6]. Il mago del Rinascimento può conoscere i reciproci accordi
e disaccordi della natura che governa il mondo, ovvero quei *consensus*
e *dissensus rerum* grazie ai quali la natura costruisce i propri *opera*,
componendo e scompaginando i corpi che la costituiscono[7]. Ciò che
il volgo considera *miracula* è oggetto di conoscenza di questo sapiente
imbevuto delle letture di quell'antica tradizione filosofica e medica
appena delineata e di ricchissimo impatto nel Rinascimento[8]. Ma le
competenze del mago non si limitano, avverte Della Porta nella prefa-
zione al volume, a una mera lettura delle fonti. I loro contenuti vanno
verificati alla luce dell'esperienza. La ricerca della "verità" configura la
metodologia di Della Porta, che associa *studium* ed *experientia* nell'indagine sui *verissima* fatti della natura, *utilia et nota*[9]. Ed è proprio
questo programma metodologico che permette all'uomo del Rinascimento di vincere in attendibilità gli scritti dei più antichi e recenti
autori: il binomio di lettura e sperimentazione consente di capire se
quanto riportato dalle fonti sia vero o falso, di testare personalmente
le narrazioni degli autori, di scoprire cose nuove[10]. In questo modo,

---

[4] Su Giovambattista Della Porta, la composizione e la fortuna del trattato *Magia
naturalis* (1558–1589), cfr. Zaccaria-Romei, 'Della Porta, Giovambattista'; Aquilecchia, 'Appunti su G. B. Della Porta e l'inquisizione'.
    [5] Della Porta, *Magia Naturalis*, xx 7, 657–663 (De lyra, et miris quibusdam eius
proprietatibus).
    [6] Ibid. i 1, 1–2; cfr. Garin, 'Le philosophe'; Shumaker, '«La magia naturale»'.
    [7] Ibid. i 2, 3.
    [8] Cfr., almeno, Zambelli, 'Il problema della magia naturale nel Rinascimento';
Copenhaver, 'Astrology and magic'.
    [9] Della Porta, *Magia Naturalis*, Praefatio, *5v–6v.
    [10] Ibid. *6v.

conclude Della Porta, 'recentiorum aetas antiquam superaverit'[11]. In realtà, la letteratura antica non era scevra da affermazioni simili, che proprio in ambito medico, e in particolare galenico, caratterizzavano il programma metodologico di associazione tra *ratio* ed *experientia*[12]. Non è forse un caso, quindi, se tra le competenze del mago rinascimentale Della Porta enunci la conoscenza dell'arte medica o, meglio, della *scientia* medica. Accanto alla filosofia, alle discipline matematiche, all'astrologia, all'ottica e alle arti meccaniche, la medicina si presenta come *congener* e *simillima* al mago. Insegna, infatti, come sono caratterizzate le mistioni dei corpi e i loro temperamenti. Mostra come comporre e applicare i corpi gli uni agli altri. Istruisce sulle proprietà di piante, metalli, minerali, pietre e gemme. Implica l'uso della distillazione alchemica e permette di scoprire continuamente nuovi ritrovati utili alla salute dei mortali[13].

Come leggiamo nel primo libro della *Magia naturalis*, i principi primi di tutte le cose, gli elementi, costituiscono i semi primigeni della natura, come il fuoco, lo spirito-aria, l'acqua e la terra. I medici dell'Antichità insegnano che la natura ha architettato la macchina del mondo secondo un disegno straordinariamente opportuno, in modo da combinare le qualità degli elementi con continuità e smussandone tutte le differenze[14]. La mescolanza delle qualità del calore, della freddezza, dell'umidità e della secchezza, la loro articolazione in qualità attive e passive secondo i principi della fisica aristotelica, la loro gradazione nella composizione dei corpi misti sono alla base delle operazioni mirabili della natura che non solo troviamo descritte nei testi antichi e recenti, ma che è possibile anche mostrare con gli *experimenta*. Si ha così conferma del principio empedocleo della concordia e della lite come fondamento dell'associazione e della dissociazione degli elementi e delle loro qualità nei corpi misti[15]. Eppure i corpi non si compongono delle sole qualità evidenti e percettibili. Come la tradizione peripatetica e i più recenti filosofi insegnano, sottolinea Della Porta rifacendosi a certo aristotelismo medievale (per esempio, il *De occultis operibus naturae* di San Tommaso d'Aquino) e al più moderno

---

[11] Ibid.
[12] Cfr., ad esempio, Galenus, *De elementis*, 2v: «Cum vero duo sint instrumenta ad horum proloquiorum inventionem, experientia scilicet et ratio». Sull'epistemologia galenica, cfr. Frede, 'On Galen's Epistemology'.
[13] Della Porta, *Magia Naturalis*, i 3, 4–5.
[14] Ibid. i 4, 7.
[15] Ibid. i 4, 8–9.

neoplatonismo del *De vita coelitus comparanda* di Marsilio Ficino o
del *De occulta philosophia* di Cornelio Agrippa, esistono qualità che
non si possono percepire, perché connaturate alla forma sostanziale
dei corpi, ma che producono effetti a tutti visibili. Queste qualità sono
caratterizzate dalla *vis formae*, tanto potente da poter essere sfruttata
come strumento di operazioni[16]. Il discorso si conclude con un rapido
panorama sulla concatenazione dei corpi in "serie" secondo il platonismo e il neoplatonismo antico[17], con l'immancabile sbocco su quella
sympathia et antipathia che si può sperimentare grazie alle proprietà
che i corpi così intrecciati e caratterizzati per forma e sostanza mani-
festano in natura. Sulla base di simpatia e antipatia, *consensus et dissensus*, i corpi si legano in mutuo connubio oppure si respingono e la
natura si diletta di questo spettacolo, frutto di quelle arcane e peculiari
proprietà che gli uomini hanno imparato a utilizzare nei loro rimedi[18].
Segue un ricco catalogo di fenomeni apparentemente meravigliosi della
natura, ma che si possono nella realtà spiegare ricorrendo ai principi
delle qualità degli elementi, occulte soprattutto, e della concatenazione
dei corpi dagli infimi ai superni in "serie" dipendenti dagli astri e in
base ai principi fisici e filosofici della simpatia e dell'antipatia[19].

Compito del mago (di ficiniana memoria) è a questo punto conoscere
gli strumenti per attrarre le virtù dei cieli e degli astri che presiedono
alle concatenazioni dei corpi e alle loro reciproche simpatie e antipatie.
Per i Platonici, la *magia* non era altro che attrazione di una cosa verso
un'altra, grazie alla simpatia tra i corpi della natura, commenta Della
Porta. Quindi, poiché il *mundus* è come un unico animale composto
di membra, dipendenti tutte da un unico *author*, è evidente che i corpi
che costituiscono la *Natura* si attraggono gli uni gli altri: come in noi il
cervello, i polmoni, il cuore, il fegato e le altre membra traggono tutte
qualcosa da tutte e godono di reciproci giovamenti e, quando una di
esse soffre, tutte ne risentono, così accade nell'animale mondano, visto
che le sue membra sono intrecciate e per simpatia (*cognatio*) si comuni-

---

[16] Ibid. i 5, 9–10. Sulle qualità occulte, cfr. Copenhaver, 'A tale of two fishes', 380–
381; Festugière, *La révélation d'Hermès Trismégiste*, VI 1, 189–196; Hutchison, 'What
happened to occult qualities in the Scientific Revolution?', 233–240; Nutton, *Ancient
Medicine*, chap. 16, 242–247; Richardson, 'The generation of disease'.

[17] Della Porta, *Magia Naturalis*, i 6, 10–13; cfr. Copenhaver, 'Hermes Trismegistus,
Proclus'.

[18] Della Porta, *Magia Naturalis*, i 7, 13.

[19] Ibid. i 7, 14–17; sulle concatenazioni e gli astri, cfr. i 8, 17–22.

cano qualità e patimenti[20]. Nei termini del più classico neoplatonismo, Della Porta identifica nell'amore (*amor*) il fondamento dell'attrazione reciproca delle membra – ovvero dei corpi – dell'animale mondano[21]. È secondo questi principi che osserviamo fenomeni quali l'attrazione esercitata dal magnete sul ferro, dall'ambra sulla paglia, dallo zolfo sul fuoco, dal sole su molti fiori e foglie, dalla luna sull'acqua[22]. Sulla base di queste competenze, l'agricoltore può preparare i campi a ricevere i benefici del cielo, così come fanno il medico che compone i farmaci e il filosofo esperto di astronomia[23].

Il vero scrutatore della natura (*naturalium rerum scrutator, et contemplator*) può allora imparare non solo a conoscere, ma anche a utilizzare le proprietà dei corpi che si attraggono e respingono, giungendo così a svelare gli arcani principi delle cose. Questo insegna soprattutto la medicina, che, più delle altre discipline, quali l'agricoltura, l'architettura, l'economia, scopre come poter sfruttare le proprietà di metalli, gemme, pietre, piante e animali osservando i fenomeni di attrazione e repulsione della natura[24]. Per esempio, con l'esperienza e l'osservazione del comportamento di animali si sono scoperte piante utili contro certi veleni, così come si sono scovate piante capaci di sanare ferite ed erbe che permettono di espellere la pituita e la bile in eccesso. Per ogni malattia particolare v'è in natura un rimedio particolare, commenta Della Porta[25]. Esistono, infatti, speciali *similitudines* tra semi, frutti, fiori, foglie, radici, astri, metalli, pietre e gemme con le malattie e le parti del corpo umano, come Dioscoride, Plinio e altri hanno mostrato con le loro opere[26]. Le citazioni delle corrispondenze tramandate da Teofrasto, Dioscoride, Galeno, Plinio, Orfeo e i *Medicorum dogmata* tra gli oggetti della natura e i morbi e le membra dell'uomo[27] ci introducono alle pagine dedicate da Della Porta alla musica: possiamo immaginare che di corrispondenze con malattie e membra del corpo umano si possa parlare anche per i suoni, che si presentano

---

[20] L'idea medica dell'uomo considerato nella sua interezza è formulata nella medicina ippocratica e ripresa nel Rinascimento, ad esempio, da Girolamo Fracastoro nel *De sympathia* (1546). Cfr. Hippocrates, 'De alim.', 23, 106; Hippocrates, 'Loc. Hum.', 1, 276–278; Fracastoro, *De sympathia*, cap. 15, 110.
[21] Della Porta, *Magia Naturalis*, i 9, 22.
[22] Ibid.
[23] Ibid. i 9, 23–24.
[24] Ibid. i 10, p. 25.
[25] Ibid. i 10, 25–26.
[26] Ibid. i 11, 28.
[27] Ibid. i 11–12, 28–31.

come "incorporei" alla percezione? Trovare tali corrispondenze permetterebbe al medico di utilizzare i suoni al pari di una pianta o di un metallo.

Parlando delle proprietà della musica, Della Porta si concentra in particolare sulla serie di casi mirabili che fin dall'Antichità attestano la capacità di agire dei suoni su oggetti animati e inanimati, anima e corpo, uomini e animali. In effetti, il capitolo settimo del libro ventesimo della *Magia Naturalis* comincia con un catalogo di *miri effectus* della musica, per passare poi all'indagine sul modo in cui questi effetti si producono[28]. Della Porta non esita, richiamandosi alla controversia sulla superiorità della musica degli antichi o dei moderni, ad abbracciare il partito di chi sostiene come la musica attuale sia più coltivata e più nobile di quella dell'Antichità. Eppure, la musica antica, ben più rozza e imperfetta della nostra, dice Della Porta, era in grado di produrre effetti straordinari, di cui la nostra sembra incapace. È risaputo che i ritmi e le composizioni possono agire sugli uomini, anche sugli animi più recalcitranti. Museo ha mostrato che il *carmen* è cosa dolcissima per i mortali e i Platonici ricordano che la musica è in grado di incantare ogni cosa che vive[29].

Il catalogo di *mirabilia* musicali, volto a dimostrare questo assunto, si concentra in primo luogo sugli effetti della musica sull'animo degli ascoltatori: da Timoteo musico che col modo frigio accendeva l'animo di Alessandro, facendolo correre alle armi, o, al contrario, cambiando il modo, lo rendeva *remollitus*, a Plutarco che racconta del potere della musica di Antigenida che faceva ricorrere alle armi; da Cicerone che riferisce di come Pitagora agiva sull'animo infiammato di amore e vino del giovane di Taormina, rendendolo pacato al ritmo dello spondeo, ad Empedocle che agiva sul suo ospite col canto. La letteratura è così ricca di episodi simili, che Della Porta si vede costretto a continuare il suo catalogo ricordando ancora l'uso della musica da parte di Teofrasto per sedare i turbamenti dell'animo e di Agamennone, che, prima di partire per Troia, aveva pensato di lasciare Clitemnestra, della cui pudicizia dubitava, sotto la custodia di un citaredo che con la sua arte la incitava alla continenza, tanto che la moglie riuscì a tradire il marito solo dopo aver fatto uccidere il musicista. Ma il potere della musica non si limita all'animo degli uomini: anche gli animali ne sono affetti,

---

[28] Ibid. xx 7, 657.
[29] Della Porta, *Magia Naturalis*, xx 7, 658.

come dimostra la storia di Arione e del delfino, e l'azione dei suoni su elefanti, cervi, cigni, uccelli e così via. In ambito medico, poi, la musica è usata come rimedio nel caso dei morsi delle tarantole di Puglia, il cui veleno è trasformato in *virus pestiferum* dai raggi cocenti del sole. È noto che anche su ferite e malattie si può intervenire grazie alla musica: Terpandro e Arione curarono gravi malattie con la loro arte, così come Asclepiade sanava i sordi e sedava le folle utilizzando il canto. Secondo Della Porta, infine, le competenze degli Antichi si erano tanto arricchite, che essi erano riusciti ad attribuire una specifica virtù a ogni tipo di *melodia*, come alla *Dorica* la prudenza, la castità e la dottrina; alla *Phrygia* l'eccitamento alla battaglia, al furore, che si ottiene suonando una *tibia*; la *Lydia* acuisce l'intelletto e induce il desiderio delle cose celesti[30].

Nell'indagine però sulla *causa* di questi fenomeni, Della Porta afferma che la ragione di tante virtù non sono i *modi* della composizione, ma la materia di cui si compongono le parti degli strumenti musicali, come le corde, i legni e le pelli. Infatti, se pure provenienti da piante e animali morti, le parti degli strumenti conservano nella loro materia le qualità (*proprietates*) di cui quelle piante e animali godevano quando erano ancora in vita. Si tratta, dice Della Porta, delle proprietà – le occulte – la cui natura ha già spiegato nel corso dell'opera, riferendosi a quanto delineato nel primo libro della *Magia Naturalis*[31]. Se la letteratura antica sin qui citata fonda l'azione della musica soprattutto sul tipo di melodie e intervalli utilizzati, per Della Porta questo bagaglio culturale deve ampliarsi alla luce della sperimentazione sul potere di certi corpi di agire su altri in base alle simpatie e antipatie della natura. Uno strumento si compone di corde, pelli, legni, ossa che derivano da piante e animali: il suo suono dipende dalle proprietà, soprattutto le occulte, di quelle piante e animali. Se infatti consideriamo solo le qualità manifeste che possiamo percepire coi sensi (calore, freddezza, secchezza e umidità), constatiamo come queste scompaiano o si modifichino in seguito a mutamenti fisiologici e biologici dell'individuo o alla sua morte. Non così quel tipo di proprietà che dipendono dalla forma sostanziale degli individui e dalla loro concatenazione in "serie" dipendenti dagli astri.

---

[30] Ibid. 658–659.
[31] Della Porta, *Magia Naturalis*, xx 7, 660.

Ed ecco che ci troviamo di fronte alla tradizione che oppone lupi e agnelli, tanto che strumenti costruiti con parti dei due animali sono in completa *antipathia*. È lo stesso tipo di antipatia che oppone cavalli ed elefanti. Se una donna incinta sente suonare una *cithara* le cui corde sono preparate con parti di serpenti, la sua gravidanza sarà messa a repentaglio. I sofferenti all'anca erano curati da *Hermenias Thebanus* al suono di uno strumento confezionato col pioppo, visto che il succo della corteccia di quest'albero cura in caso di coxalgia, come scrive Dioscoride. I deliranti per follia (*lymphatici*) si curano con l'elleboro e Senocrate riusciva a trattarli grazie a strumenti costruiti con fusti cavi di elleboro o con tibie di cavallo. E che dire di Talete Milesio, che riuscì ad agire contro una pestilenza, suonando la sua *cithara* costruita con legno di vite? Come è noto, argomenta Della Porta, vino e aceto servono a contrastare le pestilenze. Quindi, il medesimo effetto si può ricavare da suoni che provengono da strumenti costruiti con gli stessi materiali da cui traggono origine vino e aceto. E se pure quella *cithara* fosse stata costruita con legno di alloro, il risultato sarebbe stato lo stesso, visto che le foglie di quest'albero posseggono un profumo che impedisce ai contagi di diffondersi. È per la stessa ragione, continua Della Porta, che Teofrasto poteva sanare dal morso delle vipere al canto di *tibiae* e altri strumenti ricavati dal ginepro, dal frassino, dall'alloro, dalla ferula, dal sambuco, dalla vite, da ossa di cervi e così via. Possiamo ora capire, sostiene l'autore, perché e come Pitagora riuscì a sedare il giovane di Taormina: lo strumento che il filosofo utilizzava era a base di edera o di legno di mandorlo, soprattutto il selvatico, piante che grande virtù esercitano contro l'ebrietà. E così dobbiamo ritenere fosse costruito anche lo strumento con cui Timoteo governava l'animo di Alessandro[32]. È questo l'argomento che permette a Della Porta di ritornare sugli altri casi del catalogo iniziale per spiegarli alla luce della teoria dei materiali degli strumenti. Prendiamo Agamennone e Clitemnestra. Lo strumento con cui il citaredo conduceva Clitemnestra alla pudicizia era costruito di vétrice. Erano infatti di vétrice i letti delle donne ateniesi durante le Tesmoforie, atti così a soffocare i loro impulsi venerei. I Pitagorici, poi, inducevano il sonno con strumenti costruiti di legno di mandorlo o di vite, mentre eccitavano al risveglio col suono di strumenti di elleboro. Il principio della risonanza, infine, combinato con il sistema delle corrispondenze,

---

[32] Ibid. xx 7 660–662.

spiega come sia possibile che i sordi possano udire i suoni degli strumenti musicali. Cos'altro sono le corrispondenze dei corpi della natura se non un esempio di risonanza delle corde della cetra? Già Plotino, nelle *Enneadi*, e con lui il neoplatonismo ficiniano, aveva applicato al concetto di simpatia universale del cosmo l'immagine della comunicazione della vibrazione sonora da una corda ad un'altra nella stessa cetra o in cetre diverse[33]. Ora Della Porta riprende quest'immagine e spiega che la tensione delle corde di uno o più strumenti conduce all'unità, esattamente come nel corpo dell'uomo gli organi formano un'unità. Un'immagine questa che ritroviamo nella medicina galenica, dove la *consonantia* nelle lire è specchio dell'indivisibilità delle membra del corpo umano[34]. Accade quindi che il suono si possa percepire non con l'udito, ma perché le sue onde toccano altri organi, come i denti o il cervello. Si tratta di un suono percepito col gusto, piuttosto che ascoltato con l'udito[35].

Capire perché si verificano in natura tali fenomeni, significa, per Della Porta, rendere abile il *magus* nell'utilizzazione di quello strumento formidabile che è la musica per ottenere particolari effetti. I *mirabilia* musicali e medici potranno far parte del bagaglio culturale, teorico e operativo, del *magus*, esperto in primo luogo, come visto sopra, di medicina, se saranno inseriti nell'apparato teorico della magia naturale. Così sostiene Della Porta quando indica la causa del potere della musica su corpo e anima non tanto nella costruzione armonica e melodica, quanto nelle corde, nei legni e nelle pelli degli strumenti musicali, ricavati da piante e animali. Sono questi i materiali da cui la natura del suono trae la sua origine. Sono questi i materiali che caratterizzano la coloritura del suono. Inserirli nel contesto della *Magia Naturalis* permette di riportare il potere terapeutico della musica, i suoi effetti meravigliosi, nell'ambito di una concezione del cosmo basata sul principio di comunicazione simpatetica e antipatetica tra individui. Il catalogo di *mirabilia* musicali di Della Porta rivela una pluralità di fonti antiche[36], già note alla letteratura musicale del Medioevo e del Rinascimento, come dimostrano opere quali il *Theoricum Opus Musicae* (1480, ed. ampliata 1492) di Franchino Gaffurio,

---

[33] Plotino, *Enneadi*, iv 4, 41, 688; Ficino, *In Plotinum*, IV 4, 41 Plotini, dd10r.
[34] Galenus, *De sanitate tuenda*, i 5, 23.
[35] Della Porta, *Magia Naturalis*, xx 7, 662–663.
[36] Cfr., ad esempio, Boetius, *De institutione musica*, I 1, 184–187; Capella, *De nuptiis*, IX 926, 355–356; Aulus Gellius, *Noctes Atticae*, IV 13, 179–180.

le *Istitutioni harmoniche* (1558) di Gioseffo Zarlino e il *Dialogo della musica antica et della moderna* (1581) di Vincenzo Galilei[37]. Possiamo altresì dire che l'affermazione di esordio del luogo della *Magia Naturalis* sulla questione del rapporto tra musica dei moderni e musica degli antichi, con la prima incapace di produrre sugli ascoltatori gli stessi effetti della seconda, si inserisce nel contesto di vivaci discussioni della letteratura rinascimentale[38]. Il contributo di Della Porta arricchisce questo panorama grazie alla collocazione dell'attestato potere psicosomatico della musica nell'ambito della magia naturale, con un forte accento sul ruolo della medicina tra le competenze del *magus*. L'analisi delle discussioni rinascimentali sul potere dei suoni su anima e corpo non si limita, infatti, alla letteratura musicale o filosofica, ma si amplia a quella medica. Alla metà del Cinquecento sembrano delinearsi due vie d'interpretazione del potere del suono da parte dei medici. Da un lato, c'è la strada indicata dal neoplatonismo rinascimentale di Marsilio Ficino. Dall'altra, troviamo una diversa attitudine del medico nei confronti del potere del suono, vale a dire l'attitudine che viene dal versante aristotelico e che possiamo trovare rappresentata da Girolamo Fracastoro.

In opere quali il *De vita coelitus comparanda*, ovvero il terzo libro del *De vita triplici* (1489), e il Commento al *Timeo* (1496), Ficino insegna al medico-filosofo e *magus* come carpire dal cielo gli influssi benefici degli astri[39]. Bisogna in primo luogo conoscere l'unità simpatetica del cosmo, la comunicazione delle membra dell'universo grazie alla presenza dello *spiritus mundi*, strumento dell'*anima mundi*, la concatenazione degli individui secondo il principio neoplatonico delle "serie" dipendenti ognuna da un astro e la dottrina di una medicina celeste fondata sull'armonia delle sfere per individuare le *illecebrae*, le esche, che il creatore ha innestato nel mondo inferiore per legarlo al superiore. Grazie alle competenze acquisite sulla base di questo ricco bagaglio culturale e operativo il sapiente può attrarre nel mondo

---

[37] Gaffurio, *Opus*, I 1, [1–6]; Zarlino, *Istitutioni harmoniche*, I 2, 10; Galilei, *Dialogo della musica antica et della moderna*, 1.
[38] Fend, 'La teoria musicale'; Haar, 'The Concept of the Renaissance', 26–29; Palisca, 'Vincenzo Galilei'; *Idem*, 'Muovere gli affetti con la musica'; Sargolini, 'La critica di Vincenzo Galilei'; Walker, *Studies in Musical Science*, 14–26.
[39] Su Ficino e la musica, cfr., almeno, Boccadoro, 'Marsilio Ficino'; Voss, 'Marsilio Ficino, the Second Orpheus'; *Eadem*, 'The Natural Magic of Marsilio Ficino'; Walker, *Spiritual and Demonic Magic*, i 1, 1–2, 3–24.

inferiore le virtù del cielo, come il magnete attira il ferro[40]. Bisogna quindi conoscere la corrispondenza tra i corpi celesti e i gruppi di oggetti che sono indissolubilmente legati nelle "serie" neoplatoniche e che si possono dividere in sette classi generali: materie dure, pietre e metalli corrispondono alla Luna; erbe, frutta, gomme-resine, membra degli animali corrispondono a Mercurio; polvere, vapori e odori corrispondono a Venere; parole, canti e suoni corrispondono ad Apollo-Sole; immaginazione e suoi effetti corrispondono a Marte; ragione e sue deliberazioni corrispondono a Giove; intelligenza e suoi moti congiunti al divino corrispondono a Saturno. Come si può vedere da questo schema, le *voces* costituiscono la classe mediana[41]. Come da erbe e vapori si ottengono miscele atte a trattare i vari casi medici, così dai *toni*, che s'accordano alle leggi degli astri, si compongono figure sonore, accompagnate da parola e numeri armonici, che permettono di scuotere, muovere e influenzare non solo lo spirito e l'animo, ma anche il corpo. Ficino delinea una sorta d'immagine incorporea, di figura sonora, costituita da parola e numero armonico. Infatti, spiega che «concentus per numeros proportionesque suas vim habere mirabilem ad spiritum et animum et corpus sistendum, movendum, afficiendum»[42], riconoscendo al suono un potere attivo non solo su anima e spirito, ma anche sul corpo. Questo potere attivo su corpo e anima deriva al suono dalla sua origine aritmetica, armonica, ovvero dai numeri e dalle proporzioni di cui si compone, numeri e proporzioni che – insegna il *Timeo* – sono gli stessi con cui il demiurgo ha creato il corpo e l'anima del mondo e dell'uomo. Inoltre, il *concentus* è *animatus*, ovvero la *motionis efficatia* si associa alla *rei natura*[43]. Quindi, se le erbe, i metalli, le pietre e i vapori tradizionalmente in uso nella farmacopea medica hanno una certa capacità di agire, suoni e parole si rivelano molto più efficaci alla luce della loro natura aerea e mobile: 'vocales materiae ob subtilitatem suam continuumque motum...facilius consummatiusque quam succi et crassi, et ad motum ineptiores, et qualitatibus admodum discrepantes, conflantur in unum'[44]. Nel

---

[40] Ficino, *Three Books on Life*, iii 26, 386. Sul neoplatonismo ficiniano e le sue fonti, cfr., nello stesso volume, Introduction (Carol V. Kaske), 28; Copenhaver, 'Hermes Trismegistus, Proclus'.

[41] Ficino, *Three Books on Life*, iii 21, 354–356.

[42] Ibid. iii 17, 330.

[43] Ficino, *In Timaeum*, cap. 29, 1417 (*sic*: 1449).

[44] Ibid. cap. 31, 1455 (*sic*: 1451). Per echi secenteschi di quest'idea, cfr. Wuidar, 'Musique et démonologie', 72–74.

De vita coelitus comparanda Ficino può descrivere la natura del suono
e del canto, come 'aer...calens sive tepens, spirans adhuc et quodam-
modo vivens...Concentus igitur spiritu sensuque plenus'[45].

A questa tradizione risponde il versante aristotelico, che possiamo
trovare rappresentato dal medico veronese Girolamo Fracastoro e in
particolare dal suo *De sympathia et antipathia rerum* (1546). Un'opera
su simpatia e antipatia scritta da un aristotelico formatosi a Padova
non poteva non risultare intrisa di un neoplatonismo rivisitato, anzi,
inserito in una complessa trama di fisica aristotelica. Trattando dei
suoni, Fracastoro si richiama alla tradizione del *De anima*[46]: quello che
Platone racconta nel *Timeo* non è che un *poeticum quiddam* per signi-
ficare che l'anima consta delle massime perfezioni di tutte le cose del
creato[47]. Per Fracastoro non v'è affinità tra l'anima e i numeri armonici, ovvero i numeri che si trovano nei suoni. Se proprio ai numeri
bisogna far riferimento parlando di armonie musicali, continua Fracastoro, allora si potranno paragonare i numeri interi e quelli frazionari
ai suoni interi e ai suoni frazionari[48]. Il suono intero produce un'unica
nota (*vox*) nella sua integrità. Il suono frazionario è di due tipi: quello
che produce la nota per sovrapposizioni di parti e quello che produce
una nota e una sua parte. Fracastoro descrive il suono intero come
suono integro, frutto di un'unica emissione di voce oppure di più
suoni che formano un'unità, un suono distinto e gradevole, rappresentato da una nota rotonda. I suoni frazionari sono invece striduli, non
uniformi e confusi, caratterizzandosi per disuguaglianza e mancata
distinzione delle parti[49]. La descrizione dei tre tipi di suono che leggiamo in Fracastoro tace sull'apparato armonico-matematico che troviamo nei trattati di teoria musicale o nei testi filosofici neoplatonici,
come il commento ficiniano al *Timeo* (cap. 30). La lezione pitagorico-
platonica di ricerca matematica degli intervalli, unica possibile fonte
del sapere musicale[50], si stempera alla luce di un approccio improntato

---

[45] Ficino, *Three Books on Life*, iii 21, 358.
[46] Aristoteles, *De anima*, i 3, 406b26–407a9,12–13.
[47] Fracastoro, *De sympathia*, cap. 14, 98.
[48] Ibid.
[49] Ibid. (il suono dato da sovrapposizioni di parti corrisponde a quello espresso dal
rapporto superpaziente; il suono che produce una nota e una sua parte corrisponde a
quello espresso dal rapporto superparticolare).
[50] Platone, *Rep.*, vii 12, 530d–531c, 582–584; cfr. Borzacchini, 'Incommensurability', 280.

ai *Problemata* aristotelici[51], perché per Fracastoro il numero non è l'origine del suono, ma solo la rappresentazione della sua misura (*modus*): 'Numeri igitur, quatenus numeri, nihil per se faciunt ad suavitatem et molestiam in sonis, sed solum quatenus per ipsos modi sonorum notantur, qui aut distincti aut confusi et asperi ad animam pertingunt'[52]. Questo non significa negare gli effetti della musica sull'anima e sul corpo dell'ascoltatore. La musica non perde il suo potere, ma questo potere non è di ordine matematico-armonico, come voleva il neoplatonismo ficiniano, bensì fisico-percettivo. Il suono, aristotelicamente inteso nella dimensione di vibrazione e diffusione di onde[53], che non scaturisce da un intervallo ma che semplicemente si scrive come intervallo per convenzione, questo suono agisce sul corpo in base alla costituzione delle sue vibrazioni e alla affinità tra queste vibrazioni e il temperamento umorale del corpo dell'individuo.

Nel contesto ficiniano, dire che i numeri armonici dei suoni sono gli stessi dell'anima del *Timeo* e del corpo del cosmo significa affermare una corrispondenza univoca tra musica umana e musica mondana. Così, nel *De vita coelitus comparanda*, la terapia musicale è basata sulla rispondenza tra suoni e pianeti[54]. Per un neoplatonico, formatosi armonicamente alla scuola di Boezio[55], la teoria aristotelica della fisica del suono è una "descrizione" di ciò che ha origine nel numero. Per il medico Fracastoro, è il contrario: il numero descrive, indica per convenzione; la teoria aristotelica spiega ciò che avviene in natura. Se il numero o il rapporto numerico descrive il suono, ma non lo produce, allora il suono è trasmissione di onde fisiche ed esisteranno tanti tipi di suoni e di armonie quanti sono i tipi di onde. Come messo in luce da Daniel P. Walker, nel tardo Rinascimento si comincia a rifiutare il legame o, meglio, il determinismo ficiniano (platonico-pitagorico-boeziano) tra intervalli armonici, costituzione dell'anima e armonia delle sfere[56]. Viene allora da chiedersi dove collocare quelle pagine della *Magia Naturalis* di Della Porta, in cui il potere psicosomatico della musica, rilevante in campo medico, trova la sua origine non nella

[51] Aristotele, *Problemi*, xix 14, 278; 16–17, 278–280; 35, 286.
[52] Fracastoro, *De sympathia*, cap. 14, 100.
[53] Aristoteles, *De anima*, ii 8, 419b4–22, 44–45.
[54] Ficino, *Three Books on Life*, iii 21, 360.
[55] Su Boezio e la musica nel Rinascimento, Palisca, 'Boethius in the Renaissance'.
[56] Walker, *Spiritual and Demonic Magic*, iii 6, 4, 201; 7, 4, 231.

composizione armonico-melodica, ma nel colore del suono e nella materia dello strumento musicale.

Nella ricerca – dalla lunga tradizione – di una spiegazione *in naturalibus* sui fenomeni mirabili del corpo del cosmo, Della Porta riferisce le opinioni degli antichi, che si fondano sullo studio di tre principi: gli elementi, la concordia e la lite, le qualità occulte. Il cosmo di Della Porta, strutturato secondo il fondamento neoplatonico della "catene" o "serie" procliane e ficiniane, trova nel fattore della simpatia (*consensus rerum*) il motivo della coesione delle serie di individui gerarchicamente organizzati in corrispondenze di mutuo connubio. Nelle associazioni di individui sono riconoscibili però delle situazioni di discordia, di distruttività, che costituiscono il contraltare della simpatia, nella forma del *dissensus rerum*. La conoscenza dell'armonia del cosmo, regolata dal gioco di simpatie e antipatie delle "serie" neoplatoniche, permette al *magus* di padroneggiare i segreti della natura in modo che questa non presenti più fattori occulti. Gli *arcana* svelati della natura possono essere sfruttati come forma di rimedio – *remedia* – da parte del saggio mago[57]. Da queste premesse si sviluppa un lungo catalogo di *mirabilia* della natura, appartenenti al regno vegetale, animale e minerale, dall'odio tra cavolo e vite a quello tra uomini e serpenti, dall'amicizia tra uomo e cane alla paura che l'elefante ha dell'ariete[58]. In nome del binomio *auctoritas-experientia*, alle voci della tradizione medico-filosofica che spiega le ragioni fisiche delle simpatie e delle antipatie tra individui[59], il lettore della *Magia Naturalis* è invitato a confrontarsi con i libri di *Phytognomonica*[60]. Solo in considerazione dei legami di simpatia e antipatia tra le membra del cosmo delineati da Proclo nel *De sacrificio et magia*, il medico potrà far sue le virtù che si possono attrarre dal cielo e ritrovarle negli oggetti della natura per trattare i problemi della salute[61]. Metalli, gemme, pietre, animali e piante svelano i loro *arcana* al mago che sappia contemplare e osservare i fenomeni della natura alla luce della dottrina della similitudine e della simpatia, che tanta parte hanno nelle pagine di *Phytognomonica*. È così che Della Porta nel capitolo undicesimo del primo libro della *Magia Naturalis*, già citato sopra, si dedica al ritrovamento delle

---

[57] Della Porta, *Magia Naturalis*, i 7, 13.
[58] Ibid. i 7, 13–17.
[59] Ibid. i 8, 17–22.
[60] Ibid. i 8, 22.
[61] Ibid. i 9, 24.

vires arcanae grazie al principio di similitudine (*similitudo*) tra semi, frutti, fiori, foglie, radici, gemme, pietre, metalli, astri, animali e corpo dell'uomo. Ancora una volta il rinvio finale del capitolo è ai libri di *Phytognomonica*, dove il principio di similitudine, spiegato nel primo libro, sostiene l'impianto di riconoscimento delle qualità e delle operazioni proprie di ciascun vegetale e sua parte[62].

In base al panorama fin qui delineato emerge il retaggio ficiniano della *Magia Naturalis*. Resta però da chiedersi fino a che punto la ricerca sulla causalità del potere terapeutico della musica permetta di parlare in termini *solo* ficiniani. Per quanto ancora siano validi principi quali le "serie" neoplatoniche, la simpatia, l'antipatia e l'affinità tra individui, alla base degli effetti della musica sui morbi e sugli affetti non troviamo, per Della Porta, le corrispondenze tra suoni e pianeti, tra suoni e numeri armonici che, al contrario, caratterizzano la medicina celeste ficiniana del commento al *Timeo* e del *De vita coelitus comparanda*, per quanto attenta al discorso timbrico[63]. Determinanti sono invece le corrispondenze tra suoni e materiali che li producono: per Della Porta, il colore (timbro) del suono – motore dell'influsso della musica sull'ascoltatore – non dipende dal tipo di armonie e intervalli utilizzati, ma dal tipo di materiali di cui si compone lo strumento musicale: 'Sed si nos huius causam perscrutari velimus: non modiis, sed fidibus, et instrumentorum ligno, et pellibus attribuemus, quum mortuorum animalium, et succisarum arborum etiam in membris et lignis proprietates conserventur'[64]. La lezione aristotelico-fracastoriana del *De sympathia* è assimilata se solo si guardi al silenzio sul supporto teorico-matematico nella comunicazione tra musica, corpo e anima. Anche Della Porta, come può fare un Fracastoro, guarda al fenomeno, alla percezione del suono, alla sua dimensione fisica più che armonica. Ma Della Porta non rifiuta l'altro aspetto del neoplatonismo rinascimentale, ovvero la ricezione dell'idea di un cosmo simpatetico organizzato in "serie" dipendenti di individui. È proprio questa conciliazione tra percettività del suono e struttura neoplatonica del cosmo che gli permette, da un lato, di svincolare l'azione della musica su

---

[62] Della Porta, *Phytognomonica*, i 8, 16–17; 12, 22.

[63] Boccadoro sottolinea la ricerca timbrica della musica ficiniana e dei suoi epigoni cinquecenteschi, come equivalente del colore, al di là del rapporto numerico che sottende al suono, Boccadoro, 'Crase, proportion, chromatisme', 251; *Idem*, 'Musique, médecine et temperaments', 431.

[64] Della Porta, *Magia Naturalis*, xx 7, 660.

corpo e anima dall'univocità matematico-armonica che lega armonia
delle sfere e individui sublunari; dall'altro, di mantenere in piedi tutta
la portata epistemologica delle corrispondenze neoplatoniche, che
consentono di giustificare l'azione del suono e la reazione dell'ascoltatore o ricettore di quel suono secondo una costruzione organica e
prevedibile. Della Porta sembra sviluppare una sorta di "determinismo" alternativo a quello astronomico-armonico boeziano-ficiniano,
che era basato sui numeri armonici e sulla corrispondenza univoca tra
suono, numero che lo produce e numero della struttura dell'anima del
mondo. Il "determinismo" di Della Porta non è armonico-matematico,
ma fisico, quasi fisiologico, nell'attenzione per il colore del suono e la
sua capacità di agire dipendenti dalla materia dello strumento musicale. Anche se per Della Porta gli astri restano in cima alle "serie" di
individui, non è più la struttura matematica a determinare l'influsso
della musica, ma la corrispondenza dei materiali, delle qualità di cui
si compongono i corpi. La simpatia tra suono, materiale che lo produce e parte del corpo o stato morboso è così fortemente disegnata da
infastidire Athanasius Kircher, che rigetta il discorso sui materiali a
favore di un suono che informi di sé l'aria grazie alla sua costituzione
armonica[65].

Della Porta vuole trovare per i suoni un'attribuzione per *similitudo*,
incastonandoli così nel sistema delle corrispondenze che sono speri-
mentate dal sapere medico. In questo modo fornisce al mago-medico
una serie di competenze che ampliano il suo campo d'azione, con-
sentendogli di recuperare quell'efficacia terapeutica del suono – quasi
farmacologica – che, ai suoi occhi, era propria della musica antica.
Come il medico può comporre e scomporre gli oggetti della natura
e applicarli in campo terapeutico nella preparazione dei farmaci, così
quello stesso medico potrà scegliere e preparare le composizioni di
suoni, che corrispondono alle parti del corpo, ai temperamenti umo-
rali e alle diverse forme di patologia. Questa corrispondenza è basata
sul colore conferito al suono dal materiale che lo produce, quello
stesso materiale che viene utilizzato sotto forma di polvere, succo, pil-
lola e così via nelle preparazioni farmaceutiche. Solo che nel caso di
un trattamento musicale, quel materiale è utilizzato in forma di suono,
tanto che all'ascolto, dice Della Porta, il suono si può dire percepito
non con l'udito, ma col gusto ('dicique poterit non auditus sensu, sed

---

[65] Kircher, *Musurgia*, ix 8, 229–330.

gustu perceptus'), perché il suono si riproduce nel cervello (*in cerebro*) in modo ancora più dolce che all'udito. In questo modo anche i sordi possono essere trattati a suon di *lyra*[66].

BIBLIOGRAFIA

Aquilecchia, G., 'Appunti su G. B. Della Porta e l'inquisizione', *Studi Secenteschi* 9 (1968), 3–31.

Aristotele, *Problemi*, introduzione, traduzione, note e apparati di M. F. Ferrini, Milano: Bompiani 2002.

Aristoteles, *De anima*, recognovit brevique adnotatione instruxit W. D. Ross, Oxonii: e typographeo Clarendoniano 1963³.

Aulus Gellius, *Noctes Atticae*, recognovit brevique adnotatione critica instruxit P. K. Marshall, Tomus I, Libri I–X, Oxonii: e typographeo Clarendoniano 1990.

Boccadoro, B., 'Crase, proportion, chromatisme dans la théorie musicale du *Cinquecento*', in: J. Pigeaud (ed.), *La couleur, les couleurs*, XIes Entretiens de la Garenne-Lemot, Rennes: Presses Universitaires de Rennes 2007, 245–257.

——, 'La musique, les passions, l'âme et le corps', in: F. Morenzoni, J.-Y. Tilliette (eds.), *Autour de Guillaume d'Auvergne (†1249)*, Turnhout (Belgium): Brepols 2005, 75–92.

——, 'Marsilio Ficino: l'anima e il corpo del contrappunto', *Nuova Civiltà delle Macchine* 16:1–2 (1998), 36–56.

——, 'Musique, médecine et tempéraments', in: J.-J. Nattiez (ed.), *Musiques. Une encyclopédie pour le XXIe siècle*, 2. Les savoirs musicaux, Actes Sud / Cité de la Musique: 2004, 419–446.

Boetius, A. M. T. S., 'De institutione musica libri quinque', in: Id., *De institutione arithmetica libri duo, De institutione musica libri quinque*, accedit Geometria quae fertur Boetii, e libris manu scriptis edidit G. Friedlein, Lipsiae: Minerva G. M. B. H. 1867, Unveränderter Nachdruck, Frankfurt a.M., 1966.

Borzacchini, L., 'Incommensurability, Music, and Continuum: A Cognitive Approach', *Archive for History of Exact Sciences* 61 (2007), 273–302.

Burnett, C., 'Spiritual medicine': music and healing in Islam and its influence in Western medicine', in: P. Gouk (ed.), *Musical Healing in Cultural Contexts*, Aldershot, Brookfield USA, Singapore, Sydney: Ashgate 2000, 85–91.

Capella, M., *De nuptiis Philologiae et Mercurii*, edidit J. Willis, Leipzig: Teubner 1983.

Copenhaver, B. P., 'A tale of two fishes: magical objects in natural history from Antiquity through the Scientific Revolution', *Journal of the History of Ideas* 52 (1991), 373–398.

——, 'Astrology and magic', in: C. B. Schmitt (ed.), *The Cambridge History of Renaissance Philosophy*, Cambridge: Cambridge University Press 2003⁶, 264–300.

——, 'Hermes Trismegistus, Proclus, and the Question of a Philosophy of Magic in the Renaissance', in: I. Merkel and A. G. Debus (eds.), *Hermeticism and the Renaissance. Intellectual History and the Occult in Early Modern Europe*, Washington, London, Toronto: The Folger Shakespeare Library, Associated University Presses 1988, 79–110.

---

[66] Della Porta, *Magia Naturalis*, xx 7, 663.

Della Porta, G., *Magiae Naturalis libri viginti*, Amstelodami: apud Elizeum Weyerstraten 1664.

——, *Phytognomonica*, Neapoli: apud Horatium Salvianum 1588.

Fend, M., 'La teoria musicale: la concezione aritmetica di Gioseffo Zarlino e l'estetica della musica di Vincenzo Galilei', in: A. Clericuzio, G. Ernst (eds), *Il Rinascimento Italiano e l'Europa. Volume V: Le Scienze*, Vicenza: Angelo Colla Editore 2008.

Festugière, A.-J., *La révélation d'Hermès Trismégiste*, I. *L'astrologie et les sciences occultes*, avec un appendice sur l'*Hermetisme Arabe* par M. L. Massignon, Paris: Libraire Lecoffre, J. Gabalda et Cie Éditeurs 1944.

Ficino, M., 'In Timaeum Commentarium', in: Id., *Opera omnia*, con una lettera introduttiva di P. O. Kristeller e una premessa di M. Sancipriano, Torino: Bottega d'Erasmo 1962 (Basilea 1576), vol. II, pp. 1438–1466 (*sic*: 1434–1466).

——, *In Plotinum*, Florentiae: Antonius Miscominus 1492.

——, *Three Books on Life*, a Critical Edition and Translation with Introduction and Notes by C. V. Kaske and J. R. Clark, Binghamton, New York: Center for Medieval and Early Renaissance Studies 1989.

Fracastoro, G., *De sympathia et antipathia rerum*, edizione critica, traduzione e commento a cura di C. Pennuto, Roma: Edizioni di Storia e Letteratura 2008.

Frede, M., 'On Galen's Epistemology', in: V. Nutton (ed.), *Galen: Problems and Prospects*, London: The Wellcome Institute for the History of Medicine 1981, 65–86.

Gaffurio, F., *Theoricum opus musice discipline*, a cura di C. Ruini, Lucca: Libreria Musicale Italiana Editrice 1996.

Galenus, C., 'De sanitate tuenda', in: Id., *Opera quae exstant*, editionem curavit C. G. Kühn, vol. VI, Lipsiae: prostat in officina libraria C. Cnoblochii 1823, 1–452.

——, *De elementis secundum Hippocratem*, Nicolao Leoniceno interprete, in: Id., *Opera omnia. Prima classis humani corporis originem, formationem, dissectionem, temperaturam, facultates, facultatumque cum actiones omnes, tum instrumenta et loca singula complectitur*, Venetiis: apud Haeredes Lucaeantonii Iuntae Florentini 1541, 2r–9v.

Galilei, V., *Dialogo della musica antica et della moderna*, A Facsimile of the 1581 Florence Edition, New York: Broude Brothers 1967.

Garin, E., 'Le philosophe', in: E. Garin (ed.), *L'homme de la Renaissance*, Paris: Éditions du Seuil 1990, 174–192.

Haar, J., 'The Concept of the Renaissance', in: J. Haar (ed.), *European Music 1520–1640*, Woodbridge: The Boydell Press 2006, 20–37.

Hippocrates, 'De alim.', in: *Oeuvres complètes d'Hippocrate*, traduction nouvelle avec le texte grec en regard…par E. Littré, 10 voll., Amsterdam: A. M. Hakkert Editeur 1973–1989, Réimpression de l'Edition Paris 1839–1861, Tome IVe, 1978 (Paris 1844), 396–609.

——, 'Loc. Hum.', in: *Oeuvres complètes d'Hippocrate*, traduction nouvelle avec le texte grec en regard…par E. Littré, 10 voll., Amsterdam: A. M. Hakkert Editeur 1973–1989, Réimpression de l'Edition Paris 1839–1861, Tome VIe, 1979 (Paris 1849), 273–349.

Horden, P., 'Commentary on Part II, with a Note on the Early Middle Ages', in: P. Horden (ed.), *Music as Medicine, The History of Music Therapy since Antiquity*, Aldershot, Brookfield USA, Singapore, Sydney: Ashgate 2000, 103–108.

Hutchison, K., 'What happened to occult qualities in the Scientific Revolution?', *Isis* 73 (1982), 233–253.

Kircher, A., *Mururgia Universalis*, Tomus ii, Romae: typis Ludovici Grignani 1650, Reprografischer Nachdruck der Ausgabe Rom 1650, Georg Olms Verlag, Hilsdesheim-New York 1970.

Nutton, V., *Ancient Medicine*, London: Routledge 2004.

Palisca, C., 'Boethius in the Renaissance', in: Id., *Studies in the History of Italian Music and Music Theory*, Oxford: Clarendon Press 1994, 168–188.

——, 'Muovere gli affetti con la musica: teorie psico-fisiologiche antecedenti a Cartesio', *Nuova Civiltà delle Macchine* 16:1–2 (1998), 57–66.

——, 'Vincenzo Galilei, scienziato sperimentale, mentore del figlio Galileo', *Nuncius* 15:2 (2000), 497–514.

Platone, *La Repubblica*, a cura di G. Lozza, Milano: Oscar Mondadori 1990.

Plotino, *Enneadi*, Traduzione con testo greco a fronte, introduzione, note e bibliografia di G. Faggin, Presentazione e iconografia plotiniana di G. Reale, Revisione finale dei testi, appendici e indici di R. Radice, Milano: Rusconi 1999⁵.

Richardson, L. D., 'The generation of disease: occult causes and diseases of the total substance', in: A. Wear, R. K. French., I. M. Lonie (eds.), *The medical renaissance of the sixteenth century*, Cambrige: Cambridge University Press 1985, 175–194.

Sargolini, F., 'La critica di Vincenzo Galilei al misticismo numerico di Gioseffo Zarlino', *Nuncius* 15:2 (2000), 519–550.

Shumaker, W., '«La magia naturale» come forma «premoderna» della scienza', in: C. Vasoli (ed.), *Magia e scienza nella civiltà umanistica*, Bologna: Società editrice il Mulino 1976, 109–120.

Voss, A., 'Marsilio Ficino, the Second Orpheus', in: P. Horden (ed.) *Music as Medicine, The History of Music Therapy since Antiquity*, Brookfield USA, Singapore, Sydney: Aldershot, Ashgate 2000, 154–172.

——, 'The Natural Magic of Marsilio Ficino', *Historical Dance* 3:1 (1992), 25–30.

Walker, D. P., *Spiritual and Demonic Magic from Ficino to Campanella*, London: The Warburg Institute, University of London 1958, Kraus reprint (Nedeln / Liechtenstein) 1969.

——, *Studies in Musical Science in the Late Renaissance*, London, Leiden: The Warburg Institute, University of London – E.J. Brill 1978.

West, M., 'Music Therapy in Antiquity', in: P. Horden (ed.) *Music as Medicine, The History of Music Therapy since Antiquity*, Brookfield USA, Singapore, Sydney: Aldershot, Ashgate 2000, 51–68.

——, *Ancient Greek Music*, Oxford: Clarendon Press 1992.

Wuidar, L., 'Musique et démonologie au XVIIème siècle de Jean Bodin à Pier Francesco Valentini', *Studi Musicali* 36:1 (2007), 65–95.

Zaccaria, R., – Romei, G., 'Della Porta, Giovambattista', in: *Dizionario Biografico degli Italiani* 37 (1989), 170–182.

Zambelli, P., 'Il problema della magia naturale nel Rinascimento', *Rivista Critica di Storia della Filosofia* 28:3 (1973), 271–296.

Zarlino, G., *Istitutioni harmoniche*, Venetia: appresso Francesco de i Fransceschi, 1573, slightly reduced from the original, republished in 1966 by Gregg Press Limited, England.

TOMMASO CAMPANELLA (1568–1639) E LA MUSICA

Marta Moiso

English summary: Tommaso Campanella's conception of music has been influenced by Telesius and Ficinus. In Campanella's philosophy, sound-waves have physical effects and music or sounds in general are able to touch the human spirit. According to this explanation, music has mainly therapeutical aims. So, music can be used to get passions in the human spirit. In accordance with this theory, Campanella explains some practical effects of music in many of his works, but particularly in his *De Sensu rerum et magia* (first composed in 1591) and his *Theology* (composed between 1613 and 1624). These two works represent two periods and stages of Campanella's philosophy, so it is interesting to analyze how he changed his opinion about music.

Campanella e la musica: un tema che pare intrigante, se si pensa che il filosofo di Stilo è stato considerato da alcuni contemporanei un nobile ingegno, in grado di dare risposte esaurienti su qualsiasi argomento[1]. L'unico studioso che ha studiato il rapporto di Campanella con i suoni è Daniel Pickering Walker[2], i cui lavori rimangono fondamentali. Ma, per l'appassionato di cose campanelliane, non è inutile ripercorrere le tappe dell'approccio di questo filosofo alla musica, procedendo dagli anni giovanili alla maturità. In questo percorso, nei primi anni di speculazione filosofica emerge la valenza pratica e terapeutica della musica; questo aspetto lascia il posto, negli anni parigini dopo la scarcerazione, ad una prospettiva apotropaica, come ha sottolineato appunto Walker, secondo cui la musica viene utilizzata in caso di riti magici per allontanare influssi nefasti provenienti dagli astri. Per Campanella, la caratteristica principale della musica, delle parole e dei suoni in generale, è di stimolare processi fisici ed effetti curativi che hanno il fine di predisporre lo spirito a svolgere la sua funzione.

---

[1] Schino, 'Campanella tra magia naturale e scienza nel giudizio di Gabriel Naudé', 395.

[2] Walker, *Magia spirituale e magia demonica da Ficino a Campanella*, 275–320.

Nelle prime opere troviamo scarse tracce di interesse musicale, perché in esse gli sforzi campanelliani sono tesi maggiormente all'indivi-
duazione di un sistema epistemologico alternativo all'aristotelismo, di
cui percepisce le pecche e le incongruità. Così, nella sua prima opera
a stampa, la *Philosophia Sensibus Demonstrata*, non troviamo pratica-
mente accenno, nemmeno in termini pitagorici di armonia universale,
alla musica. Bisogna aspettare il *De Sensu Rerum et Magia* per vedere
accendersi l'interesse in questo ambito[3]. Nello scrivere quest'opera,
centrale per tutta la sua filosofia, Campanella attinge abbondontemente
alla cultura folkloristica della sua terra, alle credenze popolari, alle
convinzioni magiche e alle esperienze quotidiane con i fattori naturali[4]. Sono questi gli elementi che stimolano in lui il tentativo di dare
un taglio originale alla propria filosofia e di studiare le proprietà delle
cose immergendosi nella natura. Quest'ultima è basata sulla nozione
di senso mutuata da Telesio e pertanto la musica viene presa in considerazione in quanto in grado di produrre effetti *fisici* sull'ascoltatore.
È così che si crea la saldatura fra natura, magia e musica, nella trat-
tazione della quale si mescolano sincretisticamente tutti gli elementi
caratterizzanti la filosofia campanelliana: telesianesimo, ermetismo,
platonismo.

UNA MUSICA 'TELESIANA'

In tutti gli studi su Campanella emerge la radice telesiana del suo
sistema filosofico. Insieme al platonismo, appreso dalle ampie letture
giovanili, il telesianesimo costituisce l'impalcatura della filosofia campanelliana, la quale si struttura intorno alla facoltà del *sentire* concepita
come attività propria di ciascun essere. Secondo una cosmologia eredi-
tata da Telesio, Campanella descrive un universo la cui genesi dipende
dall'azione formatrice di due principi agenti, caldo e freddo, che sono
cause seconde cui Dio ha affidato la realizzazione pratica dell'ordine
cosmico presente nella Sua mente. Caldo e freddo sono contrari in
stato di perenne lotta fra loro e quindi in grado di percepirsi reciprocamente. Grazie alla sensazione l'uno dell'altro, infatti, caldo e freddo

---

[3] Giglioni, 'Magia naturale', 268–269.
[4] Lerner, *Pansensisme et interprétation de la nature chez Tommaso Campanella*;
Bortolotti, *Magia superstizione e fede nella pratica medica*; Ernst, *Tommaso Campanella*, 26.

sono attirati dal simile e respingono il contrario, generando una lotta interminabile da cui inizia l'*aeterna vicissitudo* della mutazione, della corruzione e della formazione dell'infinita varietà degli enti. Il caldo, nella ripresa campanelliana del telesianesimo, assume però da subito una funzione preminente e fondamentale, perché diventa il principio agente che "informa" la materia inerte. Nel *Senso delle cose e della magia*, Campanella si propone di individuare la serie dei processi vitali operati dal calore solare che penetra la fredda materia terrestre per imprimervi le forme dell'Idea divina[5]. Il calore diventa, una volta innestato nella materia, lo spirito di un determinato ente. Lo *spiritus* può avere finezza, sensibilità e capacità di movimento in gradi differenti. Sono proprio queste caratteristiche a rendere un ente naturale più sensibile di un altro. Per Ficino lo spirito era una sostanza utilizzabile come mezzo per le anime sensibili e conoscitive, ma non in sé dotata di capacità percettiva; per Campanella invece è proprio il nostro spirito a sentire e desiderare attraverso gli organi di senso. Insieme al principio vitale, ogni ente riceve infatti dal calore solare la quantità di sensibilità necessaria e sufficiente alla propria autoconservazione, al fine di individuare e perseguire ciò che gli è utile e fuggire ciò che gli è lesivo. Penetrando all'interno di ogni porzione di materia, il caldo, sotto forma di *spiritus* vitale, la modella e le dà forme e funzioni diverse a seconda del proprio grado di intensità. Questo grado di intensità corrisponde a quello della sensibilità, ovvero della capacità di percepire gli influssi che, espandendosi attraverso il *comune sensorio* dell'aria, provengono dagli altri corpi. Così, gli enti più freddi e duri, come le pietre o i vegetali, hanno un grado di sensibilità molto basso, ma negli organismi più evoluti, cioè gli animali e l'uomo, il caldo si organizza nella forma più complessa dello spirito, soffio caldo e sottile identificato con l'anima organica senziente. Lo spirito può conoscere fasi alterne mentre è nel corpo, perchè può essere più o meno fluido a seconda di ciò che si è mangiato e a seconda delle azioni svolte durante la giornata[6]. Se lo spirito è stanco sarà meno abbondante, ma mangiando o anche solo sentendo l'odore di buon cibo si riprenderà in fretta, ravvivandosi e vivacizzandosi. Quando poi si beve in abbondanza, il cervello si riempie di vapori e lo spirito sale tutto al capo per attenuarli, lasciando il resto del corpo privo di senso e di movimento,

---

[5] Campanella, *Del Senso delle Cose e della Magia*, 11–26.
[6] Ibid., 53–56.

così che si scivola nel sonno[7]. La magia naturale, per Campanella, deve
servirsi degli enti naturali secondo le modalità e con i fini prospettati
da Ficino: quindi per purificare o aiutare lo *spiritus* nella vicenda cor-
porea che si trova a vivere. La questione non è di secondaria importanza perché Ficino collega la propria teoria musicale con quella dello
spiritus mundi, cioè lo spirito cosmico che pervade l'intero universo e
che crea quella fitta rete di corrispondenze/influenze fra mondo celeste
e mondo sublunare che costituiscono il campo d'azione privilegiato
del mago. Considerando il mondo come un grande essere vivente,
come già Platone e i neoplatonici, Ficino indica nello *spiritus mundi* il
mezzo d'unione fra anima e corpo del mondo stesso, proprio come nel
corpo umano lo spirito fa da traduttore fra dati sensoriali, provenienti
dal corpo, e i *phantasmata* prodotti dall'intelletto[8]. Lo spirito, quindi,
collega fra loro due realtà che altrimenti rimarrebbero irrimediabilmente mute l'una all'altra, parlanti grammatiche distinte. Lo spirito
dell'animale-mondo, tuttavia, non è composto dei quattro elementi,
come invece lo spirito umano. Al contrario, Ficino stabilisce che lo
spirito cosmico è fatto di un quinto elemento o etere, che per Aristotele altro non era se non la sostanza incorruttibile di cui sono com-
posti i cieli. Tuttavia, spirito umano e spirito cosmico si assomigliano
abbastanza da consentire al primo di nutrirsi e rinforzarsi attingendo
al secondo con varie modalità. Per rendere il nostro spirito il più cele-
stiale e puro possibile, possiamo attirare gli influssi di pianeti benefici
come il Sole e Giove utilizzando animali, piante o persone soggette
allo stesso pianeta; oppure ci si può nutrire di alimenti ricchi di spirito
cosmico, servirsi di talismani – sui quali però Ficino è piuttosto
cauto – oppure utilizzare musica adatta all'astro di cui si vuole assor-
bire il positivo influsso. Questa idea si fonda sulla convinzione, di anti-
chissima origine, che uomo ed universo siano caratterizzati dalle stesse
proporzioni armoniche. Pertanto, alla musica prodotta dalle sfere celesti, corrisponde quella prodotta dall'uomo con la voce o gli strumenti
musicali. Di conseguenza, tutto ciò che ha le stesse proporzioni numeriche di un certo pianeta, conferirà le stesse allo spirito con cui entra in
contatto quelle medesime proporzioni – caratteristiche. Attraverso la
comune sensibilità, Campanella dunque fornisce una spiegazione filosofica delle simpatie e antipatie fra le cose naturali. Il senso è infatti la

---

[7] Ibid., 67–68.
[8] Boccadoro, 'Marsilio Ficino: the soul and the body of counterpoint', 99–134.

facoltà sulla quale si può far perno per modificare un ente ed ottenere determinati effetti. Questo è lo scopo dell'arte magica, che secondo l'autore ha il preciso scopo di indagare e sfruttare – per fini buoni e leciti – i legami naturali che il mago va via via scoprendo[9]. Per i rinascimentali, i principi di pensiero su cui l'azione magica di questo tipo si basa si riducono a due[10]. Il primo principio è che il simile produce il simile[11] e da esso il mago deduce che può produrre qualsiasi effetto semplicemente imitandolo. Il secondo invece è quello secondo cui due oggetti che sono stati in contatto fisico l'uno con l'altro continuano ad agire reciprocamente anche a distanza e dopo che il contatto è cessato[12]. La base antropologica di questi due principi è l'associazione di idee, nel primo caso effettuata per similarità, nel secondo per contiguità. Su questo presupposto, innestatosi sulle basi neopitagoriche e neoplatoniche, si strutturano le concezioni magiche della musica, sia per i suoi impieghi terapeutici che per quelli negromantici[13].

Nel *Senso delle cose e della magia*, infatti, viene strutturata una gerarchia di fenomeni magici, naturali e soprannaturali, secondo la quale il livello più blando del fenomeno meraviglioso è quello che il mago suscita proprio sollecitando le passioni umane[14]. In termini tecnici, tale livello riguarda tutte le funzioni relative alle capacità di muovere lo spirito umano per indurvi i sentimenti voluti[15]. Le passioni principali sono il piacere, quando lo spirito incontra qualcosa che aumenta il suo bene, e il dolore, se invece ha a che fare con qualcosa di nocivo; l'amore si identifica con la tendenza verso il bene, l'odio con la fuga dal male. Vi sono poi speranza, fede, timore, immaginazione[16]. Così, nell'opera, si trova un elenco puntiglioso degli affetti naturali che il mago deve smuovere per ottenere lo scopo desiderato. Campanella non aderisce alla convinzione che parole particolari abbiano poteri definiti, ma è senz'altro dell'idea che il suono modifica lo *spiritus* e che alcuni suoni lo animano e lo stimolano mentre altri lo debilitano[17]. L'aria, composta

---

[9] Scrimieri, 'Sulla magia di T. Campanella', 709–711.
[10] Frazer, *Il ramo d'oro*, 56–57.
[11] Campanella, *Del Senso delle Cose e della Magia*, 6.
[12] Ibid., 189.
[13] Sulla musicoterapia cfr. Boccadoro, 'Musica spiritum curat', 4–6.
[14] Campanella, *Del Senso delle Cose e della Magia*, 210.
[15] Tirinnanzi, *Umbra naturae*, 65; Zambelli, *L'immaginazione e il suo potere*, 17.
[16] Campanella, *Del Senso delle Cose e della Magia*, 212.
[17] Walker, *Magia spirituale e magia demonica da Ficino a Campanella*, 310–319 e Bolzoni, 'Telesio Bruno e Campanella', 141–169.

di corpuscoli sottili, trasporta le affezioni da un corpo all'altro e fa da
tramite ai suoni, che così possono spandersi e modificare gli spiriti
vicini. Le sue applicazioni sono dunque principalmente naturali: la
musica magica di Campanella ha il fine di disporre lo spirito a ricevere
gli influssi planetari o di purificare l'aria, piuttosto che di richiamare
i demoni o gli angeli, dal momento che essi hanno corpi spirituali
diversi dai nostri e quindi non sono sensibili al nostro stesso tipo di
musica. Inoltre, nella fisiologia campanelliana tutti e cinque i sensi si
riducono ad una questione di tatto, poiché gli organi di senso vengono
di fatto toccati in modi differenti[18]. Così, anche l'udito è tatto,

> perché dentro l'orecchio vi sta un timpanello d'aria, legato al nervo, per
> dove in quello lo spirito viene, e fuori vi sta un martelletto, e poi le cavità
> dell'orecchie che accogliono il moto dell'aria che batte il martello, e per
> esso il timpano, e per esso lo spirito [...][19].

L'organo uditivo è uno strumento che ripara lo spirito dal contatto
diretto con il mondo esterno e dal pericolo di dispersione fuori dall'or-
ganismo. Lo spirito riconosce quale tipo di corpo ha prodotto un certo
suono a seconda delle sensazioni e dei movimenti che questo suono
produce. Campanella, come già Ficino, sottolinea il movimento del
suono, ma per il domenicano non si verifica alcun contatto diretto fra
la musica e lo spirito umano: è l'aria che trasmette il proprio moto al
timpano, senza che vi sia una vera e propria commistione di sostanze.
Così, tra i suoni fastidiosi vanno annoverati quelli gravi, prodotti da
corpi grossi, che percuotono una gran quantità d'aria da cui l'orecchio
risulta investito e lo spirito, sofferente, sbattuto nella parte cava della
testa. Allo stesso modo, sono deleteri i suoni squillanti e stridenti, che
perforano l'aria e il timpano come punte, producendo lacerazioni. Al
contrario, i suoni bassi e acuti, prodotti armoniosamente dalle corde
di strumenti musicali come il liuto, conferiscono un moto regolare
all'aria, che tocca lo spirito in modo piacevole e moderato. Il suono
che deriva da questo temperato movimento dell'aria, per Campanella,
è propriamente musica, la quale si differenzia dal semplice suono
perché caratterizzata da un ritmo la cui unità di misura è, secondo
l'autore, il battito del polso umano[20]. Campanella non cita espressa-

---

18 Campanella, *Del Senso delle Cose e della Magia*, 57.
19 Ibid., 59.
20 Campanella, *Del Senso delle Cose e della Magia*, 59. Cfr. Boccadoro, 'Musique,
Médecine et Tempéraments'.

mente alcuna fonte riguardo questa teoria, ma è ragionevole avanzare l'ipotesi che egli faccia riferimento a Pitagora, che è d'altronde l'unico pensatore che il calabrese cita apertamente a proposito della musica. Piuttosto, sulla questione del ritmo è interessante notare che vi sono alcune differenze rispetto a Ficino. Secondo quest'ultimo, gli studi riguardanti musica e *spiritus* possono essere avvicinati e considerati intrecciati perché 'canto e suono sgorgano dal ragionare della mente'. La musica avrebbe, per il fiorentino, un'origine mentale, emotiva o fantastica. Per Campanella, invece, la musica nasce da un'iniziativa imitatoria che l'uomo mette costantemente in atto nei confronti dei ritmi naturali:

> Credo che il metro sia nato con il genere umano, come il canto. Non solo per gli uccelli, ma anche per l'uomo è naturale blandirsi col canto, ed emettere suoni che dispongano lo spirito alla sua funzione (...). Percependo nel parlare un certo ritmo che impressiona piacevolmente lo spirito, da esso appresero il metro, come dai suoni trassero il canto[21].

Per Campanella il suono è dunque 'movimento sentito', cioè prodotto dal moto di qualcosa che agita l'aria in un determinato modo e produce particolari onde sonore. Perciò tutti i movimenti naturali, compresi quelli degli astri, producono altrettanti suoni, o voci, che risultano musicalmente piacevoli. A questo proposito, Campanella specifica però che non a tutte le classi di enti piace lo stesso tipo di musica. Anche fra gli uomini le preferenze possono variare, proprio come si hanno gusti diversi in fatto di cibo, anche in funzione del proprio temperamento. Ecco allora che il concetto di musica viene coniugato con quello di armonia:

> e così l'aceto con l'olio fa musica al gusto, come i gravi suoni e acuti all'udito, e perché ad altri animali è dolce una cosa, ad altri amara; e pur tra gli uomini si vede che i fanciulli, per il blando spirito loro, cose dolci bramano, i vecchi, amare; alle capre la ginestra è dolce, a noi amara. Lo stesso si stima delle voci, ché l'asino gode la musica dell'asino, e l'uomo dell'uomo, e così di tutti[22].

Per Campanella, dunque, la musica produce un effetto fisico su chi ne è *toccato*. Questa idea è in contrasto con quanto sostenuto dalla teoria di Aristotele, il quale riteneva invece che la musica fosse una cosa incorporea, che penetra nel corpo umano attraverso i suoi pertugi. Contro

---

[21] Campanella, *Tutte le opere*, 1005.
[22] Campanella, *Del Senso delle Cose e della Magia*, 59–60.

questa teoria, Campanella si appella di nuovo a Pitagora e ricorda che
questi

> con la musica sanò i furiosi, Damone gli ebrii, Timoteo induceva ira o
> pietà e qual affetto voleva, Orfeo contemplazione, Terprando sanò sordi;
> la musica lidia effeminava gli uomini, la lacedemonica li facea virili e
> altri indussero castità[23].

Gli effetti della musica sul corpo e sulle passioni umane sono spie-
gati dall'autore esclusivamente dal punto di vista fisiologico e basan-
dosi sui presupposti telesiani della propria filosofia. Lo spirito viene
infatti mosso alle proprie affezioni dal caldo e dal freddo di cui sono
portatori, in misura diversa, tutti i corpi. Così, il furioso gode di una
musica particolarmente dolce perché ha l'immaginazione in stato di
agitazione per i fumosi vapori prodotti dalla malattia e lo *spiritus* scon-
volto dal calore in eccesso. Un musicista moderato e accorto può, in
questi casi, generare un suono dolce e blando che, per le sue proprietà,
distrae l'ammalato dai pensieri dai quali è ossessionato. Per godere
della musica tutto lo spirito va alla testa ed è per questo motivo che
molto spesso l'ascolto di brani musicali induce al sonno, perchè tutto
il resto del corpo rimane senza moto e senza sensibilità. Nel caso dei
'furiosi', quindi, la musica ha una funzione purificatrice perché impedisce quella produzione di spiriti in eccesso che surriscalda il corpo
e la testa e permette una dispersione dei vapori dannosi, inducendo
l'immaginazione al rilassamento. La concentrazione sul suono lascia
spazio ad una ventilazione dei vapori infetti che gravano sul cervello in
caso di malattia o di ubriacatura. Infine, diversi tipi di suono inducono
passioni diverse:

> e li suoni aspri muovono ad ira; però s'usano in guerra; i soavi a con-
> templazione, i titillanti a lussuria e mollezza; però ogni repubblica tien
> conto del canto, e con questo s'onora Dio, elevando lo spirito e l'animo
> in lui avviluppato a contemplare[24].

La musica è dunque propedeutica alla contemplazione e all'estasi, perché dispone gli spiriti a movimento straordinari. Di qui in poi, viene
istituita una connessione stretta fra gli eventi magici e meravigliosi cui
può dar vita il mago e i suoni, musicali o meno. A questo proposito,
Campanella sicuramente contrae dei debiti nei confronti della teoria

---

[23] Ibid., 60.
[24] Ibid., 60.

di Ficino, ma differenzia la propria teoria su diversi piani. Innanzi-tutto, per Campanella non vi sono differenze gerarchiche fra i sensi e, soprattutto, fra i loro gradi di efficacia sullo *spiritus*. Ficino era invece convinto che le impressioni visive siano dotate di effetti un po' meno potenti sullo *spiritus* rispetto a quelle uditive[25]. Entrambi i pensatori sono dell'opinione che lo spirito sia il mezzo atto a trasmettere ogni sensazione e che quindi tutti i mezzi di percezione sensitiva siano ad esso assimilabili. Ficino però partiva da una considerazione di fondo che Campanella scardina: cioè che l'udito sia la facoltà sensitiva che più tocca lo spirito perché si muove e trasmette movimento, men-tre la vista, pur nella sua dignità ed importanza, fornisce per lo più immagini statiche. Il movimento di cui l'udito è produttore, trasmesso dall'aria, vettore per eccellenza delle affezioni e dei moti, tocca lo spi-rito con tanta più forza ed efficacia in quanto l'essere umano ha una vita emotiva e morale composta di azioni corporee e in moti dello spirito e dell'anima. Il suono è quindi dinamico, la visione statica, ed è per questo che passioni e stati etici sono imitabili e trasmissibili dal musicista all'ascoltatore, che ne viene subito sollecitato. Non è più così per Campanella, il quale appiana le differenze fra organi di senso gra-zie alla base telesiana della propria fisiologia. Come ricordato, tutte le sensazioni, secondo il domenicano, non sono altro che espressioni differenti di un unico e solo modo di percepire, di natura tattile, con il quale il nostro spirito si mette in relazione e comunicazione con il mondo esterno. In questo modo, Campanella evita che i suoni siano gli unici effetti sensibili simili a caratteri morali (più che odori, immagini, colori etc., come ritiene Ficino), perché estende a tutti i cinque sensi la possibilità di toccare lo spirito, generando in esso movimenti.

L'efficacia della musica si basa anche nelle opere campanelliane, come nel *De Vita Coelitus Comparanda* di Ficino, sull'abilità di que-sta nel sollecitare l'immaginazione. Secondo questa teoria, i pianeti possono esercitare il loro influsso sull'attore principale dei rituali magici, la cui forza immaginativa trasferisce, per mezzo dello spirito (cosmico o umano) determinati effetti sui corpi, animati o inanimati, che possono a loro volta trasmettere un effetto di ritorno sul corpo e sull'immaginazione del soggetto iniziale. L'effetto su un essere ani-mato può essere soggettivo o transitivo, cioè rivolto ad altre persone. In entrambi i casi l'effetto può essere psicologico, quando permane

---

[25] Walker, *Magia spirituale e magia demonica da Ficino a Campanella*, 15–17.

all'interno dell'immaginazione o dell'anima, o psicosomatico, quando stimola reazioni corporee. A questo riguardo, Campanella acquisisce la certezza che i suoni possiedono capacità terapeutiche ed inducono sentimenti e passioni[26] dall'esperienza quotidiana dell'efficacia dell'arte oratoria, che può indurre il riso o il pianto nelle persone. Molti uomini politici e condottieri del passato devono i loro successi alla loro abilità nell'uso delle parole, con le quali hanno indebolito gli animi dei nemici ed instillato il desiderio di vittoria nei propri soldati, rendendoli più forti, poichè quando uno spirito nobile spande intorno la propria forza, l'aria la trasporta intorno ed atterrisce i nemici[27]. Il suono delle parole, come quello della musica, nasce per il domenicano dall'istintiva propensione umana ad *imitare* la natura, a ricrearne i ritmi elementari per trarne giovamento, per riallinearsi con essi e far in modo che lo spirito ne sia favorito e rinforzato. Riprendendo la dottrina pitagorica, Campanella specifica infine che nell'universo i suoni nel loro insieme, così come tutti gli odori e tutti i sapori, contribuiscono all'armonia universale. Per questo, anni più tardi, esprime la speranza che gli scienziati costruiscano uno strumento auricolare – equivalente uditivo del telescopio – che permetta all'uomo di sentire l'armonia delle sfere, alla quale siamo tanto avvezzi fin dalla nascita da non percepirla più[28].

Nell'ambito della rinascita culturale fiorentina, di cui Ficino è il più illustre esponente, insieme al neoplatonismo erano state riprese e ricontestualizzate alcune posizioni pitagoriche, che fanno sì che alla base del discorso sulla musica vi sia un fondamentale concetto di armonia. Anche Campanella esprime un concetto di armonia universale, declinato tuttavia secondo il telesianesimo. Per Ficino l'armonia va intesa nel contesto umorale e dei quattro elementi aristotelici e la malinconia è un ingrediente della scrittura musicale, perché la teoria degli affetti su cui quest'ultima nasce e si costruisce è l'antica dottrina dell'ethos, facente leva e perno sul valore psicologico della musica[29]. Di conseguenza, il discorso della consonanza fra soggetto e oggetto per Campanella svanisce, o meglio, è declinata in senso telesiano ed inquadrato nella spartizione telesiana fra caldo e freddo, simile e dissimile. In altre parole, Ficino riporta le caratteristiche dei diversi tipi di tem-

---

[26] Campanella, *Del Senso delle Cose e della Magia*, 198.
[27] Ibid., 198.
[28] Campanella, *Opuscoli astrologici*, 11.
[29] Boccadoro, 'Eléments de grammaire mélancolique', 25–65.

peramento ad armonie di estremi numerici consonanti; così facendo, accetta inplicitamente l'identità pitagorica fra anima e armonia basata sui quattro umori e sullo spirito responsabile delle sensazioni. La magia simpatica costruisce poi un triangolo, i cui vertici sono costituiti dall'anima del cantautore, dalla melodia prodotta e dalla facoltà immaginativa dell'ascoltatore. Il temperamento dell'ascoltatore prova piacere riconoscendo le proprie proporzioni nella melodia e soffre invece in casi di diversità. Si instaura pertanto una consonanza pura fra soggetto ed oggetto. Secondo Campanella, invece, il piacere che deriva dall'ascolto non si basa più tanto sul riconoscimento di proporzioni simili o uguali a quelle del nostro rispettivo temperamento, ma bensì sul concetto stesso di similitudine associato alla percezione di un grado di calore pari a quello del nostro spirito. Ficino, del resto, commenta il *Simposio*[30], opera in cui Platone esprimeva il desiderio di quella sintesi dei contrari che avviene solo nel superamento delle diversità, di quella unità che cercano il pari e il dispari, corrispettivi numerici del femminile e del maschile che perennemente cercano di riunirsi nella completezza dell'essere androgino. In questa tradizione filosofica, largamente ripresa dal rinascimento, l'unità è pensata quindi come un'armonia aritmetica che trova nell'ottava la sua consonanza più perfetta. L'armonia, diventava quindi sinonimo di comunicazione e transitività. Il pitagorismo, largamente ripreso dagli autori rinascimentali, riduce quindi ad un problema di consonanza tutto ciò che, nel mondo fisico e metafisico, può essere interpretato in termini di contrari[31]. L'armonia del pari e del dispari offre un modello tangibile di analisi per rendere conto di tutti i fenomeni di azione a distanza; non solo dei fenomeni fisici come la vibrazione simpatetica delle corde, ma anche di principi occulti quali le virtù delle pietre e dei pianeti, la composizione e il potere dei talismani, l'azione e la passione del simile sul simile, la comunicazione tra anima e macrocosmo, l'azione dell'anima sul corpo, l'ispirazione e la partecipazione del sensibile al mondo delle idee ed infine l'azione esercitata sull'anima e il corpo dell'uditore. In Campanella viene a mancare qualsiasi consonanza musicale stabilita da rapporti proporzionali fra corde vibranti e suoni. La consonanza musicale pensata da Campanella è relativa e nasce dalla conformità dei suoni ad un certo tipo di spirito. Egli quindi può appellarsi solo al concetto di armonia, telesianamente intesa, perché nel suo sistema

---

[30] Ficino, *Commentaire sue le Banquet de Platon*, 58.
[31] Boccadoro, 'Musica spiritum curat', 4.

viene meno la consonanza fra tempi musicali e tempi celesti tolta la
quale, tuttavia, viene a mancare una delle componenti centrali della
teoria ficiniana e rinascimentale[32]. Senza questa corrispondenza, inoltre, non è più possibile sintonizzare il proprio spirito con i movimenti
di un qualche pianeta attraverso le vibrazioni simpatiche; è solo possibile disporre il proprio spirito a ricevere gli influssi astrali. Ecco perché
per il calabrese la musica ha un effetto ridotto e più impreciso rispetto
a quanto sostenuto da Ficino. Alla base della teoria pitagorica della
musica vi era la definizione di armonia come conciliazione di forze
antagoniste[33]. Per Campanella le forze antagoniste esistono e vivificano
tutto l'universo, ma non vi è possibilità di conciliazione, perché questa
sancirebbe la fine dell'eterna *vicissitudo* che invece rappresenta la vita
del cosmo. E avrà ragione Marine Mersenne nel dire che Campanella
non sapeva nemmeno cosa fosse un'ottava[34], perchè il domenicano
fonda la propria teoria musicale su presupposti in cui l'armonia non
si configura più come il superamento dei contrari in una sintesi che
è un'unità. Per questo egli è in un certo senso un precursore dell'idea
moderna ed 'illuminata' secondo cui i fenomeni associabili alla musicoterapia non sono altro che prodotti di un *habitus*, ricordi associati
ad una particolare musica[35]. Secondo quest'idea, le virtù efficaci della
vis imaginativa saranno considerate indipendenti dall'organizzazione
dei suoni nella melodia e il senso della musica diventerà un valore
psicologico e soggettivo, elaborato sulla base di esperienze individuali
dell'uditore, in accordo con un'associazione accidentale entro cui esperienza e melodie fungono da segni evocativi (il che significa che melodie diverse possono generare lo stesso effetto, perché automaticamente
ma soggettivamente collegate dalla memoria a sensazioni provate in
situazioni simili).

I TARANTOLATI

Nel *Senso delle cose e della magia* Campanella porta una serie di esempi
in cui la musica è utilizzata per sanare malattie[36] e sostiene che l'anima

---

[32] Combarieu, *La musique et la magie*; Walker, *Music, spirit and language in the Renaissance*; Tomlinson, *Music in Renaissance Magic: Toward a Historiography of Others*; Gouk, *Music, Science and Natural magic in Seventeenth-Century England*.
[33] Boccadoro, 'Musica spiritum curat', 3.
[34] Walker, *Magia spirituale e magia demonica da Ficino a Campanella*, 315.
[35] Boccadoro, 'Musica spiritum curat', 2.
[36] Campanella, *Del Senso delle Cose e della Magia*, 199–204.

trova la musica piacevole non perché essa stessa consista di un determinato ritmo musicale, perché in questo caso dovrebbe piacere a tutti la stessa musica, ma piuttosto perché lo spirito animale è mobile, quindi ravvivato e mosso dai suoni[37]. A tal proposito, un esempio famoso e chiarificatore è quello dei tarantolati, ovvero di coloro che hanno ricevuto un morso dalla tarantola[38]. Queste persone, secondo Campanella, dovrebbero essere curate con la musica, la quale le spinge a dimenarsi nella danza e aiuta il loro *spiritus* a liberarsi del veleno introdotto nel loro corpo dall'animale, svolgendo una funzione depurativa. Campanella, denotando ampia conoscenza e testimonianza oculare del fenomeno, analizza le metamorfosi che si verificano in coloro che sono stati morsi da cani rabbiosi o dalle tarantole. I primi, passati quaranta giorni dal morso, iniziano a mutarsi e si credono cani, «languiscono e strillano» e mordono, non possono più guardare l'acqua, perché la loro immagine riflessa provoca in loro fastidio, dato che pensano di esser cani, alla fine abbaiano e muoiono da rabbiosi, dimentichi della loro condizione umana. Coloro che invece sono stati morsi dalle tarantole, si indeboliscono e a poco a poco «imbalordiscono», ballano in modo contorto e sfrenato fino a quando non crollano stremati. Grazie alla sudorazione provocata dal ballo, essi tentano di espellere i vapori infetti, ma solitamente i sintomi permangono finché permane la causa che li ha prodotti, quindi solo la morte del ragno può produrre una vera guarigione. Entrambi questi esempi evidenziano casi in cui gli spiriti acri e gli umori degli animali introdotti nel corpo umano attraverso il morso portano ad un'alterazione del temperamento e della facoltà immaginativa di chi è stato morso, il quale viene dominato dallo spirito dell'animale che l'ha attaccato e non ha più coscienza della propria condizione umana[39].

Il tema del tarantolismo non è nuovo e Campanella lo ricorda come un fenomeno tipico della Puglia. Egli non cita alcuna fonte a riguardo, ma tale credenza era ben diffusa a livello popolare ed era stata riportata negli stessi anni anche da Giulio Cesare Vanini, il quale l'aveva

---

[37] Campanella, *Medicina*, 60–61. Cfr. Mönnich e Jahncke, 'Medicine and Magic between tradition and progress in Tommaso Campanella', 32–33; Corsini, *Medici ciarlatani e ciarlatani medici*.

[38] Di Mitri, *Storia biomedica del tarantismo*, 96; *Tarantismo: transe, possessione, musica*; Cosi, 'Tarantole, follie e antidoti del sec. XVII: fra tradizione popolare ed esperienza colta', 53–111.

[39] Campanella, *Del Senso delle Cose e della Magia*, 200.

elencata fra i più tipici fenomeni magici della sua terra[40]. Ernesto De Martino non ha incluso Vanini fra i documentatori di questa pratica[41], nonostante il filosofo ne abbia parlato diffusamente e con competenza e abbia fatto derivare il nome del fenomeno dalla città di Taranto. Egli, come già Campanella, informa altresì che i morsicati sono spronati dalla musica a danze scomposte e spiega perché la danza liberi dal veleno e dai suoi malefici effetti e perché la musica ne sia rimedio. È a conoscenza anche della diversità di effetti che le morsicature potevano procurare: alcune assopivano, altre ancora facevano correre ed altre rimanere immobili e sudare, o rimettere, o delirare. I malanni erano vari, sia Vanini che Campanella sono dell'opinione che siano dello stesso numero dei giorni della settimana, perché la bestia che li causava poteva essere *ballerina, canterina, libertina, triste, muta, sorda, dormiente o tempestosa*; inoltre, essi sanno che il male causato da questi morsi torna puntualmente ogni anno nello stesso periodo in cui si è stati morsicati e che ciò si ripete ogni anno finché fosse stata in vita la tarantola[42].

Nel *Senso delle cose e della magia* viene dunque riconosciuta da Campanella ai suoni e alle parole quella forza capace di muovere lo spirito che sarà ribadita nell'accostamento fra poesia e musica istituito nella *Poetica latina*, scritta fra il 1608 e il 1613, ma pubblicata solo nel 1638 come parte della *Philosophia rationalis*[43]. In questa sede, accompagnata da una teoria dagli echi bruniani, Campanella istituisce un nesso indissolubile fra l'azione del poeta e quello del musicista: entrambi muovono lo *spiritus* degli ascoltatori/lettori al fine di causare in loro delle emozioni e quindi di vincolarli a sé. È vero che esistono linguaggi differenti, ma tali differenze sarebbero da imputare in primo luogo a diverse condizioni climatiche: ad esempio il freddo delle terre nordiche ha sempre costretto gli spiriti a percuotere l'aria per riscaldarsi, così che la loro lingua abbonda di consonanti mentre l'italiano è ricco di vocali, grazie al clima caldo e rilassante[44].

L'unico caso in cui Campanella abbandona questa spiegazione più consueta e razionale degli effetti retorici e della loro capacità di tra-

---

[40] Vanini, *De admirandis*, 444.
[41] De Martino, *La terra del rimorso*, 425–431; Bortolotti, *Magia superstizione e fede nella pratica medica*, 136.
[42] Jurlaro, 'Aspetti magici e superstiziosi pugliesi in Giulio Cesare Vanini', 383–387.
[43] Bolzoni, 'Una nuova lingua e una nuova metrica', 48–60.
[44] Campanella, *Del Senso delle Cose e della Magia*, 216.

smettere emozioni, è quello della poesia, nella quale c'è un utilizzo rappresentativo dei termini, usati come simboli, i quali possono ottenere effetti più immediati. Il linguaggio poetico è efficace, in questo senso, perché è inserito nel quadro del naturalismo campanelliano, secondo cui la parola gode di proprietà magiche perché riproduce la natura della cosa. Le parole hanno un significato intimo, ma la loro funzionalità presuppone la facoltà di sentire[45]. Il linguaggio, secondo Campanella, o almeno il linguaggio filosofico, dovrebbe garantire una sorta di conoscenza universale e costituire una forma di accesso libero e comune alla sapienza, ragione per cui questo filosofo condivide l'antico sogno di un ritorno ad una forma di linguaggio naturale ed originale, ad una grammatica che rispecchi direttamente la reale natura delle cose, in modo da recuperare tutta la loro capacità magica di agire sullo *spiritus* umano. Per questa ragione, Campanella amaramente constata che, invece, il linguaggio si è allontanato irrimediabilmente dalla forma originaria e si è inaridito fino ad essere percepito come un apparato arbitrario ed artificiale. A tale decadenza, secondo Campanella, non bisogna arrendersi e rassegnarsi in modo passivo, bensì rispondere andando alla ricerca di una grammatica filosofica che abbia la capacità di risalire direttamente alle cose e di fare i conti con le loro nature. La nuova lingua filosofica e il nuovo alfabeto dovrebbero dare espressione grafica delle forme naturali dei suoni, fornendo all'uomo uno strumento indispensabile per l'apprendimento naturale, come Campanella specifica anche nella *Grammatica*. Come ha ricordato Lina Bolzoni[46], Campanella insiste sulla necessità di un linguaggio che svolga anche una funzione pedagogica fondata sulla sua naturalità:

> Dato che non possediamo un alfabeto razionale, che imiti davvero gli strumenti vocali, e non possiamo attendercelo se non da chi istituirà una lingua novella, che imiti alla perfezione le cose con le parole e le parole con i segni grafici, sicché gli uomini imparino con facilità al solo considerare le cose, guidati dalla somiglianza, a leggere e scrivere: finché dunque i filosofi non potranno diffondere una lingua e una grafia appropriata, occorre nello scrivere valersi della solita[47].

---

[45] Guglielminetti, 'Magia e tecnica nella poetica di Tommaso Campanella', 361–400; Seppilli, *Poesia e magia*, 57.
[46] Bolzoni, 'Una nuova lingua e una nuova metrica', 59.
[47] Campanella, *Tutte le opere*, 689.

La speranza nello sviluppo di una lingua naturale si basa sulla teoria dell'imitazione della natura ed è corrispettivo al programma educativo ipotizzato nella *Città del Sole*, in cui Campanella descrive le spettacolari mura dipinte che non servono solo a proteggere la città, ma anche ad ospitare la rappresentazione di tutto lo scibile umano. Attraverso l'osservazione delle raffigurazioni pittoriche, ciascuno sarebbe stato in grado di acquisire in modo naturale un primo livello di conoscenza generale in tutte le scienze. In questo teatro, che ospita la riproduzione visiva del sapere, l'apprendimento da parte dei bambini avverrebbe secondo percorsi guidati e con più rapidità e facilità poichè basato sull'impatto delle immagini sul nostro *spiritus* e sullo sviluppo della mnemotecnica anziché sullo studio coatto di libri, nel chiuso delle biblioteche. I gironi di mura che salgono fino al tempio sono istoriati sia all'interno che all'esterno. Partendo dal basso, troviamo la rappresentazione delle scienze matematiche ed astronomiche, poi di quelle geografiche, con la descrizione di tutti i Paesi del mondo; successivamente vengono mostrati i minerali, i vegetali e gli animali e tutti i ritrovati delle scienze meccaniche[48]. Chiude bene questa serie di considerazioni sulla naturalità del sapere un pensiero ancora una volta di Lina Bolzoni: «Il filosofo, chi vuole rifondare il linguaggio, il poeta/ profeta si muovono tutti, secondo Campanella, in un'unica direzione. Li accomuna il tentativo di ricostruire la trasparenza originaria, quella per cui le parole sono il prolungamento delle cose, e le lettere dell'alfabeto rispecchiano la forma assunta dagli organi vocali nel pronunciare i suoni. Il canone dell'imitazione si tramuta nella ricerca di un immediato rispecchiamento, di un magico prolungamento del mondo delle cose nell'uomo e nelle sue forme di comunicazione e di espressione»[49].

MUSICA E TEOLOGIA

Nella *Theologia*, scritto tra il 1613 e il 1624, Campanella torna sulla questione della virtù magica insita nei caratteri, nelle lettere ed immagini, scolpite o scritte. Nel *Senso delle cose e della magia* l'interesse per la magia, e per la musica come parte della magia, era interamente naturale, negli anni successivi anch'esso viene ristrutturato alla luce

---

[48] Campanella, *Città del Sole*, 50–53.
[49] Bolzoni, *Una nuova lingua e una nuova metrica*, 58.

di un accresciuto impegno teologico. Nel XIV libro della *Theologia* l'autore è infatti più prudente e sottolinea che queste entità non possiedono la capacità di produrre effetti fisici, quali la salute o la malattia, per esempio. Allo stesso modo, suoni e parole non hanno più alcuna virtù intrinseca che li renda in grado di sviluppare fenomeni naturali per il solo fatto di essere prodotti. In questo senso, secondo Campanella, tutti i segni e i suoni non sono magici, ma semplicemente possono essere impiegati come mezzi per indurre passioni nell'animo umano[50]. Campanella si dimostra pertanto scettico, soprattutto nella più tarda opera teologica, riguardo all'effettivo potere magico di segni, simboli ed immagini, ed in generale ad un tipo di magia che faccia uso di formule incantatorie. In senso primario, le parole non sono altro che suoni, i quali muovono l'aria ed ottengono così effetti fisici sugli oggetti. Nell'opera teologica, quindi, si premura di specificare che se Dio ha eventualmente posto nelle parole determinate virtù occulte soprannaturali, allora tali parole sono di pertinenza della magia divina e non di quella umana. Bisognerà allora più ragionevolmente sostenere, dice Campanella, che le parole, dal momento che significano qualcosa, provengono dall'anima intellettiva, e come tali hanno unità con tutti gli enti dotati di cognizione. Quando vengono proferite con sentimento intenso, producono la loro azione sullo spirito di tutti, agendo in virtù di una superiore simpatia, e perciò a volte possono conseguire effetti magici. Lo scopo teologico dell'opera e probabilmente la preoccupazione di sfuggire ad accuse di negromanzia (data la facilità con cui vi si poteva incorrere e dato anche il racconto che Campanella aveva fatto nell'*Ateismo trionfato* di certe sue esperienze con gli spiriti) ispirano una condotta più prudente su queste tematiche. Ancora una volta, tuttavia, è il rapporto con Ficino e con le sue fonti a caratterizzare il pensiero campanelliano. Nel *De Vita Coelitus Comparanda* il discorso sulla musica astrologica e sulla musicoterapia si lega a doppio filo a quello sui talismani, ispirato dal commento al celebre passo delle *Enneadi* in cui veniva raccontato il rituale ermetico di attirare spiriti (demonici o angelici) nelle statue. Nell'*Asclepius* si raccontava che gli antichi avessero inventato l'arte di creare gli dei. Essendo incapaci di produrre le anime, gli uomini avevano invocato i demoni e gli angeli, raffigurandoli in statue che erano diventate oggetto di riti sacri e divini. Sull'autorità di Ermete si fondava in realtà un concetto ben

---

[50] Campanella, *Theologia*, libro XIV, 200.

più vasto e, da un certo punto di vista, pericoloso: la convinzione cioè, che l'uomo fosse in grado di scoprire la natura divina e riprodurla. Le qualità degli déi terrestri divenivano rintracciabili in erbe, pietre, odori e ogni altra sorta di elemento naturale, che ha quindi in sé un potere divino. Di conseguenza, sacrifici, inni, lodi e suoni dolci come l'armonia celeste, piacciono a queste divinità ed incidono su di esse, che sono state attirate dentro l'idolo con la ripetizione di riti sacri.

Dal commento del *liber Plotini*, Ficino traeva una teoria fondamentale per la magia rinascimentale, cioè il concetto che lo spirito celeste fosse attirabile all'interno di un corpo materiale a condizione che l'oggetto avesse una potenza adatta alla fonte celeste dello spirito in questione. Ficino usava il passo delle statue dell'*Asclepius* e gli *Orphica* per sostenere la propria teoria della magia. Senza dubbio egli si era accorto che in questa teoria era insito il rischio di accusa di idolatria e di demonologia, per questo ha cercato di difendere la propria dottrina. Egli ammetteva, ad esempio, che la magia egizia fosse illegittima, perché i demoni attirati nelle statue erano poi considerati come veri déi. Tuttavia, il fiorentino sosteneva che se, invece di adorarli, li si avesse usati come mezzi, i demoni avrebbero potuto essere accettati. In questo contensto, egli parlava più che altro di creature soprannaturali, cercando di evidenziare che la natura degli spiriti attirati dai riti magici non era sempre o necessariamente malvagia. Di conseguenza Ficino faceva saltare l'uguaglianza fra spirituale e demonico e proponeva un'opposizione fra magia demonica e magia naturale. Il mago «nero» e quello «bianco» operano sostanzialmente nello stesso modo, ma utilizzano forze diverse: inferiori e diaboliche il primo, superiori e divine il secondo. Campanella istituisce, invece, un'equazione fra spirituale e naturale, poiché grazie all'impianto telesiano della sua filosofia, tutto ciò che appartiene alla natura è vivificato dallo *spiritus*. Sempre per difendersi da possibili attacchi, Ficino citava Tommaso al fine di sostenere che la magia astrologica è incapace di produrre immagini abitate da demoni. Con questa affermazione, egli liberava dal sospetto talismani ed inni orfici. Nel *De Triplici Vita*, Ficino riprendeva l'argomento e sosteneva che le musiche proposte nelle sue opere non erano *cantiones*[51], cioè formule incantatorie per richiamare spiriti maligni e piegarli al proprio volere. Le sue musiche non erano, quindi, formule di magia negromantica: egli menzionava proprio l'uso che Ermete

---

[51] Walker, *Magia spirituale e magia demonica da Ficino a Campanella*, 61.

aveva fatto della musica per attirare gli spiriti negli idoli e citava poi anche altri usi antichi della musica per prenderne le distanze e dirsene contrario. La tattica difensiva di Ficino prevedeva, dunque, di rimettersi all'autorità di Tommaso, il quale nelle opere autentiche affermava che sostanze naturali, quali erbe, pietre etc., possono avere poteri legati alle loro affinità astrologiche e, pertanto, possono essere usate in medicina. Tommaso aveva però specificato che se si incidono lettere sulle pietre o se si accompagnano le erbe con invocazioni, se cioè si effettuano degli incantesimi, i risultati ottenuti saranno da ritenersi opera dei demoni. Anche Campanella si rifà a Tommaso in questi stessi termini, recuperando cioè la condanna espressa da Agostino riguardo gli idoli. Tommaso, inoltre, associava l'*Asclepius* alla magia e quindi, con ogni probabilità, avrebbe condannato Ficino. Tommaso, in altre parole, considerava questo genere di pratiche inesorabilmente connesse con i demoni e sospettava, pertanto, che i segni incisi sui talismani dovessero conseguire effetti particolari perché rivolti a creature dotate di intelletto e di determinate capacità. Campanella, pur richiamandosi a Ficino, nella seconda parte della sua vita sembra proprio più vicino a queste posizioni.

Nel 1626 alcuni astrologi si radunano per stilare l'oroscopo di papa Urbano VIII, iniziando a predirne la dipartita come imminente. Le voci al riguardo si diffondono ben presto a macchia d'olio, destando la più viva preoccupazione nel diretto interessato. A questi pettegolezzi, probabilmente sobillati dagli spagnoli[52], il pontefice risponde con la condanna ufficiale della pratica astrologica, sancita nella bolla *Immutabilis* del 1631, che giunge a conclusione della lunga vicenda processuale contro l'abate di Santa Prassede, don Orazio Morandi, accusato di aver ecceduto in pratiche di astrologia giudiziaria[53]. Il processo aveva avuto luogo fra il 1626 e il 1631, e aveva visto la Chiesa costretta a prendere posizioni di una certa durezza contro Morandi, perché il predecessore di Urbano, Sisto V, aveva già emanato la bolla *Coeli et Terrae* nel 1586 per vietare tutte le pratiche in qualche modo connesse all'astrologia giudiziaria. Urbano VIII, tuttavia, nel suo intimo era un fedele sostenitore dell'astrologia, solo che era stato vittima del suo stesso gioco, perché si era spesso dilettato a commissionare gli oroscopi dei suoi cardinali, facendone poi pubblicamente

---

[52] Nussdorder, *Civic Politics in the Rome of Urban VIII*.
[53] Dooley, *Morandi's Last Prophecy and the End of the Renaissance*.

pronosticare la data di morte. Ma quando viene ripagato con la stessa moneta, il papa si spaventa e chiama Campanella, che aveva fama di valente astrologo, per avere un parere sulla veridicità delle previsioni circolanti sul suo conto. Il filosofo non si tira indietro e anzi, decide di sfruttare l'occasione per convincere il pontefice di alcune idee politiche che da sempre gli stanno a cuore. Nonostante, infatti, Campanella dica di rifarsi a Ficino per una positiva applicazione dei principi magici, con il passare degli anni la sua visione politica, filosofica e magica viene colorata da una forte tensione millenaristica ed escatologica. Egli si convince che l'annuncio dell'ultima era dell'umanità sia dato anche dall'avvicinarsi del sole, sede del caldo e dell'amore, alla terra, sede dell'odio, che ne sarà distrutta. Inoltre, egli constata che tra Terra e Cielo si verificano numerosi eventi anomali che perturbano la realtà, come numerose eclissi, la comparsa di comete, la posizione negativa di Marte e Saturno, oltre ai nefasti presagi forniti dal moltiplicarsi delle eresie protestanti, dal dilagare dell'ateismo e del machiavellismo, la scoperta del Nuovo Mondo. Gli anni fra il 1628 e il 1630 sono astronomicamente travagliati: nel primo si verificano due eclissi, una di sole e una di luna, nel secondo un'altra di sole. È proprio del lento avvicinamento dell'astro solare che Campanella vuole convincere il pontefice, sul quale ricadono le speranze escatologiche del domenicano, che le aveva precedentemente affidate al monarca di Spagna e quindi a quello di Francia. Se il papa si fosse convinto della veridicità delle previsioni di Campanella e di ciò che esse comportavano, allora avrebbe permesso che missionari da lui addestrati partissero alla volta del mondo intero con l'intento di convertire le genti al Cristianesimo riformato, quel 'naturale' Cristianesimo che Campanella aveva in mente, e che doveva preparare il millennio. Dalle buone disposizioni del pontefice dipendono inoltre, cosa non di secondaria importanza, le speranze del calabrese di mantenere la libertà. Nel 1628 il papa riserva delle sedute a Campanella, ricevendolo da solo. I due devono probabilmente mettere in atto misure preventive per proteggersi dagli influssi nefasti delle eclissi. Si narra anche di riti di 'negromanzia', eseguiti di notte con candele accese. Dopo aver sigillato la stanza e purificato l'aria con spruzzi di aceto e sostanze aromatiche, nonché con il fumo prodotto dalla combustione di lauro, mirto, cipresso e rosmarino, i due addobbano la stanza con rami e festoni di seta bianca. Accendono poi due candele e cinque fiaccole, simboleggianti i sette pianeti: dal momento che l'eclissi causa una parziale diminuzione della luce, ciò serve a ristabilire l'equilibrio, come al tramonto si accende una lampada. Dato che si tratta di un procedimento basato su conoscenze di filosofia della natura, e non sulla superstizione, vengono rappresentati anche i segni zodiacali e si eseguono musiche appropriate ai pianeti Giove e Venere, per diradare le esalazioni nocive prodotte dalle eclissi. Allo stesso modo, si utilizzano pietre, piante, colori e odori attinenti ai pianeti positivi; vengono infine serviti liquori preparati secondo direttive magico-astrologiche[54]. Il confine fra l'uso buono e lecito di questo tipo di riti e la perversione demonica della magia nera è molto sottile, tanto che i talismani e le formule magiche sono considerate blasfeme. Tuttavia, Campanella ancora collega la produzione di suoni alla sfera magica, cercando, almeno formalmente, di non degenerare nell'ambito del maleficio e del demonico. Il rituale eseguito con il pontefice Urbano VIII si basava proprio sulla riproduzione all'interno di una stanza del cosmo, del mondo celeste, rappresentato come tranquillo e al riparo da ogni tipo di perturbazione per mitigare gli influssi nefasti della realtà.

È Campanella stesso a raccontare queste pratiche, nell'opuscolo *De fato siderali vitando*, stampato a Lione nel 1629. Del resto, è difficile che Campanella avesse praticato una simile forma di magia prima della sua venuta a Roma nel 1626[55]. Non ne fa menzione infatti in alcuna delle opere anteriori: né nel *Senso delle cose* né nelle due prime versioni della *Città del sole*, mentre nell'ultima, del 1637, c'è una descrizione dei Solariani intenti a pratiche di questo tipo di magia. Nel libretto astrologico, Campanella afferma che l'uomo è tenuto semplicemente a prestar fede a Dio e ad agire in conformità alle scienze che Egli ci ha dato. Per quanto riguarda il primo punto, l'autore consiglia di pregare Dio intensamente per evitare gli eventi fatali. Infatti, rivolgersi a Dio con preghiere sincere, permette spesso di evitare sventure, poiché Dio, che è più potente del fato stesso, interviene in nostro favore. Sostenere il valore della preghiera in sé può essere un modo per screditare l'immagine del Dio protestante, che non sarebbe affatto toccato o mosso nella volontà dalle nostre richieste o promesse. Ma Campanella va oltre e sostiene invece che, se si conosce la preghiera *opportuna* si può ottenere da Dio che modifichi la fortuna o il caso che attende ciascuno di

---

[54] Campanella, *Come evitare il fato astrale*, 145–147.
[55] Walker, *Magia spirituale e demonica da Ficino a Campanella*, 282.

noi[56]. Questo però presupporrebbe che le preghiere abbiano un valore effettivo e reale, cioè che abbiano un qualche potere di modifica nei confronti di Dio per il solo fatto di essere pronunciate. Ciò implicherebbe anche che le posizioni campanelliane si siano nuovamente modificate a favore di un'interpretazione forte dei poteri magici o persuasivi delle *voces*, che nel libro XIV della *Theologia* erano stati invece trattati con cautela. A questo punto, data l'oscillazione delle posizioni dell'autore in merito, si potrebbe pensare che Campanella abbia usato prudenza in sede teologica e più verosimilmente abbia espresso le proprie vere opinioni in uno scritto che non doveva essere destinato alla pubblicazione e alla divulgazione anche se si potrebbe avanzare l'ipotesi che Campanella l'abbia redatto per farlo circolare indipendentemente e in modo anonimo e clandestino[57]. Nel breve scritto su come evitare il fato astrale rimangono comunque profonde influenze ficiniane, riguardo alle quali Campanella rimanda alla propria *Metafisica*. In particolare, nella terza parte di quest'opera vi è un passo in cui l'autore parla della necessità di condurre la propria vita *celestialmente*, che non è altro che l'ideale che percorre tutto il *De Vita*[58]. Ma Campanella non si limita all'esposizione dei cardini ficiniani sulla magia e sulla teoria della musica: egli, quale ottimo intenditore della materia, fa un resoconto delle fonti ficiniane e, oltre agli *Hermetica*, espone i testi neoplatonici di Giamblico, Proclo, Porfirio. Egli riconosce dunque un'uniformità di base fra i passi salienti dell'*Asclepius* e la magia ficiniana, entrambi facenti ricorso a idoli, talismani o esseri umani. Campanella è quindi consapevole delle fonti ficiniane, anche quelle più pericolose per l'ortodossia cattolica e nonostante comprenda che alcune preghiere di Ficino sono rivolte ad angeli planetari, non sembra turbato. Probabilmente egli cerca un tipo di magia che, pur non negandone il potere, non faccia ricorso a demoni e che, in buona sostanza, sia facilmente difendibile come magia naturale. Molto più cauto, però, è l'atteggiamento nell'opera teologica. In essa, il filosofo prende le distanze proprio dall'insegnamento di Ficino, avvertendo il lettore che:

---

[56] Campanella, *Come evitare il fato astrale*, 73.
[57] Firpo, 'La stampa clandestina degli *Astrologicorum libri*', 155–169. Cfr. Formichetti, 'Il *De siderali fato vitando* di Tommaso Campanella', 199–205; Grillo, *Questioni campanelliane. La stampa fraudolenta e clandestina degli* Astrologicorum libri, 8–15; Lucchesi, 'Il *De fato siderali vitando*: varianti d'autore campanelliane in un codice della Casanatense', 15.
[58] Campanella, *Metafisica*, 195.

Le tre regole del Ficino circa la maniera di procacciarsi la vita divina sono impossibili a osservare ed intendere, però non contengono eresia, come alcuni troppo facilmente vanno dicendo. Le stelle, infatti dominano direttamente le cose inferiori compreso l'uomo (limitatamente al corpo e agli spiriti animali) e hanno con esse un legame simpatetico, ma sulla mente soltanto indirettamente, come si è spiegato tante volte[59].

Rifiutando gli esiti necessitanti del determinismo astrologico, Campanella afferma qui non esserci alcuna certezza riguardo alle influenze stellari sulla vita terrestre, ritenendo impossibile stabilire una relazione causale fra l'influsso di un astro e un dato fenomeno. In questo passo, egli insiste curiosamente sull'impossibilità di stabilire quali suoni, danze, canti o costumi dilettano o ripugnano l'uomo, così come è impossibile stabilire quale tra gli effetti giovevoli è causato dalle stelle[60]. A Ficino era rimasta, come unica linea difensiva dopo che Tommaso si era rivelato un'arma a doppio taglio, proprio la considerazione che la forma di magia da lui proposta avesse, come unico scopo, il mutamento dell'intelletto e dell'immaginazione dell'interessato. Egli non predicava atti magici volti ad ingraziarsi un demone o un angelo, ma piuttosto sistemi per intervenire sul corpo e sullo spirito del protagonista del rito. In altre parole, intonare un inno al sole non avrebbe minimamente influito sul Sole, ma avrebbe portato alla solarizzazione dello spirito della persona coinvolta. Il problema è che qualsiasi effetto dell'inno potrebbe essere prodotto da un demone malvagio, che, in quanto creatura dai poteri e dalle risorse superiori a quelle umane, potrebbe trarci in inganno. La parte relativa alla magia demonica, cioè a tutti quei fenomeni che avvengono in modo inspiegabile dal punto di vista umano, è sensibilmente accresciuta nel XIV libro della *Theologia* rispetto a quanto detto nel *Senso delle cose*, dove l'argomento era stato di fatto solo sfiorato[61]. Non è qui possibile esaminare in modo

---

[59] Ibid., 203.
[60] Ibid., 205.
[61] Lo sviluppo della tematica demonologica da parte di Campanella in opere successive non è casuale, ma dettato piuttosto dal fatto che con il passare degli anni egli si accostò sempre di più al problema. In particolare, gli anni che ruotano intorno al 1600, fino al 1604, sono segnalati da Campanella nell'*Ateismo trionfato* come quelli più significativi per la sua svolta religiosa e il conseguente avvicinamento all'ortodossia cattolica. Proprio nell'*Ateismo trionfato*, Campanella afferma di poter provare l'esistenza di una dimensione oltremondana proprio per il fatto di aver sperimentato in prima persona che esistono entità soprannaturali, quali demoni e angeli, e che possono interagire con gli uomini quando questi indulgono in pratiche magiche. E' sempre presente infatti il rischio che i demoni si intromettano nei riti e nelle operazioni magiche, specialmente quelle che ricorrono a invocazioni e uso di talismani, per i

esaustivo le infinite possibilità di azione delle creature soprannaturali
da Campanella citate e studiate, tuttavia si può segnalare che anche
gli effetti prodotti o da esseri umani in cooperazione con demoni o
dai demoni stessi sono riconducibili all'ambito del prodigio naturale.
I filosofi possono infatti facilmente individuare quando un effetto pro-
digioso nasce da magia artificiale, naturale o divina, e l'operato dei
demoni si distingue solamente perché porta cose malvagie e fa del
male, mentre i prodigi operati con l'ausilio divino si rivelano sempre
utili. I demoni, benché muniti di poteri speciali grazie al loro corpo
etereo[62], non possono rovesciare le leggi naturali – quindi nemmeno
quelle soprannaturali – che Dio ha imposto[63].

Al termine di questo *exucursus* si possono fare alcune considerazioni.
La prima è che il tema della musica, per Campanella, è strettamente
collegato a quello delle parole e delle formule magiche o guaritorie e
pertanto lo si trova affrontato, nel *corpus* campanelliano, nelle opere
naturali e mediche. La seconda, strettamente collegata alla prima, è
che quindi non si dovrebbe tanto parlare di 'Campanella e la musica'
quanto piuttosto di 'Campanella e i suoni'. Il tema del valore prodi-
gioso dei suoni e delle *voces* diventa importante in Campanella con
l'approfondirsi dell'interesse per la magia. Del resto è noto che gli
studi sulla musica e l'acustica si legano, nel Rinascimento, proprio
alle pratiche sperimentali. Queste ultime, poco sollecitate dalle scienze
che hanno, per tradizione, la specifica caratteristica di essere saperi
speculativi ed astratti, sono invece attuate dai saperi occulti e dalla
magia naturale. La differenza fra arte e *scientia* non è ancora mar-

---

loro malevoli scopi. Nel *Senso delle cose e della magia*, 215–218, la magia demonica
è presentata di sfuggita perché lo scopo principale dell'opera è di spiegare la filosofia
della natura e l'arte ad essa applicata, cioè la magia. Probabilmente la tematica demonica non è inserita come nelle opere posteriori perché il nucleo originario del *Senso
delle cose* risale addirittura al 1587, con il titolo di *De investigatione rerum*, quindi
nella fase giovanile più strettamente legata all'insegnamento telesiano, e certamente
lontana dal riconoscimento in natura di forze terze per spiegare i processi che alla
natura sola competono. La "scoperta" campanelliana dei demoni sarebbe quindi successiva e con ciò si spiegherebbe l'interesse per le loro forme di azione magica nella
Theologia e anche nella *Metafisyca*, dove è ampiamente trattata soprattutto nella terza
parte dell'opera.
  [62] La tradizione che assegna ai demoni un corpo sottilissimo e rapidissimo, fatto
di etere, risale ad Agostino, ed attribuisce a questa caratteristica la capacità di attuare
fenomeni impensabili per l'uomo che, tuttavia, non si possono assolutamente classifi-
care come miracoli veri e propri. Cfr. Agostino, *De divinatione daemonum*, cap. 3, in
Bibliothèque augustinienne 10: X, Parigi, 1952, 663–666.
  [63] Campanella, *Theologia*, XIV, 226.

cata in modo chiaro, ma le scienze non hanno nei loro programmi la 'contaminazione' con l'esperienza pratica e materiale: proprio questo aspetto, secondo Campanella, ha finito per rendere il sapere avulso dalla realtà ed incapace di dare spiegazione dei nuovi fenomeni riscontrati. Nella sua tenace avversione per l'aristotelismo, il filosofo di Stilo ha sempre tentato di scomporre la rovinosa combinazione fra teologia cristiana e peripatetismo nata, a suo dire, a causa di una contingenza storica. La mancanza di altri sistemi filosofici a cui riferirsi ha fatto sì che la Chiesa abbia indicato nelle opere dello Stagirita l'epistemologia formalmente corretta e da difendere. Ma, nel frattempo, molte nuove cose sono state scoperte: terre, stelle e pianeti, ritrovati scientifici, fenomeni naturali. Di tutto questo, secondo Campanella non si riesce a dar ragione nell'obsoleta epistemologia aristotelica e pertanto egli suggerisce una filosofia alternativa, creata dall'innesto del ceppo platonico/neoplatonico ed ermetico sul tronco telesiano. Questa originale ipotesi prevede che un posto molto importante, nel nuovo albero delle scienze che si delineava, venisse conferito alla magia naturale e alle sue implicazioni pratiche. È in questo quadro che Campanella inizia a far riferimento alla musica, intesa principalmente come strumento terapeutico. In seguito a questi approfondimenti, Campanella viene considerato un grande esperto di musica e suoni nonostante egli non sia, in verità, un gran dotto in materia. Durante l'ultimo periodo della sua vita, a Parigi, il filosofo di Stilo ebbe un colloquio con Marine Mersenne, il quale era ansioso di incontrarlo appunto per conoscerne le opinioni in materia musicale, salvo poi esserne del tutto deluso dopo aver compreso che Campanella ancora si rifaceva alle tematiche magiche dell'Umanesimo[64]. Mersenne, al contrario, avversava qualsiasi tipo di pratica magica o ricorso ad entità soprannaturale e rifiutava ogni compromesso con le attività occulte. Egli era inoltre orientato ad una sperimentazione musicale di tipo acustico. La carenza riscontrata dal francese in Campanella, e la conseguente delusione, è da addebitare alla separazione, che all'epoca si stava appena delineando, fra musica ed acustica: differenza che il domenicano doveva aver colto solo parzialmente. Bisogna invece tenere conto del ruolo significativo che Campanella ebbe nel promuovere attività di sperimentazione non contemplate nei programmi di studio tradizionali per svincolare la ricerca dal predominio dell'aristotelismo, che stava diventando di fatto un ostacolo all'incremento delle conoscenze e all'apertura intellettuale.

---

[64] Blanchet, *Campanella*, 261.

In nome della *libertas philosophandi*, il domenicano era dunque ben aperto a tutti gli esperimenti possibili: in questa inclinazione al lato pratico del sapere si trova la positiva eredità della cultura popolare. Benchè debitore nei confronti della sua terra, Campanella va tuttavia apprezzato anche per gli alti livelli raggiunti in ambito metafisico e teologico, che ne fanno uno degli ultimi grandi ingegni enciclopedici del Rinascimento italiano. La cultura popolare, dunque, anziché costituire un retaggio superstizioso, viene strumentalizzata da Campanella nel contesto magico per ampliare il raggio d'azione umana. La presenza di richiami alla sapienza popolare della terra natìa viene quindi interpretata come un positivo stimolo a fare i conti con la vita e le necessità quotidiane, a declinare la natura secondo i bisogni umani per aumentare la qualità della propria esistenza nel rispetto del mondo in quanto ordinata creazione di Dio, in cui anche la musica ha un ruolo e uno scopo.

BIBLIOGRAFIA

Blanchet, L., *Campanella*, Parigi: 1920.

Boccadoro, B., 'Eléments de grammaire mélancolique', *Acta Musicologica*, LXXVI/1 (2004), 25–65. Traduzione italiana: 'Elementi di grammatica melanconica', Editore sitoweb A.S.S.E.Psi. (Associazione per lo Studio della Storia e dell'Epistemologia della Psichiatria).

——, 'Marsilio Ficino: the soul and the body of counterpoint', in Gozza, P., *Number to sound. The Musical Way to the Scientific Revolution*, Boston: 2000, 99–134.

——, 'Musica spiritum curat', in *Handbuch der Musik der Renaissance*, A., Rifkin, J., e Schmierer, E. ed., Vol. 5, Laaber Verlag: 2008, 1–37.

——, 'Musique, médecine et tempéraments' in Nattiez, J. J., *Musiques. Une encyclopédie pour le XXIᵉ siècle*, Vol. 2: *Les savoirs musicaux*. Actes Sud, Cité de la musique: 2004. Traduzione italiana 'Musica medicina e temperamenti', in Bent, M., Dalmonte, R., e Baroni, M., *Enciclopedia della Musica. Il sapere musicale*, Torino: 2006, 361–386.

Bolzoni, L., 'Una nuova lingua e una nuova metrica', in *Tommaso Campanella e l'attesa del secolo aureo*, Firenze: 1998, 48–60.

——, 'Telesio Bruno e Campanella', in *L'Italia e la formazione della civiltà europea. La cultura civile*, Torino: 1992.

Bortolotti, A., *Magia superstizione e fede nella pratica medica*, Sommacampagna: 1992.

Campanella, T., *Ateismo trionfato, ovvero riconoscimento filosofico della religione universale contra l'antichristianesimo machiavellico*, Pisa: 2004.

——, *Del senso delle cose e della magia*, Roma-Bari: 2007.

——, *Epilogo Magno*, Roma: 1939.

——, *La Città del Sole e questione quarta dell'ottima repubblica*, Milano: 2001.

——, *Medicinalium, iuxta propria principia, libri septem*, Lugduni: 1635.

——, *Opera Latina*, II, pp. 1299–1300.

——, *Opere letterarie*, Torino: 1977.

——, *Opuscoli astrologici. Come evitare il fato astrale, Apologetico, Disputa sulle Bolle*, Milano: 2003, 63–133.

——, *Scelta di alcune poesie filosofiche*, Torino: 1982.

——, *Tutte le opere*. I. *Scritti letterari*, Milano: 1954 (unico volume pubblicato).

Combarieu, J., *La musique et la magie: étude sur les origines populaires de l'art musical, son influence et sa fonction dans les societes*, Ginevra: 1978; traduzione italiana *La musica e la magia*, Milano: 1982.

Corsini, A., *Medici ciarlatani e ciarlatani medici*, Bologna: 1922.

De Martino, E., *La terra del rimorso. Contributo a una storia religiosa del Sud*, Milano: 1976.

Di Mitri, D., *Storia biomedica del tarantismo nel XVIII secolo*, Firenze: 2006.

Dooley, B., *Morandi's Last Prophecy and the End of the Renaissance*, Princeton: 2002.

Ernst, G., *Tommaso Campanella*, Bari: 2002.

Ficino, M., *Commentaire sue le Banquet de Platon*, Paris: 2002, 58.

Firpo, L., 'La stampa clandestina degli *Astrologicorum libri*', in *Ricerche campanelliane*, Firenze: 1984.

Formichetti, G., 'Il *De siderali fato vitando* di Tommaso Campanella', in Bulzoni, *Il mago, il cosmo, il teatro degli astri*, Roma: 1985, 199–217.

Frazer, J. G., *The Golden Bough: A Study in Magic and Religion*, Londra: 1922; traduzione italiana *Il ramo d'oro: studio sulla magia e la religione*, Torino: 1965.

Giglioni, G.,'Magia naturale', in Enciclopedia Bruniana & Campanelliana, Pisa-Roma: 2006, 268–269.

Gouk, P., *Music, Science and Natural magic in Seventeenth-Century England*, Yale: 1999.

Grillo, F., *Questioni campanelliane. La stampa fraudolenta e clandestina degli* Astrologicorum libri, Cosenza: 1961.

Guglielminetti, M., 'Magia e tecnica nella poetica di Tommaso Campanella', *Rivista di estetica*, IX (1964), 361–400.

Lerner, M. P., *Pansensisme et interprétation de la nature chez Tommaso Campanella: le «De sensu rerum et magia»* (Thèse pour le Doctorat d'Etat, Université de Paris I, 1986), 2 voll.

Lucchesi, O., 'Il *De fato siderali vitando*: varianti d'autore campanelliane in un codice della Casanatense', in F. Troncarelli, *La città dei segreti. Magia, astrologia e cultura esoterica a Roma (XV–XVII)*, Milano: 1985.

Mönnich, M.; Jahncke, W. D. W., 'Medicine and Magic between tradition and progress in Tommaso Campanella', in *Medicina e biologia nella Rivoluzione Scientifica*, Assisi: 1990, 15–33.

Nussdorder, L., *Civic Politics in the Rome of Urban VIII*, Princeton: 1992.

Jurlaro, R., 'Aspetti magici e superstiziosi pugliesi in Giulio Cesare Vanini', in *Giulio Cesare Vanini dal Rinascimento al libertinisme érudit*, Galatina: 2003, 383–387.

Schino, A. L., 'Campanella tra magia naturale e scienza nel giudizio di Gabriel Naudé', *Physis*, XXII (1980), 393–431.

Scrimieri, G., 'Sulla magia di T. Campanella', in *Studi in onore di A. Corsano*, Manduria: 1970, 709–746.

Seppilli, A., Poesia e magia, Torino: 1962.

Tomlinson, G., *Music in Renaissance Magic: Toward a Historiography of Others*, Chicago: 1994.

Walker, D. P., *Spiritual and demonic magic from Ficino to Campanella*, Londra: 1958; tr. it. *Magia spirituale e demonica da Ficino a Campanella*, Torino: 2002.

Walker, D. P., *Music, spirit and language in the Renaissance*, Londra: 1985.

Tirinnanzi, N., *Umbra naturae: l'immaginazione da Ficino a Bruno*, Roma: 2000.

Vanini, G. C., *De admirandis naturae reginae deaeque mortalium arcanis libri quatuor*, Galatina: 1985.

Zambelli, P., 'L'immaginazione e il suo potere (da al-Kindi al-Farabi e Avicenna al medioevo latino e al Rinascimento)', in Miscellanea Medievalia, *Orientalische kultur und europaische Mittelalter*, Koln: 1984.

REPRÉSENTATION ÉSOTÉRIQUE ET PENSÉE SCIENTIFIQUE. LE CAS DE LA VIBRATION PAR SYMPATHIE CHEZ LES SAVANTS ET THÉORICIENS DE LA PREMIÈRE MOITIÉ DU 17ᴱ SIÈCLE

Brigitte Van Wymeersch

English summary: The first half of the 17th century is characterized by a radical change in the epistemologic conceptions. The transition from an analogical to a scientific thought is very marked in the musical domain. If numerous examples could be quoted, that of the vibration by sympathy is one of the most illustrative of this change in thought. Indeed, if the authors of the end of the 16th century and even the beginning of the 17th see in this phenomenon an inexplicable mystery, symbol of an «other thing», some of the scholars and theorists evolve from an analogical vision about this problem to a scientific conception, based on observations and experimentations, which will allow them to place, through this acoustic phenomenon, the discourse about music in the field of physical science. It is the case of Descartes, Mersenne, Peiresc, Gassendi, who all approaches this problem under various angles, to make progress its understanding towards an experimental and scientific universe.

La résonance spontanée d'une corde, – ce que l'on nomme aussi la vibration par sympathie – est un phénomène acoustique qui a frappé bien des générations de curieux. Comme son nom l'indique, ce fait s'inscrit à l'origine dans une problématique plus vaste: celle de la sympathie et de l'antipathie entre les êtres et les choses. Il a un corrélat plus ancien: le silence ou la dissonance causée par une antipathie naturelle entre les matériaux dont sont faits certains instruments de musique.

La compréhension de ces phénomènes est révélatrice de deux conceptions du monde: la première voit le monde comme un réseau de relations dans lequel les êtres et les choses résonnent les uns par rapport aux autres, tout y est lié et tout élément peut s'expliquer par un autre : c'est une épistémologie de l'analogie qui a servi bien souvent de terreau à une pensée hermétique; l'autre est une pensée rationnelle où tout s'explique par une succession de causes efficientes dont il suffit

de saisir un élément pour que le reste s'enchaîne logiquement, «selon
l'ordre des raisons»[1]. C'est un système où, selon les termes même du
père Mersenne, la démonstration remplace la comparaison[2].

Face à ce fait «troublant» – l'écho ou le silence de certaines cordes
ou membranes –, on observe toute une gamme de réactions, d'explications ou de débats qui dénotent de l'effervescence de la pensée dans
la première moitié du 17e siècle au sein des milieux intellectuels français, et qui nous renseignent sur l'ouverture de l'un ou l'autre savant
ou théoricien par rapport à la mutation épistémologique qui s'opère
alors.

Ce chapitre vise donc à mettre en lumière, à partir de cet exemple
précis, à la fois la persistance d'une lecture analogique du monde où
sympathie et vibrations font partie des qualités occultes ou révélées
des choses, et l'émergence d'une lecture mécanique où la causalité et
l'expérimentation deviennent les supports de la raison. Nous montre-
rons également comment ce fait précis lui-même a contribué à mettre
à mal une lecture analogique du monde parce que l'exploration de
ce phénomène acoustique a permis précisément d'affiner les outils de
pensée – dans ce cas ci: expérimentation et raisonnement causal –.
En effet, pour ceux qui veulent s'opposer à une explication ésotérique,
c'est un sujet rêvé pour éprouver de tels outils et s'orienter vers une
pensée différente: la vibration par sympathie est quelque chose que
chacun peut sentir, ouïr et voir et qui a des conséquences importantes,
notamment au niveau de l'accord des instruments à sons fixes et de la
justesse des intervalles. Plus que le problème physique en soi, c'est la
méthodologie mise en place pour le régler qui est intéressante. Ajoutons enfin que l'approfondissement de cette problématique a permis
d'envisager différemment un problème d'écriture et d'esthétique.

---

[1] «Ces longues chaînes de raisons, toutes simples et faciles, dont les géomètres ont
coutume de se servir pour parvenir à leurs plus difficiles démonstrations, m'avaient
donné occasion de m'imaginer que toutes les choses, qui peuvent tomber sous la
connaissance des hommes, s'entre-suivent en même façon et que, pourvu (...) qu'on
garde l'ordre qu'il faut pour les déduire les unes des autres, il n'y en peut avoir de
si éloignées auxquelles enfin on ne parvienne, ni de si cachées qu'on ne découvre»
(Descartes, *Discours de la méthode*, A.T., VI, 19).
[2] «C'est chose inutile de se servir de comparaisons lors que l'on a la demonstra-
tion» (Mersenne, *Harmonie Universelle, Livre premier des Consonances*, VI, 28).

SYMPATHIE ET ANTIPATHIE DANS L'UNIVERS:
MUSIQUE ET INIMITIÉS

Un des phénomènes célèbres de sympathie et d'antipathie dans le domaine musical est celui que Descartes lui-même rapporte au début de son *Compendium Musicae*:

> Il semble que la voix humaine est pour nous la plus agréable pour cette seule raison que, plus que toute autre, elle est conforme à nos esprits. Peut-être est-elle encore plus agréable venant d'un ami que d'un ennemi, du fait de la sympathie et de l'antipathie des passions; pour la même raison que, dit-on, la peau d'une brebis tendue sur un tambour reste muette si une peau de loup résonne sur un autre tambour[3].

La mention de cette légende au début de son tout premier écrit – Descartes n'a alors 22 ans –, contribuera, entre autres choses, à discréditer le *Compendium Musicae*, notamment auprès des grands commentateurs de Descartes[4] comme des musicologues pour ne citer que Fétis[5] ou Pirro[6].

Cette allusion que certains jugent «peu digne de son auteur»[7] le suivra longtemps. Ainsi, le deuxième exemple que donne le dictionnaire de Littré pour illustrer la définition du mot «tambour» est la citation de cette remarque de Descartes[8].

---

[3] «Id tantum videtur vocem humanam nobis gratissimam [reddere], quia omnium maxime conformis est nostris spiritibus; Ita forte etiam amicissimi gratio est, quam inimici, ex sympathia & dispathia affectuum: eadem ratione qua aiut ovis pellem tensam in tympano obmutescere, si feriatur, lupina in alio tympano resonante» (Descartes, *Compendium Musicæ*, 54).

[4] Le jugement de Fernand Alquié, dans son édition des *Œuvres de Descartes*, est assez révélateur de la façon dont il considère le *Compendium*: «De prime abord, il nous a paru possible d'éliminer ou d'abréger: les pages relatives à la musique (...) qui ne paraissent pas profondément liées à l'essentiel de la pensée cartésienne (...)» (Alquié, «Introduction» (Descartes, *Œuvres philosophiques*), 14).

[5] «Malheureusement cet ouvrage est peu digne du nom de son auteur: il parut le sentir, car il ne voulut jamais permettre qu'il fût imprimé» (Fétis, *Biographie universelle des musiciens*, 292).

[6] «Dans cet ouvrage de jeunesse, il [Descartes] fait preuve d'une étonnante crédulité. [en note:] il assure que, tendue sur un tambour, une peau d'agneau ne résonnera point, si, de l'autre côté du tambour, vibre une peau de loup» (Pirro, *Descartes et la musique*, 24).

[7] Fétis, *Biographie universelle des musiciens*, 292.

[8] «Caisse de forme cylindrique, dont les deux fonds sont formés de peaux tendues, sur l'une desquelles on frappe avec des baguettes pour en tirer des sons (...). On dit qu'un tambour couvert d'une peau de brebis ne résonne point et perd entièrement le son lorsque l'on frappe sur un autre tambour couvert d'une peau de loup, DESC. Mus. Objet» (Littré, *Dictionnaire de la langue française*, t. 4, 2137).

En fait, Descartes ne fait que mentionner une vieille fable qui apparaît très tôt dans la littérature occidentale. On la trouve dès l'époque de Charles V, que ce soit chez Nicole Oresme[9], qui lui-même la reprend de Barthelémy l'Anglais[10]. On la trouve également dans le *Songe du Vergier*, texte écrit vers 1376–78:

> Et est la guerre entre eulx [loup et mouton] si naturele, en tant que aucuns (…) veulent dire que se l'en faisset un tabour de la peau d'un mouton et de celle d'un leu il ne pourret estre de bon accort[11].

Cette légende est reprise à travers les siècles, et se retrouve assez logiquement dans la littérature ésotérique du 16e siècle, dans les livres d'emblèmes, mais aussi dans la littérature de type plus «scientifique». Ainsi Ambroise Paré, dans le chapitre où il aborde «certaines choses remerquables, qui se trouvent entre icelles [les betes], touchant leur sympathie & antipathie», la cite parmi «les plusieurs belles histoires et discours»[12]:

> Inimitiez implacables sont entre les Brebis, Moutons, Aigneaux, & les loups, voire si grandes, qu'apres la mort des uns & autres, si deux tabourins sont faicts, l'un de peau de Brebis, & l'autre de Loup, estant sonnez & frappez tous deux ensemblement, bien difficilement ne pourra ouyr le son de celuy de Brebis, tant sont immortelles les inimitiez & discordances de ces Animaux, soyent vifs ou morts. Mesmes aucuns estiment, que si un Luth ou autre instrument, est monté de cordes faictes de boyaux de Brebis & de Loup, il sera impossible l'accorder[13].

Ces problèmes de sympathies et d'antipathies sont évidemment des chapitres essentiels de la littérature magique ou hermétique. Dans sa *Philosophie occulte*, Cornelius Agrippa cite la fable des tambours dans un passage consacré aux «vertus que les choses ont pendant leur Vie, et de celles qui leur restent après leur Mort»:

[9] «Aliqui dicunt (…) quod nervus sonorum ex intestinis lupi factus nunquam potest consonare neque concordare cum nervis ex intestinis ovis facti (…). Rursum dicunt quidam quod tympnum factum de corio lupi percussum prope tympana que sunt ex ovino corio composita facit ea rumpi, destrui, seu crepari» (Oresme, *Tractatus de configurationibus qualitatum et motuum*, II, c. XVIII, 316).
[10] Barthelemi l'Anglais, *De proprietatibus rerum*, l. XVIII, c. LXIX, cité dans *Le Songe du vergier*, 479.
[11] [Evrart de Tremagon], *Le Songe du vergier*, l. I, c. CLIV, 313.
[12] Paré, *Les Œuvres d'Ambroise Paré…*, c. XXI: *de l'Antiphathie et sympathie*, 77.
[13] Paré, *Les Œuvres d'Ambroise Paré…*, c. XXI: *de l'Antiphathie et sympathie*, 78.

Il y a des choses qui ne font pas seulement ces effets sur les corps, mais même dans l'harmonie du son ; un tambour fait d'une peau de loup empêche le son d'un autre fait d'une peau d'agneau ; de la même manière un tambour fait de la peau d'un ericius marin, fait enfuir tous les animaux qui rampent aussi loin que le son s'entend ; et les cordes d'instruments qui sont faites de boyaux de loup, si on les assemble avec d'autres faites de boyaux de brebis sur le luth ou sur la guitare, l'on voit que l'on n'en peut faire aucune consonance[14].

Giambattista Della Porta ne dit pas autre chose dans sa *Magia naturalis*[15]. Et la légende figure également en bonne place dans de nombreux livres d'emblèmes, notamment celui d'Alciat, dans sa version originale ainsi que dans ses multiples adaptations et traductions françaises. Elle est alors rattaché à une autre fable, celle de Ziska, militaire vaincu qui, au moment de sa mort, demanda qu'on fasse de sa dépouille une peau de tambour lequel, lorsqu'il sera frappé, fera fuir l'ennemi[16].

---

[14] Agrippa, *La philosophie occulte ou la Magie* (1531–1533), l. I, c. XXI, 59–60 ; « L'agneau de même s'accorde toujours mal avec le loup, il l'a en horreur, il le fuit et le craint ; et l'on dit qu'en pendant la queue, la tête ou la peau d'un loup sur une étable, cela fait que les brebis s'attristent et ne mangent point, parce qu'elles ont trop peur » (Agrippa, op. cit., l. I, 52).

[15] Ainsi peut-on lire au chapitre consacré aux « de viribus, quae in vita tantum insint et quae post mortem » : « nam si lupina pelle tympanum accomodabis, inter cetera ex ovibus pulsatum audies, silentibus sonoris omnibus, & obmutescere ea faciet ; ex ursi, vel lupi corio confectum, & pulsatum longè equos abigit, & fugat. Et si ex omnibus eorum intestinis chorde in lyris tendantur, obstrepent, nec temperamentum unquam efficient » (Della Porta, *Io. Bapt. Portae Magiae naturalis libri XX*, l. I, c. XIIII, 14).

[16] « Caetera mutescent, coriumque silebit ovillum, Si confecta lupi tympana pelle sonent. Hanc membrana ovium sic exhorrescit, ut hostem Exanimis quanvis nos ferat exanimem. Sic cute detracta Ziscas, in tympana versus, Boemos potuit vincere Pontifices » (Alciati, *Emblemata*, Lyon, Mathias Bonhomme :1550, Emblema CLXXI « Vel post mortem formidolosi », 184).

Notons que cet emblème ne figure pas dans les premières éditions d'Alciat, mais apparaît pour la première fois dans la traduction espagnole de Bernardino Daza de 1549, qui comporte, en plus du corpus de base déjà augmenté des 86 emblèmes de l'édition latine de Venise de 1546, une dizaine d'emblèmes jamais édités jusque-là : « Mudo serà el ganado, y de la oveja El cuero no harà son, siendo tocado Un atambor de lobo de pelleja. Y aunque el muerto de muerto maltratado No sea, mas aun muerta ansi se aleja D'el como de enemigo. Ansi mudado Ciscas en atambor (como leemos) A los Pontifices venciò Baehemos » (*Los Emblemas*, Lyon : 1549, 253). Cette traduction espagnole fait partie du programme éditorial mené dans les années cinquante par Rouille et Bonhomme. On le retrouvera par la suite dans de nombreuses versions, et ce jusqu'au 17e siècle (*Los Emblemas*, Lyon : 1549 ; *Emblemata*, Lyon : 1550 ; *Emblemata*, Lyon : 1551 ; *Liber Emblematum…/Kunstbuch*, Franckfurt am Main : 1566/1567 ; *Emblemata / Les emblemes*, Paris : 1584 ; *Emblemata*, Leiden : 1591 ; *Les emblemes*, Geneva/Cologny :1615 ; *Declaracion magistral sobre las Emblemas de Andres Alciato*, Najera : 1615 ; *Emblemata*, Padua : 1621). (Green, *Andrea Alciati and*

Ce phénomène d'antipathie appliquée aux instruments de musique n'est pas absent des traités d'organologie. Michael Praetorius[17] ou Pierre Trichet[18] en font état, tout en s'en distançant.

Descartes s'aligne donc sur la plupart des commentaires en la matière, qu'ils soient de type philosophique, scientifique, ésotérique ou pratique[19]. Mais lorsqu'il en parle, c'est sous forme de « aiunt » : il n'affirme pas, il ne défend pas, il relate simplement ce qu'il a lu. Et l'on sait que Descartes a eu en mains ce type d'ouvrages où sont déclinés toutes les formes de sympathie et d'antipathie de l'univers, écrits magiques et occultes qui ont exercé sur le père du rationalisme une certaine fascination. En effet, dans l'histoire de sa pensée que constitue le *Discours de la méthode*, le philosophe se décrit, jeune collégien, issu

---

his Book of Emblems. A Biographical and Bibliographical Study, London: 1872; http://www.emblems.arts.gla.ac.uk/alciato. Site consulté en novembre 2008).

En 1584, un bref commentaire est adjoint à cet emblème, mais il faut attendre la version de française de 1615 pour avoir un texte plus construit. Ajoutons que le commentaire est particulièrement détaillé dans la version espagnole de 1615 ainsi que dans celle, latine, de 1621. L'édition française de 1615 complète ainsi la fable : « Nature a mis une telle haine entre le loup & les brebis, que si lon bat un tambour faict de la peau d'un loup, toutes les brebis qui l'orront, en auront aussi grande horreur, que si elles voyoyent le loup à leur queue. Si on fait des chordes des boyaux de loup, & qu'on les tende en un instrument de musique avec celles de brebis, il sera impossible d'en tirer aucune harmonie ; Si on pend une peau de loup en un parc ou estable de brebis, les brebis ne voudront rien manger ; Si on joint une peau de loup avec une de brebis, celle de brebis sera incontinent consumee & rongée. Zisque a esté un fort grand & vaillant capitaine, qui fit fort long temps la guerre aux Evesques de Boheme, Quand il voulut mourir, il commanda qu'apres sa mort on l'escorschast ; & que de sa peau on fit un tambour, lequel on feroit retenir au front de son armee. Krantze dit, que se amis luy obeirent, & que si tost que les ennemis oyoyent le retentissement de ce tambour, ils se jectoyent en fuite » (Alciato, *Les emblèmes*, Geneva/Cologny, Jean II de Tournes : 1615, Emblème XCIX, 256).

[17] Praetorius, *Syntagma musicum*, 429.

[18] « Il y aurait subjet de s'esmerveiller, si ce que l'on dit de la peau du loup estoit véritable, qu'estant appliquée sur un bout de tambour, qui soit garni par l'autre bout d'une peau de mouton, si l'on vient à battre le tambour, la peau de mouton se rompra incontinent. Ce que l'on en dit encore est beaucoup plus admirable. Que si deux tambours estoint couverts l'un d'une peau de loup l'autre d'une peau de brebis, celui-ci demeureroit muet, ou seroit assourdi, tandis que l'autre sonneroit hautement. Mais l'experience ayant faict cognoistre que c'estoint des bourdes, je ne crois pas que doresenavant on y veuille adjouter foi » (Trichet, *Traité des instruments de musique*, 240–241).

[19] Comme le suggère G. Rodis-Lewis, c'est probablement de Della Porta que s'inspire Descartes lorsqu'il rapporte cette fable. Les deux passages sont en effet sémantiquement très proches (Rodis-Lewis, « Machineries et perspectives curieuses dans leur rapport avec le cartésianisme », 466).

d'une « des plus célèbres écoles d'Europe »[20], curieux de tout, avide de tout connaître et de tout lire, sans restriction aucune :

> J'avais parcouru tous les livres, traitant de celles [des sciences] qu'on estime les plus curieuses et les plus rares qui avaient pu tomber entre mes mains[21].

Comme les définit Furetière dans son *dictionnaire* de 1690, ces sciences curieuses sont :

> celles qui sont connües de peu de personnes, qui ont des secrets particuliers, comme la Chymie, une partie de l'Optique qui fait voir des choses extraordinaires avec des miroirs et des lunettes ; et plusieurs vaines sciences où l'on pense voir l'advenir, comme l'Astrologie Judiciaire, la Chiromance, la Géomance, et même on y joint la Cabale, la Magie, etc[22].

Descartes, comme de nombreux intellectuels de son époque baigne dans ses sciences « curieuses » et il ajoutera dans son *Discours de la méthode* « qu'il est bon de les avoir toutes examinées, même les plus superstitieuses et les plus fausses, afin de connaître leur juste valeur et se garder d'en être trompé »[23].

Cette nécessité d'examiner les sciences *superstitieuses* et *fausses* pour pouvoir mieux s'en défendre, s'était imposée aussi à la Compagnie de Jésus et notamment au Père Jean François, qui fut le professeur de mathématiques de Descartes. Le père François publia en 1660 un traité sur *les influences célestes où les merveilles de Dieu dans les cieux sont déduites*, destiné à réfuter l'astrologie, la magie, et de façon générale, toutes les « sciences » qui prétendent prédire l'avenir, et ce « par toutes sortes de raisons d'autoritez, et d'experiences »[24].

---

[20] Descartes, *Discours de la méthode*, A.T., VI, 5.

[21] « J'étais dans l'une des plus célèbres écoles de l'Europe, où je pensais qu'il devait y avoir de savants hommes, s'il y en avait en aucun endroit de la terre. J'y avais appris tout ce que les autres y apprenaient ; et même, ne m'étant pas contenté des sciences qu'on nous enseignait, j'avais parcouru tous les livres, traitant de celles qu'on estime les plus curieuses et les plus rares qui avaient pu tomber entre mes mains » (Descartes, *Discours de la méthode*, A.T., VI, 5).

[22] Furetière, *Dictionnaire universel...*, t. 1er, 737.

[23] Descartes, *Discours de la méthode*, A.T., VI, 6.

[24] *Traité des influences célestes ou les merveilles de Dieu dans les cieux sont déduites ; les inventions des astronomes pour les entendre sont expliquées ; les propositions des astrologues iudiciaires sont démonstrées fausses, et pernitieuses, par toutes sortes de raisons d'autoritez, et d'experiences*. Par le P. Jean François de la Compagnie de Iesus. A Rennes, chez Pierre Hallaudays, 1660.

Descartes était donc bien informé de ces divers courants. Et si le *Discours de la méthode* condamne ces sciences, certains écrits de jeunesse démontrent la fascination du jeune Descartes pour les mouvements ésotériques qui paraissent expliquer le monde par une pensée globalisante fondée sur l'analogie. Lorsqu'il était en Allemagne, il a ainsi désiré rencontrer des membres du mouvement rosi-crucien[25], et certaines de ses notes personnelles rendent compte de sa volonté de trouver les «fondements de la science admirable»[26] qu'il parviendra à concrétiser plus tard dans une *mathesis universalis*, réglée et méthodique.

Ce cheminement intellectuel, on le retrouve chez d'autres intellectuels, notamment chez Mersenne qui, en 1623, dans ses *Quaestiones celeberrimae in Genesim*, compte cette légende parmi les «mirabiles antipathiae», et l'élargit aussi à d'autres faits, telle que la lyre qui tendue de nerfs de vipères terrorise les femmes[27].

---

[25] «La solitude de M. Descartes, pendant cet hiver [1619–1620] était toujours étoit toujours fort entière, principalement à l'égard des personnes qui n'étoient point capables de fournir à ses entretiens. Mais elle ne donnoit point l'exclusion de sa chambre aux curieux, qui sçavoient parler de sciences, ou de nouvelles de littérature. Ce fut dans les conversations de ces derniers qu'il entendit parler d'une Confrérie de Sçavans, établie en Allemagne depuis quelques tems sous le nom de *Frères de la Rose-Croix*. (…) On luy fit entendre que c'étoient des gens qui sçavoient tout, & qu'ils promettoient aux hommes une nouvelle sagesse, c'est-à-dire, la véritable science qui n'avoit pas encore été découverte. M. Descartes (…) se sentit ébranlé. Luy qui faisoit profession de mépriser généralement tous les Sçavants, parce qu'il n'en avoit jamais connu qui fussent véritablement tels, il commença à s'accuser de précipitation & de témérité dans ses jugemens. (…) Il ne crut pas devoir emeurer dans l'indifférence à leur sujet (…) Il ne luy fut pas possible de découvrir un seul homme qui se déclarât de cette Confrérie» (Baillet, *Vie de Monsiseur Des-Cartes*, l. II, c. II, 87–88).
[26] «X. Novembris 1619, cum plenus forem Enthousiasmo, & mirabilis scientiæ fundamenta reperirem &c. (…). XI Novembris 1620, cœpi intelligere fundamentum Inventi mirabilis» (Descartes, *Olympica*, A.T., IX, 179). Comme le souligne Alquié, «certains textes de Descartes sont encore pénétrés d'une sorte d'enthousiasme naturaliste et magique» (Alquié, *Science et métaphysique chez Descartes*, 5).
[27] «*Mirabiles antipathiae*. Potest etiam confirmari ex aliis rebus, quae quamtumuis esse mortuae videantur, passiones tamen & affectus proprios peculiaresque sentientis naturae inter se exercent: sic enim dum tympanum pulsas ex lupinâ pelle confectum, frangitur tympanum ex ovina pelle confectum, aut ex pelle alterius pecudis, maxime si vim au terrorem à lupo pertulit, quia passio consueta, veluti sopita excitatur, ob quam pellis contrahitur & patitur (…). Hinc vero aiunt quendam Bohemiæ regem præcepisse, ut ex eius pelle tympanum fieret, quo deterrerentur hostes, qui eum viventem timere consueuerant. Creditur etiam tympana lupina, equos & ex pelle dragonis, elephantes posse fugare: sicut sonitus lyræ ex vulpis intestinis confectae gallinas fugat; & nervi viperæ mulieribus terrorem immittunt, & contrariorum animalium chordæ in

Mais en 1636, dans *l'Harmonie universelle*, il affirme l'ineptie de cette légende, toutefois dans un raisonnement assez absurde de notre point de vue et qui laisse encore finalement toute la place à une pensée magique :

> Or il est à propos d'advertir le Lecteur de la Fable de la peau de Loup, que plusieurs croyent avoir la vertu d'assourdir la peau de mouton, ou de brebis, lorsqu'on les bat sur une quaisse en mesme temps, car on ne fait iamais les peaux du Tambour de la peau de loup, qui est tout à fait inepte, & inutile pour ce sujet, comme les Facteurs & les plus experts tesmoignent, qui maintiennent qu'il n'est pas possible d'accomoder cette espece de peau, comme il faut, sur les tambours : de sort que l'on peut asseurer que les Autheurs qui prennent cette fable pour une histoire véritable, ne se soucient gueres de la vérité[28].

Certes, il y a réfutation de cette fable chez Mersenne. Néanmoins, ce n'est pas le principe même de sympathie qu'il met en cause mais la validité de l'expérience : elle est matériellement impossible à réaliser. La fable – et ce qu'elle évoque comme arrière-fond épistémologique – n'est pas en elle-même chose étonnante, ce sont les conditions matérielles de sa mise en œuvre qui le sont. C'est une constante que l'on retrouve dans la pensée du père minime : peu importe les fondements «métaphysiques» d'un phénomène, l'expérience «physique» doit être réalisée correctement, le protocole d'expérience doit être respecté[29].

LA VIBRATION PAR SYMPATHIE : DE L'ANALOGIE À LA DÉMONSTRATION

La réfutation mersennienne de l'existence d'une antipathie naturelle entre certains tambours paraît ne pas se focaliser sur l'essentiel. Par contre, lorsqu'il aborde son corrélat, – à savoir la résonance spontanée de certaines cordes quand d'autres, accordées à l'unisson, l'octave ou à la quinte, sont mises en vibration –, le père minime tient vers 1636

---

duobus instrumentis pulsatæ obstrepunt, atque rumpuntur» (Mersenne, *Quaestiones celeberrimae in Genesim*, 1438).

[28] Mersenne, *Harmonie Universelle, Livre Septième des instruments de percussion*, 55.

[29] Notons que Furetière, dans son *Dictionnaire* de 1690, avance, pour dénigrer cette fable, la même justification fondée sur la non-pertinence d'une telle expérience : «Quand on dit que la peau du loup sur un tambour assourdit, ou fait crever la peau de mouton, c'est une fable, car on n'en a jamais fait de peaux de loup. On n'en fait point non plus de peaux d'asne, quoy que le peuple le croye» (Furetière, *Dictionnaire...*, tome troisième, 639).

un raisonnement scientifiquement correct qui est le fruit d'un cheminement intellectuel, marqué à nouveau par le souci d'une validation
méthodologique de l'expérimentation.

Comme la terminologie le prouve encore actuellement, ce problème
est, à l'époque, lié à la sympathie entre les êtres et les choses[30]. En 1634,
Mersenne en parle lorsqu'il évoque un autre phénomène observé : une
tête de brochet est mise à rôtir, et lorsqu'elle frémit dans la poêle, les
tranches de brochet qui sont restées sur le plan de travail, se mettent
à frétiller d'elles-mêmes, ce qui ne peut arriver, précise-t-il « que si les
esprits de la teste n'ont fait quelque impression sur ceux des autres
morceaux, comme fait la chorde d'un luth, laquelle estant touchée fait
trembler celles d'un autre luth qui sont à l'unisson, à l'octave, ou à la
douziesme »[31].

---

[30] Les deux problèmes – celui de l'antipathie entre deux tambours et de la vibration
par sympathie – sont également intimement reliés dans la plupart des traités théoriques du 16e qui les évoquent et ils sont insérés dans un même univers : celui des
« mirabiles naturae ». Dans le cas pris en exemple, les deux questions se suivent : « Cur
motâ chordâ vnius instrumenti, vnisona chorda alterius et non alia simul moueatur ?
Quia est sympathia idemque fundamentum vtriusque. Nam vt inter amicos est talis
affectio vt alter alterius malis dolere, gaudere bonis videatur : ita inter chordas vnisonas
est mira consensio, quae aequabiliter moto aere vnanimiter quasi vtramque mouet, et
in vtraque eundem sonum et concentum facit. Mirabilis enim est vis similitudinis in
omnibus ; nam homo hominem ; medicina humorem, adamas ferrum, chorda vnius
instrumenti chordam alterius, omne simile sibi finitimum et cognatum, abditâ proprietate similitudinis mouet.
Quae causae quòd chordae ex lupi et agni neruis factae harmonicè non concor-
dent ? Necesse est (vt ait Agrippa) omnes concentus ex conuenientibus fundamentis
procedere, si in vnum velis conuenire. Hinc illud rugientes leones, mugientes boues,
grunnientes porci chorum non faciunt ; eadem est ratio chordarum quae ex agni et
lupi fibris aut neruis fiunt. Consonantiam non habent, quippe res ex quibus fingun-
tur insitum odium habuerunt. Aquila columbam, lupus agnum dum viuunt oderunt,
cum moriuntur, illorum plumae simul cohabitare, horum nerui vnà consonare non
possunt ; ista antipathia et dissidium naturae inter homicidam et occisum, inter hir-
cinum sanguinem et adamantem, inter brassicam et virim, inter securim et vrticam
marinam, aliaque innumera naturae opera et effecta cernitur » (Case, *Apologia musices
tam vocalis quam instrumentalis et mixtae*, 70–71).
[31] « Je rapporteray seulement icy une experience qui peut confirmer leur sympathie,
si elle est veritable come on me l'a asseuré. Un grand brochet ayant esté couppé en
cinq ou six tranches, l'on en fricassa premieremnt la teste dans de l'huile, quatre ou
cinq heures apres que l'on l'eut couppé, et si tost quela teste s'eschauffa, et qu'elle
commença à se mouvoir et à sauteur dans la poëlle, les autres morceaux qui estoient
sur une table assez esloignée, se remuërent en mesme temps : ce qui n'a, ce semble,
peu arriver si les esprits de la teste n'ont fait quelque impression sur ceux des autres
morceaux, commme fait la chorde d'un luth, laquelle estant touchée fait trembler celles d'un autre luth qui sont à l'unisson, à l'octave, ou à la douziesme. Mais il faudroit
repeter ceste experience tant sur de grands que sur de petits brochets, en eloignant les
tranches, jusques à ce que l'on trouvast la plus grande distance, d'où elles se meuvent,

La vibration par sympathie d'une corde est donc placée d'emblée dans le contexte plus large des actions à distance des choses les unes sur les autres. Mais, selon Mersenne, ce phénomène de sympathie, qu'il soit piscicole ou musical, pose un problème: celui de l'expérimentation. Il faut faire et refaire cette expérience pour en comprendre les causes et les effets: pour comprendre comment ça marche, à quelle distance exacte les tranches de poisson se mettent à prendre vie, il faut reproduire l'expérience avec des brochets de taille différente, mais aussi avec une carpe, une tanche, etc. Et dans ce cas précis, ce n'est pas le phénomène de sympathie en soi qui irrite le père Mersenne, mais le fait qu'on n'ait pas mené correctement l'expérimentation. Car «il ne faut pas croire qu'une experience soit veritable, si l'on ne remarque plusieurs fois un semblable effect» et il faut que «ceux qui font des experiences y apportent la diligence qui est necessaire pour establir quelque chose de certain»[32]. C'est le même souci d'établir les raisons de la vérité à partir d'expériences menées avec exactitude, qui avait conduit Mersenne à réfuter la légende des tambours dissonants.

Au-delà de la simple anecdote, cette expérience «du brochet» montre bien dans quel contexte mental la première modernité situe le problème de la résonance spontanée des cordes. C'est un fait acoustique qui préoccupe de nombreux musiciens, savants et curieux, et qui va être l'occasion, pour Mersenne et certains de ses contemporains, d'affiner leurs outils expérimentaux, de basculer définitivement dans un autre univers conceptuel et d'entraîner par là l'art des sons vers la science acoustique.

Prenons le cas, par exemple, de Peiresc, intellectuel provençal et collectionneur, qui n'a de cesse d'informer Mersenne sur les coutumes musicales locales et orientales[33]. Cet érudit s'interroge sur la vibration

---

et observer si la mesme chose arrive aux carpes, aux tanches, et aux autres poissons, qui ont coustume de se mouvoir longtemps apres qu'ils sont couppez: et puis il faudroit esprouver si un autre morceau de brochet fait remuër la teste, ou les autres parties tant du mesme brochet que d'un autre. Car il ne faut pas croire qu'une experience soit veritable, si l'on ne remarque plusieurs fois un semblable effect, puisque le mesme phenomene peut arriver de plusieurs accidens (…). Ce que j'ay voulu remarquer afin que ceux qui font des experiences y apportent la diligence qui est necessaire pour establir quelque chose de certain» (Mersenne, *Questions inouyes ou Recréation des savants*, Question 33, 90).

[32] *Idem.*

[33] Sur l'amitié entre Peiresc et Mersenne, voir Beaulieu, *Mersenne, le grand minime*, 55–70; sur l'apport de Peiresc à Mersenne, voir Van Wymeersch, «Peiresc et la musique», 111–134.

spontanée de certaines cordes lorsque d'autres sont touchées. Il écrit ainsi à Mersenne :

> Et pour l'eccho, dont vous promettez l'artifice, je voudrois bien sçavoir ce pendant, si vous avez faict quelque experience et si vous y traittez de l'eccho du luth ou de la guiterre, que nous avons veu et ouy respondre ces jours passés, lorsqu'on en trouvoit quelque son convenable à quelq'une des cordes de l'instrument, auquel cas les cordes de mesme son faisoient paroistre leur mouvement conjointement avec la responce de l'eccho de l'instrument. Et quand on prononçoit un aultre ton accordé avec des aultres cordes du mesme instruments, les autres cordes se mouvoient aussy visiblement et l'eccho ne manquoit pas de respondre, mais quant on prononçoit un aultre ton auquel ne s'accordoit aulcune des cordes de l'instrument, toutes les cordes y demeuroient immmobiles, mais qui plus est, l'instrument, ou l'eccho, estoit sourd, et ne respondoit point du tout. Ce fut Mr le prothenotaire Aguillenquy, mon cousin, (…) qui nous fit voir ceste experiene l'autre jour à Mr Gassend et à moy, qui en demeurasmes ravys[34].

C'est donc une expérience qui « ravys » bien des gens, et de grands esprits, tels que Peiresc et Gassendi. Ceux-là n'iront pas au-delà du ravissement face à ce qu'ils considèrent encore, comme les naturalistes de la Renaissance, des *Mirabiles naturæ*.

Il n'en est pas de même pour Descartes qui avait entrevu le problème dès 1618. Il en avait discuté longuement avec Isaac Beeckman. Dans son *Journal*, ce dernier relate plusieurs expériences et observations que les deux hommes font sur la vibration spontanée des cordes, à l'unisson, l'octave ou la quinte. A contrario, constatent-ils, une corde tendue à l'intervalle de quarte n'entre jamais en vibration spontanément lorsque la corde de base vibre[35]. Mais ils en restent à une simple phase d'observation. Le phénomène reste inexplicable et n'est pas relié à d'autres faits acoustiques[36].

---

[34] *Lettre de Peiresc à Mersenne du 18 juin 1634*, C.M. IV, 177.

[35] « Observavit Renatus Picto cordas testudinis inferiores, id est bassiores, pulsas, movere evidenter ipsis consonantes acutiores ; acutioribus vero pulsis, graviores non ita evidenter moveri (…). Renatus Descartes Picto expertus est, in chordis testudinis quartâ ab invicem differentibus, unâ tactâ, aliam non tremere ; quintâ vero distantibus, unâ tactâ, aliam visibiliter & tactibiliter tremere. Quod & ipse vidi » (Beeckman, *Journal*, fol. 100ʳ–101ᵛ, 244–245).

[36] La résonance spontanée des cordes est évidemment un problème lié aux son harmoniques, mais ce lien, ni Beeckman, ni Descartes ne semblent l'apercevoir. Ils constatent l'existence de sons partiels, mais n'associent pas, en 1618, la solution acoustique de ce problème à celui des cordes sympathiques. (Bailhache, « Cordes vibrantes

Et pourtant, dès 1618, Descartes en fait la base de sa reconstruction logique et autonome du système musical. Et c'est ce qui constitue, en partie, l'originalité de *l'abrégé de musique*. Le principe du monocorde – «le son est au son comme la corde est à la corde» –, principe analogique en soi, est désormais étayé par une expérience que chacun peut refaire : c'est parce que le son le plus grave met en vibration d'autres sons plus aigus qu'il peut affirmer que «le plus grave est de beaucoup le plus puissant et contient l'autre en quelque façon»[37]. Il a atteint là une certitude acquise par une preuve d'expérience, certitude qui lui permet de transformer en axiome ce qui, auparavant, ressortissait du domaine de la simple comparaison. Ce fait acoustique est, chez le philosophe, complètement séparé de l'arrière-fond magique ou occulte que l'on trouve chez Mersenne, et pourtant, c'est dans le même traité que Descartes rapporte le phénomène étrange de l'antipathie des tambours mal accordés[38].

L'étape suivante sera de justifier, *more geometrico*, à la façon des géomètres, ce fait acoustique. Et sur ce point, la correspondance échangée avec Mersenne dans les années 1630–1631 a toute son importance, puisque c'est au fil de ces lettres que s'élaborent à la fois une pensée acoustique cohérente chez Mersenne et son cercle intellectuel, mais aussi une évolution dans le domaine esthétique qui permettre la nouvelle justification de la hiérarchie des consonances.

Si Descartes s'oriente rapidement et de façon claire hors du champ des sciences occultes, l'évolution de Mersenne est différente. Dans les

---

et consonances chez Beeckman, Mersenne et Galilée», 73–91 ; De Buzon, «Descartes, Beeckman et l'acoustique», 699–706).

[37] «De deux termes qu'on suppose être en consonance le plus grave est de beaucoup le plus puissant et contient l'autre en quelque façon. On le voit sur les cordes d'un luth : si l'une d'elles est touchée, celles qui sont plus aigües d'une octave ou d'une quinte tremblent et résonnent spontanément ; les cordes graves n'en font pas autant, du moins en apparence. La raison de ce fait se démontre ainsi : le son est au son comme la corde à la corde ; or, en chaque corde sont contenues toutes les cordes moindres qu'elle, mais non les plus longues. Donc sont contenus aussi en chaque son tous les sons plus aigus, mais non pas les plus graves dans l'aigu. Il suit de là que le terme aigu doit être trouvé par la division du grave» (Descartes, *Compendium Musicæ*, 64–66).

[38] Notons que c'est aussi à partir de cette expérience de 1618 qu'il peut affirmer la supériorité de la tierce sur la quarte : «Car j'ai reconnu par expérience sur les cordes d'un luth ou de n'importe quel autre instrument que ce soit que si l'on en touche une, la force du son ébranlera toutes les cordes qui sont plus aigües de quelque genre de quinte ou de diton, mais cela ne se produit pas avec celles qui sont distantes d'une quarte ou d'une autre consonance» (Descartes, *Compendium Musicæ*, 76).

années 1627, il reste fortement imprégné d'une conception holistique de la musique, notamment pour justifier des qualités des consonances. Par exemple, il détaille minutieusement les correspondances des intervalles avec les goûts, les odeurs et les couleurs. Dans le second livre du *Traité de l'harmonie universelle*, il veut prouver que «les sons, et les consonances sont semblables aux saveurs, aux odeurs et autres objets des sens»[39] et justifie de l'excellence des consonances ou des règles d'écriture par des associations et par des relations entre les sons et les éléments naturels. Ainsi, la quinte est associée à la graisse – c'est la plus agréable des consonances après l'octave –; la quarte est associée au salé: la saveur salée est désagréable quand elle est jointe à une saveur douce, tout comme la quarte jointe à l'octave créée une dissonance. Par contre, la quarte s'associe parfaitement à la quinte, comme le sel avec la graisse. Mersenne démontre ainsi de façon culinaire la pertinence d'un certain nombre de règles d'écriture et d'associations d'intervalles[40].

Il compare également les intervalles aux formes géométriques, ce qui lui posera problème plus tard quand il s'opposera à Kepler. Ce dernier, en effet, fonde la hiérarchie des consonances sur base de la perfection des figures planes régulières. Pour l'astronome, sa méthode pour agencer le système musical est plus conforme à l'esprit pythagoricien qu'il veut retrouver: toutes les consonances sont calculées non plus sur base de la division d'une corde tendue sur un chevalet, mais sur base de la division d'un cercle parfait, image d'une corde repliée sur elle-même. Seuls les intervalles issus de polygones «commensurables», c'est-à-dire que l'on peut inscrire dans un cercle à l'aide de la règle et du compas, sont consonants[41]. Il est impossible de construire dans un cercle un heptagone dont les côtés soient commensurables avec le rayon, tous rapports numériques dérivant du nombre 7 sont

---

[39] Mersenne, *Traité de l'harmonie universelle*, livre second, 309–312.

[40] Notons que Cardan utilise le même type d'analogies lorsqu'il évoque les intervalles musicaux. Mersenne ne cache pas sa source d'inspiration: «ainsi que Cardan a remarqué. (…) Cardan ajoute que les saveurs dépendent des planettes (…). Cardan dit qu'il n'y a que sept couleurs et sept saveurs agreables, qui répondent aux sept intervalles des consonances» (Mersenne, *Traité de l'harmonie universelle*, livre second, 310–312).

[41] Ainsi, le triangle peut diviser la corde en une partie par rapport à deux parties, mais on peut aussi comparer la partie, ou le résidu au tout : c'est-à-dire 1 à 3 et 2 à 3. Le triangle correspond donc à la quinte et à la douzième. (Kepler, *Harmonices Mundi Libri V*, 1619).

dès lors des nombres sonores dissonants, ce qui est conforme à la tradition musicale.

Si, en 1627, Mersenne rapproche les intervalles des figures, son évolution ultérieure et sa critique très précise de Kepler l'amènent à minimiser, en 1634, la façon dont il a envisagé les « rapports qu'ont les sons, les consonances et les autres intervalles (…) avec les figures, les corps Geometriques »[42]. Il veut alors marquer sa différence avec l'astronome : établir des liens entre sons et formes ne peut être qu'un jeu sans qu'on en puisse déduire le degré consonantique des intervalles. Les propos de Kepler auraient été tolérables : « s'il se fust contenté de comparer lesdites figures aux Consonances & aux dissonances par analogie, et par récréation, comme font ceux qui les comparent (…) à plusieurs choses qui se rencontrent dans la nature, comme j'ay fait dans le second livre de l'harmonie universelle »[43].

En 1627, le père Mersenne est clairement marqué par une épistémologie de l'analogie, mais dès 1634, il tend à infléchir le discours qu'il tenait alors. En moins de dix ans, on note un changement réel dans son attitude. Et la publication de *l'harmonie universelle* manifeste l'aboutissement d'un cheminement intellectuel avec pour résultat une démarche scientifique cohérente.

Aussi, dans les années 36–40, peut-il passer d'une explication « métaphysique » à une explication « physique », et cela concerne de nombreuses questions musicales. Cette position ne l'empêche pas de partir dans de nombreuses digressions qui tentent à unifier harmonieusement, via la musique, toutes les composantes de l'univers, mais fondamentalement, il affirme clairement que le principe de « sympathie universelle » n'est valable que si on n'a rien trouvé de mieux. Ainsi répondra-t-il à Peiresc à propos de l'expérience évoquée plus haut :

Je seray bien ayse de voir Mr vostre cousin pour ce qui de l'echo du luth, car je n'en ay seulement pas fait plusieurs fois l'expérience, mais je veux en donner la vraye raison dans le 3ᵉ ou 4ᵉ livre [de l'harmonie universelle]

---

[42] Mersenne, *Traité de l'harmonie universelle*, livre second, 301.

[43] « C'est pourquoy ie m'estonne comme Kepler a osé apporter la comparaison des figures avec les Consonances, pour en tirer la raison de leur nombre & de leur bonté : ce qui seroit tolérable s'il se fust contenté de comparer lesdites figures aux Consonances & aux Dissonances par analogie, et par recreation, comme font ceux qui les comparent aux costez, ou aux angles de l'Hexagone, & de l'Octogone, & à plusieurs choses qui se rencontrent dans la nature, comme j'ay fait dans le second livre de l'harmonie universelle » (Mersenne, *Harmonie Universelle, premier livre des consonances*, 86).

sans recourir à la sympathie qui n'est qu'une pure fuite des difficultez. Je luy en diray bien d'autres que personne ou peu ont apperceue[44].

La notion de sympathie est donc devenue, en quelques années pour Mersenne une fuite devant la difficulté. Et l'on trouve dans les livres sur la consonance et sur les instruments à cordes les explications promises à Peiresc. Il y explique «pourquoy les chordes qui sont à l'octave se font trembler et sonner; combien celles qui sont à l'unisson se font trembler plus fort que celles qui sont à l'Octave; combien celles qui sont touchée tremblent plus fort que celles qui ne sont pas touchées (...)»[45]; pourquoi «la chorde estant touchée fait trembler celle qui est à la quinte, mais elle fait trembler plus fort celle qui est à la Douzieme»[46].

Ces «propositions» et leurs «corollaires», il les doit, notamment, aux discussions épistolaires qu'il a eues avec Descartes depuis 1630–1631. C'est à cette époque qu'il interroge à plusieurs reprises le philosophe à la fois sur des questions esthétiques précises[47], mais aussi sur des problèmes acoustiques, comme celui de la vibration des cordes. Ces discussions alimenteront l'harmonie universelle, mais seront reprises également dans le Traité de l'homme de Descartes où l'on constate qu'il définit le son, non plus sur base de la division du monocorde, comme en 1618, mais sur base de la fréquence relative des sons, qu'il a constatée, notamment dans ses expériences menées sur les cordes vibrantes et la résonance spontanée. Outre que ces expériences présentent une avancée remarquable dans le domaine acoustique, elles permettent également à Descartes de justifier la primauté de la tierce sur la quarte et la cohérence de l'accord parfait majeur[48]. Si le discours

---

[44] Lettre de Mersenne à Peiresc du 2 juillet 1634, C.M. IV, 226; il dira semblablement dans son Harmonie Universelle: «c'est une mesme chose de respondre que les chordes qui sont à l'Unisson se font trembler à raison de la sympathie qu'elles ont ensemble, que de respondre que l'on n'en sçait pas la cause» (Mersenne, Harmonie Universelle, Livre premier des Consonances, Prop. VI, 26).

[45] Mersenne, Harmonie Universelle, Livre premier des Consonances, Prop. XIII, 52–58.

[46] Mersenne, Ibid., Prop. XXI, 67.

[47] Ces questions esthétiques concernent notamment le jugement sur le beau et l'évaluation sensible des intervalles (Descartes, Lettre à Mersenne de janvier 1630, A.T., I, 108 sq.; Lettre à Mersenne du 4 mars 1630, A.T., I, 126 sq; Lettre à Mersenne d'octobre 1631, A.T., I, 223 sq).

[48] Descartes, Traité de l'homme, A.T., XI, 150–151; Lettre à Mersenne d'octobre 1631, A.T., I, 225; Van Wymeersch, Descartes et l'évolution de l'esthétique musicale, 123–133.

cartésien est assez clair à ce sujet, les propos de Mersenne sont plus diffus et se veulent plus larges : sur de nombreux points, les questions «métaphysiques» le taraudent encore, mais il passe néanmoins progressivement d'une vision ésotérique du phénomène de résonance, d'écho, de vibration, à une conception physico-mathématique, mettant par là à mal l'appréhension d'un Kepler ou d'un Fludd, par exemple. Pour Peiresc, un des dédicataires de *l'Harmonie Universelle*, Mersenne est un de ces personnages fascinants qui a pu, selon les termes mêmes de l'intellectuel provençal «penetrer dans les secrets de la nature»[49].

Le phénomène de la résonance spontanée, de la vibration par sympathie est donc assez remarquable lorsqu'on veut examiner l'art et la science des sons face aux pouvoirs occultes.

Outre le fait que la terminologie même a été conservée au delà du contexte intellectuel qui l'a forgée, elle illustre la mutation de pensée qui s'opère dans les premières années du 17e, et de façon plus spécifique toutes les étapes de la mise en place d'une «science» de la musique au sens moderne du terme.

C'est d'abord une expérience qui «ravys», ceux qui la font et refont. Puis, des constantes s'en dégagent : telle ou telle corde vibrent spontanément, d'autres pas, et cela concorde avec l'utilisation préférentielle de tel ou tel intervalle dans la pratique musicale. C'est la première phase d'explication cartésienne qui se base dès lors sur ce phénomène pour justifier de la prééminence de tierce sur la quarte, d'un point de vue esthétique, et compositionnel.

L'étape suivante est une tentative d'expliquer ce phénomène physique, et c'est lorsqu'on est réellement dans le détail d'une explication acoustique qu'on peut alors affirmer avec Mersenne que la démonstration vaut mieux que la comparaison et que si «les hommes ont introduit la sympathie et l'antipathie, & les qualitez occultes dans les arts & dans les sciences», c'est «pour en couvrir les deffauts, & pour excuser leur ignorance, ou plustost pour confesser ingenuëment qu'il ne sçavent rien»[50]. C'est notamment l'explication rationnelle de ce fait acoustique précis qui permet à Mersenne de mettre en évidence le

---

[49] «Ne pouvant vous remercier, comme je faictz tres affectueusement de la participation qu'il vous a pleu nous en octroyer, et de la bonne volonté en mon endroict dont vous accompagnez voz faveurs, bien marry de n'avoir les notices qu'il faudroit pour pouvoir contribuer quelque chose à voz labeurs qui fust digne de voz recherches, ou pour en pouvoir juger sainement et penetrer dans les secrets de la nature que vous y descouvrez» (*Lettre de Peiresc à Mersenne du 18 juin 1634*, C.M. IV, 175–176).

[50] Mersenne, *Harmonie Universelle, Livre premier des Consonances*, Proposition VI, 26.

leurre que sont les notions occultes de sympathie et d'antipathie, propres aux naturalistes[51].

La compréhension de ce phénomène acoustique est donc révélateur d'un basculement de pensée. Mais c'est aussi un fait observé, un objet d'expérimentation, qui a permis, par son côté concret, expérimentable et audible par tous, à la fois de contrer une mentalité ésotérique, de faire progresser la science acoustique et de donner à l'art de la musique un envol vers une autre esthétique… et plus jamais, dès lors, dans les cercles intellectuels et musicaux sérieux du 17e siècle, on ne parlera de tambour qui se tait ou de brochet qui frétille.

BIBLIOGRAPHIE

Alciat, A., *Los Emblemas*, Lyon: 1549.

——, *Emblemata*, Lyon: 1550.

Alciato, A., *Les emblèmes*, Geneva/Cologny: 1615.

Alquié, F., *Science et métaphysique chez Descartes*, Paris: 1955.

Bailhache, P., «Cordes vibrantes et consonances chez Beeckman, Mersenne et Galilée», *Sciences et techniques en perspective*, 23 (1993), 73–91.

Baillet, A., *Vie de Monsieur Des-Cartes*, Paris: 1691.

Beaulieu, A., *Mersenne, le grand minime*, Bruxelles: 1995.

Beeckman, I., *Journal*, Cornélis de Waard (ed.), La Haye: 1939–1953.

Barthelemi l'Anglais, *De rerum proprietatibus*, Frankfurt: 1601.

Case, J., *Apologia musices tam vocalis quam instrumentalis et mixtae*, Oxford: 1588.

Corneille-Agrippa, H., *La philosophie occulte ou la Magie*, trad. K. F. Gaboriau, Paris: 1910.

De Buzon, F., «Descartes, Beeckman et l'acoustique», *Archives de Philosophie*, 44/4 (1981), 699–706.

Della Porta, G., *Io. Bapt. Portae Magiae naturalis libri XX*, Neapoli: 1589.

Descartes, R., *Compendium Musicæ*, trad. Fr. de Buzon, Paris: 1987.

——, *Discours de la méthode*, in: Adam et Tannery (ed.), *Œuvres de Descartes*, Vol. VI, Paris: 1982–1991.

——, *Œuvres philosophiques*, F. Alquié (ed.), Paris: 1963.

——, *Traité de l'homme*, in: Adam et Tannery (ed.), *Œuvres de Descartes*, Vol. XI, Paris: 1982–1991.

[Evrart de Tremagon], *Le Songe du vergier*, Marion Schnerb-Lievre (ed.), Paris: 1982.

Fétis, F. J., *Biographie universelle des musiciens*, Bruxelles: 1937.

François, J., *Traité des influences célestes ou les merveilles de Dieu dans les cieux sont déduites; les inventions des astronomes pour les entendre sont expliquées; les propositions des astrologues iudiciaires sont démonstrées fausses, et pernitieuses, par toutes sortes de raisons d'autoritez, et d'experiences*, Rennes: 1660.

---

[51] «car lorsque l'on connoist les raisons de ces effets la sympathie s'évanoüit avec l'ignorance, comme ie demonstre dans le tremblement des chodres qui sont à l'Unisson» (Mersenne, *Harmonie Universelle, Livre premier des Consonances*, Proposition VI, 26).

Furetière, A., *Dictionnaire universel, contenant généralement tous les mots françois tant vieux que modernes, et les termes de toutes les sciences et des arts*, La Haye: 1690.

Green, H., *Andrea Alciati and his Book of Emblems. A Biographical and Bibliographical Study*, London: 1872.

Kepler, J., *Harmonices Mundi Libri V*, Linz: 1619.

Littré, E., *Dictionnaire de la langue française*, Paris: 1863–1869.

Mersenne, M., *Correspondance du Père Marin Mersenne*, Cornélis de Waard (ed.), Paris: 1932–1988.

——, *Harmonie Universelle*, Paris: 1636.

——, *Quaestiones celeberrimae in Genesim*, Paris: 1623.

——, *Questions inouyes ou Recréation des savants*, Paris: 1634.

——, *Traité de l'harmonie universelle*, Paris: 1627.

Oresme, N., *Tractatus de configurationibus qualitatum et motuum*, Ms, early 1350s.

Paré, A., *Les Œuvres d'Ambroise Paré...divisées en vingt huict livres avec les figures et portaicts....Second livre des Animaux et de l'excellence de l'homme*, Paris: 1585.

Pirro, A., *Descartes et la musique*, Paris: 1907.

Praetorius, M., *Syntagma musicum*, Kassel: 1958.

Rodis-Lewis, G., «Machineries et perspectives curieuses dans leur rapport avec le cartésianisme», *Dix-septième siècle* (1956), 456–470.

Trichet, P., *Traité des instruments de musique*, in Fr. Lesure (ed.), *Annales de Musicologie*, (1956), 240–241.

Van Wymeersch, B., *Descartes et l'évolution de l'esthétique musicale*, Liège: 1999.

——, «Peiresc et la musique», in *Sciences et techniques en perspective*, 9/1 (2005), 111–134.

MUSICAL THEORY AND ASTROLOGICAL FOUNDATIONS IN KEPLER: THE MAKING OF THE NEW ASPECTS[1]

David Juste

A baffling problem in the history of astrology is that virtually nothing is known about the origins of its doctrines. Historians are faced with a system of interpretation of the horoscope which was already fully constructed by the second or the first century BC, and which remained fundamentaly unchanged until today. Yet neither ancient historical accounts nor the earliest extant astrological texts inform us in a satisfactory manner about how, when and in what circumstances certain characteristics came to be attributed to the planets, to the twelve signs of the zodiac, to the twelve houses and to the aspects, to name just the four major components of the horoscope. Of course, numerous attempts – ancient and modern – have been made to rationalise astrological doctrines. One such attempt is found in Ptolemy's *Tetrabiblos* (c. 150 AD), the most influential astrological treatise ever written. There, the nature and characteristics of the planets, for instance, are explained by a combination of the four essential qualities (hot, cold, dry, wet) attributed to them according to their respective distance from the Sun, so that Jupiter and Venus are beneficent 'because they abound in the hot and the moist', whereas Saturn and Mars are maleficent on account of their excessive cold and dryness respectively.[2] While Ptolemy's "physical" explanations were enthusiastically accepted by later Greek, Arabic and Latin astrologers, it is important to bear in mind that they are no more than *a posteriori* justifications for pre-existing doctrines and by no means accounts of how these doctrines actually came into being. It is safe, at least at present, to acknowledge our ignorance regarding the genesis of astrological doctrines.

The situation is different with Johannes Kepler (1571–1630). Kepler is chiefly remembered today as the founder of modern astronomy and as one of the foremost actors of the scientific revolution, but he was

---

[1] My special thanks to Darrel Rutkin for his comments on an earlier version of this article and to Hilbert Chiu for revising my English.
[2] *Tetrabiblos*, I.4–5 (ed. and transl. Robbins, 34–39). See also Riley 1988.

also – and not less – both a professional astrologer and a theoretician of astrology. With regard to the history of astrology, he is important because he invented the "new aspects" (also referred to as "minor" or "secondary aspects"), which have ever since been integrated into the astrological system. The theory of aspects was a central concern of Kepler's scientific enquiry, not only because of its practical applications to predictions, but also because it was not dissociable from his cosmology. As a result, it features in most of his scientific works, which allows us to reconstruct in detail the genesis and developments of the new aspects. The new aspects therefore become the only astrological doctrine whose origin is know with precision and certainty.

Throughout his life, Kepler produced a considerable amount of astrological texts and documents. As a district mathematician in Graz (1594–1600), as a court mathematician to Rudolf II in Prague (1601–1612) and, again, as a district mathematician in Linz (1612–1630), it was his duty to cast annual prognostications and to give personal consultations to his patrons. Kepler left over 1,000 horoscopes annotated in his hand – and these include horoscopes not only for his clients but also for his friends, members of his family and himself.[3] In his letters, he regularly addresses astrological issues and interprets configurations found in his own nativity or that of his correspondent. He also wrote three treatises devoted largely or entirely to astrology: *De fundamentis astrologiae certioribus* (1601), *De stella nova* (1606), and *Tertius interveniens* (1610, in German). Last but not least, astrology was – together with geometry and music – part and parcel of his conception of the universe, which he articulated in his two great cosmological works, the *Mysterium cosmographicum* (1596, reprinted with annotations in 1621) and *Harmonices mundi* (1619).[4]

Kepler was however not a traditional astrologer. He is indeed famous for his attempt to reform astrology, perhaps the most radical reform ever undertaken by a practitioner. In his view, most astrological doctrines have no value whatsoever, a position he summarises nicely in a letter to Thomas Harriot on 2 October 1606:

---

[3] Kepler's horoscopes have just been published in *KGW*, XXI.2b.
[4] The most important studies on Kepler's astrology are Simon 1979 and Field 1984 (a shorter version of which is Field 1987). More specific issues are dealt with by Rosen 1984, Krafft 1992, Negus 1997, Rabin 1997, Rutkin 2001, Westman 2001, and Boner 2005. On Kepler's cosmology, see Field 1988 and Stephenson 1994.

> For the past ten years, I have rejected the division into twelve equal
> signs, the houses, rulerships, triplicities, etc., all those things, retaining
> only the aspects and transferring astrology to the harmonic doctrine.[5]

Kepler then refers Harriot to his recently published *De stella nova*,
a treatise devoted to the significance of the 'new star' (supernova) of
October 1604 and whose opening chapters consist of a critical assess-
ment of astrological doctrines. There, as in all his works dealing with
astrology, Kepler's line of argument is straightforward: astrology should
be purged from all doctrines which have no natural causes. The favourite target of his criticism are the signs of the zodiac, whose divisions,
classifications, qualities and attributes are purely human conventions,
therefore arbitrary and devoid of natural significance.[6]

Only the theory of aspects escapes his criticism. But what is an
aspect? In the astrological tradition, the influence of a planet is modified according to the angle of longitude formed with other planets.
Five angles, or "aspects", are significant: the conjunction (when two
planets are 0° apart, i.e. when their longitude is identical), the sextile
(60°), the quadrate (90°), the trine (120°) and the opposition (180°).
The sextile and the trine are considered beneficent aspects (i.e. the
involved planets are friends and mix their qualities harmoniously) and
the quadrate and the opposition maleficent (i.e. the involved planets
are enemies), while the nature of the conjunction, which is not always
considered an aspect *stricto sensu*, varies according to the character
of the involved planets. Three stages can be distinguished in Kepler's
treatment of the aspects.[7]

Aspects and Musical Consonances

Kepler's first discussion on the aspects takes place in the *Mysterium
cosmographicum* (1596), in Chapter XII entitled *Division of the Zodiac*

---

[5] 'Ego iam a decennio divisionem in 12 aequalia, domus, dominationes, triplicitates
etc. omnia rejicio, retentis solis aspectibus et traducta astrologia ad doctrinam har-
monicam' (*KGW*, XV, 349–350).

[6] *De stella nova*, II–XI (*KGW*, I, 165–208), and especially III–VI (pp. 167–180) on
the signs. Of course, this kind of argumentation was not new. Attempts to reform,
or at least improve, astrological theory and practice were very much in the air in
the sixteenth century, especially after Pico della Mirandola's radical criticism in his
Disputationes adversus astrologiam divinatricem (1494). On astrological reform in the
sixteenth century, see vanden Broecke 2003.

[7] For earlier accounts on Kepler's theory of aspects, see Simon 1979, 44–48 and
169–174; Field 1984, 193–219 (and Field 1987, 147–165).

and Aspects (*Divisio zodiaci et aspectus*). The first part of this chapter discusses the relationships between geometry and music, and in particular between the geometrical divisions of the circle and harmonic intervals. In the second part, Kepler comes to astrology and points out that there is a perfect coincidence between the aspects, insofar as they are angles delimiting fractions of the circle (of the zodiac), and ratios of lengths of a vibrating string corresponding to musical consonances:[8]

Aspect	Angle	Fraction	Ratio	Consonance
opposition	180°	1/2	2:1	octave
trine	120°	1/3	3:2	fifth
quadrate	90°	1/4	4:3	fourth
sextile	60°	1/6	6:5	minor third

This idea was not new. In his *Tetrabiblos*, Ptolemy had already made a similar observation, although in passing and in rather vague terms.[9] Kepler acknowledges his debt to Ptolemy, but he goes much further. First, he notes that this relationship between consonances and aspects explains why planets that are separated by one or five signs (i.e. by 30° or 150°) do not aspect one another.[10] Secondly, and most importantly, he points out that three consonances are missing in this scheme: the

---

[8] 'Veniamus modo ad aspectus. Et quandoquidem modo ex fide circulum fecimus, facile est videre quomodo tres prefectae harmoniae pulcherrime cum tribus perfectis aspectibus comparari possint, scilicet cum opposito, trino, quadrato [symbols are given in the text]. Imperfecta vero prior B mollis ad unguem similis est sextili, cuius haec nota [symbol], quemque debilissimum esse ferunt' (*Mysterium cosmographicum*, XII; *KGW*, I, 42).

[9] 'We may learn from the following why only these intervals [Ptolemy just listed the aspects] have been taken into consideration. The explanation of opposition is immediately obvious, because it causes the signs to meet on one straight line. But if we take the two fractions and the two superparticulars most important in music, and if the fractions one-half and one-third be applied to opposition, composed of two right angles, the half makes the quartile and the third the sextile and trine. Of the superparticulars, if the sesquialter [3:2] and sesquitertian [4:3] be applied to the quartile interval of one right angle, which lies between them, the sesquialter makes the ratio of the quartile to the sextile and the sesquitertian that of the trine to quartile' (Ptolemy, *Tetrabiblos*, I.13; ed.-transl. Robbins, 72–75).

[10] 'Habemus causam (qualem quidem Ptolemaeus non dedit) cur planetae distantes uno aut quinque signis non censeantur in aspectu' (*Mysterium cosmographicum*, XII; *KGW*, I, 42).

major third (ratio 5:4), the minor sixth (8:5) and the major sixth (5:3). Transposed onto the circle of the zodiac, these three consonances would correspond to fractions 1/5, 3/8 and 2/5, that is, to angles of 72°, 135° and 144° respectively. This passage is the birth certificate of the new aspects, although Kepler is still reluctant to call them aspects at this stage. He only says that these three angles should perhaps not be neglected in the interpretation of horoscopes, adding immediately that this is a matter which would be easily confirmed by experience through observation of the weather.[11]

Aspect	Angle	Fraction	Ratio	Consonance
?	72°	1/5	5:4	major third
?	135°	3/8	8:5	minor sixth
?	144°	2/5	5:3	major sixth

Kepler's reservation about the significance of these three angles did not last. His correspondence reveals that, by 1599, he had definitively included them into the family of aspects and had already attributed an astrological symbol to each of them. In a letter sent to Herwart von Hohenburg on 30 May 1599, the aspects appear in a diagram showing the circumference of the circle of the zodiac opened up, as it were, so as to make it straight along a vibrating string (Figure 1).[12] In this diagram, the conjunction (0° or 360°, fraction 1/1, ratio 1:1), corresponding to the whole length of the string (unisson), has been added. Soon after, in a letter to Michael Maestlin of August 1599, Kepler explicitly says that the aspects are eight in number (again, including the conjunction) and that repeated observations of the weather since 1594 have confirmed the effectiveness of the three new aspects.[13]

---

[11] 'Cum igitur omnes quatuor harmoniae consonent suis aspectibus, et vero adhuc tres restent in musica harmoniae, suspicatus aliquando sum non negligendum esse in iudiciis nativitatum si planetae 72 aut 144 aut 135 gradibus distent, praesertim cum videam unam ex imperfectis habere suum aspectum. Quamvis cuilibet oculato meteororum speculatori facile patebit utrum aliqua in his tribus radiis vis insit, cum caeteros aspectibus aeris mutationes constantissima ratificent experientia' (*Mysterium cosmographicum*, XII; *KGW*, I, 42).

[12] *KGW*, XIII, 348–350. The diagram is reproduced from the original manuscript in Field 1984, 203; and Field 1987, 150.

[13] 'Sunt aspectus octo [followed by the eight symbols, the last three being those of the new aspects]. Prolixe ab experimentis et τηρήσεσι probandum esset tres ultimos

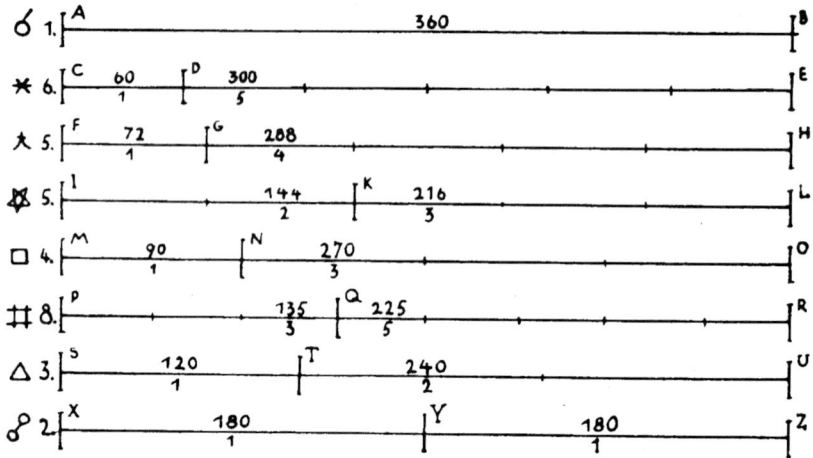

Figure 1. Aspects and musical consonances.
Letter to Herwart von Hohenburg, 30 May 1599 (KGW, XIII, 349)

THE NEW ASPECTS IN ASTROLOGICAL THEORY AND PRACTICE

In 1601, Kepler published his *De fundamentis astrologiae certioribus*, which can be regarded as his major astrological text.[14] Technically it is a prognostication (for the year 1602), that is to say a text predicting meteorological, political and other events of a general nature for the year to come. As said above, it was Kepler's duty as a mathematician to produce such prognostications and he had already done so for the years 1595–1600.[15] The prognostication for the year 1602 was however of a different nature. Here for the first time, Kepler applied his reformed astrology, whose principles are set out in the first part of the work (Theses 1–51). Moreover, the text is in Latin (unlike his

operari in meteoris ciendis. Suppetunt mihi ab annis 5 multa, cum vacuitas fuit ab aspectibus caeteris, et horum novorum aliquis solus incidit. Nam ascripsi Ephemeridibus meis omnes ab anno 94 et contuli cum annotatis tempestatibus. Si qua certitudo est in caeteris, in his quoque novis inest' (letter to Maestlin, August 1599; *KGW*, XIV, 51). Kepler briefly alludes to the aspects in relation to musical consonances in two letters of the same year, to Edmund Bruce on 18 July (*KGW*, XIV, 10) and, again, to Herwart von Hohenburg on 6 August (*KGW*, XIV, 29).

[14] *KGW*, IV, 9–35. English translation in Field 1984, 229–268.

[15] *KGW*, XI.2, 8–55 (prognostications for 1597–1599). His prognostications for 1595–1596 and 1600 are lost and he did not write any for the year 1601. For an overview of Kepler's prognostications, see *KGW*, XI.2, 459–465.

other prognostications, written in German), for he explicitly wanted to address the philosophers and 'those learned in matters of physics', whom he urged to test his new theories and the resulting predictions (see conclusion below).

From the outset, Kepler makes it clear that he will be working with natural causes of celestial influences only and rejecting 'political causes' ('cause politice'), which he regards as inadequate, imaginary, vain, false and worthless (Thesis 3). The most certain natural causes, acknowledged by all and proved by experience, are the heating power of the Sun and the humidifying power of the Moon (Theses 5–18). The Sun and the Moon transmit heat and humidity to the earth through their light (for 'nothing comes down to us from the heavens except the light of the stars', Thesis 19) and, because the nature of the light is twofold, i.e. direct (from the Sun) or reflected (from the Moon), Kepler concludes that the direct light has a heating power and the reflected light a humidifying power.[16] As for the five other planets, they have various heating and humidifying powers on account of their combination of direct and reflected light, which can be inferred from their colour (Theses 19–35).[17]

However, these premises are too general to be applied to specific predictions, at least because the planets send their rays to the earth continuously, so making it impossible to relate a specific event occurring on the earth to the influence of a specific planet. What is needed is a workable structure of interpretation. This structure will be provided by what Kepler describes as another kind of natural cause, much nobler than the physical causes dealt with so far, a cause which 'has no flavour of materiality but is concerned with forms, and not with simple form but with animate faculty, with intellectual understanding, with geometrical thought'.[18] These "nobler" causes, which are the subject of Thesis 36–48, are essentially represented by the aspects:

---

[16] Unlike Ptolemy, Kepler does not regard cold and dry as essential qualities, but only as the absence of heat and humidity (Thesis 19).

[17] For example, he writes about Mars: 'However, when black is brightly illuminated it sheds red light. This effect is seen in steel mirrors, where the white colour of the face and the black of the mirror combine to give a reflected image of a rather red face. Thus one would be entirely justified in stating that Mars possesses a black surface, since its ray is very red. Thus its reflected light is faint, and thus the planet does not humidify greatly, and is defective in humidity' (transl. Field 1984, 245–246; Thesis 28; *KGW*, IV, 18).

[18] Transl. Field 1984, 249 (I however translate "animalis" as "animate" instead of "animal"): 'Sequitur ergo alia causa; quae omnes planetas aequaliter attinet; longe,

Thus, since there are eight ratios which determine the motions, and the
action of the heavens on the earth is (as it were) a kind of motion, taking
place through the intermediary of rays from heavenly bodies which converge in the earth and make angles with one another, so the eight harmonic ratios will be translated into the sizes of these angles. The Ancient
indeed acknowledged no more than five (commonly called aspects),
namely conjunction, opposition, quadrate, trine and sextile. But reasoning first suggested to me that we should add three more, namely *quintile*, *biquintile* and *sesquiquadrate*, which experience has since repeatedly
confirmed (Thesis 38).[19]

Thus, there are eight aspects corresponding to the eight harmonic
ratios. This passage does not add much to what had been said in the
Mysterium cosmographicum; but, here, the three new aspects are named
("quintile" [72°], "biquintile" [144°] and "sesquiquadrate" [135°])
and fully integrated into the astrological machine for the first time.
The immediate implication is that the rays of light have a significant
impact on earth only when the planets are in aspect, which considerably restrains the variety and multiplicity of celestial influences. At the
same time, Kepler is aware that this system raises questions regarding the compatibility of the physical and non-physical causes, and in
particular this one: by what curious mechanism would living beings
react to celestial influences especially when the rays of the planets form
angles corresponding to harmonic ratios? The answer, put forward in
Theses 39–43, is that living beings have an unconscious or intuitive
perception of geometrical aspects, for 'every animate faculty is the
image of God practising geometry in creation, and is roused to action
by this celestial Geometry or Harmony of Aspects'.[20] In other words,
the aspects are efficient because they are perceived by a soul capable
of geometrical reasoning. Yet this resolves only part of the problem,

---

quam prior illa, nobilior; quaeque multo plus admirationis habet. Nam haec nihil
materiatum sapit, sed formae rationem habet, nec formae simplicis, sed animalis fac-
ultatis, sed intellectionis, sed geometriae cognitionis' (Thesis 36; *KGW*, IV, 21).

[19] Transl. Field 1984, 250–251: 'Motuum ergo formatrices rationes octo cum sint,
coeli vero in terras actio (vel quasi) motus sit aliquis, et contingat intermediante radio
stellae, qui in terris coeunt, faciuntque angulos: rationes ergo harmonicae octo in
dimensione horum angulorum versabuntur. Ac veteres quidem non plures quinque
receperunt (aspectus vulgo dictos) conjunctionem, oppositionem, quadratum, trinum, sextilem. At me ratio primum tres addere docuit, quintilem, biquintilem, ses-
quiquadratum: quos postmodum experientia multiplex confirmavit' (Thesis 38; *KGW*,
IV, 22).

[20] Transl. Field 1984, 252: 'omnis animalis facultas est imago Dei γεωμετροῦντος
in creatione, excitaturque ad opus suum, hac caelesti Aspectuum Geometria, seu Harmonia' (Thesis 40; *KGW*, IV, 23).

for living creatures are not responsible for meteorological and other natural phenomena, such as changes in the weather, earthquakes or tides, which are also caused by the aspects. Kepler's answer to this question is particularly original and will become a salient feature of his cosmology: the earth too must *feel* the aspects. Therefore, the earth is a living being equipped with a soul, which he justifies by saying that the earth 'has a nobler form than that which is recognised in any clod of earth. And its activities argue that this form is truly akin to animate faculties: they are engendering metals, keeping the earth warm, and sweating out vapours to beget rivers, rains and other meteorological phenomena'.[21]

The second part of the *De fundamentis astrologiae certioribus* (Theses 52–75) is the actual prognostication. Kepler provides a weather forecast for each month of 1602 and surveys other topics, such as crops, illnesses and political matters. Unlike standard prognostications, however, this one is not based on the "horoscope of the year" (that is the horoscope of the time of entry of the Sun in Aries), something he rejects in Thesis 49, and traditional astrological doctrines are ignored. Predictions are exclusively based on planetary aspects, including the three new ones which are used on two occasions:

> Towards the end of the month [of January], there is nothing to predict from the ancient aspects, though from the new ones the 21st, with Jupiter and Venus at *quintile*, will be breezy and hot, as far as Winter permits. The 24th, with Saturn and the Sun at *quintile*, will be cold, with snow and rain. The 28th, with Mars and the Sun at *sesquiquadrate*, will be sharp, with keen fierce winds, and will bring in snow. Let those who are minded to test the validity of the new aspects take note of these days (Thesis 52).[22]

---

[21] Transl. Field 1984, 252: 'Nam primo quod terram attinet, esse totius eius, quatenus tota, formam nobiliorem quam ea est quae in qualibet gleba agnoscitur, nemo negabit. Eam vero formam ex animalium facultatum genere esse, opera ipsius arguunt, quae sunt generatio metallorum, conservatio caloris terrestris, exsudatio vaporum ad fluviorum, pluviarum, caeterorumque meteorum progenerationem' (Thesis 41; *KGW*, IV, 23). The soul of the earth will receive considerable developments in *Harmonices mundi* (Book IV, Chapter 7), where Kepler makes it clear that the idea was in no way inspired by the Platonists, but by observation of the weather and the aspects only (*KGW*, VI, 265 lines 25–29). On the soul of the earth, see also Boner 2005.

[22] Transl. Field 1984, 258–259: 'Fine ex antiquis aspectibus nulli, ex novis vero d<ie> 21 quintilis Jovis et Veneris flatuosus et calidus, quantum hyems fert. D<ie> 24 quintilis Saturni et Solis, frigidus, ningidus seu pluvius. D<ie> 28 sesquiquadratus Martis et Solis, acer, subtilium et rigidorum ventorum, et pro re nata ningidus. Observent igitur hos dies, quibus est animus novos aspectus probare' (Thesis 52; *KGW*, IV, 27).

> I expect a normal April, hot at first, since Mars and the Sun are at *biquintile*... On the 10th, 11th and 12th there will be cold rain, and perhaps snow in the mountains, and the atmosphere will be unhealthy. But with a clear sky frost is still to be feared. For, apart from the ancient aspects, we have one of the new ones: Saturn and Mars are at *quintile*. There follows the most delightful mildness, with moisture...(Thesis 55).[23]

The seemingly superficial character of these predictions should not disappoint the reader. It is important to bear in mind that Kepler did not try to promote a definite system of interpretation.[24] Instead, he regarded his astrology as still purely experimental, as made plain in the conclusion, which is also a remarkable piece of document of the history of astrology and science:

> This completes what I think one may state and defend on physical grounds concerning the foundations of astrology and the coming year 1602. If those learned in matters of physics think them worthy of consideration, and communicate to me their objections to them, for the sake of eliciting the truth, I shall, if God grants me the skill, reply to them in my prognostication for the following year. I urge all who make serious study of philosophy to engage in this contest. For it concerns our worship of God and the welfare of the human race...[25]

---

[23] Transl. Field 1984, 259–260: 'Aprilem spero naturalem initio calido, ob biquintilem Martis et Solis... Die 10, 11, 12 frigidae pluviae, et vel nix in montanis, insalubris aer. At sereno coelo etiamnum pruina metui potest. Nam praeter antiquos aspectus, ex novis accedit quintilis Saturni et Martis. Sequitur amaenitas pulcherrima cum humectatione...' (Thesis 55; *KGW*, IV, 28).

[24] Kepler was fully aware of the incompleteness of his system, as it is clear in several places, for instance in Thesis 48, where he suspects the existence of another "nobler" cause besides the aspects, i.e. the harmonic movement of the planets, about which he says: 'however, these things have not yet been confirmed by experience, nor has a method yet been established by which harmonies of this kind could be investigated' (my translation: 'Sed haec tamen ab experientia nondum confirmata sunt, nec dum methodus constituta, qua huiusmodi harmoniae investigentur'; *KGW*, IV, 26 – on the harmonic movement of the planets, which will eventually become the subject of Book V of *Harmonices mundi*, see the detailed study of Stephenson). Likewise, fundamental questions are left unanswered. For example, how did Kepler differentiate a trine from a quadrate in practice? Did he follow the tradition in considering the former beneficent and the latter maleficent? How did he interpret the new aspects? We do not know because he nowhere addresses the "nature" of the aspects. We may surmise that he lacked natural grounds for doing so and it is clear that he could not have accepted the standard justification (e.g. Ptolemy, *Tetrabiblos*, I.13) that the trine and sextile are beneficent because they are geometrical relations between signs of the same sex. A study on Kepler's practical astrology is needed.

[25] Transl. Field 1984, 268: 'Haec habui in praesentia quae de astrologiae fundamentis et de anno 1602 futuro physicis rationibus dici et defendi posse putavi. Quae si physicarum rerum professores consideratione digna putaverint; suasque objectiones veritatis eruendae causa mecum communicaverint, illis ego, Deo facultatem dante,

EXPERIENCE AND CHANGE OF THEORY

It is unclear whether Kepler received feedback from other scholars after the publication of the *De fundamentis astrologiae certioribus*. What is certain, however, is that, from then on, the three new aspects definitively became part of his astrological theory and practice, as witnessed by his prognostications for the years 1603–1606 and by his *De stella nova*.[26] The first serious discussions on the new aspects seem to have arisen only a few years later. In response to a letter from Kepler of 30 November 2007, Johann Georg Brengger writes on 7 March 1608:

> You say that you have confirmed by experience, in meteorology, the existence of the additional aspects *quintile, biquintile* and *sesquiquadrate*. I myself should like to see an example of this observational material, for with such a number of variety of aspects always occurring, so that one is unsure to which of them one should ascribe a change in the atmosphere, I do not know how I should make an observational test, or even whether I should find it possible to do so.[27]

To which Kepler replied on 5 April 1608:

> I could give many examples of experience in regard to secondary aspects, but there is no time to describe my observations. So, in 1600, when from 23 April until 2 May, New Style, there were no primary aspects, and Magini's tables showed Saturn and Jupiter to be at *quintile*, on 1 May there was a very heavy fall of snow both in Prague and in Styria for Ferdinand's wedding, and the jousting had to be cancelled. From observing the heavens, it was found that during these three days Saturn and Jupiter were 72° apart.[28]

---

in prognostico anni sequentis respondebo; quem ad agonem adhortor omnes serio philosophantes. Nam de honore Dei Creatoris, et de utilitate humani generis agitur' (*Conclusio*; *KGW*, IV, 35).

[26] The prognostications for 1603–1606 are edited in *KGW*, XI.2, 61–135. In the *De stella nova*, Chapter IX is devoted to the aspects (*KGW*, I, 189–194) and the new aspects are quoted among observations reported in Chapter XI (ibid., e.g. 203 line 36 and 207 line 33).

[27] Transl. Field 1984, 202: 'Scribis te aspectus extraordinarios quintilem, biquintilem et sequadrum [symbols are given in the text] ab experientia meteorologica comprobatos habere, optarim ego huius experientiae specimen videre, nam in tanto aspectuum numero et varietate, qui semper occurrunt, ubi incertus sis cui eorum mutationem aliquam aeris adscribas, nescio quomodo experimentum capere debeam, vel etiam possim' (*KGW*, XVI, 114). Kepler is undecided regarding the spelling "sequadrus", "sesquadrus" or "sesquiquadratus" (see n. 19 and 22 above, and n. 30–33 below).

[28] Transl. Field 1984, 202–203: 'Specimina experientiae de aspectibus secundariis, plurima dare possem, sed non vacat describere observationes meas. Anno quidem 1600, cum a 23 Apr. in 2 Maii St. No. nullus esset ex primariis aspectibus, quintilis

Kepler's claim that he 'could give many examples of experience' is no boast. As we have seen (*Mysterium cosmographicum*; letter to Maestlin in 1599; *De fundamentis astrologiae certioribus*, Thesis 52 and *Conclusio*), he constantly appeals to observation and there can be no doubt that he personally checked the weather against his own predictions for the years 1602–1606. In his *Tertius interveniens* (1610), he reports that he has been carefully taking note of the weather in relation to planetary aspects for 16 years (Thesis 59) and he provides samples of these personal observations for the period 1593–1609 (Thesis 134) and again from January to March 1609 (Thesis 138).[29]

However, these repeated observations will prove the theory flawed or, at least, that there is no strict correspondence between aspects and harmonic ratios. This realisation seems to have taken place in 1607, as witnessed by his first letter to Brengger (30 November 1607), where he notes that experience has confirmed the effectiveness not only of the three new aspects, but also of the "semi-sextile" (1/12 or 30°), which he already regards as an aspect despite the fact that it has no harmonic counterpart.[30] In his second letter to Brengger (5 April 1608), he maintains his view regarding the semi-sextile, but he adds – in contradiction to what he said in his first letter – that the sesquiquadrate, which corresponds to the minor sixth, has actually no noticeable effects.[31]

---

vero Saturni <et> Iovis [symbols of the aspects and planets are given in the text] in Magino exhiberetur, 1 Maii copiosissima nix cecidit et Pragae et in Styria in nuptiis Ferdinandi, et hastiludia impedita fuerunt. Consulto coelo, inventum est iisdem diebus inter Saturnum <et> Iovem [symbols are given] esse 72° gradus' (*KGW*, XVI, 137–138).

[29] *KGW*, IV, 205, 254–255 and 257.

[30] 'Aspectus extraordinarios [followed by the three symbols], hoc est quintilem, biquintilem et sequadrum, satis ab experientia meteorologica comprobatos habeo. Sed insinuat eadem experientia non raro etiam semisextum, seu duodecimam partem circuli, cum in musica 1/12, 11/12 non gignat novam harmoniam...Igitur duodecangulum videtur ab experientia recipi inter aspectus, quamvis excludatur a musica' (letter to Brengger, 30 November 1607; *KGW*, XVI, 85). On the other hand, in his *De stella nova* of 1606, Kepler still listed the eight "usual" aspects, from which he explicitely excluded the "duodecangulum", even though it is a fraction of the circle: 'Nam aspectuum octo recipio, si conjunctio connumeretur, sextilem, quintilem, quadratum, trinum, biquintilem, sesquadrum, oppositum. Itaque etsi duodecangulum, sunt gradus 30, pars est multiplex circuli, non est tamen aspectus. Contra gradus 144 vel 135 aspectum faciunt, cum pars circuli multiplex non sint, sed superpartiens' (*De stella nova*, IX; *KGW*, I, 190–191).

[31] 'Hic igitur teneor: dixeram enim me de sequadro [symbols are given in the text] experientiam habere. Videbo per ocium sitne de hoc aspectu tam valida experientia quam valida est illa de quintile, biquintile et semisexto. Hoc quidem fateor tres

There is therefore a problem with the theory. On the one hand, these observations seem to rule out the idea that aspects are determined by music. On the other, both the addition of the semi-sextile (a division of the circle by the dodecagon) and the rejection of the sesquiquadrate would rather speak in favour of geometry. However, if the aspects are determined by geometry, then other fractions should be considered as well, for example 1/10 (36°), 1/8 (45°) and 3/10 (108°), but these are not confirmed by experience, and Kepler concludes: 'Things are not clear yet'.[32] Reflections along the same lines occur in his *Tertius interveniens* and in a letter to Nikolaus Vicke of July 1611, where he has definitively promoted the semi-sextile as an aspect and more or less abandoned the sesquiquadrate, although he continues to wonder about the existence of the latter, as well as of the "decile" (36°), "semi-quadrate" (45°) and "tridecile" (108°).[33]

---

hos quitilem, biquintilem, sequadrum ratio mihi suppeditavit (iam examinata) sed semisextum nudissima experientia contra omnem rationem. Itaque circa sequadrum experientia mea mihi ipsi fit suspecta' (letter to Brengger, 5 April 1608; *KGW*, XVI, 139–140).

[32] 'Si aspectuum eadem est causa quae harmonicarum chordae divisionum in duo secum et cum tota concordantia, tunc adsciscendi praeter veteres quintilem, biquintilem, sequadrum. Excludendus semisextus. Experientia confirmat quintilem, biquintilem, semisextum sed sequadrum confirmat obscurius et dubie. Si aspectum facit nobilitas aequationis subtensae et diametri sola, tunc excluditur sequadrus, recipitur 1/10, 2/10, 3/10, 4/10 et 1/12. Experientia confirmat 1/12 et 2/10, 4/10, hoc est semi-sextum, quintilem, biquintilem, relinquit in dubio sequadrum, 1/10, 3/10. Nondum igitur liquet' (*ibid.*, 140, and discussion at pp. 138–140; see also his previous letter (*KGW*, XVI, 85–86) and Brengger's reply (*KGW*, XVI, 114)). The whole discussion may be related to a letter from Sethus Calvisius of 23 August 1607, where doubts are raised about the relationship between harmonies and aspects (*KGW*, XVI, 46–48; see also n. 40 below).

[33] 'so hat mir doch die augenscheinliche und offenbarliche Erfahrung auch den semisextum an die handt geben, der sich mit der Music (in der ubrigen Weiß unnd Maß) keines wegs vergleichen wöllen, und hat hingegen von dem sesquadro, der sich mit sexta molli vergleichet, schlechts Gezeuchnuß geben wöllen. Darauß ich den Unterscheidt zwischen der Musica und Astrologia endtlich gemerckt, und da ich mich verwundert waromb doch ich sesquadrum, decilem, tridecilem nicht sonderlich mercke, und den semisextum so starck mercke, so doch octangulum, decangulum, et subtensa tribus decimis eben so edle und schier edlere Figuren seyen als duodecangulum' (*Tertius interveniens*, Thesis 59; *KGW*, IV, 205). When the new aspects are mentioned or discussed elsewhere in the work, the semi-sextile is omnipresent (see Theses 60, 62, 134 and 138; *KGW*, IV, 206, 207–208, 255 line 19, 257), while the sesquiquadrate is almost entirely neglected (as far as I can see, it is mentioned only once, *KGW*, IV, 206, line 12). For the semi-quadrate, see Thesis 70 (*KGW*, IV, 212 line 40 and 214 line 17). For the letter to Nikolaus Vicke of July 1611, see *KGW*, XVI, 384–385.

Kepler did not produce any prognostication between 1607 and 1616, which makes it difficult to appreciate the application of these changes in his astrological practice during those years. It is however likely that he used the quintile, biquintile and semi-sextile, as he consistently did from 1616 onwards, in his "new ephemerides" for 1617–1636 (see Figures 2–3), in his prognostications for the years 1618–1620 and 1623, and also in his correspondence.[34] The only significant change in this period seems to have been the addition of yet another new aspect, the "quincunx" (5/12 or 150°), introduced in his ephemerides from 1621 onwards (see Figure 4). In the *Prolegomena* to his ephemerides for 1617 (published in 1616), a long chapter is devoted to the new aspects, in which Kepler informs us that a number of astrologers (including Maestlin and Fabricius) have already taken them into account in their own speculations and prognostications, but he deplores their use, abuse, and even misuse of the sesquiquadrate, semi-quadrate, decile and tridecile.[35] It is clear, at that point, that music and astrology had gone separate routes and that Kepler had already in mind a new theory, based on geometry.[36]

This new theory was to be exposed at great length in Book IV of *Harmonices mundi* (1619), and especially in Chapter 5, where it takes the form of a mind-boggling system made of two definitions, three axioms and fifteen propositions.[37] Briefly stated, each aspect is defined by a pair of regular polygons (including star-polygons) inscribed in the circle of the zodiac (i.e. the "circumferential" and the "central" polygons, see Figure 5), while the power or effectiveness of each aspect is

---

[34] *Ephemerides novae motuum coelestium* (*KGW*, XI.1); prognostications for 1618–1620 and 1623 (*KGW*, XI.2, 137–229). His prognostication for 1617 is lost and he did not publish any for 1621–1622 and 1625–1630. In a letter to Vincenzo Bianchi of 17 February 1619, he resorts to the semi-sextile in his interpretation of Bianchi's nativity (*KGW*, XVII, 323 line 73). The aspects are also discussed at length in a letter to Philipp Müller in September 1622 (*KGW*, XVIII, 109–111).

[35] *Ephemerides novae motuum coelestium, Prolegomena*, IV (*KGW*, XI.1, 46–49).

[36] E.g. 'ut quae [i.e., musica] septenarii sui principia nonnulla ex ipsa rectitudine chordae trahit, cum circulus, in quo notamus aspectus, in seipsum redeat; nec possit, ut ex chordae, sic etiam ex zodiaci residuo fieri circulus alius' (*KGW*, XI.1, 48 lines 17–20) and 'magnam quidem esse cognationem harmoniis cum aspectibus, eandem utrique generi originem ex figuris nobilibus circulo inscriptilibus; aliis tamen legibus formari septenarium numerum divisionum monochordi harmonicarum, aliis itidem numerum aspectuum' (ibid., lines 29–32).

[37] *Harmonices mundi*, IV.5 (*KGW*, VI, 239–256). English translation in Aiton/Duncan/Field, 326–348.

IV.

DE NOVIS ASPECTIBVS

In compensationem omissi laboris magni sed inutilis, ego sumpsi laborem alium necessarium, hactenus fere neglectum, exquisitis 1. pluribus aspectibus, 2. congressibus Lunae cum sideribus: quorum illud Meteorologiae, hoc Astronomiae et Rei Nauticae servit; de utroque distinctè dicam.

Aspectus novos tres addidi, ⚹ Semisextum, ⧓ Quintilem et ⚺ Biquintilem, idque in omnibus planetis, praeterquàm in Luna.

Figure 2. Ephemerides for 1617, *Prolegomena*, IV.
Introduction of the new aspects (semi-sextile, quintile, biquintile).
(*KGW*, XI.1, 46)

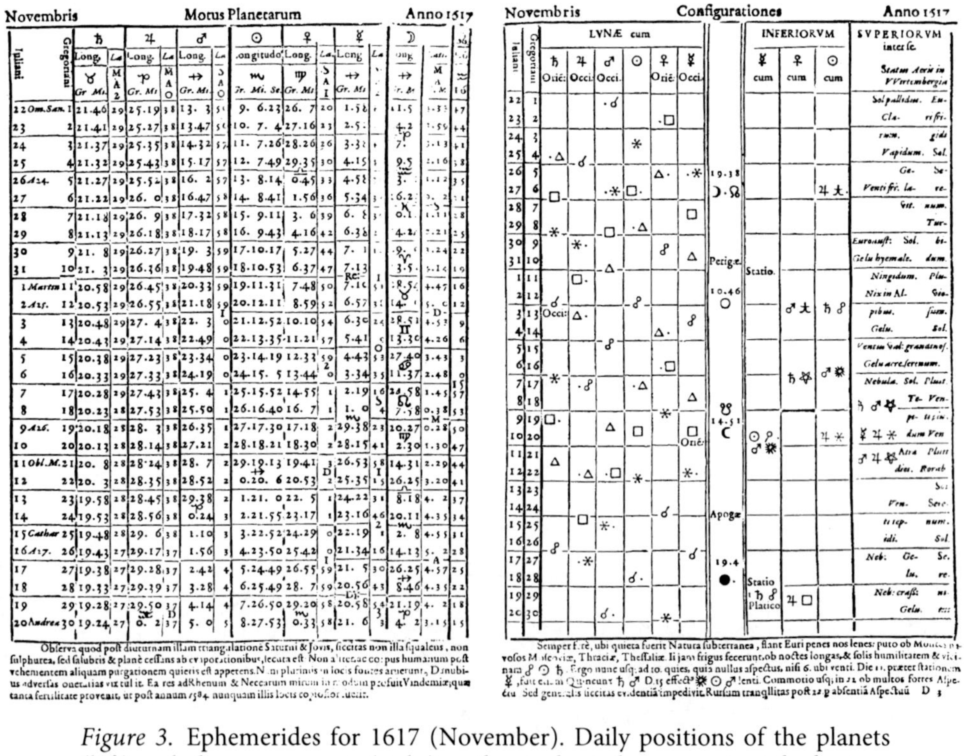

Figure 3. Ephemerides for 1617 (November). Daily positions of the planets (left) and planetary aspects (right), with astrological comments at the bottom (*KGW*, XI.1, 73).

V. Illud seorsim monendus est Lector, ab hoc anno 1621 jam porrò recep-
tum esse in Numerum Aspectuum Quincuncem, signo ⚹; Semisextum verò
qui hactenus hoc signo exprimebatur, jam porrò repraesentari hoc convenien-
tiori signo ⚹ vel ⚹. Quippe hoc erat consentaneum Prolegomenis f. 37.

Figure 4. Ephemerides for 1621, *Prolegomena,* V
Introduction of the quincunx
(*KGW,* XI.1, 142).

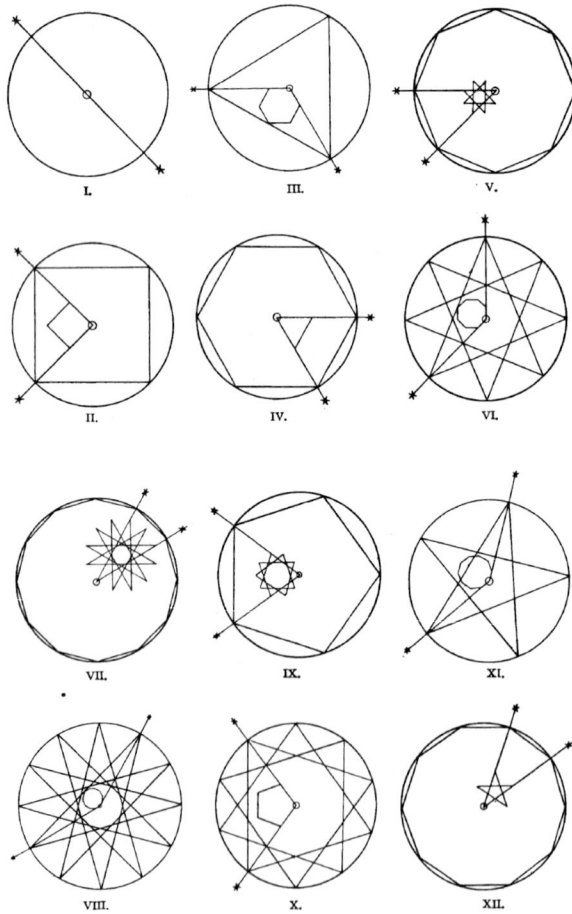

I.   III.   V.

II.   IV.   VI.

VII.   IX.   XI.

VIII.   X.   XII.

Figure 5. Aspects and polygons. I. Opposition (and conjunction) – II. Square –
III. Trine – IV. Sextile – V. Octile (semi-square) – VI. Trioctile (sesquiquadrate) – VII. Semi-sextile – VIII. Quincunx – IX. Quintile – X. Tridecile
(sesquiquintile) – XI. Biquintile – XII. Decile (semi-quintile)
(*Harmonices mundi,* IV.5; *KGW,* VI, 243).

determined by the relative "nobility" of the two polygons in question.[38] The system is then worked out through the fifteen propositions establishing both the number of aspects and their hierarchy, in five groups starting from the most influential ones, as follows:

1. Conjunction (0° or 360°) and opposition (180°)
2. Quadrate (90°)
3. Trine (120°), sextile (60°), semi-sextile (30°)
4. Quintile (72°), biquintile (144°), quincunx (150°)
5. Decile (36°), tridecile (108°), octile (45°), trioctile (135°)

Not surprisingly, this hierarchy agrees with the results obtained through experience. We note that the semi-sextile is considered as powerful as the trine and the sextile (Proposition 12), while the quincunx has been promoted to the same level as the quintile and the biquintile (Proposition 13). As to the last group, comprising the decile (or semi-quintile), tridecile (or sesquiquintile), "octile" (or semi-quadrate) and "trioctile" (or sesquiquadrate), their power is so negligible that they do not deserve a place in the ephemerides (Proposition 14). Finally, and for the sake of completeness, Kepler also mentions 'some configurations which are on the borderline between influential and non-influential', i.e. angles of 24° and 18° (Proposition 15).

Does all this still have anything to do with music? It would seem not. However, Kepler returns to that topic in Chapter 6, entitled *What the affinity is between the aspects and the musical consonances, in respect of number and of its causes.* For the main part, this chapter summarises the developments of the theory of aspects since the *Mysterium cosmographicum* and investigates the reasons why music and astrology departed from one another. Kepler repeats what he had already said in the *Prolegomena* of his ephemerides for 1617:

---

[38] Following the hierarchy of polygons set up in Books I and II. The three axioms, on which the whole system is based, read: (1) 'The arc of the zodiac circle, which is cutt off by the side of a figure or of a star [i.e., a star-polygon] which is congruent and knowable, measures the angle of an influential configuration [i.e., an aspect]'; (2) 'The angle of a figure or star which is knowable and congruent is the gauge of the angle of an influential configuration'; (3) 'The arcs of a circle, of which the figures are powerful in more, and more important, degrees of congruence and knowability, also take the more influential configurations' (transl. Aiton/Duncan/Field, 328 and 340; *KGW*, VI, 241 and 250). "Knowability" and "congruence", i.e. the two defining concepts of the nobility of a polygon, are the subject of Books I and II respectively. More details in Simon, 169–174, and Field 1984, 207–218.

> Music draws some of the basic principles of its sevenfold set from the
> actual straightness of the string, whereas the circle, in which we mark
> the aspects, returns on itself, and another circle cannot be made from the
> remainder of the zodiac as it can from that of a string.[39]

In other words, the circumference of the circle of the zodiac cannot
be equated with a vibrating string.[40] However, as was demontrated in
Book III, music also derives from noble figures which can be inscribed
in a circle, just like astrology, albeit according to different laws. This
common origin in geometry explains the coincidence, no longer perfect but still remarkable, between aspects and consonances, so allow-
ing Kepler to reaffirm the 'great affinity' ('magna cognatio') between
astrology and music.[41]

CONCLUSION

The new aspects were first brought to light by Kepler in 1596, as a
result of a scheme of correspondences between aspects and musical
consonances first suggested by Ptolemy. In that scheme, the opposition corresponds to the octave, the trine to the fifth, the quadrate to
the fourth, and the sextile to the minor third. Kepler's innovation was
to ascribe three new aspects to the remaining consonances, i.e. the
"quintile" (72°) to the major third, the "sesquiquadrate" (135°) to the
minor sixth and the "biquintile" (144°) to the major sixth. By 1601,
the three new aspects were fully integrated into his astrological theory
and practice and Kepler continued to believe in the equation aspects-
consonances until at least the end of 1606 and probably beyond.[42] His
first doubts arose in 1607–1608, when repeated observations of the
weather led him to identify a powerful aspect irrelevant to music, the
"semi-sextile" (30°), and to reject the sesquiquadrate, whose effects on
the weather had not been confirmed by experience. These discoveries
resulted, in 1619, in the formulation of a new theory, where the aspects
are explained in terms of regular polygons inscribed in the circle of

---

[39] Transl. Aiton/Duncan/Field, 351 (*KGW*, VI, 258). For the Latin text, see n. 36
above (first quotation).

[40] It is a similar objection that was raised by Sethus Calvisius in his letter of 23
August 1607 (see n. 32 above).

[41] *KGW*, VI, 260. For the Latin text, see n. 36 above (second quotation).

[42] In *Harmonices mundi*, IV.6 (*KGW*, VI, 258), he says that he changed his mind
in 1608.

the zodiac. If geometry eventually supplanted music as an explana-
tory scheme for the theory of aspects, the new aspects nevertheless
originated in musical theory. In other words, the only astrological doctrine whose origin is known with precision and certainty stems from
music.

BIBLIOGRAPHY

Aiton, E. J., Duncan, A. M., Field, J. V., *The Harmony of the World by Johannes Kepler*, Philadelphia, 1997.
Boner, P. J., 'Soul-Searching with Kepler: An Analysis of *Anima* in his Astrology', *Journal for the History of Astronomy*, 36 (2005), 7–20.
Field, J. V., 'A Lutheran Astrologer: Johannes Kepler', *Archive for History of Exact Sciences*, 31 (1984), 189–272.
—— 'Astrology in Kepler's Cosmology', in Curry, P., ed. *Astrology, Science and Society: Historical Essays*, Woodbridge, 1987, 143–170.
—— *Kepler's Geometrical Cosmology*, London, 1988.
KGW: *Johannes Kepler: Gesammelte Werke*, eds. M. Caspar, F. Hammer, V. Bialas, a.o., Munich, 1938–, 21 vols.
Kepler, *Correspondence*, in *KGW*, XIII–XVIII (1945–1959).
—— *De stella nova*, in *KGW*, I (1938), 147–356.
—— *Ephemerides novae motuum coelestium*, in *KGW*, XI.1 (1983).
—— *Harmonices Mundi*, in *KGW*, VI (1940).
—— *Horoscopes*, in *KGW*, XXI.2b (2009).
—— *Mysterium cosmographicum*, in *KGW*, I (1938), 1–80.
—— *Prognostications*, in *KGW*, XI.2 (1993), 5–264.
—— *Tertius interveniens*, in *KGW*, IV (1941).
Krafft, F., '*Tertius interveniens*: Johannes Keplers Bemühungen um eine Reform der Astrologie', in Buck, A., ed., *Die okkulten Wissenschaften in der Renaissance*, Wiesbaden, 1992, 197–225.
Negus, K., 'Kepler's *Tertius interveniens*', *Culture and Cosmos*, 1 (1997), 51–54.
Ptolemy, *Tetrabiblos*, ed. and trans. F. Robbins, *Ptolemy: Tetrabiblos*, London, 1940.
Rabin, S. K., 'Kepler's Attitude Toward Pico and the Anti-Astrology Polemic', *Renaissance Quarterly*, 50 (1997), 750–770.
Riley, M., 'Science and Tradition in the *Tetrabiblos*', *Proceedings of the American Philosophical Society*, 132 (1988), 67–84.
Rosen, E., 'Kepler's Attitude toward Astrology and Mysticism', in Vickers, B., ed. *Occult and Scientific Mentalities in the Renaissance*, Cambridge, 1984, 253–272.
Rutkin, H. D., 'Celestial Offerings: Astrological Motifs in the Dedicatory Letters of Kepler's *Astronomia nova* and Galileo's *Sidereus Nuncius*', in Newman, W. R., Grafton, A., eds., *Secrets of Nature. Astrology and Alchemy in Early Modern Europe*, Cambridge (Mass.)-London, 2001, 133–172.
Simon, G., *Kepler, astronome, astrologue*, Paris, 1979.
Stephenson, B., *The Music of the Heaven. Kepler's Harmonic Astronomy*, Princeton, 1994.
Vanden Broecke, S., *The Limits of Influence: Pico, Louvain, and the Crisis of Renaissance Astrology*, Leiden, 2003.
Westman, R. S., 'Kepler's Early Physical-Astrological Problematic', *Journal for the History of Astronomy*, 32 (2001), 227–236.

PHILOSOPHICAL INTERMEZZO

APERÇU SUR LE RÔLE DE L'HARMONIE MUSICALE DANS L'ŒUVRE DE PROCLUS

Maël Mathieu and Daniel Cohen

English summary: Synthesizing the theosophical wisdom of ancient Paganism, Proclus's work is representative of the rich conceptuality in the late Neoplatonism. In both *Commentary on the Republic* and *Commentary on the Timaeus*, his views on musical harmony appear with a real thematic coherence, based on the idea of harmony being the principle that unifies and organizes the cosmos. Harmonization of the ideal City is the starting point for classifying the species of "music" in accordance with the tetradic structure of orders in the neoplatonic apprehension of the real. As to harmonization of the universal Soul, it conforms to the mathematical structure of the diatonic mode, considered by Proclus as the pattern of the platonic dialectic: i.e. the very method for the process of philosophical thought. Philosophy itself appears, consequently, as the highest form of "music". Those considerations throw a new light on the way the philosopher conceived the exercise of his discipline.

INTRODUCTION: LE CADRE MÉTAPHYSIQUE

L'œuvre de Proclus[1], dernier successeur de Platon à l'école d'Athènes, qui tenta une mise en forme théorique et une ultime défense du paganisme antique contre le christianisme montant, se présente comme une vaste synthèse théologico-métaphysique qui récapitule la trajectoire philosophique du Néoplatonisme. Elle englobe tous les aspects du réel dans une conception systématique centrée sur l'Un ineffable et sur ses manifestations successives, qui perdent en éclat et en simplicité à mesure qu'on s'éloigne de la Source, mais qui présentent toujours, jusqu'à la Matière même, une trace, un reflet de l'Unité originaire.

---

[1] Sur la vie et l'œuvre de Proclus (412–485), voir Saffrey–Westerink, *Proclus. Théologie Platonicienne*, I, ix–lx.

Ce principe d'unité qui se manifeste à tous les stades de la procession ou manifestation universelle est la cause de l'harmonie du Tout. Cette notion d'harmonie, comme facteur de cohésion (σύνταξις) et d'unité (ἑνότης), est très présente dans l'œuvre de Proclus, bien au delà de ses applications proprement musicales. Cependant, en tant que l'harmonie musicale peut être regardée comme le paradigme de toute harmonie en général, elle est appelée à jouer un rôle didactique particulier. La notion de musique (μουσική) en tant que telle intervient principalement en deux endroits de l'œuvre proclienne : dans le *Commentaire sur la République* et dans le *Commentaire sur le Timée*. En effet, une grande partie des ouvrages de Proclus consiste en commentaires approfondis des grands Dialogues de Platon. On ne s'étonnera donc pas que la musique apparaisse surtout dans le commentaire des passages, peu nombreux, où Platon en a discuté. C'est sur cette base que Proclus a su développer ses propres considérations métaphysiques. Lorsque nous lisons les deux principaux textes de Proclus sur la musique, une certaine complémentarité se laisse analyser sans peine, malgré leurs visées assez hétérogènes à première vue.

Dans la Ve Dissertation du *Commentaire sur la République*[2], il est question de la musique en général, de ses fins, de son rapport à la politique et à l'éducation, et de la classification de ses différentes espèces, dont la plus élevée n'est autre que la philosophie elle-même, en tant que c'est elle par excellence qui contribue à harmoniser l'âme humaine individuelle aussi bien que la Cité parfaite. Les autres sortes de musique, notamment celle formée d'accords et de sons et qui s'adresse en priorité aux sens, seront alors l'objet d'un examen visant à déterminer la façon dont ils peuvent concourir, à leur niveau, à ce but élevé de la philosophie, pensée comme le sommet de l'art des Muses. On examinera donc les formes de poésie qui conviennent à la formation du caractère vertueux, les rythmes et les modes harmoniques appropriés à l'édification des âmes individuelles.

Dans le *Commentaire sur le Timée*[3], le propos de Proclus se situe dans le cadre d'une problématique cosmologique, où il s'agit d'expliquer le mode de constitution et la structure harmonique de l'Âme du Monde. Proclus développe alors, dans une section d'une densité extrême, le thème d'une rigoureuse analogie entre l'organisation de

---

[2] Proclus, *In Remp.* I, 42.16 *sq.*
[3] Proclus, *In Tim.* II, 125.10 *sq.*

l'Âme universelle, formée par le Démiurge à partir d'un mélange strictement déterminé entre les genres premiers de l'Être, et la division de l'octave en intervalles ou degrés, opération qui regarde davantage l'arithmétique que l'art musical proprement dit; aussi, la section en question commence-t-elle par un développement purement mathématique qui, pour le lecteur d'aujourd'hui, surtout s'il n'est pas familier avec les mathématiques grecques, peut présenter certaines difficultés.

Au-delà des différences d'objet de ces deux textes, il apparaît qu'ils s'inscrivent dans la continuité du thème général proclien de *l'harmonie comme principe organisateur et unificateur de l'Être*, et se complètent donc sur le plan métaphysique comme ils se complètent sur le plan de la technique musicale proprement dite. Dans le *Timée* de Platon, en effet, il est question des genres de gammes, en particulier du genre diatonique qui, pour Proclus, comme nous allons le voir, constitue l'image même de la dialectique, méthode platonicienne par excellence de la *mousikè* philosophique. Autrement dit, Proclus s'intéresse ici à la division de l'octave en intervalles définis par des proportions mathématiques. Une telle division, cependant, laisse ouvertes plusieurs possibilités quant à l'ordre dans lequel se rangeront les différents types d'intervalles retenus. Par exemple, si l'on choisit – comme fait Proclus – de subdiviser la quarte en deux tons et un *leimma*, il reste à déterminer si le *leimma* précédera ou suivra les deux tons. C'est dans le *Commentaire sur la République* que cette question sera abordée. En effet, la Ve Dissertation traite des modes musicaux proprement dits, de ceux qui conviennent ou ne conviennent pas à l'harmonisation de la Cité. Or ces modes, qui relèvent tous de ce qui a été désigné ailleurs comme le "genre diatonique", correspondent aux diverses façons d'organiser les intervalles dont se compose ce genre, pour former des gammes (diatoniques) définies. Elles apparaissent donc comme les espèces de ce genre.

Tout cela possède une signification métaphysique profonde. Puisque la structure du genre diatonique est censée correspondre à celle de la dialectique, qui est vraiment, pour Proclus, l'art de philosopher, donc d'"harmoniser" l'âme humaine, la répartition de ce genre en modes qui sont comme ses espèces reviendra donc symboliquement à distinguer entre deux usages ou modalités de la dialectique. Distinction qui n'est pas explicitement thématisée comme telle dans l'oeuvre proclienne, mais qui apparaît tout de même assez clairement dans la *Théologie Platonicienne*. Il y a ainsi, d'une part, une fonctionnalité que l'on pourrait qualifier de "démonstrative", visant à l'exposition théorique des vérités de l'ordre de l'Être et de l'Essence, et qui suit la marche "descendante" de la manifestation : 'En effet, écrit Proclus, l'enchaînement et la connexion des raisonnements imitent l'ordre indissoluble des réalités, qui toujours relie les intermédiaires aux extrêmes et qui, par le moyen des classes intermédiaires, marche vers les processions ultimes des êtres'[4]; et, d'autre part, une fonctionnalité que nous qualifierions d' "opérative", visant à la remontée vers les principes supérieurs à l'Essence, par laquelle elle élève celui qui en fait usage 'vers le Bien en soi et les toutes premières Hénades, [...] l'établit dans la compagnie des êtres réellement êtres et de l'unique Principe premier de tout [et] lui permet de parvenir enfin au Principe anhypothétique'[5].

La dialectique n'est pas seulement l'art de progresser par l'échange de répliques contradictoires, mais constitue plutôt *l'image discursive exacte* et le prolongement du mouvement universel de la procession selon lequel se déploie la manifestation ontologique, le discours total (λόγος) qui récapitule synthétiquement tout discours sur l'Un, en même temps qu'elle amène l'âme à dépasser l'ordre du discours pour expérimenter, dans la mesure du possible, l'Ineffable en lui-même.

Pour tenter de saisir cela, référons-nous une fois encore à la première partie de la *Théologie Platonicienne*, où Proclus déclare :

> Bien davantage, je crois qu'il serait avantageux pour mes adversaires d'examiner la puissance de la dialectique (τὴν τῆς διαλεκτικῆς δύναμιν) telle que Socrate la fait voir dans la *République*, et comment il affirme qu'elle couronne toutes les disciplines du savoir comme la corniche couronne le mur [...]. Elle constitue le couronnement de toutes les sciences, et vers elle mène le chemin que forment ces sciences ; à lui appartient une apparence et un semblant d'exercice, tandis qu'elle ne fait que s'élancer vers ce qui existe, usant continuellement de degrés pour s'élever, et trouve un heureux accomplissement dans la nature du Bien[6].

Ainsi, la dialectique, comme mode de la connaissance, a ceci de particulier qu'elle *fait usage de tous les autres modes*, les éclaire, révèle leur véritable fonction, et de cette façon, les subsume. Par rapport aux autres disciplines noétiques, elle est en quelque sorte investie d'un rôle de Monade, dont celles-ci sont comme les processions successives, les

---

[4] Proclus, *Théol. Plat.* IV, 27, 78.10–13.
[5] Proclus, *Théol. Plat.* I, 9, 39.10–14.
[6] Proclus, *Théol. Plat.* I, 9, 39.7 *sq.*

étapes de sa conversion vers elle-même et de son retour vers le Bien, dans laquelle elle trouve son 'heureux accomplissement'.

En effet, comme l'indique Proclus, en faisant référence à l'activité productrice du Démiurge, l'âme qui se met à "raisonner", 'descend de l'intuition intellectuelle (νόησις) vers le déroulement de l'argumentation logique et de la démonstration', ces démarches cognitives permettant de 'saisir la nature du Cosmos'[7]. C'est donc en explicitant par étapes analytiques successives le contenu d'une intuition noétique originaire infiniment simple et unitive du divin que la dialectique, imitant 'l'ordre indissoluble des réalités', déploie la totalité des ordres du réel et 'marche vers les processions ultimes des êtres'. Si bien qu'au terme de ce cheminement, le philosophe devient apte à entrer dans le mystère de la *théurgie* qui lui révèle l'expérience mystique et ineffable de la pure contemplation silencieuse de l'Un, et à saisir par la lumière de l'intuition supranoétique ce que les mythes symboliques traditionnels exposaient primitivement sur le mode synthétique et voilé.

Après cet aperçu général de la question, passons à l'examen détaillé des deux passages des *Commentaires* susmentionnés.

L'HARMONISATION DE LA CITÉ PARFAITE : LA QUESTION DE LA MUSIQUE DANS LE COMMENTAIRE SUR LA RÉPUBLIQUE

Contexte général de l'analyse de Proclus

Le *Commentaire sur la République* de Proclus se présente sous la forme de "Dissertations" indépendantes, mais qui suivent l'ordre du Dialogue platonicien. Celle qui nous intéresse ici est la cinquième, intitulée 'Opinions de Platon sur la poétique, ses différents genres, les règles les plus excellentes de l'harmonie et du rythme'. Elle est répartie en dix questions relatives à la conception platonicienne de la musique et de la poésie, de leur fonction, de leur place dans la Cité, questions que Proclus abordera une par une.

Ces dix questions ne sont pas également pertinentes pour notre propos. Les troisième et quatrième concernent des points secondaires d'exégèse. La deuxième est une réfutation de la doctrine aristotélicienne de la *katharsis*. Les première, septième, huitième et neuvième touchent, en revanche, à une problématique fondamentale dans

---

[7] Proclus, *In Tim.* I, 283.9–11.

l'œuvre de Proclus, à savoir la distinction entre la "bonne" poétique, celle qui vise un but noble et éducatif, et la "mauvaise", celle qui vise le divertissement et flatte les penchants des "masses". Proclus s'efforce en particulier de définir et de justifier la première, contre une interprétation trop littérale de certains passages de Platon, qui mènerait à un rejet pur et simple des poètes antiques comme Hésiode et Homère ; à rebours d'une telle attitude, il établira qu'en réalité ces poètes exprimaient la quintessence de la Théologie sur un mode symbolique et voilé, raison même pour laquelle leurs vers ne sont pas appropriés à l'éducation des âmes jeunes. (On retrouvera cette thématique dans la sixième Dissertation, consacrée tout entière à la défense d'Homère). Enfin, les cinquième et sixième questions, 'quelle est, selon Platon, la *mousikè* au sens vrai, et quelles les *mousikès* de second et de troisième rang ?' et 'quelle est la sorte de genre harmonique que Platon admet comme utile à l'éducation, qu'il faut donc que pratiquent les poètes en sa république, et quelle est celle des espèces de rythme qu'il choisit ?', concernent pleinement le sujet de la présente étude, et c'est elles qui retiendront surtout notre attention dans la suite.

Les formes de la mousikè

Dans cette cinquième question de la Ve Dissertation, Proclus se penche donc sur les formes de la *mousikè*. Il prend d'abord soin de distinguer la *mousikè* en général de la poétique, qui n'en est qu'un aspect particulier : 'Il semble donc, dit-il, que, ayant regardé les espèces de la *mousikè* comme multiples, [Platon] rapporte tout le genre poétique à la catégorie de la *mousikè*, mais ne renferme pas tout l'art du *mousikos* dans la poétique'[8]. Autrement dit, toute poésie est musique, mais toute musique n'est pas poésie. Toute musique n'est d'ailleurs pas non plus composée de sons, ni perceptible par les sens. Cela étant posé, Proclus distingue, d'après Platon, quatre espèces de *mousikè*.

La première n'est autre que la philosophie :

> Nous disons que c'est la philosophie même qui est la *mousikè* la plus haute (*Phédon*, 61 a3) [...] elle qui a harmonisé non pas une lyre, mais l'âme même, de l'harmonie la plus belle (*Lachès* 188 d 3), grâce à laquelle l'âme peut et ordonner tout l'humain et célébrer parfaitement le divin, imitant le Musagète même, qui d'une part célèbre son Père de chants intellectifs et d'autre part maintient ensemble par ses liens indissolubles

---

[8] Proclus, *In Remp.* I, 57.3–5.

le Monde en sa totalité, "mouvant ensemble" toutes choses, comme dit Socrate dans le *Cratyle* (405 c6 *sq.*).[9]

Ainsi la philosophie, plus haute forme de l'art "musical", n'est pas une spéculation gratuite, mais tend vers un but déterminé, qui est le maintien de l'harmonie, non seulement de l'âme individuelle, ou encore de la société, mais du cosmos tout entier, au moyen de la célébration parfaite du divin, modèle de toute harmonie. Dans la suite des développements, Proclus nous apprendra que seul mérite vraiment le nom de *mousikos* celui qui tend à cette double fin, et que de même, seul est vraiment poète celui dont la poésie contribue à ces objectifs.

La seconde forme de *mousikè* consiste dans la poésie divinement inspirée :

> D'une autre manière, Platon appelle aussi *mousikè* l'inspiration venue des Muses en tant qu'elle excite et meut les âmes à la poésie possédée des dieux (…). Car, dit Platon, l'homme saisi par les Muses n'est inspiré pour rien d'autre que pour devenir un poète, qui chante les exploits du passé et par cela excite les hommes futurs à se porter avec zèle à l'éducation.[10]

De cette inspiration procède donc une poésie sacrée qui a pour but d'inciter les hommes à la vertu au moyen d'exemples tirés des récits héroïques anciens.

De la troisième espèce de *mousikè*, Proclus affirme qu'elle 'n'est plus, celle-ci, comme la précédente, inspirée par les dieux' mais qu'elle 'n'en élève pas moins des harmonies sensibles à la beauté non perceptible de l'harmonie divine'[11]. Nous sommes donc conduits à identifier cette forme de la *mousikè* avec l'harmonie entendue en un sens purement mathématique, telle qu'elle fait précisément l'objet d'un chapitre du *Commentaire sur le Timée*. En effet, Proclus décrit le *mousikos* dont il est question ici comme 'exerçant son activité eu égard à un certain beau (τι καλλόν), je veux dire le beau consistant en accords et rythmes (τὸ ἐν ἁρμονίαις καὶ ῥυθμοῖς), et qui de là s'élève à ces accords et rythmes qui ne sont plus connus par l'ouïe, mais se révèlent à la réflexion de l'entendement (τῷ τῆς διανοίας λογισμῷ καταφανεῖς)'[12]. Dans ces accords et rythmes qui 'se révèlent à la réflexion et à l'entendement', il

---

[9] Proclus, *In Remp.* I, 57.8–16.
[10] Proclus, *In Remp.* I, 57.23 *sq.*
[11] Proclus, *In Remp.* I, 58.27 *sq.*
[12] Proclus, *In Remp.* I, 59.5–11.

n'est pas difficile de reconnaître les rapports et proportions arithmétiques dont s'occupent les théoriciens de l'harmonie.

Vient enfin la musique au sens où nous l'entendons couramment,
c'est-à-dire celle qui est formée de sons, qui s'adresse à l'âme à travers
le sens auditif. Proclus la définit comme

> celle qui éduque les caractères au moyen des accords et rythmes propres
> à conduire à la vertu, qui découvre quels accords et rythmes peuvent
> corriger les passions de l'âme et la modeler par les mœurs les plus bel-
> les en toutes actions et circonstances, quels en revanche, contraires à
> ceux-ci, rendent les âmes dissonantes en les tendant ou les relâchant et
> en les portant à la désharmonie (ἀναρμοστίαν) et au manque de rythme
> (ἀρρυθμίαν).'[13]

Nous voyons donc que cette quatrième forme de la *mousikè*, qui est
peut-être celle à laquelle nous pensons le plus spontanément en enten-
dant le mot musique, n'occupe que la dernière place dans le classement
de Proclus. Encore faut-il voir que ce n'est qu'en tant qu'elle contribue
à l'éducation de l'âme à la "vertu" qu'elle a place dans ce classement;
s'agirait-il de simple divertissement qu'elle en serait certainement ban-
nie. Ainsi, jusque dans sa forme la plus inférieure, la *mousikè* se doit
d'être encore un reflet de sa forme la plus haute, la philosophie, en
contribuant à l'ordre et à l'unité du tout.

Les genres harmoniques

Cela étant posé, Proclus va s'occuper des genres de rythmes et d'harmonies qu'il convient de retenir, au sein du dernier mode. Tel est l'objet de la sixième question, ainsi formulée: 'quels genres harmoniques
Platon admet-il que le poète doive assumer pour l'éducation des jeunes, quels rythmes le force-t-il à rechercher, dès là qu'il écarte l'emploi
de tout l'ensemble des harmonies et des rythmes, comme étant cause,
pour les caractères des élèves, d'une bigarrure étrangère aux Muses.'[14]

Nous voyons que la question est posée en fonction de la préoccupa-
tion, récurrente chez Proclus, de "l'éducation des jeunes"; en réalité,
nous verrons que la réponse possède une extension plus large. De plus,
nous remarquons qu'il considère comme acquise l'idée que toutes les
harmonies, a fortiori leur mélange, ne conviennent pas également à

---

[13] Proclus, *In Remp.* I, 59.20–27
[14] Proclus, *In Remp.* I, 60.14 *sq.*

la formation du caractère. En particulier, Proclus réprouve la "bigar-rure" (ποικιλία): attitude typiquement platonicienne, mais qui, dans la perspective du commentateur néo-platonicien, fait sens avec l'idée que le Bien se confond avec l'Un, et que ce qui se rapproche le plus de l'idéal d'unité, dont celui d'harmonie est lui-même un aspect, est toujours le meilleur.

Il va donc à présent, en se basant sur les indications de Platon, établir une classification des rythmes et des genres harmoniques. Par "genres harmoniques", il faut entendre ici ce que nous nommerions plutôt aujourd'hui des *modes musicaux*. Parmi les rythmes, il retien-dra un composé, l'*énoplien*, 'car ce mètre engendre un caractère viril et rangé en bataille'[15], et un simple, le *dactyle "héroïque"*, que Damon, l'interlocuteur de Socrate, tient 'pour être producteur de bon ordre, d'égalité et des autres biens pareils'[16]. De sorte qu' 'en vertu de l'un et de l'autre l'âme est rendue tout à la fois prompte à se mouvoir et tranquille: et ces deux ensemble, une fois bien mêlés l'un à l'autre, y introduisent l'éducation véritablement telle.'[17]

Parmi les "genres" ou "harmonies musicales", Proclus commence par rejeter comme contraire à ses objectifs 'celles qui font pleurer et celles qui concernent les banquets, dont les unes débrident l'inclinai-son au plaisir, les autres tendent la propension au chagrin'[18]. Parmi les harmonies que Damon enseignait, c'est-à-dire les sept modes diatoni-ques en usage chez les Grecs, il en retiendra deux seulement au final: le mode *phrygien* et le mode *dorien*. Encore établit-il une différence entre les deux: seul le second est considéré comme propice à l'éducation dans son sens le plus noble, c'est-à-dire à l'harmonisation de l'âme, son organisation sur le modèle du divin. En effet, dit Proclus,

> nous avons trouvé que Socrate, dans le *Lachès* (188 d2 *sq.*), dit claire-ment que l'homme vertueux, l'homme vraiment bien élevé, est celui qui a accordé non une lyre ni des instruments frivoles, mais lui-même son âme même, non selon le mode phrygien, ni non plus selon le mode ionien ou lydien, mais selon le mode dorien, qui est le seul vrai-ment grec[19].

---

[15] Proclus, *In Remp.* I, 61.2 *sq.*
[16] Ibid.
[17] Ibid.
[18] Proclus, *In Remp.* I, 61.20.
[19] Proclus, *In Remp.* I, 61.28–62.3.

On peut voir une explication de cela dans la structure même du mode dorien, caractérisé par la *symétrie*:

> la gamme du mode dorien (ἡ Δώριος ἁρμονία) manifeste la proportion de l'égalité de chaque côté du ton (τὸν ἴσον ἐφ' ἑκάτερα τοῦ τόνου λόγον ἁρμόζει): car sa progression mélodique consiste en deux tétracordes séprés par un ton. Or le principe de l'égalité (ὁ τῆς ἰσότητος λόγος) convient aux vertus des parties irrationnelles de l'âme, car il enlève et les excès et les défauts, qui appartiennent au domaine de l'inégalité.[20]

Le mode dorien grec, en effet, correspondrait en termes modernes à la gamme descendante de *Ré* (pour ce qui est de la disposition des intervalles, dont la valeur peut par ailleurs être différente). Il manifeste donc une symétrie de réflexion par rapport au milieu de l'octave, ce à quoi Proclus fait allusion ici. Ce n'est pas le cas des autres modes considérés par lui.

Quant au mode phrygien, bien qu'il n'ait pas qualité suffisante dans l'éducation, Proclus le retient comme 'adapté aux cérémonies sacrées et aux transports divins – comme d'ailleurs il [Socrate] dit clairement, dans le *Minos* (318 b6 *sq.*), que les chants d'Olympos remuent seuls ceux qui sont naturellement prédisposés à une possession divine en les mettant hors d'eux-mêmes, *mais qu'ils ne contribuent pas à l'éducation* (πρὸς δὲ παιδείαν μὴ συντελεῖν).'[21]

Sens de la classification proclienne

Rappelons que nous considérons ici deux classifications distinctes: celle des espèces de la *mousikè* et celle des modes harmoniques. Cependant, ces deux classifications sont tellement liées, notamment quant aux significations qu'il nous semble pouvoir en dégager, que nous considérerons qu'elles forment un système unique.

Ce qui apparaît le plus immédiatement c'est le thème, d'origine pythagoricienne, de la tétrade, qui revient dans toute classification portant, comme c'est le cas ici, sur la totalité des ordres de manifestation d'une idée ou d'un principe donné, par exemple l'idée de *mousikè*. Cela n'a rien de fortuit et ressortit à la conception proclienne de la symbolique des nombres, du nombre quatre en l'occurrence. C'est en effet en fonction de la structure tétradique que Proclus distingue et

---

[20] Proclus, *In Remp.* I, 62.22–27.
[21] Proclus, *In Remp.* I, 62.5–9.

organise les réalités lorsqu'il les envisage selon le complet déploiement de leurs caractères fondamentaux : 'car tout ce qui était dans la Monade primairement, unitairement et inséparablement, la Tétrade l'a montré sous forme divisée, l'ayant désormais discriminé selon le nombre et selon l'activité créatrice appliquée aux réalités inférieures'[22].

Ainsi, toute la réalité, qui consiste dans une procession graduelle à partir d'un Principe absolument transcendant et ineffable symboliquement désigné comme l'Un, se ramène pour Proclus à quatre ordres principaux qui sont, du plus subtil au plus grossier et du plus noble au plus commun : celui de l'Un et des Hénades principielles, celui de l'Intellect et des réalités intelligibles, celui de l'Âme et des entités psychiques et mathématiques, enfin celui des êtres sensibles et matériels. À ce thème de la tétrade comme moment d'un principe qui a atteint le complet développement de ses caractères propres à travers les différents ordres possibles de manifestation, appartient manifestement la présente classification des espèces de la *mousikè*, que nous avons vu s'échelonner de la plus sublime et immatérielle, la *mousikè* philosophique, à la plus commune, celle qui s'adresse directement aux sens au moyen d'accords et de rythmes. Mais à ce même thème appartient une autre classification dont des travaux récents ont montré l'importance structurante dans la pensée de Proclus : celle des "modes du discours théologique" telle qu'elle est exposée au début de la *Théologie Platonicienne* (I, 4)[23]. Nous y apprenons que le discours philosophico-théologique s'articule en quatre genres principaux, coordonnés chacun à un niveau de la réalité totale. Ces genres ou modes du discours sont le mode "mythique", qui use d'images et de figures symboliques, le mode mathématique, qui correspond aux exposés de type pythagoricien, le mode théurgique et divinement inspiré qui correspond à des textes sacrés comme les *Oracles Chaldaïques*, et enfin, la dialectique platonicienne, mode d'exposition scientifique par excellence, qui 'couronne toutes les disciplines du savoir comme la corniche couronne le mur'.

Cependant, ce que les travaux récents déjà évoqués ont également mis en valeur, est le caractère non pas simplement linéaire mais pour ainsi dire *circulaire* de cette classification, qui ressortit à la conception

---

[22] Proclus, *In Tim.* III, 106.1–4.
[23] Pépin, 'Les modes de l'enseignement théologique dans la *Théologie platoniciennes*', 1–14 ; Gersh, 'Proclus' theological methods', 15–27.

ultimement non-dualiste (au sens métaphysique) et donc cyclique (caractérisée par la *coïncidence des opposés*) du réel proclien, sur laquelle nous aurons l'occasion de revenir dans la suite de ce travail.

C'est ainsi que le discours mythique, qui, à première vue, occupe le degré le plus inférieur dans la classification précédente, révèle lors d'un examen plus poussé son ambivalence fondamentale. Selon les analyses de Proclus, les récits mythiques sont en effet de deux sortes : mythes à "finalité pédagogique", dont le meilleur exemple est fourni par les mythes "platoniciens" tel celui de la caverne, et récits mythiques à "finalité initiatique", comme ceux portant sur les dieux et les héros que l'on trouve dans les récits des "théologiens de la Grèce", Hésiode, Homère, Orphée. Si les premiers ont un statut inférieur à la dialectique et aux images mathématiques en raison de leur "manque de clarté" comparativement à ces dernières, le second type de mythes, au contraire, possède un statut éminent dans la mesure où à travers eux se dévoilent des vérités élevées sur le divin qui échappent par nature à tout autre mode d'exposition. Toutefois, les mythes symboliques n'accomplissent ce dévoilement des ordres les plus élevés du réel que moyennant une distorsion et une inversion sémantique qui nécessitent un redressement herméneutique que seule la dialectique platonicienne, par sa clarté et sa rigueur "scientifique", est en mesure d'accomplir. Ce redressement n'est cependant jamais complètement accompli dans l'ordre discursif, et la dialectique ascendante constitue en réalité une propédeutique qui mène à l'initiation proprement dite (intuition noétique) et aux actes rituels de la théurgie, par lesquels l'homme s'unit effectivement aux dieux et à l'Un transcendant.

Dans cette perspective, le mythe (initiatique, symbolique) apparaît donc comme une dialectique "concrète", tandis que la dialectique révèle son propre côté "mythique" : elle dépend elle-même, quant à sa signification ultime, des symboles sur laquelle s'exerce son activité "redressante".

D'un bout à l'autre de l'échelle de la classification proclienne des modes du discours, le mythe initiatique et la dialectique se renvoient ainsi l'image inversée l'un de l'autre, formant un cycle à l'image de l'Hénophanie universelle.

À présent, nous voyons qu'une certaine correspondance existe entre les quatre espèces de la *mousikè* et les quatre modes du discours. Au plus haut degré, nous trouvons d'un côté la philosophie, de l'autre la dialectique platonicienne, que Proclus considère comme la méthode philosophique par excellence.

Si le lien entre la seconde espèce de *mousikè* (la poésie divinement inspirée) et le mode d'exposition théurgique de la théologie est moins évident à établir, on notera que leur définition fait chaque fois appel à la notion d' "inspiration divine" et que, chacun dans leur série respective, ils ont convenance avec l'ordre des réalités intelligibles. La troisième sorte de *mousikè*, en revanche, a manifestement convenance avec l'ordre des réalités psychiques et des entités mathématiques, tout comme le mode théologique des exposés de type pythagoricien. Enfin et surtout, la dernière espèce, qui partage avec le discours mythique l'enracinement dans l'ordre le plus inférieur du réel, l'ordre sensible et matériel, présente de manière très frappante la même ambivalence que ce dernier.

Tout comme le mythe pédagogique, les mélodies composées selon le mode dorien conviennent à l'éducation des âmes jeunes, dans lesquelles elles contribuent à verser l'amour du bien et de la vertu, ayant cependant une valeur éducative moindre que les autres formes de *mousikè*, qui ne font pas principalement appel aux sens. Et tout comme le mythe symbolique, les mélodies composées selon le mode phrygien, quoique dépourvues de valeur éducative et de ce fait jugées dangereuses pour les jeunes âmes, possèdent un statut philosophique éminent lié à une vertu "initiatique" : adaptées 'aux cérémonies sacrées et aux transports divins', elles permettent, au travers d'un usage strictement encadré et réservé à l'élite, d'entrer en contact avec des niveaux de réalité qui ne se révèlent pas dans l'ordre rationnel et discursif. En sorte que cette espèce la plus inférieure de la *mousikè* qu'est la musique proprement dite se dédouble en deux sous-espèces : une qui occupe réellement le rang le plus bas de la hiérarchie, et une qui participe au contraire de la *mousikè* au sens premier et philosophique à un titre plus élevé que toute autre forme hormis cette dernière. Comme dans le cas des modes du discours théologique, les extrêmes se correspondent mystérieusement et la progression se referme en cycle.

Ceci montre à l'évidence la cohérence de la pensée de Proclus, chez qui une même structure tétradique liée à un schéma de développement cyclique ordonne la manifestation de tout principe qui se déploie à travers les multiples ordres du réel. Par la suite, nous retrouverons ce schéma à l'oeuvre dans la façon dont Proclus décrit et interprète symboliquement la structure de l'échelle musicale diatonique.

Exemple qui est bien plus qu'une application parmi d'autres, car le genre diatonique, par la relation particulière qu'il entretient avec la dialectique et que nous allons bientôt préciser, peut être tenu pour le modèle accompli de ce cycle de procession-conversion en quatre étapes auquel tout le réel se résume, et que la dialectique platonicienne imite par 'l'enchaînement et la connexion des raisonnements'.

L'HARMONISATION DE L'ÂME:
LA MUSIQUE DANS LE *COMMENTAIRE SUR LE TIMÉE*

Le *Commentaire sur le Timée* a pour objet l'examen des "dix dons du Démiurge au Monde". Les six premiers dons concernent le corps du Monde, le septième l'Âme du Monde et les trois derniers, les Astres et le Temps.

Le septième don, qui concerne l'Âme, occupe toute la deuxième partie du *Commentaire*, qui en compte trois. C'est dans cette deuxième partie que prennent place les considérations sur l'harmonie, qui décrivent l'harmonisation de l'Âme conformément à la structure du genre diatonique. Par cette expression de "genre diatonique", il faut entendre ici un certain type de division de l'octave, dont les différents modes phrygien, dorien, lydien et ionien, évoqués ci-dessus, sont autant de variantes. Mais avant d'entrer dans l'harmonisation de l'Âme proprement dite, essayons d'esquisser dans ses grandes lignes la structure de l'Âme du Monde selon Proclus.

Structure générale de l'Âme

L'Âme de l'Univers est à la fois une et triple : comme en tout être, il y a en elle l'essence, la puissance et l'activité. Mais l'essence de l'Âme elle-même est triple : on distingue en elle la *substance*, l'*harmonie* et la *forme*. Proclus a clairement défini leur rôle respectif : 'l'une définit seulement l'être, l'autre harmonise la multiplicité essentielle, la troisième maintient tout l'ensemble en son caractère propre.'[24] Cependant, il ne faudrait pas s'imaginer une séparation radicale entre les trois, car chacune comprend les deux autres selon son mode propre : 'En effet, la *substance* comporte avec elle-même la multiplicité harmonisée (τὸ

---

[24] Proclus, *In Tim.* II, 126.6–8.

ἡρμοσμένον πλῆθος) [...]. De même l'*harmonie* est, elle aussi, de l'ordre de l'essence, puisqu'elle maintient ensemble et unifie l'essence'[25].

En ce qui concerne la substance de l'Âme, elle est constituée des cinq Genres premiers, issus du *Sophiste* de Platon : Essence, Mouvement, Repos, Même, Autre, lesquels sont eux-mêmes composés de Limite et d'Illimité, qui sont des Genres divins, procédant directement de l'Un. L'Âme est donc elle-même une certaine combinaison de Limite et d'Illimité. Le Démiurge l'a constituée de deux mélanges successifs : d'abord le mélange des deux principes procédant directement de l'Un pour former les cinq Genres; puis, à nouveau, la combinaison de ces Genres pour former la substance de l'Âme.

Il est important de noter que ces cinq Genres ne sont pas séparés, mais qu'ils sont intérieurs les uns aux autres (il y a du repos dans le Mouvement, de l'altérité dans l'Identité, etc.) et sont présents en toute chose : dans l'Âme, mais aussi dans l'Intellect qui est avant l'Âme et dans le monde matériel qui est après elle. Cependant, ils ne sont pas présents en tout de la même manière. Dans la matière, ils se présentent avec une prédominance de l'Illimité, du Mouvement et de l'Autre, dans l'Intellect, ils apparaissent avec une prédominance de la Limite, du Repos et du Même. Or, l'Âme est essentiellement un *moyen terme* entre ces extrêmes (Matière et Intellect). Platon, comme le rappelle Proclus, affirme en effet (*Tim.* 35a) qu'elle est 'mitoyenne entre l'Essence indivisible et l'Essence divisée dans les corps'[26]. L'Essence indivisible' désigne ici l'Intellect cosmique, foyer unitaire où l'Âme prend sa source, comme la lumière du Soleil. Quant à l'Essence divisée dans les corps', elle désigne la totalité de l'être corporel, ce que Proclus nomme 'l'entière Essence Divisible qui entre dans tous les corps (τῆς ὅλης περὶ τοῖς σώματι πᾶσι γιγνομένης μεριστῆς οὐσίας).'[27] C'est avec ces deux extrêmes, l'Essence indivisible de l'Intellect et l'Essence divisible de la manifestation corporelle, que l'Âme communique, maintenant entre eux le lien vital qui fait de l'Univers, comme dit Platon (*Tim.*, 30b), un seul 'Vivant doué d'âme possédant l'intelligence' : l'Âme maintiendra, par sa médiété, le lien qui unit les êtres, d'une part explicitant les Causes unifiées, d'autre part rassemblant les puissances dispersées des Sensibles'[28]. C'est donc en tant que "médiété" (μεσότης), opérant

---

[25] Proclus, *In Tim.* II, 126.9–13.
[26] Proclus, *In Tim.* II, 147.23 *sq.*
[27] Proclus, *In Tim.* II, 140.13–14.
[28] Proclus, *In Tim.* II, 130.15–17.

la jonction entre l'Indivisible et le Divisible, que l'Âme contiendra les cinq Genres, de sorte qu'elle les contiendra eux-mêmes en leur degré médian, à la fois indivisible et divisé.

La division harmonique de l'Âme

L'Âme, étant à la fois une et non une, comporte des parties en nombre limité. Ces parties résultent de 'la division du tout en rapports harmoniques'[29], en commençant par l'Identité, mère de tous les rapports, car 'l'harmonie tend à s'achever dans l'identité et la communion des parties divisées (εἰς ταυτότητα καὶ κοινωνίαν τῶν διῃρημένων), et de façon générale l'harmonie veut créer de l'identité entre les choses qu'elle harmonise (ὅλως ἡ ἁρμονία ταυτοποιὸς εἶναι τῶν ἡρμοσμένων ἐθέλει)'[30].

Cette division harmonique de l'Âme est à l'image de la division de l'échelle musicale selon le genre diatonique (τὸ διατονικὸν γένος), comme nous l'explique Proclus:

> Platon a sans doute adopté le genre diatonique parce qu'il était à la fois plus fort, plus simple et plus noble que les autres, bien que le genre enharmonique semble avoir une valeur éducative plus grande. D'après mon intuition personnelle, le genre enharmonique (τὸ ἐναρμόνιον γένος) représente le système de la Vie (sc. cosmique) universelle telle qu'elle s'est répandue, en se divisant dans les corps, comme le genre diatonique représente le système de la dialectique [...]. Le genre chromatique (τὸ χρωματικόν), enfin, représente un système idéal de la nature corporelle, et c'est pourquoi il est dépourvu de vigueur et de noblesse[31].

D'après T. H. Martin, dans ses *Études sur le Timée de Platon*, un genre harmonique, chez les Grecs, était une manière de diviser la quarte, et par là même toute l'octave, puisque tous les genres avaient en commun la division de celle-ci en deux quartes séparées par un ton[32].

La particularité du genre diatonique est que la quarte est divisée en deux tons et un intervalle plus petit. Il y a cependant plusieurs espèces de diatonique, selon la valeur respective des deux tons (qui n'est pas forcément égale); l'espèce à laquelle se réfère Proclus, et que Jamblique fait remonter jusqu'à Pythagore, est le "diatonique ditonique",

---

[29] Proclus, *In Tim.* II, 167.14–15.
[30] Proclus, *In Tim.* II, 167.22–24.
[31] Proclus, *In Tim.* II, 168.29–170.8.
[32] Martin, *Études sur le Timée*, 404–405.

qui divise la quarte en deux tons égaux (tons majeurs), et un *leimma*, correspondant à notre demi-ton mineur.

En termes mathématiques, si l'on procède harmoniquement de l'aigu au grave, comme c'était le cas de Platon semble-t-il, l'octave correspond à une longueur de corde double de celle de la note de base, la fondamentale (pour une tension et une masse linéique égales). La quarte correspond à un rapport 4/3, le ton majeur à un rapport 9/8, la quinte à un rapport 3/2: on peut donc vérifier qu'une quinte vaut une quarte et un ton, étant entendu qu'additionner les intervalles revient à multiplier les rapports. De plus, on voit que le *leimma* ou demi-ton mineur vaut 4/3 : 9/8 : 9/8 (une quarte deux fois diminuée d'un ton majeur), soit 256/243. Un autre rapport important est le rapport 3/1 (longueur de corde triple de la fondamentale), correspondant à un intervalle d'une octave et une quinte. Tels sont les principaux intervalles dont se compose l'échelle pythagoricienne ou "diatonique ditonique", utilisée par Proclus. En outre, l'échelle totale utilisée par Platon allait jusqu'au rapport 27/1, correspondant à quatre octave et une quinte, soit par exemple du *Do* au *Fa* situé quatre octaves plus bas. Elle comprenait donc trente-quatre notes, soit trente-quatre rapports au total, rapports que l'on peut ramener à des nombres entiers par une multiplication appropriée, ce à quoi s'emploie fort habilement (pour l'époque) Proclus. Toutefois, les propriétés mathématiques essentielles de l'ensemble sont indépendantes de l'emploi de nombres entiers ou fractionnaires.

Le choix de division adopté par Pythagore-Platon-Proclus possède en effet des propriétés remarquables sur le plan symbolique, qui justifient pleinement, nous semble-t-il, l'intuition proclienne d'une affinité entre le genre diatonique et le "système de la dialectique", dont la finalité, telle qu'elle nous est apparue dans le *Commentaire sur la République*, est bien l'harmonisation de l'âme en accord avec ses principes divins.

Depuis longtemps, les théoriciens helléniques de l'harmonie et des nombres avaient remarqué que, lorsque deux quantités, par exemple deux longueurs, sont doubles l'une de l'autre, les quantités valant 3/2 et 4/3 de la plus petite – soit les rapports de la quarte et de la quinte –, correspondent respectivement à la *moyenne arithmétique* et à la *moyenne harmonique* des deux extrêmes[33]. En outre, l'opération

---

[33] En effet, la moyenne arithmétique de deux nombres x et y s'exprime par la formule $(x + y)/2$, la moyenne arithmétique par la formule $2/(1/x + 1/y)$ ou $2xy/(x + y)$.

consistant à diviser un intervalle en sous-intervalles égaux, par exemple l'échelle en octaves, peut être assimilée à celle consistant à insérer entre les extrêmes des *moyennes géométriques*. La moyenne géométrique, qui a pour expression m.g. = √ (x·y), peut être vue comme le principe générateur d'une suite dont les termes successifs sont dans un rapport constant, comme la suite des octaves (rapport 2/1), des quintes (3/2) ou des quartes (4/3). En effet, chaque terme d'une telle suite est la moyenne géométrique de celui qui le précède et de celui qui lui succède, comme dans la séquence 1, 2, 4, 8… où 2 est la moyenne géométrique de 1 et 4, 4 celle de 2 et 8, et ainsi de suite. Dès lors, puisque toutes les notes de la gamme de Platon sont générées au moyen de ces trois intervalles, octave, quarte et quinte (en fait, deux seulement suffisent puisque une octave = une quarte et une quinte), la construction de l'échelle se résume finalement à combler les intervalles d'une suite géométrique au moyen de médiétés arithmétiques et harmoniques. C'est bien ainsi que Proclus présente les choses:

En nous servant de ces méthodes nous arriverons à remplir systématiquement tous les intervalles des deux progressions de raison 2 et 3 par les médiétés arithmétiques et harmoniques, médiétés que le *Timée* prendra à l'intérieur de la médiété géométrique et, ce faisant, il amplifiera celle-ci par l'insertion des autres médiétés[34].

Il construira ainsi le *diagramme de l'Âme*.

Ce diagramme se compose de deux progressions géométriques de quatre termes chacune, liés entre elles par leur racine commune, l'unité. Soit, si on veut, de trois progressions, l'unité étant à elle seule la totalité des termes de la série de raison 1. Soit encore de sept termes au total, qui expriment ce que Proclus appelle le caractère hebdomadique de l'Âme, reflet de sa perfection (le nombre 7 exprimant, pour les Anciens, l'idée d'une certaine perfection): de même que l'octave est divisée en sept degrés, l'Âme, tout en étant une, est divisée en sept portions, qui comprennent la totalité des différentes classes d'êtres encosmiques en tant qu'ils restent en eux-mêmes, qu'ils font procession et qu'ils se convertissent vers leur principe: 'l'essence de l'Âme est à sept parties en tant que demeurant là où elle est, puis procédant, puis se retour-

---

Si $y = 2x$, on a donc: m.a. = $(x + 2x)/2 = (3/2)x$, m.h. = $2·2x·x/(x + 2x) = 4x·x/3x = (4/3)x$.

[34] Proclus, *In Tim.* II, 173.4–9.

nant, et en tant que cause de la procession et du retour non seulement des essences divisées dans les corps, mais aussi des corps eux-mêmes'[35]. On peut encore ranger les termes de ces progressions en un tableau à double entrée, d'un côté les raisons : 1, 2, 3, de l'autre les puissances : 0, 1, 2, 3. Les trois raisons représentent chacune un des trois moments de la manifestation de l'Un : l'unité, la manence, la dyade, la procession, et la triade, la conversion. Quant aux puissances, elles représentent les différentes ordres de réalité : la puissance 0 (unité), l'ordre parfait de l'Un ; la puissance 1, l'ordre de l'Intellect et des Intelligibles ; la puissance 2, l'ordre des êtres psychiques et des figures mathématiques ; et enfin, la puissance 3, l'ordre du sensible et des êtres tridimensionnels. Enfin, les termes fractionnaires, qui viennent combler les intervalles des séries entières, représentent dans leur variété les différentes classes d'êtres, qui procèdent toutes de l'Un selon des séries, des "chaînes" de participation, s'étendant comme des rayons à travers les divers ordres du réel : Tous ces rapports ont donc été à bon droit assumés d'avance en l'Âme, puisqu'ils déterminent toutes les sortes de participation aux espèces qui se présentent dans l'Univers, et il ne saurait y avoir d'autres principes d'association que ceux-là, puisque c'est d'après eux que tout se forme[36].

L'Âme apparaît ainsi, à l'image de l'échelle musicale, comme un système complet de rapports harmoniques. Rapport elle-même, en tant qu'elle a été décrite tout entière comme une "médiété", elle est une somme de rapports liés entre eux par d'autres rapports, appelés médiétés, une somme de rapports qui se lient mutuellement, qui se rapportent mutuellement les uns aux autres. C'est en outre une somme *parfaite*, intégrale, en ce sens qu'elle comprend l'intégralité des rapports qui unissent entre eux les éléments de l'Univers. C'est pourquoi Proclus écrit :

> Nous disons que l'Âme, qui d'une part est plus simple que les Sensibles, d'autre part plus composée que les Intelligibles, est une somme parfaite de rapports (λόγων πλήρωμα)[37].

et ajoute un peu plus loin :

---

[35] Proclus, *In Tim.* II, 205.24–27.
[36] Proclus, *In Tim.* II, 202.26–30.
[37] Proclus, *In Tim.* II, 200.21–23.

Disons donc en résumé que, de toute l'harmonie qui est dans les centres, dans les éléments, dans les sphères, l'Âme contient les rapports. C'est pourquoi nous disons que l'harmonie de l'Âme est absolument parfaite et pénétrée d'intelligence[38].

Signification des trois médiétés

Il faut revenir, avant de conclure, sur le rôle des trois médiétés: géométrique, harmonique et arithmétique, qui ont été évoquées au point précédent; car c'est là, sans doute, que se situe la clef de voûte de tout l'imposant et complexe édifice proclien de la psychogonie. Tout le diagramme de l'Âme peut être regardé comme résultant de ces trois relations mathématiques, que Proclus nomme les 'Filles de Thémis'[39], ce qui atteste leur caractère d'entités divines, plus encore que de simples relations. C'est en ce sens que l'Âme peut être dite elle-même une médiété parfaite, car elle comprend tout rapport et toute médiation: comme nous l'avons vu plus haut (III.2), 'l'Âme maintiendra, par sa médiété, le lien qui unit les êtres', tous les êtres qui composent l'Univers, sans exception. Plus originaire en quelque sorte que la division et l'harmonisation de l'Âme, sont ces trois opérations qui en sont les principes générateurs (de cette division et de cette harmonisation): 'elles sont toutes trois ce qui unifie et maintient ensemble l'essence de l'Âme'[40]. Voyons maintenant la signification de chacune d'elle.

La première et la plus fondamentale est la médiété géométrique, qui est en quelque sorte la base de toute l'échelle, puisqu'elle définit la série des octaves, que les autres médiétés viennent combler par la suite. Mieux, l'idée même d'échelle musicale, c'est-à-dire de valeurs égales revenant à des hauteurs différentes, revient à celle de progression géométrique. C'est pourquoi Proclus peut écrire:

De ces médiétés, qui sont trois, la *géométrique* (ἡ γεωμετρικέ) lie tout ce qui, dans les âmes, est de l'ordre de l'essence. Car l'essence est un rapport un qui pénètre à travers toutes choses, unissant les premiers, les moyens, les derniers, de même qu'en géométrie un seul et même rapport pénètre complètement à travers les trois termes[41] c'est-à-dire la ligne, le carré et le cube. Proclus poursuit:

---

[38] Proclus, *In Tim.* II, 211.10–13.
[39] Proclus, *In Tim.* II, 198.29 *sq.*
[40] Proclus, *In Tim.* II, 198.30 *sq.*
[41] Proclus, *In Tim.* II, 199.6–11.

La médiété *harmonique* (ἡ ἁρμονική) maintient ensemble tout ce qu'il y a d'identité divisée dans les âmes, elle établit, entre les extrêmes, une communication de rapports et de connaturalité, se laissant voir d'ailleurs plus dans les plus universels, moins dans les plus particuliers, comme l'identité elle-même. La médiété *arithmétique* (ἡ ἀριθμητική) lie tout ce qu'il y a d'altérité de toute sorte dans la procession de l'âme, étant d'ailleurs, selon l'ordre des choses, moins présente dans les supérieurs, plus présente dans les inférieurs: car l'altérité domine dans les plus particuliers, comme l'identité dans les plus universels et les plus valables[42].

Ainsi, chacune des médiétés a convenance avec l'un des trois Genres responsables de l'harmonie: l'Essence, l'Identité, l'Altérité. De même que l'Essence, qui comprend les deux autres Genres à titre premier, est en quelque sorte leur principe, de même la médiété géométrique est comme le principe des deux autres, et c'est pourquoi elle est "de l'ordre de l'essence". Par ailleurs, nous voyons que les deux autres médiétés jouent un rôle symétrique et opposé l'une de l'autre, comme l'identité et l'altérité. Proclus précise d'ailleurs: 'En outre, ces deux dernières médiétés sont dans *un rapport de réciprocité l'une à l'égard de l'autre* (ἔχουσιν ἀντιπεπόνθησιν αὗται πρὸς ἀλλήλας), comme l'identité et l'altérité, et de même que l'essence est la monade de celles-ci, de même la médiété géométrique est la monade de celles-là'[43]. Tout ce passage est d'une importance capitale. Pour bien le comprendre, rappelons quelques notions mathématiques élémentaires. Entre les trois moyennes, on démontre qu'on a toujours les inégalités

moyenne harmonique ≤ *moyenne géométrique* ≤ *moyenne arithmétique*

quels que soient les extrêmes. On comprend dès lors ce que Proclus veut dire en écrivant, à propos des médiétés arithmétique et harmonique, que 'ces deux dernières médiétés sont dans un rapport de réciprocité l'une à l'égard de l'autre'. Disposées symétriquement par rapport à la médiété géométrique, elles jaillissent d'elle comme les rayons d'un centre, ce qui renforce l'idée qu'elle joue à leur égard le rôle de "monade".

C'est en un sens plus profond, et plus rigoureux mathématiquement, cependant, que médiétés arithmétique et harmonique peuvent être dites réciproques l'une de l'autre. En effet, on montre d'après leur définition même que *l'inverse de la moyenne harmonique est la*

---

[42] Proclus, *In Tim.* II, 199.11–15.
[43] Proclus, *In Tim.* II, 199.11–22.

moyenne harmonique des inverses. Pour le voir, rappelons-nous que les expressions mathématiques de la moyenne arithmétique et harmonique de deux nombres x et y sont respectivement $(x + y)/2$ et $2/(1/x + 1/y)$. Par conséquent, si nous nommons h la moyenne harmonique de x et y, nous avons:

$$1/h = (1/x + 1/y)/2.$$

Son inverse est bien la moyenne arithmétique des inverses des extrêmes. Ceci possède une intéressante application musicale qui peut s'énoncer ainsi: *la quarte est une quinte retournée.* Nous savons en effet que la quinte (inférieure, si l'on raisonne en termes de longueur de corde) est la moyenne arithmétique de la fondamentale et de l'octave inférieure. Si, au contraire, nous prenons la fondamentale et l'octave supérieure, c'est-à-dire la corde dont la longueur vaut la moitié de celle de la fondamentale, et que nous prenons la moyenne arithmétique, nous obtenons le rapport $(1 + 1/2)/2 = 3/4$, qui est le rapport de la quinte supérieure. Inversons maintenant ce rapport, nous trouvons $4/3$, rapport de la quarte inférieure. Lequel correspond à la moyenne harmonique de la fondamentale et de l'octave inférieure, c'est-à-dire à l'inverse de la moyenne arithmétique de leurs inverses (le rapport de la fondamentale à elle-même, qui vaut 1, est son propre inverse, et celui de l'octave supérieure, $1/2$, est l'inverse de celui de l'octave inférieure, $2/1$). Les deux intervalles fondamentaux, à l'image des deux médiétés par lesquels ils sont engendrés, sont donc liés par un rapport d'*analogie inversée*. Nos considérations ne s'arrêteront pas là. Les trois moyennes possèdent encore des propriétés asymptotiques remarquables, de nature à éclairer les propos de Proclus.

Considérons d'abord fixé le terme inférieur d'un intervalle, x, et augmentons l'autre, y, indéfiniment: faisons-le "tendre vers l'infini", comme on dit en mathématiques modernes. Nous voyons immédiatement que la moyenne arithmétique $(x + y)/2$ suit la même évolution: elle tend vers l'infini, s'écartant de plus en plus du terme inférieur. Il n'en va pas de même de la moyenne harmonique $2xy/(x + y)$. La propriété tout à fait remarquable de cette dernière est que sa limite lorsque y "tend vers l'infini", est finie: un raisonnement élémentaire montre qu'elle vaut exactement $2x$. Il s'ensuit immédiatement que plus x est petit, plus la moyenne harmonique devient elle-même petite, et proche de x lui-même, à mesure que y s'éloigne. À la limite, si nous faisons $x = 0$ (ce qui correspondrait, certes, à une longueur de corde nulle), la moyenne harmonique s'annule quel que soit y.

Enfin, la moyenne géométrique a un comportement intermédiaire entre ceux des deux précédentes: lorsque y tend vers l'infini, elle en fait de même, mais infiniment moins "vite". Son rapport à y tend vers 0, ce qui signifie qu'elle devient infinie par rapport au terme fini, mais reste "finie" par rapport au terme infini. (Bien sûr, les Grecs anciens ignoraient la notion moderne d'infini mathématique, qui n'est qu'une abstraction commode. Mais ils n'en avaient pas besoin pour observer le comportement respectif des différentes moyennes lorsque l'écart entre les termes extrêmes devient important.)

À la lumière de ces considérations, nous comprenons parfaitement ce que Proclus veut dire lorsqu'il affirme que 'la médiété *harmonique* [...] établit, entre les extrêmes, une communication de rapports et de connaturalité, se laissant voir d'ailleurs plus dans les plus universels, moins dans les plus particuliers, comme l'identité elle-même. La médiété *arithmétique* [...] étant d'ailleurs, selon l'ordre des choses, moins présente dans les supérieurs, plus présente dans les inférieurs' (voir III.4 *supra*). En effet, la moyenne harmonique reste toujours plus proche de l'extrémité inférieure de l'intervalle, ce qui, transposé sur le plan ontologique, symbolise le fait que la médiété correspondante demeure plus proche des principes, de l'unité, et cette tendance augmente à mesure que le terme final s'en éloigne, va vers le multiple et le composé. Voilà pourquoi elle se laisse voir 'plus dans les plus universels, moins dans les plus particuliers'. La moyenne arithmétique, elle, a un comportement exactement inverse: plus le terme final, des deux qu'elle est censée lier, s'écarte de la simplicité et de la principialité, plus elle s'en écarte elle aussi, se laissant en quelque sorte entraîner par le terme quantitativement supérieur, c'est-à-dire qualitativement et symboliquement inférieur. Il est donc mathématiquement exact de dire qu'elle est 'moins présente dans les supérieurs, plus présente dans les inférieurs'.

Par conséquent, le pouvoir liant de la médiété arithmétique diminue à mesure que le terme final s'avance vers l'illimité de l'existence individuelle et corporelle, au point qu'elle finit par le perdre tout à fait. Au contraire, celui de la médiété harmonique ne se perd jamais, et même se renforce à mesure que les termes extrêmes s'écartent l'un de l'autre. À la limite, d'ailleurs, les intervalles qui séparent la moyenne harmonique des deux extrêmes, x et l'infini, valent respectivement, en valeur absolue, ces termes eux-mêmes : *la médiété est alors distante de chacun des termes qu'elle lie d'un intervalle qui vaut exactement ce terme.* Elle est comme un nœud qui lie chaque terme par le biais de son image identique. Dès lors, *le pouvoir liant de la médiété harmonique est le plus grand quand l'écart entre les extrêmes est maximal,* alors que l'inverse est vrai pour la médiété arithmétique. Et nous voyons par là combien Proclus a raison de dire que la médiété harmonique a davantage convenance avec l'identité, qu'elle 'établit, entre les extrêmes, une communication de rapports et de connaturalité', car c'est vraiment par elle que les extrêmes peuvent communier, que les derniers dérivés sont ramenés à leurs premiers principes. Enfin, il a raison de dire qu'elle 'fait voir en effet que les termes plus grands [qualitativement] et plus universels par essence sont aussi en puissance plus enveloppants que les inférieurs'[44].

Or c'est là un point central de la doctrine cosmologique et métaphysique de Proclus.

Comme nous avons déjà eu l'occasion de le mentionner, celle-ci repose en effet sur une hénologie intégrale non-dualiste qui se traduit ultimement par le caractère cyclique de tout procès et donc, ultimement, par la *coïncidence des opposés.* Dans cette perspective, les derniers dérivés sont en quelque sorte plus proches des principes que ceux qui occupent un rang intermédiaire. C'est là un thème important de la métaphysique proclienne. Voilà pourquoi plus noble que la médiété qui relie de préférence des êtres proches, est celle qui réunit de préférence les termes les plus opposés. Ceci en conformité avec l'axiome fondamental de la métaphysique proclienne, d'après lequel plus un être est proche de l'Un, et occupe un rang élevé dans la hiérarchie des principes, plus son activité causale porte loin dans cette même hiérarchie, ce qui signifie que les classes d'êtres les plus inférieures subissent *davantage* l'action de l'Un et de ses dérivés immédiats que celle de causes intermédiaires ontologiquement plus proches d'elles-mêmes[45].

---

[44] Proclus, *In Tim.* II, 200.1–2.

[45] C'est ce qu'exprime parfaitement J. Trouillard lorsqu'il écrit que 'les causes supérieures [...] enveloppent les inférieures parce qu'elles sont plus compréhensives, tandis que les subordonnées emploient et particularisent les plus fondamentales.' (Trouillard, *Mystagogie de Proclos*, 85). D'où le rang éminent de la médiété harmonique, image inverse de l'arithmétique, par laquelle se fait voir cette correspondance universelle des opposés.

Conclusion

Au terme de cette étude, nous espérons avoir mis en lumière la continuité du thème de l'harmonie chez Proclus, comme un discret fil rouge qui relie les deux *Commentaires*, sur le *Timée* et la *République*, et plus particulièrement les développements sur la musique contenus dans l'un et dans l'autre. Ces développements apparaissent désormais comme formant une réelle unité thématique poursuivie d'un *Commentaire* à l'autre, et qui s'inscrit dans le cadre plus vaste d'une vision tétradique de la réalité totale, combinée à une vision triadique du divin qui se reflète en chaque ordre particulier de réalité par le biais du triple aspect manence-procession-conversion propre à cet ordre. Cette sructure à double entrée est celle de l'échelle musicale diatonique dans laquelle sont pris les modes que Proclus retient comme appropriés l'un à l'éducation, l'autre aux cérémonies sacrées. C'est aussi identiquement celle de l'Âme totale considérée sous l'angle de l'harmonie, c'est-à-dire en tant qu'elle unifie, maintient ensemble, chacune à la place qui lui convient, toutes les parties de l'univers.

Cette fonction d'unification et de maintien de la totalité, qui est celle de l'harmonie comme principe cosmologico-métaphysique, est celle-la même que remplit la philosophie dans l'ordre humain et dans le cadre plus restreint de l'organisation de l'âme individuelle. On ne s'étonnera donc pas que la philosophie soit assimilée à la plus haute forme de musique, ni qu'elle ait pour modèle l'activité d'Apollon, le Musicien céleste qui toujours 'célèbre son Père de chants intellectifs'. La musique n'est donc plus seulement au service des objectifs politico-éthiques fixés par la philosophie, comme elle peut apparaître au lecteur naïf de la *République* de Platon, mais, par un renversement qui mérite d'être souligné, elle devient le modèle que la philosophie doit s'efforcer d'imiter. Avec pour conséquence que Proclus lui-même, en tant que philosophe, se pense donc comme musicien, comme le musicien par excellence. Cela implique de considérer avec attention le thème de la musique tel qu'il apparaît dans toute l'oeuvre de Proclus, notamment dans les passages dont nous avons donné ici une analyse succincte. On y découvrira sans aucun doute de nouvelles clefs pour comprendre la pensée si riche et si complexe du maître de l'École néoplatonicienne d'Athènes.

Par ailleurs, pour Proclus, qui dit "philosophie" et "méthode philosophique" dit nécessairement "dialectique platonicienne", la méthode par excellence du cheminement rationnel vers les réalités les plus hautes. On ne saurait donc être complet dans l'étude du traitement thématique de l'harmonie musicale dans l'oeuvre de Proclus sans se pencher de manière approfondie sur son idée de la dialectique platonicienne, et l'on ne saurait comprendre réellement cette dernière si on ne la relie aux conceptions mathématiques et musicales développées dans le cadre de la psychogonie. Son image mathématique, telle qu'elle apparaît dans ce cadre, est constituée par l'échelle musicale, qui procède comme elle selon le mouvement à la fois progressif et cyclique d'un développement périodique. De plus, la perfection de la dialectique implique son assimilation au genre diatonique, qui est de tous le plus homogène et qui comprend les trois médiétés, en particulier l'harmonique, par laquelle se manifeste le principe de coïncidence des opposés, en lequel réside la possibilité la plus ultime de la procession. C'est en effet grâce à lui qu'elle peut ramener les dérivés à leur Principe premier et entamer un nouveau cycle, pour que l'infinie simplicité de l'Un se manifeste dans l'inépuisable variété des formes qui l'expriment.

Enfin, comme l'Âme qu'elle harmonise, la dialectique est une unité multiple. Elle se fractionne à travers les modes du discours ou les disciplines du savoir, qu'elle tient unis comme ses propres parties, tout comme l'harmonie de l'Âme tient unies les différentes parties du Tout. À ces ordres de réalités sont coordonnés aussi bien les *modes du discours* que les formes de la *mousikè*, dont la plus haute est la dialectique philosophique proprement dite, qui fait usage des trois autres, dont elle constitue le modèle. Aussi, même dans la plus basse de ces formes, celle qui s'adresse aux sens en faisant usage de rythmes et de mélodies, il y a un reflet de la plus élevée, et même un double reflet : soit qu'elle use du mode (diatonique) dorien afin d'affiner les âmes brutes, de les former à la vertu et de les rendre aptes à l'apprentissage des vérités les plus divines, soit qu'elle use du mode (diatonique) phrygien pour conduire les âmes déjà entraînées des adeptes vers l'union effective avec le divin au cours de cérémonies sacrées qui marquent le couronnement de l'effort philosophique, la musique digne de ce nom est toujours, d'une certaine façon, dialectique platonicienne.

Par ces deux modes, qui se complètent au sein du genre diatonique, s'achève l'harmonisation de la sphère sociale et humaine, et avec elle, celle de l'Univers, qui manifeste l'unité jusqu'en ses ordres les plus inférieurs. Et lorsque le philosophe, qui est le Musicien authentique, atteint le stade ultime de son cheminement, réalisant la possibilité la plus haute de l'être humain, il achève pour lui-même l'œuvre unificatrice du père des Muses, en reconduisant l'être individuel et matérialisé à son Principe le plus universel et le plus divin.

BIBLIOGRAPHIE

Gersh, S., 'Proclus' theological methods', in Segonds, A. Ph. et Steel, C. (éd.), Proclus *et la théologie platonicienne: Actes du colloque International de Louvain (1998)*, Leuven-Paris: Leuven University Press 2000, 15–27.

Martin, T. H., *Études sur le Timée de Platon*, Paris: Ladrange 1841.

Pépin, J., 'Les modes de l'enseignement théologique dans la *Théologie platoniciennes*', in Segonds, A. Ph. et Steel, C. (éd.), Proclus *et la théologie platonicienne: Actes du colloque International de Louvain (1998)*, Leuven-Paris: Leuven University Press 2000, 1–14.

Proclus, E. Diehl, *Procli Diadochi In Platonis Timaeum Commentaria*, Leipzig: E. Diehl 1903–1906, reprint Amsterdam: Hakkert 1965. Trad. fr. Festugière, A.-J., Proclus. *Commentaire sur le Timée*, Paris: Librairie philosophique J. Vrin 1966 (Livre I), 1967 (Livres II et III), 1968 (Livres IV et V).

Proclus, *Procli In Platonis Rempublicam Commentarii*, Leipzig: W. Kroll 1899–1901, reprint Amsterdam: Hakkert 1965. Trad. fr. Festugière, A.-J., Proclus. *Commentaire sur la République*, Paris: Librairie philosophique J. Vrin 1970.

Proclus, Saffrey, H. D. et Westerink, L. G., *Théologie Platonicienne*, Paris: Les Belles Lettres 1968–1997.

Trouillard, J., *La mystagogie de Proclos*, Paris: Les Belles Lettres 1982.

QUELQUES PHILOSOPHES DU XIXE SIÈCLE ET LA MUSIQUE COMME ÉSOTÉRISME MODERNE

Jacques Amblard

English summary: First of all, the complex notion of esotericism shall be clarified. If 'esotericism' used to signify 'inwardness', or 'secrete knowledge', this text employs a more recent signification (perhaps born during the 70's and the "new age" thought), which could be more precisely *magical thought exposed with decency*. Thus, this type of 'esotericism', as a relic of the myth in the modern thought, could have appeared in the works of some great German philosophers of the nineteenth century, Kant, Hegel, Schopenhauer and Nietzsche, precisely when these authors write about music. This type of 'musical suspension' of the rational thought could even have survived during the twentieth century, which will be shortly examined as a conclusion.

Il pourrait être utile de rappeler d'abord les sens assez divers que peut revêtir la notion d'ésotérisme[1]. Antoine Faivre distingue quatre significations[2]. Or, on pourrait chercher des invariants, tenter d'articuler ces dernières entre elles, si possible par un lien logique. Dans son acception originelle, le terme renvoie à une notion de savoir *secret* en tant que réservé aux initiés. Voilà l'intériorité contenue dans *esôteros* ('intérieur'). Or, cette intériorité, sans doute, suppose également le regard vers quelque mystérieux abîme de l'intimité, occulte, à la fois

---

[1] On pourra consulter à ce sujet, par exemple, Servier, *Dictionnaire critique de l'ésotérisme*; Faivre, 'Une discipline nouvelle' ou 'L'ésotérisme et la recherche universitaire'; Riffard, *Dictionnaire de l'ésotérisme*. Pour des conceptions plus anciennes, parfois moins universitaires, on lira des ouvrages de (ou concernant) Roger Guénon (1886–1951) ou Robert Amaddou (1924–2006).

[2] 'Le mot "ésotérisme" revêt quatre significations différentes. [...] 1. Pour les libraires ou les éditeurs, "ésotérisme" sert de mot générique pour tout type de littérature relevant du paranormal, des sciences occultes, de diverses traditions de sagesse exotique, etc. 2. Le mot "ésotérisme" évoque l'idée d'enseignements secrets [...]. 3. Le mot "ésotérisme" renvoie aussi au "centre" de l'Être, celui de l'Homme, de la Nature ou de Dieu; par exemple le "Dieu ésotérique" de Franz von Baader est le Dieu caché [...]. 4. Enfin, dans notre champ de recherches, le mot "ésotérisme" renvoie à un ensemble de 'courants spirituels (hermétisme, kabbale chrétienne...), qui ont un certain air de famille.' 'Occident moderne', 961.

ineffable et commun à tout homme, finalement spirituel. Un système
ésotérique est souvent, incidemment, une théosophie. Remarquons
alors qu'un premier ésotérisme *oral* serait celui, initial, des sociétés
secrètes, un second, *écrit*, postérieur, s'associerait à une doctrine de
science ancienne écrite de façon complexe, voire cryptée : tout dépend
du secret, c'est-à-dire comment le secret est gardé (par le cénacle ou
le livre).

Un sens plus actuel et d'après Faivre : le premier sens du mot désormais, est le sens donné par les éditeurs et libraires de notre époque :
'paranormal'[3]. Permettons nous, à ce sujet, quelques commentaires.
Le fait, par exemple, que l'astrologie soit dite 'ésotérique' encore
aujourd'hui montre bien l'évolution de la notion. La lecture de l'horoscope dans le journal quotidien, même si elle ne résume pas le champ
d'application de l'astrologie contemporaine, loin s'en faut, est devenue
une cérémonie non plus secrète : non plus ésotérique mais au contraire
exotérique par excellence : commune, vulgaire. C'est peut-être la luxu-
riance même de la littérature astrologique qui finit par masquer son
éventuelle essence, qui ici devient nébuleuse de pensées d'apparence
fantaisiste, non contrôlée par une pensée unique autoritaire.

Or, cette essence pourrait même se dissimuler à dessein dans la
prolifération de ses leurres : selon quelque mécanisme de précaution
ressemblant à l'humaine *pudeur*. Esotérisme moderne – selon cette
hypothèse qui deviendra celle, principale, de ce texte – signifierait
alors 'pensée magique et désormais *pudique*'. Cette pudeur protége-
rait finalement, aujourd'hui, *toute* pensée magique des foudres scientifiques menaçant de la déconstruire en quelques arguments, dans les
sociétés modernes dominées par l'athéisme, l'épistémologie scientiste
issue du positivisme et avant lui, dès le XVIIe siècle, du courant rationaliste s'inspirant principalement du *Discours de la méthode* de Descartes, relayé au XVIIIe siècle par les Lumières puis la Révolution (et
ce que celle-ci engendra de rationalité républicaine anticléricale, d'hu-
manisme étendu au recentrage absolu sur l'humain). Puisque le XXe
siècle obéit à l'empirisme, au principe anti-métaphysique qui veut que
tout ce qui ne peut encore être démontré *a priori* soit faux, les théories théosophiques sont tout particulièrement présumées suspectes. Ce
principe de précaution (de présomption de culpabilité) paraît avoir
donné, dès lors, au concept d'ésotérisme son sens moderne : camou-

---

[3] Voir note précédente, au début.

flage (ou pudeur) du principe de magie en général dans un système sociétal qui lui est souvent hostile, ou qui pourrait le qualifier d'exclusivement populaire, de vulgaire. Ce qui a le plus modifié le sens de la notion d'ésotérisme est la révolution épistémologique du XVIIe siècle, le basculement d'une pensée analogique unitaire – incidemment magique – vers une pensée rationaliste de la dichotomie – incidemment athée, le divin ne pouvant souffrir de dichotomie. Ce qu'il fallait cacher autrefois était la raison, la science. Ce qu'il faut cacher aujourd'hui est ce qui ressemble à l'inverse : la magie, ou Dieu, ces deux derniers finissant par être assimilés. Le secret, ou du moins la dissimulation, voire seulement le fait de voiler, est resté, semble-t-il, inhérent à la notion d'ésotérisme. Mais c'est ce qu'il convient de cacher qui a totalement changé d'objet. D'autre part, la dissimulation ne protège plus le savoir de l'élite, mais au contraire du plus grand nombre. L'ésotérisme fait partie de ces notions (comme l'art ou la culture) qui se sont démocratisées avec la modernité.

'Esotérique' pourrait bien, dès lors, contenir un nouveau secret moderne, celui de dire à la fois, d'une part, 'exotérique' : soit le contraire de son étymologie, d'autre part 'déraisonnable'. Les rayons dits 'ésotériques' de nos librairies cachent une pensée principalement magique (irrationnelle et "vulgaire"). Le seul fait que ces rayons existent au vu et au su de tous montre qu'il ne s'agit plus exactement de secret mais d'habillage. L'habit est ce mot lui-même ésotérique qu'est 'ésotérisme', qui cache la populaire naïveté d'autres mots comme 'magique', 'surnaturel', 'extra-terrestres', 'voyages astraux', 'paranormal' ou 'mystique'. Cet habillage pourrait même être mieux appelé 'emballage' si l'on considère que les librairies "customisent" la pensée magique pour mieux la vendre aux acheteurs, éventuellement pudiques face aux inclinaisons populaires – magiques – de leur pensée.

Le titre de ce texte, dès lors, entend par 'ésotérisme moderne' le sens 'd'habillage de la pensée magique'. On tâchera de montrer, après quelques remarques préliminaires, que les grands philosophes allemands, au cours du XIXe siècle, développent peut-être une telle pensée magique mais sporadiquement et implicitement, avec pudeur (parfois sans doute inconsciemment), presque toujours en marge de leurs concepts habituels voire de leur système. Nous disions 'sporadiquement' car cette magie implicite s'associe souvent de façon intéressante au discours sur la musique, discours finalement dans l'ensemble rare ou du moins à tendance lapidaire et peu systématique. La musique ferait alors figure de spiritualité officieuse, déguisée, que ce déguisement fût consciemment imaginé par chaque auteur ou non. On peut noter dors et déjà que le fait que les systèmes des philosophes, quand il s'agirait d'aborder la question de la musique, en deviendraient implicitement mystiques, et perdraient alors de leur rigueur, serait rendu admissible (aux yeux des lecteurs comme des auteurs eux-mêmes) par un principe d'indulgence concernant le sujet musique, comme si l'auteur non seulement pouvait, mais se devait alors de devenir subjectif – au moins dans l'emploi d'un *style* subjectiviste ou poétique. Ce principe d'indulgence est comme un consensus culturel secret, celui qui accorderait à la musique une valeur idéale incontestable (dans l'esprit du philosophe comme dans celui de son lecteur contemporain), la valeur, si l'on veut, d'une divinité en exil, adorée secrètement mais non moins unanimement, mais valeur paradoxale puisqu'elle ne convoquerait précisément pas, bien au contraire, toute la rigueur – donc l'attention – du philosophe. Ce qui compterait pour le philosophe serait alors peut-être davantage la célébration – l'adoration, avec la complicité supposée du lecteur – de son sujet plutôt que son éclaircissement.

On constatera bientôt une certaine progression, de Kant à Nietzsche, progression d'ailleurs à peu près chronologique, progression de l'estime portée par les philosophes à la musique, estime corrélée – on le comprend peu à peu – à la magie que toute pensée musicale invoquerait discrètement, c'est-à-dire non pas secrètement (dans la mesure où tout un chacun en serait averti) mais de façon dérobée par rapport au nouveau champ scientifique, champ considérable et presque universel, à savoir celui des mots dans son ensemble. Ce qui apparaît donc notamment intéressant – cela dit en guise d'ultime remarque préliminaire – est la façon dont les philosophes, peu à peu, doivent rendre compte par les mots de ce qui échappe à ceux-ci et dès lors nier secrètement les mécanismes habituels de leur pensée[4] quand il s'agit d'évoquer la musique.

Dans l'esthétique de Kant, à l'aube du XIXe siècle, la musique ne trouve encore qu'un rôle mineur. Le philosophe, dans le § 53 de sa fameuse *Kritik der Urteilskraft* (1790), la relègue même au dernier rang des arts[5], elle qui ne 'parle que par pures sensations, sans concepts'.

---

[4] Si l'art est bien une mise en échec permanente de la raison, une 'crise pour le fonctionnement de nos discours', pour suivre Christoph Menke (cité par Jimenez, *L'esthétique contemporaine*, 93), alors la musique semble un art tout privilégié.

[5] 'Si l'on prend pour critère l'extension des facultés qui doivent coïncider dans le jugement pour produire des connaissances, la musique sera reléguée au dernier rang des beaux-arts', op. cit.

Tout au plus parvient-elle à produire 'une agréable jouissance personnelle'. Le philosophe ne semble même jamais plus prolixe, quand il s'agit d'évoquer la musique, que pour se plaindre de son 'manque d'urbanité, car [...] ses effets dépassent la limite qu'on voudrait leur assigner (et s'étendent jusqu'au voisinage), et elle s'impose en quelque sorte, portant préjudice à ceux qui n'appartiennent pas à la société de musique; ce qui n'est pas le cas des arts qui s'adressent à l'œil, puisqu'on peut toujours détourner son regard [...]. Ceux qui ont recommandé qu'on chante des cantiques à l'occasion des dévotions domestiques n'ont pas réfléchi à la pénible incommodité que ces exercices bruyants font subir au public'…

Comme le résume Alain Tirzi, dans l'œuvre de Kant la musique est 'latente et impensée'[6]. Or, voilà qui correspond déjà à ce que nous annoncions ci-dessus: 'latente' faisant figure 'd'implicite' et impensée car sans doute impensable. Le philosophe, manifestement, se permet des privautés, des remarques personnelles, affectives, peu rigoureuses en regard de la conduite logique imparable du reste de l'œuvre. Si la musique n'est pas *au-delà* de la pensée mais au contraire *en deçà*[7], il n'en reste pas moins qu'elle obtient déjà une mention spéciale qui préfigure – en négatif – sa future mission singulière.

Dans *Vorlesungen über die Ästhetik* de Hegel (ses cours d'esthétique prononcés entre 1818 et 1929 et dont la publication s'achève en 1838), la musique se hisse soudain de cette dernière place accordée par Kant à la seconde, derrière la poésie. Mais surtout elle 'renferme en soi un fond spirituel, [ce sont] toujours les mouvements intérieurs de l'âme qu'elle a à exprimer'[8]. Plus loin le philosophe se fait poète et s'exprime par métaphores, voire par allégories: il n'hésite pas à personnifier la musique, à en faire une entité pensante, capable de sentiments (d'être 'satisfaite'): 'la musique c'est l'esprit, l'âme qui chante immédiatement pour son propre compte, qui se sent satisfaite dans le vif sentiment qu'elle a d'elle-même'[9]. Finalement 'la musique, comme la contemplation de la pure lumière par elle-même, nous donne l'idée

---

[6] *Kant et la musique*, 13. Plus loin la musique apparaît 'impensée [...], ce qui en l'occurrence dans un texte est présent, mais sous une forme telle qu'une stratégie de montage, de mixage et de recoupement est nécessaire pour le mettre en lumière'.

[7] Peut-être Kant, à son époque, ne manque-t-il pas encore assez du concept magique du divin pour que la musique ne tracte secrètement celui-ci et s'en coiffe alors d'un chef idéal.

[8] Op. cit., 366.

[9] Id., 376.

la plus haute de la félicité et de l'harmonie divines'[10]. Le divin n'est pourtant pas à proprement parler un concept hégélien (mais seulement un sujet d'étude). C'est un présupposé sur lequel Hegel ne bâtit rien de sa fameuse dialectique historique. Jusqu'à preuve du contraire, sa *Phénoménologie de l'esprit* (*Phänomenologie des Geistes*) n'est pas nommément celle de l'Esprit Saint. On pourrait donc en conclure que le sujet musical, dans son œuvre, engendre un champ sémantique impersonnel. La musique semble affaiblir, mythifier son discours. Elle s'accompagne de concepts hérités (traditionnellement spirituels et notamment chrétiens), ceux de 'pureté' ou de 'lumière'. La notion de pureté parcourt tout l'Ancien Testament[11]. Quant à la lumière, éminemment biblique, c'est par exemple celle de la 'Transfiguration'[12], de la 'Naissance de Jésus'[13] ou ne serait-ce du début de la *Genèse*: 'Que la lumière soit! Et la lumière fut'.

Schopenhauer développe un discours sur la musique dans son œuvre maîtresse, *Die Welt als Wille und Vorstellung* (1818), plus précisément dans le § 52 du tome I et le chapitre 39 du tome II ('Über Metaphysik der Musik'). La musique, cette fois[14], obtient la première place dans la hiérarchie des attentions accordées aux arts par les philosophes. 'Parce que la musique ne montre pas, comme les autres arts, les idées ou degrés de l'objectivation de la volonté, mais directement la volonté *elle-même*, nous pouvons ainsi expliquer qu'elle agit directement sur la volonté, c'est-à-dire les sentiments, passions et émotions de l'auditeur, de sorte qu'elle les exalte ou même les altère. [Plus loin, elle est] le plus puissant de tous les arts, elle atteint ses fins entièrement par ses propres moyens'[15]. L'auteur, à l'instar de Hegel, personnifie la musique, fait d'elle une entité pensante, en lui octroyant des 'fins'. Or, cette entité pensante est liée à quelque *au-delà* de notre monde, 'au-delà' devant être pris dans son sens littéral. Le philosophe écrira

---

[10] Ibid., 378.

[11] Voir par exemple *Deutéronome* 14 ('Soyez purs pour votre Dieu').

[12] *Matthieu* 17, 2.

[13] *Luc* 2, 9.

[14] L'œuvre est antérieure aux *Vorlesungen über die Ästhetik* de Hegel. Nous l'avons fait figurer après ceux-ci, cependant, en raison de son engagement plus important en faveur de la musique et du fait que Hegel était de vingt-neuf ans l'aîné de Schopenhauer et que sa pensée, globalement, est antérieure.

[15] Op. cit., t. 2, 448 (édition américaine, les recherches préalables à la rédaction de ce texte ayant été menées à l'étranger, certains ouvrages comme celui-ci ont été consultés dans leur traduction anglaise et non française. Que le lecteur veuille bien nous en excuser).

ailleurs: 'la musique semble parler de mondes différents et meilleurs que le nôtre'[16]. Encore ce 'semble' peut-il signifier que l'auteur ne fait ici que s'accorder une licence poétique, s'exprimer par images. Mais dans cet exemple comme dans d'autres, on remarque que le sujet musique engendre un champ sémantique spirituel et/ou un style poétique et que dans les deux cas, il tire l'auteur hors de son domaine, de sa méthode habituelle, tel un sujet limite. Ceci est manifeste à travers cette autre opinion singulière et fameuse de Schopenhauer: 'la musique, puisqu'elle passe au-dessus des idées, est aussi assez indépendante du monde des phénomènes, l'ignore résolument, et, dans une certaine mesure, pourrait exister encore s'il n'y avait pas de monde du tout, ce qui ne peut être dit des autres arts'[17]. Une musique indépendante du monde signifie un art non créé par les hommes. Il s'agit dès lors d'une discipline engendrée par Dieu, ou à la rigueur purement métaphysique, mais cette dernière hypothèse paraît infirmée par la composante sensible (acoustique) de l'art musical. Cette opinion serait donc bien mystique mais de façon implicite: déguisée, habillée. Voilà une formulation 'ésotérique' selon le troisième sens que nous proposons ci-dessus. Notons qu'ailleurs, Schopenhauer pourra, concernant la musique, s'ouvrir d'opinions rappelant une pensée analogique ou des symbolismes courants dans les théories musicales antérieures au XVIIe siècle (généralement pythagoriciennes): 'les quatre voix ou parties de toute harmonie que sont basse, ténor, alto et soprano, ou note fondamentale, tierce, quinte et octave correspondent aux quatre degrés dans les séries des existences, donc aux règnes minéral, végétal, animal et humain'. Ce symbolisme, non plus courant à l'époque de Schopenhauer, vaut ici pour ce qu'il tracte de la pensée musicale antérieure au XVIIe siècle (par exemple dans celle de Zarlino), et de ses connotations magiques selon les canons du XIXe siècle, et donc ésotériques au sens moderne. Dans le même temps, de tels symbolismes pourront, au XIXe siècle, évoquer un univers ésotérique au sens premier du terme, c'est-à-dire survivant dans des sociétés secrètes garantes d'un savoir désormais ancien.

Nietzsche franchit encore un pas sur le chemin de la sacralisation secrète du sujet musique. Il est – ou tâche d'être – compositeur lui-même; il évoque la musique dans de nombreux ouvrages; il se définie

---

[16] *Id.*, 457.
[17] Ibid., t. 1, 257.

comme danseur; il est tout d'abord – jeune homme – entièrement *dévoué* à Wagner, avant de devenir, à la fin de sa vie, son ennemi le plus acharné. Ses premières influences majeures sont Wagner *autant* que Schopenhauer, en quelque sorte. Cette sacralisation de la musique est d'autant plus importante dans son œuvre que, par rapport à ses prédécesseurs (Kant, Schopenhauer, Hegel), le jeune penseur a davantage subi l'influence de son époque et de son culte déjà avancé du génie, notamment du génie musicien. On peut surtout parler de culte lorsque 'génie' désigne non pas seulement une *grâce* touchant un artiste à certains moments, sorte de paroxysme du talent, mais une *personne* idéalisée, supposée concernée en permanence par la dite grâce. Cet *homme-génie*, véritable magicien moderne, est typiquement 'ésotérique' dans le sens où nous l'entendons ici. Il est cette divinité débarrassée des embarras de la religion, à laquelle on voue un culte qui, s'il est libre de tout rituel (et de tout tabou grâce au caractère secret – officieux – du culte), n'en est que d'autant plus vivace au XIXᵉ siècle puis au XXᵉ siècle. Nous nus en ouvrions dans un autre texte[18].

Le jeune Nietzsche (dans *Schopenhauer pour professeur*) associe d'abord bouddhisme et culte du génie. 'Le génie cherche plus profondément la sainteté parce que, visionnaire, [...], il a vu le domaine de paix et de renoncement à la volonté, sur cette autre rive dont parle les Indiens'[19]. Durant ses jeunes années, l'idéal du philosophe, tel que formulé dans *Die Geburt der Tragödie* (1872) – première œuvre majeure – est cette musique à la fois dionysiaque et apollinienne qui alimente la pensée tragique (bientôt détruite, hélas, par le 'démon Socrate'). Partant, la musique existe avant la philosophie, selon le penseur, chronologiquement, donc, mais même ontologiquement : encore dans *Der Fall Wagner* (1888) l'une de ses dernières œuvres, Nietzsche écrira que 'plus on devient musicien, plus on devient philosophe'[20]. La musique avant même la philosophie. C'est que cet art est, pour Nietzsche, à ce point consubstantiel à la vie que le penseur en conçoit sa fameuse opinion : 'le bonheur est fait de riens! Le son d'une cornemuse. – Sans musique, la vie serait une erreur. L'Allemand s'imagine Dieu lui-même chantant des cantiques!'[21] On pourrait penser que la formulation même des idées nietzschéennes serait *musicale* de par l'emploi récurrent des

---

[18] Voir Amblard, 'L'œuvre esthétique comme œuvre limite'.
[19] *Schopenhauer als Erzieher*, 143.
[20] Op. cit., 21.
[21] *Götzen-Dämmerung*, § 33.

points d'exclamation (comme plus tard dans l'œuvre romanesque de Céline) qui accentuent l'amplitude prosodique, donc la mélodicité des fins de phrase, comme pour ré-inoculer l'affect musical dans le mot. Par ailleurs, Dieu lui-même – pour peu que Nietzsche s'identifie à cet 'Allemand typique'[22] et croit en Son existence après l'avoir maintes fois déclaré mort[23] – est ici non pas seulement identifié à la musique, mais dévoué à elle. Dieu, s'il existe, est inféodé à l'art comme l'est tout le XIXe siècle. La musique est comme au-dessus de Dieu lui-même puisque celui-ci fait l'*effort* de la pratiquer. Dieu est alors un artiste, au mieux un génie parmi d'autres, comme dans la vision de Schiller, lequel parlait des œuvres de 'l'artiste divin'[24].

Certes, Nietzsche déclara que 'Dieu est mort' et cela à plusieurs reprises[25]. Or, paradoxalement, si Dieu est mort, le divin, lui, est encore vivant, et foisonne même dans les œuvres, davantage encore que dans *Vorlesungen über die Ästhetik* de Hegel. Nietzsche écrit par exemple dans *Der Fall Wagner* : 'ce qui est bon est léger. Tout ce qui est divin marche d'un pas délicat'[26]. Voilà encore un paradoxe ésotérique au sens où nous l'entendions : Dieu doit être nommé non pas secrètement mais tout de même avec pudeur : il doit donc quitter le substantif pour se contenter de l'adjectif, à l'effet plus indirect dans la phrase, ne plus *être* (comme "est" le substantif) mais se contenter de qualifier, de façon équivoque, c'est-à-dire avoir tout de même le pouvoir de qualifier sans pour autant que son existence même soit évidente. En un sens, Dieu est ainsi, sinon annihilé, du moins exilé dans l'adjectif, non pas supprimé mais dégradé, destitué de son plein prestige, de sa présence au centre des activités humaines. Or, force est de constater que cet 'ésotérisme' charrié par la discrétion relative du mot 'divin'

---

[22] Si l'Allemand est souvent l'ennemi déclaré de Nietzsche, on peut supposer qu'ici, pour une fois, cet archétype est décrit avec sympathie. Reste à peser le terme 's'imagine' dans ce qu'il recèle d'illusion ou de juste intuition.

[23] Voir note 25.

[24] Cité par Lovejoy, *The great chain of being*, 299.

[25] Voir par exemple *Also sprach Zarathustra* (1885), 'Prologue de Zarathoustra', II, ou *Die fröhliche Wissenschaft* (1882), livre troisième, § 125 : 'Dieu est mort ! Dieu reste mort ! Et c'est nous qui l'avons tué ! Comment nous consoler, nous les meurtriers des meurtriers ? Ce que le monde a possédé jusqu'à présent de plus sacré et de plus puissant a perdu son sang sous notre couteau. – Qui nous lavera de ce sang ? Avec quelle eau pourrions-nous nous purifier ? Quelles expiations, quels jeux sacrés serons-nous forcés d'inventer ? La grandeur de cet acte n'est-elle pas trop grande pour nous ? Ne sommes-nous pas forcés de devenir nous-mêmes des dieux simplement – ne fût-ce que pour paraître dignes d'eux ?'

[26] Op. cit., 21.

s'associe volontiers à la musique. Avant d'illustrer ceci, commençons par remarquer que l'univers théologique de Nietzsche semble l'objet de conflits. 'L'âme, ça n'existe pas.', glisse-t-il dans la seconde version de *Nietzsche contra Wagner* (1888)[27], mais plus loin dans la même œuvre : 'Mon âme, un luth'[28]. On pourrait rétorquer que dans le second cas, 'âme' signifie 'sentiments' ou 'for intérieur'. Mais à cela on pourrait cette fois opposer l'autorité de la langue, de l'étymologie, qui trahit peut-être au moins l'inconscient – encore croyant ? – de Nietzsche. En tout état de cause, si l'âme existe, c'est seulement pour revêtir une forme musicale (celle d'un luth). Si Dieu est mort, dans l'œuvre de Nietzsche, c'est semble-t-il davantage l'imagerie judéo-chrétienne qui lui est associée que son essence, la nouvelle forme – secrète, ésotérique – de Dieu étant peut-être : la musique elle-même. Remarquons-le à nouveau, c'est constamment que le champ lexical traditionnel de la foi est ré-inoculé à l'univers musical, dans l'œuvre de l'Allemand. Ainsi dans *Richard Wagner in Bayreuth*, à propos du compositeur : 'c'était comme si à partir de cet instant l'esprit de la musique parlait [à Wagner] par une magie spirituelle totalement nouvelle'[29].

Dans ce qu'on pourrait appeler 'l'ésotérisme nietzschéen', si la musique revêt une forme positive absolue en prenant la place de Dieu, elle peut également devenir, à l'inverse, *diabolique*, absolument négative. Si la diabolisation d'une certaine musique pouvait sembler ordinaire au Moyen Âge, notamment du fait de l'Eglise qui redoutait parfois la musique instrumentale ou ne serait-ce que l'intervalle de triton (*diabolus in musica*), il pourrait paraître plus surprenant, en plein siècle romantique, d'aboutir à de telles mises à l'index. Si au Moyen Âge, ces diabolisations venaient facilement du fait de l'importance donnée à Dieu, diabolisations à tout propos, durant le siècle romantique elles viennent sans doute de l'importance accordée, cette fois, à la musique. On aboutit chez Nietzsche à une théosophie symétrique – ordonnée – bâtie autour de celle-ci (et non plus autour de Dieu), *musicosophie* comprenant bien et mal. Dans *Der Fall Wagner*, le maître de Bayreuth prend les caractéristiques traditionnellement attribuées au grand tentateur. 'Il n'est, dans les choses de l'esprit, rien de las, d'exténué, rien qui représente un danger mortel et dénigre le monde, que Wagner

---

[27] Op. cit., 63.
[28] *Id.*, 66.
[29] Dans notre traduction. Op. cit., 46.

ne défende en secret. C'est le plus sombre obscurantisme qu'il cache dans les voiles lumineux de l'Idéal. Il flatte tous les instincts nihilistes (bouddhistes) et les travestit en musique'[30]. Wagner est bien le grand travestisseur, celui qui maquille les œuvres du mal en œuvres du bien, rôle de faussaire traditionnellement attribué à Lucifer. Plus loin il plaint les jeunes gens qui se rendent à Bayreuth, 'au nom du Père, du Fils et du Saint Esprit wagnérien'. Il conclut alors : 'on ne peut servir deux maîtres quand l'un deux s'appelle Wagner'[31] comme il est conclu dans les évangiles à la fin de la parabole de l'intendant fidèle : 'tu ne peux servir deux maîtres. Tu ne peux servir Dieu et Mammon'[32].

En fait, Nietzsche traque non seulement la tournure d'esprit, mais la tournure de corps même instillée par la musique : en tant que danseur. Zarathoustra est défini comme danseur et c'est ainsi qu'il atteint sa 'divine légèreté'[33]. Le thème de la danse, idéal de cette œuvre testamentaire, la parcourt toute entière. Ce sont notamment ces célèbres aphorismes : 'celui qui s'approche de son but – celui-là danse'[34], ou 'et que chaque jour où l'on n'a pas dansé une fois au moins soit perdu pour nous'[35]! Peut-être la formulation la plus radicale de l'obédience de la pensée nietzschéenne à *l'esprit de la danse*, donc *a fortiori* à la musique est dans une page moins célèbre, 'ceci est mon alpha et mon oméga, que tout ce qui est lourd devienne léger, que tout corps devienne danseur'[36], à moins qu'il ne faille la trouver dans *Die fröhliche Wissenschaft* : 'Je ne sais rien qu'un philosophe souhaite plus qu'être un bon danseur. Car la danse est son idéal, son art aussi, sa seule piété, enfin, son service divin'[37]. Une fois de plus, l'adjectif 'divin' est avancé. C'est sans doute que Dieu n'est mort – insistons sur ce point – que sous certaines conditions. Or, un Dieu danseur semblerait pour Nietzsche envisageable : 'je ne pourrais croire qu'à un Dieu qui saurait danser'[38]. C'est dire que Dieu lui-même – à supposer qu'il existe pour Nietzsche, ceci reste ambigu – serait inspiré en tant que danseur, comme le

---

[30] Op. cit., 47.
[31] *Id.*, 48–49.
[32] Voir *Luc* 16, 13 ou *Matthieu* 6, 24.
[33] 'Zarathoustra le danseur, Zarathoustra le léger, celui qui agite ses ailes, prêt au vol, faisant signe à tous les oiseaux, prêt et agile, divinement léger'. *Also sprach Zarathustra*, 'De l'homme supérieur', § 18.
[34] *Id.*, 'De l'homme supérieur', § 17.
[35] *Ibid.*, 'Des vieilles et des nouvelles tables', § 23.
[36] *Ibid.*, 'Les sept sceaux', § 6.
[37] Op. cit., livre cinquième, 'De la question de la compréhension', § 381, *in fine*.
[38] *Also sprach Zarathustra*, 'Lire et écrire', *in fine*.

penseur allemand, par la musique. Cette dernière, dès lors inspiratrice de Dieu lui-même, serait alors plus que divine et comme préexistante au principe du divin, métaphysique absolue.

Reste à se demander brièvement si cette évolution de la pensée musicale allemande, ce qu'on a pu définir comme le développement d'une pensée magique implicite, a continué au XXe siècle. On ne pourra répondre ici à cette vaste question. Mais donnons quelques pistes. Force est de constater que cet ésotérisme s'est parfois propagé par sa "contraposée". Marx, dialecticien matérialiste par excellence, pour lequel toute pensée magique ne serait au mieux qu'un leurre dommageable à la classe ouvrière, n'envisage précisément, *singulièrement* pas le sujet musique (alors que la notion de musique de classe n'eût pas été absurde dans son système). Alain Badiou, dernier penseur marxiste en date, pour lequel l'art est pourtant seul apte à traduire des vérités (quand la philosophie elle-même ne le peut pas), passe la musique entièrement sous silence dans son *Petit précis d'inesthétique*, bien que le sujet apparaisse dans *Logique des mondes*. De même, si Heidegger considérait déjà que l'Être se trahissait mieux par la poésie (qu'il étudia en profondeur durant sa troisième période) que dans la philosophie, de musique il n'est peu ou pas question dans son œuvre. Implicitement, ces silences trahissent peut-être une pensée musicale (ici peut-être une crainte de la musique) encore romantique, cette pensée étant encore imaginée magique ou non envisageable.

Lorsque la pensée du XXe siècle, athée, envisage malgré tout la musique, celle-ci reste souvent une frontière, une idée de l'infini ou de l'idéal absolu, un art limite. La question n'est pas d'aborder ici, de front, le problème dans son ensemble. On se bornera à donner quelques exemples, pêle-mêle, pour conclure. Si Deleuze est incroyant, quelle peut être son idée de l'infini ? Le cosmos peut-être (seul infini "visible", concret). La musique s'identifie donc au cosmos d'après lui. Elle est 'entièrement hors du réel'[39] préfère écrire l'athée Sartre, sans doute avec admiration, la fuite du réel dans l'imaginaire étant sans doute un idéal sartrien. Dans les deux cas, la précision de vue ainsi que le *raisonnement* philosophiques semblent perdus. C'est ce que le lecteur semble attendre car la raison, face à ce sujet limite qui la met en crise, ne *doit* manifestement plus l'emporter. Question d'éthique, et non pas d'esthétique car la musique, on l'aura compris, est devenue

---

[39] *L'imaginaire*, 370.

bien plus qu'un art durant le XIXe siècle et le demeure manifestement au XXe. Alain poètise davantage encore, la musique est une 'allégresse montante d'une volonté toujours jeune', formule illuminée, peut-être même mauvaise formule, comme philosophiquement vide, qui rappelle quelque imitation hâtive de la caractérisation du divin issue des évangiles. Ailleurs: 'la musique, forme humaine la plus pure'[40], mais Alain ajoute 'la plus fragile et la plus forte'.

La plus fragile et la plus forte. Le paradoxe semble, de fait, la seule formulation possible: par la négation même de la logique. Plus précisément, la logique aime se nier par un *retournement sur elle-même*. Aussi, les formulations sont, au XXe siècle comme au XIXe siècle, volontiers "réflexives"[41], c'est-à-dire retournées sur elles-mêmes La musique partage alors avec Dieu le privilège non pas seulement rare mais exclusif d'avoir le droit de se contempler elle-même sans qu'il soit question de penser au mythe de Narcisse donc à quelque connotation morbide. Rappelons Hegel: 'contemplation de la pure lumière par elle-même'. Nietzsche, dans *Jenseits von Gut und Böse* (1885–86) écrira d'une façon analogue que 'grâce à la musique, les passions jouissent d'elles-mêmes'[42]. Alain prétendra aussi que 'le propre de la musique est de ne rien exprimer qu'elle-même'[43]. Adorno choisira, lui, cet autre paradoxe réflexif: 'le fait de la musique est de nommer le Nom lui-même'. Or, de quel nom s'agit-il? Il est surprenant de le découvrir, ainsi, sous la plume d'un philosophe marxiste – matérialiste et voilà qui nous tiendra lieu de conclusion car ceci semble expliquer 'l'ésotérisme' (comme nous l'entendions ici) du sujet musique: 'comparé au langage, la musique est un langage d'un genre complètement différent. C'est là que se cache son aspect théologique. [...] Son idée est la forme du nom de Dieu. C'est une prière démystifiée, libérée de la magie de faire survenir quoi que ce soit, le fait humain (futile comme toujours), pour nommer le Nom lui-même'[44]. Il se fût donc toujours agi pour le sujet musique de camoufler, en une 'prière démystifiée', le nom de Dieu en son sein. Les philosophes qui l'auraient compris avant Adorno auraient alors respecté le secret de cette prière déritualisée,

---

[40] Cité par Ribon, *Le gouffre et l'enchantement*, 187.
[41] 'Réflexif' doit être compris ici dans son sens mathématique, en tant qu'une loi est réflexive si 'tout élément z, selon cette loi, est en relation avec z: avec lui-même'.
[42] § 106.
[43] Cité par Ribon, op. cit.
[44] 'Musik, Sprache und ihr Verhältnis im gegenwärtigen Komponieren', 114.

et ceux qui ne l'auraient pas compris auraient relayé mieux encore qu'implicitement : inconsciemment, cette 'prière', spiritualité en diaspora. Disserter avec *dévotion* au sujet de la musique a pu continuer à poser la question de l'existence de la magie mais sur le plan affectif, inconscient, finalement sur un plan essentiel si l'on considère que le for intérieur visé par les concepts magiques est peuplé surtout d'affects, et que le personnage principal des évangiles s'intéresse traditionnellement davantage à 'l'intelligence du cœur' qu'à la raison ; cela même à des époques où l'épistémologie scientiste, de façon singulière dans l'histoire, à la question pourtant éternelle de l'existence de Dieu interdisait une réponse positive autant même qu'une simple question consciente au préalable, le plan conscient lui appartenant désormais presque exclusivement.

BIBLIOGRAPHIE

Adorno, T. W., *Ästhetische Theorie* (*Théorie esthétique*, trad. M. Jimenez, Paris: Klincksieck 1974).
——, 'Musik, Sprache und ihr Verhältnis im gegenwärtigen Komponieren' ('Music, language and composition', trad. S. Gillespie, in: *Essays on music*, Berkeley: University of California Press 2002).
Alain, *Les arts et les dieux*, Paris: Gallimard, 1958.
Amblard, J., 'L'œuvre esthétique comme œuvre limite', in: *Les limites de l'œuvre*, Aix-en-Provence: Publications de l'Université de Provence, 248–253.
Faivre, A., 'Une discipline nouvelle : l'ésotérisme', in: *Le défi magique*, t. 1 : *Ésotérisme, Occultisme, Spiritisme*, Lyon: Presses universitaires de Lyon 1994, 35–43.
——, 'L'ésotérisme et la recherche universitaire', in: *Accès de l'ésotérisme occidental*, Paris: Gallimard (Bibliothèque des sciences humaines) 1996, t. 2, avant-propos.
——, 'Occident moderne', in: *Dictionnaire critique de l'ésotérisme*, sous la direction de Jean Servier, Paris: PUF 1998.
Hegel, G. W. F., *Vorlesungen über die Ästhetik* (*Cours d'esthétique*, trad. B. Timmermans et P. Zaccaria, Paris: Librairie Générale Française – livre de poche 1997, t. 2).
Jimenez, M., *L'esthétique contemporaine*, Paris: Klincksieck 1999.
Kant, E., *Kritik der Urteilskraft* (*Critique de la faculté de juger*, trad. J.-R. Ladmiral, M. B. de Launay et J.-M. Vaysse, Paris: Gallimard – Pléiade 1985, t. 2).
Lovejoy, A., *The great chain of being*, Cambridge: Mass 1966.
Nietzsche, *Also sprach Zarathustra* (*Ainsi parlait Zarathoustra*, trad. H. Albert, Paris: Club du meilleur livre 1958).
Nietzsche, F., *Der Fall Wagner* (*Le cas Wagner*, trad. J.-C. Hémery, Paris: Gallimard – folio essais 1974).
——, *Die fröhliche Wissenschaft* (*Le gai savoir*, trad. H. Albert, Paris: Société du Mercure de France 1901).
——, *Die Geburt der Tragödie* (*La naissance de la tragédie*, trad. G. Bianquis, Paris: Gallimard 1949).
——, *Götzen-dämmerung* (*Le crépuscule des idoles*, trad. H. Albert, Paris: Société du Mercure de France 1906).

——, *Jenseits von Gut und Böse* (*Par-delà le bien et le mal*, trad. Henri Albert révisée par J. Lacoste, Paris: Robert Laffont – Bouquins 1993).

——, *Nietzsche contra Wagner* (*Nietzsche contre Wagner*, trad. J.-C. Hémery, Paris: Gallimard – folio essais 1974).

——, *Richard Wagner in Bayreuth*, in: *Nietzsche Werk*, Berlin: Walter de Gruyter & co 1967.

——, *Schopenhauer als Erzieher*, in: *Unzeitgemässe Betrachtungen* (*Schopenhauer as educator*, in: *Untimely meditations*, trad. R. J. Hollingdale), Cambridge: Cambridge University Press 1983.

Ribon, M., *Le gouffre et l'enchantement*, Paris: Buchet/Chastel 2006.

Riffard, P. A., *Dictionnaire de l'ésotérisme*, Paris: Payot 1983.

Sartre, J.-P., *L'imaginaire*, Paris: Gallimard 1986.

Schopenhauer, A., *Die Welt als Wille und Vorstellung* (*The world as will and as representation*, trad. E. F. J. Payne, New York: Dover Publications 1969).

Servier, J. (sous la direction de), *Dictionnaire critique de l'ésotérisme*, Paris: PUF 1998.

Tirzi, A., *Kant et la musique*, Paris: L'Harmattan 2003.

PART TWO

NINETEENTH AND TWENTIETH CENTURY
MUSICAL ESOTERICISM

THE MYSTERIES OF SOUND IN H. P. BLAVATSKY'S 'ESOTERIC INSTRUCTIONS'

Tim Rudbøg

This chapter is concerned with music and esotericism in the 19th century, particularly with the notion of sound in Helena Petrovna Blavatsky's 'Esoteric Instructions'. It is, however, by way of introduction deemed necessary to briefly specify these two general concepts.

Music is generally agreed to be an art form occupied with mastering and manipulating sound, "Western esotericism", however, is a much more complicated term. Even though it is not the purpose of this chapter to discuss the many complexities of the nature of "Western esotericism";[1] it should be mentioned that Wouter Hanegraaff has recently, from a scholarly perspective, argued convincingly that "Western esotericism", taken in the sense of a specific domain or field in itself, rests on a long polemical process of "othering" ideas and currents from the dominant discourses in the West[2] resulting in a reification of the concept "Western esotericism". Thus currents and ideas, which in historical reality are dimensions of Western culture and religion, have mistakenly been regarded as embodying a specific and tangible field.[3] From this point of view esotericism is not an art form with a relatively coherent history like music, but a heuristic concept which can be used in order to make sense of certain historical currents and ideas in Western culture and religion which have either direct family resemblances to each other or which have been polemically construed as belonging to the same domain by either opponents or proponents of such ideas and currents.

This chapter is therefore not particularly concerned with "Western esotericism" as a coherent field undergoing a continuous history into the 19th century, but rather with three pre-modern ideas related to

---

[1] See the following for a general overview of the concept 'Western esotericism': Faivre, *Access to Western Esotericism*. Hanegraaff, 'The Study of Western Esotericism'. Hanegraaff, 'Forbidden Knowledge'. Stuckrad, 'Western Esotericism'. Versluis, 'What is Esoteric?'. Versluis, 'Methods in the study of Esotericism'.
[2] See Hanegraaff, 'Forbidden Knowledge' and 'The Trouble with Images'.
[3] Hanegraaff, 'Forbidden Knowledge', 228.

music and cosmology, which have flourished through Western culture and were finally used in H. P. Blavatsky's Theosophy – a modern self-proclaimed form of esotericism in the 19th century.[4] Madam Blavatsky (1831–1891), herself, is well known as a controversial woman of noble Russian descent and as one of the foremost influential esotericists during the "occult revival" in the 19th century. During her lifetime she travelled throughout most of the world in search of esoteric knowledge, co-founded the well-known Theosophical Society in 1875, and wrote extensively on esotericism between 1874–1891 including her major works *Isis Unveiled* (1877) and *The Secret Doctrine* (1888), *The Voice of the Silence* (1889) and *The Key to Theosophy* (1889) as well as her lesser known 'Esoteric Instructions' (1889–1890) – dealt with in this chapter. What is also less known, in relation to music, is that Blavatsky herself enjoyed playing the piano from an early age and that she also gave piano concerts. Count Witte (1849–1915) wrote in his memoirs of her that:

> she gave pianoforte concerts in London and Paris, and afterwards became the manager of the royal choir, maintained by King Milan of Serbia.[5]

Many contemporary composers were also inspired by Blavatsky's Theosophy, such as Gustav Mahler (1860–1911), Jean Sibelius (1865–1957), and Alexander Scriabin (1870–1915).[6]

THREE IDEAS AND QUESTIONS

The three pre-modern ideas related to music and cosmology, with which this chapter is particularly concerned since they are used in H. P. Blavatsky's 'Esoteric Instructions', stem largely from the Pythagorean-Platonic tradition and its various transmutations through Western history.[7] The first is the idea of 'Kosmos' in the original Greek meaning of the word as an 'ordered whole', as an 'ornament' or the great

---

[4] It is here to be noted that from a strictly nominalistic perspective abstract ideas/concepts do not have an independent continual historical existence – I am therefore not suggesting the continual existence of the same abstract entities/ideas from Antiquity, but rather focus on how ideas have been transformed and used.
[5] Yarmolinsky, *The Memoirs of Count Witte*, 4–10.
[6] Cranston, *H.P.B.*, 495–498. On Scriabin, see Barbara Aniello's article in this volume.
[7] For an overview of translated source texts, which contain ideas that relate sound and cosmology in the Pythagorean-Platonic tradition see Godwin, *The Harmony of the Spheres*.

'harmonia'.[8] The idea that cosmos is musical in its very constitution –
from its numerical basis – has since Antiquity often been related to
the two following ideas. The second idea (or perhaps 'way of thinking') is the idea of correspondences. This idea of correspondences, or
correlative thinking, has been central to much of what has been and
is termed "Western esotericism". It can be traced all the way back
to ancient oriental sources, before entering the West through ancient
Greece; from where, after the death of Alexander in 323 BCE, it eventually spread widely.[9] The third idea is that of the power of sound
and words. Since Antiquity many claims have been made that sound,
music and words have an effect upon cosmos – and by analogy on
man, the microcosm.[10]

During Antiquity, from the legendary Orpheus down to Pythagoras,
we thus find that music (and mathematics) was regarded as an intrin-
sic ontological part of cosmos – the ordered whole. Everything had its
harmonious place in the larger whole and each part was regarded as
interactive with every other part. Nature was filled with sympathies
and antipathies, all set in harmonious proportions to each other. If
one knew the sounds of nature, one could through their powers tame
animals like Orpheus did,[11] or regulate one's life in harmony accordingly, like the Pythagoreans sought to do.

For the Pythagoreans and the Platonists, music (and mathematics)
was not just used as a formal theoretical system, but also as a practical
form of healing and purification.[12] The microcosmos – man – could
direct his life in relation to the great rhythm of a macrocosmos popu-
lated by planets, which again were regarded as embodiments of great
gods living in musical proportion to each other. If one was able to
listen carefully one could hear the unique "harmony of the spheres"
they produced.[13] If one knew the secrets of nature one could furthermore interact magically with the order of things; sounds or power
words were especially efficient for such interactions if one knew the
right intonations.

---

[8] See Fideler, 'Introduction', 20–22. Levin, *The Harmonics of Nicomachus*, 1–7.
[9] See Vickers, 'On the Function of Analogy in the Occult'. Brach & Hanegraaff,
'Correspondences'.
[10] For useful references see Frankfurter, 'Narrating Power', 457. Håkan, *Seeing the
Word*, 309 – 318.
[11] Iamblichus, 'The life of Pythagoras', 70–71.
[12] Ibid., 73–74, 84–85.
[13] Burkert, *Lore and Science in Ancient Pythagoreanism*, 357.

In the Renaissance this idea of cosmos as a musically ordered whole stemming from the Pythagorean-Platonic tradition was especially revived and embellished by influential scholars, such as Marsilio Ficino (1433–1499), Pico della Mirandola (1463–1494), Johann Reuchlin (1455–1525), Nicholaus Copernicus (1473–1543), Heinrich Cornelius Agrippa (1486–1535), John Dee (1527–1608/9), Johannes Kepler (1571–1630) and Robert Fludd (1574–1637), to name but a few of the more well known figures.[14] With the rise of the Enlightenment, the scientific revolution, and the gradual modernization of society, however, the influence of these three ideas of sound in relation to cosmology was marginalized by the dominant scientific discourses, and the "music of the spheres" was heard no more.[15]

Wouter J. Hanegraaff has discussed to what extent pre-modern ideas, similar to the three mentioned above, have survived the process of modernization and post-enlightenment culture.[16] Hanegraaff has argued that where "Renaissance esotericism" displayed a large amount of internal coherency, 19th century post-enlightenment "esotericism" lost much of that coherency in an attempt to survive in the new "disenchanted world" of secularized culture by adopting "instrumental causality" in favor of correlative thinking or correspondences.[17] Correspondences were, however, not given up completely in 19th century "occultism"[18] (to use Hanegraaff's designation for secularized esotericism). The idea of correspondences still survived, although used within a nominalistic scientific framework rather than, as in the Renaissance, within a Platonic-realist framework underscoring essential relationships.[19]

While there is no doubt that Blavatsky's Theosophy, as presented in *Isis Unveiled* (1877) and *The Secret Doctrine* (1888), to a great extent is influenced by the processes of modernization and secularization, this chapter will bring attention to the interesting observation that

---

[14] Godwin, *The Harmony of the Spheres*, 163–301.

[15] Godwin, *Harmonies of Heaven and Earth*, 112. See also Gozza, 'Introduction' and Fabbri, *Cosmologia e armonia in Kepler e Mersenne*.

[16] Hanegraaff, *New Age Religion*, 365–524. Hanegraaff does not particularly discuss the three ideas treated here, but discusses the effect of secularization on esoteric currents.

[17] Ibid, 407, 409, 422.

[18] *Idem.*

[19] Brach & Hanegraaff, 'Correspondences', 278–279. See also Hanegraaff, 'The Study of Western Esotericism', 508.

Blavatsky's practical "occultism", as it is expounded in her 'Esoteric Instructions', makes use not only of the three pre-modern ideas mentioned above, but it also does so largely within a pre-modern framework of realism.

The questions to be dealt with in this chapter are thus as follows: First, what are the "mysteries of sound" in Blavatsky's 'Esoteric Instructions', and did sound continue to be a cornerstone in Blavatsky's 19th century practical form of "occultism" as it once was in Antiquity and in what is termed "Renaissance esotericism"? And second, how did Blavatsky use the three pre-modern ideas relating sound and cosmology in the 'Esoteric Instructions', and were they used in a secularized framework of nominalism or in a pre-modern framework of realism?

ANALYSIS OF BLAVATSKY'S 'ESOTERIC INSTRUCTIONS'

Blavatsky formed the officially independent Esoteric Section of the Theosophical Society in 1888 for members who wanted to penetrate deeper into the teachings of Theosophy and practice occultism. She issued "strictly private and confidential" 'Esoteric Instructions' to the Esoteric Section's members between 1889 and 1890,[20] revealing a practical system of occult correspondences wherein special focus was put on the interrelation between sound, colour, numbers, micro-macrocosmos and levels of consciousness. It appears to have been William Q. Judge who originated the idea of an esoteric section around 1887.[21] R. A. Gilbert has speculated that the Esoteric Section was a counter-strike to the then recently founded and quite popular Hermetic Order of the Golden Dawn (1887), which experimented with practical ceremonial magic and thereby attracted many members from the Theosophical Society who longed for such a venture (as the Theosophical Society had generally warned against the practice of ritual magic).[22]

---

[20] HPB, 'E.S.T. Instructions', 479–486, 514–515. All references to H. P. Blavatsky will adopt the shortened version of her name: HPB. See also Gomes, *Theosophy in the Nineteenth Century*, 182.

[21] HPB, 'E.S.T. Instructions', 479.

[22] Gilbert, *Revelations of the Golden Dawn*, 39–40.

GNOSIS – THE AIM OF THE 'ESOTERIC INSTRUCTIONS'

The primary aim of Blavatsky's 'Esoteric Instructions' was similar to the aim of her other teachings on practical occultism:[23] to teach men and women to unite with the 'One Universal Self', to know the links by which their 'Higher Egos' are related to it,[24] and how to develop spiritual powers.[25]

In other words, Blavatsky's 'Esoteric Instructions' were oriented more toward *practice* than her other major works with the exception of *The Voice of the Silence*, which is an instructional manual for attaining enlightenment and walking the secret path of compassion.[26] In the first instruction Blavatsky makes reference to the famous utterance of the Delphic oracle: 'Know Thyself'[27] as an indication of her proposed path of practice. She states affirmatively,

> Esoteric Science is, above all, the knowledge of our [...] inseparableness from our divine *Selves*.[28]

Knowledge or gnosis of the true self thus 'above all' constitutes Blavatsky's path to spiritual union and comes quite close to Arthur Versluis' scholarly category of "metaphysical gnosis", i.e. the cessation of dualism.[29] Even though this, at first glance, might sound as though Blavatsky's 'Esoteric Instructions' are less related to Versluis' category of "cosmological gnosis",[30] or direct knowledge into the subtle structures of cosmos, and more related to what traditionally pertains to mysticism – in its endorsement of union with the divine – the interest and method of the 'Esoteric Instructions' is in fact just as *esoteric* as *mystical* if one is to use Faivre's observation that often "esotericists" are much more interested in the intermediary levels of cosmos than the mystics are.[31] To Blavatsky (macro)cosmos with its many

---

[23] See HPB, *Collected writings IX*, 99–128, 155–162, 249–261. Rudbøg, 'H. P. Blavatsky on Occultism'.

[24] HPB, 'E.S.T. Instructions', 516.

[25] Ibid., 528.

[26] HPB, *The Voice of the Silence*, 23–44.

[27] HPB, 'E.S.T. Instructions', 515–516, 528.

[28] Ibid., 551.

[29] Versluis, 'What is Esoteric?', 2.

[30] Ibid., 2–3.

[31] Faivre, *Access to Western Esotericism*, 12. See also Versluis on the difficulty of separating esotericism from mysticism in Versluis, 'Methods in the Study of Esotericism' 28–29.

levels is not a hindrance to divine union, but a significant object for obtaining it.

In the 'Esoteric Instructions' the student must, in order to reach the goal of Self-knowledge – the true object of the ancient science of Neo-Platonic Theurgy and Raja Yoga, according to Blavatsky[32] – come to know man's relation to cosmos. In order for man; the microcosm, to know himself he must know his intimate relation with macrocosm, the ordered whole of which he is a part.[33]

The teachings given in the 'Esoteric Instructions' are therefore excessively concerned with the connections or links between man and the different levels or worlds of macrocosm.[34]

> Let us study Man, therefore; but if we separate him for one moment from the Universal Whole, [...] we shall [...] fail most ingloriously in our attempt.[35]

It is however to be noted here that the practical spiritual path presented in *The Voice of the Silence* places a much greater emphasis on the obstacles, the constituents of cosmos play, in attaining enlightenment and in choosing the secret path of compassion. In this manual the disciple is not advised to learn the correspondences between himself and cosmos in order to attain union, but to walk a path of renunciation by killing out desire and by dispelling ignorance and illusion through self-mastery.[36]

The analysis presented here has thus so far shown that the general plot of the 'Esoteric Instructions' is to provide the student with intricate esoteric or metaphysical knowledge of man and cosmos – "as above, so below" – in order for him to attain the aim of divine union and the development of spiritual powers. The Instructions are therefore not simply knowledge for the sake of knowledge alone, but they are a form of cosmological knowledge, which attempts to make men and women able to unite with their "universal selves". In terms of Versluis' categories this implies that, at a profound level, the 'Esoteric Instructions' unifies "cosmological gnosis", with its ultimate aim of "metaphysical gnosis", or union with the divine, as the Instructions'

---

[32] HPB, 'E.S.T. Instructions', 559–560.
[33] Ibid., 517.
[34] Ibid., 516.
[35] Ibid., 517.
[36] HPB, *The Voice of the Silence*, 15.

insight into cosmos and man ("cosmological gnosis") leads to union
with the divine ("metaphysical gnosis").

Keeping this aim in mind, the way knowledge is given to the reader
in the Instructions is not straightforward, and there are several reasons
why this is so: first of all the 'Esoteric Instructions' were written with
deliberate blinds to obscure or keep secret the esoteric knowledge from
the uninitiated.[37] This was an often-used method by Blavatsky intend-
ing to avoid potential dangers when teaching practical occultism.[38]
Another element that hinders the reader is the fact that the knowledge
given in the Instructions was composed of ideas and elements stemming from numerous sources within Western esoteric currents, such
as Pythagoranism, neo-Platonism, Gnosticism, Hermetic astrology,
Magic, Kabbalah. This multiplicity of Western sources makes coherency difficult to grasp at first glance. Moreover, the Instructions also
draw extensively upon Oriental sources, including Raja yoga, Tantra,
Buddhism and Vedanta. Finally, a bit of modern science even enters
the mix.[39] This blend of sources and doctrines, characteristic of 19th
century 'occultism', is particularly characteristic of Blavatsky's general
style – her Theosophical discourse – because, to Blavatsky, the same
fundamental truths are to be found in all the great religious and philosophical systems of the world, behind their different cultural dresses.

THE PRACTICAL USE OF THE IDEA OF CORRESPONDENCES

In the 'Esoteric Instructions' it is difficult to separate gnosis from correlative thinking. The *practice* of correspondences becomes simply the
method or way to gnosis. In order to obtain the above-mentioned aim,
the 'Esoteric Instructions' more than anything provide numerous correspondences between all aspects of cosmos not given in Blavatsky's
other works because they were regarded as too esoteric. The student is,
however, warned not to use these many analogies on the basis of material likeness as medieval occultism and astrology supposedly did, but
instead to comprehend their spiritual or essential similarities rather
than the external ones. Or, as Blavatsky states,

---

[37] HPB, 'E.S.T. Instructions', 562.
[38] Ibid., 521–622, see also 600–603.
[39] Ibid., 542–581 as an example.

> Esoteric Science is not content with analogies on the purely objective
> plane of the physical senses [...][40] [and] esoteric philosophy [...] con-
> cerns itself pre-eminently with the essence of things.[41]

Another warning in relation to the use of analogies is that they change
with every school, so the student should learn

> the principles by their names and their appropriate faculties apart from
> any system of enumeration, or by association with their corresponding
> centers of action, colors, sounds, etc, until these become inseparable.[42]

The correlative system should thus not be taken as an external tax-
onomy applied onto the world, but used as a tool for discovering real
essential cosmological relations. These warnings clearly indicate that
Blavatsky was concerned that her idea of correspondences be taken
as mere names (nomina) and not as essences or essential relationships. As will also be elaborated further below, correlative thinking
becomes a key element in the 'Esoteric Instructions' in three ways:
First, it constitutes not only the theory of occultism, but also the practice or method of gnosis; second, it is used within a framework of
realism rather than nominalism; and third, it constitutes the compara-
tive framework or underlying system into which all the various textual
sources used by Blavatsky, such as Pythagoranism and Vedanta, are
formatted not because all names are the same in the various systems,
but because the concepts from the different systems are thought to
signify the same realities in cosmos and man.

In using the idea of correlative thinking as a method to reach gnosis
Blavatsky furthermore recommends the student of "esoteric science"
to do the following when studying the Instructions:

> Know the corresponding numbers of the fundamental principle of every
> element and its sub-elements, learn their interaction and behavior on
> the occult side of manifesting nature, and the law of correspondences
> will lead you to the discovery of the greatest mysteries of macrocosmi-
> cal life.[43]

The keys to unlocking the mysteries of "macrocosmical life" are thus
knowledge and the use of analogies, because the idea of correspondences

---

[40] Ibid., 551, see also 550, 516.
[41] Ibid., 551.
[42] Ibid., 547.
[43] Ibid., 517.

is a natural "law". It is worth noticing here that while Blavatsky makes
use of a (pre-modern) realist framework for her idea of correspondences, it is at the same time designated a "law", which clearly indicates how the idea has been modernized somewhat in the image of
natural science.[44]

According to Blavatsky the practical use of the idea of correspondences is directly related to what she terms the objects of 'Esoteric
Science'. The first object is to prove that man is in essence identical
with the Absolute principle and God in nature – the 'know thyself'
aspect discussed above. The second object is to demonstrate that man
has, potentially within himself the same powers and creative forces
that exist in nature.[45] In relation to this second object the "law of correspondences" is significant because, as Blavatsky states,

> a perfect knowledge of the correspondences between Colors, Sounds
> and Numbers is the first requisite.[46] [and] It is on the thorough knowl-
> edge and comprehension of the meaning and potency of these numbers
> [3,4,7,10], in their various and multiform combinations, and in their
> mutual correspondence with sounds [...] and colors, or rates of motion
> [...], that the progress of a student in Occultism depends.[47]

Progress in occultism and the development of spiritual powers thus
depends on knowledge of the correspondences between color, sound
and number because they contain great potency.

SOUND, ITS POTENCY AND ESSENTIAL RELATION TO COLOR AND NUMBER

Knowledge of sound, number and color is vital to occult practice, as
has been mentioned briefly above. Regarding the correspondences
between sound, color and number Blavatsky writes, further

> Esoteric Science teaches that every sound in the visible world awakens
> its corresponding sound in the invisible realms, and arouses to action
> some force or other on the occult side of nature. Moreover, every sound

---

[44] For the designation 'Law of correspondences' or 'Law of analogy' see also HPB,
The Secret Doctrine, Vol. 1 150–151, 173, 177, 585n–586n, 604; Vol. 2 197, 301.
[45] HPB, 'E.S.T. Instructions', 519, see also 625 for another version of the two
objects.
[46] Ibid., 519.
[47] Ibid., 520. The brackets are mine.

corresponds to a color and a number [...]. All these find an echo in every one of the so far developed elements and even on the terrestrial plane, in the Lives that swarm in the terrene atmosphere, thus prompting them to action.[48]

In order to understand Blavatsky's view on sound – the relation between sound and number, sound and color, and the power and potency of sound when intoned correctly – closer examination is needed before moving on to the actual cosmological significance of sound in the 'Esoteric Instructions'.

> Let the student remember that number underlies form, and number guides sound. Number lies at the root of the manifested Universe; numbers and harmonious proportions guide the first differentiations of homogeneous substance into heterogeneous elements; and number and numbers set limits to the formative hand of Nature.[49]

Number guides sound; here we find clearly the ancient Pythagorean idea that numbers lie at the root of cosmos, the ordered whole, and that these numbers also guide the harmonious or musical nature of cosmos.[50]

In regard to sound and color Blavatsky writes:

> Every impulse or vibration of a physical object producing a certain vibration of the air [...] produces at the same time a corresponding flash of light, which will assume some particular color. For, in the realm of hidden Forces, an *audible* sound is but a subjective color; and a perceptible color, but an *inaudible* sound; both proceed from the same potential substance, [...] which we call plastic, though invisible, SPACE.[51]

Several noteworthy elements are found in this quote. Blavatsky argues clearly that sound and color are, essentially, the same or that they spring from the same substance, which is space. Or, as more specifically stated elsewhere, 'color and sound are two out of the seven correlative aspects, *on our plane*, of one and the same thing, *viz*. Nature's first differentiated Substance'.[52] The difference between sound and color, then, is due to subjective or objective modes of perception.

---

[48] Ibid., 534–535.
[49] Ibid., 517.
[50] For a detailed condensation of these Pythagorean ideas see particularly Nicomachus, *The Manual of Harmonics* and *Introduction to Arithmetic*.
[51] Ibid., 620–621, see also 549, 562–563.
[52] Ibid., 620–621, see also 549, 562–563.

In regard to the idea of the magical potency of sound and the verbal intonation of sound Blavatsky, throughout the Instructions, mentions the immense potency and power inherent in sound and the key to this power, which of course is right intonation. Within Blavatsky's discourse the idea is laid out as follows: the universe itself is presented as a vibratory hierarchy of powers or forces, whose primary qualities are sound, color, and number. If man knows the right intonation of vibrations – or the secret mantras – he can control or interact with cosmos. The more spiritually developed a man is, however, the more power his intonation of sound will have.[53] Blavatsky writes, for example,

> The [Tibetan] formula "*Ōm Mani Padme Hūm*," has been chosen as an illustration on account of its almost infinite potency in the mouth of an Adept, and its potentiality when pronounced by any man.[54]

Blavatsky also warns the student, as is usual in the East, about using the mantras (intonated power-words) casually. She states,

> Students in the West have little or no idea of the forces that lie latent in Sound, the Akasic vibrations that may be set up by those who understand how to pronounce certain words.[55]

The key to right intonation is, according to Blavatsky, 'knowledge of the natural arrangement, or of the order in which syllables stand',[56] because vocal sounds correspond with musical notes, numbers, colors, forces and Tattvas and hence with the order of cosmos.[57]

The secret to the potency of sound is therefore spiritual development *and* knowledge of the correct order or scheme of intonation as well as the order of cosmos. If one can align the order of intonation and the subtle order of cosmos (primarily formed by number, color and sound), then sound can change and manipulate the elements and forces of cosmos. Blavatsky's use of the idea of the power of sound is, however, as indicated above, not only inspired by pre-modern Western currents – but also synthesizes Eastern sources integrating concepts such as Akasa, Tattva, Om, Aum, Mantra etc. into her discourse.[58] This

---

[53] Ibid., 518.
[54] Ibid., 518. The bracket is mine.
[55] Ibid., 642.
[56] Ibid., 642.
[57] Ibid., 642.
[58] The primary published source for many of these concepts mentioned in the Instructions is *Nature's Finer Forces*, a Tantric work translated in 1889 by Râma Prasâd.

brings us to the actual cosmological significance of sound in Blavatsky's instructions.

SOUND AND COSMOLOGY

In the cosmology outlined in the 'Instructions' manifested cosmos
(also termed the logos) is composed of spiritual hierarchies related
intimately to sound in the great circulatory and transformative flow of
spiritual forces through the kingdoms of nature.[59] The divine essence of
the seven primary hierarchies or "progenitors in heaven" as Blavatsky
calls them – also known as the seven sacred planets – flows through
nature in the following manner:

> [First you have] (1) color; [then] (2) sound; [and then] (3) the sound
> materializes into the spirit of the metals, i.e., the metallic Elementals;
> (4) these materialize again into the physical metals; (5) then the harmonial
> and vibratory radiant essence passes into the plants, giving them color
> and smell, both of which "properties" depend upon the rate of vibration
> of this energy per unit of time; (6) from plants it passes into the animals;
> (7) and finally culminates in the "principles" of man'.[60]

This circulation of spiritual essence is described as the circling of the
divine essence or of the spiritual forces through the seven stages of
nature – spirit becoming matter, and matter returning to spirit. From
this it seems clear that sound is portrayed as a significant stage in the
creative process of cosmos. Cosmos is continuously creative in its circulatory manifestation and it is:

> The creative force, at work in its incessant task of transformation, [which]
> produces color, sound and numbers, in the shape of rates of vibration
> which compound and dissociate the atoms and molecules.[61]

Blavatsky states that even though this subtle creative transformative
process, which produces color, sound and numbers, is invisible and
inaudible to us:

> the synthesis of the whole becomes audible to us on the material plane.
> It is that which the Chinese call the "Great Tone," or *Kung*. It is, [...]
> the actual tonic of nature, held by musicians to be the middle Fa on the

---

[59] HPB, 'E.S.T. Instructions', 550, 561, 567.
[60] Ibid., 550. The brackets are mine.
[61] *Idem*, The bracket is mine.

keyboard of a piano. We hear it distinctly in the voice of nature, in the roaring of the ocean, in the sound of the foliage of a great forest, in the distant roar of a great city; in the wind, the tempest and the storm: in short, in everything in nature which has a voice or produces sound. To the hearing of all who hearken, it culminates in a single definite tone, of an unappreciable pitch, which, as said, is the F, or Fa, of the diatonic scale.[62]

Cosmos, as it is portrayed in Blavatsky's 'Esoteric Instructions', has an anti-modern ring to it,[63] with its re-enchanted vitalistic panorama wherein everything has a distinct voice, everything produces a sound or color and is related to every other thing in a "great chain of being". Fa on the diatonic scale is the middle tone in cosmos and is the audible synthesis of the whole transformative creative process.

In relation to the unfolding and structure of cosmos, sound is also given Pythagorean geometrical dimensions. Blavatsky writes:

> In the eternal music of the spheres we find the perfect scale corresponding to the colors, and in the number, determined by the vibrations of color and sound, which "underlies every form and guides every sound,".... We may illustrate these correspondences by showing the relation of color and sound to the geometrical figures which, [...], express the progressive stages in the manifestation of Kosmos.[64]

The following diagram from the 'Esoteric Instructions'[65] gives not only the most essential correspondences found in Blavatsky's text in relation to geometry, but again shows how color, number and sound are related in the progressive stages of cosmos.

The color correspondences given by Blavatsky in this diagram are presumably derived from Louis Bertrand Castel's (1688–1757) *Optique des couleurs* (1740) in which he presented a similar set of

---

[62] *Idem.*

[63] I am not suggesting that Blavatsky's Theosophy was anti-modern, as it obviously made use of many modern ideas (see Hanegraaff, *New Age religion* and Hammer, *Claiming Knowledge*). Much of its polemical discourse is, however, directed against modernism; and its extensive use of "enchanted" pre-modern ideas makes much of its cosmology pre-modern – if not anti-modern.

[64] HPB, 'E.S.T. Instructions', 564.

[65] Diagram Source: Blavatsky, H. P., 'E.S.T. Instructions', in: Zirkoff, B. (ed.), *H. P. Blavatsky Collected Writings 1889–1890 Volume XII*, Wheaton: The Theosophical Publishing House 1987, page 564. This material was reproduced by permission of Quest Books, the imprint of The Theosophical Publishing House (www.questbooks.net). See also Caldwell, *The Esoteric Papers of Madame Blavatsky*, 395–396 for an alternative version of this diagram.

ABSOLUTE

PLANE OF
PRIMORDIAL SUBSTANCE

PLANE OF MANIFESTED
OR DIFFER-
ENTIATED MATTER

A

VIOLET (a) SI

INDIGO
LA (b) BLUE
(c) SOL

GREEN (d) FA

YELLOW
MI (e) RED
(g) DO

ORANGE (f) RE

B

(ORANGE) RED (a) DO

(YELLOW)
ORANGE
RE (b) YELLOW
(c) MI

GREEN (d) FA*

BLUE
SOL (e) INDIGO
(f) LA

VIOLET (g) SI

⊙ The Point in the Circle is the Unmanifested Logos, corresponding to Absolute Life and Absolute Sound.

△ The first geometrical figure after the Circle or the Spheroid is the Triangle. It corresponds to Motion, Color and Sound. Thus the Point in the Triangle represents the Second Logos, "Father-Mother," or the White Ray which is no color, since it contains potentially all colors. It is shown radiating from the Unmanifested Logos, or the Unspoken Word. Around the first Triangle is formed on the plane of Primordial Substance in this order (*reversed* as to our plane):

A

(*a*) The Astral Double of Nature, or the Paradigm of all forms.

(*b*) Divine Ideation, or Universal Mind.

(*c*) The Synthesis of occult Nature, the Egg of Brahmā, containing all and radiating all.

(*d*) Animal or Material Soul of Nature, source of animal and vegetable intelligence and instinct.

(*e*) The aggregate of Dhyāni-Chohanic Intelligences, Fohat.

(*f*) Life Principle in Nature.

(*g*) The Life-Procreating Principle in Nature. That which, on the spiritual plane, corresponds to sexual affinity on the lower.

Mirrored on the Plane of Gross Nature, the World of Reality is reversed, and becomes on Earth and our plane:

B

(*a*) Red is the color of manifested dual, or male and female. In man it is shown in its lowest animal form.

(*b*) Orange is the color of the robes of the Yogis and Buddhist priests, the color of the Sun and Spiritual Vitality, also of the Vital Principle.

(*c*) Yellow or radiant Golden is the color of the Spiritual, Divine Ray in every atom; in man, of Buddhi.

(*d*) Green and Red are, so to speak, interchangeable colors, for Green absorbs the Red, as being threefold stronger in its vibrations than the latter; and Green is the complementary color of extreme Red. This is why the Lower Manas and Kāma-Rūpa are respectively shown as Green and Red.

(*e*) The Astral Plane, or Auric Envelope in Nature and Man.

(*f*) The Mind or rational element in Man and Nature.

(*g*) The most ethereal counterpart of the Body of man, the opposite pole, standing in point of vibration and sensitiveness as the Violet stands to the Red.

*The Master-Key or Tonic of Manifested Nature

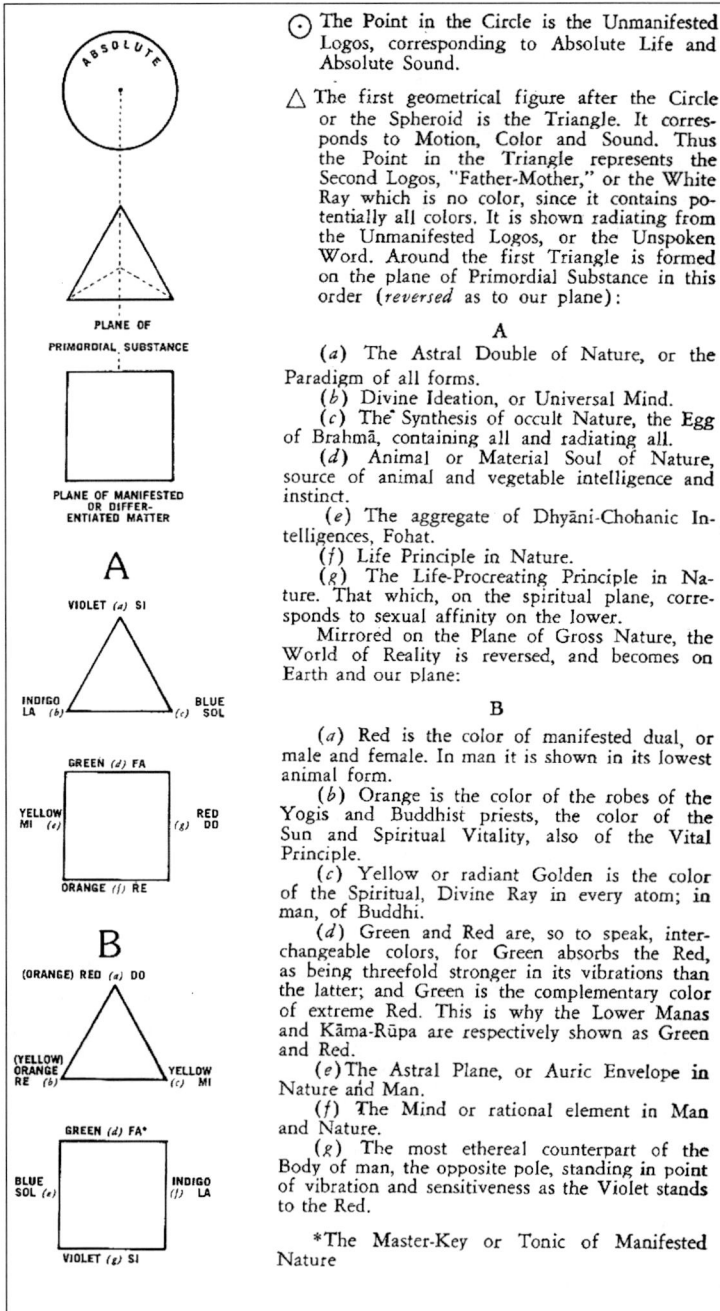

Figure 1. One of Blavatsky's esoteric depictions of the intricate cosmic correlations between Number, Color and Sound.

correspondences with the exception of 'aurore' which Blavatsky substituted by 'orange' for '(f) RE'.[66] The musical scale itself is fitted to the above-mentioned circulatory transformative cosmological processes. Blavatsky states:

> The musical scale begins from below upwards, commencing with the deep Do and ending with the far more acute Si. [...] Again, the student must also remember that these notes have to be arranged in a circle, thus showing how Fa is the middle note of Nature. In short, musical notes, or Sounds, Colors and Numbers proceed from one to seven, and not from seven to one'.[67]

Cosmos in the 'Esoteric Instructions' is fundamentally musical[68] and knowledge of sounds, colors and numbers in relation to the musical structure is essential to Blavatsky because, as shown earlier, the aim of the 'Esoteric Instructions' is to provide knowledge of the relation between micro- and macrocosm in order for man to attain divine union and develop spiritual powers. The 'know thyself' expression in practical occultism is ultimately aimed at attaining divine union; but in the Instructions divine union entails knowledge of "thy place" in the greater whole and how to interact properly with the creative process of nature.

Somewhat in contrast to this cosmological focus on sound, the *The Voice of the Silence* places a more mystical emphasis on sound. In *The Voice of the Silence* the aim of the disciple is for example to hear 'the Soundless Sound'[69] or 'THE VOICE OF THE SILENCE'.[70] This sound is the voice of man's '*inner* GOD' or 'Higher SELF'[71] which will be heard in seven different ways while progressing on the spiritual path, as follows: First like 'the nightingale's sweet voice', second as a 'silver cymbal', third like melodies of an 'ocean-spirit imprisoned in its shell', fourth as the 'chant of Vina' (an Indian string instrument), fifth as the sound of a 'bamboo-flute', sixth as a 'trumpet-blast' and finally the seventh sound 'swallows all the other sounds'.[72]

---

[66] Godwin, *Music and the Occult*, 14.
[67] HPB, 'E.S.T. Instructions', 561–562.
[68] For a similar musical conception of the cosmos see HPB, *The Secret Doctrine*, v.1 167.
[69] HPB, *The Voice of the Silence*, 1.
[70] HPB, *The Voice of the Silence*, 3, 15.
[71] HPB, *The Voice of the Silence*, 9.
[72] HPB, *The Voice of the Silence*, 9, 10.

In the Instructions man must, in order to be in unison with cosmos, fine-tune (in a musical sense) his life through practical occultism.

Inspired by both Tantric and Pythagorean sources Blavatsky pictures man, with all his subtle bodies, as a musical instrument and esoteric knowledge thus becomes the art of fine-tuning and playing this instrument correctly. For Blavatsky, this is not just an analogy. She writes,

> Our principles [the seven principles in man] are the Seven Stringed Lyre of Apollo, truly. [...] the Occultist [...] [alone] knows how to tighten them and tune his violin in harmony with the vibrations of color and sound, [which] will extract divine harmony from them. The combination of these powers and the attuning of the Macrocosm and the Microcosm, will when combined give the geometrical equivalent of the invocation "Ōm Mani Padme Hūm." This is why the previous knowledge of music and geometry was obligatory in the school of Pythagoras.[73]

The Instructions thus draw a picture of man as a musical energy system of sounds, colors and numbers to be regulated in harmony with the great energy flow of macrocosmos.[74] This was the great task of the practical occultism of the Instructions, and the idea of correspondences was the practical method used to accomplish it.

From a historical point of view Blavatsky's 'Esoteric Instructions' – being a construction and creative reformulation of pre-modern Western as well as Eastern ideas – can be said to represent a striking alternative response to an emerging "crises of faith"; the sense of cultural decay and estrangement from nature felt by an idealistic segment of modern spiritually inclined men and women largely from the growing middle class of the 19th century. This feeling was produced by an increase of materialism, secularization and rationalism, or what Max Weber has termed the "disenchantment" of the world.[75] In contrast to this unsatisfactory state of affairs, in the Instructions man is thus given an enchanted opportunity to take his rightful place in a cosmos, which is fundamentally ordered and musically harmonious by fine-tuning his own life through the regular practice of correlative thinking, spiritual knowledge and self-effort.

---

[73] HPB, 'E.S.T. Instructions', 566–567 – symbols in the quote are left out. The brackets are mine. For a similar analogy between cosmos and the Seven Stringed Lyra of Apollo see HPB, *The Secret Doctrine*, Vol.1 167.

[74] For further details see HPB, 'E.S.T. Instructions', 610–622.

[75] Max Weber, 'Science as Vocation', 155, 138–139, 142. For further details on these cultural changes in relation to the emerging occultism see also Owen, *The Place of Enchantment* and Webb, *The Flight from Reason*.

CONCLUSION

If the assumptions and observations in the forgoing analysis are correct, it can be concluded regarding the questions asked in the section entitled *Three ideas and questions* that Blavatsky in her exposition of practical occultism, as expressed in the 'Esoteric Instructions', made use of ideas similar to the three pre-modern Western ideas specified in the same said section. Cosmos, as outlined in the Instructions, is deeply related to sound/music, color and number, which are all produced in the creative transformations of nature. Cosmos is construed as a network of essential correspondences or links, which not only pertain to names and perceptible likeness, but also to co-substantiality. Correct knowledge of the essential order of cosmos and the correct order of the intonation of sound was therefore believed to have enormous potential and power.

The three pre-modern ideas relating sound and cosmology, which were marginalized during the scientific revolution and the Enlightenment, were continuously utilized by Blavatsky's largely self-styled, anti-modern form of esotericism. Theosophy, during the 19th century, therefore plays a significant role in the yet overtly unexplored history of marginal musical ideas. Blavatsky's use of these ideas, however, does not mean that they "survived" the Enlightenment untransformed/unmodernised. The above analysis has for example shown that the idea of correspondences was reformulated into a "law" and that the idea of cosmos as an ordered whole and the idea of the power of sound were synthesized with oriental ideas, stemming largely from the Orientalism of the time.

It does, however, appear that Blavatsky's use of correspondences was kept within a realist framework that was closer to pre-modern thinking than a modern scientific framework of nominalism. This realist use of correspondences thus offered a systemic coherency closer to "Renaissance esotericism" and generally formed the basis of Blavatsky's theosophical discourse in which she uses various unrelated sources – both modern and pre-modern – as examples of the same universal truths or ideas.

This chapter has outlined the central significance of what is here termed "The mysteries of sound in H. P. Blavatsky's Esoteric Instructions" in relation to the general aim of the Instructions, which was for students of Theosophy to achieve union with the divine and to develop spiritual powers. In order to reach these aims, correlative knowledge of (macro)cosmos – especially of the relations between sound, color and number – was deemed vital and the practice of correspondences became the key-method in this endeavor. Moreover, in Blavatsky's 'Esoteric Instructions' the distinction between correlative knowledge of cosmos and union with the divine merge, as do the theory of correspondence and the practice of correspondences. Put in another way, Blavatsky's 'Esoteric Instructions' revives and reformulates a central theme from the Pythagorean musical tradition by portraying man as an instrument, which through practice must be fine-tuned into the larger musical harmony with cosmos. This process of fine-tuning comprised the 'mysteries of sound' offered by Madam Blavatsky in her Instructions as an alternative to the deep-felt estrangement between man and nature caused by the modernization process in the 19th century.

BIBLIOGRAPHY

Blavatsky, H. P., 'E.S.T. Instructions', in: Zirkoff, B. (ed.), *H. P. Blavatsky Collected Writings 1889–1890 Volume XII*, Wheaton: The Theosophical Publishing House 1987, 477–713.

——, in: Zirkoff, B. (ed.), *H. P. Blavatsky Collected Writings Volume IX 1888*, Wheaton: The Theosophical Publishing House 1986.

——, *Isis Unveiled: A Master Key to the Mysteries of Ancient and Modern Science and Theology*, New York: J. W. Bouton 1877.

——, *The Secret Doctrine: The Synthesis of Science, Religion, and Philosophy*, London: The Theosophical Publishing Company 1888.

——, *The Voice of the Silence*, Pasadena, California: The Theosophical University Press, 1976.

Brach, J.-P. and Hanegraaff, W. J., 'Correspondences', in: Hanegraaff, W. J. (ed.), *Dictionary of Gnosis and Western Esotericism*, Leiden: Brill 2005, 275–279.

Burkert, W., *Lore and Science in Ancient Pythagoreanism*, Minar, E. L. Jr. (trans.), Cambridge: Harvard University Press 1972.

Caldwell, D. H., *Madame Blavatsky's Esoteric Papers: A Comprehensive Compilation of H. P. Blavatsky's Esoteric Papers*, Whitefish: Kessinger Publishing 2005.

Cranston, S., *H.P.B.: The Extraordinary Life & influence of Helena Blavatsky Founder of the Modern Theosophical Movement*, New York: G. P. Putnam's Sons 1993.

Fabbri, N., *Cosmologia e armonia in Kepler e Mersenne: Contrappunto a due*, Florence: Leo S. Olschki 2003.

Faivre, A., *Access to Western Esotericism*, New York: SUNY 1994.

Fideler, D. R., 'Introduction', in: Guthrie, K. S. (comp. and trans.), *The Pythagorean Sourcebook and Library*, Grand Rapids: Phanes Press 1987, 19–54.

Frankfurter, D., 'Narrating Power: The Theory and Practice of Magical Historiola in Ritual Spells', in: Meyer, M. and Mirecki, P. (eds.), *Ancient Magic and Ritual Power*, Leiden: Brill 2001, 457–476.

Gilbert, R. A., *Revelations of the Golden Dawn: The Rise & Fall of A Magical Order*, London: Quantum, 1997.

Godwin, J., *The Harmony of the Spheres: A Sourcebook of the Pythagorean Tradition in Music*, Rochester: Inner Traditions International 1993.

——, *Harmonies of Heaven and Earth: from Antiquity to the Avant-Garde*, Rochester: Inner Traditions International 1995.

——, *Music and the Occult: French Musical Philosophies, 1750-1950*, Rochester: University of Rochester Press 1995.

Gomes, M., *Theosophy in the Nineteenth Century: An Annotated bibliography*, New York & London: Garland Publishing 1994.

Gozza, P., 'Introduction', in: Gozza, P. (ed.), *Number to Sound: The Musical Way to the Scientific Revolution*, Dordrecht: Kulwer Academic Publishers 2000, 1-67.

Hammer, O., *Claming Knowledge: Strategies of Epistemology from Theosophy to the New Age*, Leiden: Brill 2001.

Hanegraaff, W. J., 'The Study of Western Esotericism: New Approaches to Christian and Secular Culture', in: Peter, A., Armin, W. G. & Randi, R. W. (eds.), *New Approaches to the Study of Religion I: Regional, Critical, and Historical Approaches: Religion and Reason 42*, Berlin & New York: Walter de Gruyter 2004, 489-519.

——, *New Age Religion and Western Culture: Esotericism in the Mirror of Secular Thought*, New York: SUNY 1998.

——, 'Forbidden Knowledge: Anti-Esoteric Polemics and Academic Research', *Aries* 5:2 (2005), 225-254.

——, 'The Trouble with Images: Anti-Image Polemics and Western Esotericism', in: Hammer, O. & Stuckrad, K. (eds.), *Polemical Encounters: Esotericism and its Others*, Leiden & London: Brill 2007, 107-136.

Håkansson, H., *Seeing the Word: John Dee and Renaissance Occultism, Minervaserien 2*, Ugglan: Lunds Universitet 2001.

Iamblichus, 'The life of Pythagoras', in: Guthrie, K. S. (comp. and trans.), *The Pythagorean Sourcebook and Library*, Grand Rapids: Phanes Press 1987, 57-156.

Levin, F. R., *The Harmonics of Nicomachus and the Pythagorean Tradition*, Pennsylvania: The American Philosophical Association, 1975.

Nicomachus of Gerasa, *The Manual of Harmonics of Nicomachus the Pythagorean*, Levin, F. R. (trans. and comm.), Grand Rapids: Phanes Press 1994.

——, *Introduction to Arithmetic*, D'Ooge, M. L. (trans.), London: The Macmillian Company 1926.

Owen, A., *The Place of Enchantment*, Chicago: The University of Chicago Press 2005.

Rudbøg, T., 'H. P. Blavatsky on Occultism', www.h-e-r-m-e-s.org/HPBonOccultism Article.htm 2005.

Stuckrad, K. 'Western Esotericism: Towards an integrative model of interpretation', *Religion* 35 (2005), 78-97.

Versluis, A., 'What is Esoteric? Methods in the Study of Western Esotericism', *Esoterica*, Vol. IV, www.esoteric.msu.edu (2002), 1-15.

——, 'Methods in the Study of Esotericism, Part II, Mysticism and the study of Esotericism', *Esoterica*, Vol. V, www.esoteric.msu.edu (2003), 27-40.

Vickers, B., 'On the Function of Analogy in the Occult', in: Merkel, I. and Debus, A. G. (eds.), *Hermeticism and the Renaissance: Intellectual History and the Occult in Early Modern Europe*, Washington: Folger Books 1988, 265-292.

Webb, J., *The Flight from Reason - The Age of the Irrational*, London: Macdonald & Co 1971.

Weber, M., 'Science of Vocation', in: Gerth, H. H. and Mills, C. W. (trans. and ed.) *Max Weber: Essays in Sociology*, New York: Oxford University Press 1958.

Witte, Count S. *The Memoirs of Count Witte*, Yarmolinsky, A., (trans. and ed.), *New York*: Doubleday 1921.

EVOKING THE MYSTICAL:
THE ESOTERIC LEGACY OF FERRUCCIO BUSONI

Judith Crispin

> It was my wish and principle to make the central point of my opera a figure conspicuous and proverbial in history, connected with magic and unsolved riddles. From Zoroaster to Cagliostro these figures form a row of pillars through the course of time...(F. Busoni)[1]

For the Italian-born virtuoso pianist and composer Ferruccio Busoni, the act of composing music was literally an occult practice, analogous to the incantations and evocations of ritual magic. There is much to suggest that his knowledge of occult and arcane subjects was at least as extensive as his knowledge of music.

This study will focus on Busoni's magnum opus – his unfinished *opera Doktor Faust*, which he had worked on from 1916 until his death in 1924. Busoni had jealously guarded his sketches for *Doktor Faust*, concealing them even from the students that attended his death-bed. Gottfried Galston records that as he and Busoni's sons carried the composer's coffin, Kurt Weill 'told [him] under oath of absolute secrecy the last thing that was known for certain about the tragic destiny of *Doktor Faust*. Petri, Jarnach and Weill had searched through the house and checked everything (desk and shelves): *Doktor Faust* is incomplete!'[2] *Doktor Faust* was premiered in Dresden the year after Busoni's death. The incomplete scenes had been hastily finished by Phillip Jarnach, one of Busoni's students, at the request of the Busoni family.

Further discussion of the ideas expressed in this study can be found in my book, *The Esoteric musical Tradition of Ferruccio Busoni and its Reinvigoration in the Music of Larry Sitsky: The Operas Doktor Faust and The Golem.*[3]

---

[1] Busoni quoted in Corleonis, *Ferruccio Busoni*, 109.
[2] Galston quoted in Levitz, *Teaching New Classicality*, 286.
[3] Crispin, *The Esoteric musical Tradition of Ferruccio Busoni*.

The Galston-Busoni Archive in Tennessee[4] houses a catalogue of Busoni's personal library, which was auctioned in 1925.[5] Over 1400 first edition and autographed books are listed, including an impressive array of mystical and religious texts, treatises on magic, collections of fairy-tales, and 23 different versions of the Faust story. Almost forty percent of the library catalogue is devoted to esoteric titles, including some extremely rare editions of occult texts by authors such as Cagliostro, Huysmans, Lavater, Peladan, Saint-Martin and Scott.[6] Busoni's library evidences a particular interest in the Kabbalah, from which many magical traditions are derived.

In his definitive *History of Magic*, Elphias Levi defines Kabbalah as an oral tradition that also transmits knowledge through symbols encoded within hieratic art:

> [Kabbalah was] taken from Chaldea by Abraham, communicated by Joseph to the Egyptian priesthood, ingarnered by Moses, concealed in symbols in the Bible, revealed by the Saviour to St John, and embodied in its fullness in hieratic images, analogous to those of all antiquity…[7]

For Levi, non-verbal symbols provide the degree of discretion necessitated by society's traditional hostility towards Kabbalah, while also enabling the expression of otherwise ineffable ideas.

Like his contemporary Jean Cocteau, Busoni believed that 'Art is not a pastime, but a priesthood.'[8] For him, composition was analogous to a mystical journey where the composer-priest illuminates the path for others. The notion of "musical priest" manifested in Busoni's artistic practice in two ways: firstly, in the composition of works that may be understood only with the aid of a mystic vision and; secondly, in his acceptance that the average person would be spiritually insufficient for such understanding. This belief was self-fulfilling – an artwork that

---

[4] The Galston-Busoni Archive is part of the George F. De Vine Music Library at the University of Tennessee. The archive holdings have been catalogued by Pauline Shaw Bayne, see: Bayne, *The Gottfried Galston Music Collection*.

[5] Anon., *Max Perl Antiquariat*.

[6] Cagliostro's *Secret Correspondence on the Public and Private life of Conte de Cagliostro*, Huysman's *La Bas* (which includes the first published full description of a Satanic Black Mass), Lavater's *Essays on Physiognomy and Magie: Riflessioni Sopra l'Arte Magica Annichilata*, Peladan's *Comments on Deviant Magic* (and related texts by the same author), Saint-Martin's *Natural Table of Relations Which Exist Between God, Man and the Universe*, Scott's *On Demonology and Witchcraft*.

[7] Levi, *The History of Magic*, 42.

[8] Sitsky, 'The Composer and the Anti-Composer', 14.

conveys nested symbols must also contain within itself the manner
by which they may be decoded. As the cipher is necessarily rooted in
the esoteric doctrine to which the symbol refers, it is invisible to those
unfamiliar with that discourse. This ensures that only a specific kind
of person will find the key and unlock the symbol. That Busoni con-
sciously adopted such an approach in his compositions is evidenced by
his own writings. In his *Aphorisms*, written in 1916 commemorating
the 150th year since Mozart's birth, Busoni praised Mozart's own use
of symbols, saying: 'He gives the solution with the riddle'.[9]

Towards the end of his life, Busoni became increasingly estranged
from his students, family and friends. In correspondence with Bruno
Goetz, he confided his fear that a cultural dark age was approaching in
which his musical legacy would be swallowed up if no way was found
to safeguard it:

> The handful of people who are like us will probably be the only ones who
> will really know what is going on for a long time. Things look very bad
> in the world. Maybe we'll have to live like a secret order again one day
> in order to be able to create while waiting it out. This is deeply against
> my convictions and represents a terrible danger. It all too easily becomes
> something puritan, full of vanity and darkness, produced in an unre-
> penting atmosphere.... I never liked...eliteness and preferred to live in
> a world which was free and open in every way. But what's the use when
> the world is no longer open? We must be all the more alert and not
> succumb to this danger. After all there must be someone who will save
> what is essential and pass it on. I believe in the future. I am optimistic,
> but no longer for me.[10]

Without disciples to preserve his legacy against obscurity, Busoni
embedded within his unfinished opera *Doktor Faust* a complex esoteric symbol representing the totality of his mystical conception of
music, together with the cipher by which it may be decoded. He left
deliberate clues in the score as to the location of this symbol to assist
later generations of composers to uncover it. Busoni made no secret
of his intentions, saying:

> In the case of a significant artist the first period is one of seeking
> oneself, the second is that of discovering oneself, while the third and

---

⁹ Busoni, 'Mozart: Aphorisms', 104.
¹⁰ Busoni quoted in Levitz, *Teaching New Classicality*, 82.

conclusive period often seems to be a new search for the benefit of later discoverers.[11]

In his essay 'The score of *Doktor Faust*', Busoni underscored the importance of the opera's large-scale structure, saying:

> Before anything else it was necessary to sketch out the complete plan, the larger outlines of which were previously indicated by the words, to think over the choice, distribution, and employment of means and forms (forms in time and in movement).[12]

The importance of *Doktor Faust*'s large-scale structure takes new significance in the context of Busoni's own philosophical writing. His *Sketch of a New Aesthetic of Music* advocates music that follows 'its own proper mode of growth,' directed by 'natural necessity'. Such music does not seek to *imitate* nature but, rather, can be recognised as a part of nature herself. 'Every idea' he wrote, 'fashions its own form for itself'.[13] For Busoni, specific forms naturally generate specific types of music; each composer must search for the form most likely to generate the music of their imagination. Thus, if form generates content, then an examination of form may reveal something of the content.

The first clear key to decoding *Doktor Faust* is given in the poet's spoken epilogue:

> Still unexhausted all the symbols wait
> That in this work are hidden and concealed;
> Their germs a later school shall procreate
> Whose fruits to those unborn shall be revealed;
> Let each take what he finds appropriate;
> The seed is sown, others may reap the field.
> So rising on the shoulders of the past,
> The soul of man shall close the circle at the last.[14]

Here Busoni addresses his compositional descendents, the unborn to whom he has bequeathed his legacy. As inheriting this legacy depends entirely on decoding the score, it seems likely that this stanza also provides the necessary cipher. Significantly, the stanza suggests that the score may be understood as a geometric circle. In his explanation of *Doktor Faust*, Busoni alludes further to the idea of the circle saying:

---

[11] Busoni, 'Sketch for an introduction'.
[12] Busoni, 'The score of *Doktor Faust*', 73.
[13] Busoni, 'Open letter to Hans Pfitzner', 18.
[14] 1937 Translation by Dent.

To him [the onlooker] half the circle in which the action takes place always remains hidden (as happens to the moon in relationship to the earth). Yet, in thought, the organic expanse of the circle is not dismissed, and in the play there are plenty of indications to show that the transactions continue spinning their threads behind the view...

To me it is precisely music that is qualified to encircle this circumference and in this score I have made the first attempt (not completely carried out) to create an horizon of sound, an acoustic perspective, in which I frequently allow what is sung and acted behind the scenes to sound: in this way the unseen will be revealed by the hearing.[15]

The structural use of the circle in *Doktor Faust* is connected with Busoni's speculations about the omnipresence of time. In a letter to his wife in 1911, he wrote:

I have almost found an explanation for the omnipresence of Time – but I have not discovered why it is that we humans understand time as a straight line from the past to the future, while it *must* be in all directions, like everything in the system of the world.[16]

Quoting Anatole France, Busoni re-emphasizes this idea in his essay *The Essence of Music*. The passage describes the temporal experience from the perspective of someone looking at a tree with a star sparkling above it. The light from the star is the past in relation to the tree,[17] and the tree is the future in relation to the light from the star – both are experienced in the present – integrating past, future and present within the observer.[18]

It seems possible that Busoni's opera may communicate simultaneously in two different temporal spaces – the first, in linear time, as the unfolding of sequential dramatic scenes, and the second, outside of linear time, as a circle of internal connections, inaudible but discoverable nonetheless by someone who knew how to look.

The linear form of Doktor Faust is as follows:

Symphonia
Spoken Prologue
Vorspiel 1
Vorspiel 2

---

[15] Busoni, 'The score of *Doktor Faust*', 74–75.
[16] Busoni, *Letters to His Wife*, 194.
[17] The star is the past, in relation to the tree, because its image is many thousands of years old; the light that conveys it having taken that long to travel from it's source to the observer's eye.
[18] Busoni, 'The Essence of Music', 200.

Scenic Intermezzo
Tableau 1
Scenic Intermezzo
Tableau 2
Tableau 3
Spoken Epilogue

If one arranges the various scenes of *Doktor Faust* in a circle, as shown in fig. 2, a formal symmetry is revealed. As shown in Fig. 1, the circular structure of *Doktor Faust* is reinforced by clear correspondences: the *Symphonia* (top), which begins the opera, is placed opposite to the *1st Tableau* (bottom), which begins the principal drama; the twin spoken sections, the *Prologue* (top right) and *Epilogue* (top left) are also placed opposite one another as are the twin intermezzi, the *Scenic Intermezzo* (bottom right) and *Symphonic Intermezzo* (bottom left); the two introductory scenes, *Vorspiel 1* and *Vorspiel 2* (middle right) are placed opposite to the two concluding scenes, *Tableau 2* and *Tableau 3* (middle left).

A further clue to decoding *Doktor Faust* is Busoni's stated belief that opera should combine entertainment and magical ceremony. Accepting that *Doktor Faust* takes the form of a circle, and remembering that Busoni understood music as magical practice (and an opera on Faust no less so), it seems logical to look to the Grimoires of high magic to illuminate the score. Given that *Doktor Faust* contains at least two Magic Circles, one must admit the possibility that Busoni intended the opera's circular structure as a Magic Circle.

Among the most famous of Grimoires is The *Lemegeton* of Solomon, which contains seals and evocations with which to raise demons. The best known of these seals is the hexagrammatic 'Double seal of Solomon' (fig. 3), which transmits the central hermetic doctrine: 'that which is above is as that which is below'. Other examples of magic circles based on the six-pointed star are given in figs. 4 to 7.

There are a number of discrepancies between the original and final versions of Busoni's *Doktor Faust* libretto. In the first edition from 1918, Busoni indicates his intention for the demons evoked by Faust to appear in a hexagram with Mephistopheles finally appearing in the centre. By the final version, the libretto directed that the demons were directed to appear in appear in an equilateral triangle with Mephistopheles at the apex – or, to one half of a hexagram.

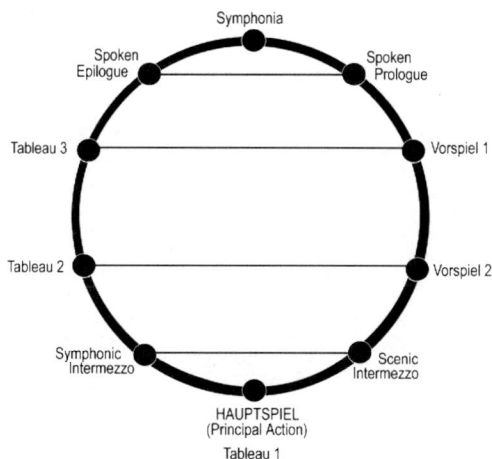

Figure 1. *Doktor Faust* as a geometric circle.

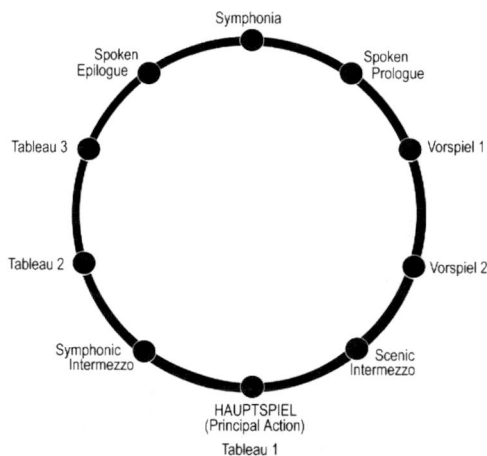

Figure 2. Formal symmetry in *Doktor Faust.*

Numerous evocation circles using a central triangular figure can be found amongst the literature of ceremonial magic, as shown in figs. 8 and 9. The *Goetic Circle of Pacts*, shown in fig. 10, is from Arthur Edward Waite's 1913 *Book of Black Magic and of Pacts*. Waite's circle seems a most appropriate choice for the appearance of Mephistopheles. While it is impossible to now establish whether Busoni was familiar with Waite's text in particular, it seems likely that his change

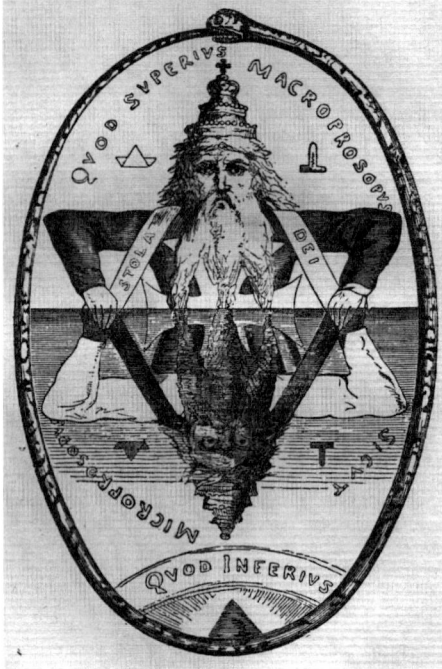

Figure 3. The 'Double seal of Solomon'.

Figure 4. Magic circle, F. Hartmann, *Magic: White and Black*, 1885.

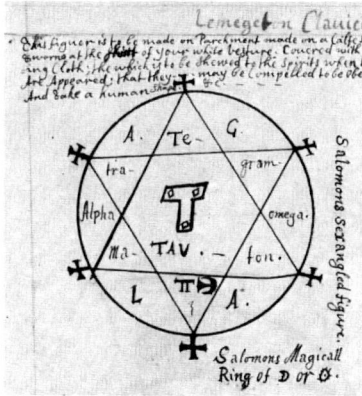

Figure 5. Hexagram of Solomon from *Lemegeten, Goetia.*

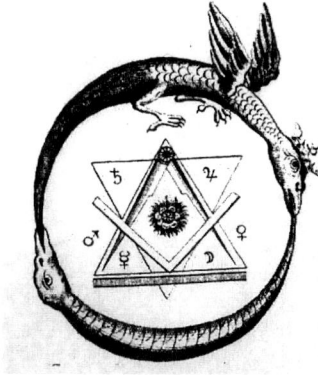

Figure 6. Alchemical Ouroboros, J. Böhme, *Des Hermes Trismegistis wahrer alter Naturweg,* 1782.

Figure 7. Grand Pentacle of Solomon from *Le Grimoire du Pape Honorius.*

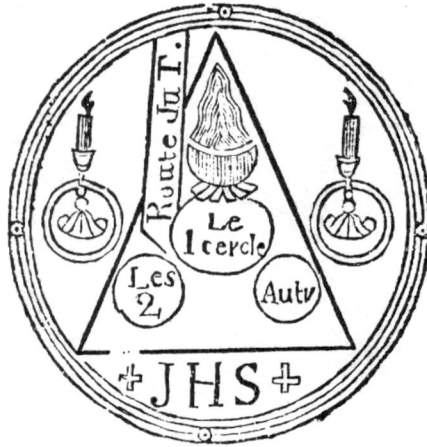

Figure 8. Triangle seal from *L'art de Calendarium Naturale Magicum Perpetuum*, 1620.

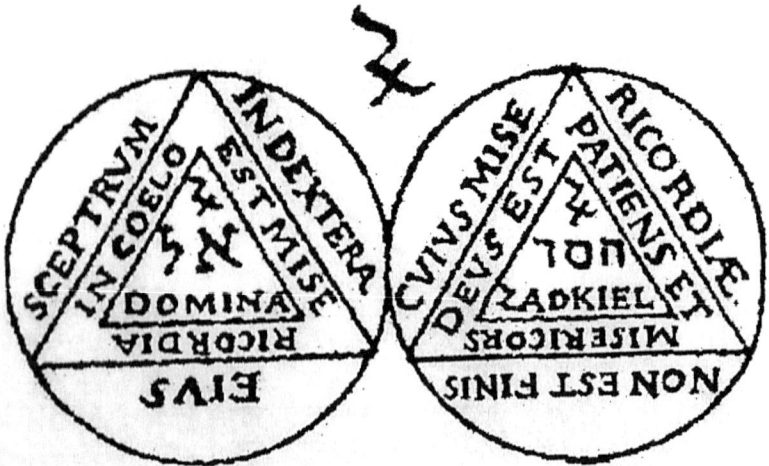

Figure 9. Zadkiel from J. Baptista Großchedel, *commander les spirits celestes, Aëriens, Terrestres, & Infernaux, Suivi di Grand Grimoire*, 1421.

of evocation circles from a hexagrammatic to a triangular configuration reflects firstly, a familiarity with specific occult discourse on the subject of demonic pacts and secondly, a desire to accurately translate a demon evocation into music rather than to create dramatic fantasy.

Like the evocation circle, one can easily find connections between the double seal of Solomon and Busoni's choice of operatic subject.

Figure 10. The *Goetic Circle of Pacts*, Arthur Edward Waite, *The Book of Black Magic and of Pacts*, 1913.

Philalethes Illustraus, an alchemical text by a Johann Michael Faust was published in Frankfurt in 1706. The engraved frontispiece clearly depicts a circle in the form of an ouroboros enclosing a six-pointed star (fig. 11). An even more striking connection between Busoni's operatic subject and the double seal of Solomon can be found in a 16th century Grimoire written by a Doctor Johannes Faust, a magician who was allegedly murdered in about 1540. Faust's Grimoire is dramatically entitled *The Black Raven: Doctor Johannes Faust's Miracle and Magic Book, or The Black Raven, or also called The Threefold Coercion of Hell*, and it contains a diagram of an evocation circle that closely resembles the seal of Solomon (fig. 12).

The rituals of ceremonial magic are alluded to on every level of *Doktor Faust*. In his book on Black Arts, Richard Cavendish records that the magician must work up to higher and higher pitches as the evocation progresses,[19] and Busoni's own evocation scene parallels this with a set of variations sung by evoked demons in increasingly higher ranges, culminating with the arrival of Mephistopheles, a high tenor.

Doktor Faust was not composed independently of Busoni's other works but draws heavily on 22 pre-existing satellite pieces composed between 1912 and 1924. The opera's scenes quote material from these

---

[19] Cavendish, *The Black Arts*, 281.

Figure 11. J. M. Faust, *Philalethes Illustratus.*

Figure 12. Evocation circle from frontispiece Doctor J. Faust, *The Black Raven.*

satellite pieces and it is possible, by mapping the occurrences of pre-existing material, to uncover hidden correspondences between otherwise unrelated scenes (Table 1).[20]

Table 1. Internal relationship of "satellite" material in *Doktor Faust*

Scenes in chronological order, and their component satellite pieces or important characteristics:	Related scenes, and their shared satellite pieces, or important characteristics:

1. *Symphonia*
    Nocturne Symphonique,
    intended for Helena's invocation
    scene, *2nd Tableau*.
	(i) *Vorspiel 1*
	        Nocturne Symphonique
	(ii) *Vorspiel 2*
	        Nocturne Symphonique
	        Bells
	        The singing of "Pax"
	(iii) *Tableau 1*
	        Nocturne Symphonique
	(iv) *Tableau 2*
	        Nocturne Symphonique
	(v) *Tableau 3*
	        Nocturne Symphonique
	        Bells
	        The singing of "Pax"

2. *Prologue*
    Spoken
	(i) *Epilogue*
	        Spoken

3. *Vorspiel 1*
    Sonatina Seconda, associated
    with the students.
    Nocturne Symphonique
    Cortège from *Sarabande and Cortège*
	(i) *Symphonia* (see above)
	(ii) *Vorspiel 2*
	        Nocturne Symphonique
	        A main act
	(iii) *Tableau 1*
	        Nocturne Symphonique
	        Cortège
	        A main movement

---

[20] A complete chart of these pieces as they occur in *Doktor Faust* can be found in Prinz, *Uberblick uber die Verflechtungen*..., 31–32.

Table 1. (cont.)

Scenes in chronological order, and their component satellite pieces or important characteristics:	Related scenes, and their shared satellite pieces, or important characteristics:

	(iv) *Tableau 2*
	      Nocturne Symphonique
	      A main movement
	      The students and the Book
	(v) *Tableau 3*
	      Nocturne Symphonique
	      Sonatina Seconda
	      A main movement

4. *Vorspiel 2*
    Sarabande from *Sarabande and Cortège,* heard when Faust leaves the circle.
    Nocturne Symphonique.
    Sonatina Brevis
    In Signo Joannis Sebastiani Magni, used for the appearance of Megaeros, the fifth spirit.
    Sonatina (in diem nativitatis Christi MCMXVII), used for the music of the 'Credo'
	(i) *Symphonia (see above)*
	(ii) *Vorspiel 1 (see above)*
	(iii) *Tableau 1*
	      Nocturne Symphonique
	      Sonatina (in diem nativitatis Christi MCMXVII)
	      A main act
	(iv) *Symphonic Intermezzo*
	
	Sarabande
	(v) *Tableau 2*
	      Nocturne Symphonique
	      Sarabande
	      A main movement
	(vi) *Tableau 3*
	      Nocturne Symphonique
	      Bells
	      The singing of "Pax"
	      A main movement
	      Evocation ritual at midnight

5. *Scenic Intermezzo*
    Edizione Minore of the *Fantasia Contrappuntistica*
    An intermezzo
	(i) *Symphonic intermezzo*
	      An intermezzo
	(ii) *Tableau 3*
	      The *Scenic Intermezzo's* opening organ solo reappears in *Tableau 3*

6. *Tableau 1*
    Concertino for clarinet and small orchestra: for the entrance of the Duke and Duchess.
    Cortège: used for the Polonaise
	(i) *Symphonia (see above)*
	(ii) *Vorspiel 1 (see above)*
	(iii) *Vorspiel 2 (see above)*
	(iv) *Tableau 2*
	      Nocturne Symphonique

Table 1. (cont.)

Scenes in chronological order, and their component satellite pieces or important characteristics:	Related scenes, and their shared satellite pieces, or important characteristics:

from Parma. *Toccata* *Sonatina (in diem nativitatis Christi MCMXVII)* *Elegy for Clarinet and Piano* *Albumleaf no.2 and Albumleaf no. 3*: for the vision of Salome and John the Baptist *Divertimento for Flute*: Devil's laughter *Tanzwalzer* *Nocturne Symphonique* *Song of the Spirit Dance*	A main act
	The conjuring of visions
	(v) *Tableau 3*
	       Nocturne Symphonique
	       Toccata
	       Albumleaf
	       A main movement
	       The presence of the Duchess

7. *Symphonic Intermezzo*
     Sarabande
     An intermezzo
	(i) *Vorspiel 2 (see above)*
	(ii) *Scenic Intermezzo (see above)*
	(iii) *Tableau 2*
	        Sarabande

8. *Tableau 2*
     Sarabande.
     Cortège.
     Lied des Mephistopheles (from Goethe's Faust), "Es war einmal ein König" [voice and orch. or piano] (March 1918): Mephisto's ballad
     Nocturne Symphonique
	(i) *Symphonia (see above)*
	(ii) *Vorspiel 1 (see above)*
	(iii) *Vorspiel 2 (see above)*
	(iv) *Tableau 1 (see above)*
	(v) *Symphonic Intermezzo (see above)*
	(vi) *Tableau 3*
	        Nocturne Symphonique
	        A main act
	        The presence of the Child

9. *Tableau 3*
     Klavierübung, No. 7: intended for Faust's death.
     Nocturne Symphonique
     Sonatina Seconda
     Toccata
     Albumleaf no. 3 and Albumleaf for flute
	(i) *Symphonia (see above)*
	(ii) *Vorspiel 1 (see above)*
	(iii) *Vorspiel 2 (see above)*
	(iv) *Tableau 1 (see above)*
	(v) *Tableau 2 (see above)*
	(vi) *Scenic Intermezzo (see above)*

10. *Epilogue* Spoken	(i) *Prologue (see above)*

As shown in Table 1, Busoni generated internal connections in four main ways:

(1) by formal design – the intermezzi are obviously related, as are the main acts and the spoken *Prologue* and *Epilogue*;
(2) by dramatic elements – the placement of evocation rituals, conjuring of visions and key characters;
(3) by musical recapitulation – the recurrent use of bells with the text "Pax", the repeated organ music from the *Scenic Intermezzo* in *Tableau 3*; and,
(4) by the careful placement of the satellite pieces *Nocturne Symphonic, Toccata, Albumleaf, Sarabande, Cortège* and the *Sonatina*.[21]

When one maps the occurrences of the satellite piece *Nocturne Symphonique*, against a structural diagram of *Doktor Faust*, the hexagram of Solomon emerges, (fig. 13)

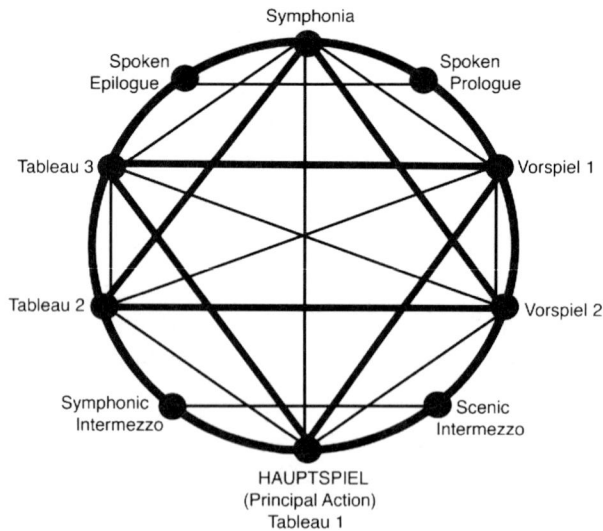

Figure 13. The hexagram in *Doktor Faust.*

---

[21] Other satellite pieces, that appear less frequently and are not used as common elements between disparate scenes, include *Prélude et étude (en arpèges) pour piano; Book two of the Red Indian Diary, Study for string orchestra, 6 wind instruments and timpani;* and *Romanza e Scherzoso* (only the *Scherzoso* is used as a satellite piece, to accompany the entry of Mephistopheles).

One may add a bisecting horizontal line to this structural diagram, (fig. 14) indicating the paired midnight evocations and appearances of the magic book. At the end of *Vorspiel 1* three students from Cracow give Faust a magical book, key and deed. The students reappear only at the end of *Tableau 2*, to demand Faust returns the book, key and deed – which he has already destroyed. The evocation ritual in *Vorspiel 2* takes place at exactly midnight, as does the evocation ritual in *Tableau 3*.

When this bisecting line is incorporated into the structural diagram, (fig. 15), clear resemblances to the Magic Circles of both Solomon and Faust are revealed (figs. 16, and 17).

Although interesting, such a conception is incomplete as all internal connections have not been included in the structural diagram. It would be misleading to simply ignore any correspondences that do not support a model of Doktor Faust as a Magic Circle. When the structural diagram is modified to include all correspondences, the resulting diagram is complex and confusing (fig. 18). Another key to understanding Doktor Faust is given by the number of dramatic scenes, of which there are ten. Central to the Kabbalistic doctrines, with which we know Busoni was familiar, is the allegorical Tree of Life depicting the ten Sephirot, or worlds, which emanate from God and the 22 paths between them (fig. 19).

If Doktor Faust is a geometric circle, it is difficult to see how its structure might relate to the Tree of Life, as two Sephirot are located in the middle of the diagram. As figs. 18 & 19 show, the structural diagram in its present form, bears little resemblance to the Tree of Life. However, the common representation of the Tree of Life, is but one of many. The Tree is also often represented as enneagrammatic circles, or chains of circles, it being necessary only that the internal connections between the Sephirot are maintained. Two different versions of the Tree of Life diagram are shown in figs. 20 & 21.

For Doktor Faust to be viable as a map of the Sephirot, two scenes should logically be relocated into the centre of the circular structural diagram. If one takes the meaning of the word intermezzo quite literally, that is as 'in the middle', then it seems quite appropriate to situate both the *Scenic* and *Symphonic Intermezzi* in the centre of the circle. The position of the *intermezzi* within the circle is easily determined with reference to table 1.

The *Scenic Intermezzo* is connected to the *Symphonic Intermezzo* and *Tableau 3*, and the *Symphonic Intermezzo* is connected to *Vorpiel 2*,

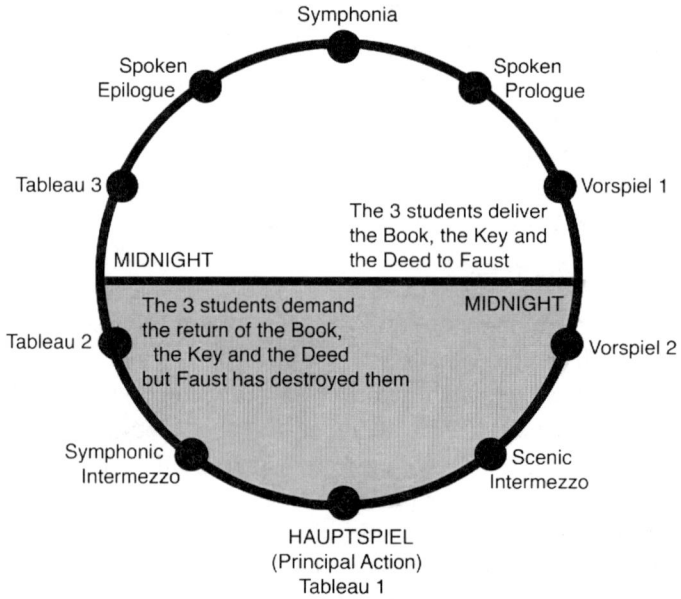

Figure 14. The bisecting line in *Doktor Faust.*

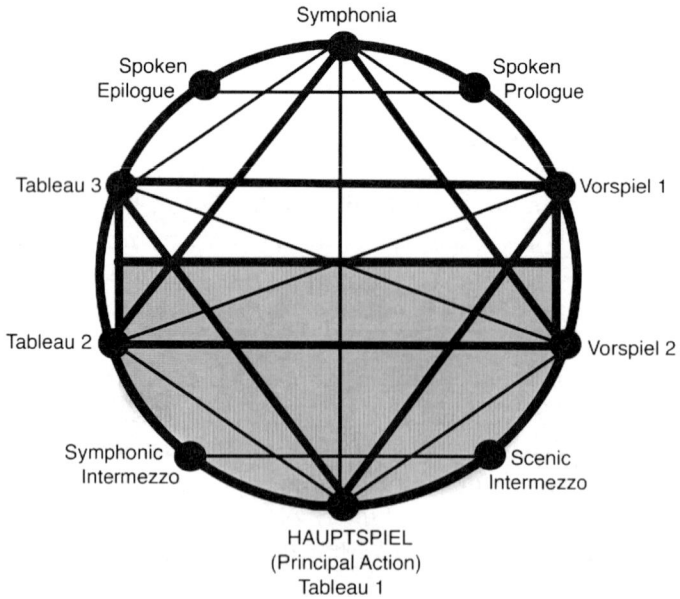

Figure 15. Structural diagram of *Doktor Faust.*

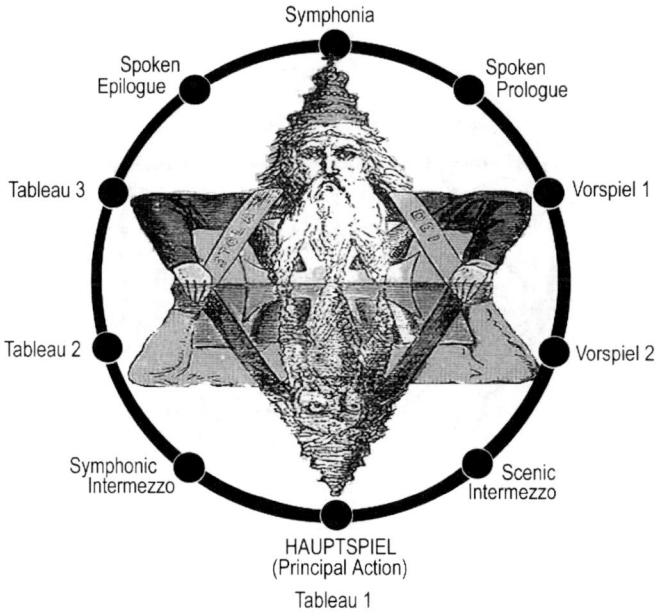

Symphonia

Spoken
Epilogue

Spoken
Prologue

Tableau 3

Vorspiel 1

Tableau 2

Vorspiel 2

Symphonic
Intermezzo

Scenic
Intermezzo

HAUPTSPIEL
(Principal Action)

Tableau 1

Figure 16. Doktor Faust as Solomon's Magic Circle.

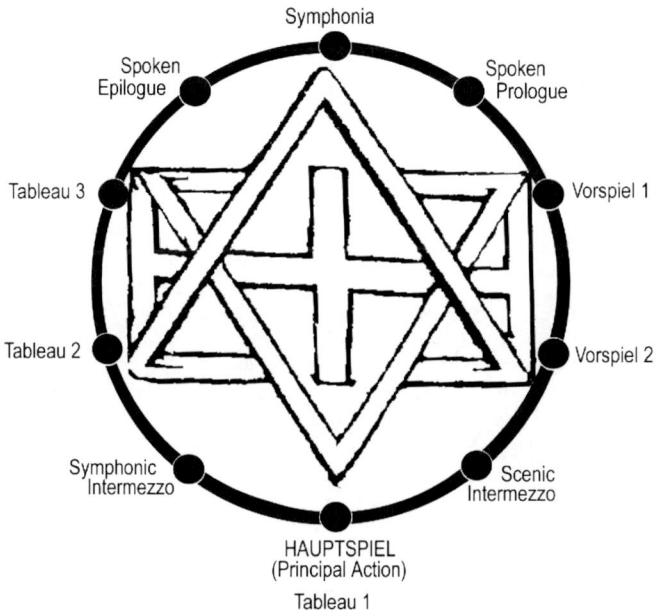

Symphonia

Spoken
Epilogue

Spoken
Prologue

Tableau 3

Vorspiel 1

Tableau 2

Vorspiel 2

Symphonic
Intermezzo

Scenic
Intermezzo

HAUPTSPIEL
(Principal Action)

Tableau 1

Figure 17. Doktor Faust as Johann Faust's Magic Circle.

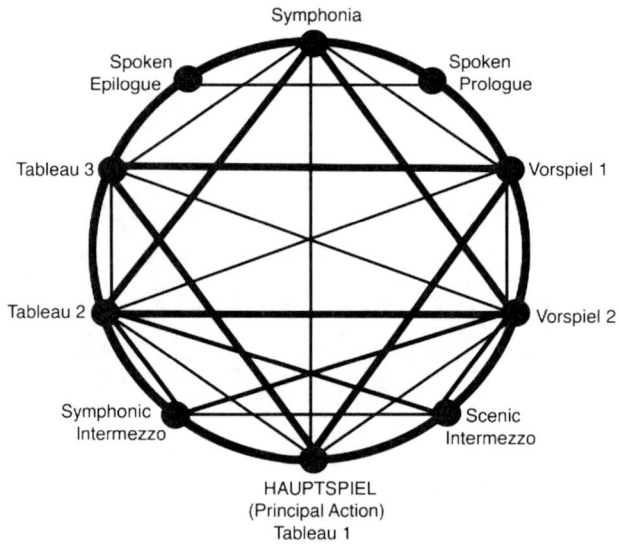

Figure 18. Correspondences of all satellite material in *Doktor Faust.*

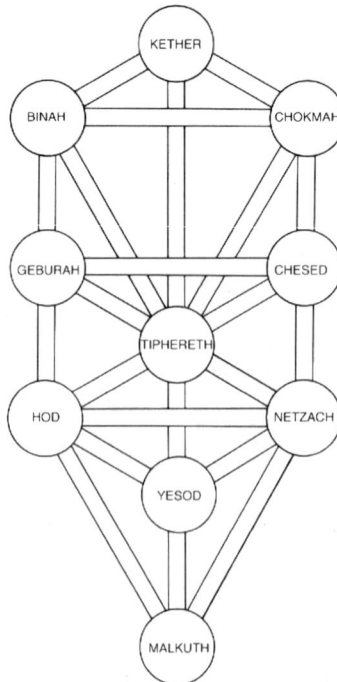

Figure 19. The Kabbalistic Tree of Life.

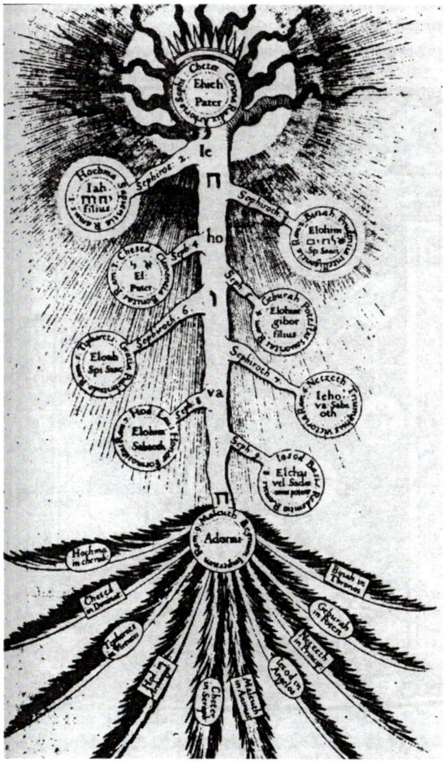

Figure 20. Arber Sephirotheca, R. Fludd, *Denuta: The Kabbalah Unveiled*, 1912.

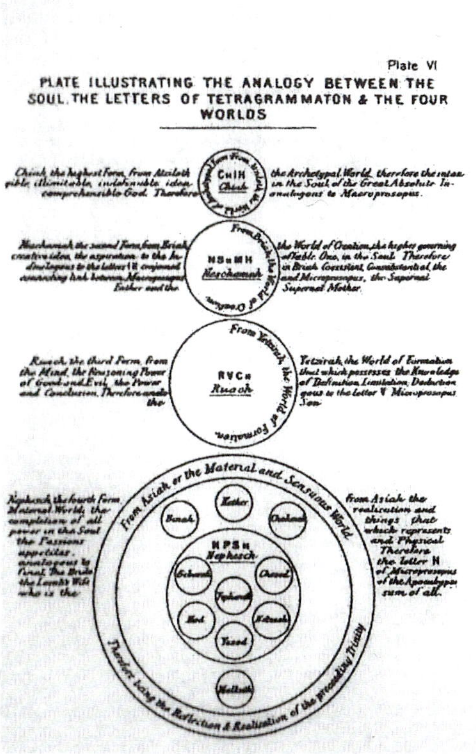

Figure 21. S. L. M. Mathers, *Kabbala Utriusque Cosmi Vol II*, 1621.

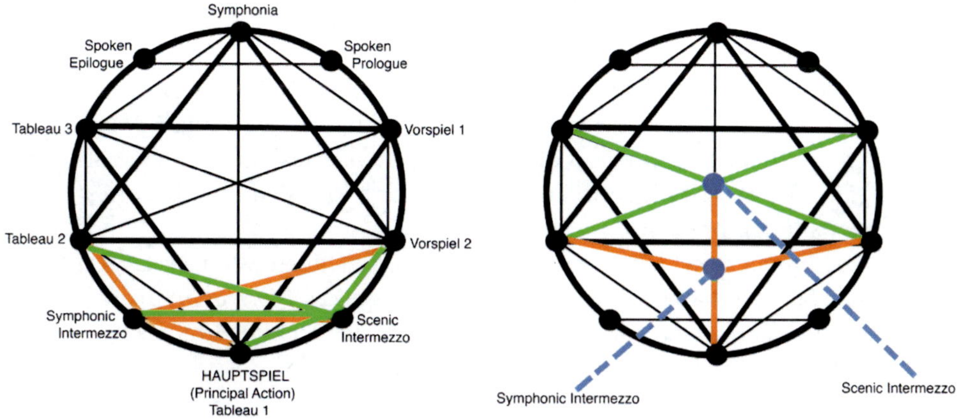

Figure 22. Scenic and Symphonic Intermezzi in the centre of the circle.

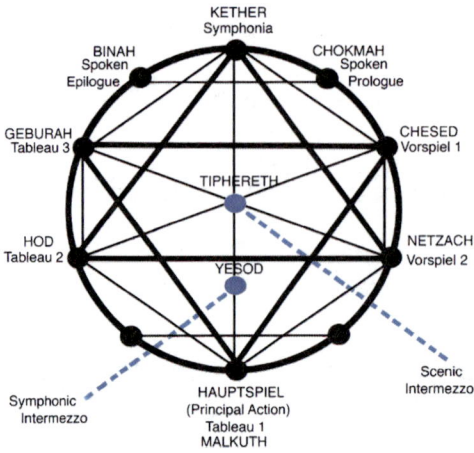 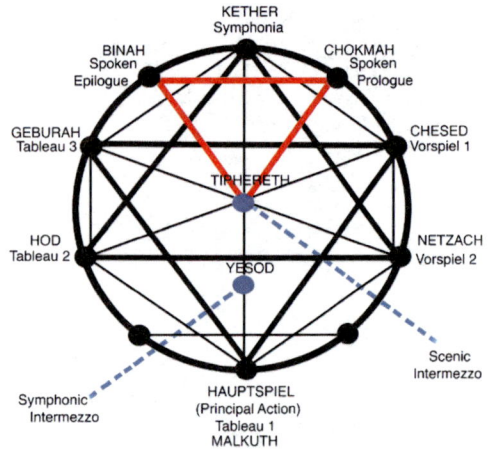

Figure 23. Doktor Faust as a depiction of
the Kabbalistic Tree of Life
(*Intermezzi* in the centre).

Figure 24. Doktor Faust with the complete
paths between Sephirot
(including correspondence between the 3
non-satellite sections).

the *Scenic Intermezzo* and *Tableau 2.* Thus, the *Scenic Intermezzo* takes
the upper position and the *Symphonic Intermezzo* the lower (fig. 22).

Two of the twenty-two paths that bridge the Sephirot on the Tree
of Life are missing in fig. 23. The structural diagram, however, might
legitimately include connections between the three scenes that include
no satellite material connections – the *Epilogue, Prologue* and *Scenic
Intermezzo.* (fig. 24) You will note that now all twenty-two paths
between the Sephirot are represented in *Doktor Faust's* structure. It is
highly unlikely, given the high degree of complexity that such a design
could have arisen unintentionally.

A visual parallel of *Doktor Faust* and the Tree of Life is given in
Fig. 25. However, there remains a problem with understanding *Doktor
Faust* as a joint transmission of Solomon's double seal and the Tree of
Life, as this appears inconsistent with existing knowledge of Busoni's
compositional practices.

Documentary evidence has revealed Busoni's tendency to base larger
works on architectural sketches. A satellite pieces for *Doktor Faust,
Fantasia Contrappuntistica*, was based on an architectural sketch
(fig. 26), which Busoni published in his edition of the work for two
pianos. In a letter to Hugo Leichtentritt, Busoni explained that this

sketch, which generated the structure of *Fantasia Contrappuntistica*, was for the Palace of Popes in Avignon.[22]

Similarly, Busoni's Piano Concerto[23] is also based on an architectural sketch (fig. 27). Unlike *Fantasia Contrappuntistica*, the structural plan of the Piano Concerto is an amalgam of architecture and Masonic symbolism. Busoni sent a copy of the architectural diagram to his wife, explaining it thus:

> This drawing enclosed is crude and clumsy, but not ridiculous. I have a little weakness for it. It is the idea of my piano Concerto in one picture and it is represented by architecture, landscape and symbolism. The three buildings are the first, third and fifth movements. In between come the two "lively" ones; Scherzo, and Tarantelle; the first represented by a miraculous flower and birds, freaks of nature; the second by Vesuvius and cypress trees. The sun rises over the *entrance*; a seal is fastened to the door of the end of the building. The winged being quite at the end is taken from Oehlenschläger's chorus and represents mysticism in nature...[24]

In an essay from 1910, Busoni states his belief that music should be presented in the manner of a Masonic ceremony or ritual:

> Music is the most mysterious of the arts. Around it should float something solemn and festival-like. The entrance to it should be through ceremony and mystery as to a Freemasons' Lodge. It is artistically indecent that anyone from the street, railway train, or restaurant, is free to clatter in during the second movement of a Ninth Symphony...The entrance to a concert hall should give promise of something unusual and should lead us gradually from secular life to the life that is innermost. Step by step the visitor should be conducted into what is exceptional.[25]

If the Kabbalistic model of *Doktor Faust* is to be upheld, it must be consonant with Busoni's practice of adapting architectural structures to musical form. Accordingly, the opera's form must be rooted in an architectural sketch and, in line with previous argument, this sketch must incorporate Masonic symbolism, the Tree of Life and the Double Seal of Solomon. Admittedly, this is a tall order, but these disparate elements are not unrelated. Solomonic magic takes its origins from the

---

[22] Leichtentritt, 'Ferruccio Busoni', 206.
[23] *Concerto per un Pianoforte principale e diverse strumenti ad arco a fiato ed a percussione. Aggiuntovi in Coro finale per voci d'uomini a sei parti.*
[24] Letter to G. Busonim July, 21 and 22, 1902. In Busoni, *Letters to His Wife*, 58.
[25] Busoni, 'How Long Will It Go On?', 182.

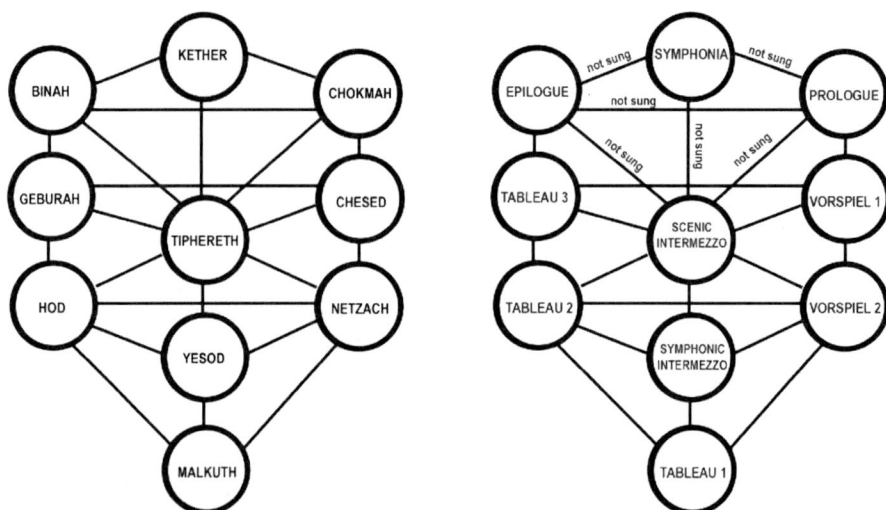

Figure 25. The connections from *Doktor Faust* as they correspond to the
Kabbalistic Tree of Life.

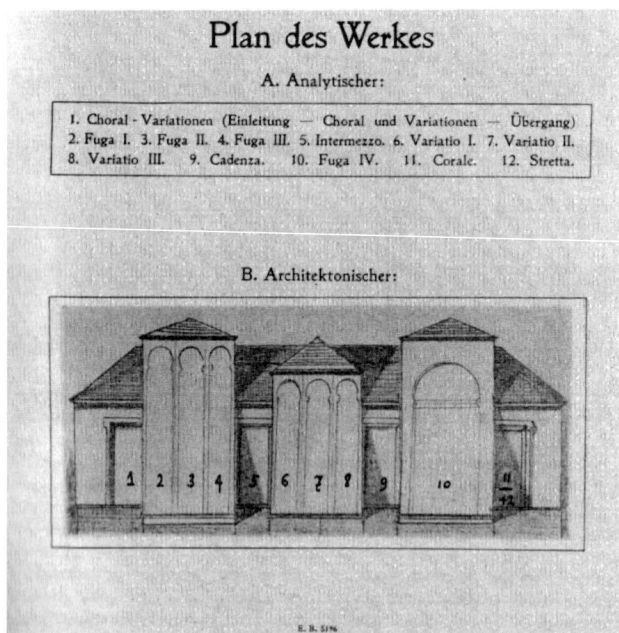

Figure 26. Architectural sketch by Busoni for *Fantasia Contrappuntistica.*

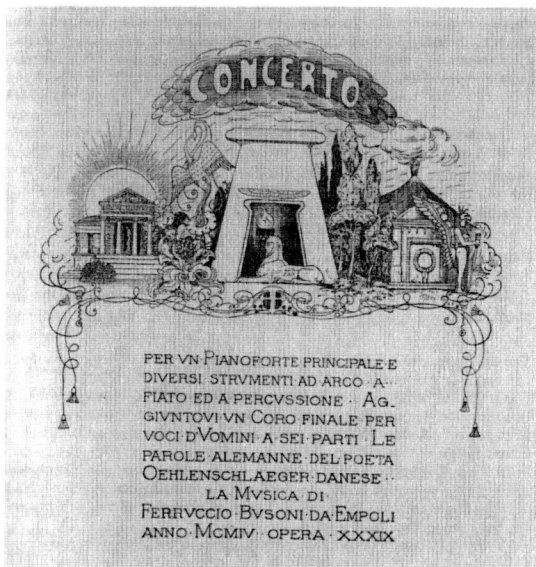

Figure 27. Architectural sketch by Busoni for his Piano Concerto.

Kabbalah and many of the *Lemegeton*'s seals refer to the Tree of Life. Likewise Solomon's writings are integral to Freemasonry, which also combines the doctrines of Zoroaster and Hermes with the Zohar.

The higher degrees of Freemasonry include a ritual that depicts the "Great Work" through re-enacting the murder of Hiram Abif, the legendary architect of Solomon's temple. In this legend, the transmutation of the spirit is allegorically represented as the rebuilding of Solomon's Temple in accordance with Hiram's plan.

The floor plan of the Temple of Solomon, as given by Kircher (fig. 28) and reproduced in subsequent Masonic publications, clearly depicts the Tree of Life. Given Busoni's interest in Freemasonry and his possession of Cagliostro's definitive Masonic text, it is not possible that he was ignorant of this floor plan. Accordingly, one may deduce that Busoni derived the large–scale structure of *Doktor Faust* from this architectural sketch.

This new conception of *Doktor Faust* underscores Busoni's conviction that musical form, determines the nature of the music it contains. Each layer of *Doktor Faust* creates a vessel specifically designed to contain supernatural force. The twin Magic Circles of Solomon and Faust, function solely as instruments for evocation – rituals by which to channel supernatural force into the physical world. The floor plan

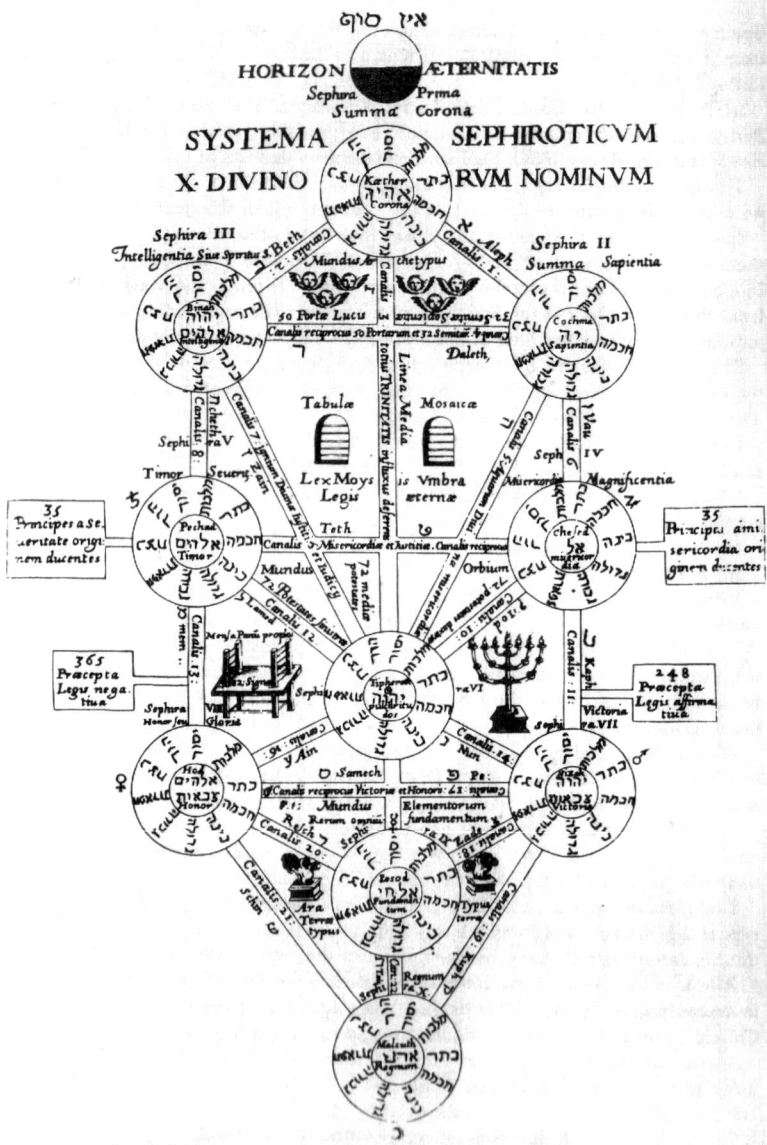

Figure 28. The Kabbalistic Tree of Life as a ground plan of the Temple of Solomon. A. Kircher, *Oedipus Aegyptiacus*, Rome.

of the Temple of Solomon, itself a representation of the Tree of Life, is therefore the perfect structure for an opera about Faust – literature's most famous evoker of demons.

In the traditions of high magic, the Tree of Life symbolises both the descent of divine power towards corporeality and, conversely, the ascent of the human spirit towards the divine (fig. 29). This symbol, in the practice of ceremonial magic, serves either to draw divine power down into the physical world, or to assist an individual human soul in becoming transcendent. Busoni believed there was a kind of doorway through which composers drew music into the world and that, potentially, through that same doorway, a human soul might literally exist the sensory world like Elijah or Enoch who ascended to Heaven without dying. It cannot now be established whether *Doktor Faust* was the culmination of Busoni's ambition to escape, like Faust, into the pages of his score – but one may be forgiven for wanting such a romantic ending to the Faustian tale of Ferruccio Busoni.

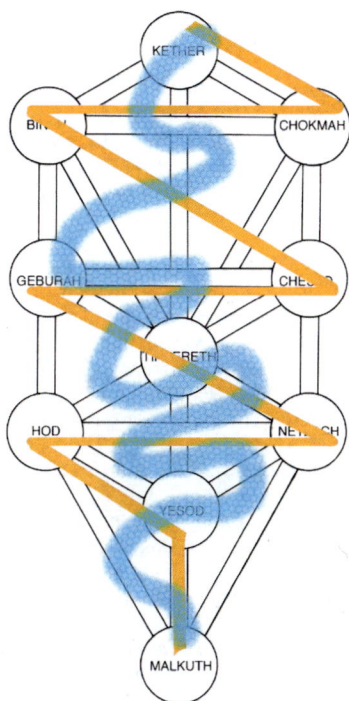

Figure 29. The Tree of Life diagram, together with the 'lightning path' (descending) and 'the serpent path' (ascending).

BIBLIOGRAPHY

D'Amico, F., 'L'utopia di Ferruccio Busoni e il Doktor Faust', in: Sablich, S. and Dalmonte, R. (ed.), *Il flusso del tempo. Scritti su Ferruccio Busoni*, Milan: Unicopli 1985, 267–71.

Anonymous, *The Black Raven: Doctor Johannes Faust's Miracle and Magic Book, or The Black Raven, or also called The Threefold Coercion of Hell*, Welz, K. (trans.), Decatur: The Knights of Runes 1993.

——, *The Key of Solomon the King: Calvicula Salomonis*, Mathers, S. L. M. (trans.), York Beach: Weiser Books 2000.

——, *Max Perl Antiquariat: Bibliothek Ferruccio Busoni*. Galston-Busoni Archive, George F. De Vine Music Library, University of Tennessee 1927.

Arias, E. A., 'Pre-Existent Material in Busoni's Doktor Faust', *The Opera Journal* XVII: 1 (1984), 5–15.

Bayne, P. S., *The Gottfried Galston Music Collection and the Galston-Busoni Archive*. Knoxville: The University of Tennessee Library 1978.

Bohme, J., *Des Hermes Trismegists wahrer alter Naturweg...*, Leipzig, 1782, reprint Berlin: Hermann Barsdorf Verlag 1915.

Busoni, F., *Sketch for an introduction to Book II of The Well-tempered Clavier*. Berlin: Breitkopf und Härtel 1914.

——, 'On the Nature of Music: Towards an Understanding of Music in Relation to the Absolute', *The Music Review* 4 (1956), 282–286. Originally published as 'The Essence of Music: A Paving of the Way to an Understanding of the Everlasting Calendar', *Melos* 1 (1924).

——, *Doktor Faust: Dichtung Und Musik*, (full score) Wiesbaden: Breitkopf & Härtel 1925.

——, 'Über Melodie. Nachgelassene Skizzen', *Zeitschrift für Musik* 97 (1930), 95–101.

——, 'The Essence and Oneness of Music'; 'Young Classicism: Letter to Paul Bekker'; 'The Future of Opera'; 'Mozart: Aphorisms;' 'The Score of Doktor Faust'; 'About Himself and His Works: Self-Criticism'; 'How Long Will It Go On?'; 'The Future of Music: Open Letter to Hans Pfitzner' and 'The Oneness of Music and the Possibilities of Opera', in: Ley, R (trans.), *The Essence of Music and Other Papers*, New York: Dover Publications 1957.

——, *Il Dottor Faust*, Wiesbaden: Breitkopf & Härtel 1960.

——, *Entwurf Einer Neuen Ästhetik Der Tonkunst, with Annotations by Arnold Schoenberg and a Epilogue by H. H. Stuckenschmidt*, Frankfurt: Suhrkamp Verlag 1974.

——, *Letters to His Wife*, Ley, R. (trans), New York: Da Capo Press 1975.

——, *Busoni: Selected Letters*, Beaumont, A. (trans.), London: Faber & Faber 1987.

Cavendish, R., *The Black Arts*, London: Pan books 1977.

Corleonis, A.,'Ferruccio Busoni: Historia Abscondita', *Fanfare* 3: January (1984), 90–117.

Couling, D., *Ferrucio Busoni: "A Musical Ishmael"*, Lanham: The Scarecrow Press 2004.

Crispin, J., *The Esoteric musical Tradition of Ferruccio Busoni and its Reinvigoration in the Music of Larry Sitsky: The Operas Doktor Faust and The Golem*, New York: The Edwin Mellen Press 2007.

Dent, E., 'Busoni on Musical Aesthetics', *Monthly Musical Record* 39: September (1909), 197–98.

——, 'Busoni's Doktor Faust', *Music and Letters* III: July (1926), 196–208.

——, *Ferruccio Busoni: A Biography*, London: Oxford University Press 1933.

——, 'Letter on Busoni's Doktor Faust', *Monthly Musical Record* 67 (1937), 113–14.

——, *Translation of the Libretto of Dr Faust, including the introduction and Epilogue*, program of the BBC concert in Queen's Hall 1937.

Evans, H. R., *Cagliostro and the Egyptian Rite of Freemasonry*, Edmonds: Holmes Publishing Group 1994.

Faust, J. M., *Philalethes Illustratus*, Francofurti ad Moenum: Johannes P. Andreas 1706.

Fludd, R., *Utriusque Cosmi maioris salicet et minoris metaphysica*, Oppenhemii, 1617–1619, reprint Kila: Kessinger 2005.

Fontaine, S., *Busoni's "Doktor Faust" und die Aesthetik des Wunderbaren*, Kassel: Bärenreiter Verlag 1998.

Großchedel, J. B., 'Calendarium Naturale Magicum Perpetuum' in: McLean (ed.), *Magical Calendar: A Synthesis of Magical Symbolism From the Seventeenth-Century Renaissance of Medieval Occultism*, York Beach: Phanes Press 1993.

Hartmann, F., *Magic: White and Black*, 1885, reprint London: Kegan Paul 1924.

Honorius, P., *Grimoire du pape Honorius: Avec un recueil des plus rares secrets*, Paris: Bussière 1995.

Joseph, A. ben, *The Book of Formation (Sepher Yetzirah): translated from the Hebrew, with Annotations, by Knut Stenring, Including the 32 Paths of Wisdom, Their Correspondence with the Hebrew Alphabet and the Tarot Symbols, with an Introduction by Arthur Edward Waite*, New York: Ktav Pub. House 1970.

Karter, J., *L'Art de commander les esprits célestes, aëriens, terrestres & infernaux: Suivi du Grand grimoire, de la magie noire et des forces infernales, du docteur J. Karter, La clavicule de Salomon, avec le vrai secret de faire parler les morts, pour découvrir tous les trésors caches…*, Paris, 1845.

Kindermann, J., *Thematisch-Chronologisches Verzeichnis der Musikalischen Werke von Ferruccio B. Busoni: Studien zur Musikgeschichte des 19. Jahrhunderts*, Bd. 19, Regensburg: Gustav Bosse Verlag 1980.

Leichtentritt, H. 'Ferruccio Busoni' *Musical Review* VI (1945), 206.

Lévi, E., *Transcendental Magic: Its Doctrine and Ritual*, Waite, A. E. (trans.), Middlesex: Tiger Books 1995.

——, *The History of Magic: Including a Clear and Precise Exposition of its Procedure, its Rites and its Mysteries*, Waite, A. E. (trans.), York Beach, Maine: Samuel Weiser 1999.

Levitz, T., *Teaching New Classicality: Ferruccio Busoni's Masterclass in Composition*, New York: P Lang 1996.

Mathers, S. L. M., *Kabbala Denuta: The Kabbalah Unveiled*, 1912, reprint New York: Arkana 1992.

Petri, E., 'How Busoni Taught', *The Etude* 58:10 (1940), 657–710.

Prinz, U. *Uberblick uber die Verflechtungen innerhalb von Busonis Originalwerk ab 1890 (mit Hinweisen auf von Busoni benutzte fremde Vorlagen)*, 1970.

Riethmüller, A., *Ferruccio Busonis Poetik*, Mainz: Schott 1988.

Roberge, M., *Ferruccio Busoni: A Bio-Bibliography*, Connecticut: Greenwood Press 1988.

——, 'The Busoni Network and the Art of Creative Transcription', *Canadian University Music Review* 11:1 (1991), 68–88.

Scholem, G. G., *Kabbalah and Its Symbolism*, New York: Schocken Books 1969.

Searle, H., 'Busoni's Doktor Faust', *Monthly Musical Record* 67: 785 (1937), 54–56.

Sitsky, L., *Busoni and the Piano: The Works, the Writings, and the Recordings*, Westport, Connecticut: Greenwood Press 1986.

——, "The Composer and the Anti-Composer", *24 Hours* July (1980), 14–15.

Sorabji, K. S., 'Busoni's Doktor Faust', *The New English Weekly* 10:25 (1937), 494–96.

Stevenson, R., 'Busoni – the Legend of a Prodigal', *The Score* 15: March (1956), 15–30.

Waite, A. E., *The Book of Black Magic and of Pacts: including the rites and mysteries of Goetic Theurgy, Sorcery and Infernal Necromancy*, 1898, reprint Chicago: The De Laurent Co., 1940.

MUSICA PIETRIFICATA, SCULTURE SONORE: ALEKSANDR SKRJABIN TRA ESTASI E TEOSOFIA

Barbara Aniello

English summary. This article proposes the challenge of reading the signs of diverse extra-musical and esoteric influences included by Skrjabin in his partitions and in his ideas about art; to capture objectively such influences transferred by Skrjabin's music trough the analysis of the partitions; to discern in the artists: sculptures, painters, poets, directors, choreographers, known by Skrjabin, the influence of his music; to trace in common theosophical readings, the *idem sentire* in base of the spiritual community between artists geographically and disciplinary away; to identify in figurative art, music, poetry or theatre the signs of common theosophical thoughts. Three are the symphonic synesthetic works of Skrjabin from 1905 to 1914: *Poem of Extase, Prometheus or the poem of fire, The Mystherium.* Influenced by theosophy, in synesthesia's history, Skrjabin represents the nodal point not only for discovering *color-sound* and the consequent innovation of the artistic performance but also because the ideal of a Art-Total.

Negli ultimi nove anni della sua vita, dal 1905 al 1914, il compositore Aleksandr Skrjabin si dedica a tre opere sinfoniche *Il Poema dell'Estasi, Il Prometeo o il poema del fuoco, Il Mysterium.* Viaggia attraverso luoghi realmente vissuti, Bogliasco, Vésenaz, Bruxelles, Mosca, Parigi, o semplicemente fantasticati, India. Questi luoghi geografici sono da intendersi più come luoghi dell'anima che come spazi fisici, quasi una "geografia-spirituale", segnata di volta in volta dall'incontro con un'arte differente, scultura, poesia, pittura, danza, teatro, che per Skrjabin rappresenta una scoperta, una fonte d'ispirazione, uno scambio, riflettendosi nella sua estetica musicale.

Quest'ultimo fecondo capitolo della vita del compositore è segnato da influenze extra-musicali e filosofiche recepite da Skrjabin nelle sue partiture e nelle sue idee sull'arte. Così, uno stesso *idem sentire* accomuna artisti geograficamente lontani che, grazie a comuni letture teosofiche, a fortuite contingenze e incontri momentanei stabiliscono contatti reciproci e riflettono nelle loro opere figurative, musicali, poetiche e teatrali i vestigi di una comune ascendenza teosofica.

Rodo, Vrubel, Blok, Andreev, Berdiaev, Baltrusajtis, Bal'mont, Taneev, Čiurlionis, Ivanov, Belyj, Koonen, Tairov, Ekster, Delville, Kandinskij, Kulbin, Marc, Baranoff-Roussiné, Picabia, Russolo, Kupka, Prampolini, Djaghilev, Inayat Kahn, D'Annunzio, Fuller, Duncan, Malevič, Matjušin sono solo alcuni degli artisti che Skrjabin incontra.

La scoperta della teosofia determinerà una svolta radicale non solo nell'universo musicale, filosofico e sinestetico skrjabiniano, ma anche in quello poetico, pittorico, scultoreo, letterario, tersicoreo e teatrale degli altri artisti con cui il compositore dialoga.

RODO E SKRJABIN, CRONACA DI UN INCONTRO

Tra i tanti scambi, cruciale per il suo approdo all'esoterismo e alla teosofia, sarà quello con lo scultore Auguste de Niederhäusern, detto Rodo, la cui cronaca è fornita da Manfred Kelkel:

All'uscita dal concerto sospetto, il musicista aveva fatto la conoscenza di un uomo d'una quarantina d'anni, lo scultore Auguste de Niederhäusern (1863–1913). "Mon nom doit se prononcer 'Nid de roses'", aveva precisato sorridente[1]. Ma lo avevano soprannominato "Rodo" perché era stato l'assistente di Rodin per 8 anni. È l'autore del monumento dedicato a Paul Verlaine eretto nel 1911 nel *Jardin du Luxembourg* a Parigi. La sua reputazione aveva un po' sofferto della sua partecipazione al *Salon des Rose-Croix*. "Il n'était pas de ce monde, c'était un occultiste!", dirà qualche anno più tardi Youri Engel che aveva assistito al loro incontro. Si era presto reso conto, infatti, che Rodo era divenuto un adepto incondizionato della teosofa russa, Hélèna Petrovna Blavatsky, che aveva fondato nel 1875, negli Stati Uniti, la Société de Théosophie con l'aiuto del colonnello Henry Steel Olcott. Il suo scopo: formare un nucleo di fraternità universale senza distinzione di razza, sesso o colore, affinché si stabilisse la pace nel mondo. Per far questo, volevano incoraggiare lo studio comparato delle religioni, delle filosofie e delle scienze e soprattutto, studiare le leggi ineffabili della Natura e dei prodigiosi poteri latenti nell'uomo. "Madame Blavatsky- proseguì Rodo che conosceva il suo soggetto sulla punta delle dita- était une prophétesse de génie qui vécut toute sa vie

---

[1] André Salmon nel 1922 riprende lo scherzoso gioco di parole: "Niederhäusern! cela s'articulait plus joliment: Niderose. Nid de rose!", in Lapaire, *Auguste de Niederhäusern-Rodo, 1863–1913. Un sculpteur entre la Suisse et Paris*, 17.

sous le signe de le surnaturel. Mariée très jeune à un général russe, elle l'abandonna aussitôt pour visiter un pays après l'autre, la Turquie, la Grèce et l'Égypte, les États-Unis où elle expérimentera l'art des 'hommes-médicine' et la magie vodou, avant d'affronter l'expérience de la mort en compagnie d'un moine tibétain." Quando ebbe finalmente diritto alla parola, Skrjabin affermò che conosceva bene l'argomento e che lui stesso aveva letto a Bogliasco una delle opere di questa donna affascinante, *La Clef de la Théosophie*, che sviluppava delle idee molto vicine alle sue. Il musicista non si sbagliava. Con l'incontro di Rodo e della teosofia, una nuova direzione prendevano le sue ricerche, che si manifesteranno presto nella scoperta della grande legge cosmica delle corrispondenze e vibrazioni universali[2].

Dal 30 giugno 1906 in poi, data del récital avvenuto a Ginevra, *La Clef de la Théosophie* diviene *le livre de chevet* di Skrjabin. L'importanza di questo testo, pubblicato per la prima volta a Londra nel 1889, lo stesso anno dell'edizione de *Les Grands Initiés* di Schuré, è attestata dal fatto che è l'unico citato esplicitamente nell'epistolario skrjabinano. Le numerose analogie tra il libro della Blavatsky e il testo letterario del *Poème*, redatto dal compositore tra il 1904 e 1906 e pubblicato nel 1907, rivelano una sostanziale adesione ai concetti teosofici fondamentali del sonno e risveglio, della lotta e unione, dell'essere e non-essere, dell'estasi e ascesi.

In effetti, Skrjabin potrebbe aver avuto un approccio diretto ancor prima che con lo scultore con le sue sculture già in occasione della magniloquente *Exposition Universelle* de Paris del 1900. Rodo vi partecipa, infatti, all'interno del padiglione svizzero, esponendo i busti in bronzo *Portrait de Georges Favon, L'Orateur*, 1900 e *Portrait de Hodler*, 1898, insieme ad alcuni frammenti del *Monument Verlaine*, 1889–1900 e ad un gruppo in marmo dal titolo molto significativo: *Les Initiés*, 1898.

I biografi di Skrjabin ricordano che quando, nel luglio del 1900, il compositore si reca a Parigi per visitare l'*Exposition*, arriva troppo tardi per assistere alla prima de *Le feu céleste* di Camille Saint-Saëns, ma visita *le Palais de l'électricité*: un autentico spettacolo pirotecnico, fatto di vetri e specchi illuminati da mille lampade gli viene incontro. Il ricordo iridescente di questa visione, unita a quella successiva delle

---

[2] Kelkel, *Alexandre Scriabine, un musicien à la recherche de l'absolu*, 119–120.

acque multicolori del lago Léman[3], si radicherà profondamente nella
memoria di Skrjabin, condizionandone le future scelte sinestetiche[4].

Un'altra occasione di incontro indiretto tra i due artisti è rappresentata dal circolo rosacrociano. È assai probabile che la conoscenza
dell'opera dell'artista sia avvenuta nell'intimità del cenacolo teosofico,
complice il *1° Salon de la Rose Croix*. Péladan, infatti, curioso scoprit-
tore di talenti e assiduo collezionatore di amicizie in campo artistico e
musicale, potrebbe aver fatto da tramite tra lo scultore e il musicista.

L'11 maggio del 1891 Sâr Péladan visita il *2° Salon de la Nationale* di Parigi e resta folgorato da una scultura in particolare. Si tratta
dell'*Avalanche* di Rodo, esposta sotto il titolo di *Génie de l'Avalanche*, riprodotta in catalogo e recensita da *l'Intransigeant* il 28 maggio. Entrato subito in contatto con Rodo, lo invita a partecipare al *1°
Salon de la Rose Croix*, il 10 marzo 1892, presente, tra gli altri artisti,
anche Delville che, conosciuto più tardi da Skrjabin a Bruxelles, sarà
un'altra figura-chiave per le idee esoteriche del maestro. Quando una
parte dello stesso *Salon* viene trasferita a Bruxelles, *Avalanche e Tor-
rent*, insieme con il *busto di Verlaine* emigrano. Delville, fondatore de
Le Cercle Pour l'Art, presenzia la sezione belga del circolo *Rose+Croix*

---

[3] Dal 1904 Skrjabin tiene un diario che rivela il suo interesse per il binomio musica-
filosofia, ma anche per la poesia e l'arte figurativa. Dopo una passeggiata a Belotte, non
lontano da Vésenaz, seduto sulla terrazza di un caffè, ammirando lo spettacolo scintillante dei colori dell'acqua del lago Léman, deciderà di annotare tutto ciò che gli passa
in testa. Il fascino per l'acqua, che ispirerà tanti artisti dell'epoca, per via dell'elemento
liquido, riflettente e cristallino, trasparente e potenzialmente multicolore, catturato
dall'occhio nell'attività instancabile di una fonte o contemplato nella statica calma
di un lago, merita qui una breve digressione. Proprio il lago Léman, in particolare, è
curiosamente al crocevia delle ricerche artistiche di un musicista, un pittore, uno scultore. Ferdinand Hodler dipingerà ossessivamente le acque multicolori del Léman, tra
il 1905 e il 1915, scoprendo, tra i suoi riflessi simmetrici, la legge delle corrispondenze
universali. Appassionato di corno delle alpi e sensibile alla musica, Rodo sognerà a
lungo di comporre con l'amico Stoecklin una *Symphonie alpestre*, da suonare su una
zattera gigante in mezzo al lago Léman. Esaltato dall'idea di realizzare un'opera d'arte
totale che riunisse scultura, musica, pittura, architettura, progetterà *Le Temple de la
Mélancolie*, ideale teatro per le sue sperimentazioni sinestetiche.
[4] L'idea di mettere le luci nel Prometeo, perseguiterà Skrjabin come un'autentica
ossessione. La visione scintillante e variopinta dello spettacolo parigino lo seduce, fis-
sandosi, indelebile, nei suoi ricordi: "cet ensemble scintillait de milliers de feux mul-
ticolores." Il ricordo della suggestiva cascata che decorava la facciata del gigantesco
château d'eau, disegnato da Edmond Paulin, farà immaginare a Skrjabin un'analoga
architettura di luce da inserire nel *Poema del fuoco*, op. 60. "Che progetti, che progetti
ho! Sapete, metterò le luci nel *Prometeo* [egli sussurrò la parola luci]. Ve lo suonerò.
Luci. È un poema del fuoco. Qui la sala cambia colori. Ora risplendono; ora si tramu-
tano in lingue di fuoco. Sentite come tutta questa musica è autentico fuoco". Bowers,
The New Skrjabin – Enigma And Answers, 203.

e illustra *Le Poème Alpestre* ai numerosi adepti del suo circolo, tra cui anche Skrjabin. Il contatto tra Skrjabin e Péladan, avverrà dunque attraverso Delville, autore del secondo circolo teosofico, filiazione di quello parigino, a Bruxelles.

Rodo pagherà molto cara la sua "tessera" di teosofo, condannato per sempre a portare l'etichetta di artista enigmatico, astruso, sibillino, incomprensibile ad un pubblico non-iniziato. La reputazione di rosacrociano, stando al racconto di Engel, non gioverà allo scultore che, bollato come "occultiste", viene stigmatizzato dalla critica e dal mercato.

Se Rodo ha il torto di essere simbolista, cosa che lo rende difficile da comprendere per quelli che non sono iniziati[5], dal canto suo Skrjabin resta un incorreggibile mistico[6].

Tacciato di ascetismo, Skrjabin subisce un analogo destino per quanto riguarda la ricezione delle sue ultime opere: è visto come un musicista bizzarro, uno Chopin russo, un Wagner malriuscito. Nel primo dei cinque luoghi dell'anima, in Svizzera, nonostante tutto e tutti, Skrjabin rivela il suo prolifico, triplice volto: come scrittore vi compone due terzi di *Prometheische Phantasien*, scrive *Notes et Réflexions, carnets inédits* e si dedica al testo del *Poème de l'Extase*; come compositore vi immagina la sua prima sinfonia sinestetica; come adepto della filosofia si nutre al congresso di Ginevra del 1904 delle conferenze di Bergson, delle dissertazioni su Fiche, Schelling e di quelle sul *panpsychisme* del professor Flournoy. Ma sarà proprio lo scultore-teosofo Rodo che nel 1906 parlerà a lungo con il musicista del testo di Elena Blavatsky, spalancando quegli orizzonti filosofici e mistici che siglano l'opera successiva di Skrjabin. Nonostante questo, la critica tende a ridimensionare Skrjabin, dipingendolo come filosofo autodidatta e ideatore di musica pura[7]. Intenzione di Skrjabin è creare un'arte messianica, su di un substrato mistico e sensuale.

Il titolo originario della prima delle sue sinfonie esoteriche, *Poème Orgiastique*, va evidentemente nella direzione del concetto platonico e nietzscheiano dell'amore dionisiaco. Skrjabin stesso lo definisce "più importante della sua Terza Sinfonia" e propedeutico per le composizioni successive[8]:

---

[5] Seippel, 'Exposition des Indépendants', 60.
[6] L'affermazione è di Plechanov in Bowers, op. cit., 58.
[7] Kelkel, 'Aleksandre Scriabine et "le charme des impossibilités"', 1988.
[8] Kachperov, *A. N. Skrjabin Pisma*, 388.

Quando spiegava gli elementi extramusicali dell'opera Skrjabin si eccitava, il suo viso si trasformava e ripeteva: "questo non somiglierà a niente di ciò che ho scritto prima d'ora. Sarà il riflesso di quello che sento e che vedo oggi: una gioia incontenibile, una festa grandiosa[9].

Nell'aprile 1906 termina il poema in versi, parallelo alla partitura, denso di quegli elementi filosofici ed extra-musicali maturati durante il periodo di Bogliasco. Ma al momento della pubblicazione, ritornato in Svizzera nel 1907, dopo una tournée negli Stati Uniti, muta il titolo, da *Poème Orgiastique* in *Poème de l'Extase*.

Il cambiamento si deve, a mio avviso, all'intervento dello scultore Rodo e alla conoscenza della sua opera. Infatti, se l'artista svizzero-francese gli aprirà le porte della teosofia e lo attrarrà verso letture occultiste[10], sarà la conoscenza diretta con alcune delle sue opere a suggerire a Skrjabin il tema, o se non altro il titolo, di tutte le sue tre opere della maturità: *Il Poema dell'Estasi, Prometeo o Il Poema del fuoco, Il Mysterium.*

Sull'importanza dell'incontro tra il compositore e lo scultore e sul ruolo di Rodo come mentore delle ascendenze teosofiche di Skrjabin la critica ha, a mio avviso, finora sorvolato. Adepto della teosofia, Rodo fin dal primo incontro lo sommergerà di informazioni e stimoli, citando il famoso testo che Skrjabin aveva già letto, come si legge nella lettera dell'8 Maggio 1905 a Tatjana.

La clef de la Théosophie est un livre extraordinaire. Tu seras étonné de constater combien il est proche de mes idées[11].

Così, dal concepimento a Vésenaz, nel dicembre 1904, presente la moglie Vera, dell'idea di una sinfonia estatica, sboccia a Bogliasco, insieme alla compagna Tatjana, la sua versione letteraria, per poi nascere a Servette, due anni dopo, nella sua forma definitiva la partitura del *Poema dell'Estasi.*

RODO TEOSOFO

Lettore accanito di Edouard Schuré, ammiratore di Wagner, autore di opere dalle intenzioni mistiche e dimensioni colossali, Rodo esegue numerose sculture tra il 1888 e 1898 di ispirazione simbolista e

[9] Hellmundt, *Musikalniyi Sovremennik*, 104.
[10] Kelkel, *Alexandre Scriabine, un musicien à la recherche de l'absolu*, 119.
[11] Kachperov, op. cit., 324.

Tabella 1. Sculture Skrjabiniane

Incrocio tra le arti	Dalla musica alla scultura		Dalla scultura alla musica	
Opere di Skrjabin	*Notturno per la mano sinistra,* op. 9 n. 1 (1894–1895)	*Poème de l'Extase,* op. 54 (1904–1907)	*Prométhée, Le poème du feu,* op. 60, (1909–1910)	*Mysterium,* (1914)
Opere di Rodo	1. *La main,* 1902 2. *Nocturne,* 1904	3. *Extase,* 1894 4. *Masque de femme,* 1898 5. *Extase,* 1904 6. *Offrande à Bacchus,* 1905,I 7. *Psyché,* 1910, I 8. *Psyché,* 1911, studio per la II versione 9. *Psyché,* 1911, II 10. *Baccante, Offrande à Bacchus,* 1910, studio 11. *Tête de femme à la bouche ouverte,* 1910 circa 12. *Offrande à Bacchus,* 1910, II 13. *Offrande à Bacchus,* 1911, III	14. *Le poème du feu,* 1908, I; II 15. *Femme à la traîne, élément du Poème du feu,* 1908 16. *Masque de Proéthée, élément du Poème du feu,* 1908 17. *Le Sarment, élément du Poème du feu,* 1912 18. *Dragon,* s.d., *élément du Poème du feu*	19. *Mélancolie,* 1893 20. *Adam et Eve,* 1906 21. *Mélancolie,* 1907[12] 22. *Temple de la Mélancolie,* 1909 23. *Paradis perdu. Désespérance,* 1909, I 24. *Paradis perdu,* 1909;1912 25. *Danseuse, Danse, Masque de la Danse,* 1910 26. *Désespérance,* 1912, II 27. *Danseuse,* 1912? 28. *Apollon,* s.d., *élément du Temple de la Mélancolie ou de L'initiateur*

---

[12] Verlaine, *Poèmes saturniens,* 1866. Melancholia è il primo dei titoli della raccolta che prosegue con *Résignation, Nevermore, Après trois ans, Vœu, Lassitude, Mon rêve familier, A une femme, L'angoisse.* Questi otto poemi esprimono una sofferenza vaga, indistinta, di cui solamente l'ultimo rivela la natura, l'angoscia.

spiritualista. A Parigi entra nel *milieu* della *Revue Wagnérienne* fondata nel 1885 da Edouard Dujardin e fa amicizia con Schuré, Mendès e Péladan. I testi di Edouard Schuré sono un grande punto di riferimento per l'opera di Rodo e per quella di Skrjabin. Schuré, oltre ad essere autore di testi teosofici, esercitava il mestiere di critico musicale. Appassionato di Wagner, dedica al compositore tedesco diversi testi e riflessioni[13]. Tra questi, *Femmes inspiratrices et poètes annonciateurs*[14] contiene la descrizione di alcune *performances* di danza, ad opera di una certa M.lle H, mantenuta in anonimato per via del contenuto *osé* dei suoi costumi e della sua coreografia. È molto probabile che la misteriosa ballerina altri non sia che Isadora Duncan[15.] Riconoscibile sotto il peplo greco, con i suoi leggendari piedi nudi e la sua coreografia non-accademica, è ritratta da Schuré quasi come una palingenesi dell'*estasi* antica greca.

UNE DANSEUSE GRECQUE RÉSUSCITÉE[16]

J'ai souvent imaginé ce que furent les danses sacrées, dans les temples de l'Inde, de l'Égypte ou de la Grèce. On sait qu'à certaines dates des représentations mimiques d'une beauté et d'une splendeur merveilleuse avaient pour but d'illustrer les plus hauts mystères de la religion. Accompagnés ou non de paroles, mais toujours soutenus par la musique, ces tableaux vivants agissaient comme une force magique sur l'âme des spectateurs par la noblesse des attitudes et l'éloquence des gestes. La forme humaine y incarnait des pensées divines. Ses mouvements traduisaient des sentiments sublimes et des idées transcendantes[17]. […] La symbolique du corps humain était la base de tout l'art grec. C'est pourquoi la

[13] Per una bibliografia essenziale dei testi dedicati alla musica da Schuré: *Souvenirs sur Richard Wagner: la première de Tristan et Iseult,* Paris: Perrin 1900; *Histoire du drame musical*, Paris: Perrin 1895; *Histoire du lied ou la chanson populaire en Allemagne. Nouv. éd. précédée d'une étude sur Le réveil de la poésie populaire en France*, Paris: Perrin 1903; *Richard Wagner: son œuvre et son idée*, 4ème éd., Paris: Perrin 1900.

[14] Schuré, *Femmes inspiratrices et poètes annonciateurs*, 239–248.

[15] Duncan Isadora (1877–1927), danzatrice e insegnante statunitense. Decisa a calcare il palcoscenico, rifiutando però l'estetica del balletto accademico, si è dedicata con passione a elaborare una sua nuova e personale forma di danza classica, dove il termine classica è da intendere come ellenica, ispirata cioè all'antica Grecia, con l'intento di esprimere i più intimi sentimenti in modo autentico e istintivo, e senza più indossare costumi e calzature costrittivi, ma lasciando vibrare il corpo, così come le onde del mare si increspano al vento, in leggere tuniche sciolte e a piedi nudi. Avendo presentato con successo alcune esibizioni in forma di concerto, danza, musica e poesia nei salotti newyorkesi, e sentendosi ormai pronta per proporle anche oltreoceano, ha quindi affrontato la grande avventura europea, destinata a farne un mito, come antesignana della danza moderna.

[16] Schuré, *Femmes inspiratrices et poètes annonciateurs*, 239–248.

[17] La danza greca si distingue per il suo carattere "sacro". Per Schuré, inoltre, riunisce in sé tutte le altre espressioni umane: la parola, la musica, il gesto, fino ad arrivare

danse fut chez eux la norme de la poésie et de la musique[18]. [...] Nous avons perdu la science, l'art et si j'ose dire la morale de la beauté corporelle, qui devrait être un des fondements de l'éducation et de l'art dramatique[19]. [...] Nul ballet, nulle danse, nul théâtre ne m'a jamais donné l'impression de ce que la sculpture nous révèle de la mimique grecque profane et bien moins encore de ce qu'elle nous fait pressentir des danses sacrées des temples[20]. [...] C'était il y a peu d'années, dans une des plus opulentes demeures de la haute finance de Paris[21]. *Danses grecques par M.lle H...accompagnée au piano par M. Bourgault-Ducoudray*[22]. On me dit que M.lle H...n'était rien moins qu'une professionnelle, mais une riche Anglaise[23], qui, toute jeune, s'était passionnée pour l'art antique.

Il carattere privato e elitario delle esibizioni di M.lle H, coincide con la biografia della Duncan.

---

all'oratoria e alla filosofia del pensiero. La danza è, dunque, il veicolo sinestetico del trascendente.

[18] Nell'atavico tema del "paragone" tra le arti, la danza è superiore alla poesia e alla musica, perché normativa di queste ultime, in quanto rivelatrice di tutto un repertorio di simboli, celati nel corpo umano.

[19] Una malinconia ricorrente accompagna Schuré, emblema dell'uomo moderno, sogna, nostalgico, una classicità perduta. Il matrimonio tra il bello e il buono, indissolubile nello spirito greco, si trova dissociato nello spirito contemporaneo.

[20] Schuré associa danza sacra e scultura, influenzando Rodo. Schuré sembra attribuire alla scultura il ruolo privilegiato assegnato alla danza. Grazie agli indizi archelogici di cui si fa portavoce, la scultura veicola e incarna lo spirito e la filosoia greca. Questo concetto sarà basilare per Rodo, nella sua esplorazione dello spirito dionisiaco greco. Per Rodo, infatti, una statua non è solo un elemento del repertorio mimico e gestuale, ma la reincarnazione di un'idea e una filosofia effigiate eternamente nel marmo.

[21] Il testo di Schuré fu pubblicato nel 1908, ma il racconto si riferisce a fatti anteriori, quindi l'ipotesi dell'*Offrande* come *d'après* della performance duncaniana è plausibile.

[22] Louis Albert Bourgault-Ducoudray (1840–1910) studiò al conservatorio di Parigi e vinse il *Prix de Rome* nel 1862. Diversamente da tanti suoi contemporanei, che diventarono solo esecutori, Bourgault-Ducoudray sarebbe considerato oggi un musicologo, o più precisamente un etnomusicologo. Il suo interesse nella musica popolare francese, greca, russa, così come per la musica orientale, lo hanno portato a pubblicare *Le Trenta melodie popolari dalla Grecia e dall'Oriente* nel 1876, *Le Trenta melodie popolari Celtiques e della Bassa Bretagna* nel 1885. Professore di storia di musica al conservatorio di Parigi dal 1878 al 1908, ebbe tra i suoi allievi Claude Debussy.

[23] Nel 1898 a causa di un incendio presso un albergo di New York dove la famiglia Duncan soggiornava, Isadora perde tutti i suoi averi, dunque, con straordinaria tenacia, convince i fratelli e la madre a trasferirsi a Londra. Dopo un periodo di totale miseria, grazie al mecenatismo della ricca signora Campbell, riesce ad inserirsi nei circoli mondani ed intellettuali della città. A Londra Isadora trascorre intere giornate nel British Museum nella contemplazione delle antiche opere di arte greca. Studia i miti greci, le posizioni e i movimenti delle figure dipinte e scolpite, si interessa all'influsso dell'arte greca sulla musica, la pittura, la danza. Nel 1900 decide di trasferirsi a Parigi, passa molto tempo al Louvre; conosce A. Bourdelle, A. Rodin, prende corpo in lei l'utopia di un'umanità danzante libera dai condizionamenti sociali, l'idea della danza come spontanea oggettivazione dei sentimenti interiori in movimenti che si susseguono generandosi l'uno dall'altro come le onde del mare.

Jamais elle n'avait paru en public. Elle réservait ses productions mimiques à des amis choisis dans son cercle londonien. Son ambition n'était
pas de reproduire telle ou telle des danses anciennes (on sait que les
Grecs en comptaient près de deux cents) mais de vivifier la sculpture
classique par une mimique expressive. Les Bacchantes et les Muses que
nous ont léguées les sculpteurs de l'Hellade et de l'Ionie ont eu des
modèles vivants. Puisqu'on peut changer des femmes vivantes en statues,
on doit pouvoir aussi changer des statues en femmes vivantes.

La danza opera un percorso inverso a quello della scultura. Mentre
questa parte dal modello per arrivare alla statua, la danza parte dalla
statua per risalire al modello, anzi per reincarnare il modello e resus-
citarlo, rendendolo "vivente".

Pour s'inspirer, la mime intelligente s'imprégna non seulement des
modèles classiques, mais également des statuettes de Tanagra et des figures des vases peints. Elle voulait, en un mot, devenir la Galathée de
la sculpture grecque, sans autre Pygmalion que sa volonté propre, une
Galathée qui trouverait dans son enthousiasme le feu nécessaire pour
transmuer le marbre en sa chair palpitante.

Ogni scultore, per Schuré ripete l'atto di Pigmaglione, attraverso il
fuoco dell'ispirazione tramuta il marmo in carne viva e palpitante.

Elle portait le péplos aux plis neigeux, chastement froncé sur la poi-
trine.[24] Les bras étaient nus. Quand elle marchait, sa jambe se dessinait
sous la draperie. Sa tête, coiffée de ses cheveux noirs comme d'un casque
luisant, rappelait plutôt le type de la Romaine que celui de la Grecque.
Ses larges yeux tranquilles lançaient de fauves éclairs à chaque mot, à
chaque sourire. M. Soldi, qui venait de nous préparer au rare spectacle
par un éloquent discours, annonça la première scène qu'allait nous jouer
l'interprète de l'art antique: L'extase de Narcisse[25].
   Le piano joue un air bucolique, une danse populaire grecque, savam-
ment arrangée par M. Bourgault Ducoudray pour les jeux de scène qui
vont suivre. M.lle H...déploie son écharpe, et, d'un coup de baguette,
la voilà transformée. Elle est devenue l'éphèbe grec, errant dans la cam-
pagne et poursuivant un songe. Ses bras étendus ou replies semblent
tour à tour les anses d'une amphore, les rameaux pliants d'un palmier
ou les ailes d'un grand oiseau de mer[26]. Devant cette apparition, éclatante

---

[24] Gli elementi del costume di scena sono identici a quelli usati nelle sue coreografie
dalla Duncan.
[25] Il soggetto del primo *tableau* è un'estasi che si fissa fortemente nell'immaginario
rodiano, soprattutto nella posa finale della *danseuse*.
[26] Il gesto di aprire o alzare le braccia, stendendole al di sopra della testa, o orizzontalmente, a mò di ali, era considerato *osé* per l'epoca, perché metteva scandalosa-
mente in mostra i seni. L'anonimato in cui Schuré mantiene la ballerina, così come il

de vie et de beauté, la salle et ses décorations, le public et ses toilettes, tout disparaît, tous les regards sont fixés sur la mime. Les plumes grises, rouges et bleues des chapeaux de femmes qui se balancent sur les velours et les ruches de dentelles deviennent immobiles. Les trophées d'armes qui brillent aux tentures de soie s'éteignent. Nous sommes aux bords e l'Alphée ou de l'Illyssus, et Narcisse est devant nous.

Il se penche à droite et à gauche en molles inclinaisons. Tour à tour, il s'enveloppe de son voile et le déroule, puis lentement, comme pris de lassitude, il le laisse pendre. Narcisse étouffe de chaleur et meurt de soif. Tout à coup il tressaille et son visage s'illumine. Il a humé la fraîcheur d'une source et découvert une rivière. Alors l'écharpe vole; il court de-ci de-là avec une grâce enivrée. On dirait qu'il respire le parfum de chaque fleur qui pousse au bord de l'eau, qu'il suit chaque vague dans sa fuite, chaque libellule dans son vol; fleur, vague et libellule lui-même. Enfin il tombe a genoux devant le clair miroir de l'onde.

Quelle merveille a-t-il donc aperçue? Sa propre image, son visage adorable, qui lui sourit et l'appelle dans son palais de cristal… Et, la tête penchée en avant, les bras ouverts, prêt à étreindre son double, Narcisse demeure immobile, fasciné dans un geste de ravissement[27].

In un'altra performance della stessa serata la misteriosa danzatrice interpreta *La Ciguë*. Al di là del racconto platonico delle ultime ore di Socrate, Schuré risalta la vibrante emozione derivante dalla visione della *danseuse*,

> La bouche ouverte, les traits tirés, la joue livide disent la terreur de l'inconnu. Si forte vibrait en nous l'émotion de cette scène revécue par la plastique impression du corps humain que nous fîmes un effort pour applaudir, malgré notre admiration. Quoique la danseuse se fût déjà relevée, des larmes coulaient de tous les yeux. […]

che è la stessa con cui Rodo scolpisce "cette figure de bacchante, ivre de toutes les ivresses, resplendit de vie et de passion". Ma è proprio nell'ultima interpretazione, quella della *Victoire de Samothrace*, che ritorna il tema dell'estasi, associato a quello dell'iniziazione e dell'offerta, raffrontabile nella baccante rodiana.

---

contesto privato dell'esibizione, spiegano l'esigenza di mantenere riservata la sua vera identità, per questioni di *bon ton*. La Baccante di Rodo, pur essendo un torso non finito e mutilo delle braccia, ripete questo stesso gesto delle braccia aperte, appena accennato, ma perfettamente intuibile per la posizione dei due deltoidi.

[27] Di nuovo il gesto delle braccia che unito a quello della testa descrive nella pantomima l'atto finale, l'estasi di Narciso. Con analoghi movimenti, Rodo effigia lo stato estatico nella sua *Offrande*.

Ses bras levés verticalement souvenaient une couronne de lauriers au-
dessus de sa tête. Une gaze blanche et transparente enveloppait cette
couronne et formait, sur la tête de la déesse qu'elle encadrait, une sorte
de tiare et flottait derrière elle comme un long voile de lumière. C'était
la Victoire absolue, mystérieuse et souveraine, sortant de l'Insondable.
Droit comme un flambeau, dans cette altitude triomphale qui sem-
blait la hausser jusqu'à l'Olympe dont elle descendait, elle parcourut
un instant l'horizon d'un regard circulaire. Enfin elle aperçut ce qu'elle
cherchait…la bataille! Alors, soudain, elle parut avoir des ailes. Les bras
étendus, elle se mit à courir en tous sens. Son voile voltigeait et se gon-
flait au vent.

Questo elemento del velo rigonfio e la posa delle braccia stese fanno
pensare alle foto della Duncan nelle sue *performances*, ma anche alla
sua collega Loïe Fuller.

Oltre ai rimandi puntuali ad altre opere di Rodo, le due *pièces* di
M.lle H., *L'extase de Narcisse* e la *Victoire de Samothracie*, forniscono
la base, a mio avviso, per l'iconografia dell'*Offrande à Bacchus* [fig. 1].

Figura 1. Rodo, *Offrande à Bacchus*, 1905.

La posa finale della ballerina che, interpretando l'estasi di Narciso, reclina la testa all'indietro e stende le braccia orizzontalmente, mentre il corpo seminudo sembra scosso da uno spirito bacchico, è identica a quella della statua di Rodo. La rappresentazione della Vittoria con la *danseuse* che spiega le braccia a mo' di ali e respinge la testa all'indietro, mentre simula lo spiccare di un volo, oltre al riferimento al non-finito dell'originale greco della Nike di Samotracia, probabile modello in pietra per la coreografia, sono elementi inequivocabilmente effigiati nella baccante rodiana. Il disegno di una *danseuse* dal torso slanciato verso l'alto e inarcato all'indietro come l'*Offrande* di Rodo, è visibile nel trattato di Émile Jacques Dalcroze, intimo amico dello scultore.

Tra estasi e teosofia

Un'analoga iconografia dell'ascesi e dell'eterno *sursum* è leggibile nella partitura dell'estasi che, nato da ispirazioni teosofiche, dipende dal modello scultoreo e rimanda alla danza. Testo di riferimento principale è *Les Grands Initiés* che, nonostante il silenzio glaciale con cui fu accolto all'epoca della prima edizione, nel 1899, conobbe molta fortuna. Rodo scolpisce diverse opere ispirate al testo, tra cui *L'Initiateur*, 1906 e *Les Initiés*, 1898. L'idea dell'estasi ricorre in Schuré associata all'idea della fecondità e della musica:

> Un jour Dévaki tomba dans une extase plus profonde. Elle entendit une musique céleste, comme un océan de harpes et de voix divines. Tout à coup le ciel s'ouvrit en abîmes de lumière. Des milliers d'êtres splendides la regardaient, et, dans l'éclat d'un rayon fulgurant, le soleil des soleils, Mahadeva, lui apparut sous forme humaine. Alors, ayant été *adombrée* par l'Esprit des mondes, elle perdit connaissance, et dans l'oubli de la terre, dans une félicité sans bornes, elle conçut l'enfant divin[28].

Nella sua interpretazione del tema dell'estasi, con *Offrande a Bacchus*, Rodo prende sia da Blavatsky, che la associa all'ascesi, all'elevazione, alla morte:

> La vera estasi è definita da Plotino: "la liberazione della mente dalla sua coscienza finita, divenendo una e identica con l'infinito". Il dott. Wilder dice che è la condizione più elevata, ma non è di durata permanente ed è raggiungibile solo da pochi, *pochissimi* individui. In realtà, è identica

---

[28] Schuré, *Les grands Initiés*, 84.

a quello stato che in India è conosciuto come *Samadhi*, praticato dagli Yogi che lo facilitano fisicamente con la più grande astinenza nel cibo e nel bere e, mentalmente, con un incessante sforzo per purificare ed elevare la mente stessa[29].

La morte è *l'estasi* finale sulla terra. Allora l'anima superiore si libera dalla costrizione del corpo e dalla sua parte partecipando alla sapienza e alla prescienza degli esseri superiori[30].

sia da Schuré, che tratta l'argomento con sfumature diverse:

> Enfin, *l'extase* se définit comme une vision du monde spirituel, où des esprits bons ou mauvais apparaissent au voyant sous forme humaine et communiquent avec lui. L'âme semble réellement transportée hors du corps, que la vie a presque quitté et qui se roidit dans une catalepsie voisine de la mort. Rien ne peut rendre, d'après les récits des grands extatiques, la beauté et la splendeur de ces visions ni le sentiment d'ineffable fusion avec l'essence divine, qu'ils en rapportent comme une ivresse de lumière et de musique[31].

Se alla base delle due visioni della Balvatsky e di Schuré vi è sempre l'idea dell'altro da sé, del fuori di sé, come trasporto dell'anima che si allontana dal corpo, l'accenno all'ineffabilità dello stato estatico in Schuré è una premessa alla sinestesia cui Rodo e Skrjabin approdano. Nell'ineffabilità delle visioni che l'iniziato esperimenta durante l'estasi, nella sua fusione con l'essere infinito, con Dio, Schuré ricorre al paragone "comme une ivresse de lumière et de musique", rendendo, per astrazione, l'idea. La statua dell'*Offrande*, "ivre de lumière et musique", e il *Poème de l'Extase* di Skrjabin derivano da questo pensiero. In numerosissimi passi de *Les Grands initiés* Schuré descrive diverse estasi, conseguenza dell'iniziazione ai misteri delle varie religioni. E' il caso dell'estasi della veggente consultata da Pitagora al tempio di Apollo:

> La voyante aux yeux fermés parla longtemps, de sa voix musicale, haletante, rythmée; puis, tout à coup, dans un sanglot, elle tomba comme morte. Ainsi Pythagore versait les purs enseignements dans le sein de Théocléa et l'accordait comme une lyre pour le souffle des Dieux. Une fois exaltée à cette hauteur d'inspiration, elle devint pour lui-même un flambeau, grâce auquel il put sonder sa propre destinée, percer le possible avenir et se diriger dans les zones sans rive de l'invisible[32].

---

[29] Blavatsky, *La chiave della Teosofia*, 32.
[30] *Idem*.
[31] Schuré, *Les grands Initiés*, 294.
[32] Ibid., 302.

Il passo è particolarmente interessante, perché unisce i concetti di estasi e armonia pitagorica, concetti-chiave per Skrjabin, che, come vedremo, creerà un'armonia per il *poème* basata sulla legge del monocordo pitagorico.

Talvolta il concetto di estasi è associato alla donna e all'eterno femmineo:

> Autour de la prophétesse se groupent des vieillards qui l'observent dans ses sommeils lucides, dans ses extases prophétiques. Ils étudient ses états divers, contrôlent ses révélations, interprètent ses oracles. Ils remarquent que lorsqu'elle prophétise dans l'état visionnaire, son visage se transfigure, sa parole devient rythmique et sa voix élevée profère ses oracles en chantant sur une mélopée grave et significative. De là le vers, la strophe, la poésie et la musique dont l'origine passe pour divine chez tous les peuples de race aryenne. L'idée de la révélation ne pouvait se produire qu'à propos de faits de cet ordre. Du même coup nous en voyons jaillir la religion et le culte, les prêtres et la poésie[33].

Ancor una volta estasi e sinestesia sono fuse insieme. Dalla visione della profetessa scaturisce un canto simile ad un recitativo, è una melopea grave, solenne, che tenta di superare i limiti della parola: "de là le vers, la strophe, la poésie et la musique". Tutte le arti derivano dunque dall'estasi, ma la prima a sgorgare da questo *status* privilegiato è sempre la musica.

Musica ed estasi caratterizzano diversi passi. Krishna, ad esempio, nato dall'estasi amorosa di Devaki, canta meravigliosamente e attira con la sua melodia les Gopis, figlie e donne dei pastori, che escono dalle loro case e cadono in estasi.

Così, dall'estasi e dal contatto con Dio, nasce la musica e con essa le altre arti e le danze sacre. Queste ultime, come abbiamo visto, messe in scena dalla Duncan, definita da Schuré "una danzatrice greca resuscitata", ispireranno iconograficamente e iconologicamente *l'Offrande* di Rodo e anche un disegno di Delville del 1915, intitolato appunto *Danse Sacrée*.

> Il donna aux unes des vinas aux cordes frémissantes comme des âmes, aux autres des cymbales sonores comme les cœurs des guerrières, aux autres des tambours qui imitent le tonnerre. Et, choisissant les plus belles, il les animait de ses pensées. Ainsi, les bras tendus, marchant et se mouvant en un rêve divin, les danseuses sacrées représentaient la majesté de Varouna, la colère d'Indra tuant le dragon, ou le désespoir

---

[33] Ibid., 37.

de Maya délaissée. Ainsi les combats et la gloire éternelle des dieux que
Krishna avait contemplés en lui même, revivaient dans ces femmes heu-
reuses et transfigurées[34].

L'iconografia delle danzatrici sacre di Schuré dalle braccia stese, mosse
come in sogno, richiama molto il torso rodiano e la *free danse* della
Duncan.

Krishna è una sorta di Orfeo che istruisce le sue baccanti, inizian-
dole alle arti e quando scompare lascia la sua essenza divina stempe-
rarsi in odori, suoni, visioni.

> Il avait disparu, ne leur laissant qu'une essence, un parfum de son être:
> les chants et les danses sacrées[35].

Secondo l'interpretazione delle religioni di Schuré dalla musica si passa
all'estasi, attraverso la passione amorosa e la contemplazione di Dio.

Nell'estasi iniziatica della sua baccante, Rodo compendia il tema
della visione interiore, per via degli occhi chiusi, e del piacere, per
via dell'enigmatico sorriso che altro non è che un grido, come spiega
Schuré:

> Le cri *d'Evohé*, qui se prononçait en réalité: *Hê, Vau, Hê* était le cri
> sacré de tous les initiés de l'Egypte, de la Judée, de la Phénicie, de l'Asie
> Mineure et de la Grèce. Les quatre lettres sacrées, prononcées comme
> il suit: *Iod – Hê, Vau, Hê*, représentaient Dieu *dans la fusion* éternelle
> avec la Nature; elles embrassaient la totalité de l'Etre, l'Univers vivant.
> *Iod* (Osiris) signifiait la divinité proprement dite, l'intellect créateur,
> *l'Eternel-Masculin* qui est en tout, partout et au-dessus de tout. *Hê, Vau,
> Hê* représentait l'*Eternel-Féminin* Eve, Isis, la Nature, sous toutes les
> formes visibles et fécondée par lui. La plus haute initiation, celle des sci-
> ences théogoniques et des arts théurgiques, correspondait à la lettre *Iod*.
> Un autre ordre de sciences correspondait à chacune des lettres d'Eve[36].

Nell'estasi in pietra, la donna di Rodo, con le labbra aperte in una fes-
sura e le labbra ripiegate all'insù, sta dunque pronunciando una formula sacra del rito dionisiaco, chiudendo gli occhi per l'abbagliante
visone della divinità.

In un altro momento del racconto, Orfeo dice all'iniziato:

> Il faut un long travail ou des grandes douleurs pour ouvrir les yeux du
> dedans.

---

[34] Ibid., 92.
[35] Ibid., 93.
[36] Ibid., 245.

Estasi e beatitudine sono associate al dolore e alla fatica, così come nel poème di Skrjabin. La perdita di coscienza, il ritorno al non-essere, la massima sintesi di umano e divino hanno come conseguenza l'annientamento, l'abisso, il nulla.

SKRJABIN TEOSOFO

La Teosofia sembra confermare, dunque, tutto quello che Skrjabin ha già in sé, in una forma asistematica[37]. Lavorando al Poema dell'Estasi, egli afferma a proposito dell'Io:

> Nell'analisi psicologica e nello studio di se stessi si può trovare qualsiasi cosa, compreso l'intero cosmo[38].

Le sue manie di grandezza con affermazioni del tipo: "IO sono DIO", "non c'è nulla che io non sappia esprimere al pianoforte"[39], non trovano una giustificazione puramente umana, sul piano del temperamento eccentrico dell'artista, ma vanno lette alla luce di un sistema filosofico che in quegli anni Skrjabin andava formando.

> Noi teosofi, quindi, facciamo distinzione fra questo cumulo di "esperienze", che chiamiamo la *falsa* (perché finta e evanescente) *personalità*, e quell'elemento nell'uomo a cui è dovuto il sentimento dell'"Io sono Io". È questo "Io sono Io" che noi chiamiamo la *vera* individualità; e diciamo che questo "Ego" o individualità interpreta, come un attore, molte parti sulla scena della vita. Chiamiamo ogni nuova vita sulla terra dello stesso Ego una *serata* sul palcoscenico di un teatro[40].
> Secondo noi l'uomo interiore è l'unico Dio del quale possiamo avere cognizione[41].

Skrjabin rovescia la sentenza del Tempio di Gerusalemme "Conosci te stesso, conoscerai Dio e l'Universo intero" in "conosco l'universo intero perché io stesso lo creo". Gli aneddoti che lo ritraggono intento a camminare sul lago di Ginevra, nell'imitazione di Cristo o mentre predica da una barca ai pescatori, fanno parte di quel periodo messianico-mistico, che è citato dai biografi con scetticismo[42]. Skrjabin

---

[37] Bowers, *The New Skrjabin – Enigma And Answers*, 130.
[38] Ibid., 66.
[39] Ibid., 67.
[40] Ibid., 47.
[41] Ibid., 70.
[42] Ibid., 62.

era convinto di possedere poteri che l'uomo moderno aveva lasciato atrofizzare nel corso dei secoli. Scopo della sua musica era risvegliare questa magia atavica insita nell'uomo. Skrjabin comincia a parlare di se stesso in terza persona, dandosi del "Lui" al posto di io:

> Io mi inchino davanti alla grande sensibilità che tu offri a LUI che dimora in me. Ora tu credi in LUI. EGLI è grande, anche se nello stesso tempo io sono povero, piccolo, debole e stanco. Ma tu mi perdoni tutto questo, perché EGLI vive in me. Io non sono ancora LUI, ma presto lo diventerò! Pazienza e credi! EGLI si identificherà in me[43].

Presto, l'idea mistica dell'arte si ricollega a quella della sinestesia. Mistico, dal greco mueyn, significa anche vicino alle labbra e agli occhi: il mistico vede e parla di verità inaudibili. Skrjabin sosteneva che le sinfonie da lui ideate, sinfonie di colori, di sensi tattili e di profumi avrebbero aiutato l'uomo a recuperare la sua vera essenza divina[44].

Lo scopo della sua musica era terapeutico. Ripeteva a Sabaneev che la musica apparteneva alle "arti teurgiche delle culture mistiche antiche perdute" e ad un certo momento della sua vita pensò di fondare una "colonia" dove avrebbe "insegnato l'estasi" e offerto dimostrazioni con l'aiuto delle sue composizioni[45]. In questo senso l'idea dell'estasi si inserisce nell'economia dell'Universo come elemento catartico e collettivo.

Si può tracciare un'evoluzione del concetto di *estasi* in Skrjabin fin dagli anni giovanili.

La prima volta che compare la parola *estasi* nella sua opera è nella *romanza per pianoforte e voce* dedicata a Natalia Sékérina, suo primo amore. Autore del testo, oltre che della musica, il giovane Skrjabin va comparando l'idea dell'estasi all'amore e alla passione:

> Ah! Que ne puis-je au fond de l'âme
> Me saisir de la tienne un seul moment,
> Dans un élan fougueux d'ivresse trouble
> Ton trop paisible cœur!
>
> L'idée sublime de la vie
> Ferait tournée ton front charmant,
> Et tout cet univers d'extase,
> Serait pour toi, ma tendre amie!

---

[43] Ibid., 67.
[44] Ibid., 113–114.
[45] Ibid., 150.

Et tout cet univers d'extase,
Serait ta chose, mon amie!

La reiterazione del verso contenente la parola *extase* dà la misura dell'importanza di questo concetto, che per Skrjabin è inseparabile dall'idea della passione amorosa. L'estasi è quindi *un élan fougueux*, une *ivresse trouble* nell'universo skrjabiniano, ma non è ancora *l'estasi cosmica* che più tardi permeerà i suoi pensieri e la sua visione dell'opera d'arte totale.

Anche in un abbozzo incompiuto di un'Opera, scritta durante gli anni di insegnamento al Conservatorio di Mosca, compare il concetto di *estasi collettiva*. Il progetto risale al 1900 e Skrjabin impiega due anni a scrivere il libretto. L'eroe-protagonista è Skrjabin stesso, musicista-poeta-filosofo:

> IO SONO IL MAGO DI UNA POTENTE ARMONIA CELESTE [...] che profonde sogni amorevoli all'umanità con la POTENZA DELL'AMORE, io creerò la primavera della vita. Troverò la pace CON LA FORZA DELLA MIA SAGGEZZA[46].

Vi sono scene ambientate in giardini magici in cui la principessa e il musicista-poeta-filosofo muoiono, come Tristano e Isotta, l'uno nelle braccia dell'altro in un'estatica felicità, ovvero l' "Atto di Estrema Realizzazione".

> Io sono l'apoteosi della creazione del mondo. Io sono la meta delle mete, il fine dei fini, annuncia l'eroe[47].

Improntata sul modello wagneriano, attraverso quest'opera Skrjabin sogna di condurre gli spettatori all'estasi. In realtà si tratta del primo passo verso le creazioni future, *Poème divin*, *Poème de l'extase*, *Prometeo, poème du feu*.

Anche il *Poème divin*, la terza Sinfonia in do minore, composta nel 1903, esprime "l'evoluzione dello spirito umano e la sua Unità con l'Universo". E' una sinfonia a programma in tre movimenti, *Lutte, Voluptés, Jeu divin*, il cui contenuto sarà scritto da Tatjana nel dicembre del 1904, seguendo le indicazioni dell'autore:

> Le *Poème divin* représente l'évolution de l'esprit humain qui, arraché à tout un passé de croyances et de mystères, qu'il surmonte et renverse,

---

[46] Ibid., 50–51.
[47] *Idem.*

aboutit, après avoir traversé le Panthéisme, à l'affirmation enivrée et joyeuse de sa liberté et son unité avec l'Univers (le "Moi" divin).

1. Luttes: C'est la lutte entre l'homme esclave d'un dieu personnel, maître suprême du monde, et l'homme puissant libre – l'Homme-Dieu. Le dernier triomphe, semble-t-il, mais c'est l'intelligence seule qui s'élève à l'affirmation du "Moi" divin, tandis que la volonté individuelle, encore faible, est tentée de s'abîmer dans le Panthéisme.
2. Voluptés: L'homme se laisse prendre par les délices du monde sensuel. Les voluptés le grisent, le bercent: il s'y plonge. Sa personnalité s'anéantit dans la nature. C'est alors du fond de son être que s'élève le sentiment du sublime qui l'aide à vaincre l'état passif de son "Moi" humain.
3. Jeu divin: L'esprit se libère enfin de tous ses liens qui l'attachaient au passé de soumission devant une force supérieure, l'esprit engendrant l'univers par le seul pouvoir de sa volonté créatrice, conscient de ne faire qu'un avec cet univers, s'adonne à la joie sublime de l'activité libre -le "Jeu divin"[48].

Alle indicazioni agogiche, in partitura, si sostituiscono quelle psicologiche e filosofiche:

Avec un tragique effroi, monstrueux, terrifiant, voluptueux, pâmé, avec ravissement et transport, extatique, languide, divin.

Anteriore al *Poema dell'Estasi*, è già qui presente l'idea associata al languore, alla voluttà, al divino.

Partendo dall'etimo greco, èx = fuori, stàsis = stato, cioè "lo stare al di fuori di sé, fuori dal proprio stato", attraverso le letture teosofiche realizzate a partire dagli anni 1903–4, Skrjabin fonde in un sincretismo filosofico il significato dionisiaco-orgiastico dell'estasi, insieme a quello neoplatonico-cristiano[49]. L'estasi dionisiaca si realizza nel trasporto dell'anima in una danza vorticosa che ne spezza l'unità, confondendone e fondendone i limiti. Dioniso è il dio della distruzione di ogni misura, l'io della libertà nel caos. L'estasi cristiana è la fusione dell'io con Dio. Secondo il filosofo neoplatonico Plotino, l'anima torna ad identificarsi con l'uno, quando penetra nell'universo, attraverso la musica, l'amore e la filosofia.

L'estasi skrjabiniana deriva dalla teoria della conoscenza della Blavatskij, per cui l'uomo che vuole scoprire la sua dimensione eterna,

[48] Hellmundt, *Musikalniyi Sovremennyk*, 58.
[49] Verdi, *Aleksandr Skrjabin tra musica e filosofia*, 54.

opera una trasmutazione dall'esterno all'interno e di nuovo all'esterno, proiettando fuori di sé l'amore:

> Fine ultimo dello spirito – l'essere assoluto – è la restaurazione dell'armonia del mondo, l'estasi[50].

Eros e creatività sono indissolubilmente legati in Skrjabin. L'atto creativo è paragonabile all'atto sessuale e lo oltrepassa. L'autore si rispecchia in questa opera, identificandosi nel protagonista, lo "Spirito". L'associazione estasi-attività-creatività è ricorrente nei suoi scritti[51]. Quando si legge nei versi entusiastici

> Finalmente ho scoperto la luce nella musica. Ho scoperto questa euforia, quest'ascesa, questa gioia che ti toglie il respiro, questa radiosa armonia che si sprigiona dall'idea della luce [...] sto galleggiando nell'estasi. Sono in grado di comporre una poesia meravigliosa.

si capisce che egli si sente un tutt'uno con la musica e con la poesia.

LA PARTITURA DELL'ESTASI

Il *Poema dell'Estasi* appartiene alla tipologia classica del poema sinfonico e della forma sonata ma, concepita inizialmente in 4 tempi, finisce per essere concentrata da Skrjabin in unico grande movimento dilatato. Dal punto di vista formale, l'analisi di Kelkel[52], che considera il "pitagorismo musicale" di Skrjabin e si basa sulla metrotettonica di Georgij Conus, restituisce i fondamenti per una profonda comprensione dell'universo matematico-filosofico skrjabiniano ed è indispensabile per l'interpretazione di quello visivo e sonoro.

---

[50] Skrjabin, *Notes et Réflexions, carnets inédits*, 55.

[51] L'azione è l'impeto, la spinta della vita. L'impeto (attività) nel suo grado più elevato è l'estasi. L'essere assoluto è estasi (*Cosa risveglia l'azione?*).
L'anima deve sfruttare la sua capacità creativa (opposizione), cioè deve inebriarsi di creatività prima di poter tornare a uno stato di pace (Bowers, *The New Skrjabin – Enigma And Answers*, op. cit., 124–125). L'anima deve desiderare l'essere assoluto, l'estasi. Come è possibile l'estasi? L'estasi è *l'apice dell'attività. L'estasi è il culmine.* Com'è possibile l'impeto più alto dell'attività? Le condizioni dell'attività: nell'ordine attuale delle cose c'è la *protesta* e il desiderio ardente del nuovo ordine. Ma questa è solo una singola figura ritmica. In forma di pensiero l'estasi è *la sintesi suprema*. Sotto *forma di sentimento, l'estasi è la somma beatitudine. Sotto forma di spazio, l'estasi è sommo sviluppo e distruzione* (*idem*). La mia gioia è così immensa che miriadi di universi potrebbero sprofondare in essa senza neppure incresparne la superficie (Ibid., 135).

[52] Kelkel, *Alexandre Scriabine et "le charme des impossibilités"*, 140–161.

> On aurait tort de croire que la musique de Scriabine puisse être com-
> prise indépendamment de sa conception du monde, et que ses idées ne
> traduisent qu'un contenu psychologique sous-jacent, peut-être intéres-
> sant pour les biographes, mais sans importance pour le compréhension
> de sa musique [...]. Etudier le matériel des formes ne peut en restituer
> les significations[53].

Kelkel divide il poema in sei sezioni:

> Introduzione: batt. 1–18
> Esposizione: batt.19–110
> Primo sviluppo: batt. 111–312
> Ripresa: batt. 313–404
> Secondo sviluppo: batt. 405–552
> Coda: batt. 553–604

Ciascuna di queste rivela un numero significativo, risultante dal con-
teggio delle pulsazioni (semiminime) contenute all'interno delle bat-
tute, come risulta dal seguente schema:

Introduzione: 36 pulsazioni	la doppia Tétrakys
Esposizione: 216 pulsazioni	il doppio della coda
Primo sviluppo 288 pulsazioni	la metà del secondo sviluppo
Ripresa 144 pulsazioni	il quadruplo dell'Introduzione e la metà del primo sviluppo
Secondo sviluppo 576 pulsazioni	il doppio del primo sviluppo
Coda 108 pulsazioni	la metà dell'esposizione e il triplo di 36

Sulla base del 36, numero magico, perché generatore di tutto il *Poema
dell'Estasi*, risultante dal doppio della somma dei numeri pari e dispari, la sacra *tétrakys* pitagorica (1+2+3+4+5+6+7+8), Kelkel scopre,
all'interno dello schema, altre relazioni numeriche, che rispecchiano le
leggi del monocordo pitagorico[54]:

---

[53] Sabaneev, 'A. N. Skrjabin', *Melos, Zeitschrift für Neue Musik*, 04/1925; Auzias,
Clefs pour le structuralisme, 221–222.
[54] La teoria della musica greca si intreccia con quella filosofico-matematica in Pitagora (VI sec. a.C.), il quale non lasciò niente di scritto, ma è noto, grazie alle testimonianze dei discepoli, che conferì alla musica un'impostazione matematica collegando i
suoni ai rapporti numerici regolatori dell'equilibrio dell'Universo Sul piano musicale,
la legge del monocordo pitagorico riflette, sul piano filosofico, quella dell'armonia
delle sfere. Pitagora scopre la teoria delle consonanze contrapposte alle dissonanze,
negli intervalli di *quarta*, *quinta* e *ottava* e per primo stabilisce la *scala armonica*
secondo tali intervalli. Nella *Scuola di Atene* di Raffaello l'attributo di Pitagora è una

rapporto d'ottava	Esposizione-Coda: rapporto 2:1 e Primo Sviluppo-Secondo Sviluppo: rapporto 1:2
il rapporto di quinta giusta	Esposizione-Ripresa: 3/2
il rapporto di quarta giusta	Primo Sviluppo-Esposizione: 4/3
e il rapporto di terza maggiore	Ripresa più Secondo sviluppo-Secondo Sviluppo: 5/4

Le 5 sezioni, generate da una prima *Introduzione* di 36 pulsazioni (tétrakys), formano la pentade pitagorica, simbolo dell'armonia universale, dell'unione uomo e cosmo, dell'amore e della conoscenza[55]. Il Pentagono regolare è antropomorfico e antropogenetico per i Pitagorici. Il numero 5 simboleggia l'uomo: 5 è la somma dei suoi arti con la testa, 5 sono le dita della sua mano e 5 è la metà della serie completa dei numeri interi da 1 a 10. La stella pentagonale esprime non solo la regolarità perfetta e completa del numero 5, ma anche

> Son dynamisme rayonnant: irradiation, énergie, créatrice, croissance, Dépassement des limites naturelles soit dans le sens du "bien", soit dans celui du "mal"[56].

---

tavoletta con un motivo numerato, simile a quello di Gaffurio, che indica la serie armonica di intervalli usati dai musicisti e talvolta dagli architetti e pittori. Il filosofo Damone (V sec. a.C.) riprende la teoria pitagorica abbinandola alla teoria dell'*ethos*, per cui ad ogni musica corrisponde un momento sociale e umano, civile e religioso. Le Muse, divinità protettrici delle Arti, incarnano il prototipo delle antiche Virtù ed inoltre il verbo greco *musichéuomai* significa "educare con armonia". In tal modo disarmonia equivale ad "asociale" mentre armonia a "bello" e "civile". Platone (427–347 a.C.) riafferma il significato etico della musica e condanna la musica edonistica elogiando quella cosmica che, come nel Medioevo, ha un valore assoluto, speculativo, in quanto considera il suono in sé. Secondo Platone il *diapason* è l'accordo costituito da tutti gli intervalli consonanti, dal grave all'acuto, armonizzati fra loro. La distinzione tra musica nobile e musica rustica era già insita nella *Repubblica* di Platone il quale condannava l'arte (*techne*) come imitazione (*mimesis*) della realtà e quindi non adatta a raggiungere la vera conoscenza (*episteme*). Nel *Timeo* il rapporto musica-anima ha un valore pedagogico in quanto i movimenti dell'anima hanno una stretta affinità con i ritmi e i modi musicali, pertanto se l'anima segue il giusto carattere (*ethos*) suggerito dalla musica non si corrompe. Nelle *Leggi* Platone indica Apollo e le Muse come guida all'educazione musicale e, infine, nel *Convito* il rapporto musica/amore è svolto secondo la teoria dell'*accordo simpatico* per il quale due anime affini, destinate all'unione, si riconoscono per mezzo di quella vibrazione interiore simile a quella prodotta tra due strumenti ben accordati dei quali uno emette il suono e l'altro vibra per simpatia.

[55] Kelkel, *Alexandre Scriabine et "le charme des impossibilités"*, 141–162.
[56] De Freitas, *515 Le Lieu du Miroir, Art et Numerologie*, 113.

Tradizionalmente quest'ultimo, il senso del male, è dato dal rovesciamento del pentagono con la punta verso il basso, simbolo di caduta e personificazione di Lucifero (*la lumière tombée*) che prende il significato di Tentatore. Un'analoga stella pentagonica stringe nelle mani, sia nella prima che nella seconda versione, il *Prometeo* di Delville [fig. 2], simultaneamente *grande iniziato* e *alter-ego* di Lucifero.

La reiterazione del numero 6 6 6, nei triplici intervalli di 6ª ascendente e discendente del tema principale nell'introduzione, fa da *pendant* con l'immagine del pentagono delle 5 sezioni dell'opera. Se nell'introduzione si ripete la cifra diabolica, tutto il poema nella sua forma pentagonale allude alla spinta dell'uomo verso l'alto, come un immenso, imperativo *sursum*, dettato dal bisogno di innalzarsi.

La lotta tra spirito del male (Satana) e spirito del bene (Uomo-Dio) è insita in questa struttura. Nel suo testo sulla numerologia, Lima de Freitas[57] chiama numero dell'Uomo-dio il 108, che corrisponde all'addizione degli angoli interni del triangolo pitagorico. Questo numero si ritrova nella coda del poema dell'estasi. Nel finale, dunque, l'uomo-Dio sconfigge il Male. L'io si identifica con Dio, sia in partitura, sia nel poema in versi, sia nello schema preparatorio di questi[58]:

> Ciò che terrorizzava
> Ora è piacere,
> E sono diventati i morsi di pantere e iene solo una nuova carezza,
> un nuovo tormento,
> ed il morso della serpe
> Solo un bacio ardente.
> E l'universo echeggia
> con un urlo gioioso
>
> Io sono!"

> Phase finale de la lutte et libération par l'amour.
> L'Homme-Dieu prend conscience de la vanité des efforts.
> Jeu libre. Ivresse de liberté. Prise de conscience de l'Unité.
> Ce qui naguère terrifiait l'esprit, s'est maintenant transformé en action.

Proseguendo l'analisi metrotettonica di Kelkel si scoprono altre relazioni numeriche.

Sommando le pulsazioni dell'Esposizione 216 e della Ripresa 144 si ottiene il 360, dieci volte 36, numero del cerchio perfetto. L'addizione tra Ripresa 144 e Secondo Sviluppo 576 dà 720, il doppio cerchio.

---

[57] Ibid., 115.
[58] Ibid., 141–142.

Quello che Kelkel ipotizza è un sistema pittorico-visuale nell'universo sonoro skrjabiniano, basato su rapporti numerici. Partendo da questo suggerimento possiamo "disegnare" nella loro sequenza esecutiva i tre cerchi

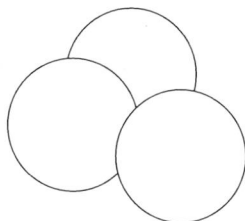

e notiamo che si ottengono tre cerchi intersecanti. Questo non è solo uno schema geometrico, ma un simbolo teosofico. Khnopff lo include nella sua criptica iconografia dell'opera *L'offerta*, 1891, non a caso esposta al *Salon Rose+croix* del 1893[59], il cui titolo è identico alla scultura rodiana. Il simbolo allude alla trinità e all'eternità. E' anche la visualizzazione della triplicità dell'uomo, formato da un corpo fisico, uno eterico e uno astrale. Lo stesso Schuré, importante tanto per Rodo quanto per Skrjabin, dice

> L'homme terrestre est triple comme la divinité qu'il reflète: intelligence, âme et corps[60].

Questa forma geometrica, nota come «trifoglio», è formata da tre cerchi intersecati, o tre lobi o foglie connesse ed era usata nel medioevo per rappresentare la Trinità. Per questo i trifogli si vedono spesso come dettagli architettonici nelle chiese.

Tornando al concetto di armonia, sappiamo che il pensiero greco ha intuito che la vera armonia si genera dalla lotta, l'ordine dal disordine, la vita dalla morte. "L'armonia – dice Filolao – si origina dai contrari, poiché essa è fusione del molteplice a concordia del discorde"[61]. Skrjabin insegue un'armonia, nel senso etimologico del termine: dal greco *armòzein* = collego, ordino, creo. Il verbo ha la stessa radice "ar" di

---

[59] I riti a carattere spirituale, soprattutto quelli riguardanti la reincarnazione, sono presenti in alcune opere di Khnopff: *Offrande, A travers les âges, Une Rêveuse, I lock my door upon myself.*

[60] Schuré, *Les Grands Initiés*, op. cit., 104.

[61] Cardini (a cura di), *I Pitagorici. Testimonianze e frammenti*, 1962.

arithmòs, che vuol dire numero. Per Platone gli stati di piacere e di dolore sono fondamentali per l'essere vivente in questo mondo, perché essi sono i modi di sentire l'armonia.

> Ha vera musica in sé colui che ha composto una sinfonia accordando l'armonia del corpo con quella dell'anima[62].

Skrjabin, inseguendo l'armonia dei contrari, tenta di unire il doppio con il triplice, il 2 con il 3, il pari e dispari. I frequenti cambi di tempo in partitura, nell'oscillazione tra binario e ternario, indicano questa utopica aspirazione ad unire gli opposti.

La quadruplice armonia pitagorica (basata sulla sacra *Tétrakys*) era stata teorizzata fin dall'inizio in questi termini: armonia fra arco e corda, fra corpo e anima, fra cittadino e stato, fra le sfere e il cielo stellato. Il rapporto di ottava e il numero 8 sono utilizzati insieme al cerchio anche nel *Poema* in versi. Se nel rapporto tra Esposizione-Coda (2:1) e Primo Sviluppo-Secondo Sviluppo (1:2), Skrjabin allude all'ottava, quello tra Esposizione-Ripresa, Ripresa e Secondo Sviluppo seguono la regola del cerchio. Nell'antichità, graficamente la *Tétrakys* era formata da 4, 3, 2, 1 punti allineati che formavano il triangolo sul quale l'adepto giurava fedeltà all'ordine.

Se si uniscono graficamente i rapporti tra la prima e le altre 5 sezioni dell'opera, secondo l'equazione 36:1, in quanto numero generatore, si ottengono i seguenti rapporti numerici 1–6–8–4–16–3 che trasposti sul piano grafico danno il *Fiore di Loto* stilizzato:

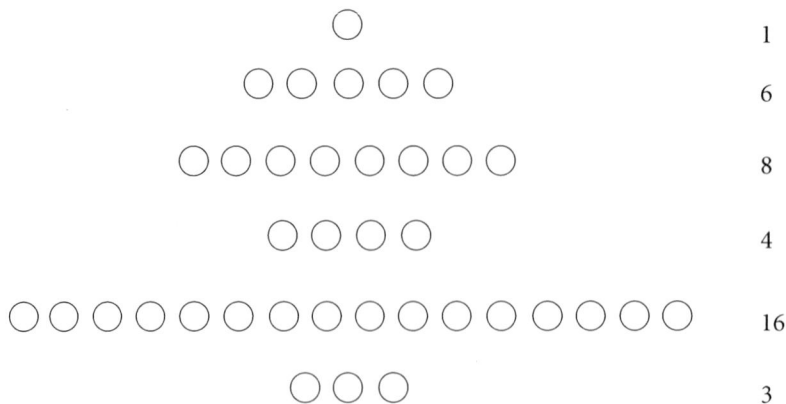

$$\bigcirc \qquad\qquad\qquad 1$$

$$\bigcirc\bigcirc\bigcirc\bigcirc \qquad\qquad 6$$

$$\bigcirc\bigcirc\bigcirc\bigcirc\bigcirc\bigcirc\bigcirc \qquad 8$$

$$\bigcirc\bigcirc\bigcirc\bigcirc \qquad\qquad 4$$

$$\bigcirc\bigcirc\bigcirc\bigcirc\bigcirc\bigcirc\bigcirc\bigcirc\bigcirc\bigcirc\bigcirc\bigcirc\bigcirc \qquad 16$$

$$\bigcirc\bigcirc\bigcirc \qquad\qquad 3$$

---

[62] Platone, *Timeo*, IX, 591.

Il fiore, riprodotto in numerosissimi pittori-teosofi, tra cui Kupka, è simbolo della rinascita e creazione. Il loto azzurro, sacro agli egiziani, di sera si chiude e si immerge sotto la superficie dell'acqua, per poi risollevarsi e dischiudersi nuovamente al mattino, divenendo facilmente un simbolo del sole e della creazione, ma anche di purificazione e rigenerazione, per via della profumatissima fragranza che lascia. Tali significati si collocano sulla stessa onda dell'estasi rigenerativa skrjabiniana. Gli esseri Luce, secondo una leggenda teosofica, abitano una regione tra le montagne innevate, le otto catene montuose, come otto sono i petali del fiore, situata tra i laghi a forma di fiori di loto. Secondo l'antroposofia steineriana, 16 sono i passi della pratica buddista della purificazione del corpo astrale. Ogni uomo è destinato, secondo Steiner[63], a purificare l'attività del corpo astrale. Tale purificazione del corpo astrale, si realizza attraverso l'Ottuplice Sentiero, la cui pratica ridesta il "fiore di loto a sedici petali", ovvero il *vishuddhacakra*, situato nella regione della gola, vicino al plesso laringo-faringeo. Questo *cakra* dà la possibilità di penetrare telepaticamente, con lo sguardo chiaroveggente, nel pensiero di un altro essere e dischiude la visione delle leggi dei fenomeni naturali. È agendo su questo *cakra*, soprattutto, che tramite la meditazione si purifica il corpo astrale, sottraendosi all'influenza negativa dei *samskâra*, delle predisposizioni psichiche prenatali, depositate nel corpo eterico o vitale. Nel percorso dell'ascesi occidentale o esoterico-cristiana descritta nell'*Iniziazione*, questo passo precede il *Il Parinirvana*, ossia la *Trasfigurazione della Luce*. Nel descrivere il Parinirvana Steiner si rifà a una leggenda birmana, assai in voga al suo tempo, secondo la quale il Buddha morì trasfigurato come in un corpo di luce[64]. In base a ciò Steiner pensa che "il Buddha sia giunto fino al punto in cui la luce divina comincia a risplendere dentro l'uomo. Quando si trova dinanzi alla morte del terrestre, egli diviene la luce del mondo". Esiste un quadro di Delville, intitolato *Le porteur de lumière*, che ripete il motivo teosofico della stella pentagonica, e uno di William Hunt, *La luce del mondo*, 1881, che fonde in una la figura di Cristo e Budda. Anche Redon rende omaggio allo stesso tema con una serie di opere tra il 1905–1910 ritraenti il Dio in versioni sempre più astratte.

---

[63] Steiner, *Iniziazione ai Mondi Superiori*, 1999.
[64] Thomas, *The life of Buddha as legend and history*, 245.

Il Parinirvana è dunque una trasfigurazione del corpo terreno in un corpo di luce. La trasfigurazione operata dallo Spirito in lotta, protagonista dell'Estasi è questa identità uomo-dio. Secondo la dottrina teosofica, durante il processo evolutivo della vita sul pianeta Terra, gli Esseri-Luce, gli Elohim, possessori e portatori dell'Idea Creativa, scrutano già tale evoluzione nel tentativo di individuare l'animale più adatto e con spiccate qualità intellettive per poterci innestare l'individualità, lo Spirito: l'*Ego Sum*. Quest'*Ego-sum* corrisponde, a mio avviso, al finale "Ja es'm" (= "Io sono") del *Poema* di Skrjabin che, tracciando una struttura "a fiore di loto" nella partitura, rende omaggio alla dimora degli Esseri Luce che hanno prescelto Lui, come uomo degno di possedere l'individualità, ossia quell'insieme di caratteristiche distintive e intellettive che lo separano dagli animali. Il fiore di loto, fortemente impregnato di simbologia teosofica, rispunta nella copertina del *Poème du feu* di Skrjabin, disegnata da Jean Delville[fig. 3]. Dal calice del fiore sorge una lira contrassegnata dalla stella di Davide, mentre il volto del martire-ribelle emerge, con uno sguardo incendiario, infiammando la quarta corda della lira. La lira di Delville ha sette corde, così come sette sono le note, i colori, i pianeti. Questi ultimi sono rappresentati da un tappeto di astri, con stelle, spirali, nebulose e raggi, su cui si stende tutto il disegno. Non a caso la fiamma dello sguardo chiaroveggente di Prometeo, accende e incendia la quarta corda che, nella partitura disseminata di intervalli di quarta, simboleggia l'uomo. Dall'estasi (fiore di loto) l'uomo-dio (Prometeo), attraverso la musica dei colori-suoni e pianeti (lira a sette corde), giunge al Fuoco della conoscenza e alla Luce della Beatitudine (Sole).

Il fiore di loto, celato nella trama musicale della partitura dell'estasi, apparendo sulla copertina dell'opera sinestetica successiva, offre una chiave di lettura a tutto tondo del panorama globale dell'universo simbolico skrjabiniano. Il *Poema del fuoco*, infatti, nato dal *Poema dell'Estasi*, è la continuazione dell'unico grande progetto, alla ricerca di un'arte totale, che nel *Mysterium* avrà il suo atto finale. L'ascetismo domina, dunque, l'opera di Skrjabin, al punto da fargli elaborare una serie di simboli mistico-musicali.

Dal punto di vista dell'organico, significativa è la predominanza degli ottoni, con la sezione rinforzata delle 5 trombe, il cui timbro chiaro e squillante è bilanciato dagli otto corni e, nella sezione dei legni, dal controfagotto e dal clarinetto basso. Saranno le trombe, infatti, a dar voce al tema ascendente dell'auto-affermazione, il tema dell'Io, che si susseguue come filo conduttore per tutta la sinfonia, dall'inizio in sordina fino al *climax* orgiastico del finale.

Figura 2. Jean Delville, Prométhée, 1907, Bibliothèque de l'Université Libre de Bruxelles.

Figura 3

La presenza delle trombe con il loro timbro solare, sigla tutta l'opera.
In accordo con Kandinskij, Skrjabin vede (o ascolta) nelle trombe, un
suono "giallo"[65]. Il *Poema dell'estasi* è vicino, in questo senso al dipinto
Concerto del 1911. Skrjabin disse una volta a Ivan Lipaev: "Quando
ascolti l'Estasi, guarda diritto nell'occhio del sole![66]"

---

[65] Verdi, *Kandinskij e Skrjabin. Realtà e utopia nella Russia pre-rivoluzionaria.*
[66] Bowers, *The New Skrjabin – Enigma And Answers*, 302.

Tra i due poli contrastanti delle trombe, solari, nel registro acuto
e i corni, scuri e tenebrosi, nel grave, si incarna una lotta dinamica,
tra slanci, tensioni, spasmi e ricadute, sintomi di una crescente eccita-
zione. È la frenesia di Bacco che si placherà solo al culmine dell'Estasi,
alla fine del *Poema*. L'aggiunta delle campane e dei campanelli arricchisce la sezione delle percussioni di una sfumatura particolare. Questi
strumenti meritano una riflessione a parte, perché intimamente legati
al misticismo russo. Nella sensibilità russa il suono delle campane è
un suono mistico: *zvon*, che in russo significa *suono*, significa anche
campana e contiene in sé tutti i suoni di tutti gli strumenti[67]. Al contrario dell'incenso che, salendo dalla terra al cielo, simbolizza il veicolo
delle preghiere dell'uomo a dio, nelle cerimonie religiose il suono delle
campane riconduce Dio all'uomo, ricongiungendo così, nel moto contrario, il cielo alla terra. La campana che riunisce in sé l'uno e il tutto,
racchiude anche emozioni contrastanti: è gioiosa e inquieta, mistica e
sinistra, festosa e minacciosa. Bowers riporta un detto popolare russo
che recita: "sentendo le campane non sapeva dove si trovava" a signi-
ficare lo stordimento e lo spaesamento mistici. Ed ecco il messaggio
del compositore: attraverso il disorientamento, lo stordimento dei
sensi, prodotto dal suono misterioso delle campane, l'uomo si prepara
a raggiungere l'estasi. Solo dopo aver attraversato tutta la gamma delle
emozioni umane, con tutti i loro contrasti, così come la campana che
contiene in sè potenzialmente il suono per eccellenza, la somma dei
suoni di tutti gli strumenti, lo spirito può raggiungere l'estasi finale.

Skrjabin inserirà campane in tutte e tre le sue opere sinestetiche.
Nel *Poema* intervengono poco prima o in concomitanza delle parti
che definirei "estatiche". Nel *Prometeo* il crescendo delle campane è
così frastornante che sembra forare l'atmosfera densa dell'orchestra.
Nell'atto Preparatorio del *Mysterium*, Skrjabin immagina delle campane che, sospese tra le nuvole dell'Himalaya, richiamano spettatori da
ogni angolo del mondo[68].

La celesta, allo stesso modo delle campane e dei campanelli, ha il
compito di sottolineare i momenti estatici del *Poema*. Inoltre, per il
suo timbro diafano e cristallino, sposta tutta l'atmosfera su coordinate
irreali, o iper-reali, d'accordo con il significato dell'estasi che fa entrare
l'adepto in una realtà *altra* da sé.

---

[67] *Idem.*
[68] Ibid., 118–119.

In uno schema sintetico del suo lavoro, Skrjabin illustra questa bipolarità, questa dialettica tra essere e non-essere.

Nella Sinfonia si scorge in filigrana questa oscillazione continua, questa periodica bipolarità, finché il moto ondulatorio non si placa nell'ascesa estatica finale. Il contrasto tra atmosfere languide, diafane e scene drammatiche, oscure è evidente. Il tema serpeggia e vortica per tutto il *Poema*, si innalza e si accresce, rallentando solo per poi riaccelerare, energico e implacabile. L'Estasi procede incessante verso un godimento infinito, che sfocia nel canto soave del clarinetto.

Dal punto di vista melodico, il poema si basa su un tema principale ascendente a intervalli in diminuzione. Nelle sue peregrinazioni, questo tema simboleggia lo Spirito che combatte tra forze oscure, incontrando zone di terrore. Gli intervalli musicali per Skrjabin contengono significati teosofici precisi: il salto discendente di *nona minore* significa la discesa dello spirito nella materia; gli intervalli di *toni interi* ascendenti o discendenti sono l'inspirazione e l'espirazione di Brama, il Creatore; il *semitono* discendente rappresenta la sofferenza umana; la *quarta* significa l'uomo; la *quinta* raffigura l'uomo-dio; la *terza* é la trinità teosofica, *corpus, anima, spiritus*, che compone l'uomo.

Dal punto di vista tematico, non si ha l'impressione di una grande varietà. Il *Poema* sembra, come qualcuno ha detto, cantare, dall'inizio alla fine, variazioni di un unico, incessante tema. Skrjabin stesso,

Tabella 2. Estasi. Unità assoluta (sintesi assoluta)

Non essere	Essere
Inerzia	Voglia di vivere
	Desiderio di vita, desiderio per ciò che è diverso
	ENERGIA[leave in caps]
Centro	Lontano dal centro
Attività centripeta	Attività centrifuga
Pace	Movimento, attività
Sonno	Risveglio
Non-distinzione	Differenziazione
	distinguere
Gravità	
Invariabilità	

tuttavia, distingue tra: Tema del tormento; Tema della volontà; Tema dell'auto-affermazione.

E' interessante vedere, tra le centinaia di abbozzi e schemi del *Poema dell'Estasi* conservati al Museo Centrale di Cultura Musicale di Mosca, le infinite versioni del tema principale, quello dell'autoaffermazione. Intonato senza posa dalle trombe, è sottoposto da Skrjabin a infinite trasformazioni. Ne cambia la tonalità, gli intervalli ascendenti mutano spesso e l'estensione supera inizialmente l'escursione dell'ottava. Anche in una versione del testo poetico, Skrjabin aggiunge un verso che non compare nella stesura definitiva: "Perché, verso cosa aneli, oh Spirito ribelle?".

Alla ricerca dell'opera d'arte totale

All'incrocio dei diversi codici linguistici, mirando a stabilire il punto d'incontro tra musica, danza, scultura e teosofia, Skrjabin si muove alla ricerca di un'opera d'arte totale, che possa incidere sul pubblico, grazie ai suoi contenuti esoterici e alle sue finalità spirituali. E' un dato di fatto, registrato nei taccuini coevi alla sinfonia, che già dal 1905 Skrjabin si interroga sull'identità vibratoria del suono e della luce e delle sue analogie col movimento, accennando al suono-colore. Sulla base della vibrazione, Skrjabin identifica con Blavatsky colore e suono, ma vibrante è anche la coscienza dell'uomo creativo. Così dalla sinestesia passa all'estasi, creando una musica da vedere, da ascoltare, da toccare, studiando la luce e l'energia pura che cercava di catturare nel suono. Una metrica dell'ascesa è rintracciabile sia nel poema in versi che in quello sinfonico che, tessuti con un identico procedimento, tramite l'accumulazione e la condensazione verbale nel primo caso e l'accelerazione ritmica e l'intensità agogica nel secondo, approdano alla beatitudine finale.

Senza considerare il veicolo della teosofia non è possibile risalire alla genesi delle sue ultime opere, né capire l'ispirazione che tocca simultaneamente artisti diversi che agiscono in diversi campi, ma che hanno in comune l'assiduità alla lettura degli stessi testi e la sensibilità per la ricerca di un'affinità tra i linguaggi delle arti sorelle.

Così, dal *Poème Orgiaque* la sinfonia skrjabiniana subisce una metamorfosi nel *Poème de l'Extase*, ovvero dalla scultura alla teosofia.

BIBLIOGRAFIA

Auzias, J. M., *Clefs pour le structuralisme*, Paris: Seghers, 1967.

Blavatsky, H. P., *La chiave della Teosofia*, Roma: Astrolabio.

Bowers, F., *The New Skrjabin – Enigma and Answers*, New York: St. Martin's Press 1973, trad. it. a cura di M. T. Bora, in *Skrjabin*, Bari, Gioiosa Editrice, 1990.

Dalcroze E.-J., *La Méthode rythmique*, Lausanne: Jobin 1916.

De Freitas, L., *515 Le Lieu du Miroir, Art et Numerologie*, Bibliothèque de l'hermétisme, Paris: Albin Michel 1993.

Hellmundt, C., *Musikalniyi Sovremennik*, (Le contemporain musical), vol. IV, 12/1915, lettera a M. Nemenova Lunc.

Kachperov, A. V., *A. N. Skrjabin Pisma*, Moscou: Izdatelstva Musika, 1965, trad. Tedesca, lettera alla Morozova, 6/8/1906.

Kelkel, M., 'Aleksandre Scriabine et "le charme des impossibilités", *Musique de Monde*, Paris: Librairie Philosophique J. Vrin 1988.

——, *Alexandre Scriabine, un musicien à la recherche de l'absolu*, Paris: Fayard 1999.

Lapaire, C., *Auguste de Niederhäusern-Rodo, 1863–1913. Un sculpteur entre la Suisse et Paris*, Zurich – Lausanne – Berne: Benteli 2001.

Platone, *Timeo*, Milano: BUR, 2003.

Sabaneev, L., 'A. N. Skrjabin', *Melos, Zeitschrift für Neue Musik*, 04/1925.

Schuré, E., *Histoire du drame musical*, Paris: Perrin 1895.

——, *Richard Wagner: son œuvre et son idée, 4ème éd.*, Paris: Perrin 1900.

——, *Femmes inspiratrices et poètes annonciateurs*, Paris: Perrin 1908.

——, *Histoire du lied ou la chanson populaire en Allemagne. Nouv. éd. précédée d'une étude sur Le réveil de la poésie populaire en France*, Paris: Perrin 1903.

——, *Les grands Initiés*, Paris: Librairie Académique Perrin 1960.

——, *Souvenirs sur Richard Wagner: la première de Tristan et Iseult*, Paris: Perrin 1900.

Seippel, P., 'Exposition des Indépendants', *Journal de Genève*, 30:11 (1891).

Skrjabin A., *Notes et Réflexions, carnets inédits*, traduction du russe, introduction et notes par Marina Skrjabine, Paris: Klincksieck 1979, trad. it. Maria Girardi e Maria Giovanna Miggiani, II (94).

Steiner, R. *Iniziazione ai Mondi Superiori*, a cura di Paola Giovetti, Roma: ed. Mediterranee, 1999.

Thomas, E. J., *The life of Buddha as legend and history*, Londra: 1975.

Timpanaro Cardini, M. (a cura di), *I Pitagorici. Testimonianze e frammenti*, Firenze: La Nuova Italia, 1962.

Verdi, L., *Aleksandr Skrjabin tra musica e filosofia*, Firenze: Passigli 1991.

——, *Kandinskij e Skrjabin. Realtà e utopia nella Russia pre-rivoluzionaria*, Lucca: Akademos & Lim 1996.

Verlaine, P., *Poèmes saturniens*, 1866, 1° vol., Paris: Léon Vanier, 1900–1902.

THE UNSPEAKABLE AND THE LAW:
ESOTERICISM IN ANTON WEBERN
AND THE SECOND VIENNESE SCHOOL

Wouter J. Hanegraaff

> [...] secret science is not what an alchemist would refuse to teach you; it is a science which cannot be taught at all. It is inborn or it is not there.
>
> (Arnold Schönberg on teaching counterpoint)[1]

THEORETICAL PRELIMINARIES

"Western esotericism" is a contested category in academic research, and will undoubtedly remain so for some time.[2] Here is not the place to go into the current theoretical and methodological debate about how this field must be defined and demarcated,[3] but a few introductory remarks are necessary to explain in what sense, in my opinion, a famous 20th-century composer like Anton Webern may be discussed within such a context.

The first point is that studying a person under the rubric of "esotericism" does not imply, by any means, that he or she must therefore be considered an "esotericist" or an adherent of an "esoteric tradition". Western esotericism is not a descriptive label, but an etic,[4] constructed, analytical category, pragmatically used by scholars as an umbrella term for gathering together a wide range of currents, personalities, ideas and even practices that have long been seen as somehow belonging together, and have tended to be marginalized in academic research.

---

[1] Schönberg, 'The Blessing of the Dressing', 386.

[2] On the field and its academic development, see Hanegraaff, 'The Study of Western Esotericism', and for a comprehensive overview of currents and personalities see Hanegraaff et al., *Dictionary of Gnosis and Western Esotericism*.

[3] For an up-to-date overview and discussion in Italian, see Grossato, *Forme e correnti*, particularly the contributions by Pasi and Hanegraaff.

[4] Briefly stated, according to current terminology in the study of religion, *emic* stands for "the believer's point of view" and *etic* for the use of scholarly, technical perspectives and terminologies. Hence we can *etically* use the modern academic term "Western esotericism" while acknowledging that many of those studied under that rubric would have identified themselves differently.

This category began to emerge in the 17th century in the context of a highly polemical discourse concerning what might be called "rejected knowledge":[5] claims of knowledge grounded in beliefs and worldviews that were in the process of being demarcated at that time, mainly by Protestant and Enlightenment historians, from what they considered to be "true" Christianity on the one hand, and "true" rational philosophy and science on the other.[6]

This ambiguous rest-category functioned as a virtual and increasingly reified waste-basket of rejected beliefs, referred to quite vaguely by a variety of names, such as "magic", "occult philosophy" or even "mysticism", and usually associated with irrational *Schwärmerei* and superstition. The term "esotericism" (first attested in 1828)[7] only gradually came to be associated with this category, largely by "occultist" authors who wanted to turn it from a negative category of exclusion into a positive label for ideas and traditions that they considered valuable: because these authors tended to reject or at least criticize mainstream Christianity and its theologies along with such things as positivist philosophy and materialist science, what was rejected by those perspectives was naturally embraced by them.[8]

Scholars studying this domain have always been, and still are, tempted to fall into the trap of reification, thereby creating confusion between historical realities on the one hand, and the imaginal invention of an "esoteric tradition" and its adherents on the other. The common result is that highly complex personalities are artificially reduced to an "esoteric" identity, whereas in fact they usually participated in a variety of contemporary discourses, only some of which could be seen as falling under the modern rubric "Western esotericism".[9] In my

---

[5] This formulation is derived from James Webb, in his pioneering studies *Occult Underground* and *Occult Establishment*.

[6] Hanegraaff, 'Western Esotericism in Enlightenment Historiography'.

[7] Matter, *Histoire critique du gnosticisme*. See discussion in Laurant, *L'ésotérisme chrétien*, 19; and Hanegraaff, 'La nascita dell'esoterismo'.

[8] Hanegraaff, 'Forbidden Knowledge', 247.

[9] For example, the 15th-century Platonic philosopher, translator, physician and priest Marsilio Ficino (1433–1499) is generally, and for excellent reasons, considered a key figure in the field of Western esotericism; but in my view it would not make sense to call him an "esotericist". The point at issue may be clarified by drawing a comparison with a completely different field of study, that of the history of homosexuality, where analogous conclusions have been drawn already since Foucault, and in which Ficino happens to play a role as well. Both homoeroticism conceptualized as "Socratic love" (theorized at length in Ficino's *De amore*) and the practice of sodomy (which he sharply rejected, but for which his city Florence was famous) are abundantly attested

opinion it is nevertheless quite possible to use that rubric as an etic[10] category without falling into such errors; but conceptual slippage and reification, leading to distortions, is easy and natural, and can only be avoided if we are well aware of the problem.

Now if we survey the most influential definitions of "Western esotericism" that are used in modern scholarly research, it seems evident to me that two elements recur again and again. The first one has to do with *claims of knowledge*.[11] Throughout the various currents discussed under the rubric of esotericism, we find a quest for higher, superior or even absolute knowledge that is believed to transcend the domains of rationality and scientific inquiry, and that claims priority over official mediators of the divine such as revealed scriptures or ecclesiastical authorities. This claim of direct, unmediated, experiential access to supreme knowledge may conveniently be referred to by the Greek term *gnōsis*, originally used in the context of ancient gnosticism and hermetism. The second recurring element is a tendency towards *panentheist cosmologies* based upon *universal interdependence*.[12] This very complex notion, which may take many forms, cannot be discussed here in detail; but briefly, two central aspects might be highlighted. On the one hand, there is the concept referred to by Jan Assmann as "cosmotheism",[13] meaning that the cosmos is permeated by divine presences; and on the other hand, the concept that all parts of this cosmos are inextricably linked to one another by means of a seamless web of "correspondences", including those between the macrocosmos

---

for the period of the Renaissance; but there certainly existed no such thing yet as a "homosexual" or "gay" *identity* (for discussion, see Hanegraaff, 'Under the Mantle of Love'). Analogously, Ficino's work is highly relevant to any history of Western esotericism, but he would never have identified himself as anything resembling our idea of an "esotericist".

[10] See note 4.

[11] This emphasis is prominent e.g. in the discursive approach to Western esotericism pioneered by Kocku von Stuckrad (*Western Esotericism*; 'Western Esotericism') and, in a very different way, my own work ('The Trouble with Images'; 'Reason, Faith, and Gnosis'). Cf. also Neugebauer-Wölk, '"Höhere Vernunft" und "höheres Wissen"'; and Hammer, *Claiming Knowledge*, ch. VI.

[12] This emphasis is prominent in Antoine Faivre's influential definition of Western esotericism (especially its first two characteristics: "Correspondences" and "Living Nature"; see e.g. Faivre, *Access to Western Esotericism*, 10–15). It is also found in von Stuckrad, 'Western Esotericism', 93 (under the rubric of "ontological monism") and Hanegraaff, 'The Trouble with Images'.

[13] See e.g. Assmann, *Moses the Egyptian*; and discussion in Hanegraaff, 'Trouble with Images', 114–120.

and the human microcosmos, which mirror one another because they answer to the same laws.

I would not go as far as claiming that these two elements define Western esotericism as a field of research; but it does seem clear to me that they play a particularly significant and central role in the various currents that, by whatever definition, are usually ranged under that rubric.[14] I will be arguing that both concepts – "gnosis" and "correspondences" for short – are of central importance to understanding the Second Viennese School, which revolutionized 20th-century music by introducing atonality and the novel technique of dodecaphony. My main focus of attention in that regard will be Anton von Webern, but as an introduction I will have some things to say about Arnold Schönberg first.

THE LAWGIVER: ARNOLD SCHÖNBERG

It is not difficult to find evidence for esoteric interests in Schönberg's works and writings. One example is his enthusiasm for the theories of his friend Kandinsky, published under the title *Über das Geistige in der Kunst* (1912).[15] Another is his admiration for Honoré de Balzac's novel *Séraphita*, based upon the teachings of the 18th century Christian theosopher Emanuel Swedenborg.[16] Yet another is the influence of Jewish kabbalah on such works as *Die Jakobsleiter* and the *Kol Nidre*.[17] But such influences, no matter how interesting they are in terms of Schönberg's personal biography, might still be dismissed as of merely anecdotal interest when it comes to his importance strictly as a composer.

To move beyond the anecdotal, we should pay attention to Schönberg's preoccupation with two central themes: *das Unaussprechli-*

---

[14] See Hanegraaff, 'The Trouble with Images'. 131–134.

[15] See e.g. Martino, 'Kandinsky, Schönberg und das Gesamtkunstwerk'.

[16] See e.g. Ashton, *A Fable of Modern Art*, 97–102; for a summary of Swedenborg's doctrine, see Hanegraaff, *Swedenborg, Oetinger, Kant*, 3–56. For a detailed discussion of the *Séraphita*-reception by Schönberg, Berg and Webern, see Gratzer, *Zur "wunderlichen Mystik" Alban Bergs*, 55–72. Around 1912 Schönberg was planning to write a large work based on *Séraphita*, to the great enthusiasm of his pupils.

[17] See e.g. Allende-Blin, 'Arnold Schönberg und die Kabbala'; Hanegraaff, 'De gnosis van Arnold Schönberg'.

che [the unspeakable] and *das Gesetz* [the law].[18] Both are central to
Schönberg's masterpiece, the opera *Moses and Aron*. This work begins
with Moses' exclamation at the sight of the burning bush: *Einziger,
ewiger, allgegenwärtiger, unsichtbarer und unvorstellbarer Gott!* [Ye
One, Eternal, Omnipresent, Invisible and Unimaginable God!] The
entire opera turns around the fundamental problem implicit in this
first sentence. Moses is driven by the numinous experience of a God
who radically transcends all human concepts, but finds himself faced
with the task of proclaiming this God to his people. Doing so seems
impossible, for he needs to use words, which can only falsify and distort this great *Gedanke* or Idea of God. And indeed, such distortions
and misunderstandings immediately occur when Aron addresses the
people in Moses' place, and turns out to be quite willing to compromise and manipulate the people by the seductions of verbal eloquence
and seductive images (*Bilder*), including the Golden Calf. For Moses,
such idolatrous compromises cannot but distort and falsify the message.[19] God is an inexpressible mystery:[20] he does not reveal himself in
the world by means of words or images, or by any kind of visible or
tangible phenomenon. Even the burning bush and the pillar of cloud
are, in the final reckoning, merely images: *Falsch, wie ein Bild nur sein
kann* [false, like any image]. In Schönberg's opera, God reveals himself
exclusively through Moses' ineffable *Gedanke* or Idea, and through *das
Gesetz*: the Law.

This unspeakable Idea and the Law as revelation of the transcendent
are straight equivalents of gnosis and the universal law of correspondences. In an unpublished essay on Hauer's theories, Schönberg wrote
the following:

---

[18] In this article, all quotations from poems or libretti, and a selected few other quotations, are given in the original followed by an English translation by the author; all
other quotations from the German are given in translation only (also by the author).
[19] For a direct application of these passages from Schönberg's opera to the problematics of monotheism versus "cosmotheism", cf. Hanegraaff, 'The Trouble with
Images', 114, 117–118.
[20] See the interesting discussion by Drummond, 'The Background, Shape and Meaning', 18–25. Drummond argues that the four mirror versions of the twelvetone row are
linked by Schönberg to the four relationships God-Moses, Moses-Aron, Aron-People,
God-people; but 'Significantly, no row-variant in the work is used to represent God, or
the Idea, Himself, for that theme is inexpressible. Similarly, Moses' relationship with
God is represented by a row-variant on a par with all the other row-variants: it is, as
Aron indicates, just another image'.

I say we are obviously as nature around us is. So that is also how our music is. But then our music must also be as we are (if two magnitudes both equal a third...). But then from our nature alone can I deduce how our music is (bolder men would say "how the cosmos is").[21]

Schönberg here describes man as a microcosm mirroring in itself the laws of the macrocosm; and music should express those laws, which for him are a direct expression of the divine "essence" of the cosmos. True insight into the cosmic "law", however, is possible only by means of direct and unmediated insight into this underlying essence. Polemicizing against "programmatic music", Schönberg insists that such insights bypass language and rationality entirely, and therefore cannot be "translated". He quotes Schopenhauer in this context: 'the composer reveals the inmost essence of the world and utters the most profound wisdom in a language which his reason does not understand, just as a magnetic somnambulist gives disclosures about things which she has no idea of when awake'.[22] Schönberg continues, however, by criticizing Schopenhauer for suggesting, inconsistently, that details of this knowledge might nevertheless be translated into our terms: on the contrary, he argues, the essence can only be perceived directly, and therefore it cannot but get lost in translation.[23] One could hardly have wished for a more exact equivalent of gnosis as direct, non-rational, superior and unspeakable knowledge.

Schönberg was convinced that as a composer, he was a conduit for direct divine knowledge, or gnosis;[24] but he had learned from painful experience that 'relatively few people...are capable of understanding, purely in terms of music, what music has to say'.[25] This small elite included his favourite pupils Berg and Webern, but most listeners and

---

[21] Schönberg, 'Kosmische Gesetze', unpublished ms dated 9 May 1923, first published in English translation as part II of 'Hauer's Theories' (1923), in: Schönberg, *Style and Idea*, 209–210. Cf. Cross, 'Three Levels of "Idea"', 29–30.

[22] Schönberg, 'The Relationship to the Text', 142. The quotation is from Schopenhauer, *Die Welt als Wille und Vorstellung* Bd. I, 3. Buch, § 52 ('...der Komponist offenbart das innerste Wesen der Welt und spricht die tiefste Weisheit aus, in einer Sprache, die seine Vernunft nicht versteht; wie eine magnetische Somnambule Aufschlüsse gibt über Dinge, von denen sie wachend keinen Begriff hat' [in: Schopenhauer, *o.c.*, 363]).

[23] Schönberg, 'The Relationship to the Text', 142.

[24] Such a conviction was not unusual. For example Johannes Brahms, much admired by Schönberg, made similar claims: 'straightaway the ideas flow in upon me, directly from God' (Abell, *Talks with Great Composers*, 21).

[25] Schönberg, 'The Relationship to the Text', 141.

critics reacted with incomprehension: as is well known, the history of the Second Viennese school is full of public scandals, with audiences beginning to hiss already during the first notes of a new piece, and concerts ending in general tumult with adherents and opponents of the new music physically attacking one another.

Like Schönberg himself, Moses in the opera was driven to despair by the abyss of translation: *es muss die Gedanke erfassen. Es lebt nur deshalb* [it *must* understand the Idea. It lives for nothing else], he complains about the people to the *Realpolitiker* Aron. Refusing Aron's road of compromise, Moses keeps pursuing the impossible: the *word* that might bridge the abyss. But at the end he has to admit defeat: *o Wort, du Wort, das mir fehlt* [oh Word, thou word, that I lack]!.[26] Thus gnosis remained what it essentially was: knowledge that cannot be communicated but can only be experienced directly. Nevertheless, it was by virtue of such knowledge that the composer was considered capable of understanding the invisible, underlying laws of the cosmos and use the laws of composition in such a way that his music would be a microcosmos corresponding perfectly to the macrocosmos.

WEBERN'S "STURM UND DRANG"

Whereas Schönberg – a Jew with a combative temperament and a strong sense of prophetic mission – had quite a bit of the Old Testament prophet in him, Webern was a Roman Catholic, an admirer of Goethe, and much more inclined towards a quiet, contemplative mysticism of nature. Nevertheless he shared Schönberg's belief in music as the privileged instrument of an ineffable gnosis, and he developed the concept of cosmic "law" with a logic even more relentless than that of his teacher. In what follows I will not attempt to trace the esoteric dimension of Webern's work in all its details (doing so would require a book-length discussion), but highlight what I see as the essential red thread.[27] In a nutshell, I will argue that on the basis of a psychological

---

[26] Here I ignore the final act, which was never put to music and in which Schönberg tried to find a solution: *Aber in der Wüste seid ihr unüberwindlich und werdet das Ziel erreichen: vereinigt mit Gott* [but in the desert you are invincible and will reach the goal: united with God].

[27] Perhaps most notably, I will not go into the relevance of the poet and artist Hildegard Jone, the exclusive supplier of texts for all the vocal works of Webern's final period. Jone has long been neglected by historians of art and poetry, and even

predisposition already present in his early years, the death of Webern's mother in 1906 was instrumental in leading him towards a persistent and almost obsessive quest for The Absolute, which found its mature expression in a spiritual ideal of abstract "purity" that came to govern his work even on a strictly technical level. Of crucial importance for this development was the metaphysics of Emanuel Swedenborg, which provided him with a framework in which "the unspeakable" of absolute spiritual reality and "the law" of universal correspondences were central.

Webern's highminded spiritual idealism and his love of the quiet and beauty of nature are already evident from the lyrics by Ferdinand Avenarius which he chose for his earliest songs.[28] After the beginnings of his music studies in Vienna and the obligatory pilgrimage to Bayreuth, Webern's meeting with Schönberg in 1904 was a turning point in his life. I find it important to emphasize that in his earliest period as a pupil of Schönberg, Webern tended to rely entirely on his (considerable) musical instincts, which were understood by him as a kind of direct divine inspiration. Very significantly, he chose for his string quartet of 1905 a motto from Jacob Böhme's *Aurora*, which he had found in a contemporary novel by Bruno Wille, *Offenbarungen des Wacholderbaums* [Revelations of the Juniper Tree], itself a typical product of the highminded Romantic idealism of the time, which exalts the soul's triumph over lower bodily desires in its quest for spiritual transcendence.[29] Böhme's description of his ecstatic illumination in 1600 is famous, and emphasizes precisely the two dimensions I highlighted as central to Western esotericism: direct revelatory knowledge by means of divine ecstasy along with a panentheist view of nature:

by specialists of Webern, but is now fortunately the focus of two recent dissertations: Reinhardt, *From Poet's Voice to Composer's Muse*, and Reinecke, *Hildegard Jone*. The nature of her esotericism and its relation to Webern's late works would require a substantial separate discussion, far beyond the scope of this article.

[28] His very first song, *Vorfrühling* (1899) could be seen as programmatic for his oeuvre as a whole: 'Leise tritt auf – / Nicht mehr in tiefem Schlaf, / in leichtem Schlummer nur / liegt das Land. / Und der Amsel Frühruf / spielt schon liebliche Morgenbilder / ihm in den Traum. / Leise tritt auf –' [Gently appear – / In deep sleep no more, / just in light slumber/ lies the Land. / And already the blackbird's early call / plays lovely morning-images / into his dream. / Gently appear –].

[29] For Wille's influence on Webern, see Gerlach, 'Mystik und Klangmagie' and *idem, Musik und Jugendstil*. That Webern copied the quotation not directly from Böhme but from Wille is shown by certain typographical details (Gerlach, 'Mystik und Klangmagie', 12). The original passage appears in Böhme's *Aurora* ch. 19 (see Böhme, *Jacob Böhme Werke*, 336–337).

> Was aber da für ein Triumphieren im Geiste gewesen, kann ich nicht
> schreiben oder reden; es lässt sich auch mit nichts vergleichen, als nur
> mit dem, wo mitten im Tode das Leben geboren wird, und vergleicht
> sich mit dem Auferstehung der Toten. In diesem Lichte hat mein Geist
> alsbald durch alles gesehen und an allen Kreaturen, selbst an Kraut und
> Gras, Gott erkannt, wer er sei, und wie er sei, und was sein Wille ist.[30]

Webern clearly identified with Böhme, but he was in for a rough awakening. While Schönberg was certainly a high Romantic in his own way, he was also known for his very stringent demands concerning formal compositional technique, and he never stopped emphasizing that, in order for great art to be produced, musical intuition must be inseparable from intellectual mastery: 'das Herz muss im Bereich des Kopfes sein' [the heart must be located in the head]. In 1906 he began to show ever more reservations about Webern's coursework, and finally told him in no uncertain terms that he would no longer accept his appeal to immediate spiritual inspiration but would insist on strict technical mastery first: 'It cannot go on like that! Once you really master the technique, you might occasionally rely on your formal instincts alone. From now on you will write wholly straight [ganz regelrecht]'.[31] Undoubtedly this reprimand was painful to Webern, but he bowed to Schönberg's authority, and years later, in 1914, sincerely thanked him for the wake-up call: 'How you have unveiled everything to me. From you I learned "what it's really all about"'.[32] Webern had to grow out of his youthful period of "Sturm und Drang" in order to reach maturity as the great composer he eventually turned out to be.

THE ENCOUNTER WITH DEATH

In september of 1906 Webern's mother died, and this was the beginning of an extraordinarily long and intense period of mourning, which

---

[30] 'But this triumph in the spirit I cannot express by the written or spoken word; indeed it cannot be compared with anything but the birth of life in the midst of death, and with the resurrection of the dead. In this light, my spirit has right away seen through everything, and in all creatures, even in herbs and grass, it has seen God: who he is, how he is, what his will is'.

[31] Webern to his friend Polnauer, in: Polnauer, 'Paralipomena', 295. See discussion in the section "Schönberg und Webern: Die Erziehung zum Regelrechten" in: Gerlach, *Musik und Jugendstil*, 105–106.

[32] Gerlach, *Musik und Jugendstil*, 106; Moldenhauer & Moldenhauer, *Anton von Webern*, 88–89.

lasted no less than seven years and came to a conclusion in 1913. In the same period, Webern met and married Wilhelmine Mörtl; and in a long series of songs based upon poems by Stefan George one can trace to an embarrassing degree how the grief over his mother and his struggle with the fact of mortality mingled in his mind with erotic, even incestuous fantasies. Webern originally planned to publish the songs as two cycles of seven, opus 2 and 4, but then changed his mind: he decided to publish only ten of them (as opus 3 and 4), in a different order, and kept back the four remaining ones, which were discovered and published by Hans Moldenhauer only as late as 1965. As noted by Albrecht Dümling, the four suppressed songs are of the same high quality as the others, but stand apart in their explicit emphasis on sensual desire and a forceful intensity, building up to a triple forte, which is absent in the rest of the songs.[33] He concludes that Webern must have kept them back to conceal some of his deepest motives; and if one restores the songs to their original order,[34] we do make some important discoveries indeed. What, then, is the secret significance of this cycle?[35]

In the immediately preceding choral composition *Entflieht auf leichten Kähnen* (op. 2), also on a text by Stefan George, we are already introduced to a tragic fall from 'berauschten Sonnenwelten' [intoxicated sun-worlds] into a realm of 'stille Trauer' [quiet mourning], and the following series of fourteen songs traces that mourning process in intimate detail. It begins with a turning-away from reality ('Welt der Gestalten lang lebewohl!' [World of forms, farewell for long!]) and the entrance into a forest of dreams, followed by 'ein Lied für dich allein' ['a song for you alone'] that mentions 'kindischen Wähnen' and 'from-

---

[33] Dümling, '"Dies ist ein Lied für dich allein"', 256–257. Actually this characterization holds true only for three of the four songs; for an explanation, see text (below).

[34] The correct order is: 1. Eingang (op. 4.1); 2. Dies ist ein Lied für dich allein (op. 3.1); 3. Erwachen aus dem tiefsten Traumes-schoosse (unpubl.); 4. Im Windesweben (op. 3.2); 5. Kunfttag I (unpubl.); 6. Kahl reckt der Baum (op. 3.5); 7. Im Morgentaun (op. 3.4); 8. Trauer I (unpubl.); 9. Ja Heil und Dank dir (op. 4.3); 10. Noch zwingt mich Treue (op. 4.2); 11. Am Bachesrandt (op. 3.3); 12. Das lockere Saatgefilde lechzet krank (unpubl.); 13. So ich traurig bin (op. 4.4); 14. Ihr tratet zu dem Herde (op. 4.5).

[35] Johnson, *Webern and the Transformation of Nature*, 95–98, provides a brief musical analysis of some of the songs in this cycle, and suggests that the diatonic is used here as the symbol of 'a distant and rarely glimpsed utopia' (98): the "paradise lost" due to the death of his mother. He mentions Dümling, but does not call attention to the narrative of mourning and recovery traced by the textual sequence.

men Tränen' ['childish illusions' and 'pious tears']. Then comes the
third, unpublished song, which introduces the combination – typical
for the period – of death and eroticism:

> Erwachen aus dem tiefsten Traumes-Schoose:
> als ich von langer Spiegelung betroffen
> mich neigte auf die Lippen die erblichen.[36]

The incestuous implications clearly suggest an Oedipus complex; and
in fact, it was only due to a psychoanalysis with no one less than Alfred
Adler, in 1913, that Webern would finally manage to process the emotional turmoil caused by his mother's death.[37]

The fourth song is about the desire for some absent person, and
is followed by "Kunfttag I", originally addressed by George to "Max-
imin" (Max Kronberger): the early-deceased "divine boy" venerated by
him and his circle. It is the only song in the cycle which cannot plau-
sibly be connected to Webern's mother, and we may assume that this
one was suppressed for a different reason: simply because, all things
considered, it did not fit the cycle.[38] The sixth song evokes an image of
desolation, isolation and the coldness of winter, but with a vague hope
for the coming of spring, which does indeed seem to have arrived in
the seventh song, where, as it turns out, the protagonist is no longer
alone: 'Im Morgentaun trittst du hervor / den Kirschenflor mit mir zu
schaun, Duft einzuziehn des Rosenbeetes' [In the morning-dew you
appear / to look at the cherry blossom with me / and inhale the smell
of the rosebed]. The first cycle of seven ends on this note of hope.
Undoubtedly, the unnamed companion stood for Wilhelmine Mörtl,
whom Webern had met just before his mother died. She got pregnant
in 1910, and the marriage took place briefly before the birth of their
daughter Amalia. What we know about Webern and his wife clearly
indicates that Wilhelmine was not only his lover but a replacement of
his mother as well.

---

[36] 'Awakening from the deepest womb of dreams: As I, overcome by lengthy reflection, inclined towards the lips gone pale'.

[37] Since opus 3 and 4 were published only in 1919 and 1923 respectively, we may
speculate that Webern decided to suppress those four songs only after the psychoanalysis had caused him to perceive the subconscious processes underlying his original conception.

[38] This explanation is strenghtened by the fact that it is the only one which, contrary
to what is suggested by Dümling (see note 33), shows neither the sensuality nor the
triple forte typical of the three other suppressed songs.

   In sharp contrast with the idyllic ending of the first cycle, the second
one (unpublished) opens again on shrill tones of despair, with evident
erotic feelings for the dead beloved ('…dass ich dich erbete – begehre
[that I beseech you – desire you]'). The protagonist desperately tries
to hold on to the deceased and keep her from leaving, but he receives
a clear answer: she tells him to let go of her, raise himself from the
ground, and get back to life. This is followed by the key song "Ja Heil
und Dank dir", where the unknown companion from the seventh song
has taken the place of the dead beloved, and is indeed leading the
protagonist back to life:

> Ja Heil und Dank dir die den Segen brachte!
> Du schläfertest das immer laute Pochen
> mit der Erwartung deiner teure Sachte
> in diesen glanzerfüllten Sterbewochen.
>
> Du kamest und wir halten uns umschlungen,
> ich werde sanfte Worte für dich lernen
> und ganz als glichest du der Einen Fernen
> dich loben auf den Sonnenwanderungen.[39]

Theodor Adorno has characterized this (mercilessly but perceptively)
as the program for a 'humiliating Ersatz-love' which insults the
beloved while professing to praise her.[40] Be that as it may, the song
was composed precisely around the time of Webern's and Wilhelmine's engagement.
   His new love notwithstanding, the protagonist long remains faithful
to the deceased, as shown by the tenth song, 'Noch zwingt mich Treue
über dich zu wachen' [Loyalty still forces me to watch over you]. The
eleventh song is a kind of intermezzo, with mournful feelings miti-
gated by the expectation of spring: 'Das Feld ist brach, der Baum noch
grau…/ Blumen streut vielleicht der Lenz uns nach' [The field lies
fallow, the tree still grey…/ Maybe spring will bring us flowers]. In

---

[39] 'Yes, praise and thank to you, who brought the blessing! / You calmed down
the ever-loud pangs / with the expectation of your dear softness / in these weeks of
mourning full of radiance. / You came, and we held each other / I will learn sweet
words for you / and, quite as if you resembled the One far away / give praise to you
while we walk in sunlight'.
[40] 'Kein Geschäftsmann liesse sich so leicht beikommen, seiner Freundin "und
ganz als glichest du der Einen Fernen" und ähnliche karge Freundlichkeiten zu sagen'
(Adorno, 'George und Hofmannsthal', 240; and see Dümling, "Dies ist ein Lied für
dich allein"', 259).

the twelfth song, which remained unpublished for reasons now easy to understand, this barren field becomes an explicit sexual metaphor: it is the body of the beloved which is being "plowed" and "seeded" at the coming of spring:

> Sei mir nun fruchtend Bad und linder Trank:
> von deiner nackten Brust das blumige Schauern,
> das Duften deiner leichtgewirrten Strähne,
> dein Hauch dein Weinen deines Mundes Feuchte.[41]

No doubt about it: the protagonist has definitely returned to life now. In the thirteenth song, his memories of the deceased one no longer evoke despair, but give comfort. The mourning process is concluded with the final song, where the protagonist resigns himself to the fact that one should not keep raking up the ashes of what has been, pointlessly trying to rekindle the fire: 'Seht was mit Trostgebärde der Mond euch rät: tretet weg vom Herde, es ist worden spät' [See what the moon advises you with a gesture of comfort: step away from the hearth. It has grown late].

Not only did the death of his mother dominate Webern's songs from 1906 to 1913, but according to himself, it dominated even his instrumental music of this period. Contrary to the image of Webern promoted by the serialists after World War II, he stated explicitly that almost all his instrumental compositions of the period were programmatic. Thus, in a letter to Alban Berg from July 12, 1912, he explained how certain experiences in his life kept moving around in his head until they turned into music 'with a quite specific connection to this experience – often up to details', and specified that, with only a few exceptions, all his compositions, including the instrumental ones, were about his mother: 'Only one summer, at the time I wrote the violin pieces [op. 7], something else has been in me as well'.[42]

---

[41] 'Now be fruit-bearing bath and a mild drink to me: / the flowery shiver of your naked breast, / the scent of your lightly twisted hair, / your smell, your crying, the moistness of your mouth'.

[42] Moldenhauer & Moldenhauer, *Anton von Webern*, 171. For additional references underpinning the significance of the death of Webern's mother in this period, see also Johnson, *Webern and the Transformation of Nature*, ch. 3.

THE QUEST FOR PURITY

The end of Webern's long mourning period in 1913 is marked not
only by his successful psychoanalysis but also by a non-musical work:
a theatre piece called *Tot* [Death] which is dominated by the influence
of Emanuel Swedenborg.

Honoré de Balzac's *Séraphita*, a novel about an androgynous angelic
being based upon Swedenborg's theories, impressed Webern at least
as strongly as it had impressed Schönberg: for example, in letters to
his teacher he calls it 'a book that is not written by a human hand'[43]
and writes that 'every sentence in it is a miracle'.[44] In 1913 Webern
was reading Swedenborg himself, and wrote about it to Schönberg:
'It leaves me breathless. It is unheard-of. I had expected something
enormous, but it is even more'.[45] The great importance to Webern of
both Balzac and Swedenborg is inseparable from his extreme preoccupation, at this time, with death, "the unspeakable" and "the absolute".[46]
The theatre piece *Tot* itself seems to have been inspired by the death
not only of his mother, but also of his cousin Theo Clementschitsch
three months earlier, and is located high up in the Alpine regions.
A man and a woman have recently lost their son and are wandering
through the mountains to get over their grief; the other two protago-
nists are the spirit of their dead son, who sometimes speaks to them,
and an angel. Apart from the written text, Webern used red ink to give
extremely precise and detailed indications for such things as lighting,
gestures and movements (sometimes there is an incredible wealth of
such instructions against only a few spoken words).

Tot is based upon an understanding of nature as a place of healing and purification. During their wanderings the couple climbs ever
higher, and this is parallelled by an increasing emphasis on how the
natural world mirrors the heavenly world above, by means of cor-

[43] Correspondence Schönberg-Berg-Webern, Wiener Stadsbibliothek, 153; letter
of November 9, 1911, here quoted according to Gratzer, *Zur "wunderlichen Mystik"
Alban Bergs*, 56 (but cf. Reinecke, *Hildegard Jone*, 269: same quotation but 'Men-
schengeist' instead of 'Menschenhand', and dated March 9, 1911). The novel had
already been translated into German as early as 1836, and a new translation by Gisela
Etzel appeared in 1910.
[44] Webern to Schönberg, March 21, 1911, as quoted in Reinecke, *Hildegard Jone*,
270.
[45] Moldenhauer & Moldenhauer, *Anton von Webern*, 179.
[46] Summaries in Moldenhauer & Moldenhauer, *Anton von Webern*, 176–183; see
also Johnson, *Webern and the Transformation of Nature*, 105–107.

respondences. For example, the man and woman speculate about the "deep significance" of the fact that the edelweiss flower, which blooms higher up and therefore closer to heaven than any other flower, already takes on the shape of the stars: these flowers, we read, are 'the final, highest greeting of earth to the region up above, to home'.[47] In the final scene, the man reads a long passage from Swedenborg, about the earliest human generation, before the flood, when man could still communicate with the angels by means of a symbolic language of nature based upon correspondences and signatures.[48] The piece ends on notes of mystical ecstasy, again with references to flowers as mirrors of heaven: 'O deepest meaning of pain, which points us to the highest felicity – Lord, oh my God – I see you'.[49]

We will see that the spiritual ideals expressed here in Swedenborgian terms became ever more important to Webern during the following years, even on the level of strictly musical technique. Webern was striving for an ideal of spiritual *purity*, associated by him with *abstraction*, and both were unambiguously related in his mind to death and transcendence: the closer one gets to the heavenly ideal, the further one gets away from the "lower" concerns of the world and the messiness of the body, including its sexual drives.[50] Webern is quite explicit about this in a very significant letter to Schönberg (July 16, 1910):

---

[47] Moldenhauer & Moldenhauer, *Anton von Webern*, 182.

[48] On the centrality of correspondences, and its relation to the alpine regions in Webern's thinking, see also Johnson, *Webern and the Transformation of Nature*, 27–35, including the quotation from a letter to Berg (July 14, 1920): 'for me, the world is grasped at the root of correspondences. The impression, which something in nature exerts over me, I grasp in the spiritual. And thus you understand my frenzy for mountain streams...the scent of flowers – the tenderness of alpine flowers – those forms of the trees "up there", that air, that rain, and so on' (o.c., 34).

[49] Moldenhauer & Moldenhauer, *Anton von Webern*, 182.

[50] At least as long as Webern's letters remain unpublished, it will be hard to find out how Webern looked at sexuality (according to Moldenhauer & Moldenhauer's analysis of the psychoanalysis, Adler focused rather on inferiority complexes: see *Anton von Webern*, 160–163); but everything indicates that for him it was and remained a taboo area *par excellence*, heavily loaded with feelings of guilt and impulses towards penance or expiation. Wilhelmine's premarital pregnancy must have been embarrassing, and his suppression of the four songs discussed above (or rather, three of them), indicates that Webern was well aware of their disturbing erotic and incestuous connotations. Everything indicates that, faced with the power of his own sexual drives, he reacted with guilty attempts at self-purification and self-chastisement. The tortured monologues of the male protagonist in *Tot* hardly require comment in that regard: 'One must whip and flog oneself, so that all the shit flies out [Man muss sich peitschen, zusammenhauen dass aller Trek aus einem fliegt], always believe that one is better –

I just believe rather that Weininger[51] is right: the human being who strips
off the characteristics of other living beings one by one, must finally also
let go of that one which propagates humanity in its animal sense [was
die Menschheit im tierischen Sinne fortpflanzt].

So that is one way: from the animal to the dissolution of material
substance as such.

I understand that with perfect clarity.

The highest peak of morality, the earthly envelope falls away. If there
is an evolution, then it can only be this one: gradually, out of the ani-
malic man [dem Tier-menschen] develops a living being that attains
knowledge, it does not need life on this earth. Thus man vanishes again,
the bodily one.

This way leads directly to God.[52]

In many letters to Schönberg and Berg, Webern kept writing long
ecstatic passages about the high alpine regions, their plants and flowers, and the purity of their atmosphere.[53] At one point he even wrote
that in the high regions of earth 'better people' must be living, although
invisible for us: 'I am sure that that exists, it must not be understood
symbolically.... So upwards upwards! That is the only thing fitting for
man. Inwardly and outwardly upwards, upwards!'.[54]

Most interesting from a musical point of view, this same movement from lower wordly and bodily concerns towards the higher,
abstract purity of the transcendent implied, for Webern, a movement
from sound to silence. One can see this already in *Tot*, where the pro-
tagonists are gradually falling silent, the closer they get to heaven.
The same tendency is illustrated by a whole series of anecdotes from
Webern's later years. While accompanying the soloist in a rehearsal
of Berg's violin concerto in 1936, right after Berg's death, Webern got
so concentrated that he gradually forgot to touch the keys. The violin-
ist still kept playing on, until Webern exclaimed ''Halt, jetzt war' ma
net beisamm!' [Stop! We weren't together anymore!]: apparently the

---

no, no, away you lust for power, arrogance, search only for the good – humility,
humility'.

[51] The reference is to Otto Weininger, *Über die letzten Dinge* (1904). On the importance of Weininger to the Schönberg circle, see Gratzer, *Zur "wunderlichen Mystik"
Alban Bergs*, 93–101.

[52] Webern to Schönberg, quoted in Reinecke, *Hildegard Jone*, 264.

[53] A good sample can be found in Reinecke, *Hildegard Jone*, 270–275.

[54] Webern to Berg (July 19, 1912), quoted in Reinecke, *Hildegard Jone*, 265; cf.
also Webern to Berg (July 12, 1912): 'Everything needed for man to thrive in a noble
manner is there, is up there. So where should man be? Up there. Up there, how that
sounds. Isn't that more than mere symbol'.

music had been going on in his head so clearly that he had forgotten the physical sounds.[55] According to a joke that circulated in Webern's circles around that time, he had now invented a new musical indication, the "pensato": a tone so unimaginably soft and tender that the musician should only *think* it.[56] Commenting on Bach's *Kunst der Fuge* in 1933, Webern wrote 'it is really almost an abstraction – or I would rather say, the highest reality'. Writing to Berg in 1929, he significantly remarked that 'I'm discovering that, at bottom, the instruments become ever more irrelevant to me';[57] and it fits the same pattern that, briefly before his death, he appears to have been busy tracing patterns of geometrical lines, circles and signs, explaining that he no longer needed to hear the music played by musicians because he could hear it internally: 'the sound is always there, and no performance could ever reproduce it so perfectly'.[58]

MUSICAL ESOTERICISM

The 1906–1913 period, dominated by the death of Webern's mother, was followed by a transitional period (1913–1917) in which we see Webern searching for a new leading theme, and a nine-year period (1917–1926) dominated by strictly dodecaphonic songs set to poems which are all characterized by their expressions of a deliberately "naive" Roman-Catholic popular piety. This period ended with two choral pieces (opus 19) based upon poems by Goethe, and in the same year Webern met the poet Hildegard Jone, who henceforth would become the exclusive source of texts for his music.

Now, it is important to realize that after the cello pieces op. 11 (1914), famous as a *non plus ultra* of brevity and musical economy, for a period of thirteen years Webern composed only music to texts. It was only as late as 1927 that he finally produced an instrumental work again: the string trio opus 20, followed in the next years by the

---

[55] Moldenhauer & Moldenhauer, *Anton von Webern*, 412; and see also the further description of these rehearsals, where Webern requested such "absolute" perfection from the musicians that even a day before the performance, he had not gotten further than the beginning of the first part.

[56] Ibid., 441 (and see further discussion on the same page, about the bizarre discrepancy between the few, fragmentary notes of the Piano Variations op. 27 and Webern's exuberant conducting gestures in rehearsing them with a pianist).

[57] Ibid., 384.

[58] Ibid., 565.

symphony opus 21 and the quartet opus 22. An important point about
this series is that in all three cases, Webern intended to write three
movements for them, but somehow did not manage to get further than
two, to his own considerable puzzlement. He writes that he felt com-
pelled by some kind of inner necessity which he did not understand
himself.[59] For the Quartet op. 22 he originally planned a third part
entirely based on a program somewhat reminiscent of *Tot* (suggesting
a mountain ascent culminating in a "Gaze into the highest region"),[60]
but to no avail. In tones of resignation, he wrote to Berg: 'again, the
"work" almost closes itself upon me ... in the exclusive opposition of
the two strongly contrasting movements ... that have already been
written. Nevertheless I keep working hard on the third one – until
my doom [Schicksal] will have overtaken me again'.[61] And indeed, a
few days later we read in his diary 'Made the decision to stay with two
movements'.[62]

The reason, I suggest, is that Webern was struggling with the problem of how to use dodecaphony for building larger musical structures
in time, and was instinctively experimenting with concepts of *polarity*
as a solution. By writing only songs and choral pieces for many years,
he had been able to evade or postpone the problem of form, because
the text provided him with a structure. But for instrumental pieces, all
the classical procedures for structuring musical time by means of an
essentially narrative sequence of thesis, antithesis and final synthesis
had vanished along with the diatonic system. The most radical solution was to deny, or at least minimize, the very *temporality* of music:
hence the extreme brevity of Webern's instrumental atonal pieces
before 1927, with the cello pieces opus 11 as the ultimate example. I
would suggest that this brevity signals an intuitive understanding on
Webern's part that the ultimate logic of atonality implied a collapse
of narrative structure, and pointed towards the theoretical endpoint
of a non-narrative and therefore non-temporal music taking place in
a single moment without extension. Or in other words: a music that
could only attain perfection by falling silent. Opus 20–22 represent
an attempt at avoiding such a conclusion by replacing the narrative
dialectics of thesis/antithesis/synthesis by a non-narrative and there-

[59] Ibid., 289, 293, 385.
[60] Ibid., 382.
[61] Ibid., 385.
[62] Ibid., 385.

fore non-temporal dualism: thesis and antithesis holding one another
in the balance without an attempt at resolution or synthesis (significantly, even Webern's early concept of three movements for op. 21
was already based upon a programmatic opposition of "Sun" against
"Moon", with a variation part in the middle).[63] Of course, neither of
these "solutions" could ever be satisfactory: the former was a dead end
because it implied the end of music, the latter was a straitjacket that
condemned the composer to writing only two-part pieces characterized by extreme oppositions of mood or expression.

Schönberg's own solution to the problem had been a stroke
of genius. As is well known, the dodecaphonic system essentially
replaced the concept of musical time by a new concept of *musical
space*, and Schönberg's argument was made with explicit reference to
Swedenborg:

> *The unity of musical space demands an absolute and unitary percep-
> tion.* In this space, as in Swedenborg's heaven (described in Balzacs
> *Seraphita*)[64] there is no absolute down, no right or left, forward or back-
> ward. Every musical configuration, every movement of tones has to be
> comprehended primarily as a mutual relation of sounds, of oscillatory
> vibrations, appearing at different places and times.[65]

Such a notion of space in heaven can indeed be found in Swedenborg, whose speculations in that regard must therefore be recognized
as an important influence on the development of dodecaphony.[66] The
underlying idea was that anything existing in external reality corresponds with an "internal" reality that is both ontologically more
real *and* far more abstract in nature. Against that background, it is

---

[63] Ibid., 293.

[64] As remarked by Gratzer, *Zur "wunderlichen Mystik" Alban Bergs*, 73, Balzac's
novel does not actually contain such a description of Swedenborg's heaven. Schönberg
must have found it in Swedenborg himself.

[65] Schönberg, 'Composition with Twelve Tones' (1941), in: Schönberg, *Style and
Idea*, 223 (emphasis in original).

[66] See especially Swedenborg, *Heaven and its Wonders and Hell*, # 141–153, and cf.
191–199. See also Hanegraaff, *Swedenborg, Oetinger, Kant*, 54–55, quoting *Secrets
of Heaven* 3638, 3641: 'all communities in the other worlds…maintain their own
constant position in relation to the Lord, who appears to the whole of heaven as the
sun. What is surprising – and hardly any will believe it, since they cannot understand
it – is that the communities there maintain this same position in relation to *everyone* there. No matter where you are, which way you turn, or how you move around,
communities that appear on your right are always on your right, and those on your
left are always on your left, even when you turn your face or move your body from
quarter to quarter…'.

important to emphasize that although Schönberg clearly shifted the emphasis from a temporal framework for music to a spatial one, he was actually describing a metaphysical realm beyond both time *and* space. Swedenborg was explicit in emphasizing that motion, in heaven, was not a change of place but a change of "inner state".[67] This is highly important for understanding Webern's motivations in embracing the concept: what he really wanted was to write music that would stand in the strictest possible correspondence to (and hence would approximate as closely as possible) an "eternal" and "infinite" metaphysical reality beyond the (Kantian) space/time restrictions which ruled the material world and historical time.[68]

Against this background, Webern's initial attempt at creating musical structure by means of polarity eventually led him from the crude "dualism" of opus 20–22 to a much more subtle concept of *complementarity*, within a broader context of universal *correspondences*; and in this development he was directly inspired by Swedenborg's concepts as well as by the organismic speculations of Goethe's mature *Naturphilosophie*.[69] To replace the tension between consonant and dissonant within diatonic music, some principle of polar tension was needed within the dodecaphonic system too. And this was easy to find, for actually, the "musical space" consisting exclusively of semitones is only seemingly indifferentiated: even single tones are already "polarized" all along, due to the inherent tension between the perfect consonance of the octave and the relative dissonance of the other harmonics. In a long, detailed and technical argumentation which cannot be summarized here, Angelika Abel has demonstrated that this was the starting point for Webern to try and apply Goethe's concept of a law of complementary to the writing of music.[70] Goethe had observed that the eye automatically complements colours by their opposites (green by red, orange by blue and so on), so as to achieve "wholeness", and therefore described colour as 'die gesetzmässige Natur im Bezug auf den Sinn des Auges' [lawful nature with reference to the visual sense]. Webern transposed this argument to music: 'since there is only a grad-

---

[67] E.g. Swedenborg, *Heaven and Its Wonders and Hell*, 191–192.
[68] On the relation between Swedenborg's metaphysics and Kant's philosophy, see Hanegraaff, *Swedenborg Oetinger, Kant*, 87–107.
[69] On the hermetic backgrounds to Goethe, see the 2–volume standard work by Zimmermann, *Das Weltbild*; and Zimmermann, 'Goethes Verhältnis zur Naturmystik'.
[70] Abel, *Die Zwölftontechnik Weberns*; and cf. Abel, 'Musik als Sprache'.

ual but not an essential difference between colour and music, one can say that music is lawful nature with reference to the hearing sense'.[71] Abel argues that on the Goethean assumption that the ear "demands" intervals to be complemented so as to achieve "wholeness", Webern's twelvetone rows were structured specifically so as to highlight the complementarity between e.g. major septh and minor second, major third and minor sixth, and so on.

Furthermore, Webern combined a Swedenborgian concept of correspondences with Goethe's concept of the *Urpflanze* [Archetypal Plant] to develop the idea that a piece of music should be a perfect microcosmic mirror of the macrocosm. About the model of the *Urpflanze* he was quite explicit:

> Theme in unison; and all the rest is based upon this idea, it is the archetypal form. Unheard-of things happen, and nevertheless it is always the same thing again. You see now what I'm driving at – Goethe's *Urpflanze*: the root is really no different from the stem, the stem is no different from the leaf, the leaf again is no different from the blossom: variations of one and the same idea [Gedanke]...No matter where we cut the piece [of music], always we can observe the same sequence of tones.[72]
>
> With this model [of the *Urpflanze*] and its key, one can keep inventing plants into infinity.... "The same law will be applicable to all other living things"...*Isn't that the essential core of our law of twelve-tone rows?*[73]

Webern's concept of the correspondence between hidden laws operating on the natural, spiritual and musical levels is demonstrated perhaps most clearly by his fascination with the phenomenon of magical squares, which he saw as perfect examples of universal order and symmetry grounded in a spiritual reality beyond time and three-dimensional space. That the famous SATOR/AREPO square

---

[71] Webern, *Wege zur neuen Musik*, 11.

[72] Ibid., 56. Note that exactly the same "holographic" concept, including even the metaphor of "cutting", is found already in Schönberg's "Verhältnis zum Text" of 1912: 'Thence it became clear to me that the work of art is like every other complete organism. It is so homogeneous in its composition that in every little detail it reveals its truest, inmost essence. When one cuts into any part of the human body, the same thing comes out – blood. When one hears a verse of a poem, a measure of a composition, one is in a position to comprehend the whole' ('The Relationship to the Text', 144).

[73] Letters to Reich (*February* 28 and July 31, 1942), as quoted in Moldenhauer & Moldenhauer, *Anton von Webern*, 523 (emphasis in original). Cf. the quite analogous discussions in *Wege zur neuen Musik*, culminating again in the conclusion 'And that is the meaning of our composition style' (o.c., 42ff).

```
S A T O R
A R E P O
T E N E T
O P E R A
R O T A S
```

is based upon a Christian message (the letters can be rearranged so
as to produce a double Pater Noster + Alfa/Omega in the form of a
cross)

```
                        A
                        P
                        A
                        T
                        E
                        R
        A P A T E R N O S T E R O
                        O
                        S
                        T
                        E
                        R
                        O
```

seems to have been first discovered in the 1920s,[74] and if Webern ever
learned about it, it will certainly have impressed him greatly. What we
do know for certain is that Webern used the square as the structural
basis for his Konzert op. 24 (1934), even to such an extent that its final
part is a literal (one might even say "mechanical") transcription of
it. This has been demonstrated in detail by several musicologists, and
therefore need not be explained here again.[75]

Concluding Remarks

I have argued that on the basis of a psychological predisposition
already present in his early years, the death of Webern's mother in
1906 was instrumental in leading him towards a persistent and obsessive quest for The Absolute, which found its mature expression in a

---

[74] The discovery seems to have been made independently by three persons
(C. Frank, F. Grosser, and S. Angrel) in 1924 and 1927 (see Moeller, *The Mithraic
Origin*, 44ff, as quoted in Neuwirth, 'ROTAS – SATOR', 461–462 and 472 nt 5).
[75] Cohen, 'Anton Webern and the Magic Square'; Neuwirth, 'ROTAS – SATOR'.

spiritual ideal of abstract "purity" that came to govern his work even on a strictly technical level. As part of this project, Schönberg's basic concepts of an unspeakable, supra-rational "gnosis" and a universal cosmic/divine law were adopted by Webern on his own terms: he understood them not in Jewish and kabbalistic terms, but in terms of an esoteric Naturphilosophie strongly influenced by Swedenborg and Goethe. Far from being of mere anecdotal interest, these dimensions are of basic importance to understanding Webern's development as a composer, particular after 1926. Contrary to what was claimed by the serialists of the post-war period, the extremes of musical abstraction that characterize Webern's mature work are grounded not in some wish to "rationalize" musical language, but rather, in a spiritual world-view that may convincingly be categorized as "esoteric".

BIBLIOGRAPHY

Abel, A., *Die Zwölftontechnik Weberns und Goethes Methodik der Farbenlehre: Zur Kompositionstheorie und Ästhetik der neuen Wiener Schule* (Beihefte zum Archiv für Musikwissenschaft 19), Franz Steiner: Wiesbaden 1982.

——, 'Musik als Sprache: Über Webern und Goethe', *Neue Zeitschrift für Musik* 12 (1983), 10–13.

Abell, A. M., *Talks with Great Composers*, G. E. Schroeder: Garmisch-Partenkirchen 1964.

Adorno, T. W., 'George und Hofmannsthal: Zum Briefwechsel 1891–1906', in: Adorno, *Prismen: Kulturkritik und Gesellschaft*, Suhrkamp: Frankfurt a.M. 1959.

Allende-Blin, J., 'Arnold Schönberg und die Kabbala', in: Heinz-Klaus Metzger & Rainer Riehn (eds.), *Musik-Konzepte: Sonderband Arnold Schönberg*, Edition Text + Kritik: München 1980, 117–145.

Ashton, D., *A Fable of Modern Art*, Thames & Hudson: London 1980.

Assmann, J., *Moses the Egyptian: The Memory of Egypt in Western Monotheism*, Harvard University Press: Cambridge Mass. / London 1997.

[Böhme, J.], *Jacob Böhme Werke* (Ferdinand van Ingen, ed.) (Bibliothek der frühen Neuzeit 6), Deutscher Klassiker Verlag: Frankfurt a.M. 1997.

Cohen, D., 'Anton Webern and the Magic Square', *Perspectives of New Music* 13 (1974/1975), 213–215.

Cross, C. M., 'Three Levels of "Idea" in Schoenberg's Thought and Writings', *Current Musicology* 29 (1980), 24–36.

Drummond, J. D., 'The Background, Shape and Meaning of Twelvenote Music: An Examination via Moses and Aron', *Soundings* (1973), 18–25.

Dümling, A., '"Dies ist ein Lied für dich allein": Zu einigen Motiven von Weberns Textwahl', in: Heinz-Klaus Metzger & Rainer Riehn (eds.), *Musik-Konzepte Sonderband Anton Webern*, vol. I, 256–257.

Faivre, A., *Access to Western Esotericism*, State University of New York Press: Albany 1994.

Gerlach, R., 'Mystik und Klangmagie in Anton von Weberns hybrider Tonalität: Eine Jugendkrise im Spiegel von Musik und Dichtung der Jahrhundertwende', *Archiv für Musikwissenschaft* 33 (1976), 1–27.

Gerlach, R., *Musik und Jugendstil der Wiener Schule 1900–1908*, Laaber-Verlag: Laaber 1985.

Gratzer, W., *Zur "wunderlichen Mystik" Alban Bergs: Eine Studie*, Böhlau Verlag: Wien / Köln / Weimar 1993.

Grossato, A. (ed.), *Forme e correnti dell'esoterismo occidentale* (Viridarium 5), Medusa: Milano 2008.

Hammer, O., *Claiming Knowledge: Strategies of Epistemology from Theosophy to the New Age* (Numen Book Series 90), Brill: Leiden / Boston / Köln 2001.

Hanegraaff, W. J., 'De gnosis van Arnold Schönberg', *Vooys: Tijdschrift voor letteren* 7:1 (1988), 28–37.

——, 'The Study of Western Esotericism: New Approaches to Christian and Secular Culture', in: Peter Antes, Armin W. Geertz & Randi R. Warne (eds.), *New Approaches to the Study of Religion I: Regional, Critical, and Historical Approaches* (Religion and Reason 42), Walter de Gruyter: Berlin & New York 2004, 489–519.

——, 'Forbidden Knowledge: Anti-Esoteric Polemics and Academic Research', *Aries* 5:2 (2005), 225–254.

——, 'The Trouble with Images: Anti-Image Polemics and Western Esotericism', in: Olav Hammer & Kocku von Stuckrad (eds.), *Polemical Encounters: Esotericism and its Others*, Brill: Leiden / Boston 2007, 107–136.

——, *Swedenborg, Oetinger, Kant: Three Perspectives on the Secrets of Heaven*, Swedenborg Foundation: West Chester 2007.

——, 'Under the Mantle of Love: The Mystical Eroticisms of Marsilio Ficino and Giordano Bruno', in: Wouter J. Hanegraaff & Jeffrey J. Kripal, *Hidden Intercourse: Eros and Sexuality in the History of Western Esotericism*, Brill: Leiden / Boston 2008.

——, 'Reason, Faith, and Gnosis: Potentials and Problematics of a Typological Construct', in: Peter Meusburger, Michael Welker & Edgar Wunder (eds.), *Clashes of Knowledge: Orthodoxies and Heterodoxies in Science and Religion*, Springer Science & Business Media: Dordrecht 2008, 133–144.

——, 'La nascita dell'esoterismo dallo spirito del Protestantesimo', in: Alessandro Grossato (ed.), *Forme e correnti dell'esoterismo occidentale* (Viridarium 5), Medusa: Milano 2008.

——, 'Western Esotericism in Enlightenment Historiography: The Importance of Jacob Brucker', in: Andreas Kilcher (ed.), *Constructing Tradition: Means and Myths of Transmission in Western Esotericism*, Brill: Leiden / Boston 2009.

——. (ed.), in collaboration with Antoine Faivre, Roelof van den Broek & Jean-Pierre Brach, *Dictionary of Gnosis and Western Esotericism*, 2 vols., Brill: Leiden/Boston/Köln 2005.

Johnson, J., *Webern and the Transformation of Nature*, Cambridge University Press: Cambridge 1999.

Laurant, J-P., *L'ésotérisme chrétien en France au XIXe siècle*, L'Âge d'Homme: Lausanne 1992.

Martino, V., 'Kandinsky, Schönberg und das Gesamtkunstwerk', in: *Okkultismus und Avantgarde: Von Munch bis Mondrian 1900–1915*, Schirn Kunsthalle: Frankfurt 1995, 562–577.

Matter, J., *Histoire critique du gnosticisme, et de son influence sur les sectes religieuses et philosophiques des dix premiers siècles de l'ère chrétienne*, 2e éd., revue et augmentée, Strasbourg / Paris 1843.

Moeller, W. O., *The Mithraic Origin and Meanings of the Rotas-Sator Square*, Leiden 1973.

Moldenhauer, H. & Moldenhauer, R., *Anton von Webern: Chronik seines Lebens und Werkes*, Atlantis: Zürich 1980.

Neugebauer-Wölk, M., '"Höhere Vernunft" und "höheres Wissen" als Leitbegriffe in der esoterischen Gesellschaftsbewegung: Vom Nachleben eines Renaissancekonzepts im Jahrhundert der Aufklärung', in: Monika Neugebauer-Wölk (ed.),

Aufklärung und Esoterik (Studien zum achtzehnten Jahrhundert 24), Felix Meiner: Hamburg 1999.

Neuwirth, G. , 'ROTAS – SATOR', *Österreichische Musikzeitschrift* 35:9 (1980), 461–472.

Pasi, M., 'Il problema della definizione dell'esoterismo: Analisi critica e proposte per la ricerca futura', in: Alessandro Grossato (ed.), *Forme e correnti dell'esoterismo occidentale* (Viridarium 5), Medusa: Milano 2008.

Reinecke, T., *Hildegard Jone (1891–1963): Untersuchungen zu Leben, Werk und Veröffentlichungskontexten. Zugleich eine Studie zu einigen Figuren im Denken Anton Weberns und den von ihm vertonten Texten*, Peter Lang: Frankfurt a.M. etc. 1999.

Reinhardt, L., *From Poet's Voice to Composer's Muse: Text and Music in Webern's Jone Settings*, unpubl. Ph.D. dissertation, The University of North Carolina at Chapel Hill 1995.

Schönberg, A., *Style and Idea: Selected Writings* (Leonard Stein, ed.), Faber & Faber: London 1975.

——, 'The Relationship to the Text' (1912), in: Schönberg, *Style and Idea*, 141–145.

——, 'Hauer's Theories' (1923), in: Schönberg, *Style and Idea*, 209–213.

——, 'Composition with Twelve Tones' (1941), in: Schönberg, *Style and Idea*, 214–245.

——, 'The Blessing of the Dressing' (1948), in: Schönberg, *Style and Idea*, 382–386.

Schopenhauer, A., *Die Welt als Wille und Vorstellung*, in: *Sämtliche Werke* I (Wolfgang Frhr. von Löhneysen, ed.), Wissenschaftliche Buchgesellschaft: Darmstadt 1974.

Stuckrad, K. von, *Western Esotericism: A Brief History of Secret Knowledge*, Equinox: London / Oakville 2005.

——, 'Western Esotericism: Towards an Integrative Model of Interpretation', *Religion* 35:2 (2005), 78–97.

Swedenborg, E., *Heaven and Its Wonders and Hell: Drawn from Things Heard and Seen*, Swedenborg Foundation: West Chester 2000.

——, *Secrets of Heaven*, Swedenborg Foundation: West Chester 2008.

Webb, J., *The Occult Underground*, Open Court: La Salle, Illinois 1974.

——, *The Occult Establishment*, Open Court: La Salle, Illinois 1976.

Webern, A., *Wege zur neuen Musik* (Wille Reich, ed.), Universal Edition: Vienna 1960.

Wille, B., *Offenbarungen des Wacholderbaums: Roman eines Allsehers*, 2 vols., Leipzig 1901.

Zimmermann, R. C., *Das Weltbild des jungen Goethe: Studien zur Hermetischen Tradition des Deutschen 18. Jahrhunderts*, 2 vols., Wilhelm Fink: München 1969 / 1979.

——, 'Goethes Verhältnis zur Naturmystik am Beispiel seiner Farbenlehre', in: Antoine Faivre & Rolf Christian Zimmermann (eds.), *Epochen der Naturmystik: Hermetische Tradition im wissenschaftlichen Fortschritt*, Erich Schmidt: Berlin 1979, 333–363.

MUSIC, MAGIC AND POSTMODERN HISTORICAL METAFICTION: HELMUTH KRAUSSER'S 'MELODIEN' (1993)

György E. Szönyi

It is well known that in the protomodern period music was studied as part of the cosmic order and theories of music were connected to astronomy, mathematics and other, superior forms of natural philosophy. In the Renaissance, from Francesco Giorgi's *De harmonia mundi totius* (1525) to Johannes Kepler's *Harmonices mundi* (1619) music was discussed within the framework of the Great Chain of Being as well as the universal correspondences. In a world, which was looked at and interpreted through analogies and correspondences, it was only natural that music was also associated with magic, sympathetic as well as ceremonial.

Having all the above in mind as a background, my paper is going to deal with a modern novel, Helmut Krausser's *Melodien oder Nachträge zum Quecksilbernen Zeitalter* (1993) which may be classified as postmodern historical metafiction, touching upon alchemy, mystical-magical theories and praxis of music, and other occult lore of the early modern period. The historical narrative is framed by a story of modern academics studying all this with various purposes.

THE PROTOMODERN THEORETICAL FRAMEWORK

If we examine protomodern theories of music we can arrive at a typology according to which the esoteric properties of music are related to three connecting areas: first is the interconnectedness of musical proportions and the structure of the cosmos; second is the idea that music has magical creative energy, and even the cosmos was created by divine music; finally, the third is related to the physical or psychological power of music over human individuals.

The idea that musical and cosmic harmony are of the same kind roots in ancient Greek thought. According to tradition it was Pythagoras who for the first time discovered that a musical scale on a monochord coincides with strict arithmetical and geometrical proportions. As on a 13th-century Cistercian manuscript (from Alderspach,

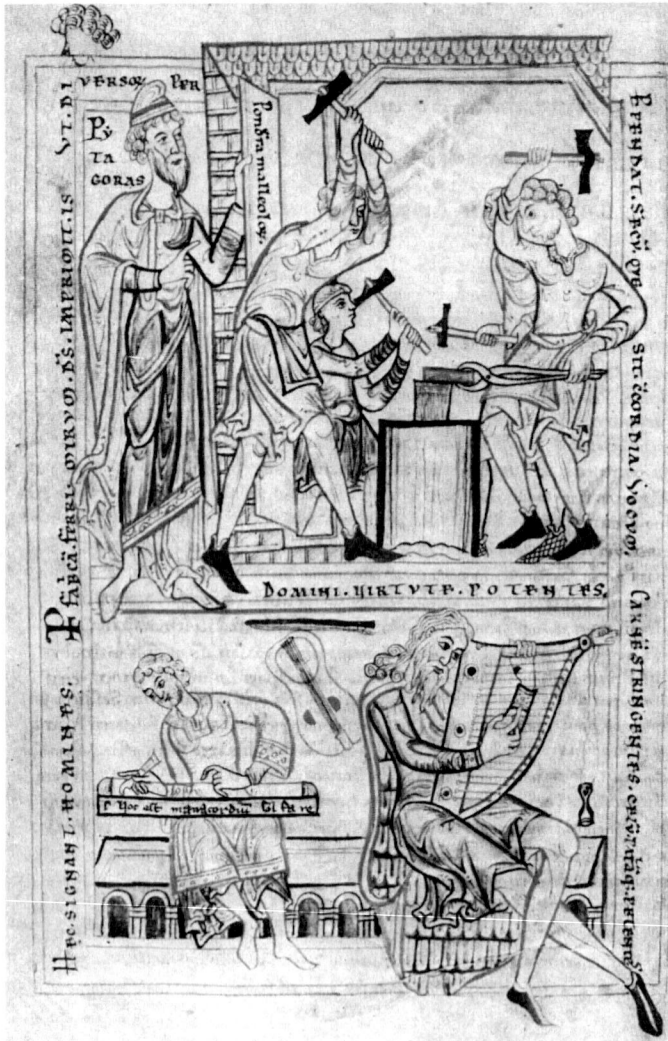

Figure 1. Pythagoras discovers the musical proportions. C13 MS, Cistertian monastery, Alderspach. Reproduced from Peter Gülke, *A középkor zenéje* ([*Mönche, Bürger, Minnesänger*, Leipzig, 1975] Budapest: Zenemükiadó, 1979), fig 16.

Germany) one can see Pythagoras giving advise how to create a proper monochord following the rules of mathematical proportions.

This idea lead Robert Fludd to propose in his *Utriusque cosmi historia* (1617) that the whole universe has been created and functions as a gigantic, cosmic monochord.

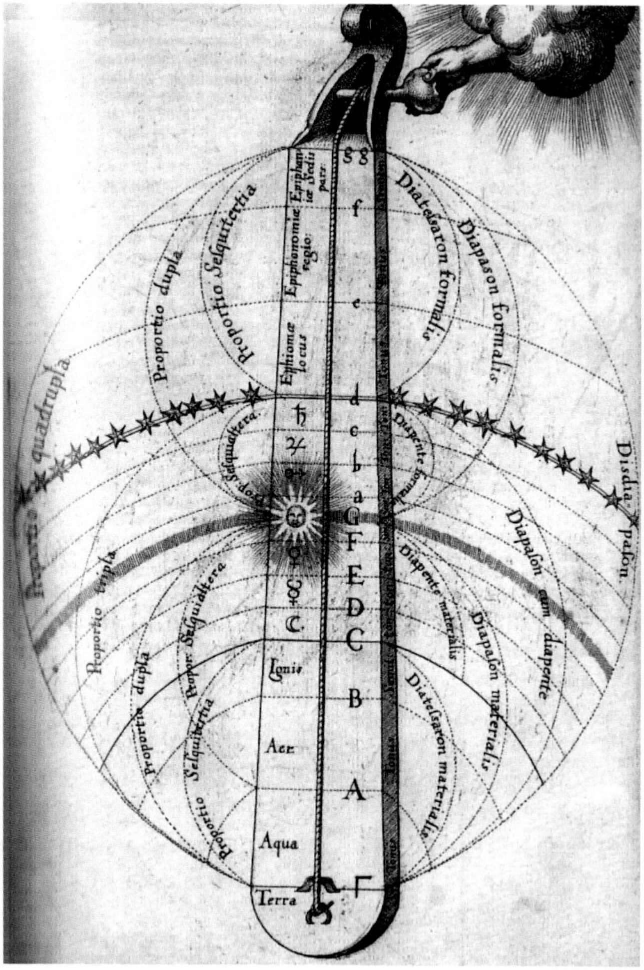

Figure 2. The Divine Monochord. Robert Fludd, *Utriusque Cosmi Historia* (Oppenheim: Johann Theodor de Bry, 1617), 1a: 90. Courtesy of the Somogyi Library, Szeged.

For such concepts one could find confirmation in the writings of ancient philosophers. As Alexander of Aetolia wrote: "The seven spheres give the seven sounds of the lyre and produce a harmony [i.e. the octave] because of the intervals which separate them from one another."[1] Or one could cite the great Renaissance magus, Heinrich

---

[1] Quoted by Tyson in Henry Cornelius Agrippa, *Three Books of Occult Philosophy*, 337.

Philofophiæ partitio.

```
                                              ⌠Diuinic⁹ infpirata & eft The
                                              │ ologia vera in veteri ac no
                            ⌠Methaphifica.    │ uo teftamento tradita
                            │ & hæc aut eft  ⟨ Humanius cõquifita quam
                            │                 │ Ariftoteles Auicenna &c.,in
                            │                 │ multis libris defcripfere.
                            │                 ⌊Arithmetica
                            │ Mathematica   ⌠Geometria     integrantes
                            │ cui⁹partes funt⟨Mufica        quadruuia
            Realis.q̄        │                ⌊Aftronomia
            ⌠rufus in      ⟨
            │               │                ⌠Phifícorum
            │               │                │ De cœlo & mundo.
            │               │                │ De generatiõe & corruptiõe
            │               │                │ Methaurorum
            │               │                │ Mineralium
   ⌠Theorica │              │ Phificã fiue na⌠De elementis
   │ fiue fpecu│            │ turalem .fub q̄│ De Anima
   │ latiuam  │             │ & Medicía the⟨ De animalibus & plantis
   │ Et eft aut│            │ orica cõtinef &│ De fenfu & fenfato
   │          │             │ tradif in libris│ De memoria & reminifcētia
   │          │             │                │ De Somno & vigilia
   │          │             │                ⌊De iuuentute & fenectute
   │          │             ⌠Grammatica      ⌠De refpiratiõe & infpiratione,
Philofo/    │  Rational   / Rhetorica &     │ De nutrimento & nutribili
phia diui  ⟨   ⌊cuius par⟨ Lógica cõftiui   │ De fanitate & ægritudine
dicitur in  │   tes funt  \ entes Triuiu.    │ De motu cordis
            │                               ⌊De morte & vita. Et multa
            │               ⌠Ethica.          aliis breuitatis caufa hic præ
            │    Actiua q̄  / Politica         termiffis.
            │    ⌠tradif in⟨ Iconomica
            │    │          \ Monaftica
            │    │           Sub his utruncq̄ ius continetur.
   Practicam│   ⟨
   ⌠q̄ eft aut⟨  │
            │    │           ⌠Lanificum
            │    │           │ Armatura
            │    Factia cu  │ Nauigatio
            │    ius ptes ft⟨ Agricultura
            │    artes Mc/  │ Venatio
            ⌊    chãicq̄ fcq̄) Medicina
                             ⌊Theatrica
```

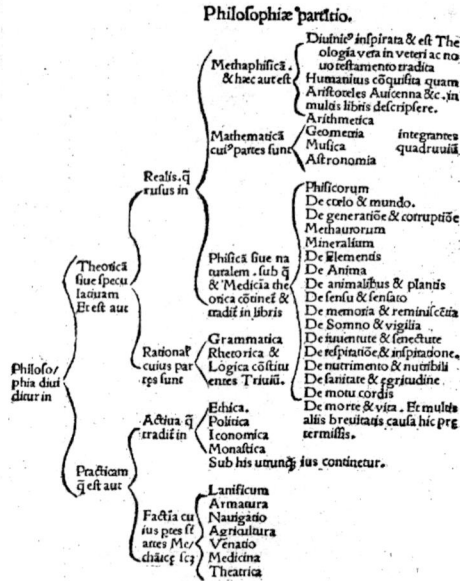

Figure 3. Music in the hierarchy of philosophy and mathematics. Gregor Reisch, *Aepitoma Omnis Phylosophiae, Alias Margarita Phylosophica, Tractans de omni genere scibili* (Argentina: Grüninger, 1504). Courtesy of Herzog August Bibliothek, Wolfenbüttel.

Cornelius Agrippa, who, following Plutarch suggested "Moreover we shall not deny, that there is in sounds a virtue to receive the heavenly gifts; if with Pythagoras and Plato we thought the heavens to consist by an harmonical composition, and to rule and cause all things by harmonical tones and motions."[2]

Accordingly music, in the medieval system of sciences, was placed next to arithmetic, geometry and astronomy, fitting in the system of the quadrivium.

Undoubtedly the greatest synthesis and most grandiose effort to prove the relationship of cosmic order and musical harmonies was done by Johannes Kepler. His first try to explain the harmony of the world was based on geometry. In his *Mysterium cosmographicum* (1596) he observed that the five Platonic solids (cube, tetrahedron,

---

[2] This resounds in Plutarch's *Moralia*: 'For Pythagoras, Archytas, Plato, and many others of the ancient philosophers, were of opinion, that there could be no motion of the world or rolling of the spheres without the assistance of music, since the Supreme Deity created all things harmoniously.' See Plutarch, *On Music* 44, in Plutarch, *Morals*, 1:134.

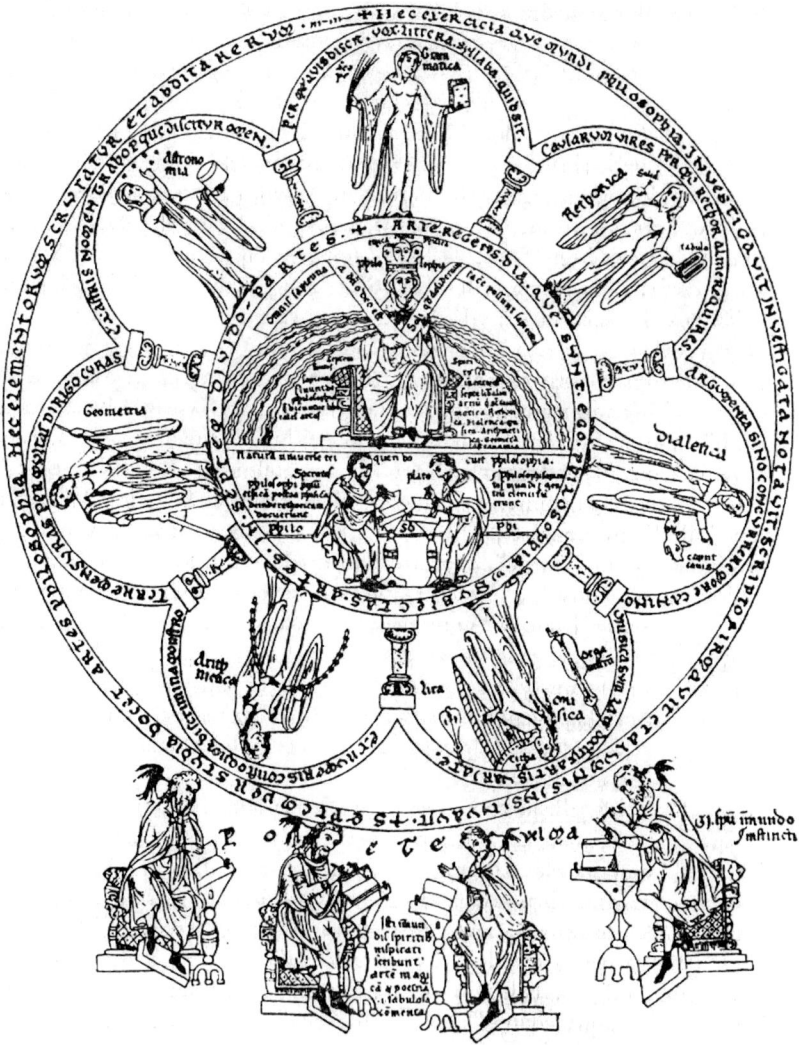

Figure 4. Music among the Seven Liberal Arts. Illustration from "Hortus deli-
ciarum" of Herrad von Landsberg, C12. Reproduced from Gülke, *A középkor
zenéje,* 105.

octahedron, dodecahedron, icosahedron) could be imagined as fitting
between the spheres of the planets.

A few years later Kepler himself disproved his original theory by
discovering the elliptical course of the planets which could not accommodate the solids any more. However, as a modern scholar of esoteric
harmonics, Rudolf Haase explains, Kepler never gave up his ambition

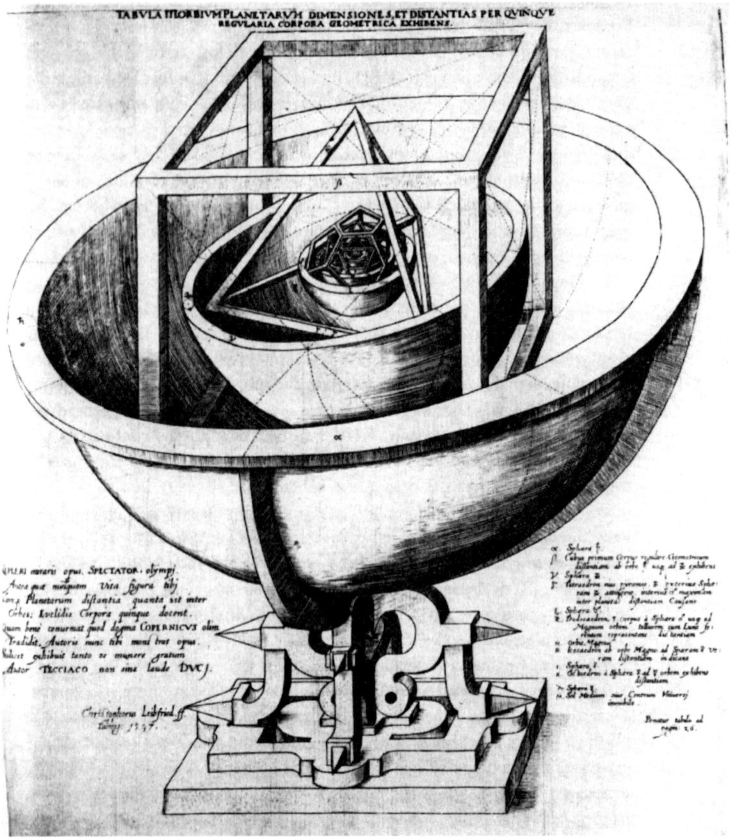

Figure 5. Johannes Kepler, *Mysterium cosmographicum* (1596). Reproduced from Allen G. Debus, *Man and Nature in the Renaissance* (Cambridge: Cambridge University Press, 1978), 93.

of acquiring the ultimate key to world harmony![3] In 1609 Kepler published his *Astronomia nova* which contained his first two laws. The third famous law – *"The squares of the orbital periods of planets are directly proportional to the cubes of the semi-major axes (the 'half-length' of the ellipse) of their orbits"* – had to wait until 1619 and quite significantly it was published as the fifth chapter of his book, called *Harmonices mundi*. Kepler in fact considered this law as a proof for world harmony since he discovered that the proportions between the

---

[3] Haase, 'Kepler's World Harmony', in Joscelyn Godwin ed., *Cosmic Music*, 111–31.

orbital periods and the distances from the sun correspond to musical harmonies. For his calculations Kepler, like Pythagoras, used a monochord.

After having furnished the proof of world harmony, Kepler concluded his book by a prayer, giving thanks to the Creator: "You see that I have now accomplished the task to which I was called. I have applied to it all the powers of my spirit bestowed upon me by You. To those who will read my treatise I will have revealed the magnificence of Your works."[4] As one of the peculiar outcomes of Kepler's investigations, the astronomer managed to create planet-tones, polyphonic musical phrases, even formulated a hypothesis for how the harmony of all the planets together must have sounded on the first day of creation![5]

This leads us to the second category of our typology outlining relationships between esoterism and music. Kepler's ideas may have inspired some rather grandiose, Baroque theories in the seventeenth century according to which the creation itself was a musical act. John Dryden's beautiful poem, "A Song for St. Cecilia's Day" is well known from 1687:

> FROM harmony, from heavenly harmony,
> This universal frame began:
> When nature underneath a heap
> Of jarring atoms lay,
> And could not heave her head,
> The tuneful voice was heard from high,
> 'Arise, ye more than dead!'
> Then cold, and hot, and moist, and dry,
> In order to their stations leap,
> And Music's power obey.
> From harmony, from heavenly harmony,
> This universal frame began…

Even more overwhelming than Dryden's mighty line is Athanasius Kircher's visualization (in his *Musurgia universalis*, 1650), according to which the creation functioned like a huge organ, from its pipes exhaling the accomplishments of the six days.

A particularly complex and intriguing illustration explaining the cosmic, musical and mythological relationships can be found in an early print, serving as the title page to Frachino Gafori's *Practica musicae* (Milan, 1496). At the top of the page Apollo can be seen on his throne,

---

[4] Quoted by Haase, 'Kepler's World Harmony', 115.
[5] Haase, 'Kepler's World Harmony', 118.

Figure 6. The Creation as Musical Act. Athanasius Kircher, *Musurgia universalis* (Roma, 1650), 2:366. Courtesy of Somogyi Library, Szeged.

surrounded by the three Graces (Euphrosine, Aglaia, and Thalia). In
the left-side medallions there are eight of the Muses (Euterpe being
responsible for music) and on the left side of the snake – the central
axis of the picture – one finds the names of the strings and chords of

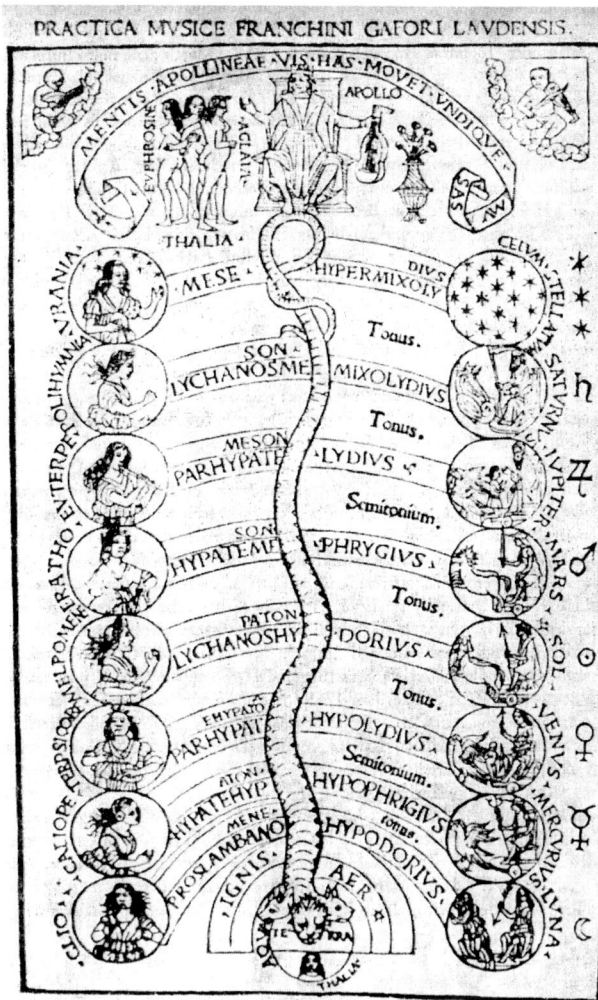

Figure 7. Franchino Gafori, *Practica musicae* (Milan, 1496), title page. Reproduced from Howard M. Brown, *A reneszánsz zenéje* ([*Music in the Renaissance*, Englewood Cliffs, NJ: Prentice Hall, 1976] Budapest: Zeneműkiadó, 1980), 383.

the lyre. On the right side the tones and semitones of the musical scale are listed (Ionian, Dorian, Phrygian, Lydian, Mixolydian, Aeolian, Locrian), next to this list in medallions allegorical representations of the planets can be found, accompanied by their signs that also refer to the basic set of metals. In the middle, a three-headed snake descends from the throne of Apollo through the eight celestial spheres and the musical octave down to the four elements biting into the silent earth.

The identity and meaning of this monster was clarified by Panofsky as a companion of the Egyptian god Seraphis, the three heads representing time: past, present and future.[6]

Interestingly, Gafori's book was mostly concerned with practical aspects of music and its performance, having little in common with

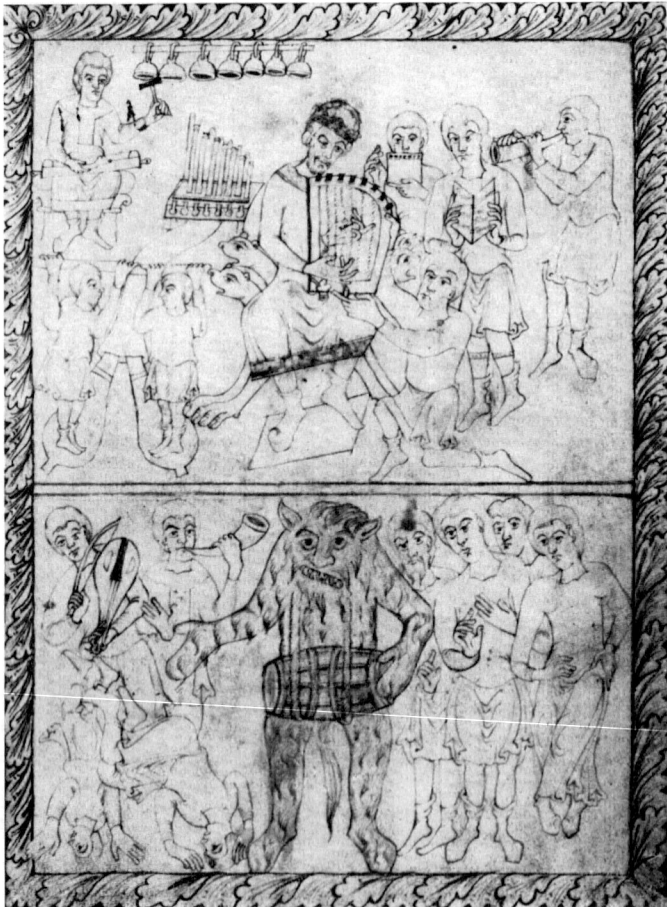

Figure 8. Scientia & usus. King David with musicians. C12 MS, Reims. Reproduced from Gülke, *A középkor zenéje*, fig. 14.

---

[6] Panofsky, 'Titian's Allegory of Prudence', in his *Meaning in the Visual Arts*, 194. This famous title page has been interpreted by other leading iconologists, too: Warburg, 'I costumi teatrali per gli intermezzi del 1589', in his *Gesammelte Schriften*, 1:271, 412–14; Seznec, *The Survival of the Pagan Gods*, 140–42; Wind, *Pagan Mysteries in the Renaissance*, 46–48, 112–13. A more recent interpretation: Haar, 'The Frontispiece of Gafori's *Practica Musicae* (1496)', *Renaissance Quarterly* 27:1 (Spring, 1974), 7–22.

the highly theoretical title page. The difference between "usus" and "scientia" is strikingly illustrated by a 12th-century French illumination from Reims: the latter is represented by King David and his harp, while "usus" means barbarous music produced by a monster.

This fascinating image has important implications in relation to our novel under discussion, but before touching upon it let me mention the third category of my typology of music and esoterism: the magical, healing power of music.

Cornelius Agrippa is again straightforward about the matter:

> Musical harmony is not destitute of the gifts of the stars. Whilst it follows opportunely the celestial bodies, doth wonderfully allure the celestial influence, and *doth change the affections, intentions, gestures, motios, actions and dispositions of all the hearers*, and doth quietly allure them to its own properties.[7]

Figure 9. Under the Zodiacal sign of Venus, nude lovers revel in a tented tub while listening to erotic feast music...(16th-century woodcut). Reproduced from Madeleine Pelner Cosman, "Machaut's Medical Musical World," in Cosman ed., *Machaut's World. Science and Art in the 14th Century* (New York, 1978, Annals of the New York Academy of Sciences 314), fig. 14.

---

[7] Agrippa, *Three Books of Occult Philosophy*, 333 (Book 2:24, 'Of Musical Harmony'). Emphasis mine.

Figure 10. C16 Germanic health spa, bathers listening to a jester's viol. Reproduced from Madeleine Pelner Cosman, "Machaut's Medical Musical World," fig. 12.

Figure 11. Erotic bath festivity entertains five couples. Reproduced from Madeleine Pelner Cosman, "Machaut's Medical Musical World," fig. 15.

A lot of premodern illustrations give testimony about this property of music. We see images of feasting, ritual and/or erotic bathing and various medical scenes which cannot be complete without musicians being present and attracting celestial influences.

Especially the first 16th century woodcut is interesting, which shows ritual bathers and musician framed by the signs of the zodiac.

Madeleine Pelner Cosman characterized this musical-medical-magical world as follows: "Music pervaded medieval medical practice and theory in astounding manner. Not only was music prescribed for good digestion and for bodily preparation before surgery, but also as a stimulus to wound healing, a mood changer, and as critical accompaniment to bloodletting. Specially composed medical music (the *shivaree*) graced the wedding chamber to assure erotic coupling at the astrologically auspicious moment."[8] The "medical musician" shows a sleeping patient being cured by the sound of music, the next image has a similar topic with the motto: "Sonare et balare."

This musical-magical world picture echoes in the writings of the Renaissance neoplatonic philosophers as well as the magical doctors, such as Ficino or Paracelsus. Their explanations seem to struggle with Plotinus' research question raised in connection with the problems of the soul:

> There is a class – rhetoric, music, and every other method of swaying mind or soul, with their power of modifying for better or for worse – and we have to ascertain what these arts come to and what kind of power lies in them.[9]

Here is the hypothetical answer of Paracelsus:

> Art, science, and skill exist only to be conductive to joy, peace, unity, purity, respectability. This is also true of music. It is the remedy of all who suffer from melancholy and fantasy, disorders that ultimately make them desperate and solitary. But music has power to hold them in human company and preserve their minds; it drives out the spirit of witches, demons and sorcerers.[10]

---

[8] Pelner Cosman, 'Machaut's Medical Musical World', in M. P. Cosman and Bruce Chandler ed., *Machaut's World*, 1.

[9] Plotinus, *Enneads*, IV.4.31. Quoted from: Plotinus, *The Enneads*, 317.

[10] Paracelsus, 'Von den hinfallenden Siechtagen (de Caducis, Epilepsie)', in Paracelsus, *Sämtliche Werke*, 8:292–3. English translation: Paracelsus, *Selected Writings*, 133.

Figure 12. A medical musician bows his viol, playing soothing melody to the sleeping patient. Repr: Madeleine Pelner Cosman, "Machaut's Medical Musical World," fig. 5.

Although Ficino also wrote about the healing power of music, for my present interest he is more significant as the Renaissance theoretician of Orpheus, the Theologian-musician. D. P. Walker devoted his book, *The Ancient Theology* largely to the career of Orpheus from the fifteenth through the eighteenth centuries,[11] and with this we have arrived at Helmut Krausser's second major theme in his *Melodien*: the myth of Orpheus. It is time to turn to the novel finally.

THE HISTORICAL STORY LINE

According to the rules of "postmodern historical metafiction" Krausser's novel is self-referential, intertextual, category-defying, pastiched,

---

[11] Walker, *The Ancient Theology*.

Figure 13. "Sonare & balare," the healing power of music. Picture book of Verona, C14. Reproduced from Gülke, *A középkor zenéje*, fig. 44.

hopelessly mixes fact and fiction, and, first of all, impressively oscillates between two plot lines and two time frames: one in the Renaissance and Baroque periods, the other is contemporary to the time of writing. For the sake of clarity I am going to separate the two plot lines from each other and first summarize the historical narrative.

The novel starts with the career of Castiglio of Florence, a Renaissance humanist and renegade medical doctor-turned-magus. After various adventures and travels (which included meetings with Heinrich Cornelius Agrippa and Johannes Trithemius) Castiglio ended up at the mini-court of Gianfrancesco Pico in Mirandola and became the prince's alchemist. His real research project was to compose magical music that could transfer power and compel humans to follow the intentions of the magus. Because of a mishap Castiglio and his disciple-assistant, Andrea, had to leave Mirandola (they failed to force by their music a pious local girl to make love with the lustful old prince). Having taken shelter in the Abbazia of Pomposa, Castiglio finally manages to complete seventeen magical melodies.

With these in their bags and in their hearts, the magus and assistant proceeded toward Ravenna, but, unfortunately, on the way some vagabonds killed Castiglio. Thus Andrea became the inheritor of the melodies. At the market place in Ravenna he started singing them and the result was miraculous healings. The city was turned upside down, and the Inquisition without hesitation arrested Andrea as a dangerous heretic; first they cut his vocal chords in order to prevent him from further singing, then he was soon executed. Before the fatal morning the abbot of Pomoposa visited him in the prison and Andrea gave him the scores of the melodies.

From this point on the Renaissance story line becomes scattered: it is hinted that the melodies were discovered and used by Palestrina, Gesulado and Allegri. Finally they came into the hands of Marcantonio Pasqualini (1614–91), the leading male soprano of the seventeenth century. By this time nobody remembered Castiglio, on the other hand, Andrea, the transmittor of the melodies became a mythical character, identified with Orpheus, who was also martyred by a jealous and mad mob, having his body torn to pieces, thus having put an end to his musical art. The analogy with Orpheus became significantly meaningful for Pasqualini, who was a castrato and the partner of the homosexual Allegri. Pasqualini could not stand women and projected his hatred onto female singers who threatened his glory and career.

When he reads the story of Orpheus in Ovid's *Metamorphoses* (Book 11: "The Death of Orpheus"), a great metamorphosis takes place in himself:

> While reading this grandiose poem I experienced a metamorphosis. I have become the new Orpheus, the singer, who tames wild beasts. I have understood that the spirit of the God lives on and reincarnates – from adept to adept. There is always one governor staying on the Earth in order to guard the mystery, the signs of beauty.[12]

---

[12] Since there is no English translation of this novel, I give the text in my translation. Book 6.6, 'Vita Pasqualini, 1635–40' in Krausser, *Mágikus dallamok*, 683.

And he transfers the dangerous role of the maenads to his female colleagues in the theatre because he feels that the secret melodies of Andrea, now in his possession, are endangered by female singers.

> I perfectly well knew where were strolling the maenads of my own age. They were standing next to me on the opera stage, full of hatred in their eyes, how gladly would they have torn me into pieces and shared my body among themselves. Finally something had to be done about it: somebody had to put an end to the abuse of the melodies and revenge that horrible crime.[13]

Thus Pasqualini becomes a terrible pervert and uses the melodies to accompany his dreadful sadistic human sacrifices and dark "Orphic" rituals performed in the cellar of his house in Rome. I cannot go into the details of Krausser's abject-oriented description of the revengful and ritualistic execution of the opera singers, performed by Pasqualini and other members of his secret society, called the ONTU (meaning "Orpheus numquam totus ultus," that is Orpheus has never been fully revenged); instead, I turn now to the contemporary story line.

The Contemporary Story Line

There is no single narrator, however the main hero of the contemporary line is Alban Täubner, a young travel writer and photographer who, due to a mismatch in Siena, Italy, gets entangled in an extraordinary and horrifying story of research and scholarly rivalry. The object of this academic enterprise is the fate of the magic melodies that had been composed by the mentioned Castiglio, then handed down to the great Italian Renaissance composers, Palestrina, Gesualdo and Allegri, finally to fall in the hands of the monstrous Pasqualini.

The serious historical research pursued by high-minded academics turns into a crazy competition and race for glorification among some scholars: Jan-Hendrik Krantz, the Swedish professor of mytosophy; Nicole Dufrés the feminist historical psychologist; Doctor Mendez, the frustrated South-American anthropologist; and Lupu Stancu, the maffioso and bibliophile librarian who steals manuscripts from Italian collections and sells them to the competing scholars. They all ruthlessly struggle with each other for every document and piece of evidence in

---

[13] Ibid.

order to reveal the story of the magic melodies. Similar to *Foucault's Pendulum*, the narrative turns into a multiple nightmare, and Täubner finally finds himself locked up in a madhouse. This outcome leaves the reader in utter uncertainty about the reality of the previous happenings of the novel, thus fulfilling the requirements for historiographical metafiction.

Apart from the engaging plot and powerful characters, the construction is also the work of a virtuoso writer. In addition to the two intertwining story lines, "documents" are also inserted to create multiple layers of action and narration. We learn about Gesualdo's life from a fictitious manuscript of a German professor that had been stolen by Krantz from the widow of the renowned scholar. On the other hand, Pasqualini's life and perverted Orphic cult are revealed from his own autobiography (*Vita Pasqualini*), and the self-apologetical narration, while step by step shedding light on the monstrosity of that character, utterly shocks the reader.

POSTMODERN HISTORICAL METAFICTION

When postmodern fiction turns to historical topics, the result is historiographical metafiction, a strange product that – in the words of Victoria Orlowski –, "through its play upon 'known truth' [...] questions the absolute 'knowability' of the past, specifically the ideological implications of historical representations. In its process of redefining 'reality' and 'truth' historiographic metafiction opens a sort of time tunnel."[14] Krausser's *Melodien* perfectly fits this definition. It is structured in such a way that in the contemporary story line the presentation of the research of the competing scholars constantly reshapes, redefines the past. This technique is similar to what Umberto Eco employed in his *Foucault's Pendulum* and one more connecting link between his and Krausser's novel is the penetrating irony and sarcasm. Nevertheless, historiographical metafiction, and, even more, metafiction that features esoterism as its main topic, cannot exist without the ultimate uncertainty, called "the uncanny" by theorists. The uncanny is the heart of the fantastic, not knowable and not explainable as opposed to many "technical" fantasies of science fiction. One of the

---

[14] Orlowski, <http://www.english.emory.edu/Bahri/Metafiction.html>, access: 2005–06–25.

archetypal examples of the uncanny is Gregor Samsa's metamorphosis in Franz Kafka's famous short story.[15]

In the *Melodien* the miracles of the magical music in Andrea's performance constitute the most uncanny element. There is no logical explanation for the curative success of the melodies just as well as there is no logical explanation of that horrifying Walpurgis night of witches that Castiglio witnesses among the Northern Italian hills on one of his journeys. These elements suggest that there is a reality outside language, something that is impossible to tell, at least not in our discursive ways of communication. This reality is conncted to the sub-semiotic sphere, very often the abjected body on the one hand, and to the supercelestial spheres on the other. In this respect Krausser connects the question of the magic melodies to some Renaissance theories of language and music.

The writer is very well versed in the Renaissance neoplatonists. He extensively uses the works of Ficino and Agrippa, and suggests that music is the archetypal, ur-language of mankind, what is more, Castiglio comes to the conclusion that this most ancient music was inaudible and his task is to make it accessible through the melodies.

The idea of the inaudible archetypal music has survived the Renaissance and can be found in Rudolf Steiner's antrophosophical philosophy, too. Later in the twentieth century it was professionally expanded in the works of the Steinerist musicologist, Hans Erhard Lauer.[16] His ideas are recalled by the following recognitions of Castiglio:

> There still exists the ur-music and its melodies need not to be discovered, only made audible. This ancient music during the centuries has been buried under the noise of human music, musicians with their artificial embellishments, like a Babylonian cacophony, covered it. Humans have forgotten about the archetypal music which was the beginning of everything.[17]

Castiglio's speculations which lead him to compose magical music recall the ambition of the Renaissance magi (such as Lodovico Lazzarelli,

---

[15] On historiographical metafiction and the uncanny see: Waugh, *Metafiction*; Onega, 'British Historiographic Metafiction', 92–103; Orlowski, 'Metafiction' (see the previous note); Freud, *The Uncanny*; Royle, *The Uncanny*.

[16] Hans Erhard Lauer, 'The Evolution of Music', in Joscelyn Godwin ed., *Cosmic Music*, 168–229. See also, Rudolf Steiner, *The Inner Nature of Music*.

[17] *Melodien...*, Bk 2, Ch 8 (in the Hungarian edition p. 192).

Guillaume Postel, or John Dee) to find the *lingua adamica* the perfect divine language, which was lost at the time of the Fall:

> The scale contains twelve semitones – a divine number, having all sorts of consequences. It is certain that one can find correspondences between sounds and words, melodies and sentences. Music is language. Divine language, its comprehensibility is not limited by borders. This language has grammar and rhetorics – where does it come from? Who created this language? [...] If we were able to discover the rules of this divine lan-

Figure 14. Andrea Sacchi (1599–1661), "Marcantonio Pasqualini Crowned by Apollo" (1641, New York, MET). Reproduced from http://www.metmuseum. org/TOAH/ho/09/eusts/ho_1981.317.htm. Access: 2008–10–03.

guage, wouldn't it be possible to devise such melodies that could enchant the souls deeply and entirely?[18]

A SHORT CONCLUSION

Thus, in spite of its multiple ironies, the elements of the uncanny in the novel serve to create an impression that he Renaissance/Baroque story line offers a strong morale, otherwise quite common in esoterically-oriented narratives: namely, the noble idea of magical deification or *exaltatio* becomes corrupted, and due to hubris and thirst for power, the magus becomes a monster. This morale in fact is mirrored in the contemporary narrative, when the scholars, out of rivalry, vanity, and jealousy, also become cruel and inhuman, only to loose their dignity.

In conclusion, let us have again a look at the "scientia & usus" picture, in contrast to the idealizing painting of Andrea Sacchi from 1661: "Marcantonio Pasqualini Crowned by Apollo". In both pictures the monstrous and the miraculous are side by side, in Sacchi's painting represented by the satyr Marsyas whose tortured state and bagpipe represent inferior music. I would emphasize that the uncanny in (post)modern fiction occupies precisely that liminal space between the two, which in other contexts might be reserved for rational explanations.[19]

BIBLIOGRAPHY

Agrippa, Henry Cornelius, *Three Books of Occult Philosophy*, tr. James Freake (1651); ed. Donald Tyson, St. Paul, MN: Llewellyn Publications 1997.

Cosman, Madeleine Pelner, 'Machaut's Medical Musical World', in M. P. Cosman and Bruce Chandler ed., *Machaut's World. Science and Art in the Fourteenth Century*, The New York Academy of Sciences 1978, Annals of the NY Academy of Sciences 314.

Freud, Sigmund, *The Uncanny* (*Das Unheimliche* 1919), London: Penguin 2003.

Haar, James, 'The Frontispiece of Gafori's *Practica Musicae* (1496)', *Renaissance Quarterly* 27:1 (Spring, 1974), 7–22.

Haase, Rudolf, 'Kepler's World Harmony', in Joscelyn Godwin ed., *Cosmic Music. Musical Keys to the Interpretation of Reality. Essays by Marius Schneider, Rudolf Haase, Hans Erhard Lauer*, Rochester, Vermont: Inner Traditions 1989, 111–31.

---

[18] Op. cit., 193.

[19] See Attila Kiss and György E. Szönyi, 'The Iconography of the Fantastic', in Márta Baróti-Gaál, Attila Kiss, György E. Szönyi ed., *The Iconography of the Fantastic*, 7–21.

Kiss, Attila and György E. Szönyi, "The Iconography of the Fantastic: An Introduction," in Márta Baróti-Gaál, Attila Kiss, György E. Szönyi ed., *The Iconography of the Fantastic*, Szeged: JATEPress 2002, 7–21.

Krausser, Helmut, *Melodien oder Nachträge zum Quecksilbernen Zeitalter*, München: List 1993.

——, *Mágikus dallamok*, Budapest: Európa 2001.

Lauer, Hans Erhard, 'The Evolution of Music Through Changes in Tone-Systems', in Joscelyn Godwin ed., *Cosmic Music*, Rochester, Vermont: Inner Traditions 1989, 168–229.

Onega, Susana, 'British Historiographic Metafiction' (1990), in Mark Currie ed., *Metafiction*, London: Longman 1995, 92–103.

Orlowski, Victoria, 'Metafiction', <http://www.english.emory.edu/Bahri/Metafiction.html>, access: 2005–06–25.

Panofsky, Erwin, 'Titian's Allegory of Prudence', in E. Panofsky, *Meaning in the Visual Arts* (1955), London: Penguin 1993.

Paracelsus, Theophrastus Aureolus Bombastus, *Sämtliche Werke*, ed. Karl Sudhoff and Wilhelm Matthiessen, Munich: O. W. Barth 1922–25.

——, *Selected Writings*, ed. Jolande Jacobi, Princeton: Princeton University Press 1951, 1973, Bollingen Series 28.

Plotinus, *The Enneads*, tr. Stephen MacKenna, abridged, intr. and notes John Dillon, Harmondsworth: Penguin 1991.

Plutarch, *Morals*, ed. William Goodwin, London: S. Low 1870.

Royle, Nicholas, *The Uncanny*, Manchester: Manchester University Press 2003.

Seznec, Jean, *The Survival of the Pagan Gods*, New York: Panteon 1953.

Steiner, Rudolf, *The Inner Nature of Music and the Experience of Tone* (1923 in German), tr. Maria St. Goar, Spring Valley, NY: Anthroposophical Press 1983.

Tyson, Donald, 'Introduction', in Henry Cornelius Agrippa, *Three Books of Occult Philosophy*, tr. James Freake (1651); ed. Donald Tyson, St. Paul, MN: Llewellyn Publications 1997.

Walker, D. P., *The Ancient Theology. Studies in Christian Platonism from the Fifteenth to the Eighteenth Century*, London: Duckworth 1972.

Warburg, Aby, 'I costumi teatrali per gli intermezzi del 1589', in A. Warburg, *Gesammelte Schriften*, Leipzig: Teubner 1932, 1:271, 412–14.

Waugh, Patricia, *Metafiction: The Theory and Practice of Self-conscious Fiction*, London: Routledge 1984.

Wind, Edgar, *Pagan Mysteries in the Renaissance*, New Haven: Yale 1958.

INDEX

Aries Book Series

Texts and Studies in Western Esotericism

Editor-in-Chief
Marco Pasi

1. Szulakowska, U. *The Sacrificial Body and the Day of Doom*. Alchemy and Apocalyptic Discourse in the Protestant Reformation. 2006. ISBN 978 90 04 15025 6
2. Barnes, K. *The Higher Self in Christopher Brennan's* Poems. Esotericism, Romanticism, Symbolism. 2006. ISBN 978 90 04 15221 2
3. van Helmont, F.M. *The Alphabet of Nature*. Translated with an introduction and annotations by A.P. Coudert & T. Corse. 2007. ISBN 978 90 04 15230 4
4. Geffarth, Renko D. *Religion und arkane Hierarchie*. Der Orden der Gold- und Rosenkreuzer als Geheime Kirche im 18. Jahrhundert. 2007.
   ISBN 978 90 04 15667 8
5. Paracelsus (Theophrastus Bombastus von Hohenheim, 1493-1541). Essential Theoretical Writings. Edited and translated with a Commentary and Introduction by A. Weeks. 2007. ISBN 978 90 04 15756 9
6. Hammer, O. and K. von Stuckrad (Eds.) *Polemical Encounters*. Esoteric Discourse and Its Others. 2007. ISBN 978 90 04 16257 0
7. Hanegraaff, W.J. & J.J. Kripal (Eds.). *Hidden Intercourse*. Eros and Sexuality in the History of Western Esotericism. 2008. ISBN 978 90 04 16873 2
8. Heidle, A. & J.A.M. Snoek (Eds.). *Women's Agency and Rituals in Mixed and Female Masonic Orders*. 2008. ISBN 978 90 04 17239 5
9. Wuidar, L. (Ed.). *Music and Esotericism*. 2010. ISBN 978 90 04 18267 7
10. Huss, B., M. Pasi & C.K.M. von Stuckrad. *Kabbalah and Modernity*. Interpretations, Transformations, Adaptations. 2010. ISBN 978 90 04 18284 4